A LIE
TOO BIG
TO FAIL

To
Robert F. Kennedy, Jr.
and
Munir Sirhan

who have courageously sought
the truth about what happened to
their loved ones on June 5, 1968

———————

Feral House
1240 W Sims Way #124
Port Townsend Wa 98368

*A Lie Too Big to Fail: The Real History of the
Assassination of Robert F. Kennedy*
ISBN 978-1-62731-070-3
Copyright © 2018 Lisa Pease

10 9 8 7 6 5 4 3 2

Design by Unflown

A LIE TOO BIG TO FAIL

The Real History of the Assassination of
ROBERT F. KENNEDY

Lisa Pease

FERAL HOUSE

ACKNOWLEDGEMENTS ix

PREFACE xiii

INTRODUCTION xvii

EVENTS

HOPE 1

NIGHTMARE 27

TRAGEDY 63

PREPARATION 89

TRIAL 135

ANALYSIS

REINVESTIGATIONS 197

TOO MANY HOLES 255

SUSPICIOUS OTHERS 291

MIND GAMES 375

MISSION: POSSIBLE 455

INDEX 506

I urge you to learn the harsh facts that lurk behind the mask of official illusion with which we have concealed our true circumstances, even from ourselves.

Our country is in danger: not just from foreign enemies, but above all, from our own misguided policies—and what they can do to the nation that Thomas Jefferson once told us was the last, best, hope of man.

There is a contest on, not for the rule of America, but for the heart of America.

—Senator Robert F. Kennedy, Kansas State University, March 18, 1968

ACKNOWLEDGEMENTS

"Sensible people keep asking if it is really worth the time and effort to dig into the difficult past in this difficult way. Some time ago, near the beginning of this long journey, I tried to explain my own reason for pressing ahead. 'Assassinations of national figures are not ordinary murders,' I wrote. 'When bullets distort or nullify the national will, democracy itself has been attacked. When a series of such events changes the direction of the nation and occurs under suspicious circumstances, institutions seem compromised or corrupted and democratic process itself undermined.' It was Robert Kennedy's special gift that he understood the new realities of power in this country and could make people believe that if they roused themselves to the effort they could, as he liked to put it, 'reclaim America.' Perhaps that helps explain why the pain of his loss remains so great after so long a time."

—Congressman Allard Lowenstein,
Saturday Review, February 19, 1977

I STOOD ON THE SHOULDERS OF GIANTS WHEN I STARTED LOOKING into this case. Former FBI agent Bill Turner and former journalist Jonn Christian first opened my eyes to the numerous discrepancies in the government's case against Sirhan Sirhan. Robert Blair Kaiser's book made me curious about Sirhan's mental state at the time of the shooting. Dr. Phil Melanson's work brought provocative witnesses into view.

I am indebted to the archivists at the California State Archives who put up with my numerous requests and made key records available to me. I am grateful to the news organizations that donated footage of the event to the libraries at the Paley Center for Media in Los Angeles (formerly the Museum of Television and Radio) and UCLA. I watched dozens of hours of video from the event and listened to dozens of hours of taped witness interviews, many of which had never been transcribed, to find some of the new information you'll see in these pages.

I'm grateful to the folks who maintain the Mary Ferrell Archives, a collection of files from various government agencies relating to our secret history. The FBI, CIA, LAPD and Los Angeles County files there were invaluable, as were the Sirhan trial transcript and related court filings.

Thank you, Los Angeles Public Library. I had only a passing interest in this case, having focused my attention on the assassination of President John F. Kennedy. But one day, while looking for something else, I stumbled upon a drawer full of reels of microfilm from the Robert Kennedy investigation. The tapes were unlabeled, so I put a reel into the machine at random. I was immediately impressed by the number of reports of suspects beyond Sirhan, including one who had been handcuffed at the scene. I knew these files had only been released four years earlier and suspected there was a wealth of information that had not surfaced in the few books on the case that had been published to date. My suspicion proved to be well founded, as you will see in this book.

Special thanks go to all members of my family as well as the friends and coworkers who urged me to continue even when completion of this journey seemed a distant fantasy.

Munir Sirhan gave me insight into the shoddy way the defense team treated the family of Sirhan Sirhan and has shown a deep passion for justice as well as a broad knowledge of the intricacies of this case. He also gave me three bags of the best lemons I have ever tasted, fresh off his backyard tree.

The most surprising and welcome development of all was being able to discuss the case with Robert Kennedy, Jr. Of all the members of the Kennedy family, Bobby has long been the truest heir to the legacy of his father and his uncle John. Bobby is an attorney, an environmental activist, and the co-founder and President of Waterkeeper Alliance. I was impressed with Bobby before I met him. But I was even more impressed after discussing the case with him and seeing how quickly his mind worked, how easily he grasped concepts that others had shown trouble understanding. In turn, he taught me about some legal aspects of this case, as well as how to make perfect corn on the cob! I will be forever grateful to our mutual friend, author David Talbot, for connecting us.

David also made possible my second meeting with John Meier, whose interesting story about what he learned while working for Howard Hughes greatly informed my work. Or maybe I should thank John, who told David he wouldn't meet with him unless David brought me along. I was devastated to learn that David had suffered a stroke as I was nearing the finish line on this book. I hope by the time you are reading this that he has fully recovered.

Paul Schrade became a treasured ally over the course of our many encounters. Not only did I get to know him through this case, I got to know him from political events all over Los Angeles. Whenever there was a group that needed support, he was there. He is a gem of an activist on all sorts of progressive issues, and his tenacity in calling for reinvestigations of this case has been unparalleled.

Posthumous thanks go to Adel Sirhan, who called me after one of my first articles on the case to find out for himself if I were sincere and honest. He told me I passed his muster, but I never got to meet him in person as he died shortly after.

I learned so much about the ballistic evidence from Lynn Mangan that I must posthumously thank her too. She spent decades examining the evidence in the case, and hosted me at her place in Reno for a few days to explain to me what she had learned. She generously shared not only her research but also her world-class collection of miscellaneous historical artifacts.

Posthumous thanks go to Carl McNabb as well, a former CIA operative who quit the agency in disgust and in later years attempted suicide. We took an instant liking to each other, and he shared some information with me he had not shared with others. He was a sensitive and charming man whose genuine concern for the world touched me. In Bill Turner's and Jonn Christian's book, he appears under the name "Jim Rose."

Posthumous thanks are also due Gordon Novel, another CIA operative who led quite a darker life than Carl. Almost in spite of himself, he provided me some valuable information about this case and others, along with some terrifically entertaining lies. He was the most colorful speaker I have ever encountered, with a vocabulary more befitting a Damon Runyan novel than an assassination investigation.

Thanks to Cyril Wecht and his son Ben for providing me the opportunity on several occasions to share my knowledge with others at conferences sponsored by the Wecht Institute at Duquesne University. Thanks to Jim Lesar and all the people at the Assassination Archives Research Center who have hosted me at conferences in Bethesda, Maryland, as well (and who posted my testimony to a United Nations inquiry regarding the 1961 death of U.N. Secretary Dag Hammarskjöld). Posthumous thanks to John Judge, who gave me my start as a speaker at Coalition on Political Assassinations (COPA) conferences in Dallas and Washington, D.C. I'm grateful to have met and learned much about the research process from incredible historians at these conferences, including Bill Turner, John Newman, Gary Aguilar, Bill Davy, Jim Douglass and others. I met the maker of the documentary *The Second Gun*, Ted Charach, at a couple of these conferences as well. I also shared the stage with Oliver Stone, whose film *JFK* made possible the release of so many important files, at a couple of related events.

I must offer special thanks to Jim DiEugenio, my former partner in *Probe Magazine*, a journal we co-edited for several years that illuminated information from files released through the JFK Act. Our goal was to tie the past to the present, to show the through-line of history. Jim approached Adam Parfrey about publishing a "best of" volume of past articles, which you can find under the title *The Assassinations: Probe Magazine on JFK, MLK, RFK and Malcolm X*. Jim has encouraged me to write this book for years. I repaid that favor by giving Jim the awful task of reading the longest version of this manuscript, and over the winter holiday season, no less. I relied on Jim's good judgment to help me excise less-than-critical information from the present volume. Whatever remains must be blamed solely on me.

Thank you, Adam Parfrey, for being absolutely fearless and passionate about bringing the darker parts of our past to light in both of these books. Sadly, Adam passed away just as we were making final edits to the book. I will forever miss his voice in the world on this and other subjects.

My sincere thanks go to everyone who has ever said a kind word to me about this project—whether in person, online (thanks, Twitter family!), on radio shows, in documentaries, at conferences, and in other venues. Your support has carried me when the difficulty of telling this story grew nearly unbearable.

Final thanks go to you, dear reader. You showed the curiosity it takes to become informed in a world that wants to keep you ignorant. I hope you come away from this feeling empowered. Because once you learn how a magic trick works, you can never be fooled again.

PREFACE

I AM NOT OLD ENOUGH TO REMEMBER THE DAY PRESIDENT JOHN F. Kennedy was shot in Dallas. But I remember seeing thousands of people waving at Robert Kennedy's funeral train as it passed through their towns. I remember thinking, even as a young child, that the best politician of my lifetime was already gone. As a child, that was a terribly depressing moment. As an adult, I've yet to shake that feeling.

I learned to distrust the media while serving as Governor Jerry Brown's assistant during his presidential run in 1992. I would attend events, and then see the way the media reported on them. Huge crowds were dismissed as "a handful of supporters." The large protests at the Democratic Convention, where I walked the floor as a delegate, went unreported entirely. Liars were given time on *Nightline* while truth tellers were relegated to the alternative media. At the end of the campaign I volunteered for a time with Fairness & Accuracy In Reporting (FAIR) because I was so incensed at how dishonestly the media reported on major events. I started paying attention to bylines, not just headlines. Who in the media could be trusted? Who could not?

I started to wonder about other major events. If someone other than Oswald had killed President John F. Kennedy, would the media have told us? If someone other than Sirhan had shot Senator Robert Kennedy, would the media have covered that up?

My first Internet search ever, in the pre-World Wide Web days, was "JFK assassination." I found an online group where the assassination of JFK was discussed in minute detail. I plunged head first into an argument there that lasted five years. I realized right away I was outgunned in terms of being able to cite data in defense of my positions. So I went to a local library and found a full set of the Warren Commission volumes of testimony and documents that accompanied the report. I started reviewing newspapers on microfilm, and even found some FBI files at the local library that related to the JFK case. I went from being a curious reader to an active researcher in short order.

The more I learned about the JFK assassination, the more I wondered what happened to RFK. I read every book published on the case, including some obscure ones rarely cited. And then one day, I opened "the wrong" drawer in the library and found, to my amazement, microfilm of the LAPD's and FBI's investigation into the RFK assassination. At the time, those files had only been released four years earlier. I knew only a handful of people, at best, had looked at those files. I realized I might find things in that data that no one else had found. And I did, as you'll soon see.

Similarly, many witness interviews were never transcribed. I listened to hours of audio tapes, some recorded at extremely low volumes. I also went through a number of video archives throughout the Los Angeles area and found interesting nuggets that have never been reported before that dramatically contradict the official version of events.

The official story is deceptively simple. A young Palestinian immigrant named Sirhan Bishara Sirhan shot Senator Robert Kennedy in front of numerous witnesses in a narrow serving area called "the pantry" at the Ambassador Hotel just after midnight on June 5, 1968. Senator Kennedy had just won the Democratic presidential primary the night before in California and was walking through the pantry on his way to a room where the print media reporters were waiting. He never made it that far. Five other people were wounded during the shooting. Sirhan was tried and convicted in a trial and sentenced to death.

But even in the early days after the assassination, conspiracy theories were forming. Weren't there too many holes in the victims and the doorframes in the pantry to have come from a single gun? A bullet pictured in a newspaper was one bullet too many for the official scenario to work, as a housewife pointed out, to deafening media silence. Witnesses to evidence of conspiracy were told they could not speak to reporters per a judge's order. A film about a second gun that had entered the case raised numerous questions about the validity of the authorities' conclusions about the case. A criminalist from Pasadena with a lot of credibility wrote a report demonstrating that two different guns had been fired in the pantry, meaning Sirhan could not possibly have acted alone. Others pointed to the fact that witnesses uniformly put Sirhan in front of Kennedy, but Kennedy was shot from behind.

The discrepancies in the case led to a formal re-examination of the evidence. A panel of experts examined the bullets to determine if more than one gun had been used. But the public was told of only a single key finding—that the panel found no evidence proving that a second gun had been used. They were not told other key data, such as the fact that the panel could not match *any* of the victim bullets to Sirhan's gun. And while the panel did discover one deliberate deception, they missed the much larger deception operation that had been pulled on them, as you will learn in this volume.

It has often been said that one lie begets another. Nowhere is that more evident than in this case. Each time one lie was exposed, another lie had to be concocted to explain the previous lie away. Those who protected the lies ascended to higher positions of power. Those who challenged the official story would be shot at, sued, or marginalized as "conspiracy theorists," a frame the CIA promoted to its media assets in 1967 when New Orleans District Attorney Jim Garrison was investigating suspects in the JFK assassination case with deep connections to the CIA.

It really is a crime to marginalize the few who have spent years trying to find the truth about this and other cases, who have given generously of their time and resources, who view such research not as a hobby or a gruesome pastime but as an important part of participating in what's left of our democracy. Each person bears a responsibility to pass an accurate understanding of the past to future generations so that the country and humanity can successfully advance. When we turn our backs on the truth, either through lies or indifference, we are ruining our own future. Without an accurate understanding of where we've been, we can't understand where we are, or where we're going.

"Who controls the past controls the future," Eric Blair wrote under his pseudonym of George Orwell in his book *1984*. No one understood that better than Blair, who was himself an intelligence agent. He originally named his book *1948*, because he saw so clearly where the dictatorial impulse led, and how "perpetual war for perpetual peace" was not just an idea but already in motion after World War II ended.

The Cold War was a blanket term for what was in effect a series of resource wars. Who would control the oil supplies around the globe? Who would control the rare earth minerals that made flight, computers and cell phones possible? We will perhaps always be involved in resource wars unless we recognize that nearly every international conflict is about resources, and that ideology is simply the fig leaf used to hide that fact.

Both JFK and RFK understood this. Both actively sought to stop the plundering of the poorer nations by the rich. In doing so, the Kennedys put themselves at odds with powerful people who drove the economy, controlled the media, and ran covert operations. Both brothers paid a high price for their efforts to make the world a better, fairer place.

I didn't plan to write a book when I started on this journey. I just had an intense, personal curiosity. I wanted to understand what happened for myself. But as the years went by and I read the books of others on the case, the gap between what I was learning and what appeared in print began to weigh on me. Reluctantly, I realized I had a responsibility to share what I had found.

Thank you for being brave enough to open this volume. It takes a certain amount of courage to challenge the status quo, to dare to have a thought that differs from what the media screams at you daily. The media usually provides facts, but not always the clarifying context. Facts without context can become lies. "He robbed a bank" is a lot different from "He robbed a bank because his kid was being held hostage." While both statements could be technically accurate, the first statement is closer to a lie if the second statement is true. Context matters.

After 25 years of research, I now believe I understand what happened at the Ambassador Hotel that night. I believe the truth about these events informs our current political situation. And I believe *you* have a part to play in this story as well. The truth can set us *all* free. Read on. Then find me on Twitter (@lisapease) and tell me what you think.

INTRODUCTION
by James DiEugenio

THE ASSASSINATION OF ROBERT KENNEDY IN LOS ANGELES ON
June 5, 1968, is perhaps the most ignored American historical milestone in the
second half of the 20th century. In fact, virtually no historian recognizes it as
such. Which is odd since it is clearly a marker in two ways. First, his murder
climaxed a series of four major assassinations in less than five years. Preceding his
assassination were those of his brother President John Kennedy, Malcolm X, and
RFK's friend and colleague Martin Luther King. All four of these deaths were caused
by gunfire, and were redolent with suspicious circumstances. It was impossible
to delineate the truth about the actual facts pertaining to them since, in each
case, a cover-up ensued almost immediately afterwards. In an earlier book, Lisa
Pease and I co-edited an anthology from *Probe Magazine* called *The Assassinations*,
which tried to demonstrate the commonalities between the four cases.

The second way in which Senator Kennedy's death is a watershed relates to
the outline above. His murder marked the end of an era: it was the premature
death of the Sixties. I do not mean that as pure numerology, but in the sense that,
in June of 1968, Robert Kennedy represented the last great desperate hope for
the social and political activism of that remarkable decade. When he was killed,
it was killed. Or as Jean Genet reportedly said, "America is gone." It is difficult to
understand what that means unless one is old enough to have lived through the
era. And fortunately—or unfortunately—I was. No feature film or documentary

I know of has ever been able to encapsulate the energy, the idealism, the sense of empowerment that so many people felt from 1961 to 1968.

And Robert Kennedy—from the beginning—was right there in the middle of it.

RFK became the first Attorney General to rigorously enforce the Supreme Court's *Brown v. Board* decision, and the Civil Rights Acts of 1957 and 1960. He had planned on breaking the walls of discrimination by using those legal tools to file civil actions showing that the states of the former confederacy were circumventing federal law. To do so, he hired dozens of new lawyers in his civil rights department, and almost a score of researchers to secure data proving his charges. The Attorney General filed almost twice as many civil cases in 12 months as his predecessor had *in eight years!*

This was such a drastic change from the Eisenhower/Nixon regime that it gave ballast to civil rights groups, and it inspired individuals to defy the status quo in the South. Why? Because they knew the Attorney General would do all he could to protect them. This was the case at the University of Mississippi with James Meredith, and at the University of Alabama with Vivian Malone. Robert Kennedy had Meredith escorted to and from class by two federal marshals during his student career at Ole Miss. Governor George Wallace brought in almost nine hundred state troopers to block Malone from entering his university. The Attorney General brought in General Creighton Abrams with three thousand federal troops. After that nationally televised showdown, it was Robert Kennedy who encouraged his brother to go on network TV to give his epochal civil rights address.

As John Bohrer notes in his book *The Revolution of Robert Kennedy,* the Attorney General understood that what he had done for the moral cause of civil rights had extracted a huge political price: He had lost the South for his brother's 1964 campaign. He therefore drafted a letter of resignation to remove the impact his legacy would have the following year. He did this on November 20, 1963. Therefore, his brother did not have the opportunity to act on it. But such is the stuff of moral and political heroism.

But it was not just on the domestic scene where RFK proved his mettle. After the CIA hoodwinked his brother into launching the Bay of Pigs invasion, President Kennedy put the Attorney General on the White House panel to find out what went wrong with Operation Zapata. The experienced lawyer found that, as his brother suspected, the CIA had deceived the president. They had lied to him about its possibility of success, and then banked on JFK ordering in the navy to avoid a humiliating defeat. When RFK confirmed this, with the advice of his father's friend Robert Lovett, the Attorney General recommended firing CIA Director Allen Dulles. But after listening to Lovett, the brothers went further and terminated the entire upper level of the Agency: Dulles, Deputy Director Charles Cabell, and Director of Plans Richard Bissell. When is the last time something like that happened? Who was terminated over the catastrophe of 9-11?

How accurate was Robert Kennedy about the Bay of Pigs? It's always nice for a prosecuting attorney to get a written confession. As scholar Lucien Vandenbroucke later discovered in the Dulles archives at Princeton, Allen Dulles posthumously provided just that. In notes prepared for a magazine article, he admitted that such was his strategy: knowing the operation had little chance of success, he wanted President Kennedy to commit American military forces into Cuba. In 1984, when Vandenbroucke published an article in *Diplomatic History* on the subject, Bissell also confessed to this hidden agenda.

As more than one author has noted, after this, Bobby Kennedy became one of the president's closest foreign policy advisors, going as far as serving as his back channel emissary during the Berlin Crisis in 1961, the Cuban Missile Crisis in 1962, and in the implementation of the withdrawal from Vietnam in 1963.

Because of his position as First Ambassador, RFK understood what his brother had been attempting to do after the missile crisis, which was to form a rapprochement with both Russia and Cuba. After his brother's death RFK conveyed a message to the Soviets that JFK's plan for relaxing tensions would have to be placed on hold during President Johnson's administration; but he himself would soon resign, run for political office and then the presidency, at which point it would be continued.

For reasons minutely explicated in this book, that did not occur. But the real point is this: when one adds to the above his nine years as a congressional chief counsel before he became Attorney General, and his three and a half years as a senator afterwards, was there a better post-World War II candidate for president than Robert Kennedy? And if there was not, what does his loss represent to this country?

If the historians do not understand that loss, those around the event in 1968 certainly did. His funeral mass in New York was watched by over 100 million spectators via television. At that funeral, SDS leader Tom Hayden and Chicago Mayor Richard Daley both choked back tears. Jackie Kennedy had wept over his casket at a private wake, something she did not do over her husband's death. Two million people lined the railroad tracks to bid their final farewells as his corpse was transported back to Washington to be buried near his brother at Arlington Cemetery. When it got there, hundreds of spectators from King's last crusade, the Poor People's March, came to pay their respects. As Arthur Schlesinger revealed in his biography of Robert Kennedy, it was the senator who had given King the idea to bring the poor to Washington in order to force Congress to act. Which is one of the reasons King had decided to endorse RFK over Eugene McCarthy.

Robert Kennedy was the buffer that kept people like Hayden and Daley from savaging each other; he was the inspiration that made students and peace activists believe the Vietnam War would now end, who made King think that once that occurred, he would finally get economic progress in addition to civil rights. It all came asunder at the Ambassador Hotel in June of 1968. We then saw the results in August in Chicago, where the Democratic Party unraveled and caused the election of the anti-RFK, Richard Nixon. Vietnam went on for four more years and expanded into Laos and Cambodia, the latter invasion provoking one of the worst genocides of the twentieth century. Thus the tragic arc of the decade was completed. It began with a Camelot period of hope and ambition; after 1963 it shifted into the angry sixties of Selma and massive antiwar demonstrations; after RFK, it dissipated into an escape into the drugs and rock music of Woodstock.

But as Congressman Allard Lowenstein eloquently asked: Why did so many intelligent people accept Sirhan as the lone killer of Robert Kennedy? To the point that they could not imagine the solution being anything else?

Because the Robert Kennedy case became known as the Open-and-Shut Case. After all, there were dozens of witnesses who saw Sirhan with a handgun firing at the senator from the front. Therefore he had to have been guilty. And this is the pretext the LAPD and the district attorney's office used to snap on the cover-up—*for the public.* But as this book reveals, there was a lot to conceal to make the Open and Shut Case appear credible.

But what Lisa Pease shows in even more careful detail was the fact that Sirhan Sirhan did not get anywhere near the defense he was entitled to. Contrary to what people understand it to be, Sirhan's trial was not about the question of his culpability in the murder at the Ambassador Hotel the night of Bobby Kennedy's electoral victory in California. It was really about the state of mind of the defendant at the time of the shooting. As this book shows, Sirhan resisted this angle of defense. So much so that he said in frustration he had planned the whole thing for twenty years. From before he would have entered kindergarten, had he been in America then. Sirhan never got a trial on his guilt or innocence in the RFK case. His defense team assumed he was guilty. In this they were worse off than the prosecution. As the book shows, they at least understood the problems with the evidence. Sirhan's lawyers never explored those problems.

As noted, the trial was really about Sirhan's state of mind at the time of the shooting. Therefore, psychologists were allowed to spend hours on end with the defendant. More than one person observed how easily Sirhan was hypnotized. All the psychologists who have examined Sirhan have noted how quickly and deeply he could be sent into a trance state. And also how resolutely he would deny he had been hypnotized once he snapped out of it. The few people who studied the case began to reread the novel by Richard Condon published in 1959, *The Manchurian Candidate.*

Having lived in Los Angeles for nearly four decades I understand that during most of that interval it has really been a one-newspaper town, dominated by the *Los Angeles Times.* One can measure the *Times'* honesty and credibility by what editor Shelby Coffee ordered his staff to do to the late Gary Webb's stories on the importation of crack cocaine into Los Angeles through dealer Ricky Ross. (If you are not familiar with that episode, see the fine film *Kill the Messenger.*) At the time of the RFK murder, the *Times* was owned by the Chandler family. All one needs to know about that fact is that Harry Chandler was the model for the John Huston character in the classic film *Chinatown*. The scheme depicted in the film—the funneling of water to the San Fernando Valley from the Owens Valley—actually occurred.

Thus the *Times* was instrumental in the defeat of Upton Sinclair in his race for governor in 1934, and they backed Richard Nixon from the start of his career. They had always been close to the LAPD, and they fell into line on the RFK case. But it was not just the *Times*. Ben Bradlee and the *Washington Post* also did what they could to discredit those who thought something was wrong with the evidence in the case. Because of this media cover-up, most of the public does not know very much about the evidentiary problems in the case.

This book makes a quantum leap forward, in both the explication of the crime and the cover-up. Lisa Pease has found new evidence that is too abundant to list here. Some of it no one even knew existed. Some of it surprised even someone as jaded as myself. On one key item, she called me up at night and told me to come down to the library she was at to see it. It was so exculpatory of Sirhan that she thought it would soon disappear, and if so she needed someone to bear witness. I will not try to summarize the case presented here, but I will say this: if Sirhan ever got a new trial, this book could be used to set him free. I doubt a prosecutor would even bring a case once he examined its contents. Former California Attorney General and now Senator Kamala Harris would have been humiliated in court. Which explains why she resisted reopening the case.

Lisa Pease has labored long and hard on the Robert Kennedy case. She has been researching in the archival documentation and calling witnesses for 25 years. She had to. When a cover-up is this systemic it makes it hard to get at the truth. And it is a shame that a private citizen with limited resources had to take it upon herself to do so.

As her book shows, the RFK case was never an open-and-shut case. In fact, the Robert Kennedy case is more clearly a conspiracy than the John Kennedy case. As some have said: One does not need to commit the perfect crime to escape detection. One only needs to control the cover up. Which includes the mainstream media, which, disgracefully, is all too eager to tag along. Ms. Pease demonstrates that paradigm in a way that no other author has before. As I noted, the murder of Robert Kennedy was a milestone in American history. This book is a milestone in the literature on that case.

A LIE
TOO BIG
TO FAIL

HOPE

"This country is going to kill another Kennedy.
And then we won't have a country."

DRIVING THROUGH PRE-DAWN LOS ANGELES ON JUNE 4, 1968, veteran reporter Jack Newfield saw an inspiring sight. Large numbers of African-Americans, Mexican-Americans, and blue-collar workers were already in lines at polling places, waiting for their chance to vote for Senator Robert Kennedy in the Democratic presidential primary. By the end of the day, the turnout in Watts and East L.A. would surpass Beverly Hills, upending the longstanding political maxim that the poor don't count because the poor don't vote.

Kennedy had forged this unusual coalition through what Newfield wrote was the best political platform he had ever heard. "It's class, not color," Kennedy had explained during his successful Indiana primary campaign a few weeks earlier. "What everyone wants is a job and some hope."[1]

Hope had been dealt a body blow during Kennedy's Indiana campaign. On April 4, 1968, Dr. Martin Luther King, Jr., had been assassinated on the balcony of the Lorraine Motel in Memphis by a sniper.[2] King had been killed on the one-year anniversary of his first speech challenging the U.S. role in the war in Vietnam, a speech that changed his enemies from racists to the national security state.

---

1   Jack Newfield, *RFK: A Memoir* (New York: Thunder's Mouth Press, 2003), p. 8.

2   A civil trial in 1999 found that James Earl Ray, convicted for assassinating King, did *not*, in fact, kill Martin Luther King, and that government and "persons unknown" played a role in King's death. Jim Douglass attended every day of this trial and wrote an account that is included in *The Assassinations: Probe Magazine on JFK, RFK, MLK and Malcolm X* (Los Angeles: Feral House, 2003).

Despite pleas from his staff, fearing for his safety, to skip the Indianapolis event, Kennedy went to his prearranged rally, threw out his prepared speech, and delivered a hastily crafted one instead. As he informed the crowd of King's death, he pleaded for understanding, not hatred and violence. He reminded them his own brother had also been killed by a white man. And while ghettos all over the country burst into violent riots at the news, the ghettos of Indianapolis remained quiet that night.

The following day, with violence across the country still echoing, Kennedy quoted President Lincoln, warning that "Among free men ... there can be no appeal from the ballot to the bullet; and those who take such appeal are sure to lose their cause and pay the costs."[3] Years later, Newfield would describe how King's death became a turning point for Kennedy:

> Kennedy sought the Presidency in 1968, he said, and believed, because of the war in Vietnam. But Dr. King's murder, preceded as it was by Johnson's abdication and the start of peace talks, enabled Kennedy to glimpse the deeper roots of America's internal disease and to imagine himself as the healer of that disease.
>
> Kennedy had for several years been tormented by the poverty and unhappiness of the other America. But it was only campaigning for the Presidency, feeling the love for him among the poor, seeing his huge vote margins from slum districts, that showed Kennedy that his passion for the poor was reciprocated.
>
> This did not happen in one moment. It was perceived in action during the final weeks of Kennedy's life, as he spoke about poverty and racism, as he campaigned among the poor, and gradually came to comprehend how much he meant to them, and to understand that his career was no longer the private property of the Kennedy family, but that it also belonged to the dispossessed who cheered him with such hopes and voted for him in such numbers.[4]

Numbers were just what Kennedy needed today. He was still recovering from a defeat in Oregon the previous week. He'd lost in part due to a Drew Pearson column that ran the Friday before the election, which accused the Senator of having bugged Martin Luther King. President Johnson had leaked the story, with Hoover's permission, to Pearson.[5] The truth, however, was more complicated.

Kennedy had approved the wiretapping of King because he wanted to

---

3   Newfield, p. 249.

4   Newfield, pp. 250–251.

5   Evan Thomas, *Robert Kennedy* (New York: Touchstone, 2000), p. 379.

prove to FBI Director J. Edgar Hoover that King was not the Communist threat the Bureau believed him to be. Kennedy authorized, with King's knowledge, a wiretap on the phone line in King's office and home.[6] What Kennedy never approved was the bugging of King's hotel rooms. Kennedy handled the issue poorly with the press, and Senator Eugene McCarthy seized on it immediately. The result: Kennedy lost in Oregon.

Kennedy found the loss strangely freeing. Now, no one could accuse him of riding on the coattails of his assassinated brother, President John F. Kennedy. He'd win or lose on his own merits.

The morning of the primary, June 4, 1968, Robert Kennedy slept in. The day before, Kennedy had campaigned in Los Angeles, San Francisco, Long Beach, Watts, San Diego, and Los Angeles again. He had covered 1,200 miles in 12 hours before spending the night at the Malibu beachfront home of John Frankenheimer.

The choice of Frankenheimer would prove ironic. Frankenheimer had directed the film *The Manchurian Candidate*, in which a U.S. soldier is captured in Manchuria, hypnotized by Communists, and sent back to the U.S. to be used as a mind-controlled assassin. Before the next 24 hours were over, a consultant to that film would suggest on the radio that Robert Kennedy's assailant had been hypnotically programmed. Shortly before his death, that consultant would also claim to have been the assailant's hypnotist.

Kennedy hadn't even wanted to run for president in 1968, initially. He had feared his candidacy might split the Democratic Party if he ran against President Lyndon Johnson, giving the race to the Republican nominee. But Senator McCarthy demonstrated that the fissure already existed by his strong showing in the New Hampshire primary.

Kennedy wasn't certain McCarthy would be a strong enough candidate to compete against the presumed Republican nominee, former Vice President Richard Milhous Nixon, in the fall election, so he considered throwing his hat in the ring. He was still undecided when his friend (and John Kennedy's former speechwriter) Richard Goodwin put on a recording of the recent Tony Award-winning musical *Man of La Mancha*. When the song "The Impossible Dream" came on, Kennedy shouted from another room, "Turn that damn thing off. If you keep playing it, I might run for president."[7]

Kennedy formally entered the race on March 16, 1968. Two weeks later, President Johnson stunned the nation by saying that he would neither seek nor accept the nomination.

---

6   Arthur Schlesinger, *Robert Kennedy and His Times* (Boston: Houghton Mifflin Company, 1978), p. 360.

7   Richard Goodwin, *Remembering America : A Voice from the Sixties* (Boston: Little, Brown and Company, 1988), p. 479.

"Pick one out, they're all good dances," John Fahey said to a shapely girl in her late twenties who had come up beside him. The two stood looking at dresses in a store window in the lower lobby of the Ambassador Hotel, about 15 feet from a sign pointing up the stairs to the "Kennedy Reception" to be held later. It was about 9:30 in the morning.[8]

The girl asked Fahey if he knew where the hotel's post office was. Fahey didn't even know the hotel *had* a post office, so the girl walked off.

The Ambassador Hotel was like a city unto itself, containing a concourse of shops, bars, restaurants, the popular Cocoanut Grove nightclub, and yes, even a post office. But Fahey knew little about the hotel except the location of the coffee shop, designed by celebrity architect Paul Williams.

The hotel straddled two "ground-floor" levels due to a small hill at the eastern and southernmost ends. You could enter at street level, walk up or down a staircase, and still exit at street level, as if you were in an Escher print.

When Fahey had arrived at the hotel that morning, he had parked in the back lot on the southern side and hurried through the southeast entrance, as he was late for a breakfast meeting with a colleague. As he neared the entrance, two men caught Fahey's attention, because although they looked Spanish, the foreign language they were speaking wasn't Spanish.

From the upper lobby, Fahey had descended the spiral staircase to the lower lobby. He had been looking for his colleague when he had stopped in front of the store window and had his moment with the girl.

Figuring he had missed his colleague, Fahey walked into the coffee shop, sat at the gracefully swooping counter, and ordered a cup of brew. A few minutes later, the woman joined him at the counter. Fahey asked her about herself. Her answers were surprisingly strange.

She was from Virginia, she told him. But when he started questioning her about Virginia, she said she wasn't really from Virginia, but New York. When he asked about New York she mentioned Iran. Or Iraq. He wasn't sure, later. She also mentioned Beirut, Cairo, Eilat, and Aqaba.

The girl asked for Fahey's name, where he worked, what he did for a living. Fahey answered and asked what she was doing at the hotel.

"I don't want to get you involved," she said.

---

8   This portion of Fahey's story comes primarily from Fahey's interview conducted 6/12/68 by journalist Fernando Faura, a 24-page document found in the Los Angeles Police Department's Special Unit Senator (SUS) files. Specific quotes are from the Faura interview unless otherwise noted. Robert Blair Kaiser called this man "Robert Duane" in his own book to protect his identity. A few other authors on the case borrowed Kaiser's pseudonym of Robert Duane for Fahey as well.

Some have unfairly discounted Fahey as crazy because he referred to his talks with Eugene McCarthy, a reference, they thought, to Senator Eugene McCarthy. It's clear, however, from the tapes, transcripts, and FBI files that Fahey was referring to the FBI Special Agent who interviewed him, whose name was Eugene B. McCarthy.

One of Fahey's employers referred to the fact that Fahey's "honesty was unquestioned." The man does not seem capable of having invented the story he told.

"What do you mean, you don't want to get me involved?" Fahey asked.

"If I tell you too much they're liable to be watching me."

"Who?" Fahey asked.

"I don't know if I can trust you," she said.

Fahey noted she seemed very nervous, so they moved to the privacy of a table, where they ordered breakfast. He asked for her name, and she gave him a few different ones, explaining, "I can't go by my real name."

"I think we're being watched," she added.

Fahey looked around and saw what seemed to be the older of the two men he had passed on his way into the hotel watching them from outside the coffee shop window.

"Is there something I can help you with?" Fahey asked the girl. She told him she had to get to Australia to get away from certain people, and that she needed a passport. Fahey couldn't help with that. He had been in the service and hadn't needed one. He had no idea what you'd need to get one.

"Well, I know how to get a passport," she said, surprising Fahey. She told him that she could get a deceased person's name, use that person's Social Security number, write to their place of birth, get the birth certificate, and get a passport made with that information.

Fahey had initially assumed the girl was a troubled prostitute. Her comments, however, put things in a different light. His bigger surprise came with her next question. Could he come to the hotel tonight, to the winning reception, to watch them get Mr. Kennedy?

"What do you mean?" Fahey asked.

"Well, they're going to take care of Mr. Kennedy tonight."

At this, Fahey felt uncomfortable and wanted to leave, "but being a gentleman, we were having breakfast and I didn't want to cut it off or dump her. She told me that we were being watched and I did see this guy watching us."[9] He told her he had business up the coast. She invited herself along.

Fahey started to pay for breakfast but the girl beat him to it. She pulled out a wallet that had, to Fahey's surprise, a number of large bills—$50 and $100 bills. Still, Fahey felt strongly that a gentleman should pay, and he did.

He started to lead her out but she knew a different way, taking Fahey up a staircase he'd never seen before that led to the back parking lot. They got into Fahey's car and drove up the coast, past where Robert Kennedy was still sleeping.[10] The marine layer locals call "the June gloom" hung over the coast like a shroud.

---

9   Transcript of interview of John Henry Fahey by journalist Fernando Faura, 6/12/68.

10   At this point, the LAPD and FBI versions of what Fahey and the girl did for the next seven hours diverge. They converge again at about 7:15 P.M. that night. Fahey's day-long encounter with this girl will be detailed in depth in a later chapter.

It was late in the morning before Kennedy awoke. He phoned Dick Goodwin and invited him come out to Malibu to join his party, which included six of his ten children, his wife Ethel (then pregnant with their eleventh child), Theodore White, and Fred Dutton.

Despite the cloudy sky, Kennedy took his children to the beach. As the kids played, Kennedy and White discussed coastal pollution, the disappearing kelp beds, and which ocean was better—the Atlantic or the Pacific. (Naturally, Kennedy preferred Cape Cod.)

While Kennedy and his children were swimming, a large wave suddenly swept over his son David, pulling him out to sea. Kennedy dove into the dangerous surf to rescue him. Both could have died. A few tense moments later, Kennedy rose from the waves, bruised above one eye, clutching David.[11]

At the Ambassador Hotel, an unkempt, 47-year-old William F. Crosson, an Army Sergeant who had served in World War II, kept approaching the hotel desk in the lobby, where Donald Reinke and Gail Farrar worked, to complain about the lack of security there.[12] He mentioned how someone could hide behind the cameras and that they, presumably the Kennedy party, should be careful. Farrar got the impression that Crosson knew something was going to happen there.[13]

Crosson asked for a floorplan of the hotel but was refused. He took a sheet of paper, drew his own map, and gave it to Reinke. "He is going to die," Crosson said.[14] Neither Reinke nor Farrar got the impression Crosson was making a threat. He seemed genuinely concerned.

When Goodwin arrived at Frankenheimer's home, he found Kennedy stretched over two chairs by the pool, his head hanging limply, his body motionless, Goodwin felt a sudden rush of fear. Then he realized the Senator was only sleeping. He returned to join the others at the buffet. "God," Goodwin thought, as he served himself food, "I suppose none of us will ever get over John Kennedy."[15]

---

11   Theodore White, *The Making of the President 1968* (New York: Atheneum Publisher, 1969), p. 210.

12   SUS records list him as both Crosson and Crossen. The correct name is Crosson. Army rank and information comes from his 1969 obituary listed at www.locategrave.org/l/416580/William-Frederic-Crosson-CA, accessed 1/9/13. Comments from Farrar and Reinke come from SUS interviews of Farrar and Reinke. The SUS cardfile for Crosson has mistaken information in it, as is shown by cross-referencing with the other records. "Farrar got the impression ..." from LAPD interview of Reinke and Farrar on June 8. Both of them correctly identified Crosson from his photo.

13   Farrar's impression was noted in SUS I-85, which was Reinke's interview summary. The person who wrote the report noted: "Photos of Wm. Crossen [sic] were taken to witnesses (Reinke, Donald and Farrar, Gail) and both identified Crossen as the man who had left the floor plan. ... Miss Farrar states (Crossen [sic]) gave her the impression that he knew something was going to happen."

14   "He is going to die" statement from Officer T.B. Roberts in his property report, where he quoted Reinke's recollection of what Crosson had said.

15   Goodwin, p. 535.

Robert Kennedy himself was not immune from such thoughts. "I can't plan," he had said some months earlier. "Living every day is like Russian roulette."[16]

The campaign had shared a similar scare the day before. Monday morning, as Robert Kennedy's motorcade had worked its way through a crowded street in San Francisco's Chinatown, someone had set off a string of firecrackers. Kennedy and the rest in his party thought someone was firing at them. As Newfield recounted:

> The memory of Dallas flashed through the minds of the press. Was it happening again? … Ethel Kennedy, terrified, crouched down. But Robert Kennedy didn't flinch. He kept cool, refusing through will to show fear, shaking hands, waving to the people … The whole incident took perhaps ten seconds, but the next day we would all remember it, remember how close to the surface of our consciousness Dallas had been all along, how we all had a secret fleeting premonition of how the last passionate passage of Robert Kennedy might end. We remembered how John Lindsay of Newsweek had warned us … "This country is going to kill another Kennedy. And then we won't have a country."[17]

As the early projections started to come in, Kennedy joined Goodwin and White in Frankenheimer's living room. CBS projected that Kennedy would win 49% of the vote to McCarthy's 41%. "If only we can push up our percentage a point or two," Kennedy lamented, hoping to cross the 50% threshold. "We talked idly," Goodwin would later note, "as if the big victory were already in—not because we were sure, but because that's the only way politicians can talk." [18]

Thane Eugene Cesar, a self-described plumber at Lockheed's "Skunk Works" facility where the CIA's "Top Secret" spy planes were made, arrived five minutes late for his second job at the Ambassador Hotel. Cesar had signed up to moonlight as an after-hours security guard for Ace Guard Service barely a week earlier.[19] Dressed in his gray Ace uniform, Cesar reported to Fred Murphy, his commander and a former LAPD lieutenant, and William Gardner, the head of the Ambassador Hotel's unarmed, brown-suited security force, who was also a retired LAPD lieutenant. Gardner had asked for the additional help from Ace after realizing he was likely understaffed for the large turnout expected.

In Malibu, Kennedy and Dutton clambered into John Frankenheimer's Rolls-Royce Silver Cloud. Frankenheimer sped so fast down the Santa Monica

---

16   Newfield, p. 31.
17   Newfield, p. 286.
18   Goodwin, p. 536.
19   Philip H. Melanson, Ph.D., *The Robert F. Kennedy Assassination* (New York: S.P.I. Books, 1991), p. 85.

Freeway toward the Ambassador Hotel that it caused Kennedy some alarm. "Take it easy," Kennedy said. "Life is too short."[20]

As night settled in, the Embassy Room filled past capacity. Some 1,800 people milled about, chatting as they awaited the results of the California primary and what many believed would be Senator Kennedy's victory speech. Firemen and security officers shooed away supporters and campaign workers from the overflowing Embassy Room doors, pointing them instead to the smaller Ambassador Ballroom downstairs.

North of the eastern half of the Embassy Room and parallel to it ran a small food preparation area that would become known as "the pantry." The room contained three steam tables lined up along an east-west axis on the north side and a gargantuan ice machine that covered a large portion of the south side. It was not well guarded. Kennedy worker Judy Royer complained of having to constantly clear the room. Only campaign workers and press people were allowed in that area, but every time Royer entered, unauthorized people were present. Royer was concerned because this room was very close to where Kennedy would be speaking.

The Embassy Room rippled with excitement with each primary update. NBC reported that McCarthy was ahead in the initial count, while CBS predicted a strong Kennedy victory. Kennedy's biggest rival for the nomination, Vice President Hubert Humphrey, wasn't on the ballot in California. He was accumulating delegates the old-fashioned way, by lobbying them directly. He planned to make a play for delegates at the convention in Chicago.

Due to a newly installed IBM computer voting system, the vote counting had proceeded more slowly than usual. In the past, ballots had been counted by hand at the precincts all day so the tallies were nearly done by the time the polls closed. The tallies had then been called in and summarized at the county registrar's office. With the computerized system, however, the ballots had to be driven by truck from each precinct to the central computer in the IBM building, which happened to be across the street from the west end of the Ambassador Hotel. There, the new punch card ballots were fed into a computer to get the count. The new process significantly delayed the count.

In Suite 511, Kennedy and his aides strategized. Senator George McGovern called from South Dakota to give Kennedy an update on the primary results there. McGovern told him that Kennedy had received more votes than Humphrey and McCarthy combined. He had won both the Native Americans' and the farmers' votes.[21]

---

20   Robert Blair Kaiser, "R.F.K. Must Die!" : A History of the Robert F. Kennedy Assassination and Its Aftermath (New York: E. P. Dutton & Co., Inc., 1970), p. 15.

21   Schlesinger, p. 913.

Down the hall, in Suite 516, Pete Hamill, Jack Newfield, Budd Schulberg, Jimmy Breslin, John Frankenheimer and another 25 or so members of the press gathered. "There were no laptops, or cell phones, or BlackBerrys, or cable-television news either. So telephones rang insistently in the suite, were picked up, and names were called in stage whispers," Hamill recalled.[22] Hamill talked for a while to Frankenheimer about his film *The Manchurian Candidate*.

"Do you think it could happen in what is laughingly called 'real life'?" Hamill asked.

Frankenheimer smiled nervously as he glanced at the suite's door. "Yeah."[23]

As the crowd in 511 grew, people spilled into the hallway. At around 9 P.M., Kennedy walked out into the hallway and was immediately besieged.

"I like politics," Kennedy said to the reporters. "It's an honorable adventure." Kennedy asked if anyone knew whom he was quoting. No one did.

"That was Lord Tweedsmuir. Does anybody here know who he was?" Again, silence. Kennedy told them Lord Tweedsmuir was John Buchan, a Scottish statesman whose novel *The Thirty-Nine Steps* was used as the inspiration for Alfred Hitchcock's famous film of the same name.[24]

Kennedy retreated to his room. On and off, Kennedy mingled with the crowd in his suite until he had to leave for an interview with Roger Mudd of CBS.

Several floors below, in the Embassy Room, Sandy Serrano, a Hispanic 21-year-old "Youth for Kennedy" co-chair for the Pasadena-Altadena area, enjoyed the vodka and orange juice drink a friend had purchased for her. To escape the heat in the room, Serrano walked out the room's southwest fire escape exit, descended the metal fire escape and reentered the hotel's Sunset Room to listen to the "Viva Kennedy" band.

Somewhere above Serrano in the hotel, Roger Mudd grilled Kennedy on live TV.

"And you would not be willing to join with Mr. Humphrey in order to help the Democratic Party win—"

"In what way?" Kennedy interrupted.

"As Vice President," Mudd replied.

"In what order?" Kennedy responded, smiling.

"Well, I," Mudd laughed, caught off guard. Kennedy smiled broadly. Mudd asked if Kennedy would consider taking the second slot.

"No I wouldn't …. I'd be glad to help the Democratic Party, I believe in the Democratic Party. In what way, I'd have to work out … particularly if Richard

---

22   Pete Hamill, "June 5, 1968: The Last Hours of RFK," *New York Magazine*, May 18, 2008, nymag.com/news/politics/47041/, accessed November 29, 2015.

23   *Ibid.*

24   Newfield, p. 291.

Nixon is the nominee of the Republican Party, which I think is unacceptable to the country. And I have strong disagreements … with Hubert Humphrey and the positions he espouses, particularly what he said this week—that he'd step aside if Lyndon Johnson then decides that he wants to run."

"You thought that was fairly shoddy politics, I take it?"

Kennedy smiled and blinked when Mudd said "shoddy."

"No, there again—Roger!" Kennedy smiled and blinked again. "I think you're either in it, or you're not."

"Are some of the delegates that are listed as leaning or even committed to the Vice President, are they 'squeezable'? Are they solid?"

"Roger!" Kennedy gasped, almost blushing. "Your language! I don't like either of those expressions."

"Well … isn't that the way you talk—behind closed doors?" Mudd pushed.

Kennedy shook his head, talking over Mudd, who was starting to laugh. "I don't. I don't …. Probably somebody else does …." He would, of course, make an effort to win over the delegates, Kennedy acknowledged.

"Thank you, and I'll work on my language for the next time, Senator," Mudd ended, chuckling amiably.[25]

Throughout the interview, Kennedy came across as poised, charming, bright, and most of all, presidential. "If he looks like that for the rest of the campaign," Goodwin thought as he watched, "we might win."[26]

Michael Wayne, a 5'8" young man in his mid-twenties with dark, curly hair, sideburns and an olive complexion, tried to get into the Embassy Ballroom but was turned away. He walked unchallenged through the kitchen pantry instead and into the press area in the small Colonial Room just across the hall from the east end of the pantry. There, he managed to beg a "Kennedy Election Night Press" pass and a similar badge that read, "Kennedy for President – Press."

Wayne was not a member of the press.

Wayne clipped the two badges together with a PT-109 tie clasp he had already obtained from Robert Kennedy two weeks earlier at another event at the Ambassador Hotel. He had traded a PT-109 clasp in his possession for one Kennedy had been wearing. Wayne took two Kennedy posters, found his way to Kennedy's fifth-floor suite, walked brazenly through the open door, and begged a second PT-109 tie clasp from a worker there. He ordered a Scotch and water at the bar in the suite.[27]

Wayne was not a Kennedy supporter. He was not even a Democrat.

25   Quotes are excerpted from Mudd's CBS footage of the interview, June 4, 1968.
26   Goodwin, p. 538.
27   FBI interview of Michael Wayne, 7/8/68.

Elsewhere in the hotel, at around 9 P.M., a girl in a "white dress with dark blue polka dots" tried to beg a press pass off of Conrad Seim, a 50-year-old photographer. He would remember her later for her persistence and her funny nose, which he thought may have been broken at some point. She was between 5'5" and 5'6" tall, between 25 and 30 years old, Caucasian, with an olive complexion and dark brown hair.[28]

Between 10:00 and 10:30 p.m, Mrs. Eve Hansen and her sister Nina Ballantyne went up to a bar on the lower level of the hotel. They were approached by a Caucasian girl with a "turned-up nose," 25 to 26 years old, wearing a white dress with black or navy blue polka dots approximately the size of a quarter.

"You'll never get served at this end of the bar," the girl told them. "I've been waiting up at the other end, I know." The girl offered to bring them drinks. But Hansen told the girl essentially, watch this, got the attention of the bartender, and ordered drinks. The girl walked away for a bit and then returned with their drinks a few minutes later and offered a toast to "our next President," without naming whom she had in mind. Hansen noticed three dark-haired men sitting against a wall nearby and wondered why they were lurking there, in the dark.[29]

Around 11:15 P.M., Murphy moved Cesar from the eastern pantry door to the western one, nearest where Kennedy would soon be speaking. Cesar's job was to make sure no one without the appropriate credentials got into the pantry. But a number of people who had no business being there would enter the pantry under Cesar's watch.

By 11:30 P.M., the crowd in the Embassy Room was getting restless. It was very hot, and by now, the victory was obvious. They started chanting "We want Kennedy!" and occasionally, "We want Chavez!"

Cesar Chavez was the charismatic founder of what became the United Farm Workers (UFW). Earlier in the year, Chavez had conducted what would be the first of many "hunger strikes" to draw attention to the plight of the immigrant farmworkers in the pesticide-polluted grape fields. He had broken his 25-day water-only fast by accepting bread from Robert Kennedy, who had come to his side to support what Chavez was fighting for.

Kennedy had first encountered Chavez in conjunction with Kennedy's work on the Migratory Labor Subcommittee of the Senate Labor Committee. He had flown to California to attend some hearings on a strike Chavez had organized.

When a local sheriff who had arrested some lawfully picketing farmworkers spoke, Kennedy let the sheriff have it with both barrels. "This is the most interesting concept ... How can you go arrest somebody if they haven't

28   LAPD interview of Conrad Seim, 7/1/68.
29   LAPD taped interview of Eve Hansen, 6/17/68.

violated the law? ... Can I suggest during the luncheon period that the sheriff and district attorney read the Constitution of the United States?"[30]

Kennedy hadn't endeared himself to law enforcement with his comments, but the farmworkers loved him, and by day's end, the feeling was mutual. Kennedy defended the farmworkers against the charge that they were Communists, telling the press they were simply struggling for their rights.

"Robert didn't come to us and tell us what was good for us," Dolores Huerta, Chavez's lieutenant and the farmworker's chief negotiator, explained later. "He came to us and asked two questions ... 'What do you want? And how can I help?' That's why we loved him."[31]

Chavez had been both grateful and protective. "He shouldn't go too far," he had warned Huerta, "because it's only going to hurt him."[32] Chavez and Huerta were both at the hotel that night to share the upcoming victory with their beloved ally.

On and off, the crowd in the Embassy Room launched into what had become the unofficial campaign song, a Woody Guthrie classic, slightly altered:

This man is your man. This man is my man.
From California to the New York Island.
From the redwood forest to the Gulf Stream waters
This man is Robert Kennedy.

Let us stop the fighting, start reuniting
Increase our labors, to help our neighbors.
This nation needs now a man who leads now
That man is Robert Kennedy.

He walks with all men. He talks with all men.
In times of crisis he is the right man.
For peace in our land, for peace in all lands
The man is Robert Kennedy.

At some point during the celebration, a copy of these lyrics would end up in the pocket of a short, dark, curly-haired, olive-skinned young immigrant who was about to become infamous.

Upstairs, Kennedy talked briefly to Budd Schulberg, the screenwriter whose film *On the Waterfront* had won him an Academy Award. After the Watts riots

---

30   Schlesinger, p. 791.
31   *Ibid.*
32   *Ibid.*

in 1965, Schulberg had formed the Watts Writer's Workshop and the Douglas House Theater.

"I think you touched a nerve," Kennedy told Schulberg. "I think that workshop idea of yours is a kind of throwback to the Federal Theater and Writers Project of the New Deal. ... We have to encourage not just mechanical skills ... but creative talent. ... on a national scale ... I'll do what I can,"[33] Kennedy continued but was interrupted by the Speaker of the California Assembly, Jesse Unruh. Kennedy's victory was clear, and his margin was substantial. It was time to go down to speak to the crowd. As he left the room, Pete Hamill remembered the mood was light, "almost giddy."[34]

When Kennedy and his aides left his suite and proceeded to the elevator, Michael Wayne followed. Kennedy asked if the elevator opened to the lobby. He had nearly been mauled by crowds recently and hoped to avoid wading through them. Uno Timanson of the Ambassador Hotel's staff took Kennedy instead to the freight elevator, which opened into the kitchen area. Wayne and the press went down in a second elevator nearby.

Kennedy and his entourage walked through the kitchen into the pantry. There, Michael Wayne got Kennedy to stop and sign one of the two posters he was carrying.[35] Kennedy proceeded into the Embassy Ballroom to make his acceptance speech, with his entourage following closely behind.

It was midnight, in more ways than anyone could have known at the time.

"We want Kennedy! We want Kennedy!" The crowd's chants were deafening as Kennedy tried to get a word in. "Thank you very much," he said for the third time as he waited for the crowd to calm down. His wife Ethel stood next to him on the stand. He began by congratulating Los Angeles Dodgers pitcher Don Drysdale, who had just completed his sixth straight shut-out. "I hope we have as good fortune in our campaign," Kennedy said, a comment whose irony would only be evident after the fact. Drysdale's run would end in his next game. Kennedy's run would end in the next room.

Serrano returned to the Embassy Room after hearing rumbles of "He's here!" But the room was so thick with people, and it was so hot inside that Serrano took to the southwestern fire escape a second time and sat about halfway down the steps. She reveled in the moment. She had worked very hard on his campaign.

Serrano had originally met Robert Kennedy in D.C. in 1965. He had stepped

33   Schlesinger, p. 914.

34   Pete Hamill, "June 5, 1968: The Last Hours of RFK," *New York Magazine*, May 18, 2008, nymag.com/news/politics/47041/, accessed November 29, 2015.

35   This moment is captured in news footage and in a photo available at the California State Archives. See also Houghton, p. 153.

on her foot in an elevator by mistake and she had shoved him away. She'd kept a copy of the speech he had given that night, a copy he had provided to her.[36]

As she rested there, two young men and a young woman came up the stairs. "Excuse me," the girl said as the trio walked past her and up into the back of the ballroom. The two men could have been Mexicans, Serrano thought. In the darkness of night, they both appeared to have dark hair—one with straight hair and the other with curly hair. The taller one was maybe 5'7", a little overweight, with straight hair and wearing a gold sweater. The curly-haired guy was a few inches shorter than his companion, and seemed "borracho," she thought. Not drunk. Just messy...something. She couldn't put her finger on it, but he just didn't seem to fit in with the upbeat, well-dressed crowd.

The girl was in her mid-twenties, had light skin, was about 5'6" tall, and had a good figure. Her dark hair was done up in a bouffant, and she didn't appear to be wearing much makeup. She had a funny, turned-up nose. The girl wore black shoes and a white dress with dark polka dots.[37]

In the same southwest corner of the ballroom where the trio entered the Embassy Ballroom, Mary Whalen and her friend Felicia Messuri, both married to NBC executives, noticed a 6' tall, heavy-set, swarthy man in his forties in a maroon coat. He held something to his face that looked like a leather-covered small transistor or radio. Messuri thought his manner indicated a "sense of urgency."[38]

Kennedy thanked all who had helped on his campaign, joking with the crowd by calling his brother-in-law Steve Smith, who was running his campaign, "ruthless." Kennedy also expressed his gratitude "to my dog Freckles, who's been maligned."[39]

"And—I'm not doing this in the order of importance, but I also," Kennedy broke and chuckled as he realized what he'd just done, "want to thank my wife Ethel." The crowd went wild. "Her patience during this whole effort is," he said, turning from the crowd to say to her face, quietly and sincerely, "fantastic." She acknowledged his thanks with a beaming smile.

He thanked Chavez, Huerta, and Paul Schrade, the western regional director of the UAW. He thanked the students and others who had worked so hard on his campaign. He acknowledged the support of the African-American community,

---

36   FBI transcript of Serrano's televised interview with Sander Vanocur on 6/5/68.
37   LAPD interviews of Sandy Serrano on 6/5/68 at 2:35 A.M. and 4:00 A.M.
38   FBI 6/25/68 Airtel from SAC, New York to Director, concerning the 6/19/68 FBI interviews of Felicia Messuri and Mary Whalen.
39   While campaigning in Oregon a little over a week earlier, McCarthy had launched into a challenge regarding Freckles, Kennedy's beloved spaniel. "I have a dog. I think he's a better dog than his. My dog's name is Eric. I think that's a better name for a dog. There was another cocker spaniel that got involved in politics," McCarthy said, alluding to Checkers, the dog Nixon referenced in his famous 1952 speech. "Cocker spaniels have a hard time getting to the White House." New York Times, 5/26/68. Kennedy felt the need to respond in his victory speech. "Franklin Roosevelt said, 'I don't care what they say about me, but when they start to attack my dog ....'"

particularly Rafer Johnson, a former Olympic decathlon champion, and Roosevelt "Rosey" Grier, a former Los Angeles Rams defensive tackle, both of whom were serving as unofficial bodyguards. After the thank yous, he turned to the crisis facing the nation: the deep divide between those with the power and those without it.

"What I think is quite clear, is that we can work together, in the last analysis. And that what has been going on within the United States over the period of the last three years—the divisions … whether it's between blacks and whites, between the poor and the more affluent, or between age groups or on the war in Vietnam, that we can start to work together. We are a great country, an unselfish country, and a compassionate country, and I intend to make that my basis for running …. The country wants to move in a different direction. We want to deal with our own problems within our own country, and we want peace in Vietnam." A loud cheer burst out.

"My thanks to all of you, and now it's on to Chicago and let's win there." He flashed a victory sign and brushed the hair from his forehead.

The crowd cheered for a long time, whistling and hooting, waving hats, and chanting.

Just steps away in the pantry, Vincent DiPierro, an 18-year-old waiter and political junkie,[40] waited. DiPierro had not been scheduled to work that night, but his father, Angelo DiPierro, the senior Maître d'Hotel, had told him of Kennedy's appearance. Vince had arrived shortly before midnight in the hopes of shaking the Senator's hand.

In the pantry, Vince noticed a person who looked "sick," a short, Hispanic-looking young man with curly hair holding his hand to his stomach. But Vince's attention was momentarily diverted by a dark-haired, attractive girl with a good figure and a funny nose in a white dress with black polka dots. The curly-haired man said something to the girl as he stood on a tray rack, and she smiled. Vince thought the girl seemed to be "holding" him.

To thunderous cheers of "We want Bobby," Kennedy started to exit the stage to his right but was called to the left since his next destination, as decided by Fred Dutton during his speech, was the Colonial Room, where the newsmen of the printed press were working. The quickest way from either side of the stage to the Colonial Room was through the pantry. But by exiting to the back of the stage instead of the left, Kennedy was not following his unofficial bodyguard, former FBI man Bill Barry, who was waiting stage left. Barry had planned to walk in front of Kennedy to protect him. But Kennedy was now far ahead of him, unprotected from the front, as Barry pushed through the crowd, trying to catch up.

---

40   Vincent DiPierro told me of his interest in politics and how he had once interviewed President Kennedy for his school paper.

Karl Uecker, a hotel maître d', grabbed Kennedy's right wrist and led him east toward the pantry. As they passed through the swinging double doors at the west end of the pantry, Ace guard Cesar took hold of Kennedy's right elbow, guiding him forward.

Reporters Richard Drew and Boris Yaro were at the door as Kennedy entered. Yaro raised his camera. "Hey, Boris, you missed him," Drew said as Kennedy walked by. Drew and Yaro followed Kennedy into the pantry.

Cesar pushed people away with his free right hand if they got too close. Rosey Grier walked behind them, with Ethel and Paul Schrade trailing Grier. Taped to the wall was a hand-lettered sign that said "THE ONCE AND FUTURE KING."[41] The tiny room at that moment held, by the LAPD's count, 77 people.

At the eastern end of the room stood several people, including Michael Wayne; a girl in a polka-dot dress; a short, olive-skinned curly-haired man; and a teenage volunteer named Lisa Urso, who focused her attention on Kennedy as he approached. [42]

Kennedy's progress through the room was slow. He kept breaking from Uecker and Cesar to shake hands with many of the staff in the room, including Vince DiPierro, Martin Patrusky, and busboy Jesus Perez. Kennedy passed the large ice-making machine to his right, stopped again, and shook the hand of busboy Juan Romero. The room's three steam tables were lined up ahead and to Kennedy's left, along the northern side of the little room.

Vince DiPierro saw the young man who had been talking to the girl in the polka dot dress climb down from the tray rack at the east end of the ice machine, on the south side of the room, and cross north toward the Senator.

Uecker reclaimed Kennedy's right hand and turned to go. As Kennedy turned to follow Uecker, Romero noticed a young man approaching Kennedy. One of the waiters nearby, Martin Patrusky, saw a smile on the young man's face as he crossed the room. Urso saw the man from behind as he moved between her and Kennedy. As the young man moved his arm across his body, her first thought was that he was reaching out to shake Kennedy's hand.

Then she realized he was reaching for a gun.

Photographer Yaro saw two men standing next to the Senator move off to the right as the shooting began.

Richard Lubic, a TV producer, was an arm's length from the Senator when he saw an arm with a gun point at Kennedy's head. He didn't see a face, only a hand with a gun.

Frank Burns, a personal advisor to Speaker Unruh who was behind Kennedy

---

41   Kaiser, p. 25.

42   All witness comments in this chapter are taken from interviews they gave the LAPD and/or the FBI, unless otherwise noted.

with his eyes fixed on his back as the shooting started, focused on an arm and a gun to his right that was close to the Senator.

Uecker heard a pop and saw what looked like little bits of paper falling. Burns and Romero felt searing sensations on their cheeks. Urso and Vince DiPierro saw the flash of the first shot.

Kennedy threw up his hands, staggered, and twisted left.

Booker Griffin, publicity director for the Negro Industrial Economic Union, had entered the pantry at the eastern end just before the first shot. He heard two sounds that he didn't think of as shots until he saw a man with a gun. When he saw Kennedy throw up his hands, Griffin ran forward to help him.

Uecker felt Kennedy slip from his grip as he heard what he realized was a second shot. He turned back in time to see Kennedy throw up his hands and twist to his left.

Richard Drew thought someone lowered Kennedy to the ground. Dun Gifford, an administrative assistant to Robert's brother Edward, thought Kennedy fell unaided to the ground. Cesar reported that he had grabbed the Senator as they both fell. Cesar's clip-on tie lay on the ground next to Kennedy's outstretched hand, as if Kennedy had somehow pulled it off.

Roger Mudd said he was with Ethel at that moment. "And we heard these shots. It was like Hades—this screaming that was going on. It was absolutely unworldly. It was awful. You weren't prepared for it. … Jim Wilson, one of the TV cameramen, was absolutely going out of his mind. He was so frustrated, so frozen."[43]

Several besides Kennedy were hit by stray bullets. Schrade, who was just behind Kennedy, was shot in the forehead and collapsed to the ground. William Weisel, a 30-year-old ABC associate director, took a bullet in his abdomen. Nineteen-year-old Ira Goldstein was hit in his left hip. Seventeen-year-old Irwin Stroll received a bullet in his left shin. Elizabeth Evans was struck in the head.

Juan Romero knelt down to help Kennedy. A bystander handed Romero a rosary,[44] which Romero pressed into Kennedy's hand, wrapping it around his right thumb so it wouldn't slip off. Both DiPierro and Romero heard Kennedy ask, "Is everybody okay?"[45]

After the shots stopped, Lubic saw that the guard to his left was holding a gun that was pointed at the floor.[46]

---

43   Jerry Oppenheimer, *The Other Mrs. Kennedy*, (St. Martin's Press, 1995), p. 439.

44   In later years, Juan told reporters he had the rosary in his pocket, but in his FBI statement, which he signed, he said "A white man, age unknown, handed me a rosary and said, 'Keep this, Mr. Kennedy.'" FBI statement of Juan Romero, 6/7/68.

45   Juan Romero's numerous statements and Vince DiPierro's FBI statement of 6/7/68.

46   David Talbot, *Brothers*, p. 374. When Lubic later expressed concern to the LAPD that the guard had his

From the Embassy Room, the shots sounded like little more than balloons popping. Suddenly, screams shattered the celebration. People near the pantry door snapped to attention at emerging news. Necks craned and strained, looking in the direction of the pantry. Within seconds, a strange mixture of stunned silence and sporadic screaming ensued.

George Green had just entered the pantry from the west end when he heard popping sounds. He saw a girl in a polka dot dress and a tall, thin man running away from him. He noticed them because they seemed to be the only ones intent on getting out of the pantry, while everyone else was trying to get in.

Evan Freed, a freelance press photographer, was at the east end of the pantry when the shooting began. As people tried to leave the pantry, he found himself pinned at the east end. He also saw a girl that he thought was wearing a polka dot dress and a tall, dark-haired male companion run through a door to his right, out of the pantry. The door to his right led north into the main kitchen.

Ace guard Jack Merritt was near the front doors to the Embassy Ballroom, just outside the east end of the pantry when someone yelled that Kennedy had been shot. He drew his gun and ran into the pantry just in time to see a girl in a white dress with dark polka dots accompanied by two men, a tall, dark-haired man and a "short" male, run out of the pantry through a northern exit, into the main kitchen.

From the kitchen there were a number of ways out. One could go downstairs and out the building. One could cut through the lobby, behind or into the Embassy Room or into the Gold Room which connected with the Embassy Room. One could also reenter the pantry at the west end, and from there, enter the Embassy Room, and exit out the southwestern fire escape door. While traveling from the west end of the pantry to the southwestern fire escape exit himself, to ask the guard at the bottom of the fire escape to call an ambulance, 13-year-old Ronald Panda noticed a girl in a white dress with black polka dots and a ruffled collar in the Embassy Room. He wouldn't have seen her if she was behind him. Clearly, she was in front of him.

On the fire escape steps, Serrano heard what she thought were six backfires from a car. She looked around for the car making this noise. Seconds later, two of the three people who had passed her earlier came running down the stairs. The girl in the polka dot dress came first, followed closely by the man in the gold sweater. They nearly stepped on Serrano. The girl was shouting, excitedly, "We shot him! We shot him!"

Serrano asked, "Who did you shoot?"

---

gun pointed at the floor and not at the shooter, Lubic was cut off, told it was none of his business, and told not to talk to anyone else about this.

"Senator Kennedy!" the girl said as the two ran down the stairs and out into the darkness toward the back parking lot.

Serrano didn't believe it at first. She climbed down to the hotel's ground-floor level and asked a guard at the Ambassador Room (below the Embassy Room) if Kennedy had been shot. "You're drunk," the guard said, blowing her off. She next asked a group of people down there if they'd heard if Kennedy had been shot. "You're crazy," they told her. Despite their responses, Serrano had the feeling something was terribly wrong.

In the same southwest corner where the girl in the polka dot dress and the man in the gold shirt had just exited, the man who had been holding what appeared to be a radio or transistor to his cheek turned to Mary Whalen and Felicia Messuri, who had been sitting on a packing crate at the rear of the ballroom, and told the two women words to the effect, "You've seen me here all evening, haven't you? You witnessed the fact that I was standing here when the Senator departed. Remember, you have seen me here. Don't forget." Then the man disappeared. Messuri felt he was "trying to establish he was in her view when Senator Kennedy was shot."[47]

During the shooting, while pinned at what was likely the southeast end of the pantry, Freed saw a curly dark-haired man run out the door to his left chased by a person who was yelling, "Stop him! Get him!"

William Singer saw a man pushing his way through the crowd, carrying a rolled-up poster over a yard long, about 4" to 6" in diameter, with something black inside. Several people were now saying, "Stop that man!"

Joseph Klein and Patti Nelson were just outside the Embassy Room in the main lobby when they saw a man running out of the pantry carrying a package. Patti thought she saw a gun inside what appeared initially to her to be a blue canvas type of cloth that "could well have been a gun case." She described seeing "about six inches" of "a wooden stock of a rifle or a shotgun" protruding from the blue canvas. She was "quite sure that the wood that protruded from this blue canvas was definitely the stock of a gun."

Klein also thought he saw an object wrapped in some sort of blue material. The object appeared to be larger at one end than at the other. Klein tried to chase the man but he disappeared out the door. "My God, he had a gun and we let him get by," Klein said.

Steve Fontanini, a photographer for the *Los Angeles Times*, saw a man running through the lobby and, thinking he might have been the shooter, gave chase.

---

47   FBI 2/25/68 Airtel from SAC, New York to Director, concerning the 6/19/68 FBI interviews of Felicia Messuri and Mary Whalen.

Gregory Ross Clayton, a Rafferty campaign worker, was in the lobby on his way to the Embassy Room when he heard what sounded like firecrackers. Suddenly, he saw a man running out and heard someone yelling "Stop that man," so he chased and tackled him. Clayton recognized the running man as one of four men he had seen in a group with a woman in a polka dot dress earlier that night by the lobby fountain.

Ace security guard Augustus Mallard ran over and helped Clayton subdue the man. Mallard handcuffed him, a moment photographer Fontanini captured on camera. Mallard turned the man over to the police, who quickly learned his name was Michael Wayne.

Inside the pantry, the struggle continued. By the third shot, Uecker grabbed the small gunman and threw his right arm around the young man's neck. Uecker grabbed the gun hand in his left and tried to point it away from the crowd. Another maître d', Edward Minasian, grabbed the shooter around the waist. Uecker swung the man around and pushed him down onto the steam table.

Rosey Grier joined the struggle, trying to wrestle the gun from the shooter's hand. Rafer jumped in as well, as did several others, including Barry and Burns.

Robert Healy, a reporter for the *Boston Globe*, saw four or five flashes and heard the same number of shots. He jumped up on the steam tables and ran to the end, where he saw a struggle going on at his feet. It struck him as unusual that a man as large as Rosey Grier was having so much trouble getting the gun from such a small man.

Barry got the gun out of the shooter's hand and put it on the steam table, but the gunman grabbed it right back. Someone pounded the gunman's hand on the table, and the gun fell out. Reporter Boris Yaro reached out and grabbed it, but another man ripped it from Yaro. Amazingly, that gun—or *some* gun—found its way back into the suspect's hand, despite the fact that several large men were then holding him.

Andrew West, the news director for radio station KRKD, had entered the pantry just as shots were being fired. He instinctively turned on his tape recorder and captured the scene vividly. West would later tell the FBI he couldn't identify the shooter because his attention had been focused entirely on the gun, as his broadcast made clear:

> Senator Kennedy has been shot ... Oh my God ... I am right here and Rafer Johnson has hold of the man who apparently has fired the shot. ... He still has the gun—the gun is pointed at me right at this moment. ... Get the gun ... Get the gun ... Get his thumb ... Get his

thumb … Get a hold of his thumb and break it! … That's it, Rafer, get it. … OK now hold on to the gun.[48]

Grier finally wrested the gun from the shooter. Joseph LaHive tried to take it from him, but Grier held on until Rafer Johnson came up, at which point Grier and LaHive released the gun to Rafer. Rafer wisely refused to give the gun to anyone on the scene. He wanted to take it to the police himself.

Bystanders were pummeling the shooter. Speaker Unruh moved quickly to ensure no one killed the suspect before they figured out what had happened.

"We want him alive," La Hive and Grier yelled. People were vividly aware of how Jack Ruby shot Lee Harvey Oswald in Dallas just four and a half years earlier.

"We don't want another Oswald!" Unruh yelled.

"We don't want another Oswald!" West echoed.

On the stage of the Embassy Room, a man pushed his way to the microphone asking, "Is there a doctor in the house?" Men and women screamed and shouted, as Steve Smith asked people from the podium to "Please clear the room" so that medical people could get to the Senator and the other victims.

Dr. Stanley Abo, whose wife was a campaign worker for Kennedy, had already made his way into the pantry. He stopped at Paul Schrade, whom he mistakenly thought was Steve Smith, then moved on to Kennedy and knelt down beside him. Kennedy had a problem with one eye, but otherwise seemed "quite lucid," but his breathing was shallow and his pulse was slow. Kennedy looked around for his wife and called her name several times.

Dr. Abo felt for the wound and soon found a hole in the head just behind the right ear. He worried the slow pulse might be due to intracranial pressure, so he pressed his finger on the wound to stimulate the bleeding to relieve cranial pressure and to prevent blood from clotting there.

Kennedy grimaced in pain. Ethel found her way to his side, bringing a bag of ice, which Abo took and applied to Kennedy's head. "Oh, Ethel," Abo heard Kennedy say.

Elsewhere in the hotel, Lillian Butler, a hotel phone operator, called the police department. "This is the Ambassador Hotel. Do you hear me?" Butler queried.

"Yeah," Wayne G. Hathaway, a Communications Division officer, replied from Parker Center. "I hear you."

"They have an emergency … they want the police to the kitchen right away."

"What kind of an emergency?"

"… I don't know, honey," Butler replied. "It's some kind of an emergency. I don't know what happened. You know we have a Kennedy here tonight."

---

48   LAPD transcript of West's broadcast.

"Big deal!" Officer Hathaway said with obvious disdain.

"Do you want me to find out what it is?"

"Yes, please."

"Hold on." Ruby Ford then came on the line.

"Uh, my banquet maître d' reported that Senator Kennedy has been shot."

"He's been shot?" Hathaway asked in a very different—almost plaintive—tone. "What's the address there, please?"[49]

LAPD Sergeant Paul Sharaga was literally driving past the back of the hotel when, at 12:23 A.M., he heard a call about an "ambulance shooting" at the Ambassador. Sharaga turned quickly into the back parking lot and began setting up a command post.

During Kennedy's speech, Don Weston, a driver for the Kennedy party that night, had left the hotel to line the cars up to take the Kennedy party to a popular club downtown. He had tried to listen to Kennedy's speech on the radio, but there was a problem with his antenna. He got out of the car to fix it, leaving the door open so he could hear the radio. Suddenly he heard someone asking for a doctor. He realized he needed to make room for an ambulance and backed up his car just as the first policemen arrived.

Weston heard a group of people at the back of the hotel talking to the police about a man whom they saw running out the back parking lot. Some people in the crowd pointed in the direction the man had gone, and two policemen took off after him.[50]

Sergeant Sharaga apparently received this information, because he immediately broadcast a description of a suspect just before 12:29 A.M.: "Description suspect of shooting at 3400 Wilshire Boulevard, male Caucasian, 20 to 22, 6'2", very thin build, blond curly hair, wearing brown pants and shirt. It's a light tan shirt. Direction taken unknown." A response came back that the suspect was in custody, but when Sharaga asked for confirmation, he was told, "Unable to determine whether actual suspect is in custody or person in custody is the suspect."[51]

Jim Busch, a Students for Kennedy volunteer, had pulled into the parking lot on the southern side of the hotel with his sister Andrea and their friend Richard Rittner just as Kennedy's speech, which they had been listening to on the radio, was ending. They were still listening when they heard a commotion, followed by

---

49   Excerpted from the LAPD's transcript of the call, which the author checked against an audio recording of the call. In his book *The Killing of Robert Kennedy*, Dan Moldea mistakenly records the officer's name as "G.W. Hathaway," but the LAPD's cardfile shows him as Wayne G. Hathaway. Moldea also attributes the whole call out to Ruby Ford, but the LAPD's Final Report attributes the first half of the call to switchboard operator Lillian Mary Butler.

50   LAPD Interview of Don Weston, 9/12/68.

51   Communications between Sharaga, other officers and LAPD HQ are taken from the LAPD radio transcripts.

Smith's call for a doctor. Suddenly, the three noticed a male and female hurrying past their car. Jim threw his arm out to stop the man. The woman, wearing a long dark coat, hurried past and stopped a few feet away. Jim asked the man what had happened, and the man said he'd just shaken the Senator's hand when a man stepped forward, pulled a gun from his trousers, and fired at Kennedy.

Just then, they saw five patrol cars pull up. Andrea felt there was something strange about these two, so the trio told Officers J.J. Fedrizzi and L.E. De Losh enough to lead them to believe that the male and female were possibly fleeing the scene. Rittner described the male as "Mexican," about 5'9" and stocky, and the girl as having dark brown or black medium-length hair.[52]

De Losh immediately asked the Communications Division to seal off the area and broadcast the following "suspect" descriptions: "No. 1, male Latin, 30 to 35, 5'9½", stocky, wearing a wool hunter's hat with a small brim. No. 2, described as a female Caucasian. No further description."[53]

LAPD Chief of Detectives Robert A. Houghton was on vacation in Yosemite. He had left instructions for how he could be reached in an emergency, but no one apparently followed those instructions. In his absence, Inspector John Powers, the acting commander of the LAPD detectives, took control of the crime scene and gave primary authority to the nearby Rampart Station.

Several officers responded to the Ambassador call immediately, including Officers Travis White and the young police academy graduate he was training, Arthur Placencia. When they entered the pantry, they found Rosey Grier lying on the suspect to hold him down. Frank Burns had the suspect's legs and Uecker had the small man in a headlock. Unruh was keeping people off the suspect so no one could kill him before he stood trial. Officer White asked who had the gun. Somebody indicated Rafer had it, so White asked for the gun, but Johnson refused to turn it over at that point, possibly because he wasn't sure these were actual policemen. Rosey Grier didn't want to release the suspect to the police,[54] but White and Placencia were finally able to pry the suspect free.

One officer present as White and Placencia took the suspect away, Randolph Adair, told Dan Moldea years later, "The guy was real confused. It was like it didn't exactly hit him what he had done. He had a blank, glassed-over look on his face—like he wasn't in complete control of his mind at the time."[55]

As the officers put the suspect in the car, Jesse Unruh jumped, uninvited, into the car with him. The police car sped three miles in three minutes to transport the suspect from the Ambassador Hotel to the Rampart Station.

---

52   LAPD interviews of Richard Rittner on June 6, 1968 and August 21, 1968.

53   SUS Final Report. The initial report from these witnesses appears to be missing from the record, and a later account from these witnesses appears to have been, if not altered, at least edited.

54   Dan Moldea, *The Killing of Robert Kennedy* (W. W. Norton & Company, 1995, 2006 edition), p. 47.

55   Moldea, pp. 47–48.

The suspect was "very cool," and said nothing but "yes" to questions Officer Placencia put to him about understanding his rights, wishing to remain silent, and wishing to have an attorney present. The only time he said anything else was when Unruh asked the suspect the question everyone wanted answered: "Why did you shoot him?" The LAPD recorded the response as: "You think I'm crazy so you can use it as evidence against me?"[56]

In the car, the rookie Placencia flashed lights in the suspect's eyes. Placencia thought the suspect's pupils looked dilated and wondered if he was under the influence of alcohol or a drug. Placencia's partner, the more experienced White, redid this check when they arrived at the station a few minutes later, because Placencia had only looked at the suspect's eyes to make his assessment. White checked the suspect's eyes, then Placencia's, for comparison. White reported that the suspect's eyes behaved normally, that the man did not appear to be intoxicated.

When they reached Rampart, although the officers placed the suspect in the Breathalyzer room, the suspect was not given a Breathalyzer test. White left to inform the watch commander of their arrival. Unruh waited with the suspect until he was transferred to Interrogation Room B.

At 12:30 A.M., Kennedy was rushed by ambulance to Central Receiving Hospital, a police hospital which serviced criminals and victims of crime (and later became the site of a new Rampart police station), where Dr. Faustin Bazilauskas and Dr. Albert Holt examined him. Dr. Holt found two bullet wounds and recommended brain surgery and suggested getting Dr. Henry Cuneo.

Minutes later, the police radio chatter indicated confusion. One officer asked if there was a command post set up and if the suspect was in custody. Another officer responded, "He left there approximately five minutes ago. He was taken into … custody in the police car, and there was another suspect being held within the building, and I sent Nunley into—"

"One suspect in custody. One suspect in the building. Is there a supervisor at the station?" asked the first officer.

At the command post, Sharaga continued to communicate with Control. "Until I establish or at least have been informed at the C.P. [Command Post] that the suspect is in custody," Sharaga broadcast, "request you repeat the broadcast

---

56   SUS Final Report, 194. If the quotation is accurate, and not everything in the *Final Report* is, the punctuation is odd. If another question mark is added, i.e., "You think I'm crazy? So you can use it against me?" the double question implies that the person knew he was guilty and chose to remain silent. If no question marks had been used, the statement indicates that the suspect feared people would think he was crazy and therefore blame the crime on him. Punctuation matters, and without a recording, it's impossible to state with surety whether the ending question mark belonged there. With only the ending question mark, the meaning is unclear.

of suspect description I gave earlier this evening. Repeat at least every ten minutes on all frequencies."

Another officer responded. "The description we have is a male Latin, 25–26, 5'5", bushy hair, dark eyes, light build, wearing a blue jacket and blue Levis and blue tennis shoes. Do you have anything to add?"

"That's not the description I put out," Sharaga objected. "The description I put out was a male Caucasian—20 to 22, approximately 6' to 6'2", sandy blond curly hair, and wearing brown pants and a light tan shirt."

Several times throughout the first 90 minutes after the shooting, Control noted to Sharaga that his radio was "breaking up."

Ethel, Pierre Salinger, astronaut John Glenn and several of Kennedy's friends and aides gathered at Central Receiving Hospital, where Kennedy had been brought by the police. Kennedy was given oxygen and fed intravenously. But it was clear Kennedy would need brain surgery, which Good Samaritan Hospital was better equipped to handle, so Kennedy was transferred. There, Kennedy was given a tracheotomy to help his breathing. Two minutes later, Kennedy stopped breathing and was immediately put on a respirator.

The police prevented unauthorized personnel from entering the sealed fifth floor containing the Intensive Care Ward where Robert Kennedy was being examined. Several times, the police had to turn back people clad in hospital-type clothing. Not even other doctors were allowed in the ward without permission.[57] Their barricade was so effective they nearly prevented Dr. Henry Cuneo, one of Los Angeles' best brain surgeons, from reaching the Senator.[58]

Outside Good Samaritan, a somber crowd gathered. People lit candles, cried, prayed, and held their breath as they waited for word from the men battling to save his life.

Some 270 miles away, secluded in his private penthouse suite at the Desert Inn in Las Vegas, the eccentric billionaire Howard Hughes tuned in to watch the only TV station still broadcasting in his area at that hour, the CBS affiliate that he owned. He had watched Kennedy's victory speech and was still watching when the report came in that Robert Kennedy had been shot. He would watch the continuing coverage nearly nonstop for the next 26 hours.

---

57   SUS Final Report, p. 27.

58   Kaiser, p. 52.

NIGHTMARE

"I was concentrating on him because I saw the gun going like that, so I didn't really look around at that point. If I hadn't seen the gun, I probably would have looked a little more."

THE PROSPECT OF A SECOND KENNEDY ASSASSINATION WAS A nightmare. People were spread out all over the grounds of the hotel screaming and crying. Crowds of people gathered at the fountain the lobby of the Ambassador Hotel, sobbing and praying. Some dipped their hands in the water from the fountain and crossed themselves in the Catholic tradition.

Inside the Rampart Station, Sergeant William Jordan, the Night Watch Detective Commander, was dealing with a different kind of nightmare. He had been utterly unable to identify the suspect in custody. The dark, young, curly-haired "Suspect No. 1" had no identifying information on him—no business card, no wallet. And the suspect wasn't helping.

"What is your name, sir?" Sergeant William Jordan, the Night Watch Detective Commander, asked the suspect. The suspect did not answer.

Unable to determine if the suspect had been read his rights, Jordan gave the suspect the official admonition required in the wake of the Supreme Court ruling in the case of *Miranda v. Arizona* in 1966.

"I have to advise you that you have the right to remain silent; that if you give up the right to remain silent, anything you say can be used against you in a court of law; you have a right to an attorney and have an attorney present during any questioning; and if you desire this and cannot afford one, one will be appointed for you without charge before any questioning. Do you understand your rights?"

"Is this of the—what the officers told me in the car?" the suspect queried.

"I have no idea, sir, at this point, what you were told."

Jordan started to repeat the Miranda admonition but was interrupted by another officer on an administrative matter. The suspect asked Jordan to start afresh a third time. Jordan obliged. The suspect also asked Jordan for his name, even though Jordan had already given it. It was as if Jordan's words were simply not being recorded in the suspect's brain.[59] The suspect finally said he wished to remain silent. Jordan said he'd count the money from the man's pockets but the suspect did not wish to speak even to confirm the count.

At the Ambassador Hotel, Lieutenant Robert Sillings, the watch commander, arrived at Sergeant Sharaga's command post and assessed the situation. Many of the evening's guests wanted to leave, but the police wanted to talk to everyone, so Sharaga ordered arriving officers to create a perimeter around the hotel. Arrangements were made to bus witnesses to the Rampart Station for interviews.

Two members of the LAPD's Intelligence Division tried to segregate witnesses who had seen or heard something in the pantry from the rest of the witnesses. They took Juan Romero, Vince DiPierro, and other pantry witnesses to the Gold Room, a small room adjacent to the large Embassy Room.

Confusion reigned. According to a contemporaneous LAPD log, at 12:50 A.M., Lieutenant Sillings said on TV that the suspect, a 6'4" male Caucasian, was in custody.[60] The suspect Jordan was interviewing, however, was a foot shorter. Another log item stated the suspect had been shot in the leg. The suspect taken from the pantry had not been pierced by any bullet, although his ankle had been twisted in the struggle.

According to someone from Administrative Services at the Rampart Station,[61] there were "several suspects in custody." For the next 20 minutes, repeated references to the "other suspects" in custody were broadcast over police radio.[62]

---

59   These and all further quotes from the suspect and his interviewers are excerpted from the LAPD and FBI transcripts of the taped interviews conducted in the early morning hours of June 5, 1968, as well as the tapes themselves. There are some minor variations between the FBI and LAPD transcripts. Tapes of these sessions are also available from the California State Archives.

60   LAPD Intelligence Division Log of June 5, 1968.

61   LAPD call signs represent the division, the unit, and the officer type. "2 Henry," the code for the person who made this report, means someone from the Rampart division (2) who works in administrative services (Henry). Sergeant Sharaga's call number, 2L30, meant he was also from Rampart, was a lone officer (L) and was likely a field supervisor (numbers ending in 0 indicate a field supervisor, except for 10, which indicates the watch supervisor). "Adam" represents a two-man patrol car. "Boy" represents a two-man van. Call-sign information from www.freqofnature.com/frequencies/ca/losangeles/lapd.htm, which no longer exists as of April 2017, which credits former LAPD dispatcher Harry Marnell with providing much of the information.

62   LAPD radio transcripts and Philip Van Praag's transcription of additional LAPD radio traffic. Van Praag constructed equipment that allowed him to copy the LAPD's original 20-track tape recording at the California State Archives and separate out the 20 tracks. His transcription of the first 20 minutes after the shooting appears in an

LAPD Captain Hugh Brown and Detective Inspector John Powers arrived at the Rampart Station at 1 A.M. to find the suspect still unidentified. This troubled them:

> Thoughts of accomplices were much on the minds of both Brown and Powers. Had the man they were holding really been alone? Could it possibly be a foreign conspiracy? Could it be the first in a series of assassinations planned in the midst of national election campaigns in order to paralyze the entire nation? Or was this perhaps the second? Just two months had gone by since Dr. Martin Luther King, Jr., was murdered. As yet, there was no suspect in that killing. Could it possibly be the third? Dallas, Memphis, Los Angeles?[63]

Jordan was arranging to transfer the suspect from Rampart to the newly opened Parker Center downtown when he was handed a note with Sharaga's description of a 6'2" blond suspect. Jordan wondered if the suspect he had been questioning was, in fact, the actual—or only—shooter.[64]

At Rampart, LAPD detectives Michael McGann and Robert Calkins, who had only just arrived themselves, interviewed Rafer Johnson:

> I thought it was a balloon, the first shot, because I didn't see anything. I looked and then the second shot, I saw smoke and I saw like something from a—like a—the residue from a bullet or cap, looked like a cap gun throwing off the residue. And when I saw that I ... fought my way through .... By the time I got there ... the fellow had—I don't know how many shots. I couldn't count them, to tell you the truth, but I know it was like four or five.[65]

Sergeant Calkins asked Rafer where the guy was shooting from. "The guy was standing right in front of him," Rafer answered. This information caused a stir in the room,[66] presumably because the police knew by this time that Kennedy had been shot from behind.

McGann asked for the gun. Calkins inspected it. "Fired every one of them," he said. "No wonder everybody's laying on the ground." McGann and Calkins focused on the type of gun:

---

appendix in the book he and Robert Joling, J.D., wrote and self-published in 2008, called *An Open and Shut Case.*

63 Houghton, p. 32. Note that Houghton didn't mention the possibility of a domestic conspiracy.

64 Houghton, p. 14.

65 LAPD interview of Rafer Johnson, 6/5/68. Although the transcript indicates this conversation took place at Parker Center, other records make it clear that this conversation transpired at the Rampart Station, where Calkins and McGann interviewed witnesses all night.

66 The LAPD transcriber noted unintelligible overtalk at this point.

> McGann: We have an Iver—
> Calkins: Iver-Johnson—
> McGann: Iver-Johnson Cadet, model 55-A
> Calkins: More of these goddamn guns kill more people—
> McGann: Model number 50—number 56-SA. The serial number
> is H53725—
> Calkins: Eight shots expended.[67]

Calkins asked Rafer, "Everybody's interested—real, real big. Now, is this conspiracy? Is there more than one guy, and what do we have to prove it? That's the big deal now, so—"

"In other words, is there anything to make you believe there was another person there?" McGann interrupted.

"No," Rafer said, but he immediately qualified his answer:

> I wouldn't—not me. See, maybe—Rosey's a little taller than I am and
> was a little closer to the Senator. ... I heard the second shot and I
> saw people start to move and I just pushed my way through ... I was
> looking at the guy at this point and I didn't notice what was around. I
> was just trying to get to him. ... I really ... couldn't tell you anything
> about the people around at that point. I just wasn't looking.[68]

McGann took him through the whole event again, right up until he saw the second shot. "And then you immediately saw this cloud of smoke coming from where this suspect, who you ultimately took the gun away from, was standing?"

Rafer repeated that he had seen smoke as well as something else. He reported seeing "these particles flying in the air like, you know, expended—"

Calkins cut him off before Rafer could finish with the likely word "caps." From Rafer's description, it sounded as if the suspect was firing blanks, not bullets. When a blank is fired, a wad of paper—the "cap" that seals in the gunpowder—burns quickly, creating a little shower of paper ash residue from the expended cap. "It was your opinion at that time that somebody was firing a gun, is that right?" Calkins asked in an apparent effort to eliminate that possibility.

"Yeah, I thought it was a gun at that point," Rafer responded. "I still wasn't sure, but I just wanted to get up there, you know, and see what was going on."

"Anything else at all that you can think of that happened regarding the suspect or possible other suspect, or—anything that was said that led you to believe that there would be another suspect possibly involved?

---

67   LAPD interview of Rafer Johnson, 6/5/68. Neither Calkins nor McGann identified the model of the gun booked into evidence. The gun in evidence is a 55-SA.

68   LAPD interview of Rafer Johnson, 6/5/68.

"No, nothing," Rafer responded, but again, he qualified his statement: "I was concentrating on him because I saw the gun going like that, so I didn't really look around at that point. If I hadn't seen the gun, I probably would have looked a little more."[69]

At the Ambassador Hotel, KTLA reporters Larry Scheer and Stan Chambers described the scene. Scheer told the camera, "I understand—and it is purely hearsay—that there were…four men back there that were apparently waiting for the group to come out. Whether they were caught or escaped, I do not know."

Chambers reported: "Out here on the floor of the ballroom, we did not hear the shots, but we were told that there apparently were four men back there. One man who was standing near me a few minutes ago indicated that he saw four flashes—he thought there were flashbulbs. They may have been shots from a gun."[70]

On NBC, Joseph LaHive described what he heard: "I was directly behind the Senator, about three or four people behind him, when I heard the firecracker barrage of shots come off. We knew that it wasn't balloons cracking or anything—it was drastic—so we plowed through." He joined in the struggle with the suspect. "We wanted just to make sure that the suspect was not hurt any more than being held so he would be available for questioning rather than the incident that happened before," LaHive said, referring to the fact that Lee Harvey Oswald had been murdered while in police custody.

LaHive thought the shooter might have been Filipino and 30 years old. "I didn't even see the other suspect," he said, referring to reports of others. "I only saw the one suspect."

"It was almost like rapid fire. The guy must have just squeezed them off as fast as he could. … [I]f there were two people, that would account for the seemingly [sic] sequence of shots."[71]

At 1:30 A.M., Cartha DeLoach, Assistant to J. Edgar Hoover, the Director of the FBI, responded to a request from Ted Sorenson and Pierre Salinger to provide protection to the Kennedy family at their home. DeLoach also advised Los Angeles FBI Supervisor William Nolan that under no circumstances should the FBI "give the impression that we are investigating this matter,"[72] an odd statement for a high-level crime in which the suspect hadn't even been identified. That position would change in a few hours. Attorney General Ramsey Clark asked the FBI to

---

69   LAPD interview of Rafer Johnson, 6/5/68.

70   Both the Scheer and Chambers quotes are taken from KTLA footage I reviewed at the UCLA Film & Television Archive. A man was interviewed on camera who said he saw two flashes that he thought were flashbulbs, so it is unclear where the "four" number came from unless the comment was made off camera or by some other witness.

71   NBC footage.

72   FBI memo from Cartha DeLoach to William Nolan, 6/5/68.

investigate the crime under the Civil Rights Act of 1968 and the Voting Rights Act of 1965. An FBI codename of KENSALT ("Kennedy Assault") was designated for their investigation.

At Good Samaritan, X-rays were taken of Kennedy's head, neck, chest and right shoulder, all of which had been penetrated by bullets. One bullet had passed harmlessly through his clothing at close range at a steep upward angle. Another had passed through his chest from back to front at a similarly steep upward angle and exited his body.[73] A third bullet had entered his right armpit and lodged in the base of his neck. But the fourth bullet was the one that was worrying the doctors: it had shattered in his brain.

Kennedy's prognosis was "extremely poor,"[74] and the doctors knew they were dealing with an "absolute disaster."[75] Nonetheless, they began to prep Kennedy for surgery.

Outside the hospital, people gathered, holding signs, praying that Kennedy would recover.

Two miles away, Sergeant Robert E. Lindblom[76] of the Los Angeles Sheriff's Office led a squad of deputies, which included Lieutenant Beto Kienast, Sergeant John Barber, Deputy Walter Tew, and Deputy Tom Beringer, into the Embassy Ballroom. There, they met LAPD Sergeants Jones and Rolon. Together, these LAPD and LASO officers "formed a 'wedge' and ... cleared the crime scene. Newsmen and their equipment were moved only by the sheer number of officers and deputies."[77]

Inside the pantry, Beringer saw a man in a tuxedo "trying to take a bullet out of the wall with ... a silver knife," ostensibly "for a souvenir."[78]

After someone pulled the 4"x¾" pine wood door jamb casing off the front of the swinging doorframe, photographs were eventually taken by the FBI of two holes in the center divider and two other holes in the southern door jamb. The photographs showed that the holes were circled and labeled by Tew.[79] According to Barber, Tew may have marked the holes, rather than leaving them for the LAPD, on the assumption that the Sheriff's office would conduct the primary investigation. "[T]here were so few blue suits [LAPD

---

73   Some authors have tried to claim these were shallow angles. But photos of Dwayne Wolfer standing in Kennedy's position while Coroner Thomas Noguchi tries to hold up rods matching the entry holes of the coat with the spots where Kennedy was hit make a mockery of that claim. These photos can be seen in the Turner and Christian book.

74   LAPD interview of Mrs. L. Omer, R.N. 6/5/68.

75   Kennedy medical report by M. Bowles, p. 10.

76   The SUS Final Report (p. 207) spells his last name Lindblom. Dan Moldea lists his last name as both Lindblom (p. 66) and Lindbloom (p. 59 et al).

77   SUS Final Report, p. 207.

78   Moldea, p. 235.

79   Moldea, p. 234.

officers] there that we were really the only police in that area" for a period of about 10 to 15 minutes.[80]

As the men finished clearing the pantry, LAPD Sergeant Jones recalled seeing what he "thought might have been a bullet hole in a door jamb."[81]

At the Rampart Station, Calkins and McGann interviewed Dick Aubry, who worked part-time for the Negro Press Bureau. Aubry had been walking in front of Kennedy through the pantry. Aubry saw a short Caucasian male in a dark sports coat, about 25–26 years old, kneeling on the table, getting down as he passed him. Aubry had just reached the end of the first steam table when he heard something. He heard one shot, then five more in a spurt. "I thought it was Chinese firecrackers … it was just a constant … pow, pow, just cracking like a little bag of potato chips or something." He saw a flash, "like a little spark."

"Did you see this guy with the flashes coming out of his hand?"

"Oh yes," Aubry replied. He described how the gunman was six or seven feet in front of Kennedy at the time. "It was just the flashes I saw. I thought I saw somebody throw a firecracker right at him."

"Did you get … any indication at all that there was anybody helping this assailant who shot the Senator?"

"Booker Griffin asked me, should we take off after the other cat like this, and my first impulse was to say, 'yes,' but …"

"But by then it was all over?"

"Yes. But Booker said, 'Did they get the other guy?'"

Calkins and McGann took down the little information Aubry had on Booker Griffin, the publicity director for the Negro Industrial Economic Union. Despite this provocative information indicating a possible accomplice which the LAPD received from Griffin on June 5, the LAPD would not interview Griffin again until late July, and then only after Griffin had provided his own account in a local newspaper.

The FBI, however, didn't wait that long. Griffin told the FBI a few days later of a 6'2" Caucasian male he had seen a few times that night in the company of the suspect and currently in custody.[82] Other witnesses would provide similar accounts, which sounded remarkably like the suspect Sharaga had been seeking in his earliest broadcasts.

Over police radio, an officer asked if another suspect was still being sought. Control responded by rebroadcasting Sharaga's description of the 6'2" Caucasian male suspect. Sharaga added "Code 2 on that," indicating that the information should be given urgent attention.

80   Moldea, p. 234.

81   Moldea, p. 66.

82   FBI interview of Booker Griffin, dated 6/11/68.

Two minutes later, Inspector Powers got on the radio and asked Sharaga, "Where did you get your information on this second suspect wanted on the broadcast?"

"The second suspect came from a witness who was pushed over by this suspect," Sharaga replied. "Witness and his wife—we have name and address. The Juv[enile] officers who were collecting witnesses initially have a sheet of paper with the name and address of this witness."[83]

"What proximity to the shooting were these people?" Powers asked.

"They were adjacent to the room."

"Disregard that broadcast," Powers said. "We got Rafer Johnson and Jesse Unruh who were right next to him and they only have one man and don't want them to get anything started on a big conspiracy. This could be somebody that was getting out of the way so they wouldn't get shot. But the people that were right next to Kennedy say there was just one man."

Either Powers had been misinformed or he was deliberately misrepresenting, as neither man had said that, and Rafer had twice noted that, due to his focus on the man with the gun, he didn't look around to see whether others were involved. But Sharaga had no way of knowing that and dutifully followed Powers' orders.

"2L30 to Control, disregard my broadcast. A description male/Caucasian 20 to 22, 6' to 6'2"—this is apparently not a correct description. Disregard and cancel."[84]

Ironically, at nearly the same time that Sharaga's description was cancelled, two Juvenile officers, perhaps the ones to which Sharaga had just given the name and address of two witnesses shortly before, broadcast a description of a "male Latin" and a "female Caucasian" wanted "as suspects."[85] Despite Powers' best efforts, the door to conspiracy was about to be pushed wide open.

Deputy District Attorney John Ambrose was approached by Sandra Serrano as he stood outside the hotel's main entrance. She told him how a young man in a gold sweater and a girl in a polka dot dress had come by her saying "We

---

[83]   For years, Sharaga has maintained that an elderly Jewish couple told him of a girl in a polka dot dress fleeing the scene saying "We shot him." No evidence exists in the LAPD's record of this. Phil Van Praag, a sound engineer who examined a tape of the shooting in the pantry that will be discussed later, told me that the police radio was recorded on multi-track drums which would be nearly impossible to alter without some obvious sign. Several tracks were recorded simultaneously, so a splice or edit would have affected all tracks. I believe Sharaga may have confused this event—the report of a tall sandy-haired man escaping—with one relating to the girl in a polka dot dress. Sharaga, years later, told Art Kevin in an interview that he had taken down the name of the couple and handed it over on paper to other LAPD officers. Sharaga associates Powers saying "don't want to get them started on a big conspiracy" with the polka dot dress story, but on the police radio transmission, Powers' statement clearly refers to Sharaga's broadcast of a tall blond man. That said, there is still some backup for Sharaga's belief that he talked to a man and a woman who alerted him to another man and woman, a point which will be discussed later in this book.

[84]   Excerpted from the radio communication log, SUS files.

[85]   The description of this APB is as noted in the Final Report, p. 21. The original APB has never surfaced, although numerous references to it exist.

shot him." He took her contact info and walked her down to the Gold Room.[86]

Before Serrano appeared on the television, Vince DiPierro, who had overheard Serrano describe a woman in a polka dot dress, volunteered to Ambrose that he, too, had seen a girl in a polka dot dress in the pantry just as the shooting was starting.[87] Serrano and DiPierro had a brief exchange of not more than a few seconds before an officer interceded and said they should not talk to each other.[88] Nearly immediately, according to Ambrose, NBC's Sander Vanocur pulled Serrano aside and put her on camera.[89]

Ambrose asked one of the officers if that was a good idea, letting a witness talk to the press before the police had heard her story.

"I guess there's nothing we can do about that now," the officer told Ambrose.[90]

On live TV at about 1:30 A.M. Pacific Time,[91] Vanocur asked Serrano to recount what she had seen and heard. The distraught Serrano told the pre-dawn national audience:

> Serrano: Well, he, he—everybody was in the main room, you know, listening to him speak and it was too hot, so I went outside, and I was out on the terrace, and I was out for about five, ten minutes, you know, I started to get cold. And then, you know, and everybody was cheering and everything, and then I was standing there just thinking, you know, thinking about how many people there were and how wonderful it was. Then this girl came running down the stairs in the back, came running down the stairs and said, "We've shot him, we've shot him." Who did you shoot? And she said, "We've shot Senator Kennedy." And aft—she had—I can remember what she had on and everything—and after that a boy came down with her. He was about twenty-three years old and he was Mexican-American because—I can remember that because I'm Mexican-American—and I says, "What's happening?" And all of a sudden all these people start coming down that back end, and I walked in, and I was by the bar area and nobody seemed to know anything about it, and I thought well, you know, maybe I misunderstood or something.
>
> Vanocur: Wait a minute. Did this young lady say "we"?
>
> Serrano: "We," she said.

86   SUS Final Report p. 206.

87   LAPD interview of John Ambrose, 6/10/68. Ambrose did not know the young man's name, but from his description it is clear he is referring to Vincent DiPierro.

88   Author's interview with Vince DiPierro in 2005. DiPierro emphasized that he and Serrano had not compared notes on the polka dot dress or any other aspects of the girl. There was no time. According to DiPierro, their brief exchange transpired in less than 30 seconds. Serrano asked DiPierro if he had seen a girl go by saying "we shot him," and he told her had not.

89   Some records indicate this happened around 1:30 A.M. and others at 2 A.M.

90   LAPD interview of John Ambrose, 6/10/68.

91   Time is from Brad Johnson, former CNN producer, who collected live footage from the event.

Vanocur: Meaning, "We, the Mexican-Americans"?

Serrano: No. She was not of Mexican-American descent. She was not. She was Caucasian. She had on a white dress with polka dots. She was light-skinned, dark hair. She had black shoes and she had a funny nose. It was, it was—I thought it was really funny. All my friends tell me I'm so observant.[92]

When she finished, the police wanted to question Serrano at Rampart Station. Serrano asked Ambrose to come with her. She also asked him to call her aunt and uncle to tell them she was all right. Ambrose made the call and then drove to Rampart to join Serrano, but when he arrived, the police told him he was not needed.[93]

Back at Parker Center, in Room 318, the suspect faced John Howard of the Los Angeles County District Attorney's office, Jordan, Sergeant A.B. Melendres (another detective from Rampart), and George Murphy from the D.A.'s office. Like the others before him, Howard informed the suspect of his rights. "Do you understand your rights, first of all?"

"Yes. I think that I shall remain incognito," the suspect replied.

Howard gave the suspect his number and asked him to call any time, day or night, if he wanted to reach him. Howard explained what was ahead for the suspect.

"You will be booked. That's a legal procedure. Fingerprints, pictures taken, everything like that. After that time, I'm sure you will be able to clean up."

Oddly, the suspect seemed not to care about any of that. He wanted to talk about something else. "How long have you been with the D.A.'s office, Mr. Murphy?" the suspect asked. "Remember Kirschke?"

A year earlier, Los Angeles Deputy District Attorney Jack Kirschke had been found guilty of two counts of murder for killing his wife and her lover, a charge Kirschke had vigorously denied.

Howard wondered why the suspect was so interested in the Kirschke case. He told the suspect they'd take up the subject again and ended the conversation.

At the Ambassador Hotel, the LAPD criminalist who had presented key evidence at Kirschke's trial, Officer DeWayne Wolfer, reported to Sergeant James MacArthur in the pantry. Wolfer had called in LAPD photographer Charles Collier and Sergeant William Lee to help him. Collier was assigned to photograph, among other items, "bullet holes."[94] For the next few hours, Wolfer and his team, on behalf

---

92   LAPD transcript of the broadcast. I added some punctuation to the transcription to make her statement more readable. The added punctuation does not alter the meaning of the text.

93   LAPD interview of John Ambrose, 6/10/68.

94   LAPD interview of Charles Collier, 10/7/68.

of the LAPD's Special Investigation Division (SID), scoured the scene of the crime, collecting what evidence they could and photographing anything of significance.

Outside the Ambassador Hotel, Deputy H. J. Foster, who had been patrolling the patio area east of the Palm Court, saw a man step out of the bushes. Foster asked him what he was doing there. The 24-year-old Terry Lee Fraser became nervous and evasive and denied walking in the bushes. Foster apprehended Fraser and took him to the Sheriff's command post at the IBM building for questioning, where he released him to Sergeant D.G. Fossey's custody, who contacted Sharaga by radio.[95] Sergeant Davis of the Sheriff's office wanted an LAPD unit to meet him at the IBM unit to interview this suspect. Sharaga responded that there'd be about a five-minute delay getting officers to the building.

Sharaga then tried to notify Lieutenant Sillings that a Sheriff's unit at the IBM building had "some people to be interviewed" and asked if they should be brought back to the Command Post. But immediately after Sharaga mentioned sending officers to the IBM building, Sharaga's Command Post communications went out for the next 21 minutes.[96] Someone had left a microphone on that interfered with the Command Post's channel.

Officer A.D. Bollinger and LASO deputies Wernicke and Foster brought Fraser to the Command Post. After Sharaga's communications were restored, Sharaga asked Shillings over the radio, "What they believe is a suspect—do you want him in there or do you want him taken to Rampart?"

"Take him to Rampart," Sillings responded. Fraser, the third known suspect apprehended that night, was taken to the Rampart Station, where he was fingerprinted, photographed, interviewed, and held until 6 A.M.[97]

Back at Rampart Station, McGann and Calkins interviewed Thane Cesar, the security guard who had been at Kennedy's right elbow when the shooting started. Cesar told them he worked days at Lockheed but also did assignments for Ace Security. He gave them his manager Tom Spangler's home number, as Spangler was the one who had asked him to come to the Ambassador Hotel that night. Today, people's home number and work number are often the same, a cell phone number. But in the 1960s, people had different landline numbers for their workplace and home. It was odd then that Cesar had Spangler's home number at the ready, but not his office number.

Cesar described that when Kennedy had entered the pantry after his speech, Cesar had grabbed Kennedy's right elbow with his left hand and stayed with him.

---

95   Final Report, p. 211.

96   LAPD Radio logs.

97   Fraser's strange story will be covered in a later chapter. It's worth nothing that although I call Fraser the "third" suspect arrested, as we saw from the radio traffic, additional "other suspects" may also have been in custody.

As they had reached the first steam table, Kennedy turned to his left. "When he did, my hand broke loose—sort of broke loose from his arm, and, of course, I grabbed it again because people were still all over the place. ... I just happened to look up and that's when I seen—all I could see was an arm and a gun. ... And I reached for mine, but it was too late. He had done fired and when he did, I ducked because I was as close as Kennedy was, and from what I can remember, from what I did, I grabbed for the Senator[98] and fell back and when I hit—there's iceboxes right here...and I fell against that and then the Senator fell right down in front of me."[99]

According to Cesar, the gunman was "standing behind the camera crews and all I could see was his hand and the gun." Cesar didn't think it sounded like a .38 and guessed the gun was a .22. Cesar didn't recognize the gun, saying he'd seen only the end of the barrel. He suspected the gunman was short because he hadn't seen his face—only an arm sticking out from the crowd.

At 2:15 A.M., the primary suspect was booked at the Central Jail, charged with 217 PC—Assault with Intent to Commit Murder.[100] In the nearby police headquarters, Jordan, Howard and Murphy sat down with Jesse Unruh. "I must have been 20 to 30 feet behind him," Unruh said, as he entered the pantry. "I heard this crackle of what I thought was [sic] really firecrackers, and I don't really quite remember how many reports there were. I'd guess—it sounded to me like somewhere between five and ten—but there was such a sharp crackle that I couldn't distinguish the individual reports." He hadn't seen the actual shooting.

At Rampart Station, Calkins and McGann continued to interview witnesses. Estelyn Duffy had been with her friend Joseph LaHive (whom NBC interviewed earlier) in the hallway between the stage and the swinging doors through which Kennedy entered the pantry. Kennedy entered the pantry just ahead of them, after which Duffy heard what she later learned were shots. "They weren't real loud, sounded like a whip going." She told them, "I thought I heard at least ten shots.... It wasn't one or two. It was a lot of shots."

The suspect's gun could only hold eight bullets.

At the sound of the shots, LaHive had rushed into the room and joined the struggle to get the gun from the suspect. He told Calkins and McGann, "in my own rash conclusion at the time...this many shots couldn't have come from this little revolver."

The police were particularly interested in obtaining any photos from the event. Did the police want the photos so they could do a thorough investigation?

98   LAPD interview of Thane Cesar, 6/5/68. The transcript here says "I grabbed for the center" but I think that was a phonetic mistake. I believe he said "Senator."
99   LAPD interview of Thane Cesar, 6/5/68.
100   Final Report, p. 310.

Or did the police want to control all photographs lest something suggesting a conspiracy leak out?

High school student Scott Enyart had been standing on a table in the pantry, waiting for Kennedy so he could take his picture, when the shooting began. He took pictures "while the shots were being fired" or "maybe a little afterward," he wasn't sure. He jumped up on one of the steam tables so he had a good view of the room. Enyart mentioned his friend Brent Gold was there with him, taking pictures as well. Enyart wanted to know if he'd get his pictures back, stressing they were very important to him. He was told he might get back prints or negatives, but the police weren't sure which. McGann gave him his card and told Enyart to call back "maybe Thursday or Friday" and they'd let him know the status of his pictures. Forty years later, Enyart would win a lawsuit against the LAPD over this film, but as the film was ostensibly being returned to him, it was stolen from the courier's car.

Hotel maître d' Eddie Minasian told Calkins and McGann he had been standing to the right of Kennedy and slightly in front of him as the shooting began. Kennedy had just finished shaking someone's hand when a man came up and reached around his left. He fired two or three shots before Minasian and Karl Uecker grabbed him. Uecker had been ahead and to the right of Kennedy by about four to five feet, according to Minasian. He had been leading him through the pantry but Kennedy broke away to shake hands. Minasian said Kennedy "took a step back to shake hands with personnel"[101] when Minasian saw someone reach around past Uecker with a gun. He "saw two shots fired" and then Uecker grabbed him. Minasian jumped forward to help but turned to look back. He saw Paul Schrade fall, then Kennedy. He helped Uecker subdue the suspect.

Calkins asked which hand the gun was in, and Minasian said the man's right hand. The man was standing to the front left of Kennedy when he fired. "It sounded like firecrackers going off."

Calkins showed Minasian the gun and asked if that was the one he remembered. It looked similar, Minasian said. Minasian said Rafer Johnson kept asking "Why did you do it?" and the shooter kept answering, "Let me explain."

Minasian pointed Uecker out to Calkins and McGann, as Uecker was sitting just outside the room where they were talking.

When Calkins and McGann interviewed Uecker later, Uecker confirmed the shooter was "right in front of me" and that both of them were in front of Kennedy. "I think he must have covered the gun with something, paper or something, 'cause the first [sic] I didn't see no gun; then I saw something white, either paper or something, and I heard a shot.... I didn't even realize at the first shot that it was a gun but by the second shot, I turned around and saw Kennedy

---

101   LAPD interview of Edward Minasian, 6/5/68.

falling down out of my hand and then at the time that I realized it must have been a gun, then I grabbed him...."[102]

McGann asked, "Did he sort of reach around you to shoot the Senator?"—information he had just heard from Minasian.

"Yes, I think he was right in front of me because the way he—he was right in front of me, right in front. He turned around and shot with his right hand."

McGann showed him the gun and asked if the gun "appears to be similar to the one you saw?"

"I tell you the truth, I don't think it was that big, but could be. I really don't—"

"You're not sure?"

"No, I'm not sure because I didn't pay too much attention to the gun."

Both Minasian and Uecker described the man's suit as a "work suit," that was "dark" and "blue." "I thought it was one of our banquet workers because he had a blue suit on, a dark suit on," Uecker explained. "I thought it was one of the busboys, one of the housemen."

The suspect the police had been interviewing had been apprehended wearing a light blue velour shirt that zipped at the neck over a light shirt, with light blue denim pants.

Jesus Perez had seen the suspect in the pantry for about a half-hour before Kennedy had walked through there en route to the stage. The suspect had asked several times whether Kennedy would be coming through there, but Perez couldn't answer because he didn't know.

Perez said the gun he had seen was quite large. When Calkins and McGann showed him the gun and asked if that was the size he remembered, Perez said, "No, I think it's bigger than that." He indicated with his hands how big the gun had looked.

"You thought it was about a foot long, a foot?"

"Yeah."

Perez described the suspect as a bit taller than himself. Perez was only 5'2". When the police asked Perez if he'd recognize him if he saw him again, Perez said, "I don't want to get involved because, you know, I don't have no [protection] in the street...You get me in the street, they are going to [unintelligible] me."[103] Apparently, Perez feared retribution from some unidentified conspirator.

Elsewhere at Rampart, Sergeant Jack Chiquet and Sergeant Henderson of the homicide division interviewed Sandra Serrano about the girl in the polka dot dress. Serrano described how she had been standing on the fire escape stairs outside the southwest exit from the Embassy Ballroom, when "a girl in

---

102   LAPD interview of Karl Uecker, 6/5/68.

103   LAPD transcripts of recorded interviews with Jesus Perez, 6/5/68.

a white dress, a Caucasian, dark brown hair, about five-six, medium height" with "black polka dots on [her] dress" walked up the stairs past her. With the girl was "a young man" about 23 years old "who had on a white shirt, a gold sweater, and he was of Mexican-American descent." A third man "had on rather messed-up clothes" and "a lot of hair. He looked like he needed a haircut or something. And to me he looked like … somebody who, you know, just never looks right." She described the third man as Mexican-American, between 5'2" and 5'5" tall.

Serrano described how, about 15 to 20 minutes later,[104] the girl and the male in the gold sweater came running back out with the girl saying "We shot Kennedy." Serrano described calling her parents and how she didn't know if Kennedy had really been shot until she heard people in the hallway outside her phone booth confirm that Kennedy had been shot and was in critical condition. She ended the call with her mother abruptly to find out about Kennedy's condition.

Henderson asked if she had heard gunfire. "Yes," she said, adding immediately, "I didn't know it was a gun. I thought it was the backfire of a car."

Henderson asked for more details on the girl. Serrano said the girl had a "funny nose," "turned up like…a pixy [sic] nose." She appeared to be 23–26 years old, 5'6" inches tall, 122–127 pounds, with short hair and brown eyes. She didn't seem to be wearing a lot of makeup. Serrano was very specific about the dress: it was a "white voile dress with black polka dots on it and a bib collar."

Henderson asked for more details on the man in the gold sweater, Serrano remember his hair was "greasy," "long on top," and "combed straight. It was very straight…." The sweater was a cardigan, he was wearing dark pants. His height was about five-five or five-six, and she guessed his weight to be around 160 pounds.

After her interview concluded, an All Points Bulletin (APB) was issued to all agencies requesting information on a "female Caucasian 23–27, 5'6", wearing a white voile dress with small black polka dots, three-quarter sleeves, and wearing heels" and a "male, Mexican-American, 23, wearing a gold sweater."[105] As word of this female suspect spread, the LAPD and FBI began asking all witnesses if they had seen a girl in a polka dot dress.

As Robert Houghton, the LAPD Chief of Detectives, would later note, this

---

104   LAPD 6/5/68 2:35 A.M. interview transcript of Sandra Serrano. At the start of the interview she said she saw the girl came running down two to three minutes "later," but in the same interview she makes it clear the interval was 15–20 minutes. I believe she meant she saw the girl and her companion again two to three minutes after she heard noises that made Serrano assume Kennedy had just come down. More likely, the commotion she heard was stemming from the news Kennedy had been shot.

105   I have not seen a copy of this particular APB, mentioning the girl's male companion, in the official record. It was captured for posterity, however, in Robert Houghton's account of these events in *Special Unit Senator* (p. 31). Houghton's co-author, Theodore Taylor, was given unprecedented access to LAPD records to write his account. Ironically, because of this, the LAPD in later years had no case in arguing for continued withholding of their files, since they had already been shared with civilian Taylor. I found several copies of a second APB, mentioning the girl but not the male in the gold sweater, issued not long after this one, which remained in effect for several days. I

information made the suspect's silence even more disturbing:

> The first four hours are the most crucial in any homicide investigation; if the guilty are not apprehended or identified by then, they may never be found. It has proven true in case after case.
>
> [Captain] Brown knew very well that the "polka-dot girl" and her "boy friend" [sic] could be north of Santa Barbara by now, or heading toward the Arizona line, or within the time factor, already across the Mexican border. The All Points Bulletin would reach agencies in every direction, covering California and parts of Arizona and Nevada."[106]

Brown's and Houghton's professed concerns didn't manifest, however, in what followed. Within a few hours, the APB regarding the girl in the polka dot dress and the male in the gold sweater had been altered. The reference to a young man in a gold sweater disappeared. The APB for the girl in the polka dot dress, however, would remain in effect for two more weeks.[107]

At 3 A.M., Howard rushed back to Central Jail. The suspect had asked to talk to him. Howard was hoping the suspect was ready to reveal his identity. The suspect, however, simply wanted to talk more about the Kirshke case. The suspect was interested not in the specifics but in the philosophical issue of how the man had found himself at the end of the same law he had used to convict others. He discussed this question with Howard and Jordan:

"When you are the prosecutor and you want the other man's life—you're thirsty—you're hungering for his blood, and yet you are thrown in his position... how would you want... the man that's prosecuting you to react?"

"Oh, I don't know. I'd—let me ask you this. How much do you think?"

"I asked the first question," the suspect replied, seizing control of the conversation. "You answer first."

Jordan said people expect fairness and justice. The suspect went on to ask another extraordinary question: "Supposing a defendant was in fact innocent of an accusation of—whatever you call it, and Jack Kirschke demanded his life as restitution for his crime or the thing—the wrong he did...Would you consider...that a request for his life would in some way recompense the innocent lives that he had requested?"

Jordan and Howard both recognized that something extraordinary was going on here. The suspect, who had ostensibly just killed the second Kennedy with presidential aspirations in five years, was calmly discussing the philosophy of justice. Something about all of this prompted Howard to switch gears and ask a

---

have no doubt that Taylor was quoting verbatim from the actual APB.

106   Houghton, pp. 31–32.

107   This APB can be found in the LAPD's files.

very different question of the suspect.

"You know where we are now? I've told you you've been booked."[108]

"I don't know," the suspect responded, justifying Howard's question.

"You are in custody. You've been booked. You understand what I've been—"

The suspect interrupted with something unintelligible, followed by, "I have been before a magistrate, have I or have I not?"

"No, you have not," Howard responded. "You will be taken before a magistrate as soon as possible. Probably will be tried. ... You're downtown Los Angeles in the Central Jail. ... This is the Main Jail for the L.A. Police Department. You'll be booked into a cell.... Do you understand where you are?"

"As long as you say it," was the suspect's strange response.

Howard tried a last time to elicit the man's name. "If I were going to call you something, what would I call you? George, or Pete, or what?"

The suspect said to call him John Doe, having learned of that generic name from one of his LAPD guardians. The suspect asked about Howard's daughter and if she would attend Vassar. Howard, however, was only interested in getting on with the case, and left, saying he was going to go back to sleep "because I am inherently lazy."

"Inherently," the suspect echoed, teasing, "You shouldn't be a D.A.'s assistant."

The suspect asked Howard if he ever played the stock market. "Tell me about it, you seem to be wealthy enough to ... want to speculate in it."

"I don't know anything about it," Howard responded.

"Really?" the suspect asked. "Gee, I mean in legal cases, how—I mean, doesn't the stock or the finances come in at all?"

"There are much darker things than that that come in," Howard said cryptically. "You'd be surprised."

Howard prepared to leave, making certain that the suspect had his number, but also making clear he didn't want to come back for no reason. "As I told you, I'm that lazy...."

"Inherently," the suspect remembered.

"Inherently," Howard reiterated.

"Really, how would you, say, judge a man who is inherently lazy and yet so thriving and wanting to be on the job to impress his superiors? ... And yet this guy claims and professes to be inherently lazy. He should go out and exercise—you've got a lot of it here," the suspect said, apparently referring to Howard's rotund gut.

"He knows how to hurt a guy," Jordan said to Howard.

At Good Samaritan, Dr. Cuneo and others began a surgical attempt to clean Kennedy's brain of bullet fragments and to restore what mental and physical

---

108   The LAPD transcript notes this is Howard speaking. An FBI transcript says this is Jordan speaking. I believe the LAPD transcriptionist made more accurate identifications, so I am attributing quotes based on the LAPD transcripts.

functions they could. The surgery would last just over three hours.

Outside the hospital, a growing contingent of supporters prayed that the Senator would live.

At Rampart, Sergeants Chiquet and Henderson interviewed Los Angeles Rams tackle Roosevelt "Rosey" Grier, who had been functioning as an unofficial bodyguard for Kennedy.

"When I located him he wasn't firing." Grier saw a gun was beside the suspect on the steam table. "I don't know if it was another weapon, or the same one," Grier said, raising an interesting issue that neither Chiquet nor Henderson showed any interest in pursuing. Chiquet was preoccupied with another question.

"Did you at any time see a female near him wearing—also of Latin extraction—wearing a polka dot dress?"

"No, I didn't see her."[109] Like Rafer Johnson, Grier hadn't been looking around. Grier had been focused on keeping the suspect from killing anyone and keeping anyone from killing the suspect.

Officer Frank Foster tried his hand with the suspect whose life Rosey may well have saved. The suspect had turned to a new topic: the "Boston Strangler," the nickname given to a man who confessed to strangling several women to death between 1962 and 1964, and the title of Gerold Frank's 1967 book about the case.

"Well, I'm only topically familiar with that, with the whole story about him, not with the individual himself; so how does it go?" the suspect asked. "Have they found out his name? I mean the guy who done this?" Foster told him the man's last name was DeSalvo.

It's odd that the suspect seemed not to know the name of the guy who did it, since "Di Salvo," ostensibly a phonetic version of DeSalvo, was written in an odd, repeated manner on a page in a notebook belonging to the suspect that the police would soon confiscate.

McGann and Calkins interviewed Martin Patrusky, a hotel waiter who had been in the pantry when Kennedy came through. He shook Kennedy's hand and saw him shake the hands of his friend and fellow waiter "Vincent" (DiPierro), a girl in a white dress (Robin Casden), a busboy (Juan Romero), and then "all of a sudden, there was just a matter of maybe four or five feet from us, I heard like somebody throwing firecrackers, and all that I seen was this guy standing from—there's a tray rack on the opposite side of the steam table and all I seen was the guy moved over and he looked—there was like two people in front and the guy looked like he was smiling and he looked like he was going to shake

109   LAPD interview of Rosey Grier, 6/5/68.

hands with him and he reached over like this and then the firing just started and the next thing I know I looked at Vincent and I seen Kennedy starting to go down on his knees and I looked at Vincent and his glasses all of a sudden come up with blood."

Patrusky thought the suspect's pants were "black with blue checks in them." (DiPierro would describe the pants as light blue with black checks in them. The suspect in custody was wearing blue jeans.) "I think he had a blue jacket but when I seen him later when they were pulling him away, all I saw was the white shirt. He thought the shooter was 28 to 30 years old, "Mexican or Puerto Rican or Cuban" and a little taller than himself. Patrusky was 5'4". The suspect in custody was 5'4½" but only 24 years old.

As the morning ticked by, the witness accounts continued to paint a strange picture. Sergeants Chiquet and Henderson interviewed Freddy Plimpton, wife of George Plimpton, a famous writer and Kennedy supporter who had become the first editor-in-chief of *The Paris Review*, a European literary magazine that the CIA had funded in the hopes of persuading the continent to support the American establishment's point of view on foreign affairs.[110] Freddy described hearing "what sounded like yesterday in Chinatown," referring to the firecrackers that scared the Kennedy group in Chinatown in San Francisco two days earlier. She described how she was ahead and to the right of Kennedy, saw him shake a busboy's hand, and saw someone push in close and fire a gun, who was then pushed down on the steam table nearby. She thought the suspect might have been Filipino and in his early thirties. She thought he had been wearing white, like so many of the kitchen staff, but she was told by others the shooter had not been in white, and she was "just very confused about that right now."[111] She had not actually seen the shooting, "but from his position and his posture," she "just assumed that he was the guy that fired."

McGann and Calkins interviewed Michael Lawrence Wayne, the man caught running from the pantry with a rolled-up poster in his hand that some witnesses thought concealed a gun.

Wayne described how Kennedy had signed a poster for him when Kennedy had passed through the pantry to get to the stage to give his speech. He was still in the pantry when Kennedy came back through after his speech.

"And I heard a sound, I guess like backfires. I wasn't quite aware of it until I heard some more of them and there was a commotion. 'He's been shot. He's been shot.' And I saw the—I believe he was wearing, I can recognize if I saw it, he was wearing like a blue jacket." Wayne described how a group descended on the suspect

---

110   Joel Whitney, *Finks: How the CIA Tricked the World's Best Writers* (New York: OR Books, 2016), pp. 1-2.

111   LAPD interview of Freddy Plimpton, 6/5/68.

and pushed him onto the steam table. "I was in shock for a minute, and then I ran into the Press Room, which was the Colonial Room. ... And I tried to call an operator to call the police, what have you, and all the phones had the lights on, you cannot call out, so I ran outside the Colonial Room this way to go ask what happened, you know—so I can't talk about it so I don't, you know—in other words, not out of fear, but I just thought it would be best rather than that to cause panic."

"Uh hum."

"So I ran out towards—I believe there's another room on this side—that was not the main room. And there was a waiter there and I asked him, 'Where's the telephone?' And he pointed it out so then I ran out and there was a security guard and I asked him, 'Can you get me to the telephone, can you get me to the telephone?' and he cuffed me, thinking I may have been the suspect, and I was detained by security for about an hour and a half."

McGann asked if he was with Scott—he couldn't remember the last name, and thought it might have been Egert. He was referring to Scott Enyart, who had taken pictures in the pantry. Wayne remembered speaking to Scott but didn't know him. McGann asked Wayne if he had taken any pictures. "No, I didn't. I didn't have my camera tonight."

"No pictures, huh?" McGann queried again.

"No, sir."

"Hum, he seemed to think you took some pictures down there."

"No, it was the other guy that did."

"Who was that?"

"That was another guy downstairs, downstairs right now."

"That took some pictures, huh?"

"Yes. I believe they have his roll of film out here."

"Other than this Scott?"

"I don't know his name, like I said. There was at least one person that took photographs."

McGann returned to the main subject. "Can you identify this suspect again?" Yes. "What kind of gun would you say it was?" Wayne said "maybe it was a .22." He knew it was a handgun of some sort.

"A small gun or a large gun? In other words, a long barrel or a short barrel?"

"I think it was a short barrel. I remember about three years—more than that—about five years ago, I went with a friend to the Las Vegas Police Rifle Range and I did some—I shot a few shots with a .38. I remember the sound was rather loud."

"Uh huh."

"And when I was in the Boy Scouts they had a .45 exhibition once and it was fantastically loud."

"Uh huh.

"Yet these shots were not really loud. I was right on top of it, but they didn't sound that loud. I would assume, you know, if I was to make assumptions, it was a smaller size gun, which is confirmed, I guess."

McGann asked if he could describe the suspect. He said he could identify him if he saw him in the same clothes. McGann pressed for details. What nationality did he appear to be?

"Well, they said on the radio, and I would concur, he was a Mexican."

About what age? Wayne "really couldn't say," adding, "Young. I mean I've heard things on the radio."

"About how tall?"

"About my height."

"How tall is that?

"I'm 5'8". Probably, maybe a little taller." That was odd. Wayne was at least four inches taller than the suspect in custody. While he described the suspect as having dark and curly hair, he couldn't remember the color of his eyes.

"How about the shirt or upper clothing?"

"Well, I saw the photograph out here, but I'd have to see a color shot of what he was wearing to be positive. … I think I could be positive if I saw it on him."[112]

Around 4 A.M., Jordan returned to the suspect's cell and performed the role of official taster, taking a sip of coffee in front of him to prove it was safe to drink. Jordan knew enough not to ask the suspect any more about the crime. The suspect simply shut down and refused to say anything when asked about those topics. But Jordan and the rest hoped in casual conversation the subject would divulge something that might enable them to ascertain his identity. Jordan asked if he could discuss the Kirschke case a bit more.

"Surely, surely. … I'll hear anybody," the suspect said. "I'm a good listener but a hell of a lousy talker."

"You're a lousy talker," Jordan repeated as the room erupted in laughter at the irony. The chatty suspect had expounded at length on a number of subjects, just not the one the police most wanted to discuss.

The suspect, Jordan, and Murphy discussed the philosophy of prosecution, how far you can go with the evidence, how you try to avoid prosecuting innocent people. Jordan asked the suspect if he would work hard to convict a person he really believed to be innocent. The suspect's answer was strange:

"I don't really know. You're asking me this question as if you're putting me—you're giving me the responsibility of something so fantastic that it's beyond my mental and physical ability to—to—to cope with, really."

Jordan responded, "I don't think it's beyond your mental ability. I think you've got a lot of mental ability. I think you have been putting us on a little bit here."

The suspect turned to Murphy. "What's he talk about, Mr.—"

"See, right now, … you're doing it. You're very sharp."

"Well, if you mean that as a compliment or a—"

"I mean that as a compliment."

The suspect complained about his knee hurting. It had been injured during the struggle. Murphy suggested the suspect put his foot up on the table, where his own apparently were. "No, no, no, no, no, no, no. Sorry, your relaxation is my desire," the suspect said, causing some laughter.

As the conversation regarding the need to find out if people were innocent or guilty before prosecuting, as a matter of conscience, was winding down, Murphy offered, "I can assure you, you're going to get a fair shake. … Your treatment has been all right up 'til now?"

The suspect joked, "I was lavished with your company. … I would say most merrily entertained, in this whole building, maybe."

Murphy replied, "Well, you're the star of the show."

"Better take acting, no?" the suspect joked back.

Jordan chimed in. "Well, what is it—who was it? Shakespeare said the whole world is a stage."

"That's right," the suspect said, "And everybody—"

"—everybody's an actor," Jordan paraphrased, before excusing himself to check on something.

The suspect described to Murphy how people can't really play a part, how eventually they will be found out, an odd thing to say for one who was at that very moment playing a part, trying to avoid being found out. He then talked about whether juries could be fair or not, without discussing how or why he would soon be facing one.

When Jordan returned, the suspect asked why Jordan had been gone for so long. Murphy replied that it was a mystery and that in investigations, sometimes things got tedious. The interesting part, continued Murphy, was finding out "exactly who John Doe is. That's what we're really interested in."

"Really, you know, that's beautiful. Beautiful. Maybe we should keep it interesting."

"We have to, I guess. … You're just sort of matching wits with us."

"You know, there's a horse named that," the suspect said, dropping the first genuine clue to his identity.

"What?" Murphy asked.

"Matching Wits."

Given the slight size of the suspect, the police could have considered that the young man in front of them had been a jockey or, in this case, an exercise boy.

Howard, who was not the least bit lazy that night, inherently or otherwise, ducked into a room at Parker Center where Sergeants Patchett and Melendres were asking more questions of Serrano regarding the girl in the polka dot dress. Was the dress tight-fitting? No. What kind of gold was the girl's male companion's sweater? "Autumn gold," Serrano replied. Her description of the third man closely resembled the suspect in custody.

After listening to what Serrano had to say, Howard stepped into another room, where Sergeants Patchett and Melendres were interviewing the 19-year-old Vincent DiPierro.

DiPierro said there were two people between him and Kennedy, and Patchett asked if, just before the shooting started, there were still two people between him.

"No, at this time … there was no one in front of me."

"You were on Mr. Kennedy's left side or right?"

"Right side, near the ice machines."

Patchett then asked a question that indicated he knew Kennedy had been shot from behind. "And who was to your left?" If DiPierro had been facing east, he would have likely been right next to the actual shooter.

"Oh, a crowd of people," Vince said, indicating the people crowded into the area behind a white divider with plastic flowers on it behind the west end of the ice machine. Vince had been facing north, not east, so the shooter would have been more ahead of him than to his left.

DiPierro noted that the suspect caught his attention when he crossed toward Kennedy. He figured he was going to shake Kennedy's hand, but instead the man "kind of swung around and he went up on his—like on his tiptoes—and he stuck over with the gun and he shot, you know, and the first shot I don't know where it went, but I know it was either his second or third one that hit Mr. Kennedy and after that I had blood all over my face from where it hit his head."

Vince described seeing the suspect before the shooting, a young man (23 to 28 years old), "an ordinary Latin," approximately 5'4", slender, with dark, wavy hair. "I didn't really take notice of his hair. All I could see was the gun, you know, and he had a stupid smile on his face."

Could he recognize him again if he saw him?

"Yes, definitely."

Was there any question in his mind?

"No, none at all, because I'll never forget the way he looked at me," DiPierro said. "When I saw him first, there was a girl behind him, too. I don't know if you need that. There were two people that I saw."

Patchett stopped DiPierro. He wasn't interested in hearing about the girl yet. He wanted to hear about the male that DiPierro had seen shoot Kennedy. DiPierro described the suspect in custody. The clothing he described was not an exact match, although it was close. DiPierro said the man had a powder-blue sport coat on that buttoned. The suspect in custody had worn a light blue velour top that zipped at the neck.

Vince described a small gun—not more than an inch longer than a ballpoint pen, that was "not black, but blue … it's a real dark blue." When DiPierro first saw the man, he thought he was sick in some way. He was bent over. "He looked as though he were crouched." He was standing on a tray rack, about four inches off the ground. "The only reason he was noticeable was because there was this good-looking girl in the crowd there."

"[W]as the girl with him?"

"It looked as though, yes."

"What makes you say that?"

"Well, she was following him."

"Where did she follow him from?"

"From—she was standing behind the tray stand because she was up next to him on—behind, and she was holding on to the other end of the tray table and … it looked as if she was almost holding him."

DiPierro said the guy got off the tray stand and approached the Senator, but the girl stayed with the tray stand. "I glanced over once in a while. She was good-looking so I looked at her."

"What was it in your mind that makes you think they were together …?"

"He turned when he was on the tray stand once and he had the same stupid smile on, you know, and then he kind of turned and said something. I don't know what he said."

Howard asked, "You did see him speak to her?"

"He turned as though he did say something, whether he said anything—"

"Did she move her mouth like she was speaking to him?"

"No, she just smiled."

Howard asked if she was smiling from what the man had said to her or whether she was smiling because she saw the Senator approach. DiPierro said yes to the former and no to the latter, adding, "she looked as though she was sick, also." Howard didn't ask if she, too, was bent over, holding something, the explanation DiPierro had just given when he said the other man looked "sick."

DiPierro's description of the girl was very close to the description Sandra Serrano had just given: a Caucasian girl in her twenties, with brunette hair that fell just above her shoulders, a "good figure," a "nice dress" that was white with "either black or dark violet polka dots." and "a kind of a bively [sic] like collar."

"A what kind of collar?"

"A thing that goes around like that. I don't know what they call it," DiPierro said, describing a bib-like collar.[113]

DiPierro noted that her hair was "puffed up a little." She seemed to be the only person with the suspect at that moment. He hadn't noticed what she did

---

113   The transcriptionist noted that "bively" was a phonetic translation. I believe he said a "bib-like" collar

during the shooting because he "forgot about her and everything else but the gun."

DiPierro described seeing the flash of the first two shots and how "after the second one, I couldn't see, because I had blood all over my face....I got smashed up when the guy fell on me, when he fell down right on top of my hands."

Vince was certain the man he had seen on the tray stand was the same one caught in the act of shooting at Kennedy.

Patchett ended the interview, but after a "discussion off the record," Patchett asked a few more questions. "Okay, just to sum this up. What's the first thought that comes in your mind as far as the appearance of this man that had the gun?"

"The stupid smile … It was kind of like an envious smile, like ah, you know, villainous—I don't know how to describe it."

Vince wasn't the only one to notice a smile on the suspect's face during the shooting. At Rampart, Yoshio Niwa told Sergeants McGann and Calkins the suspect was smiling. "I was so excited and upset, and he was smiling."

"That's hard to understand, isn't it?" Calkins asked Niwa.

"I don't know why," Niwa responded, clearly disturbed by the incongruity.

"Can you think of anything else … that might help?"

"That's all I could think I think [sic]. I didn't see the other two, the one woman and a guy I didn't see at all."

"How do you know there was another woman?"

Niwa explained he had heard second-hand that there had been a woman and another man with the shooter. He thought he had heard it on the news.

McGann and Calkins spoke next to 17-year-old "room service bus boy" Juan Romero. Romero was the last to shake Kennedy's hand. Kennedy then took two steps away, and "all of a sudden I just seen somebody jumping up, no jumping, you mean, you know, just going over, reaching over … I felt something like burning, like, you know, like when you throw out firecrackers and some—"

"Powder burns?" Calkins interrupted.

"Powder burns, something like that. I see it burn there, I saw it all."

McGann and Calkins showed him the gun Rafer had given them. "Yes, it looked something like that."

"Did you miss me?" Jordan asked as he returned, joking that the suspect likely didn't, which appeared to offend the suspect, as the suspect clearly liked Jordan.

Jordan asked if the suspect's name might be Jesse. There was radio chatter that a suspect named "Jesse Greer" had been picked up and was on the way to Rampart just before Jordan's anonymous subject was captured.[114] The suspect

---

because that matches what he described here and that's also what he said to the Grand Jury two days later.

114   The Emergency Control Center Journal in the LAPD records states: "Possible suspect JESSE Greer, male

was happy to adopt the name Jesse in place of John. Neither matched his real name, but his captors didn't know this yet.

The suspect asked for more coffee, adding, "Please ... if it's no inconvenience at all."

"What could be inconvenient at 4:30 in the morning?" Jordan responded dryly.

"Is it 4:30 or 5:00, quarter to 5:00?"

"Quarter to 5:00," Murphy responded.

"Are you sure it's a quarter to 5:00? I had that feeling," the suspect said.

"You mean you can tell what time it is?" Murphy asked, surprised. There were no clocks in the room and the man wore no watch.

Jordan and Murphy separately asked what kind of work the suspect did. "Oh, whatever you want me to do," the suspect answered. "Really, everything fascinated me in life, you know. ... [By] trying to specialize in one thing ... you're just jeopardizing your knowledge and appreciation of whatever else there is ... When ... I watch a barber, sir, I just stand and watch that barber for hours. I—from the time I'm watching him I want to be nothing but a barber. You know, if I'm watching a dentist, boy, he fascinates me, and I want to be him. I was talking to Frank [Foster, an LAPD officer] here a while ago. The way he talked, you know ... I was very fascinated, and, you know, I was sort of superimposing myself in his position for temporarily."

The suspect was describing a strangely permeable mental state, one in which an external reality merged with his own, but the officers didn't pick up on this. Their sole focus remained on identifying the suspect.

Jordan was called away and learned that a key found in the pockets of the suspect opened a car parked nearby that belonged to Robert Gindroz, a chef at the Ambassador Hotel.[115] He returned, certain he finally had the man's correct identification.

"You have been through Jesse; you have been through John [Doe]. What about Robert Gene Gendroz or Jendroz?"

"Hell, that's a good name. Jendroz."

"It's a nice name. And your car?"

"Cadillac?"

"No."

"Rolls-Royce?"

"You're in the general area," said Jordan wryly. "How about a Chrysler?"

"Beautiful."

Cauc., en route Rampart Station (info received from Jesse Unruh)." But there's no evidence Unruh supplied the name.

115   Although this key bothered the LAPD and the press for a while, I've never found this episode particularly important. I once opened someone else's car, accidentally, thinking it was mine, using my own car key.

The suspect owned a 1956 De Soto, but Jordan had no way of knowing this yet, and he thought he had him, this time. He asked the suspect if he recognized Gindroz's address, noting that it was just off Mulholland.

"Where's Mulholland?" the suspect asked. Mulholland Drive is a famous ridge-top road that separates Beverly Hills from the San Fernando Valley. Most people who live in the central part of Los Angeles would have used or crossed that road at some point, so Jordan found this answer not credible.

"Come on now, you've been real good up to now, but I think you're—I'm going to charge you with overacting a little bit." But the suspect lived in Pasadena, as Jordan would eventually learn, which is nowhere near Mulholland Drive. The suspect did recognize the person with that name, though.

"Mulholland, there was a hell of a civic leader in his day, wasn't it? … Wasn't he the founder of the water project? … I read it one time in Griffith Park…."

"This guy misses nothing, you know," Jordan said to Murphy. "I tell you he'd be a hell of a partner to have." Jordan was only partly buttering him up. In the trial that would follow, Jordan described him as "extremely intelligent."

Murphy was more interested in finding out if the suspect was Gindroz. "Do you drive a '58 Chrysler?"

"Do I drive one? I can drive any car you want to put me in." Imagine the cops' frustration at a suspect who parried every question in this manner. It is to the credit of all the LAPD officers who interacted with the suspect in these first few hours that none of them lost their temper.

Jordan tried a different approach to the question. "Have you driven one, let's say, in the last 12 hours?"

"A—that make of car? I don't really know. I don't remember. I don't know."

"You are being truthful with me now?" Jordan asked.

"I swear to God—I swear to God on that."

Jordan explained to Murphy. "[He's] been very truthful. … If … he doesn't like the question, he won't answer me, but he's truthful when he does answer, I'll say that."

A few minutes later, Jordan asked the same exact question again. "You're repeating the question, sir. Please don't," the suspect said. Repeating a question is a standard interrogation tactic because it literally bores the subject into answering "fully and candidly."[116] Had the suspect been taught to resist interrogation?

The suspect continued to surprise the officers with his knowledge. Most suspects apprehended at crime scenes were, at best, undereducated. This one talked about a Chinese saying about how even a trickle of water would eventually erode the hardest stone. Jordan misunderstood and thought the suspect was referring

---

116   Bobby Ghosh, "Beyond Waterboarding: What Interrogators Can Still Do," *TIME*, April 28, 2009 via www.time.com/time/nation/article/0,8599,1894432,00.html, accessed 7/10/12, quoting from the Army Field Manual.

to Chinese water torture, but the suspect corrected him. Murphy suggested the suspect must have done a lot of reading. The suspect said any grammar school book would have that information. "Possibly so," Jordan said, "but I dare say if we lined up a hundred thousand people out here ... we wouldn't find too many that would remember it."

Jordan didn't want to let the possible Gindroz identification drop. "Robert Gene Gendroz [sic]... do those three names together ring a bell with you as anybody you know or have met?"

The suspect answered in a strange way: "I honestly don't know. I don't think so. I might meet in the future. [sic] I might never, you know, or I might have met him, you know, but forgot that I met him."

I might have met him but forgot that I met him. The suspect had just succinctly described how one might behave under the influence of hypnosis.

"I doubt if you have forgotten too many meetings in your life," Jordan said.

"Now why do you say that?"

"Well, just because you don't strike me as the kind of person that forgets."

"Well, I don't forget. I don't forget," said the man who just a short time earlier couldn't remember if he had been before a magistrate or not, or what kind of car he had driven in the last 12 hours.

After Murphy and Jordan left the suspect, Frank Foster returned and conversed with him some more. "Are you married, were you married?"

"I don't think so," the suspect said.

"Oh, you're not divorced, huh?"

"I don't know."

"How do you mean you don't know?"

Incredibly, the suspect truly didn't seem to know at that moment whether he was married or not. It was as if he wasn't so much keeping his identity hidden as he was trying to hide the fact *that he truly didn't remember, at that moment, who he was.*

At hospitals from Huntington Beach to Encino, the other shooting victims were being treated. Bullet fragments were removed from the heads of Elizabeth Evans and Paul Schrade and given to the LAPD. Dr. Max Finkel removed a bullet from Ira Goldstein's thigh, marked its base with an "X" and placed it in a glass jar, which was later given to the LAPD. An "identifiable lead bullet"[117] was removed from Bill Weisel's stomach and given to LAPD Officer L.M. Orozco, who marked the base with his initials, "LMO." Officer E. Kamidoi collected a bullet removed from the middle of Irwin Stroll's lower left leg. According to the LAPD evidence log, the bullet was "not marked for ID due to odd shape but traced in Kamidoi's notebook." Miraculously, after all those shots, everyone was still alive, for the moment.

---

117   LAPD interview of Dr. William B. Neal, 8/2/68.

"I thought this place was bugged," the suspect said. Jordan and Murphy had confirmed to the suspect earlier that all his conversations were being recorded, and that the mirror in the interview room was a two-way mirror. Foster did not know of those conversations, however, and lied.

"Not this place. You try to imply too many things. You're trying to think … you're the big notorious criminal."

"No, no, please forgive me if I give you that kind of implication," the suspect said, confounding Foster's expectations. There would be no *Sic Semper Tyrannis* here.

The suspect shifted painfully in his seat.

"Your leg hurt you?" Foster asked.

"Kind of."

"How did you hurt it?"

"I don't know."

"Did you fall down or something?"

"No."

"When did it happen?"

"I don't remember."

"You don't remember?" Foster asked again, clearly disbelieving him. The suspect had been caught in the act of firing a gun. His leg had been hurt in the struggle. *How could anyone not remember that?* It's not like he had anything to gain by lying about that—there were plenty of witnesses to the struggle that injured him in the pantry. Yet, throughout every discussion that night, the suspect evinced a genuine hole in his memory not just for the events of the night, but even, to some degree, about who he was.

"You from the L.A. area?" Foster asked.

"I don't know," the suspect replied.

"What are you going to do when you get out of this deal?"

"I don't know. Try to correct whatever I work for."

Foster and the suspect chatted about the law, the need for justice to be delivered equally to the lowliest as well as the mighty (at which point the suspect asked to shake Foster's hand) and of the need to be gentle in one's authority. Like Murphy and Jordan, Foster was impressed with the man's intellect. "You've had … more education than just high school, haven't you? … I mean … you're not any person that is of low intelligence."

"Thank you, thank you. Well, really, you're too generous," the suspect replied, deferring modestly.

"Well, maybe … you're just the victim of circumstances," Foster offered.

"Beautiful," the suspect replied.[118] The suspect noted that Foster didn't fit

---

118   "Circumstances" is not in the official transcript, but when this tape was played at the trial, both the defense and prosecution agreed that was the next word. Trial transcript, p. 6162.

the stereotype of a policeman.

"I hope you think of me as just another human being," Foster said.

"We're all puppets," the suspect replied, with more truth than he could have understood in that moment.

When District Attorney Evelle Younger learned that the suspect had asked for an attorney, he told Inspector Powers and Police Chief Tom Reddin that the suspect should not be questioned further.[119]

Back at the Ambassador Hotel, reporter Robert Wiedrich examined the pantry. The *Chicago Tribune* had flown its 20-year veteran crime reporter Wiedrich to Los Angeles immediately following the shooting. When he entered the pantry in the wee hours of the morning, he found MacArthur and others from the LAPD still examining the scene. To his surprise, the police were uncharacteristically chatty. The police pointed him to Karl Uecker, whom he interviewed.

Uecker told Wiedrich how he had led Kennedy through the pantry, how he kept breaking away, and how Uecker kept retrieving his hand to pull him eastward. Just before the shots, Uecker had retrieved his hand and turned to go, "and then it happened. I heard a pop, I saw what looked bits of paper flying [*sic*]."[120]

Wiedrich added: "MacArthur said what Uecker thought was paper probably was ceiling insulation scattered by a first wild shot." That was a bizarre comment to interject, especially since it didn't match a single witness statement. The few witnesses with a clear view of the subject and his gun said the gun was pointed straight at Kennedy's face when the first shots went off, before Uecker grabbed the gunman. Perhaps MacArthur was as aware as Calkins had been of what "bits of paper" in the air indicated: that the suspect had been firing blanks, not bullets. But Uecker said that after the first shot, he had grabbed the suspect around the neck and hurled him to the right, away from Kennedy, who was falling to the ground on his left. If Kennedy or, as some witnesses asserted, Schrade had been hit by the first shot, the first shot could not *also* have hit the ceiling and caused the tile to crumble.

Wiedrich noted a wooden strip of molding with holes in it that had been pulled off the door jamb and asked the policemen about it. He recorded their answers in his article:

> On a low table lay an 8-foot strip of molding, torn by police from the center post of the double doors leading from the ballroom. These

---

119   LAPD interview of Inspector J.W. Powers, 10/2/68.

120   Robert Wiedrich, "'Felt Him Fire Gun,' Hotel Worker Says," *Chicago Tribune*, June 6, 1968.

were the doors through which Sen. Kennedy had walked, smiling in his moment of victory.

Now the molding bore scars of a crime laboratory technician's probe as it had removed two .22-caliber bullets that had gone wild.[121]

No one could have known, at that early point, that had even a single additional bullet been found; that meant at least two guns had to have been fired. No one knew yet that seven bullets would be recovered from six victims and that multiple holes would have to be accounted for in the pantry's ceiling. So the police told Wiedrich, accurately, that two bullets had been removed from the wood molding.

It would be ridiculous to assert that the police were lying or mistaken about bullets being recovered from the center divider. Wiedrich could see the holes with his own eyes. The police knew that anything they said would be repeated. They knew they were talking to a reporter. It's likely the police told Wiedrich the truth simply because they didn't understand at that point that they should have lied. They didn't know yet that two bullets in the molding were two bullets too many to have been fired from the suspect's gun.

Kennedy's surgery ended at 6:20 A.M. on June 5, 1968, and the long wait began. Dr. Cuneo told Frank Mankiewicz and Steve Smith that the next 24 to 36 hours would determine whether he'd live or not.

Mankiewicz asked what Kennedy's condition would be if he lived. Cuneo told them there had been damage to the brain. He would likely be deaf in one ear, his vision would be affected, his face might be partially paralyzed, but "the higher centers of his brain" seemed unaffected. "He would still be able to think and reason." Kennedy was taken from surgery and laid on an ice blanket designed to lower his temperature to reduce the stress on his heart and lungs. At lower temperatures, the body needed less oxygen to survive. Ethel sat at Kennedy's side, holding his hand.[122]

Chief Reddin scheduled a press conference for 7 A.M. The police had little to report. They did not know the suspect's identity. The point of the press conference, however, was not to inform the press but to create a diversion so that the suspect could be transported to the Hall of Justice nearby. The specter of Lee Harvey Oswald's assassination while in police custody was ever-present.

At 7 A.M., the still unidentified suspect was booked as "John Doe" and charged with six counts of "Assault to Commit Murder." Judge Joan Dempsey Klein set the bail at $250,000 but ordered the suspect held without bail until identified.

---

121   Robert Wiedrich, "'Felt Him Fire Gun,' Hotel Worker Says," *Chicago Tribune*, June 6, 1968.

122   Kaiser, pp. 82–83.

The suspect was then turned over to the Sheriff's Department.

Chief Reddin told the media, who did not realize the suspect was no longer in the building, that the suspect was "extremely articulate," had "an extensive vocabulary," and expressed himself well. Asked what he meant by "extremely articulate," Reddin slightly misquoted the suspect. "I prefer to remain incommunicado," Reddin said, which caused a follow-up question of whether that was a quote from the suspect or Reddin's comment on the matter. The room rang with laughter.[123]

Reddin described the man in custody as "Very cool, very calm, very relaxed." Asked if the man was mentally stable, Reddin replied, "Oh yes," adding, "He's very calm and relaxed and quite lucid in what he talks about, but he won't talk about the case."

Someone asked if the man was under the influence of anything whatsoever. "Absolutely not," Reddin replied. Asked specifically whether there was any evidence that the suspect was on drugs or under the influence of alcohol, Reddin reiterated, "No narcotics, no evidence of any type of narcotic use, no evidence of any use of alcohol."

Asked whether there had been other shooters, Reddin wouldn't rule out the possibility of conspiracy, but said that no one else was being sought (which wasn't true, as the APB for the girl in the polka dot dress was still in force and would be for nearly three more weeks).

Throughout the press conference, Reddin's delivery was calm, articulate, and professional, until he came to one particular question. He had just explained that the LAPD was checking with other agencies for any information they might have on the suspect— "the immigration service, the CIA, the Bureau of Customs, Social Security, the Post Office department—"

"Why the CIA, Chief?" a reporter asked.

Suddenly, Reddin became visibly rattled and nearly choked as he tried to get the agency's name out. "The C-A … the C-A … the C-I-A has types of information that might help us identify who the person might be. We'll give them his picture." Reddin regained his composure shortly after, but it was a bizarre break—and the only such break—in an otherwise seamless presentation.[124]

At the nearby Hall of Justice, Chief Public Defender Richard Buckley talked briefly to the suspect. The suspect asked to speak to someone from the ACLU. In fact, the ACLU was already on the case. Shortly after the shooting, the president of the Los Angeles branch of the ACLU had woken Abraham Lincoln Wirin and

---

123   Quotes from the press conference come from the videotape I viewed at the UCLA Film & Television Archive.

124   *Ibid.* You really have to see this to believe it. Reddin literally almost choked on the CIA's name and looked incredibly uncomfortable at having to say the agency's name out loud or that the name had been highlighted at all.

urged him to police headquarters to talk to the suspect. Wirin had sent a telegram to Mayor Sam Yorty and Police Chief Tom Reddin to request access.

As the LAPD's press conference was winding down, over at Good Samaritan Hospital, about halfway between downtown and the Ambassador Hotel, Frank Mankiewicz addressed the media, who were clamoring for an update on Kennedy's condition. He didn't tell them all he knew. If he died, what did it matter if he might have been cognitively or physically impaired?

Further down Wilshire Boulevard, LAPD photographer Charles Collier completed his work at the Ambassador Hotel and returned to the SID photo lab. Officer DeWayne Wolfer returned to Parker Center for more equipment. At 10:30 A.M., the floor of the pantry was swept for debris related to the crime.

The floor may not have been swept very carefully, because the next day, Robert Alfeld, an assistant sound man for the Cocoanut Grove, found three shell casings under the ice machine. They were long rifle expended shells. He knew a lot about guns and noted the shells had firing pin indentation marks on their bases. He showed them to his boss, the head electrician, Paul Dozier. Alfeld thought perhaps someone had been playing a morbid joke. Alfeld put them in a drawer of a desk he shared with Dozier and promptly forgot all about it. When the FBI questioned him a couple of weeks later, distracted by the shooting itself and his father's recent death, he didn't think to mention them. It wasn't until he saw a news article years later indicating there might have been two shooters that he realized the significance of this. He gave a deposition regarding the shells to Vincent Bugliosi.[125] The shells disappeared into history. If the shells weren't planted as a joke, that was three more shells than the suspect's gun could have held, as all eight shells were still in the gun when it was turned over to the police.

The search for the suspect's identity was starting to bear fruit. The gun that had been taken from him at the scene was traced to a man named Albert Leslie Hertz. Albert's wife told the police Albert had given the gun to their daughter, Dana Westlake. Dana had, in turn, given the gun to George Erhard, her neighbor in Pasadena at the time, somewhere between December of 1967 and February of 1968. The police caught up with Erhard in the early morning hours of June 5 and asked him what had become of the weapon. He told the police he had sold it to a guy he knew as "Joe" who worked at Nash's Department Store in Pasadena.

At Nash's Department Store, the young man Erhard thought of as "Joe," whose real name was Munir Sirhan, stopped into the employee breakroom before

---

125   Statement given by Robert Alfeld to Vincent Bugliosi on 11-16-75, in the Exhibits to a Request for a Grand Jury, www.maryferrell.org/showDoc.html?docId=99873&search=alfeld#relPageId=802&tab=page.

work and caught the end of a brief report on the Kennedy assassination. When a picture of the suspect flashed, Munir thought that could be his brother Sirhan Bishara Sirhan, whom he hadn't seen since the previous morning. Munir, who had taken the bus to work, asked his boss if he could borrow his car to go to the police. He drove home and woke his brother Adel, and together they drove to a Pasadena police station and asked for a newspaper. The station didn't have one, so they picked one up at a newsstand a couple of blocks away. There, on the front page, was a picture of their brother.

Munir dropped Adel back at the station to identify the suspect and got permission to return his boss' car to Nash's. An investigator met Munir when he arrived.[126] The gun had just been traced to him. Munir asked to be taken to the same station where Adel was. They arrived just after the police had taken Adel to the Sirhan home. The police did not arrest Adel, but they had read him his rights, which unnerved him.[127] Adel gave them permission to search the premises, which was not his to give, as his mother, not Adel, owned the house.

Led by LAPD Sergeant William E. Brandt, the police found a handbill to a McCarthy rally, information about the Rosicrucians and the occult, a brochure advertising "mental projection" and a 4"x9" envelope from the U.S. Treasury on which someone had scrawled "RFK must be disposed of like his brother was" and a second handwritten comment that said, simply, "Reactionary." They also found three spiral-bound notebooks filled with handwriting and doodles, most of which pertained to his classwork at Pasadena City College.

Scrawled all over one of the pages in a bizarre, repetitive fashion, were the words "RFK must die," followed by "I have never heard" and "pay to the order of."

Munir was taken to Rampart Station for questioning. There, Munir explained that his brother had been a member of ROTC in high school, so he was accustomed to using guns. He said Sirhan wanted to practice shooting a gun but didn't want to borrow one at a shooting range. Munir quoted his brother as having said "I don't want to get involved. I don't want a signature," which was odd, because one day prior, Sirhan's name had been logged into the registry at a shooting range in San Gabriel, where several witnesses would report having seen Sirhan firing a handgun throughout June 4, the day of the primary.

Munir and Adel gave officers the broad strokes of Sirhan's life. He had been born in Palestine, moved with the family to Pasadena, and attended high school and junior college in Pasadena. He had worked with a horse trainer as an exercise boy but left after a bad fall from a horse that resulted in an injury. He had

---

126   Kaiser says it was "some gentleman from the FBI," p. 88. The Final Report says "Investigators took [Munir] into custody]" (p. 316) and later notes that Officer J.D. Evans and Sgt. G.R. Harrison brought Munir to the Pasadena police station. The Final Report refers to "FBI Agent Sullivan," first name not mentioned, as being present at the search of Sirhan's Pasadena home.

127   Kaiser, p. 88.

worked as a clerk in a health food store in Pasadena.

The notebooks and other items from the Sirhan residence were taken to Rampart Station and booked into evidence right after bullet fragments recovered from Kennedy's head during surgery. The bullet fragments and notebooks were turned over to FBI Special Agent E. Rhoad Richards at 3 P.M. by Sergeant Brandt.[128]

At Parker Center, Wolfer spent the day examining the gun and the recovered bullets. Earlier that morning, Wolfer and his crew had run string through several bullet holes in the ceiling, attempting to determine bullet trajectories. After these were photographed, Wolfer's team removed some of the ceiling tiles and took them to Parker Center, where Wolfer's log indicates that he performed chemical and microscopic examinations of them.

Dr. Marcus Crahan examined Sirhan, who was now back in his cell. The suspect was shivering. Dr. Crahan asked Sirhan if he was cold.

"Not cold," Sirhan replied.

"You mean you're having a chill?" Crahan persisted.

"I have a very mild one," Sirhan said.[129]

Sirhan would later experience a similar chill coming out of hypnosis induced by a member of his defense team.

Sheriff Peter Pitchess dropped by to see Sirhan the morning of June 5. He wanted to ensure Sirhan understood that his complicity with procedures was necessary for his safety. Sirhan asked what rights he had, beyond his Miranda rights. After a brief conversation, the Sheriff left, but something stuck with him enough to express to Undersheriff William McCloud that their "very unusual prisoner" was "a young man of apparently complete self-possession, totally unemotional."[130]

All day, the FBI and LAPD heard from a number of witnesses with many strange stories to tell of people who had seen or heard something relating to the assassination. The only thing that was immediately clear is that this case would take months to investigate. There were literally thousands of witnesses to be interviewed. Yet the police were already telling everyone that Sirhan was the sole participant in the crime.

As night fell on June 5, Kennedy seemed to be stabilizing. But by the end of the night, his "heart tones had weakened." Friends and family conducted a

---

128   Property report notation between evidence items 37 and 38.
129   Kaiser, p. 89.
130   Kaiser, p. 55.

grueling watch as the life slowly ebbed from the man intimates called "Bobby." By 1:27 A.M. on June 6, Kennedy had no pulse, no heart sounds, and was not breathing. Tubing to assist his breathing was removed.[131]

At 1:44 A.M., Robert Francis Kennedy, at the young age of 42, officially passed away.

Jackie Kennedy came out first, with "this terrible unreal smile," supported by a man at each elbow. "He had to improve after surgery," Mankiewicz explained, but "He never did." With tears in his eyes and still wearing his blue Kennedy button, Mankiewicz added, "But God, he gave it a fight. Twenty-five hours. God he gave it a fight."[132]

---

131   LAPD interview of Mrs. L. Omer, R.N., 6/5/68.

132   Joe McGiniss, "Long, Grim Vigil at the Hospital – Then It's Over," *Philadelphia Inquirer*, June 7, 1968.

TRAGEDY

"He made light in everybody.
Now he is dead and all is dark."

AS NEWS OF ROBERT KENNEDY'S DEATH SPREAD, GRIEF SWEPT across the nation. Flags were flown at half-mast. In Los Angeles, drivers left their lights on all day in tribute. President Johnson declared the upcoming Sunday a national day of mourning.

"Robert Kennedy affirmed this country—affirmed the decency of its people, their longing for peace, their desire to improve conditions of life for all," President Johnson said, as he urged people to "join hands and walk together through this dark night of common anguish into a new dawn of healing unity."[133]

Robert Kennedy's body was placed on one of the several planes that served as Air Force One when President Johnson was aboard. It was the same plane that several of his brother's cabinet members were on when they learned of President Kennedy's death.

At the airport, tear-streaked faces pressed against the chain-link fence as some two thousand people sought a last glimpse of the man who might well have become President. Waiting inside the plane were two women who knew more than anyone what Kennedy's wife Ethel was feeling. Jackie Kennedy and Coretta Scott King had come to be by her side. And the women weren't the only ones grieving. Frank Mankiewicz wrote of the deep grief of the last of the Kennedy brothers:

---

133   *Los Angeles Times*, June 7, 1968.

> After the California primary as I left the hospital room—and RFK—
> for the last time, I noticed Ted Kennedy standing by the sink in the
> adjoining bathroom, in semidarkness. I had never seen—nor do I
> expect ever to see again—a human face so contorted in agony. Ted's
> face twisted, his eyes unseeing and beyond tears, beyond pain, truly
> beyond any feeling I could bring myself to describe, a sight impossible
> to banish from memory.[134]

At Elysian Heights School in Los Angeles, 11-year-old Maedon Lau crafted perhaps the most eloquent statement of all: "He made light in everybody. Now he is dead and all is dark."[135]

Where world leaders saw tragedy in the passing of this young man who cared so passionately about justice for all people, Howard Hughes saw only opportunity. He pulled out one of his numerous yellow writing pads and scrawled a message to his top lieutenant, Robert Maheu, instructing him to move quickly to hire the Kennedy organization.

Hughes was in some big legal battles, and who better than the indomitable Kennedy machine to help him? First they would mourn, but eventually they'd realize they still needed to feed their families. Hughes wanted to capture the whole organization intact to fight his mounting political battles over nuclear testing in Nevada. It wasn't that Hughes cared about the environment. He worried about how the tests would affect his *personal* health and fought to get the tests stopped or at least moved out of state.

He managed to snag one of Kennedy's top lieutenants, Larry O'Brien, after convincing him he was going to support Hubert Humphrey, with whom O'Brien had accepted a job. Hughes likely didn't tell O'Brien he was also backing Nixon. Hughes just wanted to own the next president, regardless of political affiliation.

Maheu, at the request of Howard Hughes, also offered Paul Schrade a place at his Spring Mountain ranch in Las Vegas to stay while he was recuperating from his head wound from the pantry shooting, an offer Schrade accepted. Schrade was already friends with one of the few people Hughes trusted and spoke to in person, John Meier (not to be confused with Johnny Meyer, a publicist, who also worked for Hughes).

LAPD Chief of Detectives Robert Houghton wrote in his book *Special Unit Senator* that he didn't learn of the shooting until the morning of June 6. He had been vacationing in the wilds of Yosemite Valley in Northern California, far from televisions, radios, and telephones. It wasn't until his wife talked to someone

---

134   Frank Mankiewicz and Joel Swerdlow, *So I was Saying … : My Somewhat Eventful Life* (New York: Macmillan, 2016), p. 159.

135   *Los Angeles Times*, June 7, 1968.

along a trail that they learned what had happened. Houghton drove to a store in Wawona and called his office from a pay phone. Houghton's initial thought was that this was a conspiracy. "There was a pattern of a 'hired killer' here rather than murder on impulse, for whatever reason," Houghton wrote later, citing Sirhan's lack of identification and the large amount of cash he was carrying.[136]

The autopsy of President John F. Kennedy had been one of the most poorly documented autopsies ever conducted. Dr. Thomas Noguchi, the coroner for Los Angeles County, was determined that Robert Kennedy's autopsy, in contrast, be completely professional.

Six years earlier, Dr. Noguchi, who had emigrated from Japan to America in the fifties and joined the Los Angeles coroner's office in 1960 as a deputy medical examiner, had found himself staring at the naked body of Marilyn Monroe, whose death by drugs raised serious controversy. Had she committed suicide? Had someone murdered her?[137] Dr. Noguchi's examination led him to the conclusion that she died of an accidental overdose of self-administered medication.

Now, Dr. Noguchi found himself in front of another beloved and famous figure taken too soon. Noguchi had read a great deal about Robert Kennedy. He took the unusual step of asking that Kennedy's face be covered while he worked so he would not be distracted by his own grief.

The day before, Noguchi had contacted the forensic community's version of INTERPOL, the International Reference Organization in Forensic Medicine (INFORM), founded in 1966 and located in Wichita, Kansas. INFORM stored computer records on forensic cases from across America so similarities across state borders can be more readily tracked, and so the science of forensics can be improved through shared knowledge. At INFORM, Noguchi reached the organization's founder, Bill Eckert.

"Take command of the examination right there in Los Angeles. Fight off any pressure to remove the body to Washington. No Dallas this time," Eckert told Noguchi. After President Kennedy's assassination in Dallas, the President's body had been forcibly removed from the medical professionals at Parkland Hospital at

---

136   Houghton, p. 89.

137   There has long been talk that in some way, Robert Kennedy may have been involved in Monroe's death. But the facts do not bear this out. Robert Kennedy was at an American Bar Association meeting in San Francisco at the time. Robert Kennedy and Marilyn were friends. They met the night Monroe sang her famous, breathless performance of "Happy Birthday" to President Kennedy. As Robert Kennedy's biographer Arthur Schlesinger explained in his biography of Robert Kennedy, "Robert Kennedy, with his curiosity, his sympathy, his absolute directness of response to distress, in some way got through [to Marilyn Monroe.] She called him thereafter in Washington, using an assumed name. She was very often distraught."

Lawford dismissed claims of an affair between Robert Kennedy and Marilyn Monroe as "garbage." Even Monroe herself told her masseur Ralph Roberts she'd heard such rumors and that they were not true. "I like him, but not physically." (Schlesinger, p. 591).

gunpoint and transported back to Bethesda, Maryland, where a team of inexperienced pathologists had conducted the autopsy under the command of, among others, the CIA-connected Rear Admiral Calvin B. Galloway.[138] Neither Eckert nor Noguchi wanted to see that happen again. "This time, bring Washington to you," Eckert advised.[139]

Noguchi contacted the director of the Armed Forces Institute of Pathology, the AFIP. The director told Noguchi that three experts were standing by and would take a supersonic military jet to Los Angeles in the event of Kennedy's death, and he asked Noguchi if he'd mind if one of the experts was Colonel Pierre Finck, who had participated in President Kennedy's autopsy. Noguchi had no objection. The other two were Commander Charles J. Stahl, III, and Dr. Kenneth Earle.

At 8:49 A.M., Noguchi removed a bullet from the back of Kennedy's neck. This bullet had not been life-threatening but was lodged near his spine, so the doctors did not see a need to remove it while Kennedy was still alive. He inscribed "TN31" on the base of the bullet and gave the bullet to Sergeant Jordan, who gave it to Officer Leroy M. Orozco, who logged it into evidence with the provision that the Crime Lab be notified it was available to test against the "arrestee's weapon."

Charles Collier, who had photographed the pantry for Wolfer, photographed the autopsy as well. Years later, copies of these photos would inexplicably turn up in the possession of James Angleton, the CIA's infamous 25-year counterintelligence chief.[140]

The autopsy ended at 9:05 A.M.[141] The official write-up of the autopsy, however, would not enter the record for many months, literally days before the trial was initially set to begin. The obvious reason for this appears to be that the autopsy results, as you will soon see, did not support the official story of events.

Wolfer's log for June 6, 1968, shows his shift ended twice that day: once at 4 P.M. and again at 1 A.M. the following morning. What happened in the interim to keep him there so late?

Wolfer received the non-fatal bullet Noguchi had retrieved from Kennedy's neck in good condition at 3:15 P.M., per his log. He had received the gun the day before. His next step was to do what any criminalist would do: ensure that the bullet he was handed came from the gun in custody. Wolfer fired test bullets from the gun recovered in the pantry. Although it is not noted in his log, we

138   Admiral Calvin Galloway was a point of contact for anti-Castro Cubans wishing to join the CIA's anti-Castro effort, according to Felix Rodriguez in his book *Shadow Warrior* (New York: Simon and Schuster, 1989), pp. 46–48.

139   Thomas T. Noguchi, M.D., *Coroner* (New York: Simon and Schuster, 1983), p. 94.

140   Jefferson Morley, *Our Man in Mexico: Winston Scott and the Hidden History of the CIA* (University Press of Kansas, 2008), p. 282. I was also told this information by a former CIA operative named Carl McNabb years earlier.

141   The medical report M. Bowles in the LAPD files states the autopsy finished at 9:05 A.M. An FBI memorandum of 6/6/68 states it ended at 11:05 A.M., which is incorrect.

have to presume he attempted to make a match between the Kennedy bullet and the test bullet. Yet nowhere in his detailed log is such a comparison indicated. Wolfer clocked out at the end of his shift at 4 P.M.

For some reason, Wolfer returned to the lab for a second session that night. The reason for his return was probably related to the next item in his log: his 9 P.M. "comparison of the Kennedy bullet and Goldstein bullets." What he found was not noted in his log, nor is there mention in the log of a photograph comparing two bullets (called a photomicrograph, as it was taken through a type of a microscope) that was taken in his lab that night and deliberately kept secret for years. Whatever the reason, his activity around this entry kept Wolfer at the lab until 1 A.M.

Seven years later, a panel of experts would uncover a deliberate deception in this photo. It would take many more years before one intrepid researcher would discover an additional layer of deception that even the experts had missed.

On June 7, 1968, Deputy District Attorneys John Howard, Morio Fukuto, and John Miner brought witnesses before the Los Angeles County Grand Jury to tell the story of the assassination as they understood it to date, which wasn't well.

Kennedy's death was the first topic. Miner asked Dr. Cuneo to point to the place where a bullet had entered Kennedy's head. "The bullet entered approximately in the midportion of the right mastoid process, right—just in back of the right ear."[142]

Coroner Noguchi gave the specific cause of death as "gunshot wound of the right mastoid, penetrating the brain." He also described two other gunshot wounds, neither of which would have proved fatal. Kennedy had been shot four times: three shots had entered his body, and a fourth shot had passed through his clothing.

Noguchi numbered the shots "Gunshot Wound 1," "Gunshot Wound 2" and "Gunshot Wound 3," taking care to note that number was purely for identification purposes and was not intended to designate the actual shot order. A fourth shot to Kennedy, which passed through his coat but did not penetrate his body, was not discussed.

The fatal shot, Gunshot Wound 1, entered behind Kennedy's right ear. Gunshot Wound 2 entered the back of the right armpit, "and the Gunshot Wound 2 [sic] was also found very close, approximately—it's about half inch below the Gunshot Wound Number 2," Noguchi said, confusing the Foreman. Miner clarified that there were two separate wounds under the right armpit, within a half-inch of each other, e.g., the lower of which was being designated Gunshot Wound Number 3.

Miner asked Noguchi to describe the path of the bullets through the body. Noguchi explained that the bullet in Gunshot Wound Number 2 penetrated

---

142   All quotes in this section come from the Grand Jury transcript unless otherwise noted.

tissue and muscle both in a "right to left direction" across Kennedy's back and in an "upward, and back to front direction." This bullet, which entered under the armpit, exited at the front of the right shoulder at a steep upward angle. The track of Gunshot Wound Number 3, Noguchi stated, was "almost parallel … to the Gunshot Wound Number 2 pathway," except that this bullet "was found lodged in the area called the sixth cervical vertebra and slightly to the right … at midline, the lower portion of the back of the neck." This was the bullet Noguchi had marked and given to the police.

Miner handed Noguchi Grand Jury Exhibit 5-A, an evidence envelope which carried a bullet. Noguchi examined the bullet and confirmed this was the bullet he had personally pulled from Kennedy's neck. Miner asked how Noguchi could tell it was the same bullet.

"Well, I placed my identifying mark, T.N., my initials, and [the] last number of a Medical Examiner Coroner's Case Number 68-5731 so I placed '31,'—it is very clearly visible on the base of this bullet," Noguchi explained.

Under Miner's questioning, Noguchi explained it was "unlikely" that the bullet retrieved from Kennedy's neck had caused Kennedy's death. Bullet fragments had been recovered from the fatal wound, where the bullet had entered from an inch behind the right ear and shattered inside Kennedy's brain. This was the fatal shot. Noguchi described seeing "blackening discoloration, indicating what we call powder tattooing and still grayish black powder deposited on the surface of the edge of the right ear, and this was about one inch in longest dimension."

Miner said he had no further questions. But a juror did, and evidently the wording of the juror's question, which does not appear in the transcript, caused Miner some concern, for Miner interceded.

"Before we look at the Grand Juror's question, Mr. Foreman, may I reopen my examination of this witness?" Miner asked. The Foreman consented.

Miner asked Noguchi, "Do you have any opinion as to what might have been the distance from which that bullet was fired?"

Noguchi qualified his response first by saying he had not been able to fire the gun, but "the position of the tattooing and the powder on the edge of the right ear indicate that the … muzzle distance was … very, very close." Miner pressed him for the maximum distance the gun muzzle could have been to produce those patterns. "I don't think it will be more than two or three inches from the edge of the right ear," Noguchi said, but he added that he would like to study this further before answering it definitively.

"I think that the question—one question asked by a Grand Juror was answered," Miner said. After an additional question, Noguchi was dismissed.

Something must have nagged at Miner, however, because he followed Noguchi into the hall and asked him had he meant inches or feet, regarding Kennedy's head wound. If Noguchi had misspoken, Miner indicated, Noguchi might want to change his testimony.

"My goodness, it's an inch, not feet, because of the black powder behind the ear," Noguchi responded. [143] Miner didn't press the matter. But the fact that Miner asked the question suggests that Miner understood the significance of the autopsy evidence: none of the witnesses had put Sirhan close enough to have fired a shot from that close a range.[144] Years later, at a 1974 hearing, Noguchi noted that he didn't have to concern himself with witness testimony—only the physical evidence.[145]

Noguchi was smart enough to understand he had better be able to back up his assertion with harder proof. That afternoon, while the Grand Jury proceedings were still continuing, Noguchi surprised a lab technician with a request for seven pigs' ears.

On June 10, Noguchi had lab technicians attach the pigs' ears to muslin-covered "skulls," which were then fired upon by an LAPD officer at the Police Academy on June 11.[146] He found an exact match to the powder pattern on Kennedy's head at one position, proving the gun muzzle must have been "one inch from the edge of his right ear and three inches behind the head."[147]

At 10 A.M. on June 7, not far from the room where the Grand Jury sat, U.S. Attorney William Matthew Byrne, Jr. hosted a high-powered interagency meeting.

Several of the government officials involved in this meeting would go on to fame and fortune. In addition to Inspector Powers and a couple of deputy chiefs from the LAPD as well as William Lynch, head of the Criminal Division under U.S. Attorney General Clark, Byrne met with Warren Christopher, then the Deputy Attorney General under U.S. Attorney General Ramsey Clark and later Secretary of State under President Jimmy Carter; and Chief Deputy District Attorney Lynn D. "Buck" Compton, who was later appointed to the Second District Court of Appeals by then-Governor Ronald Reagan, and whose World War II exploits as part of the U.S. Army's 101st Airborne Division were immortalized in the HBO series *Band of Brothers*. Byrne himself later presided over the Daniel Ellsberg trial regarding the leaked Pentagon Papers, two years after having been appointed as a judge to the U.S. Federal Court.

Also at the meeting was Evelle Younger, the Los Angeles District Attorney.

143   Moldea, p. 92.

144   Some authors have quoted Lisa Urso, who said Sirhan fired his gun at "point blank range." But in a reenactment for the LAPD, Urso made clear that *her* definition of "point blank range" meant a *few feet*, not an inch.

145   Testimony of Thomas Noguchi at a Los Angeles Board of Supervisors hearing, May 13, 1974.

146   In his book, Noguchi said the tests occurred "the next day." They did occur the day after the pigs' ears arrived. But in DeWayne Wolfer's log, the muzzle test preparation happened on June 10, and the shooting test conducted with Noguchi occurred on June 11.

147   Noguchi and DiMona, *Coroner*, p. 103.

Earlier in his career, Younger had run the FBI's National Defense section before being "co-opted by the Counterintelligence Branch of OSS for service in the Far East."[148] The OSS was the forerunner to the CIA. Curiously, John Garrett "Gary" Underhill, an OSS small arms expert who had done "special assignments" for the CIA, blamed the CIA's "Far East section" for the assassination of President John F. Kennedy. Underhill died in a "suicide" that appeared to be a murder.[149] The CIA did admit to planning assassination plots in the Far East against the Chinese leader Chou En-lai, [150] Indonesia's leader Achmed Sukarno,[151] and Prince Norodom Sihanouk of Cambodia.[152] Desmond Fitzgerald had run the CIA's Far East Division from 1957 to 1962, after which he headed up the Cuban Task Force which was tasked by President Kennedy to find a way to overthrow, but not kill, Castro, a point we'll return to much later.

Byrne's group discussed jurisdictional responsibilities of their respective agencies, how information would be exchanged among agencies, and "ramifications in investigations which might engulf areas of the Mid-East."[153]

What ramifications did they fear? One year earlier, Egypt and Israel had been gripped in what became known as the "Six-Day War." And just as the Cuban Missile Crisis, one year before President Kennedy's assassination, had almost led to nuclear war, the Arab-Israeli conflict, one year before Robert Kennedy's assassination, almost turned nuclear as well.[154]

One year to the day before Robert Kennedy was shot, Israel had launched a preemptive strike against what they asserted was the threat of imminent attack by Arab forces from Egypt, Syria and Jordan. The popular young Egyptian leader Gamal Abdel Nasser had expelled UN advisors from the Suez Canal zone in May 1967. Israel read that as preparation for an attack on Israel, so Israel struck first. In preparation for their attack, Israel had also attacked the American intelligence ship U.S.S. *Liberty*, professing not to see the American flags it was flying nor the clear markings that it was an American vessel. The Israelis quickly struck against Egyptian air forces, crippling their ability to respond. Israel then seized control of the Golan Heights, Sinai Peninsula, and the Gaza Strip. The Soviets immediately threatened the U.S. that if it did not pressure Israel to immediately

---

148   Richard Harris Smith, *OSS: The Secret History of America's First Central Intelligence Agency* (Berkeley, University of California Press, 1972) pp. 20–21.

149   James DiEugenio, *Destiny Betrayed: JFK, Cuba and the Garrison Case* (New York: Sheridan Square Press, 1992, First Edition), pp. 27–30.

150   Schlesinger, *Robert Kennedy and His Times*, p. 481.

151   Testimony of Richard Bissell to the Church Committee, June 11, 1975, p. 60.

152   David Pallister, "Leaders on the CIA's hit list," *The Guardian*, March 20, 2003, via www.theguardian.com/world/2003/mar/21/usa.davidpallister, accessed September 16, 2015.

153   LAPD interview of Inspector Powers, 10/2/68.

154   Isabella Ginor, "How Six Day War almost led to Armageddon," *The Guardian*, June 9, 2000, via www.theguardian.com/world/2000/jun/10/israel1, accessed September 16, 2015.

cease military actions, the Soviets would attack Israel.[155] Israel, for its part, was hurriedly trying to complete the building of its first nuclear weapon.[156] By 1968, President Johnson may well have feared that discovering some sort of Arab-led conspiracy might have led to a nuclear conflict in the Middle East.

After President Kennedy's assassination, when evidence surfaced suggesting (falsely) that Lee Harvey Oswald was a Communist, President Johnson told the Warren Commission (which should have been named the Dulles Commission, after its most active member, the deposed CIA chief Allen Dulles) that he didn't want to find a conspiracy that might lead to war with the Soviet Union. If any of the participants in Byrne's meeting willingly participated in a cover-up of aspects of conspiracy, it's possible a similar inducement was provided, that blaming the Arabs might lead to a nuclear confrontation in the Middle East.

At the end of this meeting, a second meeting was scheduled, to include Chief Houghton, DeWayne Wolfer, and others, for June 9.

Back at the courthouse, Officer Travis White described to the Grand Jury entering the pantry at the direction of people in the hotel and seeing eight to ten people holding down a suspect on a steam table. He guessed there had been between 75 to 100 people in the pantry when he entered.

Although it took several people to subdue the suspect in the pantry, Officer White said the suspect gave them no trouble at all once they got to him, and he did not struggle when they put the handcuffs on.

The first shooting witness to testify was 17-year-old Irwin Stroll, who appeared in a wheelchair, as he was still recovering from the gunshot wound to his left leg. Irwin had been asked to guard the northernmost of the two swinging doors at the west of the pantry. Sergeant Albert La Vallee had earlier introduced into evidence a diagram showing the layout of the pantry he had made in his official capacity as the officer in charge of the Survey Unit in the Scientific Investigation Division (SID). Howard had Irwin show the Jurors where he had been standing, the northwest door of the pantry, and marked his location S-1. A security guard covered the southernmost of the two swinging doors, marked S-2.

Irwin was just outside the northwest pantry door as Kennedy and his party came through. Two press people beat him to the door. As he followed them into the pantry, he heard something "like firecrackers, just pop, pop, pop, all over the place—and smoke." He pushed Ethel Kennedy to the floor and covered her. He felt "a kick in the knee" but then saw blood, and realized he had been shot. He didn't see the shooter.

---

155   *Ibid.*

156   Press release "Untold Nuclear Dimension of the Six-Day War," issued 6/7/07 from the Arms Control Association, citing Avner Cohen, *Israel and the Bomb* (Columbia University Press, 1998).

Other pantry witnesses followed. Jesus Perez was so nervous on the stand that Deputy D.A. Fukuto asked him to "relax a bit." Perez identified a picture of Sirhan as the person he had talked to about half an hour before the shooting. Sirhan had asked Perez three or four times if Kennedy would be coming through that area. Perez had been near the first steam table on the western end, and Sirhan had come and gone from that position.

Vincent DiPierro testified that he had stayed at S-2, the southern door at the west end of the pantry, right next to where Stroll was standing. Howard asked if DiPierro had seen a "young chap there though at that time, like a guard," because Stroll had described talking to a guard there.

"Yes, he had glasses. I recall he was wearing glasses, dark-rimmed glasses." When the Senator came through on his way to speak, this person asked DiPierro to help hold people back.

When Kennedy returned to those doors after his speech, roughly 15 minutes later, DiPierro followed him into the pantry. The Kennedy party walked through door S-1, which was propped open and which opened from the pantry into the hallway between the stage and pantry area. DiPierro pushed through door S-2, which opened from the hallway into the pantry. He was about five feet from Kennedy when DiPierro reached the ice machine. There, he noticed "a girl and the accused person standing on…a tray stacker…. Whether or not the second person was involved, I don't know."

DiPierro described that the tray stacker was "four or six inches off the ground."

"If I stood on it, I'd have a six-inch height advantage?" Howard asked.

"Yes, sir, you would." Even if there were trays on the stand, because the trays were oval, DiPierro explained, one could still get a foothold.

DiPierro told the jury that the only reason he noticed Sirhan was because "there was a very good-looking girl next to him." Howard asked why he noticed "the fellow" next to the girl. "Because he was grabbing on with his left hand … [to] part of the tray holder. … he looked as though he was clutching his stomach, as though somebody had … elbowed him." DiPierro said Sirhan was in a "semi-crouched" position.

"From that moment on, I just looked at the girl, and I saw him get down off the tray stand. And when I went to turn, the next thing I saw was him holding a gun. He kind of moved around Mr. Uecker … He kind of motioned around him and stuck the gun straight out, and nobody could move. It was—you were just frozen; you didn't know what to do.

"And then I saw the first powdering or plastering. When he pulled the trigger, the first shot, Mr. Kennedy fell down."

"How close to the Senator was the suspect when this gun started firing?" Howard asked.

"Four feet—four to six feet." DiPierro added that he thought the suspect must have been "on his tiptoes" to shoot around Mr. Uecker, who was "quite huge." DiPierro heard five shots but acknowledged there could have been more. He got blood all over his face and glasses. "And then the man that got shot in the head fell in my arms," he said, referring to Paul Schrade. "And then the other boy that got shot in the thigh [Ira Goldstein], he fell on top of me, and they pushed me down, they fell on top of me."

Asked if he had seen what happened to the Senator before DiPierro himself fell, DiPierro said, "The first shot, he kind of reared back very, very sharply. ... Both hands went up like that," he said, matching what other witnesses had described or would soon describe, of how Kennedy threw his hands up to shield his face at the time of the shooting.

Asked to describe the suspect's post-shooting behavior, DiPierro said, "Well, the suspect turned almost immediately ... he was trying to escape. He tried very, very hard to get away."

Howard showed DiPierro Grand Jury Exhibit 7, the gun retrieved in the pantry, and asked if that was the gun he remembered. "The same gun," DiPierro said, adding, "the reason is it had the funny little corkscrew here."

"That is in front of the gun, below the barrel?"

"Yes, sir. It's the same thing I saw."

DiPierro described the shot sequence: "The first shot was definitely a distinct shot. I mean, it was a pause in between the next three. It was three rapid ones that were fired. The first one I saw, you know, I was stunned after that."

Howard brought DiPierro back to the girl he had seen with Sirhan. Howard asked if DiPierro could identify her if he saw her again.

"I would never forget what she looked like because she had a very good-looking figure—and the dress was kind of—kind of lousy ... It looked as though it was a white dress and it had either black or dark purple polka dots on it.

"It kind of had—I don't know what they call it—but it's like—looked like a bib in the front, kind of went around."

"A lace dickey, probably," a Grand Juror offered.

"It was the same as the clothing," DiPierro clarified. "And then she was—she—the person who is accused of shooting him was—like I say, they were both on the—standing together."

"Back of the tray stand?" Howard asked.

"Yes ... he looked as though he either talked to her or flirted with her because she smiled. This is just before he got down. ... Together, they were both smiling. As he got down, he was smiling. ... In fact, the minute the first two shots were fired, he still had a very sick-looking smile on his face. That's the one thing—I can never forget that."

One of the jurors asked DiPierro to describe the facial characteristics of the girl. "She had dark hair that was cut … just above the shoulders. … And it just kind of looked like it was messed up … She could have changed that—she could have come with curls. I don't know, it was just messed up at the time.

"Her face—facial expression, she had what looked like a short nose. She wasn't too—facially, she wasn't too pretty; she was not that pretty. …

"And like I say, figure—she had a very good figure."

Howard asked DiPierro to describe the dress. "It was a white dress and it had either black or dark purple polka dots on it. It kind of had—I don't know what they call it—but it's like—looked like a bib in the front, kind of went around. It's like that," he said, indicating with his hands.

Howard asked DiPierro how all the non-kitchen staff got into the kitchen, given that there were guards at both ends of the pantry. DiPierro himself had been challenged by a guard, but a fellow worker had said to the guard "He is with the hotel." DiPierro had no answer, but stated most of the people in the pantry seemed to be press people.

Ira Goldstein took the stand next. A young reporter for *Continental News*, Goldstein had initially entered the pantry because someone said there were sandwiches there. He did not notice Sirhan there. While inside, the Senator entered just as Ira was walking west. The woman he was with, Robin Casden, shook Kennedy's hand, and then Ira and his companion continued on. He heard shots just seconds after he passed Kennedy. He thought it was balloons popping, but by the second or third sound he realized someone was shooting at Kennedy. He didn't turn back to look. He stepped over Irwin Stroll, who was wounded already, and felt a bullet graze him. Then a second bullet hit him in his left thigh. Like DiPierro, he heard about five shots, but said there could have been more. Goldstein staggered to the wall and fell against DiPierro.

Goldstein added, unprompted: "By the way, the shots had the same tone to them. I don't think they were from two guns, two different guns. … They sounded the same."

Officer Arthur Placencia testified next. He didn't even know whom the suspect had shot when he apprehended him. He described how in the car, the young man refused to give his name. Officer Placencia read him his rights and asked if the suspect understood them. The suspect was silent, so Placencia read them again. This time, the suspect mumbled something. Placencia read him his rights a third time and asked him "Do you understand your rights?" The suspect said yes, and indicated he wished to remain silent. Officer Placencia then asked, "Do you wish an attorney present?" When the suspect indicated that he did, Placencia asked him no more questions.

Next up was Karl Uecker. Howard asked Uecker, who had a noticeable German accent, to slow down a bit when he spoke so the transcriptionist and jury could process what he was saying. Fukuto showed Uecker the drawing of the pantry, and Uecker described taking Kennedy's hand to lead him into the pantry. Kennedy had turned almost immediately after entering to shake someone's hand, causing Uecker to lose his grip. Uecker retrieved Kennedy's hand and led him a few steps further, to the west end of the steam tables, when Kennedy again turned, breaking free to shake a dishwasher's hand. Uecker grabbed him one last time and turned to walk eastward. Then, said Uecker, "something rushed on my right side. I—at that time I didn't recognize what it was, paper or white pieces of things."

Uecker heard the first and second shots, felt Kennedy fall from his hand, and noticed a shooter to his right. He threw his right arm around the shooter's neck and pressed him up against the steam table.

"While I was holding the hand where he had the gun in, I was trying to get the point of the gun as far as I could away from the part where Mr. Kennedy was laying. ... I was trying to push the gun away ... where I didn't see too many people, while he was still shooting."

Fukuto asked Uecker how many shots he had heard.

"I couldn't heard [sic] too clearly, but I thought it was five or six, but I was hitting his hand on the steam heater as hard as I could, with my left hand, I had him right here on the wrist, and hitting my left hand on the heater to get rid of the gun."

"He has his gun in his right hand?" Fukuto asked.

"In his right hand, yes."

"And you grabbed him with your left hand?"

"The left hand, yes, and had the right arm around his neck. I was standing there and he was shooting and I could feel when he was turning his hand towards the crowd, that's why I pushed all over the steam table as far as I could, to almost to the end of the steam table."

Uecker had pushed the suspect down backwards onto the steam table.

"And then I saw some hands coming over, reaching for the gun. I don't know who it was." Uecker hollered at his partner Eddie Minasian to "Get the police."

Asked again how many shots he thought he had heard, Uecker said "there was six shots—six—could be seven."

Fukuto asked how many times the gun went off before Uecker grabbed the suspect.

"Twice" was Uecker's unequivocal reply.

"Twice that you know?"

"I must have grabbed the arm by the third shot."

Fukuto showed him the gun and asked how it compared with the one he had seen in the pantry.

"I don't know too much about guns, but I think it was about this size. ... The gun was not bigger than this one."

"I understand, you can't say it's the same gun?" Fukuto probed.

"I couldn't tell you it was the same gun because I was too busy to keep him in my headlock."

Amazingly, at Sirhan's trial, Uecker was the one asked to verify that Sirhan's gun was the one used in the pantry. Amazingly, no one on Sirhan's defense team quoted this back to Uecker on the stand in rebuttal of that identification.

Fukuto was ready to dismiss Uecker, but the foreman indicated one of the jurors, Mrs. Meyers, had a question, which was read by Mr. Fukuto:

"How far was the suspect from Senator Kennedy and yourself at the time that the first shot took place?"

"How far?" Uecker said, thinking. "As far as my left hand can reach because I remember I was trying to pull him [Kennedy], and the man who shot [Sirhan], I could feel him [Sirhan] coming around me ... I could feel that the gun was about this far," Uecker said, indicating a distance, "when he shot, right from me, from my right."

"Your body was in between this person's body and—"

"—and Senator Kennedy."

"And his arm reached over your body when he fired—"

"Around me, around me, not over me."

Edward Minasian testified next. He told nearly the same story as Uecker, but from a slightly different angle. After Kennedy stopped to shake hands, both Minasian and Uecker turned back also and took a step toward Kennedy. As Minasian turned his head to the left to look back toward the west, he described how through his "peripheral vision" he "noticed someone dart out from this area, dart out and lean against the steam table."

"And I saw a hand extended with a revolver, and I saw the explosion of the cartridges out of the ... revolver."

Howard asked to what portion of the Senator's body the gun was pointed.

"I would say the revolver was at the suspect's shoulder height."

"Could you tell how close to the Senator the barrel of that gun would be?"

"Approximately three feet."

"Was there one shot at this time or more than one shot?"

"I heard two shots. ... They were very, very deliberate shots. There was just a slight pause. It was a bang-bang cadence, and after the second shot, why, as I said, I saw the flash of the cartridges being discharged, and immediately there were several other people in that area behind the Senator, and I just pushed into Karl Uecker."

"It seemed to be that the gentleman standing behind the Senator [Paul Schrade] fell first," Minasian added. "And the Senator was kind of staggering a little bit, and then seemed to be that that was the order that they fell." (Other witnesses would later say Kennedy fell first, then Paul. Clearly, they fell nearly simultaneously.)

Howard asked how many shots he heard in total.

"I thought he emptied the revolver, and there were quite a few—I know the first two were deliberate, and the others came in quick spurts so—"

"[I]f there were two—was that before anyone touched the suspect or the person shooting?"

"Yes, sir."

"After that, people started grabbing?"

"Right."

"And there were then shots fired after that, is that correct?"

"That's correct."

"Were those shots fired in the general direction of the Senator?"

"I doubt it because the Senator at that time was—well, the suspect was shooting from this … end of the table. And I don't see how he could have been shooting at—and we had him and his arm somewhere on this steam table here. And I doubt if it was in the same direction as the first two shots."

At this point, the Grand Jury broke for lunch.

The Grand Jury reconvened at 2 P.M., and Howard questioned Harold Burba. Burba was a fireman with the Los Angeles Fire Department assigned to the Photo Bureau, where he occasionally took photos "when requested by other agencies, such as the Fire Prevention Bureau." (In a statement to the FBI later that day, Burba stated he had gone to the Ambassador Hotel at the request of the Fire Prevention Bureau "to take pictures of any violations of fire regulations.")

Burba told the Jury that he was in the pantry about 30 minutes before Kennedy came through. Howard asked Burba "What is the first thing that you noticed or heard that was unusual?"

"I think the first thing that attracted my attention was the gunshots sounded like a cap pistol to me."

"What did you do when you heard those shots?"

"Well, I was looking in that direction and saw the flashes, and I jumped up and started over in that direction. And there was such a big crowd around, that I—my second thought was, 'my job is to take pictures,' so I went back and got my camera and started taking pictures."

Howard showed Burba Grand Jury exhibits 3-A and 3-B, large photos of Sirhan as he was being apprehended. Burba said he had witnessed the man depicted in those photos walk in with Kennedy's party the first time he entered the pantry, en route to the stage to speak. Burba said this man noticed his attention because "he appeared to be looking all around him instead of looking ahead, as all other members were." The prosecution had called Burba because his account suggested premeditation—a key component the County would have to prove to convict Sirhan.

Burba noticed the man who was "looking all around him" was holding a rolled-up poster—"I thought maybe it was a Kennedy poster, or something. And he was holding it in both hands." Burba described the roll as two feet long and "possibly three—three—three to four or five inches in diameter." He saw the man hold this object up, twice, at two different times. "The only reason it caught my eye was because it was the same object. I wondered about it as he passed by, what it was. … I saw the poster, as if he was holding it up, to get it out of the way, or something. At least, I saw the poster up in the air."

Neither Burba, nor the grand jurors, nor the prosecution had any way of knowing that Burba was actually describing Michael Wayne, not Sirhan. Burba himself didn't learn that until a month later, when the LAPD showed him a photo of Wayne, at which point Burba stated it was Wayne, not Sirhan, that he saw walking with the rolled-up poster looking around suspiciously. Instead of proving premeditation, Burba's testimony proved only that sworn testimony is not necessarily accurate, however honestly given. Burba swore to what he *thought* was true. But it wasn't the truth at all. This would not be the last time an untruth entered the court record as an uncontested "fact" that wasn't.

Henry Carreon spoke next. He was a playground director for an elementary school but was also studying police science at East Los Angeles College. He had gone to a shooting range in Fish Canyon in the San Gabriel Mountains, several miles east of the Pasadena area, with another man, David Montellano, on June 4, the day of the presidential primary. They were there from about noon to 2 P.M.

Under Howard's questioning, Carreon described seeing a shooter, "about five feet away," who was shooting very rapidly with a revolver. On the range, Carreon explained, "you are supposed to shoot and pause. … Usually, the range officer goes up to an individual shooting in this manner and he will inform them that it's not supposed to be done on the range. So this attracted our attention."

Carreon was asked if the man shown in the same photos that had just been shown to Burba was the same man he had seen on the range. Carreon said it was.

Carreon related how David went over and asked the man shooting what type of revolver he was using. The man said it was a .22 caliber gun. But when Carreon asked him the same question, he got an odd response: "At first, he paused. He didn't say anything, like as if I wasn't—didn't even exist. And then I asked him again. … And he said, 'An Iver Johnson.'" The man then turned the pistol around and showed it to him.

Howard asked if he had noticed how many shells the man had fired and what type of ammunition he had used. "I'd say three to four hundred empty casings," Carreon replied. (No one ever reported Sirhan buying that much ammunition, ever.) Carreon also quoted David as having asked, "Isn't that a special type of bullet?" because the man "had just one box aside from all these other—that it's called the mini-magnum; and this type of bullet, when it penetrates on an object, usually tears and splits out into different directions where the regular bullet of a .22 caliber goes in a hole, and when it goes into an object, it will come out the same size." While Mini-Mag bullets can shatter on impact, they don't always. In this case, it's interesting that of all the bullets fired in the pantry, that the only one that shattered was the one that entered Robert Kennedy's brain.

Howard handed Carreon the gun Rafer Johnson had turned in. "This is it," Carreon said. Howard asked was there any other conversation.

"I think the individual asked David, 'How do you hold your gun to get better accuracy because this gun doesn't have a sight on it?' … It didn't have a sight where David's did."

Two jurors had questions. Was anyone allowed to shoot on that particular range? Yes. Was a fee required? No. Was it crowded that day? No. Was there a range master that day? Yes. But the range master, Everett Buckner, who would have a very interesting story to tell about what he had seen on the range that day, had not yet been interviewed.

Dr. V. Faustin Bazilauskas described the wounds of the other people shot that night. The first victim he saw was a young man (Irwin Stroll) with a shin injury. (He did not appear to know that a bullet was recovered from Stroll's leg, and the Grand Jury did not learn of this.) Elizabeth Evans had a bullet lodged in her forehead that had penetrated about an inch and a half into her scalp, but she was lucid and hadn't required immediate treatment. A bullet had penetrated William Weisel's left abdomen but Dr. Bazilauskas didn't know how deeply. All of these victims were sent out to neighboring hospitals for treatment. He remembered a "young fellow" named "Goldstein" who had a bullet lodged in his "upper thigh, near the hip."

Dr. Bazilauskas' initial notes on Paul Schrade said the wound was "superficial," but it was already bandaged, and he did not probe the wound. He simply determined Schrade's condition was neurologically sound, and he sent him to another hospital for treatment. Schrade had said, according to Dr. Bazilauskas, "I'm not bad, Doctor. Work on the others." According to the doctor's notes, the wound was "in the vertex," i.e., the top portion of the skull. (A bullet was subsequently removed from the top of Schrade's head and not at "the center of his forehead," as Officer DeWayne Wolfer's 7/8/68 report would wrongly attest,[157] but Dr. Bazilauskas appeared to have no knowledge of this either when he testified.)

Charles Hughes testified that a "Chrysler products" key was found on the suspect and given to Hughes by Officer White. Hughes noted that Officer White had put his initials on the evidence, and Hughes read the serial number into the record. He had given the key to Lieutenant Albin Hegge at about 4:30 P.M. on June 5. Oddly, this evidence did not come to the court in an evidence envelope. It came in Hughes' pocket.

Hegge testified that he had received the key from Officer White initially, but had returned it to White, who then gave it to Hughes, who gave it back to Hegge. Howard asked if he had obtained a search warrant to search the car which this key fit. He had.

"What type of automobile did you search?"

"I searched a '56 Chrysler Sedan," Hegge said.

But that wasn't Sirhan's car. The Chrysler, a '58 model, had been Robert Gindroz's car. Sirhan drove a '56 De Soto. As we saw earlier, the key to Sirhan's car also opened the door to Gindroz's car. The jury was not informed of this.[158] Hegge moved seamlessly to describing what was in Sirhan's car, and how he had found a wallet inside "the glove compartment of the '56 De Soto which I searched."

"Just a minute," the Foreman interjected. "He first called it a Chrysler. Now it's a De Soto. Which is it?"

"It is a De Soto," Hegge replied.

Hegge's testimony shows how easy it is, even for the police, to mix and match evidence, even when testifying under oath on the stand. This, too, would happen repeatedly in this case.

Along with the wallet, Hegge found a box of Mini-Mag ammunition, as well as two "expended" slugs. Howard asked him "When you say 'expended slugs,' what does that mean?'"

"This is the lead portion of the bullet from a—that has been fired."[159]

Why would anyone fire a bullet and then retrieve the bullet and put it in

---

157   I know this personally because Paul Schrade took my hand and placed it on his wound, which was just forward of the center of the top of his head, well back from the hairline. That's not the "forehead," which is characterized in *Medscape Reference* as "the upper third of the face." See emedicine.medscape.com/article/834862-overview, accessed 2/8/13. The wound Schrade had me touch was at the vertex, just as Dr. Bazilauskas had said.

158   The LAPD later said the lock in Gindroz's car was defective and that any number of keys could have opened it.

159   Oddly, when the FBI examined these two "expended slugs" the following day, they came to a different conclusion:

"Regarding the two spent bullets found in the vehicle registered to Sirhan Sirhan, one is not capable of being examined as it is flattened out, appearing to have hit a piece of metal or rock. The other one has not been subjected to ballistics examination but from visual observation indicates that it had been removed from its casing without being fired." FBI report of 6/8/68, LAFO #56-156, Sub File X-1, Volume 4, p. 1082.

their car? It's not like it could be used again, and Sirhan was no bullet collector. Had someone planted bullets retrieved from the pantry doorframes in Sirhan's car in the hopes of tying him to the shooting?

A couple of miles from the courthouse, FBI photographer Richard "Dick" Fernandez[160] and FBI Special Agent Al Greiner were busy at the Ambassador Hotel. Frans Stalpers, the Assistant Manager of the Ambassador Hotel, had arranged for them to photograph interiors and exteriors of the Ambassador Hotel. At this time, Greiner was the Los Angeles Photographic Squad Supervisor. Greiner would eventually become the number three man in the Los Angeles office.[161] Under Greiner's supervision, each photo was captioned with a letter and a number, and a map of the hotel was marked and inserted in sequence to indicate exactly what portion of the hotel was depicted in each photo.

By the time Fernandez took the pantry photos, the wood facing that had been in front of the doorframes had been removed not just from the doorframe but from the pantry altogether, leaving the FBI without crucial evidence.[162] Even so, Fernandez took close-up photos of the four holes in the doorframes—two in the center divider and two more on the left side of the southernmost door at the west end of the pantry. The photos were captioned—unequivocally—"bullet holes."

But the Grand Jury wasn't told that in addition to the seven bullets re-covered from the five shooting victims, four bullet holes had been found in the doorframes. They also weren't told that the LAPD had already identified at least three additional bullet holes in ceiling tiles. And the one man in a position to know about all of these bullets and holes did not tell them this when he testified.

Under Fukuto's questioning, DeWayne Wolfer provided his background. "I am a police officer for the City of Los Angeles, assigned to the Scientific Investigation Division, Crime Laboratory, where I act as a criminalist, and among my criminalistics duties is that of firearms and ballistics expert." He received a Bachelor's Degree from the University of Southern California, where he was a pre-med student. He had a background "in the field of chemistry, physics, and all types of laboratory technique courses."

---

160   Greg Roberts, "Police Supress [sic] LAPD Intelligence Records," *Hollywood Press*, dated "9/10–9/20/76" per the notation on the clipping in the FBI's LAFO file, Sub-H, Volume 6 and Greg Roberts, "County Supervisors Ward and Hahn to Visit Sirhan in Soledad," *Hollywood Press*, 5/27/77. Greg identifies the photographer as "Dick," and other records identify the photographer as Richard Fernandez. Most authors on this case have mistakenly credited Greiner for the photos.

161   Greg Roberts, "County Supervisors Ward and Hahn to Visit Sirhan in Soledad," *Hollywood Press*, 5/27/77.

162   This is deduced from the fact that the LAPD photo list included pictures of the wood frame facings, but the FBI photo list did not. The facings were known to have removed and placed in LAPD custody. The absence of photos of the molding in the otherwise comprehensive FBI list is circumstantial evidence that the moldings were removed from the scene before June 7. They do not appear in any of the FBI photographs in this set.

Wolfer described how, after being assigned to the SID Laboratory in January 1951, he went to "all of the major firearms factories" to study weapons. He "manufactured barrels and all parts of guns to study the basis of—upon which we make our identifications." He made "similar and like studies at all of the major ammunition factories." He was also a part-time assistant professor at California State College at Long Beach, where he taught criminalistics. He also taught "the criminalistics subject matter" at USC, UCLA, and a number of smaller colleges.

"I have testified hundreds of times involving firearms and ballistics matter in our courts here in the State of California," he added. He had "published papers" regarding these matters.

Fukuto asked Wolfer to describe how he could tell a particular bullet came from a particular gun. Wolfer explained:

> In the barrels or the rifling of the weapon there is what we call imperfections which scratch the bullet as they cross these imperfections. These imperfections produce in the bullet a series of valleys and ridges which we call striation marks ...
>
> We would take and fire the gun into a water recovery tank so that the bullet entered the water and was stopped with little or no damage. We would then recover that bullet and place it under what we call a comparison microscope, which is simply two microscopes with one eye piece. We place the bullet that we test fire through the suspected weapon on one stage of the microscope and the bullet, such as the—such as a Coroner's bullet or the evidence bullet on the other stage of the microscope.
>
> Then, as we look through the common eye piece at both of these bullets, we would be able to see lines on one bullet, on one side of the microscope, and lines on the other.
>
> We would try to line them up ... if we can line up a majority of the lines, we can say it was fired from this revolver and no other.

Fukuto directed Wolfer to Exhibit 5-A, the bullet Noguchi had retrieved from the back of Kennedy's neck and on the base of which Noguchi had inscribed his initials. Had he seen that before? Wolfer answered yes, he had seen that bullet the day before.

When asked when he had seen the gun presented as Grand Jury Exhibit 7, Wolfer responded:

"I first saw this revolver on or about June the 6th of this year."

"That's yesterday, too?"

"That's yesterday, too."

Wolfer may well have inadvertently told the truth here, for reasons that will become clear in a later chapter. But if that were the truth, then the gun the Grand Jury was looking at wasn't the one Rafer Johnson had brought to the police after the shooting, as Wolfer had first seen *that* gun on June 5. As Fukuto started to ask the next question, Wolfer suddenly realized his serious mistake.

"Actually, no, I saw it in the latter part of June the 5th, in the afternoon."

Fukuto asked Wolfer if he had made test shots from Grand Jury Exhibit 7.

"I did."

"Do you have the test shots with you?"

"I have some of the test shots, but not all of the test shots."

Wolfer handed Fukuto an evidence envelope with test bullets in it. This item was marked as Grand Jury Exhibit 5-B. What was in evidence envelope 5-B? Four spent slugs, Wolfer told him.

Were markings found on them? Yes. Did Wolfer compare these markings to the bullet labeled 5-A, the bullet retrieved from Kennedy's neck?

"I did."

"And from your comparison of the two bullets, were you able to form any opinion as to the bullet 5-A?

"I was."

"What is that opinion?"

"That the bullet in People's 5-A here, marked the bullet from Robert Kennedy, was fired in the exhibit, the revolver here, People's Exhibit Number 7 at some time. Yes, it was fired in the weapon."

"Any question about that?"

"No."

"So that the gun that fired Exhibit 5-A was Grand Jury Exhibit Number 7, is that right?"

"That's correct."

But that was misleading, if not outright perjury. In 1971, under oath, Wolfer would reveal that *none* of the four bullets he submitted to the Grand Jury as Exhibit 5-B had been successfully matched to the Kennedy neck bullet.

Wolfer claimed other bullets *not* submitted to the Grand Jury *did* match the Kennedy bullet, despite the lack of evidence of that in any of Wolfer's detailed logs. Wolfer would testify that Fukuto had given him permission to keep some of the bullets, and that Wolfer had put those bullets—which he alleged *did* match to the bullet from Kennedy's neck— in a manila envelope, a plain envelope or a paper bindle, depending on which of these conflicting answers Wolfer gave you wish to believe.[163] He then returned to his office, where he put this all-important evidence in his desk drawer, locked only with his desk drawer lock. And the kicker? Those three remaining bullets would be placed at some later date in an

---

163   Lynn Mangan, *Sirhan Evidence Report*, p. 20. On June 16, 1971, Mangan found that Wolfer told Commander Beck for a Board of Inquiry that he had stored the test bullets in "a paper bindle" in his pocket until

envelope dated June 6 but marked with *a gun number that did not match Sirhan's gun.* The gun with *that* number wouldn't officially enter the case, according to Wolfer, until June 11.

But the Grand Jury would learn none of this. Their session concluded just before 4 P.M. The Grand Jury issued an indictment of Sirhan Sirhan, and the scramble to prepare the cases for the prosecution and the defense began in earnest.

On the East Coast the next morning, June 8, a mile-long line of mourners waited to say their final goodbye to Senator Robert Kennedy. Kennedy family, friends, and politicians of various stripes, including ex-Vice President Richard Nixon and current Vice President Hubert Humphrey, gathered at St. Patrick's Cathedral in New York as friends and strangers were allowed to file past the casket. The ceremony was broadcast live.

Ted Kennedy, who had lost all three of his older brothers, gave a moving eulogy. He opened with a short statement of his own:

> On behalf of Mrs. Kennedy, her children, the parents and sisters of Robert Kennedy, I want to express what we feel to those who mourn with us today in this Cathedral and around the world.
>
> We loved him as a brother, and as a father, and as a son...Love is not an easy feeling to put into words. Nor is loyalty, or trust, or joy. But he was all of these. He loved life completely and he lived it intensely.

Ted quoted from a eulogy Robert had given at their father's memorial service to show the true nature of Robert Kennedy:

> What it really all adds up to is love—not love as it is described with such facility in popular magazines, but the kind of love that is affection and respect, order and encouragement, and support. Our awareness of this was an incalculable source of strength, and because real love is something unselfish and involves sacrifice and giving, we could not help but profit from it. ...
>
> [My father] tried to engender a social conscience. There were wrongs which needed attention. There were people who were poor and needed help. And we have a responsibility to them and to this country. Through no virtues and accomplishments of our own, we have been fortunate enough to be born in the United States under

---

he got back to his office, at which point he put the bindle in his desk drawer and locked it. But a few days later, on June 29, 1971, Wolfer told John Howard, also for the Board of Inquiry, that he had placed the test bullets in "a plain envelope." On September 9, 1971, Wolfer told Barbara Blehr in a legal case the bullets were placed in a "plain manila envelope."

the most comfortable conditions. We, therefore, have a responsibility to others who are less well off.

Ted then quoted extensively from Robert's "Day of Affirmation" address in South Africa, which he gave on June 6, 1966, two years to the day before he died. No other speech so clearly elucidated just who Robert Kennedy was and what he cared most passionately about, and why he had the kind of enemies who would stop at nothing to keep him out of power:

> There is discrimination in this world, and slavery, and slaughter, and starvation. Governments repress their people; millions are trapped in poverty while the nation grows rich and wealth is lavished on armaments everywhere. These are differing evils, but they are the common works of man. ... But we can perhaps remember—even if only for a time—that those who live with us are our brothers; that they share with us the same short moment of life; that they seek—as we do—nothing but the chance to live out their lives in purpose and happiness ....
>
> Some believe there is nothing one man or one woman can do against the enormous array of the world's ills. Yet many of the world's great movements, of thought and action, have flowed from the work of a single man. A young monk began the Protestant reformation; a young general extended an empire from Macedonia to the borders of the earth; a young woman reclaimed the territory of France; and it was a young Italian explorer who discovered the New World, and the 32-year-old Thomas Jefferson who claimed that "all men are created equal."
>
> These men moved the world, and so can we all. Few will have the greatness to bend history itself, but each of us can work to change a small portion of events, and in the total of all those acts will be written the history of this generation. It is from numberless diverse acts of courage and belief that human history is shaped. Each time a man stands up for an ideal, or acts to improve the lot of others, or strikes out against injustice, he sends forth a tiny ripple of hope, and crossing each other from a million different centers of energy and daring, those ripples build a current that can sweep down the mightiest walls of oppression and resistance.

The "ripples of hope" quote would eventually be inscribed on a wall near Robert Kennedy's grave at Arlington Cemetery, where he lay not far from his brother John's grave. Ted continued, quoting a passage Robert had spoken that described the essence of Robert's character:

Few are willing to brave the disapproval of their fellows, the censure of their colleagues, the wrath of their society. Moral courage is a rarer commodity than bravery in battle or great intelligence. Yet it is the one essential, vital quality for those who seek to change a world that yields most painfully to change. And I believe that in this generation, those with the courage to enter the moral conflict will find themselves with companions in every corner of the globe.

Ted quoted Robert's admonition that "the fortunate among us" needed to resist "the temptation to follow the easy and familiar paths of personal ambition and financial success so grandly spread before those who enjoy the privilege of education" and that we will all "ultimately be judged … on the effort we have contributed to building a new world society and the extent to which our ideals and goals have shaped that event." Ted finished the long excerpt from the Day of Affirmation address with this passage:

The future does not belong to those who are content with today, apathetic toward common problems and their fellow man alike, timid and fearful in the face of new ideas and bold projects. Rather it will belong to those who can blend vision, reason and courage in a personal commitment to the ideals and great enterprises of American Society. Our future may lie beyond our vision, but it is not completely beyond our control. It is the shaping impulse of America that neither fate nor nature nor the irresistible tides of history but the work of our own hands, matched to reason and principle, that will determine our destiny. There is pride in that, even arrogance, but there is also experience and truth. In any event, it is the only way we can live.

"That is the way he lived," Ted told the crowd in the church and the live television audience all over the world. "That is what he leaves us," adding, as he started to choke up:

My brother need not be idealized, or enlarged in death beyond what he was in life, to be remembered simply as a good and decent man, who saw wrong and tried to right it, saw suffering and tried to heal it, saw war and tried to stop it.

Those of us who loved him, and who take him to his rest today, pray that what he was to us and what he wished for others will someday come to pass for all the world.

Ted ended his eulogy with a line Robert used frequently in his stump speeches, a paraphrase of a quote from the famous Irish playwright and Socialist George Bernard Shaw:

> Some men see things as they are and say, "Why?" I dream things that never were and say, "Why not?"

After the ceremony, Kennedy's casket was placed on a funeral train that proceeded, slowly, to Arlington. The bier was raised onto chairs so the nearly two million people lining the tracks could see the coffin as they waved their last goodbyes.

When President John Kennedy was killed, people expressed immense grief. When Martin Luther King was killed, grief turned in many cases to anger. But when Robert Kennedy was killed, there seemed to be a sort of finality that left only despair. As Jack Newfield poignantly noted:

> Now I realized what makes our generation unique, what defines us apart from those who came before the hopeful winter of 1961, and those who came after the murderous spring of 1968. We are the first generation that learned from experience … that things were not really getting better, that we shall not overcome. We felt, by the time we reached thirty, that we had already glimpsed the most compassionate leaders our nation could produce, and they had all been assassinated. And from this time forward, things would get worse: our best political leaders were part of memory now, not hope. The stone was at the bottom of the hill, and we were alone.

After Robert Kennedy was killed, the Democratic Party became a shadow of its former self. Six of the next nine presidents would be Republicans. It would be 22 years before a Democrat was elected to two full terms in office. The political left, after the assassinations of President John Kennedy, Martin Luther King Jr., Malcolm X and Senator Robert Kennedy, had been beheaded. After the Democratic Party's 49-state loss to incumbent President Richard Nixon in 1972 (in a campaign so deceitful and dishonest that President Nixon was eventually forced to resign), the Democrats abandoned their core base—union laborers, minorities and blue-collar workers—and started catering to the Wall Street crowd instead. It would be 48 more years before an independent Senator from Vermont named Bernie Sanders ran on the kind of platform that used to define the Democratic Party in the 1960s.

PREPARATION

*"It's unbelievable how many damn holes there are in
that kitchen ceiling."*

AS THE COUNTRY—AND INDEED, THE WORLD—REMAINED RIVETED
on how tragedy had hit the Kennedy family yet again, the LAPD scrambled to
figure out how to conduct such a large investigation. The FBI, on the other hand,
showed no hesitation, having been through this before. Within a few days, the
FBI had flown more than one hundred agents to Los Angeles to jump-start their
KENSALT inquiry.[164]

The FBI was pulling triple duty, as it was concurrently investigating not only
Robert Kennedy's assassination but also those of his brother John and Martin
Luther King, Jr. as well. The same day that thousands of people waved Robert
Kennedy's funeral train a last goodbye, James Earl Ray, the alleged killer of King,
was apprehended at the London Heathrow airport.[165] And although the Warren
Commission had issued its report four years earlier, the FBI was, at the moment,
tracking New Orleans District Attorney Jim Garrison's case against Clay Shaw, a

---

164   Houghton, p. 87.

165   Two people sharing the alias James Earl Ray was using appear to have been arrested under the same
alias that day. I recounted this bizarre episode in *The Assassinations*.

In 1997, Dexter King, one of Martin Luther King, Jr.'s sons, met with James Earl Ray and asked him, "Did you
kill my father?" Ray said he didn't, and Dexter King replied that he and his family believed Ray on this point.

In 1999, the King family brought a civil suit against Loyd Jowers, who claimed he had been involved in a
conspiracy to kill Martin Luther King. The jury found that a conspiracy that involved government people, not James
Earl Ray, had killed King.

New Orleans resident and former Army major,[166] whom Garrison believed had played a role in President Kennedy's assassination. Garrison's growing thesis was that the CIA worked with Clay Shaw, anti-Castro Cubans and others in New Orleans and Dallas to kill President Kennedy and blame Oswald for the deed.

The FBI wasn't the only agency tracking Garrison's investigation. The CIA was sending agents to infiltrate Garrison's office in New Orleans as well. The only reason we know this is that in the 1970s, the House Select Committee on Assassinations had open access to CIA records relating to the assassination of John Kennedy, and some very good investigators did some incredible work. There has been no such access to or investigation of CIA records relating to the Robert Kennedy assassination. We do know, however, that the LAPD and CIA were in communication about the case, as you will see later.

Several LAPD leaders commented about how they wanted their investigation to stand up to historical scrutiny. They fully expected either a "Warren Commission" type of body to be appointed or a future Congressional committee investigation. They wanted to leave no stones unturned, no witnesses uninterviewed. But was this evidence of the LAPD's diligence in getting to the bottom of what happened? Or was this effort aimed at discovering evidence of conspiracy before anyone else did so that the LAPD could either disprove it or cover it up? It's not a wild question. Cover-ups are as American as apple pie. Teapot Dome. Watergate. Iran-Contra.

To some, the notion that Sirhan acted alone seemed incongruent with the known facts. Concerned citizens wrote the FBI, asking questions such as this one:

> How did Sirhan know that Sen. Kennedy was going to go out through the kitchen…? Had this been planned? Apparently, Sirhan was *waiting* in the kitchen so he must have *expected* the Senator to go that way. He was *ahead* of him, not following him.
>
> This seems to point to someone in the hotel organization who could have suggested to a Kennedy aide that this route would be a good one for the Senator to take. Perhaps you can find out from the aides *who suggested* that Kennedy take that way out of the hotel? [Emphasis in the original.][167]

---

166   See the chapter "The Hidden Record" in Bill Davy, *Let Justice Be Done*. Garrison believed but could not prove that Clay Shaw was a CIA asset. Years later, released CIA files showed the CIA granted a "Covert Security Approval" for the use of Clay Shaw under project QK/Enchant, a project which has not, as of the time of this writing, been declassified. Shaw was also briefed by the CIA both before and after trips to Latin America. See Davy's full book for an excellent exploration of the evidence suggesting Clay Shaw did play a role in the president's assassination. There is a great deal of evidence that Shaw knew Oswald and had helped set up the assassination of President Kennedy, much of which came out during his trial, but some of which was stolen from District Attorney Garrison's office. For another excellent account of the Garrison investigation, see Jim DiEugenio, *Destiny Betrayed*.

167   Letter from a person whose name was redacted by the FBI to the FBI HQ office in Los Angeles, dated 6/13/68. FBI RFK-LA-56-156 VOL.04-SER.751-0950.

Some witnesses, some of Sirhan's lawyers and family, and government officials had their lives threatened. In a few cases you'll read about later, witnesses were shot at. After California Attorney General Thomas Lynch criticized Mayor Yorty for making claims about Sirhan before he had been tried, five threats were made on his life: one to his office, three to the Los Angeles office of Governor Ronald Reagan, and one to the District Court of Appeals in Los Angeles.[168] When death threats are made it doesn't matter to whom they are made. Ronald Reagan and everyone in the chain of command between Los Angeles and the Governor's office got the message: look too closely into this case and you could die. That is one possible explanation for the cowardice government officials exhibited when confronted with evidence of conspiracy in this case.

What follows is only a short summary of what the LAPD and FBI did during this period. Similarly, the defense team's efforts will be told only in the broadest outline. Many problematic details from their efforts, as well as the CIA's subterranean role in this investigation, will be examined in more depth in later chapters.

On June 8, DeWayne Wolfer's top priority was proving that Sandra Serrano couldn't have heard gunshots from the fire escape at the back of the Ambassador Hotel. Never mind that Serrano never *claimed* she heard gunshots, but had only acknowledged the possibility when the police suggested that's what she had heard. She thought she had heard backfires. But that wasn't the point. Her story of seeing a woman in a polka dot dress fleeing out the back of the hotel was already featured in papers across the country. The quickest way to stop that story would be to shoot down Sandra's credibility on *any* point, however small. So this straw man was created, which Wolfer sought diligently to demolish.

Wolfer took a gun to Long Beach State College, fired it at various distances and measured the decibels. He determined, easily, that Serrano could not have heard gunshots from where she sat. *Which* gun he used for this test, however, would later become a matter of surprising importance.

In the early hours of June 9, Chief Houghton, Inspector Powers, Wolfer, and other LAPD leaders prepared for the interagency meeting that was to immediately follow. Houghton asked Lieutenant Charlie Hughes to brief them on the case so far.

Hughes spoke of the enormous backlog of interviews: thousands of witnesses known to be at the hotel that night had yet to be identified. Despite there being approximately four thousand people the police had yet to interview, Hughes evidenced the sentiment of all when he said, "I don't expect we'll have much trouble proving *who* did the killing—it's finding out *why* he shot the Senator, and whether there was more than one man responsible."[169]

---

168   Gladwin Hill, "Woman is sought in Kennedy death," *The New York Times*, June 7, 1968.
169   Houghton, pp. 93–94. It's worth nothing that neither the tape nor the transcript of this meeting,

Hughes went through some of the initial evidence that appeared to suggest a conspiracy. The fact that the key in Sirhan's pocket fit Gindroz's car was dismissed as "one of those crazy coincidences." Sandra Serrano's story was dismissed primarily on two issues: she had not mentioned the girl in the polka dot dress when she had called her mother right after the crime, and, thanks to Wolfer's experiment the day before, she couldn't have heard shots from her distance from the pantry. Based on those points, and the general unbelievability of a woman running out yelling "We shot him," Hughes concluded Serrano's story "looks pretty thin, so far." But, Hughes noted, the FBI had was still interested because another witness, Vincent DiPierro, had placed a girl in a polka dot dress with Sirhan moments before the shooting. "That's what's convincing the Bureau" that there might be something to Serrano's account, Hughes explained.[170]

Houghton asked what had caused Mayor Sam Yorty to state, the morning of the shooting, that Sirhan was a Communist. McCauley explained that he had been at Rampart when Yorty had come in mid-morning on June 5. He described how Yorty had flipped through one of the notebooks found in Sirhan's bedroom, found a comment in there that looked like a statement from Karl Marx, about workers having nothing to lose but their chains, and took that as proof that Sirhan was a Communist. In addition, Sirhan's car was frequently seen near the DuBois Club, which the police had deemed a Communist outpost. But it turned out the car was parked there by Sirhan's brother Adel, who borrowed it when he played music at a club nearby. And the text was likely related to one of Sirhan's college courses, like most of the other entries in his notebook.

In fact, no evidence ever surfaced, then or later, that Sirhan was in any way a Communist. But at that point in time, little was known with certainty, and despite the fact that such an accusation was guaranteed to prejudice potential jurors, Yorty's statement hung out there in the public mind, unchallenged.

Due in part to Yorty's outburst, Judge Arthur Alarcon had issued an order that the defense and prosecution must refrain from making any evidence public in order not to prejudice potential jurors. The order only applied to attorneys for the defense and prosecution, police, grand jurors, subpoenaed witnesses and others connected with the case in an official capacity. It was never meant to keep witnesses from talking to the media, although the police told witnesses they couldn't talk to anyone about what they knew. The "Alarcon order" effectively silenced witnesses, even long after the order had served its original purpose.

---

which Houghton's co-author, Joseph DiMona, evidently had access to, have surfaced in the records made public on this case. That said, I have no reason to believe any of these quotes are fabricated or inaccurate, and the records DiMona quoted that I could verify matched the record. Clearly, some records were lost or destroyed.

170   Houghton, p. 94.

At 10 A.M. on June 9, the five-hour interagency meeting commenced. Ten LAPD members joined William Lynch; Matt Byrne; Evelle Younger's deputies Buck Compton, John Howard, John Miner, and George Stoner; Captain Clifford Montgomery of the Sheriff's office intelligence division; Stewart Knight from the Secret Service; and William Nolan from the FBI. Lieutenant Hughes recapped his earlier summary, then Wolfer took the floor.

"I'll give you all I have ... there's still a lot of work to be done. We've been over the kitchen area twice, and we're going at least one more time. It's unbelievable how many damn holes there are in that kitchen ceiling." (A few photographs from the LAPD's investigation show at least five ceiling tiles had been removed, presumably for further investigation.) "Even the doors have holes in them," Wolfer continued, "which can be mistaken for bullet holes."[171]

It must be noted that there is no evidence to support Wolfer's assertion that the holes in the pantry doorframes were *not* bullet holes, as the doorframes with the holes in them were destroyed after the trial, and Wolfer kept no notes of the investigations he claimed to have performed on them. He noted in his log that he performed "X-rays of door-jam," [sic] but no X-rays were ever presented, nor does the log indicate what the results were. This is problematic, because as we've already seen, several members of the LAPD and FBI noted bullet holes in the pantry doorframes. One LAPD officer even saw someone dig a bullet out of a hole with a knife. If there was even just *one* bullet hole in the pantry doorframes or walls, that meant a second gun had been used. Wolfer had already accounted for the eight bullets Sirhan's gun could hold. Two bullets were found in Kennedy, and five other bullets were removed from the other five pantry victims. Wolfer also had to explain the three bullet holes found in the pantry ceiling tiles. He concluded that two bullets had entered the ceiling, and one of them had hit something and ricocheted back down into one of the victims. But a third bullet had evidently entered the ceiling and stayed there. This bullet was never recovered.

The LAPD's and County's entire case for Sirhan being the lone shooter hangs on Wolfer's credibility in this regard. So it's important to consider his credibility on this matter before continuing.

If Wolfer told the truth when he said no bullet holes were found in the pantry, then the Sheriffs who had first circled and labeled the holes had been fooled, veteran *Chicago Tribune* crime report Robert Wiedrich's account of bullets having been removed from the doorframes—provided to him by experienced members of the LAPD in the pantry immediately after the shooting—had been incorrect, the FBI photo captions that indicated those holes were bullet holes were

---

171   Houghton, p. 97. Although Houghton's co-author was provided access to the transcript of this conversation, the public has never seen this document, or many of the documents referenced in Houghton's book. I have no reason to doubt the authenticity of the documents, although I question how fully they have been represented. Houghton's privileged access was a key point in a lawsuit that forced the opening of many, but not all, of the files on this case to the public.

incorrect, and the statements of FBI and LAPD officers—who described seeing not just bullet holes but a bullet in one of the holes and a bullet being removed by a man in a suit—were also incorrect. Were all these people, whose accounts were entirely consistent with each other despite having never met or talked to each other, incorrect? Either *all those highly qualified witnesses were wrong*, or Wolfer was.

For those who cannot fathom that a member of the LAPD could be so dishonest, consider the Rampart Division scandal that erupted in the late 1990s. A group of officers from the same Rampart Division that handled the initial investigation into Robert Kennedy's assassination were found to have committed perjury on the stand and planted evidence on people to obtain, in some cases, false convictions. The wrongdoing was eventually found to have spread far beyond the Rampart Division. Members of the LAPD's crime lab were also implicated. The scandal was so big and represented such entrenched corruption that *eight years of court-ordered federal oversight of the LAPD ensued.*

How, then, are we to assess Wolfer's credibility, given how all-important his assertion regarding the pantry bullet holes is to this case? Fortunately, we don't have to. The California Court of Appeals already did that for us. The Court railed against Wolfer's actions and testimony in the Kirschke case, stating he had "negligently presented false demonstrative evidence in support of his ballistics testimony," that "Wolfer's acoustical testimony was false," and that "his testimony on qualifications as an expert on anatomy was also false and borders on the perjurious."[172] In other words, the Court of Appeals stopped just short of calling Wolfer a liar. I believe the Court chickened out and should have said what the evidence clearly shows. Bear that in mind with everything Wolfer said and did over the course of this case. In the law there's the principle, "false in part, false in whole." And given Wolfer's long tenure with the LAPD, as well as his engagements as an instructor of crime scene forensics, it's difficult, if not impossible, to argue that if he were wrong, he was simply mistaken. It makes more sense that Wolfer was deliberately lying in the Kirschke case to gain a conviction.

So it would hardly be out of character for Wolfer, a member of the LAPD's crime lab, to dissemble about what he knew in the Robert Kennedy case as well. We saw in the previous chapter how he essentially told an untruth to the Grand Jury about the bullets he had turned in, claiming to have made a match between test bullets and the Kennedy neck bullet, a match he would later deny regarding those same bullets.

None of this means Wolfer was directly or even indirectly involved in any conspiracy to kill Kennedy or that had any idea who the actual conspirators were. It could simply have meant he saw gaps and felt the need to improvise to smooth the police's way to a speedy conviction of the only identified shooter.

---

172   *In re Kirschke 53 Cal. App. 3d 405*, law.justia.com/cases/california/calapp3d/53/405.html, accessed 9/1/13.

However, an alternate possibility cannot be ruled out: that conspirators planned the assassination in Los Angeles because they knew they had a trusted contact in DeWayne Wolfer.

Similarly, it's hard to believe FBI agent Nolan didn't know by this time that a photographic supervisor and photographer from the FBI had already captioned their photographs of the doorframe holes in the pantry as "bullet holes." It strains credulity that Nolan would attend a meeting as the official FBI representative without having informed himself as to the core evidence uncovered to date.

Another meeting participant who had reason to believe there was more than one shooter was Deputy District Attorney John Miner. When Wolfer mentioned to the group that the shot that killed Kennedy had to have been fired from "less than one inch" from Kennedy's head, Miner confirmed Wolfer's conclusions. But what Miner didn't say, even though he apparently understood, was that no witness had put Sirhan close enough to Kennedy to have fired those shots. Remember how at the Grand Jury hearing, Miner had asked Noguchi if he'd change his testimony to say feet, not inches. Such a change would have brought Noguchi's testimony in line with that of the pantry witnesses. Miner clearly understood this was an issue. But there is no evidence that Miner brought this issue to the attention of the meeting participants.[173] Miner, too, seemed not to want to raise any evidence that could prove a conspiracy had been at work.

Why would anyone want to hide evidence of conspiracy? There are innocent and sinister answers to that question. Consider the simplest one: it's much easier to prosecute a single person for a crime than multiple individuals. And only one person had been arrested. Did the LAPD or D.A.'s office want to look incompetent, letting other conspirators go free? It was simply easier to ignore or hide evidence of multiple shooters. For whatever reasons, innocent or sinister, that, as we will see, is what the LAPD and D.A.'s office did in this case.

Similarly, Sirhan's legal representatives weren't interested in finding out whether Sirhan acted with others. And Sirhan, for his part, proposed no alternative. He had no conscious memory of events in the pantry. He named no co-conspirators. In the absence of a memory to the contrary, Sirhan accepted what he was told: that he had fired a gun in the pantry and killed Kennedy. As one of his original defense team members would say to me years later, how could a lawyer hope to save his client's life by arguing he had participated in a conspiracy to kill Kennedy?[174] The easier argument was to assert that Sirhan was experiencing some sort of temporary insanity.

---

173   I can only go by what DiMona quoted from the tapes or transcripts which he had, which do not appear to have been made available to the public, if they even still exist. Like several other critical records, these seem to have disappeared without a trace. If Miner did raise this point, DiMona or Houghton did not include it in the excerpts quoted in *Special Unit Senator*.

174   Robert Blair Kaiser, via email.

What about the FBI? Wouldn't it have been an impartial party? Not necessarily. For example, when the FBI traced the ammunition used in the assassination of President Kennedy to a batch ordered by the U.S. Marine Corps for weapons that the Marine Corps did not possess, an FBI agent's memo said that fact gave rise to the "obvious speculation that it is a contract placed by the CIA with Western under a USMC cover for concealment purposes."[175] The FBI never told the public this. The document describing this part of the story was only released as part of a broad FBI dump of files related to the Kennedy assassination many years later, where it has remained largely invisible.

The media, too, largely avoided suggestions of conspiracy. For one, little of the vast evidence of conspiracy was known at the time. But there was another reason as well. A little over a year earlier, the CIA had sent a dispatch to its media assets at home and worldwide encouraging the framing of any conspiracy evidence in President Kennedy's assassination as a "conspiracy theory," as if a conspiracy could never be real, but only ever a theory, and laying out alternate explanations to use instead. These explanations (such as that people couldn't keep something so big a secret, for example) are still echoed in the media coverage of both Kennedy assassinations at the time of this writing.[176] (It's worth noting one would not be allowed to work for the CIA unless one *could* keep such big secrets for life.)

Truly, there wasn't a single official investigator in this case or mainstream media spokesperson who had a motive to find a conspiracy, and many motives not to find one. That, by far, is the simplest explanation for what happened next, as a general rule. In other words, you don't need to believe that any of the people who covered up evidence of conspiracy were part of the conspiracy or had any idea whose conspiracy they were covering up. It was simply not in their best interests to find a conspiracy. It's important to understand that mindset from the outset. People will rarely find what is inconvenient for them to discover, even when it's staring them in the face.

That said, it's important to look specifically at what was buried or deliberately misrepresented, and by whom. For a few individuals, these innocent explanations may no longer suffice.

In the June 9 interagency meeting, Wolfer claimed that at least three of the victim's bullets "definitely" came from Sirhan's gun:

> [W]e have three bullets that definitely come [*sic*] from the gun taken
> from Sirhan, one from Kennedy's sixth cervical vertebra, one from
> Goldstein and one from Weisel. At this point I can't be too sure about

---

175   FBI memo from (FBI Lab employee Roy) H. Jevons to (FBI Lab head Ivan) Conrad, December 2, 1963, www.maryferrell.org/mffweb/archive/viewer/showDoc.do?mode=searchResult&absPageId=692546.

176   CIA dispatch dated 1/4/67, NARA Record Number: 104-10404-10376, www.maryferrell.org/mffweb/archive/viewer/showDoc.do?docId=3167&relPageId=1.

the rest of the ballistic evidence. We have bullet fragments from Kennedy's head, but right now all I can say for sure is that they're mini-mag [sic] brand ammunition—the same kind Sirhan is supposed to have bought, and the kind that's in the other victims.[177]

This comment was, like so many others of Wolfer's, disingenuous. Wolfer kept a log of his various tests and examinations. Nowhere in his detailed log does he mention comparing bullets taken from Kennedy or any victim to bullets test-fired from Sirhan's gun. The omission, if indeed there was such a test, is bizarre in light of how *acutely* aware Wolfer was that the record would likely be examined in the years to come. And it's difficult to argue that Wolfer was simply sloppy, given how meticulously he recorded other events that transpired. How could he simply have forgotten to record the most important evidence of all?

Wolfer also appeared to be, at best, confused when he stated that bullet "fragments" removed from Evans' head were of the same "Mini-Mag" ammunition that had fragmented in Kennedy's brain. While the evidence log reports "fragments" were recovered, a surprising number of records referred to the Evans "bullet," not "fragments." An FBI report refers to the "bullet," not fragments, taken from Evans' head. A Pasadena Police report indicates "The bullet entered the scalp of the forehead, just below the hairline ... X-rays indicate that the bullet flattened itself against the skull. ... [the doctor] decided to leave the bullet in the scalp and have a surgeon remove it later...."[178] Dr. John Garner, who retrieved the "bullet," gave it to "Lt. M. K. King" of the Pasadena Police Department.[179] Evans herself later sought the "bullet" for a souvenir. Wolfer *even contradicted himself* on this point: his official report on the bullets stated that *a bullet*, not fragments, had been recovered from Evans' head.

The FBI report added a twist as well: "The bullet causing the wound to Mrs. Elizabeth Evans cannot be entered into evidence as continuity of the bullet [i.e., the chain of possession] has been lost."[180] Had the chain of possession truly been "lost," indicating extreme sloppiness in the most important case the LAPD had ever investigated? Or had the chain of possession deliberately been broken to prevent the Evans bullet from being examined? If the Evans bullet had been of a different ammunition type than the bullet retrieved from Kennedy's body, that would also have been strong evidence that two gunmen had been firing in the pantry and reason enough to swap the "bullet" with "fragments," thereby preventing future bullet comparisons.

---

177   Houghton, pp. 97–98.

178   Pasadena Police report on Evans, Elizabeth Y., bearing the correct (at that point in time) chart of PC 217, Attempt [sic] Murder, June 5, 1968.

179   LAPD interview of Dr. John T. Garner, 7/31/68.

180   FBI interview with [redacted] of the LAPD Detective Division, conducted by [redacted] at the LAFO on 6/8/68. FBI files, Sub-file X-1, Vol. 4, p. 1082.

Shortly after the interagency meeting, the LAPD began constructing a separate unit, initially dubbed "Special Operation Senator" to investigate the assassination. Captain Brown was asked to assign two lieutenants to head the group. Within two days, the unit would be renamed "Special Unit Senator," (SUS) perhaps because the term "special operation" has often been used to denote an intelligence operation.

Houghton "specifically recommended" only one person to Captain Brown: Manny Pena.[181] Why did Houghton want Pena there so badly?

Lieutenant Manual Pena had been a member of the LAPD for 22 years. He taught criminal investigation at a local college. Pena was trilingual in English, French and Spanish, and "had connections with various intelligence agencies in several countries."[182] Ironically, Pena had some peripheral involvement with the investigation into the assassination of President John Kennedy, specifically regarding the ordering of the sight on the rifle that Oswald had allegedly used to assassinate President Kennedy.[183]

Despite his apparent qualifications, Pena was an odd choice, as he had retired in 1967 in a publicly reported ceremony at the Sportsmen's Lodge in the San Fernando Valley in 1967. According to an article in the *San Fernando Valley Times*,

> Pena retired from the police force to advance his career. He has accepted a position with the Agency for International Development Office of the State Department. As a public safety officer, he will train and advise foreign police forces in investigative and administrative matters. After nine weeks of training and orientation, he will be assigned to his post, possibly a Latin American country, judging by the fact that he speaks Spanish fluently.[184]

During the Senate ("Church Committee") and House ("Pike Committee") investigations into the CIA's domestic and foreign activities, we learned that the Agency for International Development (AID) often served as a front for CIA activities and officers. FBI agent Roger "Frenchy" LaJeunesse, a Los Angeles FBI agent deeply involved in the KENSALT assassination investigation, told his friend and former FBI agent Bill Turner that Pena had gone to a "'special training unit' at a CIA base in Virginia," and that Pena had "done CIA special assignments for a decade, mostly under AID cover." Pena's own brother told reporter Stan Bohrman that Manny was proud of his service to the CIA.[185]

---

181   Houghton, p. 103.
182   Houghton, p. 103.
183   Warren Commission Hearings, Vol. XXII, p. 528.
184   *San Fernando Valley Times*, 11/13/67, quoted in Turner and Christian, p. 64.
185   Turner and Christian, p. 65.

When Betsy Langman, an actor and journalist who later married writer Budd Schulberg, asked Pena in 1977 if AID was connected to the CIA, Pena told her, "not to my knowledge."[186] Given how public the knowledge was that AID provided cover to CIA activities by that time, and given Pena's work for them, Pena's answer is simply not credible, unless he *was*, in fact, working for the CIA. If he were a CIA employee or contract agent, that is what he would have *had* to say. All CIA employees and agents must sign a secrecy agreement in which they promise never to divulge their work for the agency or any of the agency's secrets. If they violate this oath, they can be stripped of all retirement benefits, fined and even prosecuted. One CIA insider, E. Howard Hunt, notorious for his role in the Watergate affair, even said the CIA had an assassination team that ended the life of CIA employees who gave away CIA secrets.[187] If anyone can keep a secret forever, it's a CIA employee or asset. If they couldn't, they wouldn't be employed there.

For whatever reason, Pena's stint with AID was cut short. Fernando Faura, a local journalist on the police beat, asked him why he had returned when he saw him back at the LAPD after the assassination. Pena told him the job wasn't what he had hoped it would be.[188] Pena denied in later years that his return to the LAPD had anything to do with Robert Kennedy's assassination. The problem there is, if he *had* come back to help the CIA in some way regarding the assassination, he would have said the same thing. He would never have been allowed to admit to his CIA work without violating his secrecy oath, so his denial isn't useful evidence. The man who would function as Pena's close partner on Special Unit Senator, Sergeant Enrique "Hank" Hernandez, also had ties to the CIA and was involved in their police training activities in Latin America.[189]

While Pena and Hernandez were getting started with the newly formed Special Unit Senator (SUS), Sandra Serrano and Vincent DiPierro were brought, separately, to the LAPD to look at a set of polka dot dresses the LAPD had purchased. Each was to identify the dress that most closely matched the dress of the girl each

186   O'Sullivan, p. 406.

187   John M. Crewdson, "Hunt Says CIA Had Assassin Unit," *New York Times*, December 26, 1975.

188   Turner and Christian, p. 66. Fernando Faura clarified in an email to Lisa Pease on 4/9/16 that he had not seen Pena at the LAPD in "April," as the Turner book states, but only when he was turning the Fahey tapes over to the LAPD. Faura allowed that perhaps Turner or Christian had found evidence that Pena had returned in April, but as of 4/9/16, both had passed away so I was unable to question them on this point.

189   See additional details in Lisa Pease, "Sirhan and the RFK Assassination Part II: Rubik's Cube," in DiEugenio and Pease, *The Assassinations*, p. 572. See also Ralph Schoenman, "RFK's assassination: The beat goes on," *The Baltimore Sun*, 5/28/95 and Turner and Christian, p. 66: In 1963, Hernandez "played a key role in Unified Police Command training for the CIA in Latin America" and received a medal from the Venezuelan government.

This CIA document, describes the problems in Venezuela, the likely formation of a unified police command, and the need for training, which, as of mid-1963, had been inadequate: www.foia.cia.gov/sites/default/files/document_conversions/89801/DOC_0000261026.pdf. The new training referenced, conducted by the CIA, may well have been the very training Hernandez was involved with.

had seen with Sirhan. DiPierro remembered the dress as being "form-fitting" with a "wide collar" and Serrano recalled the dress was "A-line" (fitted at the top but looser at the bottom) with a "bib collar." Serrano remembered the sleeves as being ¾-length (mid-forearm) but DiPierro thought the sleeves were shorter. Serrano picked out dresses three and six as being the most similar to the dress she had seen. DiPierro picked out dresses four and seven.

The LAPD would later make a big deal of the differences between their identifications. But since none of the dresses were an exact match, it makes sense that the witnesses would not necessarily agree on which dress was the most similar. But both said that the dress was white with dark polka dots, form-fitted on the top, with a bib-like collar and sleeves. In addition, both would tell the authorities, in different words, that the girl had a "very shapely" (Serrano) or "good" (DiPierro) figure and a "turned-up" (Serrano) or "pug"[190] (DiPierro) nose. They both described the girl as a Caucasian with brunette hair in her mid-twenties. And both described her in the company of someone whose description matched Sirhan's.

After this session, Serrano was taken back to the hotel by FBI Special Agent Richard Burris, Deputy D.A. John Howard and Dan Johnson, another Deputy D.A. She was shown the stage area where Kennedy had spoken, and then shown the route Kennedy had taken to enter the pantry. They informed her there were some 1,100 people in the room between where she had been sitting and where the shooting had occurred and told her the distance was about 170 feet. They then mentioned that she had reportedly heard six gunshots, a few seconds after which a girl in a polka dot dress ran out saying "We shot him." Burris then asked if she still felt she had heard gunshots. Serrano replied "she had never heard a gunshot in her life and never claimed she heard gunshots," a true statement.

Burris told Serrano the FBI had interviewed her mother and that her mother had said Serrano hadn't mentioned anyone connected with the shooting. Serrano told Burris she "always had difficulty communicating with her mother" and that she had asked to talk to her father, but that her father was too upset over the shooting and didn't want to talk.

Had Burris reviewed her statements, he would have realized that Serrano wasn't even convinced when she called her mother that Kennedy *had* been shot, but that she had heard confirmation of that while on the call, at which point Serrano promptly ended the call.

Burris then asked why in her television interview she hadn't mentioned seeing the same woman who ran down the stairs going up the stairs with Sirhan. "It was pointed out to her that the fact that she claimed one of the men going up the stairs was Sirhan Sirhan was the most significant part of the incident described by her."

---

190   LAPD's transcript of Vince DiPierro's July 1, 1968 session with Hernandez.

Serrano then accused the people present of lying and trying to trick her. As Professor Phil Melanson wrote later, "Either Burris and his colleagues woefully misunderstood the sequence of events, or they actually *were* trying to trick her. Miss Serrano had not witnessed Sirhan's arrest and his picture had not yet been flashed on TV when she went briefly on camera with NBC."[191] She did not, at the point of her TV interview, understand the significance of the third man. And she *did* mention the third person in her earliest official interview, at 2:35 A.M., shortly after that broadcast and before she ever saw a photo or video of Sirhan. She accurately described his clothes before having been shown his picture.

John Howard then asked if she would take a polygraph. She said she would, and Howard then asked her to reenact what happened on video "to avoid any misunderstanding on anyone's part on what she claimed to have seen." Serrano agreed under one condition: that someone not connected with the investigation be present as a witness. By the end of the video, Serrano was "very upset" and "could not continue and requested to be taken home." Unfortunately, this video appears to have disappeared from the record.[192]

Ironically, that same day, John Ambrose, the Deputy D.A. whom Serrano had talked to before her on-air interview, gave statements separately to the LAPD and FBI, in which he recounted to both how Serrano had told him she had seen a young man in a gold sweater and a girl in a polka dot dress run by with the girl yelling, "We shot him." He mentioned that he had contacted Rampart detectives and left a message about how another witness had also mentioned seeing a girl in a polka dot dress but that no one had ever called Ambrose back for the details. He closed his statement by adding that "Sandra Serrano impressed me as a very sincere girl who had been a dedicated Kennedy fan, not interested in publicity in any way."[193]

Ambrose wasn't the only one vouching for Serrano. Another volunteer for Kennedy's campaign who had known Serrano for some time described her as "a reliable, level-headed" and "responsible person."[194]

The next day, Serrano called Burris at the L.A. FBI office. She had been contacted by someone claiming to be FBI, and she wanted to know if it was a legitimate contact. She also advised that she had changed her phone number and that any further contact should go through one of two attorneys she had lined up to support her.

---

191   Melanson, p. 241.

192   Brad Johnson, a former CNN producer who has aggressively sought copies of all video in this case, was unaware of this video when I contacted him about it, and he initially doubted it had been made. Shane O'Sullivan, whom I also contacted, expressed the same doubt. However, the documentation clearly states a video was made. It appears this video has been lost, hidden, or destroyed, begging the question of why it was destroyed. Was Serrano too credible?

193   LAPD interview of John Ambrose, June 10, 1968, www.maryferrell.org/showDoc. html?docId=99848&#relPageId=391&tab=page.

194   FBI interview of David Kal Haines, 6/11/68.

On June 11, Houghton went on a self-described covert mission to Sacramento "ostensibly to testify before the Criminal Procedures Committee on Senate Bill 203 [but] actually, to interview and solicit the cooperation of key people of State Government in connection with the Kennedy investigation."[195] There, Houghton met with several who would rise to enormous positions of power in later years.

One was Edwin Meese, the legal advisor to California Governor Ronald Reagan. Meese told Houghton, confidentially, that all the resources of the Governor would be made available to the LAPD. Meese would later be investigated on charges that he deliberately covered up President Ronald Reagan's involvement in the Iran-Contra affair. Reagan himself would, in a few years, be a member of the Rockefeller Commission, formed by President Gerald Ford (a former member of the Warren Commission, who later received CIA funding during his Congressional career[196]) to investigate the CIA's illegal domestic activities.[197] The media charged the panel was so loaded with CIA friendlies that the commission would produce nothing more than a "whitewash," a prediction that essentially came true. It was Congress' lack of confidence in the independence of the members of the Rockefeller Commission that caused the Senate and House to form their own separate investigations of the CIA.

Houghton also contacted Warren Christopher, who, years later, would serve as President Carter's Deputy Secretary of State and head the "Christopher Commission," which looked into police brutality in the LAPD in the wake of the Rodney King beating. Houghton wanted Christopher, who was then Deputy Attorney General of the United States, to find out whether the process of getting information from the FBI to the LAPD could be sped up. The current process required that FBI reports from the Los Angeles field office be forwarded to the office of the U.S. Attorney General in D.C., and then returned to the FBI's Los Angeles field office and the local U.S. Attorney General's office before being turned over to the LAPD.[198]

Houghton also contacted Christopher to "solicit his office's assistance in establishing local liaison with CIA."[199] Why the LAPD was seeking local liaison with the CIA at this early stage, and why Houghton went to Christopher, as

---

195　SUS Daily Log of Commander, Detective Bureau in Investigation of Robert F. Kennedy assassination, Commander Houghton, June 11, 1968 entry.

196　Larry DuBois and Laurence Gonzales, "The Puppet and the Puppetmasters," *Playboy*, September 1976.

197　President Ford was himself the instigator for the three investigations of the CIA due to a clumsy comment he made at a luncheon with reporters. When challenged regarding his appointments to the Rockefeller Commission, Ford said he needed people who could be trusted, lest the commission dig up some of the darker operations of the CIA, like "assassinations." He tried to censor himself, after the fact, by adding "That's off the record," but it was too late. The media ran with it, and the Senate and Congress, fearing Ford's Rockefeller Commission would be little more than a whitewash, created select committees to investigate the CIA, which became known, respectively, as the "Church Committee" and "Pike Committee" after their leaders Senator Frank Church and Congressman Otis Pike. See Daniel Schorr's account of this in his book *Clearing the Air*.

198　Daily Log of Commander, Detective Bureau in Investigation of RFK Assassination, SUS files.

199　Daily Log of Commander, Detective Bureau in Investigation of RFK Assassination, SUS files.

opposed to an official CIA representative, is not stated. Months later, Houghton suggested to Captain Brown "that he have Goliath work on Sirhan background re traumatic injures [sic]." "Goliath" was a codeword used by law enforcement agencies to refer to the CIA.[200] The LAPD would later openly acknowledge getting CIA help on Sirhan's childhood in the Middle East during the traumatic period that ended with the formation of Israel in the land formerly known as Palestine. They did not, however, mention additional assistance the CIA provided the LAPD in other areas of their investigation, which will be discussed in a later chapter.

By June 12, SUS was in motion, staffed largely by officers with previous backgrounds in military and intelligence work.[201] Pena moved quickly to take control of the FBI's relationship with the LAPD. He wanted access to anything and everything they were discovering relating to either Sirhan or "anything suggesting or eliminating possible political conspiracy and anything of a local nature supporting or eliminating any intra United States or local conspiracy." The FBI reported that Pena had communicated that "it is necessary for him to know whether this information is forthcoming from the FBI or whether the LAPD will have to make its own arrangements to obtain same." The FBI's record of this request notes that "Lt. Pena further advised that there would be no distribution of LAPD material until he personally had a chance to review this material."[202]

A flow chart showed how information was routed through Special Unit Senator. Information was gathered by various officers on the investigative team, but all information came to Pena for his personal review. He was the only one who got to see all the pieces. On Pena's sole authority, avenues of investigation could be pursued or shut down. If anyone wanted to control the investigation of the Robert Kennedy assassination, one needed simply to control Lieutenant Manny Pena.

Similarly, Pena's close associate Hernandez, who was promoted to Lieutenant during this investigation, was the sole arbiter of witness veracity. He alone could decide who was telling the truth and who was not, based on his polygraph sessions. These "lie detectors," however, are provably misnamed. Innocent people can fail to pass a polygraph test. And pathological liars, those with special training, and a small percent of the general population can "beat" the machine, i.e., tell a lie without indicating abnormal stress on the machine. Lastly, the integrity of the operator is key to a successful session. A faulty or dishonest operator can cause the person being tested such stress that a truth-teller can be made to look like a liar. Similarly, a dishonest operator can lessen the sensitivity of a machine such that

200   John Newman, *Oswald and the CIA*, p. 253.

201   SUS files. Each of the SUS staff had a bio on file within the LAPD. See my article "Sirhan and the RFK Assassination Part II: Rubik's Cube," in DiEugenio and Pease, *The Assassinations*, p. 571, for a quick summary of some of these. See the SUS officer files for their backgrounds.

202   FBI memo from SAC, Los Angeles to [redacted], dated 6/13/68.

a liar can look like a truth-teller. There are other concerns as well. Poor wording of questions and too many questions can adversely affect the usefulness of the test. For all these reasons and more, most states do not allow use of polygraph evidence in court. The primary use of such a machine is simply to scare criminals into a confession.

Given that Hernandez was the sole person responsible for polygraphs in this case, it's worth evaluating his credibility before continuing. If Hernandez is credible, we should give his assertions some weight. But if he himself has veracity issues, then we should not trust his pronouncements on the veracity of others.

We don't have a California Court of Appeals record on Hernandez to quote. Instead, we have the tapes of his lie detector sessions. None are more incriminating to Hernandez's credibility than his session with Sandra Serrano, although what he did with Serrano he did to others with evidence of conspiracy as well. His treatment of Serrano was a sort of template that he repeated with others as needed. Allow me to set the stage.

When Pena and Hernandez joined the investigation, like Wolfer, their first area of focus was discrediting Serrano's account of the girl in the polka dot dress running from the hotel saying "We shot him." According to Houghton, "Pena knew that as long as Miss Serrano stuck to her story, no amount of independent evidence would, in itself, serve to dispel the 'polka-dot-dress girl fever' which had by now, in the press and public mind, reached a high point on the thermometer of intrigue. She alone could put the spotted ghost to rest."[203]

Pena suggested Hernandez take Serrano out for an "SUS-bought steak." Houghton describes the evening as follows:

> Hernandez called for Miss Serrano, and over dinner they talked about what she had seen and heard after the assassination at the hotel. She still insisted her original story was true. Hernandez asked if she would be willing to undergo a polygraph examination. She readily agreed, and after dinner they drove to Parker Center...."

From Houghton's description, this all sounds very friendly. But the facts paint a different picture. Serrano only agreed to the meal on the condition that her aunt Cecilia Magdaleno ("Maggie," to Serrano), whom she lived with, be in attendance. After a heavy steak meal, and two drinks, which Hernandez—an officer of the law—bought for the underage Serrano, at roughly 8 P.M., Hernandez brought Maggie and Serrano into a room and strapped Serrano into his polygraph machine.

With Serrano's aunt Maggie in the room, the session started innocently enough. Serrano asked why she should have to take a polygraph when it's not

---

203   Houghton, p. 120.

allowed to be used in a court of law. Hernandez told her she had been misinformed, which was partly true. A few states unfortunately *do* permit the use of polygraph evidence, although most do not, for the reasons noted above.

Hernandez tried to get Serrano to close her eyes, but she refused. He gave her an introduction to how the polygraph worked. He asked her to answer every question he was about to ask with "no." He would list street addresses and ask if they matched her parents' address. He instructed her to answer no to all of the questions, i.e., to deliberately lie when he came to the right address. Then he would show her he was able to determine when she lied. When he got to the correct address and Serrano said "no," Hernandez said "Okay, that's the first untruthful answer you've told me." This might seem impressive, but this information was likely already available to him. Then he turned to her aunt and explained he needed to talk to Serrano "by herself if that's all right with you. You can wait at the door." Serrano didn't want her aunt to leave, but Serrano reluctantly agreed to continue the session, given that she was already strapped into the chair.

The transcript of this session, excerpted below, doesn't capture the full impact of the audible record. Interested parties should obtain a copy of the full session on tape from the California State Archives. As disturbing as this is to read, it's worse to hear. It's so distressing that one of Serrano's cards in the LAPD's master cardfile index of the investigation says, "Do not play or have transcribed without permission of Capt. Brown." What you are about to read was an interview that, for reasons that will become obvious, was never intended to be made public.

With Serrano strapped in a chair, alone and without support, Hernandez began his interrogation of Serrano. The session would last roughly two and a half hours.

Hernandez began by playing "good cop." He told her she looked better in person than in a picture he had of her on the back steps. He said he had interviewed "19 other girls that have made statements regarding what they observed on that night," implying that 19 other girls had opened up to him. He told Serrano he liked her and that she was a "very intelligent girl" and that he thought she was "going to go somewhere" in her life.

He then mentioned not wanting this to turn out like Dallas and the Warren Report, which—even by 1968—was considered a flawed investigation that left many questions unresolved.

Before he got very far, Serrano interrupted to ask who would learn of the results of this session. "I don't want any of this stuff just made public," she said.

Hernandez sidestepped her question, saying "No, I give you my" but before he said "word," he changed his statement. "We're not dealing for publicity in this thing."

Hernandez refocused her on their session, stressed he needed "yes" or "no" answers only, and asked her to stop fidgeting.

"I'm going to ask you some questions now. Answer me truthfully to the best of your ability. Is your true first name Sandra?"

"No."

"Is your true last name Serrano?"

"Yes."

"If I ask you questions about the Ambassador Hotel, will you tell me the truth?"

"Yes."

"Do you believe that I will be completely fair with you throughout this examination?"

"No."

"When you told the police that a girl with a polka dot dress told you she had shot Kennedy, were you telling the truth?"

"She didn't say we had shot Kennedy. She said, 'We shot him.' I don't know if she was saying we, you know, her."

"Okay. Did a girl in a polka dot dress tell you that, 'We have shot Kennedy'?"

"A white dress, black polka dots," Serrano clarified.

"Did a girl in a white dress with black polka dots tell you, 'We have shot Kennedy'?"

"Yes."

"During the first 19 years of your life, do you remember lying to an FBI agent?"

"No."

"After Kennedy was shot, did you lie to an FBI agent?"

"No."

"On election night, at the Ambassador Hotel, did you yourself see a girl with a white dress with black polka dots?"

"Yes."

"Is there some other question that you're afraid I will ask you during this test?"

"Like what?"

"Have you tried to answer all my questions truthfully?"

"If possible."

"You can relax now. Okay, remember I told you to try and answer all my questions with one word, yes or no."

"Yeah, but they can't be answered like that."

"Well, then we'll review them, okay? Are you afraid right now?"

"I'm not afraid, I just don't like it."

"No, no, you're afraid. You're afraid. You see, I talk to many, many people." Hernandez clearly *wanted* her to be afraid.

But she wasn't afraid. Not yet. She had an ace up her sleeve. "May I ask you something? When you asked me what my name was, what did it turn out?

"Sandra?"

"Yeah."

"That you said no, it was meaningful to me. I think you had a different name or you use a different name, whatever it is. I'm not concerned with it though. I'm not concerned with it." But he should have been, because Sandra had just proved to herself that Hernandez couldn't distinguish a lie from the truth, because Sandra *was* her real first name, and she had just fooled him. Hernandez suddenly realized what had happened.

"Look, if you're not convinced yet that this thing works—" and he went back to the top of his act. "I like you as a person."

Serrano put the lie to that right away. "I think it was rotten in the beginning because you never mentioned it to my aunt that we were gonna take a polygraph."

"Oh yes I did. I told her this morning," Hernandez said.

"She said you just wanted to talk to me, 'cause I asked her."

"Well Sandy, uh, Sandy, look," Hernandez fumbled.

"It was never mentioned, and I think that's rotten."

"She was in here during the test," Hernandez lied, as no pertinent questions were asked until after her aunt had left the room and the official polygraph session hadn't even begun yet.

"Yeah, yeah, I know that, I think this is rotten though. But anyways, go ahead. You know, we're here, we can't do anything about it, let's go and get it done with, that's the way I feel about it now."

In a nutshell, everything that followed stemmed from that one moment. Serrano knew this was all a set-up, but she also realized she was stuck. The LAPD were never going to stop questioning her until she gave them what they wanted. And she knew what that meant: a retraction. She tried to play along as nicely as she could, to give Hernandez an out. But she clearly didn't want to have to lie to do so.

Hernandez asked her, "Do you think that I'm being fair and honest with you?"

"I'm sure that you're a fair and honest person, but the job you have to do may not be fair and honest."

Hernandez twisted this to imply Serrano meant that investigating the "death of a Senator" was a "rotten job." Serrano tried to explain.

"I understand that … what the public might seem, think is wrong and everything is really the right thing and this is a job and it has to be done…"

"Do you know why it has to be done?" Hernandez asked.

"Because if this is greater than what it seems to be right now, it could cause a big hassle between countries. You know, it could possibly lead to another war," Serrano answered, showing an astute understanding of how the world worked. Clearly, Serrano felt this was a conspiracy the police needed—for whatever reason—to cover up.

Hernandez couldn't let that stand, however. He told Serrano the people they needed to be concerned with were "the family of Senator Kennedy. They'll never know, until people come forward and are truthful with this thing—"

"Yeah, I know."

"Because they don't know. And they want to find out what happened to their father. The kids do. Ethel wants to find out what happened to her husband. This isn't, this isn't a silly thing."

Serrano saw right through him. "Oh, I know it's not a silly thing, but don't come with this sentimental business, let's just get this job done."

Hernandez interrupted her here, breaking her rhythm, not letting her finish, and claimed he was only interested in the truth. She told him to leave the Kennedy family out of it, because it was an emotional subject to her.

Hernandez backed off for a moment. He asked whether she was left-handed, whether she was born in Ohio, and other innocuous questions before returning to the main subject. When he questioned her, Hernandez insisted on using the wrong set of words. Serrano consistently stated, in every interview, that the words were, "We shot Kennedy," not "We have shot Kennedy." Whether this reflected deliberate deception or ignorance on Hernandez's part is anyone's guess. How can one "truthfully" answer such a question?

Hernandez repeated the same questions over and over, slightly reworded, and followed them up with "did you lie" or "did you make up the story" to several of the questions.

No matter how he approached the question, Serrano stuck strongly to her story. So Hernandez moved on to his next approach.

"Sandy, I'm not gonna ask you any more questions, not a single one. I do want to talk to you like a brother. Look, I don't know what religion you are. I'm Catholic. Are you Catholic?"

"I don't believe in religion."

Hernandez tried another approach. Three times in a row, Hernandez told her "I talked to 19 girls" and added, the last time, that "there's been only two girls that I really believe loved Kennedy. ... that I really sincerely [believe] did it, not for publicity...but because they were sorry about what happened and they loved President Kennedy, uh, Senator Kennedy. And I think that you're one of these girls, and I sincerely believe this. So what, here's what you have to think about right now."

"Uh huh."

"I think you owe it to the late Senator Kennedy, to come forth, be a woman about this. If he, and you don't know and I don't know whether he's a witness right now in this room watching what we're doing in here. Don't shame his death by keeping this thing up. I have compassion for you," said the man trained by the CIA to interrogate prisoners in foreign countries.[204] "I want to know why you did what you did. This is a very serious thing."

"But I seen those people!"

"No, no, no, no Sandy!" Hernandez said, his voice and temper audibly rising. "Remember what I told you about that you can't say you saw something when you didn't see it?"

"She said that to me," Serrano replied emphatically.

"I can explain this to the investigators where you don't even have to talk to them and they won't talk to you. I can do this. I can sit down with you and your aunt in the next room and I can guarantee you that nobody will ask you one more question about this," Hernandez lied. He was not in a position to promise that to anyone.

"I want you to be able to rest yourself, after what I'm telling you right now, because you know it's true. I want you to be able to go home and rest. I don't know if you've been sleeping well at night or not, I don't know this. But I know that, as you get older, one of these days, you're gonna be a mother. You're gonna be a mother, you're gonna have kids, and you know that you can't live a life of shame, knowing what you're doing right now is wrong."

Despite the intense psychological pressure, Serrano continued to fight back. "I don't feel I'm doing anything wrong."

"Well maybe you don't feel it, but when you get older you will. And you see here, you see here, Sandy, not to get sentimental, but I personally loved Kennedy as a man. … I knew the man. I had lunch with him. He gave me a commendation that I relish very much. It's one of my most favorite mementos now, one of my more prized mementos."

"Uh huh."

"So don't have these fellows that are investigating this thing looking for somebody that you know you didn't see. We have enough of a problem nationally to determine what actually happened, and we can't be putting that power chasing this thing that you say you saw. Probably somebody else saw something, I don't know, but what you're talking about, what you say you saw is not true. And I can guarantee you this, Sandy, and believe me, and I'm talking to you with complete honesty, that after you leave this room, if you want to tell me *why* it is that you made up this story, I can assure you that nobody else will talk to you about anything."

For over an hour, Serrano gamely hung on. "I know what I saw."

"You might want to be pushing it off with a smirk on your face, with a smile,

204   Ralph Schoenman, "RFK's assassination: The beat goes on," *The Baltimore Sun*, 5/28/95 and Turner and Christian, p. 66: In 1963, Hernandez "played a key role in Unified Police Command training for the CIA in Latin America" and received a medal from the Venezuelan government.

but you know that deep inside—"

"I remember seeing the girl!"

"No. No, I'm talking about what you have told here about a person tell you 'We have shot Kennedy.' And that's wrong."

"That's what she said!"

"No it isn't, Sandy."

Can you imagine what it would be like to hear a policeman tell you, at 20 years old, with alcohol in your system, at a late hour, strapped into a lie detector, with the only person you trust locked outside, without a lawyer or anyone else present, that you didn't hear and see what you actually saw and heard? Would you have had the guts, the moral courage to hold on?

"Lookit, lookit, I love this man!" Hernandez said, his temper showing.

"Don't shout at me," Serrano bravely asserted.

"Well, I'm trying not to shout. But this is a very emotional thing with me too, you see."

Hernandez was struggling but Serrano still had the upper hand. He tried again to play on her emotions: "If you love the man, the least you owe him is the courtesy of letting him rest in peace, and he can't rest. I don't think I could rest knowing … do you think maybe he could watch us right now?"

"No."

Hernandez tried to offer her a way out. "I think probably somebody misquoted you from the beginning, is what I, I don't know. Somebody misquoted you, one thing led to another, before you knew it, maybe it wasn't even your fault that somebody put, started putting this thing on the television and everything. But if that is the case, well tell me about it. It's very easy to redeem, but it isn't easy to redeem something that's like a deep wound that will grow with you like a disease, a cancer."

"Uh huh."

"So did somebody misquote you…?"

"Yes and no. There was this girl coming, and she was coming down the stairs and she had said, 'We shot him, we shot him.'"

"Sandy, don't. It's like a disease, I know what I am telling you. … I am saying that nobody told you, 'We have shot Kennedy.'"

"Yes, somebody told me that 'We have shot Kennedy.'"

"No," Hernandez bizarrely insisted. *He wasn't there. How could he know?* Anyone interested in an honest investigation would have stopped arguing with Serrano and started looking in earnest for the girl she had clearly seen and heard. Anyone even half honest would at least have suggested simply that she had misheard and left it at that. But Hernandez had something far more sinister planned.

"I'm sorry, but that's true. That is true."

"Let this thing that is gonna grow with you and is gonna make an old woman out of you before your time come out of you before it is...Look, I'll tell you something, I personally have talked to many people, and I respect, it takes a hell of a lot of person, a lot of guts, for an individual to say, 'Okay, I'm sorry that I did this.'"

The wine, the dinner, the hour, the restraints, and the big man in front of her who made it clear that the session would not end until she changed her story started wearing on Ms. Serrano. She sighed audibly, looking for a way out.

"It's, it's...it's a whole mess of things..."

Hernandez encouraged her to go on.

"It's too messed up, even I can't remember what happened anymore." She was willing to concede to being confused, but Hernandez wanted more.

"You know nobody told you, 'We have shot Kennedy.'"

"No," Serrano contradicted emphatically. "Somebody told me, 'We have shot Kennedy'. ... I'm not going to say, 'No, nobody told me,' just to satisfy anybody else."

"No, just the truth to satisfy yourself. No one else," Hernandez said, immediately contradicting himself with "To satisfy the family, the remaining family." He played the emotional card over and over. "The Kennedys have had nothing but tragedy here since first President Kennedy and now Senator Bobby Kennedy... now, what next? They have enough, at least it's a consolation to them and I'm certain, and you mark my words, that one of these days, if you're woman enough, you will get a letter from Ethel Kennedy," Hernandez lied again, promising things that would never happen. "Personal. Thanking you for at least letting her rest on this aspect of the investigation. There's somebody told me that, honest. No, really." Hernandez tried pathetically to bribe her with something he could never promise. "No, no, look, Sandy. And I'm not going to put words in your mouth," Hernandez lied again, trying desperately to do just that. "But I want you to tell me the truth about the staircase. Nobody on that staircase, what you're telling me here, told you that there was a woman that told you that 'We have shot Kennedy.'"

Serrano sighed but refused to give in.

"A woman told me, 'We have shot Kennedy.'"

Hernandez had just run what could best be described as an interrogation session and the woman had not budged. Serrano 1, Hernandez 0. So Hernandez essentially started the session over, from the top, as if working from a script. She was an "intelligent woman," he told her again. Her whole life lay ahead of her. He had interviewed 19 girls and two had finally been brave enough to say they had made it up. If she really loved the Kennedys, she would stop telling "this lie." And a second time, nothing he tried worked.

"It happened," Serrano persisted.

"No, it didn't happen," Hernandez asserted.

"Maybe not all of it, but it happened."

He tried to suggest she had gotten this statement from someone else. She refused that as a possibility as well. Serrano 2, Hernandez 0.

Hernandez paused for a smoke. He offered her a stick of gum, which she refused. "How about some Sen-Sen" (mint candies). He pushed hard. "Come on, let me give you something."

"I don't want any, now don't bug me. ... Leave me alone."

"The only time that you will be left alone," Hernandez started belligerently, then interrupted himself, perhaps remembering he was being taped. "You tell me what happened out there and I can assure you that nobody else will—"

"I don't know what happened," Serrano said.

Now that she was thoroughly tired, upset, and rattled, Hernandez ran the session a third time.

"When did you first hear that Kennedy had been shot? Let's start there."

"I was outside."

"Who told you?"

"A girl!"

"What did she say?"

"We shot him."

"No, that's not the truth, Sandy."

This is what psychological torture looks like. You don't have to abuse someone physically to torture them mentally and emotionally. Under the pen name of George Orwell, in *1984*, Eric Blair wrote, "Freedom is the freedom to say two plus two is four." Serrano was given no such freedom. She knew what she had seen and what it meant. And Hernandez was not going to stop until she gave him a full retraction.

Frustrated and tired himself, Hernandez called Sandra Serrano "Cathy" at this point, by mistake. Serrano thought he was referring to Cathy Fulmer, a 19-year-old girl who had worn an orange scarf with white polka dots on it at the hotel the night Kennedy was killed. Fulmer had been seen by several witnesses emerging from the west end of the pantry after the shooting saying "they shot Kennedy" or "they killed Kennedy." Fulmer had offered herself up to the police as the possible lady in the polka dot dress the media had mentioned. But a scarf is not a dress, and when Serrano was taken to view Fulmer, Serrano instantly confirmed Fulmer was not the girl she had seen.

"It wasn't Cathy Fulmer. But it was a Kathy," Hernandez said.

Hernandez may have been thinking of Kathy Lentine, who had come to the hotel as part of the Students for Kennedy group with six other teenage girls: Karen Pasalich, Liza Miller, Terri Trivelli and Jeanette Prudhomme and Irene Gizzi and 14-year-old Katherine "Katie" Keir. What these girls saw gave enormous credence to Serrano's account.

Kathy Lentine was separated from Miller and the group when she saw at the Ambassador Hotel "someone who resembled Sirhan Sirhan" with dark curly hair, jeans and a light blue top talking to a man who looked similar, but a little taller with a stockier build, who was wearing a "gold" or "toast" colored top.[205] This sounded just like the man Serrano had seen with the girl in the polka dot dress and Sirhan.

Jeanette Prudhomme told the LAPD that while in the Sunset Room she had seen two "grubby-looking" men sitting together, one of whom looked like Sirhan. The second man was wearing a gold shirt. They caught her attention because they did not appear to be properly attired for the event. Later that night, she saw the man in the gold shirt talking to a girl in a "white dress with black polka dots approx. one inch in size" who was about 5'6", with brown "shoulder-length" hair.[206] Again, this backs up what Serrano had seen.

Irene Gizzi had also noticed a trio of two males and a female because they didn't seem properly attired and "didn't seem to fit the exuberant crowd" as they stood and talked together in the lobby of the hotel off to the right in an area that was "lesser lit." One of the males looked like Sirhan and wore blue jeans and a light top. The second male was a "possible Latin" with a medium build, "dark sun-bleached hair," and a "gold-colored shirt." The girl, whose dark hair was combed up and hanging down in love locks, wore a white dress with black polka dots.[207]

Four of the girls had separately described seeing a man who looked like Sirhan in the company of a man in a gold sweater or shirt. Three had mentioned seeing a girl in a white dress with black polka dots in the company of the same two men.

One girl in this group, however, would add the most important detail.

Katherine McKensie "Katie" Keir was interviewed on June 5 by Van Nuys detectives. She told them she had seen Sirhan and "one male Caucasian, approximately 22 years old, 5'11"/6'0" tall, sandy hair, medium olive complexion," in a short-sleeved "goldish colored" shirt, who looked "grubby," and a light-skinned female in a white dress with black polka dots, with her dark brown hair "fixed in love locks all around" in the Sunset Room, which was one floor down from

205   LAPD interview record of Kathy Lentine, date unreadable due to the poor quality of the photocopy.
206   LAPD interview of Jeanette Prudhomme, 6/5/68 and 8/8/68.
207   In her LAPD interview summary of 8/6/68, Irene Gizzi reportedly said the dress was white with "unknown color" polka dots. But in her original interview of 6/6/68, Gizzi said the girl was wearing a "white dress with black polk-a-dot."

the Embassy Ballroom. "They were walking around looking at everyone and were quite obvious to others in the room, due to their dress." Keir lost track of them for a bit, "then observed them when another room was opened for air." After losing them a second time, Keir walked outside the Sunset Room and stood on a platform next to "an adjoining stairway," the very fire escape stairs where Sandy Serrano was sitting, when Keir saw "the girl in the white with black polk-a-dot [sic] dress running down the stairs" yelling "We shot Senator Kennedy." [208]

Serrano was never told that other witnesses had corroborated her observations of the trio of men, or that one in particular had witnessed her exchange with the girl in the polka dot dress.

"I thought that's what she said. I'm sure that's what she said. I mean, maybe they, she said, 'They shot him, they shot him.' I don't know." Serrano was starting to crack under the pressure.

"*If you don't tell me the truth, Sandy, they're gonna want to talk to you again and again.*" Hernandez's point was clear: these sessions would never end until Serrano changed her story.

"I'm ready to tell everybody to go to hell," the strong young woman defiantly said. But after more questioning, Hernandez finally got her to slip up.

"I was outside and some girl with a white dress on—"

Hernandez jumped on the "white dress" even though Serrano tried to add that "I think it did have polka dots on."

One last time, Serrano said the girl said "We shot him." "And that's the honest-to-God-truth," Serrano emphasized, adding, "and you can put it on your thingamajig machine and—"

"All right, you say a girl with a white dress told you—please, please don't make yourself a liar, don't have this piece of machinery here—"

And then Hernandez claimed that the test had not actually started. Of course it had started. Several times. He just wasn't getting the responses he needed. Now that he had her thoroughly upset, guaranteeing the machine would indicate extreme stress, which is read as a deceptive response, he asked her more formal questions. When he asked her, "Did a girl in a white dress tell you, 'We have shot Kennedy?'" she still answered yes, adding later, "I'm sure there was a girl in a white dress."

It still took many more minutes before Hernandez could coax her into the statement he was looking for. He started telling the story for her.

"First, you tell them that the person said 'We shot Kennedy,' and now you say you don't know whether they said 'we' or 'he.'"

"Uh huh."

"You say that girl was wearing a white dress with black polka dots. Now you

---

208   Van Nuys and LAPD interviews of Katherine Keir, 6/5/68 and 8/7/68, respectively.

know it was a *white* dress. That's number two. Then you said you saw two people coming down. ... But there were more than two people coming down."

Hernandez was telling the story the way he wanted to hear it. Under duress, Serrano starting caving in. "I don't know what happened. I don't know what happened."

Hernandez then went in for the kill.

"When this publicity was put out initially didn't you say, wait a minute, that's not true? Why? I know the answer, but I want you to tell me." He was basically saying that Serrano had lied, but he wanted the explanation for the lie in her own words.

Serrano started blaming the police for having "messed" her up, including Ambrose. Hernandez encouraged her, telling her she was being a "woman about this" now. "I'm proud of you," he said as Serrano finally started backpedaling. She mentioned how "some boy" (Vince DiPierro) had said something about a girl in a polka dot dress.

During her "confession," however, Serrano revealed something interesting: while she was at the police station "until six o'clock the next morning," someone tried to break into the house where she lived. "That really convinced me, you know."

Now that, at 10:15 P.M., Serrano was clearly willing to say anything to get free and go home, Hernandez once again indicated that the actual polygraph session hadn't started yet. He wanted to bring in a stenographer. Serrano clearly didn't want to rely on a police stenographer and insisted on a tape recorder, not knowing everything she was saying was already being taped. Hernandez made a show of bringing in a recorder and tried to get her to drink something, offering her a coffee or a Coke.

"I don't drink Cokes, just milk. ... Let me out."

Then the transcriber records an unintelligible whisper ending with "home."

But home was still a few lies away. Hernandez wasn't letting Serrano go until she not only retracted what she said but "explained" why she had changed her story. He homed in on the dress.

"Did you describe this person as being a female in a white dress?

"Right."

"And then sometime later, you heard some kid mention something about a white dress and polka dots—is that right?"

"Right."

"Was this where you got the idea or where somebody misquoted you?"

"I don't know. I guess. I don't know."

"No earlier, you said, somebody had quoted as you as saying that you had seen this same woman, who you saw with the white dress, that then was described as a white dress with black polka dots and which, in fact, was only a white dress that you saw?"

"Uh huh," Serrano said noncommittally.

"Right. Is that right?" Hernandez had to force the issue.

"Yes."

"And then somebody misquoted you or stated that you had said that this girl had told you to the effect, 'We have shot him.'"

"Uh huh. Right."

Then Hernandez told a whopper of a lie. "And in effect what you have told me previously is that this person told you 'he shot Kennedy' or 'they shot Kennedy'; is that right?"

Serrano was unwilling to flat-out lie, but she tried to play along. "Uhm, something about shooting Kennedy, yeah."

In the end, Serrano was willing to say only that having heard what other witnesses had said might have confused her or polluted her memory. But she had told an incredibly consistent story to each person she talked to—to Ambrose, to Sander Vanocur, to officers of the LAPD and agents of the FBI.

Hernandez insisted she had gotten the idea that the woman was in a polka dot dress from DiPierro.

He would next force DiPierro, through a similar session, to admit he had gotten the idea that the woman was in a polka dot dress from Serrano.

Any honest person would have to find Hernandez's treatment of Serrano unprofessional and *not* an effort to determine the truth about what Serrano had seen. Author Robert Blair Kaiser noted that "Hernandez was too eager. ... It was poor police work simply to wish [the girl in the polka dot dress] away, but that is exactly what the LAPD was doing."[209]

Sergeant Sharaga had stronger words for Serrano's treatment at the hands of Pena and Hernandez when I talked to him: "They should have gone to jail for what they did to her."[210]

Hernandez conducted a similarly bizarre lie detector session with the young Vincent DiPierro on July 1, 1968. DiPierro had reported a girl in a white dress with dark polka dots "holding" Sirhan just before Sirhan stepped out and fired his gun. Hernandez got DiPierro to say he had not seen a girl in a white dress with dark polka dots next to Sirhan, despite the fact that DiPierro had told that to the police in his first interview and had repeated it many times since, including to me when I interviewed him in 2006.

I won't quote his session here. It would be redundant. Suffice it to say the

---

209   Kaiser, p. 155.
210   Author's phone interview with Paul Sharaga in 2005.

17-year-old DiPierro was no match for the heavily experienced Hernandez. Interested parties should listen to the audio, which is available at the California State Archives. I took a tape of this session to DiPierro in 2006 and played a particular section for him. "They're putting words in my mouth," he said, clearly surprised. He had never heard the tape before. "I did not know that," he said, shaking his head and repeating, "I did not know that."[211] The teenage DiPierro didn't know he had been manipulated, but the adult DiPierro spotted it right away.

Hernandez's goal was made clear in the entry for this day in the official SUS Daily Summary: "Vincent DiPierro broken down on polka-dot story."

The police didn't stop there. They wanted to put the story of the girl in the polka dot dress to permanent rest. DiPierro was shown pictures of various women and had him pick out the one who looked most like the girl in the pantry. DiPierro picked out Valerie Schulte, who didn't match DiPierro's original description in any way. She was blonde, not brunette. She was on crutches, something DiPierro would have noticed. And she was wearing a green dress with yellow lemons of increasing size, not polka dots. But Pena and Hernandez told everyone they had "found" the girl in the polka dot dress.

When I interviewed DiPierro years later, I showed him his original description of the brunette in the white dress with dark polka dots, which he confirmed. Then I showed him a picture of Valerie Schulte. He readily acknowledged that that was not the dress of the girl he had seen in the pantry. But that's what Schulte had worn in the pantry. In other words, DiPierro confirmed, clearly, she was not "the girl in the polka dot dress" he had initially reported. He said he picked her out only because her face was similar, and he had been shown only headshots. He said that Deputy D.A. Howard had told him that if he said Schulte was the girl with Sirhan in the pantry, "we'll stand by you." DiPierro seemed proud that he had picked out a girl who had actually been in the pantry, saying words to the effect that the other women pictured might have been policewomen, and that he was pleased he had successfully chosen an actual pantry person. But it was equally clear this was not the girl he had originally seen. In fact, when I showed him a picture of an attractive, voluptuous woman from behind, in a fitted white dress with black polka dots, with shoulder-length hair, who much more closely matched his original description, he literally shuddered in front of me, as if recalling something unpleasant. (This photo was staged by journalist Fernando Faura and ran in his paper, the *Hollywood Citizen News*, with one of his stories. When I showed DiPierro a drawing Faura had made from John Fahey's description of the girl, DiPierro had no visible reaction at all.)

---

211   The portion of the tape I played for DiPierro does not appear to have been transcribed. The transcript from that same date picks up after the pressure had been brought to bear on DiPierro. In-person interview with DiPierro on 5/6/06. Other comments in this section come from phone interviews with DiPierro prior to our meeting. He would not let me tape our meeting.

DiPierro told me he passed two lie detector sessions and didn't break down until the third. At that point, he said he was in tears and just said whatever they wanted to hear.

DiPierro told me he believed Sirhan acted alone. But everything else he said belied that. He had been very fearful of meeting me in person. DiPierro told me he had carried a gun for protection for ten years after the assassination. It took several phone conversations before he finally agreed to meet with me in a public place. When we met, he said his girlfriend had been afraid I might kill him and had urged him not to see me. If he really believed Sirhan had acted alone, why was he so fearful? Sirhan was in jail. Who would want to kill him?

As we discussed the pantry events, he was noticeably shaken, and even teared up a few times. It's still a difficult moment for him to relive, something I've noticed with the other pantry witnesses I have talked to. He had nightmares about the shooting for ten years after the event. The police wouldn't even let him wash the blood off his hands before they interviewed him. He had to sit for hours with blood caked on him. He expressed a sense of guilt, as if there was something he could have done, should have done, to prevent Kennedy from being killed. I assured him that of course he couldn't have known what was about to happen, that it was not his fault.

As we were finishing our conversation, he mentioned how he was afraid that the mob might have wanted to take him out, another indicator that he believed Sirhan wasn't the only party involved. He said that FBI people had come to his home and said they'd protect him, which made him feel safe. Late in the conversation, DiPierro mentioned something about his personal data not being easily findable on the Internet at that time, and said that was part of "my deal with the FBI."

"What deal with the FBI?" I asked him in amazement.

He was silent for a few moments, perhaps realizing he had said something he shouldn't have. Then he changed the subject. I didn't press. I don't know what it's like to be in the shoes of someone who witnessed something like that and I refuse to pass judgment on people's choices in that regard. We parted shortly after that.

Hernandez had been gentler with DiPierro than with Serrano and some others because the police needed to preserve DiPierro's credibility so he could identify Sirhan as the shooter at the trial. And few witnesses put up Serrano's level of resistance. John Fahey was one of the rare exceptions. He was the one who had driven up to Oxnard with a girl who told him "they" were going to "take care of Kennedy" at "the winning reception" that night. He reported how, as he had driven this woman up the coast, his car had been followed. At one point he pulled off the road and one of the cars pulled off with him. He started to get out of the car to confront his follower when he saw the girl eyeing his car keys. Afraid she might steal his car, he got back in. Fahey told a consistent story several times over a period of months. The journalist Fernando Faura even arranged to have Fahey polygraphed by Chris Gugas, who said Fahey passed the test with flying colors. But this was a problem for the LAPD, which had to quash all evidence of conspiracy. So the LAPD insisted Fahey submit to Hernandez's polygraph. As with Serrano, Fahey eventually told Hernandez what he wanted to hear so he could end the process. Hernandez, of course, deemed Fahey a liar, even though no reasonable person who listened to Fahey on tape could come to that conclusion.

When Hernandez took on Everett Buckner, the range master from the gun range where Sirhan had been seen firing a gun the day of the primary by several witnesses, Buckner buckled faster than most, and Hernandez embellished the rest. Like Serrano, DiPierro and Fahey, Buckner's story indicated a conspiracy.

Ten days after the Grand Jury hearing, Buckner told the LAPD that Sirhan had arrived at the gun range at about 9:30 A.M. the morning of June 4 and taken up a position at the pistol range at the far west end of the range. After firing nearly one hundred rounds, Sirhan walked back to the control tower and asked Buckner for some .22 caliber ammunition that would not misfire. Buckner sold him some hollow-points. At some point after Sirhan returned and was firing, he saw Sirhan engage a white female, 5'7" to 5'8", 130–140 pounds, with shoulder-length blonde hair in conversation. She was wearing a light-colored "one-piece dress" with a full skirt. To the FBI, Buckner described her as attractive with a rather husky build.

Buckner told the LAPD the woman had arrived at the shooting range with a slim man more than 6' tall, and that the two had gotten into an argument, with the tall man saying to the woman, "Goddamn it, you've got to learn how to fire this gun today." Buckner told the FBI that the woman had a pistol and the man had a rifle. Buckner walked over to tell the man with the rifle he had to go to the rifle area, that he couldn't stay in the pistol area. Buckner said he asked the tall man, "Aren't you going to help your wife set up her target?" The tall man replied angrily, "She's not my Goddamn wife" and walked off to the rifle range.

The woman asked Buckner to assist her with firing, saying something like "This is the first time I have shot this gun, but I have to shoot it today." Buckner said she had a very small gun which he thought was a .22, with a pearl handle. Buckner declined to help, explaining it was against the rules for the range master to assist customers. A little while later, he saw Sirhan appeared to be assisting the woman, making gestures with his hands, pointing at the sight, for a few minutes. Suddenly Buckner heard the woman say, "God damn you, you son of a bitch. Get out of here or they will recognize us." Then he lost track of Sirhan.

The LAPD's contempt for Buckner shows on the cover sheet to his interview, which states "Buckner...has been running off the mouth [sic] to Time Magazine." Buckner was shown the Alarcon order and told, essentially, to shut up.

Just as he had with Serrano, when Hernandez polygraphed Buckner, Hernandez told Buckner he could not have heard what Buckner was certain he had heard.

"Why did you say to all these other people ... that the woman had told Sirhan something to the effect, 'Get away from me...somebody will recognize us.' Why did you say this before?"

"Because I thought that's what she said."

"But you know that's not what she said; is that right?"

"That is true. I don't know what she said."

In his summary of his session with Buckner, Hernandez wrote that Buckner "admitted that he never heard any woman saying anything to Sirhan at the range on June 4, 1958," which is not at all what Buckner had said, according to the transcript. Buckner had insisted many times during his questioning that the woman really had said something like "get away, they'll recognize us." "I think she said that. I still think she said that," he reiterated in his session.

The day after he talked to the LAPD, Buckner, who had been the range master for the past two months, was suddenly fired for allegedly drinking on the job. Nonetheless, the prosecution would find him credible enough to put on the stand as a witness.

There was another witness that partially backed up what Buckner had reported. A note in the LAPD's case preparation files states the following:

> On 6-28-68, Officer Thompson interviewed James J. Thornbrugh. His statement substantiates statements of others witnesses with one exception—Thornbrugh stated he thought Sirhan was with a girl and was showing her how to fire. He describes this female as Mexican or Latin descent, 22 to 23, 5-2 to 5-4, dark brown, shoulder-length hair, dark complexion. He was uncertain if it was Sirhan giving her this instruction or another male standing near Sirhan's position.
>
> A re-interview is to be scheduled with Thornbrugh and if necessary a polygraph examination will be requested.[212]

During Thornbrugh's polygraph session, he noted that he hadn't recognized Sirhan at first due to his messed-up, bruised appearance right after the shooting. but "after he had cleaned up and bruises or whatever was on his face was gone,

---

212   LAPD report from Sgt. M.J. McGann and Officers J. Mount and C.B. Thompson to Lt. Pena, July 5, 1968, page 6.

then he looked exactly like the person I saw out there." At the start of the session, Hernandez didn't seem to know what information he was there to test. When Thornbrugh said he could not be sure Sirhan had been talking to the woman, rather than probing Thornbrugh's memory to seek out the truth of what had happened, Hernandez let Thornbrugh go.[213] Hernandez's sole purpose, it seemed, was to get witnesses to reject anything they said that suggested a conspiracy.

The LAPD would later claim Sirhan had talked to a woman named Claudia Williams. But Claudia and her husband had not gone to the range until late afternoon, and both Buckner and Thornbrugh had seen Sirhan with the girl much earlier. In fact, Thornbrugh left the range a couple of hours before Claudia showed up.

Perhaps the most damning evidence against Hernandez is his uncharacteristically *friendly* treatment of Michael Wayne, the man who had been handcuffed after fleeing the pantry immediately after the shooting.

As you'll learn in a later chapter, Wayne lied to various parties throughout the night about who he was, who he knew, and what he was doing at the hotel that night. If anyone deserved a harsh session, it was Wayne. But Hernandez bent over backwards to let Wayne off the hook. He asked Wayne if he had ever been arrested, and when Wayne said yes, Hernandez told him that, since it happened when he was a juvenile, he could say "no."

When Hernandez asked if Wayne was running for a phone booth when he made his hasty exit from the pantry, Wayne answered "no" during the test. But after the test, when the polygraph was no longer tracking his responses, Wayne said he answered "no" because he wasn't looking for a "phone booth," just a phone. Someone then falsely typed in the transcript of his session that Wayne had answered the question "yes," which he didn't, according to the tape of his session.

Hernandez declared from the test results that Wayne had told only the truth. But if Wayne had said no because he was uncomfortable with the wording, 1) why didn't he speak up at the time, as others did when asked something they wanted clarified, and 2) why didn't that show up as deception in his results? And if his answer did indicate deception, why did Hernandez so readily accept Wayne's weak explanation after the fact? It makes more sense that Wayne told the truth the first time, leaving no reaction on the machine, and then lied about his reason after the test ended. Either way, the LAPD should not have rewritten the test answer to "yes," since that's not what Wayne actually said.

If Hernandez's motive was to prevent a conspiracy from being revealed, all of his sessions, including his softball one with Wayne and his tough ones with Serrano, DiPierro, and others with evidence of conspiracy, make sense. Without that motive, it's hard to find any reasonable explanation for Hernandez's selective treatment of witnesses or inaccurate reporting of what they said.

---

213   LAPD transcript of polygraph session of James Thornbrugh by Lt. Enrique Hernandez, July 18, 1968.

Pena, too, was less than honest in the way he handled the evidence. There were over 20 witnesses to a girl in a white dress with dark polka dots acting suspiciously, frequently in the company of someone who looked like Sirhan. But rather than trying to follow these leads, after Serrano was forced to retract her statement, Pena went through his stack of files on the girl and wrote, with his thick black pen on the interview cover sheets, "Polka Dot Story Phony" and "No further Int." ("no further interviews").[214]

Another common notation found on the cover sheets of interviews that had allegations relative to conspiracy: "Do Not Type." The LAPD sent officers with tape recorders hidden inside suitcases into the field for interviews (which explains the low sound quality of many of the interviews). Not all of these were transcribed, and in a disturbing pattern, several of the interview cover sheets or cardfile notations marked "Do Not Type" no longer have corresponding tape or paper interviews on file.

The FBI, too, was not above covering up or simply altering what witnesses had said in their interview summaries. Nina Rhodes-Hughes, one of the pantry witnesses, had told Professor Philip Melanson that her FBI statement was filled with lies. She reiterated this point to me in 2012 when I showed her a copy of her statement at a little café near Beverly Hills. She assured me she had told the FBI she heard 12–14 shots, but her FBI interview summary said she had heard only eight.[215] Rhodes-Hughes also told me she had heard shots coming from two different places in the pantry, one ahead of her to her left and another to her right, a point to which we'll return in a later chapter.

Similarly, after FBI agents interviewed Darnell Johnson on June 6, he told them he saw a girl in a white dress with black polka dots standing with four guys who appeared to be together, one of which Darnell identified as Sirhan from photos the FBI showed him. The FBI's response? At the bottom of this interview report, William Nolan wrote, in capitalized letters, "DO NOT COVER THIS LEAD AGAIN."[216]

While the authorities were busy explaining away, burying and avoiding evidence of conspiracy, Sirhan's defense team started to coalesce. The ACLU's Chief Counsel in Los Angeles, Abraham Lincoln (A.L.) Wirin had first asked that the chief public defender, Wilbur Littlefield, take over for Sirhan's initial public defender. But Wirin also asked that a private attorney be assigned to represent Sirhan. Judge Alarcon would not assign one.

---

214   Some researchers have mistakenly suggested that, because Pena's handwritten notes are scrawled on some interview summaries dated June 6 and 7, that Pena's involvement in the case was nearly immediate. But Pena's comments were clearly added after Hernandez had obtained Serrano's "confession," because his handwritten comments use Serrano's statement as a justification to close those files.

215   Interview of Nina Rhodes-Hughes, 5/24/2012.

216   FBI Memo from Nolan to SAC 56-156, 6/6/68.

Wirin was considering asking Grant Cooper, a high-profile Los Angeles attorney, to represent Sirhan when Robert Blair Kaiser, a stringer for *Time* magazine who had covered the Second Vatican Ecumenical Council (more commonly known as "Vatican II"), called to ask Wirin if he could speak to Sirhan. Kaiser mentioned that he had recently spoken to Grant Cooper. Wirin asked Kaiser if he would ask Cooper to take on Sirhan's defense.

Seeking help from Cooper seemed a no-brainer. He was a well-known, highly esteemed lawyer in the Southern California area. Not one of his clients had ever been put to death. He was a former president of the California Bar.

The choice not to use a public defender seems equally obvious to anyone who has not been inside the justice system. After all, isn't the fact that an attorney is highly paid a sign of their competence? Not necessarily. A public defender has an advantage that the private attorneys often do not: they know the habits of each Deputy D.A. they face, as they encounter them almost daily in the course of their work. Private attorneys don't usually have that level of familiarity. The public defenders also know the judges and the police department, what kind of evidence a certain judge is likely to allow, and how best to present a case such that it gets a fair hearing.[217]

Of course, Sirhan had no idea that a public defender might be better than a private one, so he did what most people would have done: he took Cooper.

Cooper, however, was busy defending a man involved with mobsters in a card-cheating scandal at the Friars Club. And one of the men involved in the Friars Club case was not just any mobster. He was Johnny Roselli, who had worked with the CIA on plots to kill the Cuban leader Fidel Castro. Cooper agreed to take Sirhan's case and to work for free on the condition that someone else represent Sirhan until Cooper's Friars Club case concluded.

Kaiser presented Cooper a list of potential lawyers who could serve as a proxy until he could be more fully involved. From the list, Cooper picked Joseph Ball, who had been a senior counsel for the Warren Commission, as one of his first choices, but Ball wasn't interested. Cooper didn't know Luke McKissack, another name on the list (and a man who became Sirhan's lawyer in later years). Cooper recognized the name Russell Parsons, however, and chose him. LAPD records note, without further explanation, that Parsons also went by the alias "Lester Harris," perhaps from his days as a mob lawyer. Parsons, who was well past the "69

---

217   I had a chance to see this up close as a juror on a conspiracy trial in Los Angeles. I was amazed to see how much more clearly the public defender presented her case than the Deputy D.A. presented hers. The public defenders on that case and another I sat for were so sharp that I asked a clerk of the court if these were the exception, or if all public defenders were that good. The clerk told me that the public defenders in Los Angeles were, on the whole, exceptional.

years" he joked he was to the press, agreed to help "the poor devil in trouble."[218]

Parsons brought in Michael McCowan to serve as his investigator. As an ex-LAPD officer, a former Marine and a former law student, McCowan seemed, on the face of it, a good choice.

Kaiser also ended up as a member of the defense team in exchange for exclusive journalistic access to Sirhan so he could write a book. He agreed to share a portion of his book advance in exchange for this access. Curiously, in Tennessee, a similar pattern was playing out. William Bradford Huie was given exclusive access to James Earl Ray by his defense team in exchange for a share in the profit of Huie's book.

The final member to join the defense team was New York lawyer Emile Zola "Zuke" Berman." Berman was the son of Russian-Jewish socialist revolutionaries who named him after the famous author Emile Zola who had exposed the unjust conviction of Alfred Dreyfus in his famous essay "J'Accuse...!" Berman had been an intelligence officer in the Army Air Corp's China-Burma-India theater. And though he was not classified as a flying officer, he flew on missions in the Far East.[219]

On the face of it, Sirhan had a powerful, experienced team to help him. In reality, however, McCowan was a convicted felon on parole who offered to serve as an informant to the LAPD on the Sirhan case,[220] Berman had a drinking problem, and Cooper was facing possible disbarment after having been caught red-handed in possession of a stolen Grand Jury transcript during the Friars Club case.

From the start, the defense team's stated goal was simple: to get Sirhan a punishment less than death. They asked the court to appoint various medical and psychological experts to attempt to determine whether Sirhan had any physical or mental disability that led him to commit the act.

The prosecution had exactly the opposite goal: to prove that Sirhan was of sound mind and body at the time of the assassination, that he was capable of distinguishing right from wrong, and that he willfully, premeditatedly committed the crime. They, too, needed psychological experts.

There was also a third party that had an interest in this case that also had

---

218   Klaber and Melanson, p. 26.

219   John C. Stevens, *Court Martial at Parris Island: The Ribbon Creek Incident*, (University of South Carolina Press, 2007), p. 68.

220   One of several such mentions of McCowan's offers to help the LAPD can be found in the Daily Summary of Activities report entry for November 1, 1968, written by Lt. Keene: "McCowan was in, saw Hernandez. Michael professed cooperation and indicated he'd obtain needed background information from family. He wants photos or maps showing kitchen and location of witnesses." Three days later, on November 4, Captain Brown's entry in the Daily Summary noted, "Made decision to decline McCowan's offer of help in obtaining miscellaneous information from family, information is not worth what he would want in exchange. It also raises the specter of 'dealing with the enemy,' which could embarrass the investigation at a later date." Despite this, another three days later, on November 7, McCowan called the LAPD to give them a heads-up that the FBI was about to interview Sirhan's family. McCowan also met with Hernandez on November 7, as Keene reported November 12 in the Daily Summary, and fed Hernandez derogatory information on Sirhan's brothers.

the goal of proving Sirhan sane: Arab nationalists. The Israeli-Palestinian conflict was about to explode, and some in the Arab community felt Sirhan, who was probably set to lose his life anyway, could be a spokesman for their cause. The Arab nationalist element also wanted to prove Sirhan sane to emphasize the political nature of his act.

Not one of these parties could claim "getting to the bottom of what happened" as a motive. That's not how our legal system works. It's all about which facts support one's case, not which facts inform the historical truth of the event.

The problem for all parties was that no obvious motive presented itself. Juries are persuaded more by stories than facts. So both the prosecution and the defense needed to come up with a compelling narrative. If Sirhan's motive were publicity, why did he claim no memory of the crime? If it was a political act designed to make a statement against U.S. support for Israel, why did Sirhan not say anything about that at the time, or shortly thereafter? Why did it take his defense team, essentially, to suggest that angle? Sirhan had no reason to pretend to have forgotten. He was sure to be in jail for life and likely to be put to death. If he had a motive, why not reveal it now?

In a notebook seized from Sirhan's bedroom after his arrest, across one particular page was scrawled, over and over, down nearly the entire page, "RFK must die. RFK must die." Why? The prosecution would argue that was proof of deliberate premeditation of the crime. The defense would argue the repeated writing showed Sirhan was mentally ill.

Sirhan could not remember writing that notebook entry, which was dated May 18. Oddly enough, on May 18, tourists in Israel heard that a radio report claimed Senator Robert Kennedy had been shot. Had a plot that had been expected to succeed failed that day?

John Lawrence, the director of Federated Americans against Israeli Racism, an advocate for Arab causes and an anti-Zionist, wrote Sirhan a letter, which Sirhan received on June 10, 1968, urging Sirhan, in essence, to claim his act as a response to the injustice facing Palestinians at the hands of the Israelis but backed by the American government. Lawrence told Sirhan that Robert Kennedy had encouraged the U.S. to send 50 jets to Israel, which Lawrence characterized as "jet bombers."

When Kaiser asked Sirhan why he had written "RFK must die," Sirhan had said he must have done it in response to a documentary he saw which mentioned the bombers. The problem was, the entry in the notebook was dated May 18. The statement itself was not made until May 26, and was not televised or written in local papers. News of the statement may have been heard over the radio, but regardless, the statement, however Sirhan first learned of it, came nearly a week after the notebook entry. The first article Kaiser found that contained this information was in the *New York Times* of June 7, in the article Lawrence clipped and sent to Sirhan.

Sirhan was disturbed by the notebook entries when he was first shown them. "All this repetition!"[221] Sirhan exclaimed. Even the existence of the notebook made no sense to Sirhan in the context of a supposedly premeditated act. "I don't understand. Why did I leave the notebook behind?"

Having no memory of the crime, Sirhan grappled with his options: either he killed Kennedy willfully, against his own morality, or he had somehow killed Kennedy unwittingly, a notion that frightened him. Perhaps he did what most people would do: he chose to believe he had some strong reason for committing this crime. Sirhan said at one point, he'd rather "die and *say* I killed that son of a bitch for my country"[222] than claim he was mentally unbalanced. To that point, Sirhan urged his lawyers to plead him guilty, an option his lawyers refused initially because it would leave him no recourse for any appeal later.

Three of the defense team members suspected something more was at play. Parsons, Berman and Kaiser expressed at different times the possibility that someone else was involved. But Cooper had no intention of mounting a defense by claiming there was a conspiracy involved. In the end, both the prosecution and the defense bent over backwards to minimize the jury's exposure to any evidence of conspiracy.

The FBI and LAPD were also puzzled, as they had trouble finding people who could testify to the kind of rage that's usually associated with killers. They tried hard to find someone who would claim Sirhan was a violent person. But nearly everyone described Sirhan as polite, respectful, and friendly.

Jack Davies, a former employer of Sirhan's when Sirhan worked at a gas station, told the FBI that "Sirhan was an excellent worker and never caused any trouble around the station, was friendly to the customers, and seemed dedicated to his work. ... He advised that Sirhan was very polite to the customers, attention, showed an outstanding personality, and one of the best employees that has worked for him...."[223] Sidney McDaniel, who worked with Sirhan under Davies, also said "it was hard for him to believe that Sirhan could do this." Yet another employee at this station, Chester Yashuk, noted that when a security guard who collected the money at night was overly profane, Sirhan asked him to tone it down. The guard tried to pick a fight with Sirhan, but Sirhan "became very meek and would not fight this guard."

---

221   Kaiser, p. 324.
222   Kaiser, p. 345.
223   FBI interview of Jack Davies taken 6/7/68, dated 6/12/68.

Another former employer, Clarence Copping, said Sirhan was "an outstanding employee, an excellent worker," and that "at no time did Sirhan ever express any of his political views or nationalistic leanings in any manner." Copping, like nearly everyone the LAPD and FBI interviewed, said that "when he was notified that Sirhan was the person suspected of shooting Senator Kennedy, it was very hard for him to believe." Wayne Brantley, who worked with Sirhan while he was working for Copping, said Sirhan "did not indicate any emotional disturbance over the situation in Israel, and no particular animosity toward any individual or group."

William Beveridge, who had employed Sirhan as a part-time gardener a few years earlier, also said Sirhan was "quiet, well mannered, and studied very hard. He did not discuss politics and did not in any way express resentment toward any individual or group. He appeared to like the United States and enjoyed living in this country. At no time did he display any temperament or show violence."

When Henry Peters, a man who had worked with Sirhan at a health food store in Pasadena and who tutored Sirhan on the Bible in Sirhan's home, whom his mother said was the only "friend" Sirhan invited home in the months prior to the assassination, was asked by Hernandez about Sirhan, Peters said, "I cannot say anything against him. He was a really nice boy." Asked if he had ever seen Sirhan express a temper, Peters said, "I'd have to lie.... No, he didn't. ... We were just dumbfounded...." Sirhan had a run-in with his employer at the Pasadena store, but Peters sided with Sirhan in the dispute. These are not cherry-picked examples. These represent the vast majority of comments people made about Sirhan.

You can cherry-pick a few examples of people who saw Sirhan in an angry state. The one topic that definitely animated Sirhan was discussing the Palestinian-Israeli conflict, which had erupted into what became known as the Six-Day War in 1967. But even in those animated discussions, no one ever indicated that Sirhan's rage ever remotely rose to a level that indicated a capacity to kill.

Sirhan's legal team sought help from mental health professionals to attempt to determine, after the fact, his mental state at the time of the shooting. There are five possible explanations for Sirhan's claimed memory loss, and these are not mutually exclusive:

1. He had physical brain damage that prevented the physical recording or recall of that memory.

2. He was lying.

3. He was drunk or drugged.

4. He had a psychological impairment that prevented the recording or recall of that memory.

5. He suffered from post-hypnotic amnesia. People who have been hypnotized to a deep stage often have no memory of what transpired under hypnosis. This is not true of those who have been only lightly hypnotized, who remember everything that happened under hypnosis.

Dr. Eric Marcus, appointed by the court to examine Sirhan, found there was no abnormal brain activity that would indicate any physical damage. And neither the defense nor the prosecution could prove Sirhan was lying regarding his memory loss. Even Sergeant Jordan, who had interviewed Sirhan for a long time after his arrest, had told another officer he was convinced Sirhan was being truthful to the facts he could remember. Similarly, Sirhan's defense team could see how anguished Sirhan was by his lack of recall. It did not make sense that he was making up a memory loss as a defensive technique.

Neither the defense nor the prosecution could successfully argue that Sirhan was under the influence of alcohol or drugs at the time of the shooting (although the defense team would try), as the LAPD had convincingly ruled that out. LAPD Chief Reddin had told the media at the initial press conference after Sirhan's arrest that they had "definitely" ruled out the possibility that Sirhan was under the influence of alcohol or some other substance. And not one witness mentioned alcohol on Sirhan's breath, slurred speech, bloodshot eyes, or any other of the normal indications of alcoholic intoxication.

That left only two options—that Sirhan either was psychologically impaired or had been hypnotized. Ironically, the explanation that fits the evidence the best is also the one that sounds the craziest to a layperson: that Sirhan was under hypnosis, a point to which we'll return in a later chapter. But if Sirhan had been hypnotized by an outside party, that would indicate a co-conspirator, and as we've already seen, neither the defense nor the prosecution had a motive to explore a conspiracy and strong reasons not to. So from a practical standpoint, that left both sides with only one real choice: that Sirhan was mentally impaired in some way. This, then, became the sole point of the trial. Was Sirhan so crazy he could not be held accountable for his actions? Or was he only partially impaired, and therefore capable of legal premeditation? To answer that question for their respective cases, the defense and the prosecution hired psychologists to examine Sirhan.

Showing premeditation was the prosecution's primary goal. To that effect, they focused on Sirhan's activities at the gun range earlier in the day. They wanted to paint a picture of a would-be assassin practicing for his eventual target.

But one point about the firing range episode bothered LAPD Chief of Detectives

Houghton. *Not one* of the more than 40,000 shell casings the FBI gathered from the firing range had been matched to Sirhan's gun. As Houghton wrote in his book *Special Unit Senator*, shell casings are "branded with the indentation mark of the firing pin, a brand as unique and infallible in matching spent shells to the guns which fired them as fingerprints are in identifying people."[224] So it should have been an easy matter to find at least one shell that could be definitively matched to Sirhan's gun. That no match had been made concerned Houghton enough to discuss it in his daily log:

> One hole that has been overlooked that should be checked was discovered in this reading. The FBI, within a day or two after the Kennedy assassination, sent agents to the Pistol Range in San Gabriel and they gathered some 40,000 shell casings which were forwarded back to the FBI Crime Lab. They threw up their hands, and at our request, the brass was sent back to us. Wolfer reports he examined all of these casings and could not connect any of them to Sirhan's gun. This means that if Sirhan shot several hundred rounds at the San Gabriel range, either he took the brass with him or someone else picked it up. Neither of these conclusions appears at this time to make sense. More investigation is needed. There is a possibility that Wolfer really did not examine all of this brass (this should be checked) or that the FBI still has brass in Washington (this should be checked.)"[225]

A few years later, Houghton wrote that Wolfer really did check the shells, but was unable to find a match.[226] An LAPD progress report states Wolfer examined "37,815 shell casings" but could not match even one to Sirhan's gun.[227]

Despite the autopsy report having been completed just days after the shooting, the LAPD did not provide a copy to the defense team until November of 1968, when the trial was supposed to begin. In retrospect, the LAPD kept a tight hold on the autopsy report for obvious reasons. If you put the witness statements and the autopsy report side by side, it is clear Sirhan was not standing where the shooter had to have been. All the witnesses put Sirhan in front of and facing Kennedy. All the bullet wounds in Kennedy came from behind him. Perhaps the LAPD hoped Cooper and his team wouldn't have time to read the report before the trial. But since Cooper was still wrestling with his own legal troubles, the trial was delayed until January.

---

224   Houghton, p. 266.

225   August 27, 1968 entry in the daily log of the Commander of Detectives for the Bureau of Investigations.

226   Houghton, p. 266.

227   SUS Final Report, p. 842.

The delay gave Kaiser time to read and comment on the report. Kaiser told me he wrote a memo to Cooper explaining that there was a serious issue with the distance. All the witnesses who saw both Sirhan and Robert Kennedy together placed Sirhan's gun muzzle, on average, at about three feet from Kennedy. But the autopsy report showed that the four shots that hit Kennedy—three that entered his body and one that passed through the top of the right shoulder of Kennedy's jacket without entering his body—were all shot from not more than six inches behind him, with the fatal shot coming from a distance of not more than one inch. Cooper simply ignored this evidence, however, as he did all evidence that might have pointed to conspiracy.

Meanwhile, Sirhan's defense team was still trying to construct a plausible motive. In an attempt to get Sirhan to remember the events of the pantry, Bernard Diamond, a psychiatrist and assistant Dean of Phrenology at the University of California at Berkeley, put Sirhan under hypnosis in a series of meetings to attempt to get Sirhan to reenact the events of the pantry. But even under hypnosis, Sirhan failed to remember exactly what had happened, despite what, as we will see later, were extremely leading suggestions.

Diamond also noted that Sirhan evinced great emotional distress when his childhood in Israel was discussed. Sirhan had lived in an area that received heavy bombing during the 1948 Arab-Israeli conflict that ended with the creation of the new state of Israel. A sensitive young boy to begin with, he had witnessed heinous atrocities that had left permanent scars in his psyche. This, then, over Berman's objections, became the defense's case: the shooting was an act of temporary insanity, inspired by Kennedy's support for sending bombers to Israel.

Cooper did something strange as the trial approached. Normally, the medical and psychological examinations of a defendant are kept private. According to California law, the prosecution's psychiatrist could only comment on the defense witnesses' presentations in court and are not allowed to examine the defendant directly. This is to protect the defendant's privacy. But Cooper decided that Sirhan was so obviously disturbed that the prosecution's psychiatrist, Dr. Seymour Pollack, would clearly see that. To that end, Cooper staged a meeting on February 2, 1969 of all the medical and psychiatric personnel who had examined Sirhan so they could exchange notes and perhaps reach a common verdict. It was a hell of a gamble. If they all agreed Sirhan was crazy, perhaps a trial could be avoided and Sirhan unanimously recommended to a mental institution. That would guarantee he would not be put to death, and given that that appeared to be the defense team's sole goal, that makes some sense. But if Cooper's gamble went awry, it could set the stage for a death penalty verdict. To the dismay of all the participants, Pollack refused to offer his conclusions as to Sirhan's state, saying that he had not yet made up his mind.

While Judges Alarcon and Richard Schauer had presided over pre-trial hearings, in October 1968, responsibility for the case transferred to Judge Herbert V. Walker, a former Chief Deputy District Attorney for Los Angeles. A white-haired near-septuagenarian, Judge Walker was known for his big bushy eyebrows as much as for his position. Sirhan's lawyers had approached Judge Walker several times about pleading Sirhan guilty. Then, just days before his trial was to begin, something shocking happened. While Pollack would not state his conclusions to the defense team, he apparently convinced the prosecution their case would be best served by allowing Sirhan to plead guilty.

On the morning of February 10, 1969, District Attorney Evelle Younger told the Judge:

> I understand that the defendant is prepared to plead guilty and accept a life sentence ... We favor it, Judge, and the law requires your approval. ... [And] now that we have gotten our psychiatrist's report, a man whom we have great confidence in, we are in a position where we can't conscientiously urge the death penalty, number one. Number two, we don't think under any circumstances we would get the death penalty even if we urged it and number three, we don't think we can justify the trial under those circumstances.
>
> It appears that the result is a foregone conclusion. *Our psychiatrist, in effect, says that the defendant is psychotic and his report would support the position of the defense because of diminished capacity and the death penalty wouldn't be imposed.* ... Are we justified in going through the motions of a trial, a very traumatic and expensive trial, when we say we can't conscientiously ask for the death penalty anyway? We don't think we are.[228]

The jury would never hear *those* words. They'd hear something quite different.

Cooper told the Judge he'd be willing to plead to first degree murder to avoid the death penalty. In other words, Cooper was willing to concede completely the culpability of his client leaving him no option for appeal, on the premise that he was saving his client's life.

In a less political case, the Judge would likely have accepted such an offer. But in this case, Judge Walker said:

---

228   Sirhan Trial Transcript, pp. 2651–2652. The following dialog is excerpted starting from this point in the transcript.

Gentlemen, I have a great deal of respect for all of you, as you know … but the ramifications of this thing, I think, should be thoroughly given to the public. I appreciate the cost. I appreciate the sensation, but I am sure it would just be opening us up to a lot of criticism by the people who think the jury should determine this question.

We have a jury and whatever expense is incurred from here on out would only be negligible with what I think would be incurred if we did otherwise. Obviously, in open court, if there was a plea of murder, then you could have a trial to determine the degree and the penalty, that would be all right [sic] with me. …

I don't let the public influence me, but … there are a lot of ramifications and they continually point to the Oswald matter and they just wonder what is going on because the fellow wasn't tried.

The "Oswald matter" referred to the fact that Lee Harvey Oswald was killed by Jack Ruby while in the custody of the police before he could be brought to trial, a move many—even at that early point—read as a sign of a conspiracy working to silence Oswald. The irony of putting a man not in control of his mental faculties into a trial situation that could result in his death, thereby silencing him, too, apparently never crossed Judge Walker's mind.

Cooper offered, "If we had first degree, we could put on a very skeleton outline of the case at the time of plea instead of submitting reports, and we could put witnesses on to testify."

"Well, then they would say that it was all fixed, it was greased, so we will just go through with the trial," Judge Walker replied.

John Howard suggested the record of this conversation be sealed.

"It should be sealed, don't you think?" the Judge asked Cooper.

"Yes, by all means," Cooper responded.

But Younger argued this point. "I don't think your Honor is right. I don't want to argue with you publicly or privately, but I am inclined to think our position should be made a matter of record." The Judge had no objection.

Younger still wanted to agree regarding the penalty. "I do think the one thing we could do would be the penalty, because we are burdened with it from our psychiatrists."

"I am not concerned about your organization," the Judge responded. "I say if they come out with second degree, that is it, and that is what the jury does. I don't think psychiatrists should determine the outcome of a lawsuit."

"Well, they have been for years," Younger said.

"I am not going to argue it any further, gentlemen. My mind is made up."

Both the prosecution and defense agreed that Sirhan should not be given the death penalty. Both feared if the case went to a jury, that's what would happen. Judge Walker feared that by not putting the case to trial, the public would suspect a cover-up. But by putting a defendant up for a penalty both sides agreed would be both unfair and likely, hadn't the Judge essentially guaranteed that which he most feared?

In summary, the LAPD and FBI came up with an extraordinary amount of evidence of conspiracy, much of which will be discussed in later chapters. But both the LAPD and FBI, for reasons that could have been as simple as wanting to wrap this up quickly, either ignored this evidence or tried to cover it up.

But Deputy District Attorney John Howard had heard direct evidence of conspiracy, as you learned, when he listened to both Serrano and DiPierro discuss separately, and within minutes of each other, a suspicious girl in a polka dot dress in the company of Sirhan.

Members of the defense team, too, had voiced concerns about evidence indicating a conspiracy, but since they couldn't imagine a conspiracy in which their client could be innocent, they, too, ignored that evidence.

Fearing the public would cry "cover-up" if no trial were held, Judge Walker overrode the joint agreement of both the prosecution and defense and possibly guaranteed what could have been the most permanent cover-up of all: the death of Sirhan Sirhan.

What happened next was not a trial to determine the truth of what happened in the pantry but a "show trial" staged for the purpose of putting evidence of Sirhan's culpability into the record, attempting to dismiss any evidence of conspiracy that had already been made public, and providing an appropriate punishment.

Had Sirhan had a defense team brave enough to follow the evidence *wherever* it led, the trial that followed would have unfolded quite differently.

TRIAL

"Most of what ails our criminal justice system lie[s] in unwarranted certitude on the part of police officers and prosecutors and defense lawyers and judges and jurors that they are getting it right, that they simply are right. Just a tragic lack of humility of everyone who partici- pates in our criminal justice system."

TRIALS ARE MEANT TO BE ADVERSARIAL AFFAIRS, WHERE ONE SIDE argues for a person's guilt regarding specific charges and the other side argues for a person's lack of guilt (as opposed to "innocence") regarding those specific charges. The entire judicial system is predicated on the belief that through such an adversarial proceeding, the truth will emerge.

In reality, this is not always the case. The prosecution gets the first opening argument and the last rebuttal, so the prosecution has an advantage in any trial. In a long trial, the prosecution can build their case for days or weeks before the defense has much to say about it. Although jurors are admonished not to form an opinion until both sides have been heard, it's human nature to do so. The defense can challenge the prosecution and cross-examine the witnesses to attempt to keep the defense's case alive, but if the defense attorneys are too aggressive in their questioning, this can turn off the jury before the defense has even been able to call its first witness.

When I sat on a jury, I was appalled that our elected foreman's first words at the beginning—not the end but the beginning—of deliberations were, "We all agree he's guilty, right?" There had been no discussion yet of the evidence. No deliberations. Just an assumption that everything the prosecution had said must be true and everything the defense said must be false. Fortunately several of us disagreed. But even so, it was one of the more disturbing moments of my life, because it proved the fallibility of our legal system. Dean Strang, a defense attorney and adjunct professor at the University of Wisconsin made an astute comment about such assumptions in 2016:

> Most of what ails our criminal justice system lie[s] in unwarranted certitude on the part of police officers and prosecutors and defense lawyers and judges and jurors that they are getting it right, that they simply are right. Just a tragic lack of humility of everyone who participates in our criminal justice system.[229]

In Sirhan's case, not only was there a tragic lack of humility by all involved, but there was the perception that Sirhan was definitely guilty because Sirhan had essentially admitted as much. Most people believe that innocent people do not confess to crimes they did not commit. Sirhan's defense team, from the start, encouraged Sirhan to accept responsibility for a crime he had no memory of committing, claiming that to do otherwise would weaken his case, as it would appear he was simply lying.

In one of the numerous ironies in this case, in 1966, Grant Cooper had penned an article for the *Los Angeles Times* titled "Confessions, Cops and the Courts" that opened with a story of a man named George Whitmore, Jr., who had confessed to two murders and a rape after the police found a photo of one of the victims on him. But a woman stepped forward and said the picture was of her, not any of the murder victims, causing "an enterprising young prosecutor" to question the confession. In the end, Whitmore was exonerated. Cooper quoted the prosecutor as having said, in answer to the question of why someone would confess to a crime they didn't commit, "Call it what you want—brain washing, hypnosis, fright. They made him give an untrue confession."[230] In the article, Cooper listed five cases where false confessions were made and overturned. Years after the Sirhan trial, Cooper signed a sworn statement saying had he been aware of the evidence of conspiracy, he would have mounted a different defense. But evidence of conspiracy had entered the record early and often. Cooper simply ignored it.

Provably then, people *do* confess to crimes they didn't commit, for a variety of reasons. In a scholarly study of cases from 1971 to 2002, Steven Drizin and Richard Leo "identified 125 false confession cases between the years of 1971 and 2002 by combing through electronic media and legal databases, police reports, trial transcripts, articles and books. The study focused on proven false confessions—those that dispositive evidence objectively established were indisputably false because the confessor could not possibly have been the perpetrator of the

---

229   Keith A. Findley, "'Making a Murderer' shows that our justice system needs a healthy dose of humility," *Washington Post*, January 15, 2016.

230   Grant B. Cooper, "Confessions, Cops and the Courts," *Los Angeles Times*, October 2, 1966.

crime." In addition, the Innocence Project documented that, of the first 225 cases where a person was exonerated of their crime through DNA evidence, 23% of the convictions were based on false admissions of guilt and 52% were based on invalidated or improper forensics.[231]

"Improper forensics" is the generous term to describe what happened in Sirhan's case under Wolfer's watch. In fact, less than a month before the trial, the FBI had turned down the request from LAPD to confirm the LAPD's analysis of the evidence in this case.[232] That's not surprising, given that the FBI's findings were already at variance with the LAPD's, notably about the presence of bullet holes in the frames of the pantry doors, which inflated the total bullet count from the LAPD's eight to at least twelve. By agreeing to reexamine the LAPD's evidence, the FBI would have been put in the awkward position of having to reject the findings of their own professionals or reject those of the LAPD's, which would have called the entire case against Sirhan into question. Neither the defense nor the prosecution could have welcomed such a move. In fact, both the defense and the prosecution made sure the jury never learned there was any question about Wolfer's veracity, or that any of the physical evidence in the case might not have been as presented.

In this particular trial, there were substantial factors that prejudiced the jury from the start. The public had been told from the first day that Sirhan was guilty, that there was no question of his guilt. Indeed, Sirhan himself had never claimed to be innocent. He claimed only to have no memory of the crime, but he accepted that he "must" have committed it because a number of witnesses saw him fire a gun at Kennedy.

To compound the matter, the fact that Sirhan's lawyers had considered pleading him guilty to murder in the first degree in an effort to spare his life appeared in the *Los Angeles Times the day before the trial began*, before the jurors had been sequestered.[233] The front page headline screamed, in large, capitalized type "above the fold," i.e., in the part seen from every newsstand, "SIRHAN GUILTY PLEA NOW APPEARS LIKELY." In addition, there had been a radio report on one of the major local radio stations to the same effect.

The morning of the trial, Judge Walker brought the jurors in one by one to ask what they had seen or heard about the plea. Ten of the twelve jurors had heard something about this, either directly or indirectly from family or friends.

---

231   Amelia Hritz, Michal Blau, and Sara Tomezsko; "False Confessions," Cornell Law School on Social Science and Law website, courses2.cit.cornell.edu/sociallaw/student_projects/FalseConfessions.html, accessed March 15, 2015.

232   After the FBI turned them down, LAPD sought help from the Los Angeles County Sheriff's office. SUS Daily Summary of Activities, January 29, 1969.

233   Dave Smith, "Sirhan Change of Plea Seen Likely," *Los Angeles Times*, February 12, 1969.

One of the jurors, Ronald Evans, said he had heard on the radio that the lawyers for Sirhan might plead him guilty. Cooper asked him, "Don't you feel now ... that it would be very difficult for you to find a verdict of second degree or manslaughter?" "Yes," Evans had answered. "Well, if I understood that broadcast, it said he was going to plead guilty to murder in the first degree. Then it would be hard to bring in a verdict of second degree or manslaughter." Judge Walker asked Evans if he were told that weren't true, that the newsman had been speculating, could he keep an open mind? Yes, Evans said, he could. But no one then followed up to tell him that *wasn't* true (because, of course, it *was*), yet the man was allowed to remain on the jury. (Evans didn't finish the trial though, as his father died during closing arguments. Evans was replaced by an alternate juror.) The other jurors who had heard something about the plea promised it would not affect their judgment. But how could it not?

In addition, the defense team stipulated up front to the jury in their opening statement that their client, Sirhan Sirhan, had killed Robert Kennedy. The only point of this trial was to determine Sirhan's state of mind at the time. Had he willfully, premeditatedly killed Senator Robert Kennedy, or had some mitigating factor, such as mental illness, played a role? Normally, given that both sides agreed, this would have been merely a penalty hearing. But Judge Walker wanted the *appearance* of a full trial, fearing the public would demand no less. But what the public would have demanded, had they understood what was being concealed, was a procedure leading to the truth of what had happened.

When evidence indicating a conspiracy did leak out in court, despite the defense and prosecutions' efforts to conceal it, it was either ignored or quickly mitigated by the prosecution or, more often, by Cooper, Sirhan's lead defense attorney. As we saw in the previous chapter, arguing that Sirhan was part of a conspiracy was believed to be a sure way to guarantee a harsher verdict for the defense (as it would presumably demonstrate premeditation) and a nightmare for the prosecution (as it would demonstrate incompetence, in that the other conspirators got away). Even a third party that tried to take over Sirhan's defense, the Action Committee on Arab-American Relations, saw this trial only as a way to gain publicity for their cause in Palestine. They, too, had neither Sirhan's nor history's best interests at heart, but rather an agenda of their own to pursue.[234]

The fact is that the truth of what had actually happened in the pantry never had an advocate in that courtroom. The system simply isn't built to expose conspiracies that benefit neither the prosecution nor the defense. And at some point we have to seriously consider a darker possibility: that the cover-up was deliberate, that one or more people on both the prosecution and the defense fully understood there was a conspiracy, and that those who knew agreed to

---

234   "Sirhan Offered New Defense Team," *Los Angeles Times*, 2/13/69.

keep it concealed. That's actually the simplest explanation for all that happened at the trial.

On February 13, 1969, at the Los Angeles Superior Court building in downtown Los Angeles, the "people," i.e., the District Attorney's office, put forth their opening statement about Sirhan's guilt in the shooting of Robert Kennedy. A camera hidden in an air conditioning unit transmitted the proceedings to a separate room used as an overflow room for the media.[235]

The Judge told the jury that an opening statement is not evidence. In fact, nothing attorneys said, whether from the prosecution or the defense, could be considered evidence. Attorneys can only provide the framework for the case. Sworn witnesses produce evidence. It's up to the jury to decide if those sworn witness statements are actually facts. It should go without saying that just because someone swears to something under oath doesn't mean it's the truth. That's why perjury charges exist.

All dialog in this chapter is from the trial transcript unless otherwise noted. In some cases I have excerpted testimony without ellipses and presented witnesses out of order to make a more coherent presentation, a luxury neither the defense nor the prosecution had.

David Fitts began his opening statement to the jury with Sirhan's purchase of a gun and bullets. Fitts described how Sirhan had bought "Mini-Mag," hollow-point bullets from Larry Arnot at the Lock, Stock & Barrel Gun Shop in Pasadena on June 1, 1968.

Fitts did not, of course, inform the jury in his opening statement that Arnot had told both the LAPD and FBI that he saw two other men with Sirhan when he purchased the ammunition, nor that the owner's wife, Donna Herrick, also recalled seeing three men who had talked to Arnot that day. Herrick remembered them because the same three men had been in her shop a couple of months earlier inquiring about tank-piercing ammunition. Arnot, Herrick, and her husband Benjamin all told their stories to the FBI.

The FBI had tried to get Arnot and the Herricks to identify Sirhan's brothers as the two men with him, but not one of the three would make that identification. But all three were certain Sirhan was one of the three men.

Predictably, since they had evidence of conspiracy, Hernandez had polygraphed both Arnot and Donna Herrick and concluded they were lying. Predictably, like Sandra Serrano, both were adamant they had not lied. Predictably, none of this information reached the jurors.

---

235   UPI story in *The Bryan Times*, 1/8/69, raising the question of whether the trial was also recorded on videotape.

To address distances, Fitts introduced a scale mockup of the pantry area of the Ambassador Hotel and nearby areas to help orient the jury to the various positions of witnesses who had seen Sirhan that night at various places in the hotel and in the pantry at the time of the shooting. The exhibit was divided into a grid of two-inch squares, each representing a two-foot-by-two-foot square, so witnesses could specify their positions with a letter and number. Fitts told the jury that most witnesses put Senator Kennedy at about 13-E on the grid.

Using this grid made it easy for witnesses to point to where people were in the pantry, but it also obscured distances. Sirhan and RFK could have been placed in the same square by witnesses, but the jury wouldn't know from that whether they were an inch apart or two feet apart. People in adjacent squares could have been four feet apart. The transcript, too, could not capture *where* in the squares witnesses pointed to. The transcript was the only record that was, at that point, sure to be made public, and both sides made sure they asked no questions that would expose the distance and positioning issues between Sirhan and Senator Kennedy to the trial jury, although witnesses sometimes volunteered this information. Whether it was intended as such or not, it was a clever trick that apparently worked, as no jurors or, for that matter, journalists, questioned the distance issue during the trial.

Fitts told the jury that Judy Royer had shooed Sirhan out of the pantry earlier that night. This was not true, as Royer had provably shooed *Michael Wayne* from the pantry, not Sirhan, although Royer had shooed Sirhan out of a different area a couple of hours earlier that night. In doing so, Fitts amply demonstrated why judges have to remind people that nothing a lawyer says can be considered a fact.

Fitts named several people whose hands Kennedy shook as he crossed the pantry. He described how Sirhan crossed from the serving tray rack by the ice machine across to the serving tables where Kennedy stood, raised his gun and fired. Then Fitts stated something else that was provably untrue, but which the defense team neglected to challenge: that Sirhan shot Kennedy at "point blank range." *No credible witness ever placed Sirhan close enough to get his gun muzzle within an inch of Kennedy's head.* Witnesses who saw a gun close to Kennedy could never identify the shooter as Sirhan, and those who saw both Sirhan and Kennedy made clear they were feet, not inches, apart. Frank Burns said the gun was "very close to Kennedy," but oddly, while looking at Sirhan to his right, he felt "a burning sensation on my left cheek," indicating a gun had been fired on his left, where he wasn't looking.[236] Another witness, Lisa Urso, who had seen both Sirhan and Kennedy at the same time, Sirhan fired at "point blank" range. But when the happy police staged a reenactment in

---

236   LAPD interview of Frank Burns, June 19, 1968.

the pantry, Urso disappointed them by making clear that by "point blank" she meant two to three feet away.

When Fitts started to mention the notebooks from Sirhan's room, Cooper registered an objection. Before the trial, Cooper had told the Judge the notebooks had been illegally obtained. While Sirhan's older brother Adel gave the police permission to search Sirhan's room, Adel was not the property owner. The mother was, and she had never given permission for that search. Judge Walker agreed to sustain the objection but noted he was not ruling on the admissibility of the evidence, and that he would rule on that later if an objection were entered at that time.

Fitts assured the jury "the defendant was not to any extent whatsoever under the influence of intoxicating liquor." Fitts ended his opening statement with this:

> In conclusion, ladies and gentlemen, the evidence in this case will show that defendant Sirhan Sirhan was alone responsible for the tragic incidents at the Ambassador Hotel in the early morning hours of the fifth of June; that he acted alone and without the concert of others. I thank you very much."

In essence, Fitts had just summed up the hidden agenda for this trial. The trial wasn't about Sirhan's penalty. The point of the trial was to prove that Sirhan had acted alone. In other words, the trial was aimed at the public, not the jurors. Any evidence of conspiracy was avoided or disputed, often via an assertion from Hernandez that the witness had been lying. (Had the jury heard Hernandez's questioning of Sandra Serrano, no doubt they would have found Hernandez's assertions less compelling.)

Fitts was a crafty jurist. He took up the full day so the jury would go home with nothing but his story circulating uncontested in their brains. The defense did not appear to understand the psychological advantage this presented Fitts, or surely they would have planned better when Fitts pulled off the same feat again during closing arguments.

Judge Walker adjourned the trial for the day with the admonishment he would reiterate nearly every day over the nearly three-month period of the trial. He told the jury to disregard everything they heard on radio or television or read in the media and to keep an open mind until the very end.

On the next day, the one Jewish lawyer on Sirhan's defense team, Emile Zola "Zuke" Berman, pleaded the case for the Palestinian Arab defendant. He told the jurors Sirhan was "an immature, emotionally disturbed and mentally ill youth."

"No, no," Sirhan murmured, rising from his chair to interrupt. He desperately did not want to be painted as mentally ill, despite the fact that that was the defense's strategy for saving him from the death penalty. Sirhan felt if he had to go down for a crime he didn't remember committing, it should at least stand for something, and he had settled on the Palestinian-Israeli conflict as his motive.

"Talk to him, Mike," Superior Court Inspector William Conroy said to Michael McCowan, who pushed Sirhan back into his chair with both hands and whispered to him as Berman continued. Later in the day, Parsons told reporters that "like most mentally ill people," Sirhan "doesn't like to be told he's mentally ill. He doesn't like it when I tell him."[237]

Berman summarized Sirhan's upbringing in Palestine. He was only three years old when war broke out in the wake of the United Nations resolution to divide Palestine into Jewish and Arab portions. The Jews agreed to the UN plan, but the Arabs did not, and the day after the Jews declared their new state of Israel, the Arabs launched an attack. Sirhan's street, Berman told the jury, "became the dividing line between the Jews on one side and the Arabs on the other." Berman described to the jury how Sirhan and his family were driven from the place of his birth:

> One night, the very building he lived in became a machine gun nest, and on another night, his very home was bombed.
>
> On the Saturday before Easter of 1948, Sirhan and his mother, father, brothers and sister crawled out of their home in the early dawn, with gun shots echoing all about them, to a temporary safety in an Orthodox Christian Convent in another part of the city.
>
> They never went back.

He described how the impressionable three-year-old Sirhan saw "a little girl's leg blown off by a bomb" and "went into a spell. He stiffened. His face became contorted. He was out of contact with reality and lost all sense of where he was or what was happening to him." He described another time when a bomb exploded and Sirhan went into a trance from which he did not return for four days. Sirhan went to the Lutheran Church School run by Arab Christians. He came to America, Berman told the jury, with his family when he was 12 years old.

Then it was Berman's turn to tell an untruth. He said Sirhan always felt and reacted like he was an outsider. But Sirhan had previously told his defense team, "I was raised here. My whole mind is engulfed in the American way of life, American line of thinking...I'm a Christian. Their language [Arabic] I don't speak

---

237   Dave Smith, "Sirhan Protests as His Attorney Describes Him as Mentally Ill," *Los Angeles Times*, February 15, 1969.

very well. Hell, I'm an American. That's the way I look at myself."[238] One of the psychologists brought in by the prosecution to evaluate Sirhan's responses to various psychological and intelligence tests would concur with Sirhan, testifying that his responses were more American than foreign.

Berman told the jury Sirhan wanted to be a diplomat, but he didn't get the necessary grades and was dismissed from college. Berman did not tell the jury that Sirhan was dismissed from college because of numerous absences incurred while he took care of his older sister who was dying of leukemia, or that the failing grades were a result of his absences, not his scholarship.

Berman described how, without a college education, few avenues for employment were open to Sirhan. He worked a night job at a gas station and bet some of his earnings at the racetrack in the hopes of striking it rich. He got a job as an exercise boy at a thoroughbred ranch near Corona, California. He hoped to become a jockey, but he had a horrible accident where he was thrown from a horse and injured.

"He complained about headaches, became more irritable, brooding, quick to anger, and preoccupied with fanatical obsessions of hatred, suspicion and distrust," Berman said, stretching the truth far beyond what any witness had said or would ever say.

Berman described how on June 2, 1967, just three days before a war broke out in Israel, Sirhan had written something Berman believed showed Sirhan to be crazy. The jury likely found it evidence of something else. Berman quoted a "Declaration of War Against American Humanity" from the very notebook Cooper had, the day before, tried to suppress:

> The victims of the party in favor of this declaration will be or are now the President, Vice-President, et cetera, down the ladder. ... The author of this memorandum expresses his wishes very bluntly that he wants to be recorded by history as the man who triggered off the last world war to ever be.

"And there were such other writings, clear evidence of diminished capacity," Berman said before Judge Walker cut him off.

"Mr. Berman, you are getting into argument now."

"We expect to prove this," Berman replied, but Walker told him now was not the time for argument.

Berman then revealed the essence of the defense's case: Sirhan, upset by the war in the Middle East, turned inward, seeking an internal power that could be

---

238   Kaiser, pp. 275–276.

manifested physically. "For example," Berman told the jury, "he would concentrate on a hanging lead fishing sinker and make it swing back and forth with the power of his mind. He would concentrate on a candle flame and make it dance, first to the right and then to the left." While this may seem like a bizarre claim to make in the present era, in 1968, the question of whether some people could move objects with their minds was the subject of Soviet experiments,[239] CIA curiosity and public credulity.

"Then came another heavy shock. In late May and early June of 1968," Berman told the jury, "Senator Kennedy, whom he admired and loved, said during the campaign, in essence, that if he were president, he would send 50 Phantom jets to Israel."

Berman explained that's when Sirhan turned back to his mental powers as a way to express himself through mental acts, not physical ones. "Sirhan will tell you himself from this witness stand that he never thought he ever would kill Kennedy," but in a "disturbed mental state, intoxicated and confused," he did.

"There is no doubt, and we have told you this from the beginning, that he did in fact fire the shot that killed Senator Kennedy," Berman told the jury inaccurately, adding,

> The killing was unplanned and undeliberate, impulsive and without premeditation of malice, totally a product of a sick, obsessed mind and personality.
> At the actual moment of the shooting, he was out of contact with reality, in a trance in which he had no voluntary control over his will, his judgment, his feelings or his actions.[240]

Berman told the jury he did not expect them to take his word at face value, but that he would bring forth experts to support this assertion. "Sirhan did not have the mental capacity" under California's legal definition of premeditation to have committed this crime with "malice aforethought," a legal requirement.

Berman closed by reminding the jurors that the prosecution gets to present all its witnesses first, and asked them to keep an open mind and wait for the defense to present its case before making up their minds.

The trial was organized by the prosecution and the defense into essentially four segments: the crime and arrest, acts of apparent premeditation, Sirhan's

---

239   A compelling video from 1968 of a Soviet woman named Ninel Kulagina apparently moving objects simply by concentrating on them can be found at www.youtube.com/watch?v=ZMj_bgzCUw8. Uri Geller claimed he could bend spoons with his mind, while others claimed it was merely sleight of hand. Would it surprise the reader to learn that Uri Geller was befriended by James Angleton, then the CIA's head of counterintelligence?

240   Sirhan trial transcript, p. 3058.

life to that point, and the evaluation of Sirhan's' mental state by psychological and medical professionals.

The People's first witness was Sergeant Albert La Vallee, who took the jury through the scale model he had built of the Ambassador Hotel so they could get a sense of the layout and pantry area. I drew the picture in Figure 1 (not to scale) to similarly orient the reader.

Karl Uecker was called to the stand to confirm the model's layout, and established that television cameras were along the southern side of the Embassy Ballroom.

He told the jury how he'd been leading Kennedy by hand, how Kennedy turned, breaking his grip, and that Uecker grabbed Kennedy's right hand with Uecker's left and started forward. As he turned forward, he felt someone between him and the first steam table. He heard what he thought was a firecracker and looked back at Kennedy and saw him falling away as he heard a second shot. "And then I realized someone was following me with a gun," Uecker said. Uecker placed himself "two feet" from Kennedy at this point, which puts Sirhan at least two feet away since Sirhan was parallel to Uecker at the time of the first shot. When Sirhan slid between him and the table and fired his gun, Uecker threw his arm around him in a headlock.

Howard had Uecker examine the gun. "I recognize the number, yes, H58725."

H58725. That's what the official transcript says. Both the prosecution and the defense reviewed these transcripts daily and made *numerous, detailed* corrections of each day's testimony. *They were especially meticulous with physical exhibits.* Did no one notice that the actual gun recovered from Sirhan, according to the contemporaneous police records, was *H53725*, not H58725? Several witnesses were asked by the LAPD to read, on tape, the gun's serial number, so we know for certain the gun turned in after the shooting was gun H53725. Three and eight don't sound the same, nor are they near each other on the keyboard, so it's hard to explain that as a mere "typo." Was the number correctly recorded? Had a different gun been used at the trial? Amazingly, Wolfer's testimony, as you'll see later, would support that notion. Recall too that Uecker had said he hadn't paid much attention to the gun. So if the gun at the trial was not the one in the pantry, that would explain why Uecker, who barely noticed it, was asked to identify it instead of Rafer Johnson, who had it on his person for some time before he gave it to the police.

Cooper cross-examined Uecker briefly to establish the presence of large mirrors in the Embassy Ballroom foyer. The mirrors would play a role in the defense's case. Uecker established there were floor-to-ceiling mirrors on the

Figure 1: Drawing of the pantry area

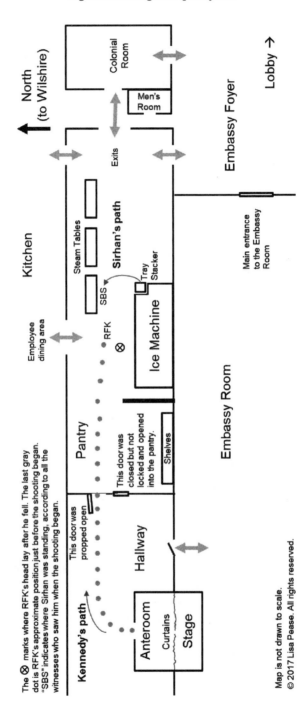

south wall of a little foyer that led from the lobby into the Embassy ballroom.

By getting Uecker to say it took all his strength to subdue Sirhan, Cooper established something else the defense hoped to prove: subduing the little would-be jockey Sirhan required all of the 190-pound, five-foot-ten Uecker's strength. In other words, Sirhan exhibited an unnatural level of strength, relative to his small size, in the pantry. Despite laying this foundation with several witnesses throughout, none of the defense team would make this point strongly in their closing arguments, that the fact that this small man could hold off Rosey Grier, a football player, Rafer Johnson, an Olympic athlete, and others much taller and heavier than Sirhan, was a strong indicator that Sirhan was in a hypnotic state. Feats of superhuman strength under hypnosis have been routinely noted.

Had Cooper wanted to challenge the notion that his client killed Senator Kennedy, Uecker gave him an opening. When Cooper asked for Uecker's "best estimate" of how many shots had been fired before Uecker deflected Sirhan's gun, Uecker said "three shots" (after originally telling the police he grabbed Sirhan's gun hand and swung it out of the way after the first or second shot). But Kennedy had been shot *four* times from behind (with one of those passing through his suit without entering his body), and, as Wolfer would soon testify, at a distance of not more than a few inches at best, meaning *at least one* of the close-range shots that hit Kennedy had to have come after Uecker grabbed Sirhan, a fact neither the defense nor the prosecution pointed out to the jury. Uecker had, by all witness accounts, pulled Sirhan's gun further away from, not closer to, Senator Kennedy.

Howard questioned Maître D' Ed Minasian. Minasian had been walking just to the right of Kennedy, when he felt him pull away to shake hands with people. He saw "the arm extended with a revolver and he had reached around Mr. Uecker. ... I saw the explosion of the shells and I saw the Senator raise his arm practically in front of his face and then the second shot went off..." After that shot, Minasian tried, with Uecker, to grab hold of Sirhan. Minasian was certain Uecker grabbed Sirhan after the second shot. Minasian clarified that it was the second shell that he saw "explode." Minasian described how the first shots "were in a bang-bang cadence." Then there was "a pause" of "possibly two or three seconds," and then more shots. "I would say a total of five or six shots."

Under cross-examination, Cooper had Minasian read his original statement to the LAPD to refresh his memory and got Minasian to admit he had not seen *Sirhan* fire a gun—he had seen *an arm* reaching around, and "personally saw two shots fired," a contradiction from what he had said just a short time earlier about seeing only the second shot's "explosion."

Minasian made clear, under Cooper's questioning, that Sirhan never "dropped" the gun. "It was taken out of his hand" during the struggle but Sirhan grabbed the gun (or at least *a* gun) again during the struggle.

Cooper also pointed out how, in his initial statement to the police, Minasian had described the suspect as "running" toward himself, something that would have been physically impossible for Sirhan, since Sirhan had been witnessed walking to his spot, standing still and firing at Kennedy when Uecker put a headlock on him.

Minasian was not the only witness to have seen someone he thought was the shooter running in the pantry. Virginia Guy, a reporter in the pantry, had her tooth chipped by something in someone's hand who came running from Kennedy's direction past her. Both Guy and Minasian assumed this was Sirhan. But this person was not Sirhan, as you'll learn in a later chapter.

Cooper and Fitts both realized Minasian's remembrance opened the door to conspiracy rather than closing it. Cooper asked Minasian hadn't he "just assumed that he [Sirhan] came running? Because you weren't able to see, were you, sir?"

"As I say, through my peripheral vision. If I said 'running,' I was mistaken; I obviously couldn't see anyone; but I saw a dart or another quick movement from the side, from my side."

This raised a second problem. Sirhan wasn't to Minasian's side. He was in front of him. Minasian was walking forward with Kennedy to his left, so the person had to be running at Minasian from his right to appear in his "peripheral" vision. Yet witnesses who had a clear view of Sirhan said he walked over as if to shake Kennedy's hand and then stopped and fired. If someone ran up to or darted at Kennedy, it wasn't Sirhan.

Fitts asked, "This darting, do you have anything in mind other than a gun being outstretched when you describe a darting motion?"

"No sir."

"I think that clears that up," Fitts said. But it didn't. Holding a gun in an outstretched fashion has nothing to do with running or darting.

Howard questioned tall young Juan Romero next, the busboy who had been captured in a photograph by Boris Yaro kneeling next to the wounded Kennedy in the pantry. He described shaking Kennedy's hand and then catching sight of a person he thought "couldn't wait to shake his hand." But then the person put his arm up and fired. "I seen he was right in front of him," Romero said. He dropped down to help Kennedy "and put my hand to the back of his head and tried to give him some, whatever I could, aid, some aid; that is about all I could do."

"But you saw someone coming toward the Senator; was this a male or a female?" Howard asked.

"It was a female," Romero replied in his instinctive response.

"A man?" Howard prompted quickly.

"It was a man," Romero said.

Romero told Kennedy, "Come on, Senator, you can make it; Mr. Kennedy, you can make it." Romero said Kennedy tried to respond, and Romero thought he said, "Everything is all right, everything is okay." (This may be an error in the transcription. To reporters, Romero had said he thought Kennedy had asked, "Is everyone okay?") Someone came up and put his coat under Kennedy's head. Someone handed Romero a rosary, which he pressed into Kennedy's hand.

When Ethel came up, Romero got out of the way and went to see what had happened to the shooter. "I couldn't tell right away, because everybody had covered his body, including his head."

When the two previous witnesses had been asked to identify the shooter from the pantry, both had pointed to Sirhan. But when Juan Romero was asked to identify the shooter, Romero said he didn't think he saw the shooter in court. Cooper said, "Stand up, Mr. Sirhan," clearly trying to cue Romero that this was the guy on trial for shooting Kennedy, but Romero held firm. "I don't believe that's him."[241]

Neither the defense nor the prosecution brought up the fact that right after the shooting, when Sgt. Calkins asked if Romero would be able to identify the shooter if he saw him again, Romero had said, confidently, "Yes, I would." No one dared consider that perhaps Romero *could* identify the shooter he had seen, and that it was *not* Sirhan.

Parsons cross-examined Romero. "What happened when you heard the shot?"

"Well, at first I thought it was something outside like a firecracker or somebody busted a balloon, then I felt the powder burning here."

"The side of your face?"

"Yes. Then I saw the guy and I pushed him around. Then I had him on the table, so then I went down to try to protect him [Senator Kennedy]."

No one asked whom Romero pushed down on the table, since he had already failed to identify Sirhan twice in the courtroom.

"How many shots did you say you heard?" Parsons asked.

"Approximately four shots," Romero responded.

"Did they all happen one right after another?"

"Well, they were less than three seconds apart."

"And when you looked around, you saw a man lying on the counter, did you not, on the steam table?"

"Yes."

Romero saw a man being held on the third steam table from Kennedy at that point. "This person, Mr. Sirhan, when you saw him there, did he appear to be smiling?" Parsons asked.

"He was smiling or either was just making a face," Romero responded.

241   Sirhan trial transcript, p. 3193.

No one followed up to ask why, since he clearly recognized Sirhan as the guy under the pile of bodies on the steam table, he hadn't identified Sirhan as the shooter. Perhaps both the prosecution and defense realized that was a door better left unopened.[242]

Vince DiPierro mentioned how he was stopped at the swinging doors to the pantry by a security guard, but was let in when a fellow kitchen employee told the guard DiPierro could come in. DiPierro crossed through to the little area between the pantry and the stage and waited for Kennedy with Martin Patrusky, his fellow waiter, "and a gentleman with dark glasses" (he likely meant dark glass *frames*, as he had said in an earlier interview) standing "on the other side."

"Did he appear to be a Kennedy worker?" Howard asked.

"Yes, sir, he had a badge."

Having a badge did not indicate the person was a legitimate member of Kennedy's staff. Michael Wayne had obtained Kennedy badges even though he was not a member of the staff. Clearly, others could have obtained Kennedy credentials as well. And there was no Secret Service protection for candidates in 1968. It was Robert Kennedy's assassination that changed that policy.

When Kennedy entered the pantry, he went through the propped-open northern swinging door at the western end. DiPierro pushed his way through the southern door, which opened to the inside and had not been propped open. At some point before he shook Kennedy's hand, he saw Sirhan on the tray rack at the eastern end of the ice machine.

"The same person I had seen standing on the tray rack had come out around Mr. Uecker," DiPierro said. Howard had DiPierro indicate where this happened and he indicated the westernmost corner of the three steam tables. "At that time … I observed … a flash that came out of the gun."

Howard asked DiPierro, "Now, how close to the Senator was Mr. Sirhan when he produced the gun?"

DiPierro answered, "I would say within two feet to eight feet."

If anyone on the jury, which had heard in the opening statement just the day before that the gun had to have been no further than an inch from Kennedy, noted this discrepancy, there is no record of it.

---

242   I finally reached Romero as the book was going to press and asked him why he didn't identify Sirhan as the shooter. He said he really didn't see the shooter's face so he didn't want to identify the wrong man under oath and potentially send an innocent man to prison. It's also important to note that, as with other witnesses, Romero's current memories have occasionally contradicted his earlier statements. For example, he now says he handed Kennedy a rosary from Romero's own pocket, but originally and at the trial, he said someone else handed him the rosary to give to Kennedy. Romero is clearly an honest person. But honest people can still make mistakes. I trust what he said immediately after it happened over what he said dozens of years later. Alison Winters wrote a book called *Memory* which describes how flawed memory can be, and how it can change over time. For that reason, I have given greater credibility to witnesses' earlier statements than to later ones, which may have been colored by additional information.

DiPierro confirmed that Uecker grabbed Sirhan after the second or third shot, again, well before Sirhan could fire the four shots that hit Kennedy (one of which passed through his clothing without entering his body).

"Did you see what movement the Senator made...?" Howard asked.

"He threw his head and hands started to go up as if to grab his head. He made a sudden jerking motion and he let go of Karl's [Uecker's] hand and I guess it was after the second shot. It would be after the second shot he let go of his hand. The first shot, he still had a hold of his hand and he started to pull and then the second shot was fired and both hands went up."

"Then what happened to the Senator?"

"He started falling and then the third shot was fired and he hit the ground just prior to the third shot." (How, then, did Kennedy get shot from close range four times?)

When asked if there was "something about" Sirhan that made DiPierro notice him, DiPierro mentioned that the girl near Sirhan had drawn his attention. In his first interview he described how the two seemed to be together, how Sirhan appeared to say something to the girl that made her smile, and how she appeared to be holding him. Now, many interviews with law enforcement and the prosecution later, DiPierro said the girl who was wearing a "polka dot dress" was "not definitely by him," but only "in the area of him."

When Cooper asked if the girl and Sirhan had talked, DiPierro said, "Whether he conversed with her or whether he just looked at her, I could not say. It looked as though he looked over where he could have just been, a natural impulse, by human nature to look at a pretty girl."

"In other words, he looked toward her?" Cooper asked.

"For a split second," DiPierro replied.

"Did she look toward him?"

"I believe she did."

"Then what happened?"

"Then the Senator turned to me and I shook hands with him and I lost sight of her."

DiPierro reported he stayed focused on Kennedy's head until he saw a commotion involving Uecker. Then he saw the gun being fired.

Cooper asked DiPierro to describe the color of the dots on the dress. "Black," DiPierro replied. What color was her hair? DiPierro said he did not "recall," which is not legally the same as saying "I don't remember." You might actually *remember* something but *choose* not to *recall* it at the present moment. Cooper wasn't going to let that stand.

"Do you remember in a statement you said it was brown...brunette?"

"Brunette, possibly dark brown," DiPierro acknowledged.

This was important, because in the papers, the police had promoted Valerie Schulte, a blonde in a cast for a broken leg who had been wearing a green dress with yellow lemons on it as "the girl in the polka dot dress." The prosecution was about to do the same thing here at the trial.

Cooper wanted to damage DiPierro's credibility, so he quoted from his session with Hernandez where DiPierro had responded to Hernandez's challenge that "you have told me now that there was no lady you saw standing next to Sirhan?" with "That is correct."

"Did you so testify?" Cooper asked DiPierro.

"Yes, I did."

Cooper than quoted Hernandez's words to DiPierro: "What I think you have told me is that you probably got this idea about a girl in a black and white polka dot dress after you talked to this Sandy Serrano?" "Yes, sir, I did" the transcript of DiPierro's earlier session read. Cooper seemed as eager as Hernandez to shut down anything that pointed at the suspicious presence of a girl in a polka dot dress in the pantry. Walker allowed Cooper to read the following into the record:

> Q [Hernandez] You did not see a girl in a black and white polka dot dress standing beside Sirhan on that evening?
> A [DiPierro] No.

On redirect, Fitts, who probably sensed the jury's likely confusion on this point, asked DiPierro, "Are you telling us in substance there was a girl standing near Sirhan at or near the time of the shooting, sir?"

"Yes, sir."

"With a polka dot dress?"

"Yes."

Fitts entered three black and white photos of Valerie Schulte—in a "polka dot dress" says the transcript, but the dress actually showed lemon-shaped objects, albeit in black and white—into the record as Exhibit 10-A. He added four more color photographs of Schulte as Exhibit 10-B.

"Do you recognize that individual as anyone you have ever seen before?"

"Yes, I believe I saw her that night," DiPierro said truthfully. But Fitts needed a different answer.

"Are you telling us that this appears to be a picture of the girl you saw in the pantry at or near the time of the shooting?"

"Yes, but I believe she had darker hair than that."

"I didn't hear the answer, your Honor," Cooper interjected.

"He said, 'but I believe she had darkened her hair,'" Judge Walker replied, which was a strange perversion of what DiPierro had said.

"In any event," Fitts said, before losing the jury's comprehension on this thread, "she seems to be a pretty blonde in the pictures, doesn't she?"

"Yes, she does."

Fitts and Cooper both then suborned perjury from DiPierro.

"Other than the difference in the color of the hair that you noticed, does she seem to be the girl?"

"Yes, I would think she would be."

Cooper asked, "Is that the girl you think you saw in the pantry?"

"I believe it was," DiPierro said.

"And is that the dress she was wearing at the time?"

"As to the dress, I do not recall. I can say it was, but I'm not sure."

"You have described a dress with black polka dots, is that correct?"

"Yes."

"This picture," Cooper pressed, holding up a color photo of Schulte in her green lemon-decorated dress: "this particular picture that has the colored photographs...what color would you say it is?"

"They are yellow polka dots on a green background."

By no stretch would anyone in fashion call those obviously lemon-shaped ovals "polka dots." Cooper understood this, and showed the photo to the jury. But he did not explain what this meant to the jury. Nor did he explain his reason for wanting to discredit DiPierro. He had already admitted Sirhan was guilty. The only reason to discredit DiPierro would be due to his public profile regarding the girl in the polka dot dress.

For his part, DiPierro *knew* Schulte was not the girl he had seen with Sirhan, as he made clear to me when I interviewed him years later in Toluca Lake, a modestly upscale suburb in the San Fernando Valley. He told me flat out that was not the dress of the woman he had seen with Sirhan, nor did Schulte have the brunette hair he had seen. Looking similar is not the same thing. He told me, however, that Howard had said he would fully support DiPierro if he identified the blonde Schulte as the girl in the polka dot dress.[243]

Jesse Unruh, like most other witnesses, thought firecrackers were going off at first, not a gun. "It seemed to me there was a little pause between the first crackle explosion and the later crackle, but it would have been relatively close... it seems to me that there was a momentary pause between the first three and the last five or the first four and the last four."

Fitts prompted Unruh, "And you indicated you heard some eight reports?"

"I couldn't count them. It could have been six, eight *or ten*, but it seems to me a relative definite string of explosions and then a short pause, and then

---

243   Author's in-person interview with Vincent DiPierro, May 2006.

another string." Ten, of course, was too many for Sirhan's gun to have held. But no one told the jury this.

Fitts prompted Unruh to say he had heard Sirhan say "I did it for my country" by referring him to his FBI report.

Under cross-examination from Berman, Unruh said the shots sounded like firecrackers. Berman reminded him he had told the FBI the shots sounded like balloons popping. Why Berman felt it was important to get that into the record isn't clear. For some reason, Berman also felt it was important to establish that Unruh never saw Sirhan with the gun in his hand.

On redirect, Fitts asked Unruh if he thought at any point Sirhan appeared intoxicated. Berman objected, feeling Unruh was not qualified to make an opinion, but the Judge allowed the question. "Mr. Unruh, you have on some occasions in your life perhaps observed some people who are under the influence of intoxicating drink, that sort of thing?"

"The defendant seemed as normal as you would expect one to be under such anguishing circumstances. I thought later on during the course of the evening he was considerably calmer," Unruh said, an important observation that was corroborated by other witnesses.

The defense was planning to argue that Sirhan was—as incredible as it sounds—both drunk and in a state of self-induced hypnosis at the time of the shooting. Unruh's observation was a supporting piece of data that Sirhan was indeed in some kind of hypnotic trance.

Judge Walker, perhaps understanding this, derailed this track immediately. "The question was with respect to his sobriety. Did you believe him to be under the influence of intoxicating liquor or did you not believe him to be under the influence of intoxicating liquor?"

"I didn't even think about it at the time. In observation now, I would have to conclude that the evidence I observed would lead me to believe he was not."

Despite the fact that arguing Sirhan was drunk was a key tenet of the defense's case, the defense team was unable to find a single witness who could attest that Sirhan was in a drunken state. At best, they found only people who saw him with a drink in hand, without knowing what was inside the glass or how many he had. Sirhan believed he had drank four Tom Collinses. But the defense was unable to find anyone who could corroborate more than seeing him with a Tom Collins glass in hand with a milky liquid and some red item that looked like a candy or a cherry inside.

Roosevelt "Rosey" Grier was called next. Fitts showed him the gun H58725, (which, if the number was accurately recorded, was not the gun taken from Rafer Johnson at the police station after the shooting), People's Exhibit 6, and asked if it was similar to the one Grier remembered seeing.

"Yes, but it doesn't, the gun—it looked like it was older than this one."

Fitts claimed he didn't hear Grier and asked him to answer again.

"I said, 'It is similar, sir.' Of course, I wouldn't be able to tell whether it was the identical gun."

"But does it look different?" Fitts asked, still hoping for a better answer.

"Other than it is clean, and this other one looked like it was dirty."

Grier was not making a positive identification. And guns are not supposed to be cleaned when taken into evidence. Evidence should be sealed and left untouched until the trial. But Fitts couldn't let Grier's lack of an ID stand. "In any other respect except cleanliness, it doesn't seem to be any different?"

"It doesn't seem to be any different," Grier repeated.

Having finally gotten the answer he wanted, Fitts moved on and asked if Grier could identify the shooter in the courtroom. Grier said "Yes," but before he could point him out, Cooper interjected, "Stipulate it is the defendant, your Honor." Cooper was clearly hoping to avoid another Juan Romero situation. Cooper also said he would so stipulate to any witness, going forward, but Judge Walker didn't like that and told Cooper to let the prosecution try its case the way it wanted.

Grier testified that he gave the gun he took from Sirhan's hand to Rafer Johnson.

Cooper had only one goal on cross-examination. He established that Grier was a 6'5" defense tackle, roughly 290 pounds, and a "pretty strong fellow."

Jesus Perez told the jury something that would have supported the case for Sirhan's innocence, had anyone dared to follow his testimony where it led. Perez heard the first shot coming from approximately the position of 17-D. Kennedy was at about 13-E, and each grid square represented two feet. There were three squares between 13-E and 17-D. Perez essentially put the first shot at a *minimum* of six *feet* from Kennedy, yet Kennedy was shot four times from a distance not greater than six *inches* (and not more than an inch for the fatal shot). Given that Perez was nearly shaking hands with Kennedy and had a clear view of Sirhan, his testimony on this point should be given significant weight. The jury, of course, was likely not doing the math, and no one pointed the problem out to them.

Frank Burns told the jury he had gotten just past Kennedy when Kennedy stopped to shake hands with two people in white kitchen uniforms. Burns was looking back to his left when he heard "the noise, a ripple of what was a gun, and it sounded like firecrackers." A "string of shots," Burns said, "without any real long pauses in between."

"When you heard the sound of gunfire, what did you do?"

"The first thing I did was to look toward the sound, the noise, and at that time, all I really saw that I recall was an arm holding a gun. There … was a hand stretched out with the gun in it and I very vividly recall seeing that. I immediately looked in the direction of the Senator and he had thrown up his head and was falling and spinning at that time.

"I then glanced back and at that time, that was the first time I saw the person."

What neither the defense nor the prosecution pointed out to the jury was that Burns essentially just said he turned his head three times—once to see the gun and an arm (but not the shooter), once to look back toward Kennedy, and a third time, at which point he saw the shooter fully. If the gun had been the inch from Kennedy's head necessary to create the powder burns found on his scalp by Coroner Noguchi, Burns would not have had to look in two different directions to see both the gun and Kennedy. Clearly, there was some space between Kennedy and Sirhan during the first two shots, after which Karl Uecker and others grabbed Sirhan.

"He was aiming the gun down at the Senator as he was falling." When Kennedy collapsed backward, Sirhan was still in front of Kennedy. Kennedy fell on his back, not his stomach, so at no point was his backside exposed to Sirhan. Yet all the shots in Kennedy and through his clothing were made in a back-to-front and right-to-left fashion. Sirhan was ahead of Kennedy and slightly to Kennedy's left, making those angles impossible.

When Fitts questioned Valerie Schulte, the girl the police and prosecution tried to paint as the girl in the polka dot dress, he asked her something that wouldn't have helped the prosecution's case had the jury been paying close attention. Fitts asked where she was standing, where Kennedy was standing, and where the shooter was standing. Valerie said the arm with the gun was "approximately three yards, something like that, from the Senator." Three yards is nine feet away. She saw the man "from his shoulders up." She had seen his face, but she did not feel she could make a positive identification of the man she had seen with the gun. Like Romero, Schulte, too, refused to identify Sirhan as the man with the gun that she had seen, even when he was pointed out to her in the courtroom.

Cooper cross-examined Officers Placencia and White pretty hard about their respective tests of Sirhan's eyes. When Placencia said he "couldn't recall" whether Sirhan's eyes were dilated or not, Cooper handed him a copy of his original statement "for the purposes of refreshing your recollection" and asked him again, "Did you not observe that his pupils were real wide?"

"Yes, sir."

"When you flashed the light in his eyes, did the pupils react to the light?"

"I can't recall, sir."

Cooper then read Placencia's earlier statement into the record that Sirhan's pupils "didn't" react to the light at all and that "His pupils were real wide."

Dilated pupils that don't react to light can be a physical indicator of a hypnotic state.[244] But Cooper did not make that point to the jury.

"Did you make that statement in response to those questions at that time?" Cooper asked.

"Yes, sir," Placencia responded.

"In other words then, his pupils did not react to the light, did they?"

"No, sir."

"All right. Now what did that mean to you as an officer?"

"That he was under the influence of something."

"In other words, it meant to you that he was under the influence of a drug or alcohol, isn't that true?"

"Yes, sir."

Howard asked on redirect, "Did you ever smell any odor of alcohol on the defendant?"

"No, sir."

Cooper asked a barrage of questions about why Sirhan was put in the Breathalyzer room if no test was to be performed there. But it appears that no tests were done because no tests *needed* to be done. Had Sirhan been intoxicated, surely *at least one witness would have noticed* and commented on this to the police. But not one witness mentioned smelling alcohol on his breath, seeing him stumble or maneuver clumsily. Not one witness said Sirhan appeared red-faced or had bloodshot eyes. And on redirect, Howard established Placencia smelled no alcohol on Sirhan.

White said that in the car, Sirhan had appeared to White to be "very frightened. He was in terror." But after a few minutes, "he regained his composure and he was quite calm."

White claimed that after he and his partner brought Sirhan into the Breathalyzer room, he darkened the room and then passed a flashlight across first Sirhan's eyes, then Placencia's eyes. White thought the pupils contracted at the same rate, and was of the opinion that Sirhan was not under the influence of alcohol.

White's memory was clearly muddled for this period. He first testified that Sirhan had been placed in Interrogation Room A, where he conducted the eye test, after which he went in search of a key to Interrogation Room B, where

---

244   "To perform the following feats will, I imagine, be found above the power of the most accomplished imposter: to keep the pupils dilated, without the use of drugs, in passing from darkness into sunshine.... The dilation and insensibility of the pupil are recorded in my first case, and have since been frequently seen." James Esdaile, M.D., *Mesmerism in India* (London: Longman, Brown, Green and Longman, 1846), quoted in Dr. Milton V. Kline, *The Roots of Modern Hypnosis: From Esdaile to the 1961 International Congress on Hypnosis* (Xlibris Corporation, 2006), published posthumously.

See also Carl Sextus, *Hypnotism, Its Facts, Theories and Related Phenomena, with Explanatory Anecdotes, Descriptions and Reminiscences* (New York: H.M. Caldwell Co., 1893), p. 148. "During the whole experiment, the pupils of the eyes of the subject were also considerably dilated, even if we allowed him to look straight at the light."

Sirhan was ultimately moved. But a couple of minutes later, White said Sirhan was first placed in Interrogation Room B, and then moved to A.

When Cooper asked him what Placencia had said after his own eye test, White said that Placencia told him "he thought that his pupils were unusually large." Cooper also elicited that White had not made a mention in his only report on the incident that he had conducted an eye test at all. Cooper also pointed out Lieutenant William Jordan's report, written after an interview with White in August, two months after the events, that "White believes that he checked Sirhan's eyes with his flashlight," an odd wording, as if Jordan himself didn't believe White had performed the test. Cooper read into the record the following exchange between Jordan (Q) and White (A):

> Q   By the look on his face, being that of terror, to use your adjective, would you describe that for me?
>
> A   Well, when we first encountered him, he was laying on his stomach on the preparation table for food; and myself, I can tell when a person is in just sheer terror, his eyes are widened, he had a pale look to his face. ...
>
> Q   You say his eyes were widened?
>
> A   Yes. I mean they were wide open, not in a relaxed manner at all. They were very alert at this point.
>
> Q   Did you take a close look at his eyes at any time?
>
> A   I believe it was either at the arrival at the station or in the station itself that I took, I checked the reaction of his pupils.
>
> Q   How did they react, Officer?
>
> A   They were very near normal at that point because I meant to check him later, after he was able to calm down. Lots of times when a person is frightened or surprised they don't have normal reactions to their pupils. They dilate automatically, and he—I was meaning to go back and check them after he was able to calm down, but I was never able to. He was transferred to Central Jail before I was able to recheck them.[245]

Cooper pressed: "When you said this statement on September 13th, Officer, that they were very near normal, I take it you meant by that, did you not, that they weren't completely normal?"

"Yes, sir," White responded.

"And because they weren't completely normal, you attributed the reaction you got to his fright, is that right?"

"To the experience he had just gone through, yes."

---

245   Sirhan trial transcript, pp. 3857–3859.

"In other words," Cooper pressed, "they didn't react the way a normal person's eyes would react, did they? ... They were 'very near normal' but they weren't normal, is that right?"

"Yes, sir."

"Why did you feel it was necessary to check his eyes again?"

"For a double check."

"As a matter of fact, you didn't give him any eye examination on that morning, did you?"

"Yes I did."

Cooper had no further questions, and Fitts declined the opportunity to reexamine White.

The prosecution moved to witnesses they felt showed premeditation on Sirhan's part. Of course, if someone was controlling Sirhan through hypnosis at the scene of the crime, someone was likely controlling Sirhan before the crime as well, creating a pattern of activity designed to produce the appearance of premeditation and guilt.

This isn't just idle speculation. In a footnote at the end of his chapter on the CIA's known experiments with hypnosis in his book *The Search for the Manchurian Candidate*, former State Department officer John Marks related the comments of a CIA veteran of the agency's MKULTRA mind control program. The veteran CIA officer described how easy it would be for a hypnotist to set up someone to be a patsy. The hypnotist would offer suggestions that seemed innocuous, out of context (go to a range, do some target practice, go to a party at a hotel). "The purpose of this exercise," the anonymous informant told Marks, "is to leave a circumstantial trail that will make the authorities think the patsy committed a particular crime."[246]

Fitts questioned Everett Buckner (misspelled Edward Buckner in the transcript) to establish Sirhan's presence at the firing range on June 4. Buckner said Sirhan had asked to buy "some shells that will not misfire" at the range. Buckner sold him "one box."

Cooper wanted to establish that Sirhan was at the gun range until 5 P.M., but Buckner said Sirhan came in at 9:30 A.M. or 10:30 A.M. and was only there "two or two and a half" hours. Cooper didn't like that answer, and kept pressing.

"Isn't it true, sir, that he arrived about noon and remained until five o'clock in the afternoon? And remained there until you closed?" Cooper said.

"He did not remain there until we closed," Buckner said.

"All right. And I take it then that he didn't arrive about noon?"

"As near as I can remember, he arrived about ten or ten-thirty."

---

246   Marks, *The Search for the Manchurian Candidate*, p. 204n.

Cooper continued to needle him, pointing out any discrepancy in this statements regarding the time. Then he revealed perhaps the true reason for his heckling.

"Now, you have a kind of vivid imagination, do you not, sir?"

"No, sir."

"Well, let me ask you this," Cooper said. "Didn't you tell the police at one time that there was some lady with him?"

"No, sir. I said that some lady came and he helped show her how to shoot."

"And didn't you say that that lady had said to him, 'Get out of here, God damn you, somebody will recognize us'?"

Buckner said he wasn't sure what she had said, but "it sounded like that."

Cooper then brought out the report from Hernandez on Buckner's lie detector session. This was the prosecution's witness being attacked, but Fitts didn't object initially. Neither did Judge Walker, although lie detector evidence is not admissible in California courts. It seems all three forces—the defense, the prosecution and the Judge—wanted to discredit Buckner on the record regarding that one statement that lent credence to a conspiracy. This incident showed again the real purpose of the trial: to attempt to introduce and then explain away any evidence of conspiracy that had already been made public. Buckner's comments had been quoted in the media, so they needed to be put to rest, even if it required using the dishonest Hernandez to do it.

Fitts let Cooper point out to the jury that Buckner had "lied" (per Hernandez) on the question about the woman's statement. Buckner said that was the only question he was deemed to have "flunked." Once that was in the record, Fitts objected and Judge Walker added, "certainly, any testimony about lie detector tests is objectionable and the objection will be sustained." Fitts asked why Cooper was even bringing this up, since the prosecution had no plans to introduce that statement. It was a direct question to which Cooper had no direct answer. Given how Cooper's own legal troubles were hanging over his head like a dagger throughout the trial, the simplest explanation could be that Cooper was following someone else's orders on this point. Although Cooper wanted to establish Sirhan was at the range until 5 P.M., and Buckner was interfering with that, Cooper had other ways to challenge that witness rather than bringing up the woman and her alleged conversation with Sirhan, something Fitts clearly would rather have left off the record entirely. But if Cooper's goal was not so much to defend Sirhan as to discredit any evidence of conspiracy, his continued questioning along this line made sense.

Cooper asked Buckner about the statement and how when talking to Hernandez, he "admitted that statement wasn't made."

"I didn't admit it wasn't made," Buckner said correctly. "I admitted I could have misunderstood it, the conversation."

And with that, Cooper was done. Buckner's statement about the woman had been reported in the papers. It seemed Cooper really wanted the media to hear that Buckner had, if not retracted it, significantly watered it down.

Two shooters from the range on June 4, Henry Adrian Carreon and his friend David Montellano, testified about encountering Sirhan there. Carreon described how the firing range was laid out in a straight line, broken by the range office. To the left of the office, facing the targets, was the pistol range. To the right of the office was a rifle range. Carreon heard someone shooting "rapid fire" which "was abnormal" so he walked over to see who was doing it. "I expected the range officer or someone working there in the place to come over. They usually come up and stop them, as you are not supposed to shoot like that."

Carreon described how his friend David came over from the rifle range and the two of them approached Sirhan. David asked Sirhan what kind of gun he was using, but Sirhan didn't respond initially. Carreon asked him a second time "and he didn't [answer], I wondered what the story was on the guy, if he was trying to avoid us." Cooper moved for that to be stricken and Judge Walker agreed. Carreon said something similar and again the Judge struck it and asked the jury to disregard Carreon's conclusions about why Sirhan responded the way that he did.

Sirhan did talk to them a bit, but he seemed to answer some questions and ignore others. David wanted to know why he had a box of Mini-Mag ammunition on his bullet stand. "David said, 'Well isn't it for better accuracy at long range?' And he didn't say anything. At times when we were speaking, he just didn't answer us." Was Sirhan in a trance state at the range?

Under cross-examination, Parsons got Carreon to recall that his friend David had said that Sirhan wasn't a very good shot. David testified right after, and confirmed that Sirhan wasn't hitting his target.

Twice, David alluded to Sirhan's gun holding nine rounds. But the gun Rafer Johnson had taken from the pantry to the police could only fire eight rounds. If Sirhan had used a different gun at the range, that would explain why nearly 40,000 shells from the range could not be matched to the gun with the serial number H53725, the gun Rafer Johnson turned over to the police after the shooting.

Ronald Williams was next. He claimed his wife Claudia was the woman who had a discussion with Sirhan. He claimed that Buckner, the range master, was there until closing at around 5 P.M., and that Sirhan was, too. So either Buckner was incorrect or Williams was, as they could not both be accurate. Curiously, one of the main FBI Special Agents on the case, Amedee Richards, wrote a report of this event for the FBI that supports Buckner, not Williams. Richards' report put Sirhan at the range between roughly 11 A.M. to 3 P.M.[247] The FBI had interviewed

---

247   FBI report by Amedee O. Richards, Jr., December 4, 1968.

20 people from the range that day, including Claudia, before Richards came to that conclusion.

Williams testified that he arrived about an hour before closing, which, if Richard's report is correct, means he couldn't have run into Sirhan. Claudia Williams said essentially the same thing when she followed her husband on the witness stand—that they had arrived about 4 P.M. and that she had had an innocuous conversation with Sirhan. Is it possible she had talked to someone who merely looked like Sirhan? Is it possible she wasn't the woman Buckner was referring to?

Claudia said Sirhan was firing rapidly. In direct contradiction to what David Montellano had said, Claudia said Sirhan was a good shot, that his shots were hitting close to the target, and that his gun was easy to shoot. Sirhan would later testify that his gun's sight was off and he had to adjust for that when shooting. Sirhan would also testify that the man next to him was the one rapid-firing, that it took him time to press and release the gun. Sirhan didn't know what time he left the range.

Michael Saccoman had also been at the range that day, and testified that Sirhan's gun had a "black plastic grip" and "a cheap paint—very little finish on it." (Other range witnesses described Sirhan's gun handle as black or blue.) He identified the gun in court as the gun he had seen at the range. Oddly enough, on color video of the press conference on June 5, 1968, where the gun was shown, the handle of the gun retrieved from the pantry was clearly brown.[248]

Saccoman said he and Sirhan talked for about 45 minutes. They fired each other's guns. At one point, Saccoman reported Sirhan told him he was planning a hunting trip, and Saccoman said you couldn't use a pistol for hunting because it was against the law to use pistols for hunting. "He asked me why, and I said to the best of my knowledge and belief, it is because of the accuracy. And then he said, 'Well, I don't know about that. It could kill a dog.'"

Sirhan would vigorously deny having said that, although he did remember a casual conversation about hunting small animals. If Sirhan said that, it appears he meant it quite literally, and not as a reference to Senator Kennedy.

Previous to June 4, Sirhan had apparently been to the Corona Police range. The prosecution called Officer Harry C. Starr, the assistant to the range master at the Corona Police pistol range, which was open to the public for one dollar. Starr confirmed that Sirhan's name appeared on the register there. (People's Exhibit 70). The date appeared to be "6/1," i.e., Saturday, June 1, 1968. The shooter had clocked in around 12:15 P.M. and left about 3 P.M. Starr was at the range at that time. Starr had spoken to the shooter by that name, but when

---

248   Video of the press conference can be viewed at the UCLA television archives.

Sirhan was pointed out to him in the courtroom, like Juan Romero and Valerie Schulte before him, Officer Starr failed to identify the Sirhan in the courtroom with the Sirhan he had talked to at the range: "I can't truthfully say that that is the man, that is, I picked out a picture that resembled the man, but I cannot say that he is the man."

Cooper had offered to stipulate that Starr saw Sirhan at the range, but Howard had rejected it. When Starr failed to identify Sirhan as the shooter from the range, however, Cooper again offered a stipulation, and this time, Howard took it.

Returning to pantry witnesses, Howard called George Plimpton to the stand. Plimpton did not see Sirhan fire, but he joined the struggle to get the gun from Sirhan. Berman asked didn't Plimpton believe "for the size of a man he was, that he was showing great strength?"

"I think it surprised us that we could not remove the gun as easily. Yes, he was very strong."

"In connection with that, [what] do you remember saying to the Sergeant or whoever it was that you were interrogated by: 'Tell us all about his eyes'? Did you go on to say that they were dark brown and enormously peaceful eyes?"

"Yes, I remember saying that," Plimpton confirmed.

Berman asked Plimpton to describe further what he meant by that.

"He struck me, with a circle of people around him, as compared to the rest of us, enormously composed. The rest of us, of course, given this sudden tragedy were not as composed. His reaction seemed startling to me because in the middle of a hurricane of sound and feeling, he seemed almost peaceful, and I had the sense, if I am allowed to say this sort of thing—"

"I don't want to ask you for your sense," Judge Walker interrupted. "I just want a description."

"That is what I mean 'peaceful.' He seemed purged."

Larry Arnot of Lock, Stock & Barrel testified that Sirhan had bought "Mini-Mag" ammunition from "CCI" that was ".22 Long Rifle HP" on June 1, 1968. Arnot said HP stood for "hollow point."

"Approximately 3:30 in the afternoon, three individuals entered the store, walked to the portion of the store where the ammunition was stored. I approached them, asked them if I could be of assistance, and in turn was given the request for ammunition."

Fitts interrupted Arnot's account. "If the Court please, I don't think I'm going to let this one go any further. If I may take this witness in my own way at this time?"

Can you guess why Fitts stopped his witness here? That's right. Fitts wanted to stop and discredit the evidence of conspiracy Arnot had just introduced.

"Mr. Arnot, do you recall having a conversation with Lieutenant Enrique Hernandez of the Los Angeles Police Department with reference to selling ammunition to three individuals?"

"Yes."

"And isn't it a fact that Mr. Hernandez had some conversation with you with respect to this business of selling the ammunition as reflected on that sales slip to three persons who walked into the store?"

"Yes."

"Then he put you on the so-called polygraph, the lie detector, isn't that true?"

"Yes."

"And he indicated to you with reference to the sale of what is reflected on that slip that you were confused?"

"Yes."

"And then you ultimately told Mr. Hernandez that …you had mixed up with a sale to three other people and were in your own mind trying to connect it with the sale to Sirhan. Isn't that right?"

"I don't remember those words."

"Did you ultimately tell Mr. Hernandez that so far as that particular transaction reflected People's 22, that you didn't remember Sirhan and you didn't remember anything other than that you had filled out that sales slip with respect to a sale?"

"Yes."

Cooper cross-examined him in a similar vein.

"Why did you say you sold it [the ammunition] to three persons then?"

"I didn't say I sold it to three persons, did I? I just said three persons entered the store."

No one asked why he initially felt the three people were together, and the jury was not told that two others, the store owner and his wife, had also thought two men were with Sirhan at the time of this transaction.

The grilling of Arnot proved once again that the trial wasn't about the truth of Sirhan's involvement so much as to attempt to discredit, in the guise of a trial, all public evidence of conspiracy. Had Sirhan had a proper defense, someone would have played the tape of Sandra Serrano's session with Hernandez for the jury. That would have kept the prosecution from injecting his assessment every time they had a witness they wanted to discredit.

On February 20, out of the hearing of the jury, Cooper brought up an article that had appeared in the *Los Angeles Times* that morning, and moved, not for the first time, for a mistrial. The article was headlined, "Possibility of Guilty Plea by Sirhan Now Appears Remote." While Judge Walker assured Cooper that the jury, which was now sequestered, would not see that article, Cooper had a different point to make. The article mentioned "everything that we said in chambers," meaning, it could only have come from someone in that conversation. He was gently accusing the prosecution of leaking to the press.

"Well, let me say that I gave some of that information myself," said Judge Walker. "I told them the plea had been offered and I had refused the plea, but that I would take a plea on first degree and that the jury could try the penalty."

"I assign your Honor doing that is misconduct," Cooper said, a comment he indicated was offered "without rancor."

"Your Honor, now, I am representing a client and I feel that in fairness, please, I feel that your Honor should not have done it for the reason, first, that we asked that the remarks in connection with that were supposed to be sealed, and it was my understanding they were sealed, so this wouldn't be made public. And there was discussion about making it known, which your Honor indicated at that time that it was not to be made known."

Judge Walker wanted to move on, but Buck Compton spoke on the same issue. He was certain no one from the D.A.'s office had discussed the possible plea deal with the local *Los Angeles Times* reporter who sat just outside the D.A.'s office. But Compton was surprised that it was the Eastern press, specifically *Newsday*, and not the *Los Angeles Times*, which had broken the story first. Compton stated that four people from the *New York Times* and *Time* had asked him questions about California law. "In their questioning, they evidenced a great deal of knowledge about what had gone on in chambers before they came to see me. ... The point I'm trying to make is that the Eastern press apparently has some source of information that is better than or equal to the *Los Angeles Times*, and we have no connection with the Eastern press...." Compton resented the implication that any information had come from the D.A.'s office. But perhaps the D.A.'s office had been tapped by someone—or some intelligence agency—back east?

Cooper had the "impression from a reading of the article" that the information had come "from Evelle Younger himself." Cooper had a strong argument for a mistrial, but he didn't press his advantage at all, saying only, "I have made my motion, if your Honor please, and I assume your Honor is going to overrule it."

"I had the same story—the story was given to me," said Judge Walker, "that your man, your investigator-writer, was the one who did it."

"Kaiser?" Cooper asked.

"I don't believe that," the Judge assured Cooper, "but I'll check it out."

But Cooper wasn't done. He was also upset by an appearance Compton had made on TV the night before. Compton brought up something that Cooper had objected to during questioning. The prosecution had tried to hint at Sirhan's status as an immigrant, not a citizen, and the Judge had overruled it. "You said you were seeking to develop was the fact that he was an alien in possession of a gun. You shouldn't have done that, because the very purpose of making an objection is to keep that kind of thing from the jury."

Cooper added that even though the jury was sequestered, "when leaks occur, you don't know how far the water will leak."

Judge Walker offered to bar spousal visits in an effort to further protect the jurors from outside information, but Cooper said that would be "cruel and unusual punishment" to the jurors. In the end, not only did Judge Walker not recuse himself and declare a mistrial, he instead said that the transcript of *this* session, too, would be made available to the press. "It's only a matter of your making a motion for a mistrial and my denying it," Walker said.

"Then it spreads like ripples going out. Your very objective is defeated. It's the only remedy that is available to us as lawyers—the very doing of it, if it's going to be made public, is defeated. ... May the record show we vigorously oppose this being made public, a matter of public record, until all the proceedings are over."

Judge Walker asked what Compton thought. Compton felt it was important to leave it all on the record, an ironic note, given that a portion of conversation just prior to this had been conducted "off the record" in the official transcript, "sealed by the Court."

"Your Honor, please," Cooper begged. "In that connection with plea bargaining, it is always a secret matter." But Walker had a strange sense of what should be kept secret and what should be made public in this case.

The next day, Judge Walker called both the prosecution and the defense to the bench to discuss another leak. Someone had leaked unedited transcripts to the *New York Times* and the *Los Angeles Times*. Rather than trying to find out who was leaking the court documents, Walker wanted to ensure that the other media were also then given transcripts, saying it was not fair for those organizations to have an advantage over the rest. But unedited transcripts also contained things that, upon editing, the Judge could seal, such as continuing discussions around a plea bargain. Walker's behavior was bizarre in this matter. He seemed more interested in making the proceedings of the court public than he was in preserving the rights of the defendant. There may have been a method to his madness, as we'll see later.

The strange figure of Michael Wayne received mention at the trial. Judy Royer, the secretary to the former Governor Pat Brown, told Howard that about one to two hours before the speech, she saw Sirhan in the anteroom behind the curtains of the Embassy Ballroom stage. She asked him to leave the area because he had no press or staff badge and had no reason to be there. She believed he exited into the Embassy Ballroom. She accurately described Sirhan's clothing.

Cooper must have known that Royer had also spoken to Michael Wayne. He showed her a picture from *Life* magazine of Michael Wayne talking to Senator Kennedy in the pantry without explaining to the jury who he was.

"Is this not the individual you saw...?"

"No, it is not."

"You're sure of that in your own mind?"

"Yes, I know that person."

Cooper said he had no further questions, but Howard said, "Well, there may be some questions, but we will wait, your Honor."

As if taking his cue from Howard, Cooper said he did have another question for Mrs. Royer. Cooper apparently had read pantry witness Robert Klase's statement. Klase overheard Royer talk to Michael Wayne. Klase told the LAPD that Wayne had told Royer "he had part of an autograph of Senator Kennedy and the Senator told him he would finish signing it when he came back through the kitchen. Judy made him leave the pantry area at that time." Klase himself had shooed Sirhan from the pantry. Klase had not been called as a witness, probably because he said Sirhan had entered with a group of people, not alone.[249] Cooper showed Royer the picture of Michael Wayne from *Life* magazine, People's Exhibit 33, where Wayne was shown talking to Senator Kennedy on Kennedy's way out to the stage to give his speech.

"Did you ever ask the individual that is in the photograph that is apparently talking to Senator Kennedy ... to leave any portion of the area on the evening or night of June 4 or early morning hours of June 5?"

"Yes, I did, the pantry area." Royer said she saw Wayne enter the pantry from the eastern double doors when the Senator was speaking.

Cooper asked why she had said she knew this person.

"I had seen him around political headquarters and rallies." Was Wayne stalking Kennedy? As you'll see in a later chapter, Wayne's politics were the polar opposite of Kennedy's.

Howard put Wayne's name into the official record by asking Royer if the name "Michael Wayne" meant anything to her. "No, it doesn't," she replied.

Wayne came up again when Howard questioned the other shooting victims in the pantry. Ira Goldstein described how he had walked the length of the pantry from the west nearly to the east end. He turned back and walked west. About midway, Ira told the jury "I was stopped by an individual who asked me if I would like to trade press badges with him." The individual had not been wearing the badge, but had taken it from his pocket. It was a green Kennedy press or staff pass. The man wanted to trade it for Ira's "yellow Embassy Room press badge."

Cooper showed Ira Goldstein the picture of Michael Wayne in People's Exhibit 33 and asked if he had seen him before.

"Yes, sir. This is the person that I was speaking to about the press badge."

Cooper, the lead defense counsel for Sirhan, had been given a gift. Here was a man who looked so much like Sirhan that witnesses had confused the two, who may well have been stalking Kennedy before the assassination, who had been loitering in the pantry just prior to the shooting, and who had been seen running out of the pantry suspiciously afterwards. But Cooper had rejected a conspiracy defense, so this information just hung out there, unexplained to the jury, who surely had no understanding of why Wayne had even been mentioned.

The most damning evidence for premeditation came from the prosecution's least credible witness: Alvin Clark, the garbage collector who worked on Sirhan's street. Fitts asked Clark to recall a conversation he had with Sirhan shortly after Martin Luther King's death.

According to Clark, Sirhan "was upset somewhat" about King's death. Clark claimed Sirhan asked him who he was going to vote for in the primary, and when Clark said Kennedy, Clark claimed Sirhan said "What do you want to vote for that son-of-a-bitch for? Because I'm planning on shooting him."

Under cross-examination, Berman asked Clark if the FBI had visited him in September 1968 and asked him to testify. "Just answer yes or no," Berman said. But Clark said something off script: "Well, I didn't want to testify," implying the FBI had put some pressure on him to do just that, a statement which caused Judge Walker to interject.

"I'll tell you what you do, if you will, please. Listen to the questions that are asked of you, and then answer. Don't volunteer."

Berman got the "yes" he was looking for, and continued. "And did you tell whoever asked you that question that you would not want to take the oath because you hated Sirhan so much that you would do anything to see him convicted, did you say that?"

"Yes, I did."

According to the FBI report of Clark's interview, which was available to Sirhan's defense, Clark had said he wanted to "kill" Sirhan.[250] Berman could have done something with that information. Instead, he said, "I have nothing else."

Fitts, on the other hand, wanted to ask one last question:

"Have you told the truth here, sir?"

"Yes, I have," Clark replied.

Sirhan turned to Parsons and whispered, "He's a liar."[251] When Sirhan took the stand for his own defense, he claimed Clark's statement was "utterly false."

And Sirhan was likely right. What neither Sirhan nor his defense team knew, or brought up if they knew, was that the LAPD had withheld critical information on Alvin Clark. According to the LAPD's Daily Summary of Activities log for October 31, 1961, Lt. Keene reported the following:

---

250   FBI interview report of Alvin Clark, 6/11/68, p. 3.

251   UPI, "Witness' Story of Sirhan's Plans," *San Francisco Chronicle*, 2/22/69.

> Interesting development in the case of Alvin Clark, the Pasadena
> rubbish collector. The D.A. sent an ace investigator, Charles Lawrence,
> to re-interview Clark and establish better rapport (Clark's been hard
> to get along with). Lawrence returned from Pasadena and reassured
> Howard that he and Clark were soul brothers and everything was fine.
> A short time later Clark called the Pasadena PD and beefed Lawrence,
> said he was being harassed by the D.A. and the police!! [sic] Clark has
> several prior arrests for ADW, burglary and child molesting and this
> would help explain his abrasive attitude.

It could also have explained the leverage someone in law enforcement may
have wielded over Clark to get him to testify when he didn't want to, and to
perhaps tell an untruth to ensure he wouldn't go back to jail again, that would
have the added bonus of convicting the man Clark wanted to "kill," believing
him to be the one responsible for Robert Kennedy's death.

The jury would never learn this important context.

On Friday, February 21, Judge Walker, the prosecution and the defense
gathered in chambers again for what would prove to be a remarkable and
disturbing session.

The first topic was *yet another* leak. The *Los Angeles Times* had run a page-one
wire service story that morning headlined "Possibility of Guilty Plea by Sirhan
Now Appears Remote." Judge Walker asked around and was told the story had
been written and filed by George Lardner, Jr. of the *Washington Post*, who had
been in attendance for the trial. The *Post* and the *Times* jointly owned the wire
service that ran the story.

The article focused, for the third time in just over a week, on the discussions
around a guilty plea. The repetition seemed designed to prejudice not just the
jury but the public at large. The report also made reference to psychiatric reports
that had not yet been introduced into evidence.

Cooper and Judge Walker felt there should be an investigation to find Lardner's source. Walker asked the City Editor who Lardner's source was. But when
the City Editor asked, Lardner said he would share the source if he could, "but I
can't." Cooper believed the source was probably former OSS man and current
District Attorney Evelle Younger.

"Well, it could only be two sources," Judge Walker said. "It's either the
prosecution or the defense."

"Well, there is a third one I wasn't aware of until yesterday," Cooper said,
referencing the Judge's admission to leaking court documents the last time such
a story surfaced.

There was a fourth possibility no one appeared to consider. The CIA might have been tapping the Judge's chambers as well. The CIA has been known to illegally spy on Congressional members, plant janitors, secretaries and gardeners at the White House, and bug rooms where lawyers discussed cases with their clients.[252] It would be in keeping with the CIA's activities then and now if they had been bugged Judge Walker's chambers. However, given Evelle Younger's OSS past, that was likely not necessary.

Cooper asked Walker where he got the report that Lardner had written the story. Walker told him to ask the District Attorney, Evelle Younger. Fitts said "we will invite investigation" to determine the source of the leak to Lardner.

Lardner was an interesting figure who was concurrently covering the trial of Clay Shaw in New Orleans, whom the District Attorney there, Jim Garrison, had accused of colluding in a CIA-sponsored plot to kill President Kennedy. The stories of the Sirhan trial and the Clay Shaw trial often appeared next to each other in newspapers.

In an odd twist, Lardner had talked to the man who could have been one of Garrison's most important witnesses, David Ferrie, the very night that Ferrie either died, committed suicide, or was killed, depending on whose evidence you believe. The coroner reported that Ferrie died of a brain aneurysm, but given that he had just asked to speak in private to Jim Garrison, and given that there were suicide notes around, that Ferrie may have been forced to write or that may have been written for him, some suspected foul play. "I suppose it could just be a weird coincidence that the night Ferrie penned two suicide notes, he died of natural causes," Garrison had said in his 1967 *Playboy* interview.[253]

Lardner had reported that "Ferrie was certainly living when I said good-bye to him Wednesday shortly before 4:00 A.M.," but New Orleans Coroner Nicholas Chetta thought, based on the body's condition, that Ferrie had to have been dead earlier than that.[254]

The CIA had reason to fear what Ferrie might have known or said. Ferrie, whose CIA alias was "Hugh Pharris," had been involved in anti-Castro operations. He had been captured in a photo at a picnic with Lee Harvey Oswald when Oswald was training to fly in the Civil Air Patrol. (Interestingly, an acquaintance told me the CIA had attempted to recruit him when he himself was learning to fly with the Civil Air Patrol.)

---

252   The CIA's spying on Congress will be explained in detail in a later chapter. That the CIA had White House gardeners, secretaries and janitors on their payroll was exposed by the Pike Committee in their censored report, which was leaked to the *Village Voice* and later published in book form in the UK. The CIA's role in bugging lawyers the rooms where 9/11 terrorism suspects met with their lawyers has been detailed in a number of sources, including a Reuters report of February 11, 2015 and a Human Rights Watch report of February 21, 2013.

253   "Playboy Interview: Jim Garrison," *Playboy*, October 1967.

254   "Ferrie Death Probed, Link to 'Plot' Is Denied," *Washington Evening Star*, February 23, 1967.

In the last official memo from the District Attorney's staff on Ferrie before he died, Ferrie expressed a desire to talk to Garrison alone and asked Lou Ivon of his office to call him. Ferrie said he wanted to look Garrison in the eye to see how serious he was about Shaw's case. Ferrie said he didn't believe the magic bullet theory. In short, Ferrie sounded like he was on the verge of confessing. Years later, one of Jim Garrison's investigators, Lou Ivon, told Oliver Stone Ferrie *did* confess, which led to the memorable scene played by Joe Pesci in the film *JFK*. While some have disputed Ivon's late-stage remembrance, the same parties have not disputed the final memo in which Ferrie asked Lou Ivon to talk to him and expressed a desire to meet with Garrison alone.

In any case, the CIA had a provable interest in Garrison's investigation. The head of the CIA's counterintelligence branch, James Angleton, appeared so concerned he had his staff do background checks on Garrison's jurors, a move that might have been a first step toward jury tampering. The CIA was so concerned with Garrison's case that they had asked their media assets in 1967 to do all they could to discredit those who came forward with "conspiracy theories."[255]

It's not surprising, then, that the journalist assigned to the Sirhan case from the *Post* was one whose reporting had been, on the other Kennedy assassination, favorable to the CIA's version of events. It's not surprising that same journalist would break a story that could only have come from a leak inside the D.A.'s office or the Judge's chambers (or a wiretap).

Lardner, being the *Post*'s national security reporter, no doubt had sources in the CIA, as did nearly all national security reporters of prominence. Then as now, the CIA controlled which journalists got prime stories, helping to raise the most subservient to grand positions and helping to oust journalists who told too many of their secrets. *San Jose Mercury News* reporter Gary Webb learned this when he tried to tell the truth about the CIA's role in Los Angeles drug trafficking. *New York Times* reporter Sydney Gruson, who had a history of dogging the CIA, learned this years earlier when Allen Dulles had him removed from his post in Guatemala so he could not report on the CIA's coup about to take place there.[256] Those who kept the Agency's secrets were rewarded with leaks and scoops. Those who exposed the Agency's wrongdoings were not.

While the leak was cause for concern, it was not the most important issue to be discussed in this meeting. "May we raise a couple of other problems about the progress of the case as we now envision it?" Fitts asked. "I think a couple of

255   CIA Dispatch from Chief, WOVIEW to Chiefs, Certain Stations and Bases, April 1, 1967, with handwriting that says "This was put together by Ned Bennett of CA [Covert Action] staff, in close connection with CI/R&A [Angleton's Counterintelligence/Research and Analysis staff], NARA 104-10404-10376, viewable at www.maryferrell.org/showDoc.html?docId=3167&relPageId=2.

256   Tim Weiner, "Role of C.I.A. In Guatemala Told in Files Of Publisher," *New York Times*, www.nytimes.com/1997/06/07/us/role-of-cia-in-guatemala-told-in-files-of-publisher.html, June 7, 1997.

these things can be discussed at this time, so we will have some ground rules in mind, so we won't suffer any unnecessary embarrassment in court." ˑ

Fitts mentioned "Larry Sloan, our handwriting expert," and problems with "some of the signatures or the writing *which may or may not be in question* in this case…with respect to the whole question of the admissibility and the relevance of some of that handwriting—I am referring specifically now to the notebooks …."[257]

The admissibility was an obvious issue. The notebooks had been retrieved from Sirhan's bedroom without his or his mother's permission. The defense argued that Sirhan's brother Adel did not have the requisite legal standing to allow the search. But more important was Fitts' statement that some of the writing might have been "in question." If there were a question whether Sirhan actually wrote all of the text in the notebooks, that would indeed affect the notebooks' "relevance."

And in fact, there was a question. In Lieutenant Pena's "Progress Report" dated July 3, 1968, nearly a month after the crime, Pena reported, "To date the suspect has not been made on handwriting. The written material obtained at suspect's home was forwarded to the FBI in Washington DC, but they were unable to make a determination on the specimens submitted." In other words, neither the LAPD's nor FBI's handwriting experts could prove Sirhan had written all the material in his notebooks based on the other documents they had collected of Sirhan's handwriting.

Cooper, predictably, let that issue drop. But that statement, coupled with what came next, should have given him grave pause.

"It is our intention now," Fitts told the group, "to call DeWayne Wolfer to testify with respect to his ballistics comparison." Then Fitts added something stunning: "Some of the objects or exhibits that he will need illustrative of his testimony will not, because he is being taken somewhat out of order for reasons that we will come to later, will not have adequate foundation, as I will concede at this time."

Some of the objects or exhibits will not have adequate foundation, as I will concede.

"You mean the surgeon took it from the body and this sort of thing?" Cooper asked.

"Well, with respect to the bullets or bullet fragments that came from the alleged victims, it is our understanding that there will be a stipulation that these objects came from the persons whom I say they came from. Is that right?"

"So long as you make that avowal, there will be no question about that," Cooper replied.

If that was all there was to it, Fitts would have stopped there. But he felt compelled to add one more thing, for a very serious reason.

---

257   Sirhan trial transcript, p. 3957.

"We have discussed the matter with Mr. Wolfer as to those envelopes containing those bullets or bullet fragments; he knows where they came from; the envelopes will be marked with the names of the victims and I will pick those up in order and ask for a stipulation that this is the bullet or bullet fragment from, let us say, Elizabeth Evans."

What Fitts was saying, had Cooper been paying close attention, is that *the bullets were currently in unmarked envelopes,* and that Wolfer would say which envelopes contained which bullets, *and then the envelopes would be marked accordingly.* This is far from standard procedure. Bullets and other evidence are supposed to be marked and sealed immediately upon receipt to prevent evidence tampering. Instead, this gave the impression it was the D.A.'s office or Wolfer that was doing the tampering.

To make matters worse, Cooper had been *specifically warned that Wolfer had a credibility issue.*[258] Shortly before the trial began, William Harper, a well-respected criminalist from Pasadena, contacted Cooper to warn him about Wolfer. Harper had examined the evidence in the Kirschke case and found Wolfer's testimony deceptive, an opinion with which, as we've already seen, the California Court of Appeals concurred.[259]

Harper had told Cooper to challenge all evidence from Wolfer because he was simply not to be trusted on those matters. "He gives them what they want," Harper told Cooper, meaning, Wolfer's concern for the truth was not as great as his concern for serving the LAPD's top ranks. "Wolfer is not competent," Harper had said. "He will do what's expected of him."[260]

If you were charged with a crime, would you appreciate your attorney simply stipulating to evidence the prosecution admitted might be somewhat problematic? Especially after your attorney had been warned by a credible source not to trust the person presenting the unsupported evidence? Wouldn't you want your attorney to instead challenge that evidence and possibly get you off on a technicality (if you were guilty) or to demonstrate to the jury there had been evidence manipulation (if you were innocent)? Instead, Cooper stipulated to everything Fitts asked for. The incriminating handwriting in the notebook may not have been Sirhan's, said the prosecution. The bullets were without adequate foundation and may have been substituted. But Cooper stipulated to it all.

---

258   Letter from Grant Cooper to Roger S. Hanson, Esquire, November 3, 1972.

259   Opinion by Thompson, J., with Wood, P.J. and Lillie, J., concurring, 53 Cal. App. 3d 409, Crim. No. 26380. Court of Appeals of California, Second Appellate District, Division One. December 2, 1975, law.justia. com/cases/california/court-of-appeal/3d/53/405.html, accessed October 4, 2015.

260   Klaber and Melanson, p. 79. Their sources were Lynn Mangan and Lt. Booth, both of whom had conversations with Cooper regarding Harper's conversation. Mangan was undoubtedly notified of this even by Harper himself, as she was a friend of Harper's and discussed the case at length with him on a number of occasions, per my own conversations with Lynn Mangan. See letter from Grant Cooper to Roger S. Hanson, Esquire, November 3, 1972 re Cooper's admission that Harper had warned him "that Wolfer could not be relied on."

Some authors have argued that Cooper served his client faithfully. It's possible that was Cooper's sincere intention. But one would be hard pressed to defend Cooper's choices at this unusual and important meeting.

On the afternoon of Monday, February 24, 1968, Wolfer took the stand. Asked if he were a sergeant, Wolfer said "No, just a police officer." Before Fitts asked Wolfer any questions, Fitts entered into evidence an evidence envelope containing an expended bullet, marked People's 47. Fitts asked Cooper to stipulate that "this expended bullet was removed from the vicinity of the sixth cervical vertebra of Senator Robert F. Kennedy at the time of the autopsy which was performed upon him." The prosecution had presented a number of witnesses to establish the chain of possession of Sirhan's gun. But for a bullet retrieved from Kennedy, no witnesses were called.

At the Grand Jury hearing, the bullet had been handed to Noguchi for inspection, and he said his marks were on the bullet. Why was that not done here? Couple this with the discussion in Judge Walker's chambers about not being able to prove the bullets came from the people claimed, there's a strong likelihood—which will be added to in the next chapter—that the bullet presented in court was not, in fact, the bullet retrieved from Kennedy.

The bullet envelope, whatever it contained, was entered into evidence as People's 47. Table 1 shows the reference number for bullets and fragments entered into evidence during Wolfer's testimony. Cooper stipulated to all of them.

Had Cooper or anyone on the defense team paid close attention to the FBI's information, the "bullet fragments" from Elizabeth Evans' head should have been contested. In the previous chapter, we saw that the FBI had reported that the Evans bullet "cannot be entered into evidence as continuity of the bullet has been lost." Sirhan's attorneys had every right to challenge the admissibility of this evidence, but they did not.

Fitts told the jury these stipulations would save "even more" than "a couple days' testimony" from witnesses to establish the chain of possession—"About 20 witnesses," Fitts said. But no one explained to the jury that without such a chain, the evidence presented might not actually be the evidence it was represented to be.

Fitts had Wolfer expound upon his credentials, not noting the odd fact that a guy with such credentials who had worked with the LAPD's crime lab for over 15 years would still be "just a police officer," not a sergeant, not a lieutenant.

Fitts had Wolfer discuss a large blow-up of the bullet fragments. Cooper interrupted and asked if Wolfer had a smaller version of those pictures. Cooper asked to approach the bench and told Judge Walker he thought the bullet pictures and the pictures of Kennedy that were also to be introduced were "highly inflammatory." Once again, Cooper offered to stipulate to all the evidence Fitts was about to present. But was this motivated by a desire to serve Sirhan, or something else?

Table 1: Trial exhibit numbers for the bullets

PEOPLE'S EXHIBIT	DESCRIPTION (stipulated to but not proven in court)
47	Bullet retrieved from Kennedy's neck during the autopsy
48	Two vials containing bullet fragments removed from the head of Senator Kennedy
50	Two bullet fragments retrieved from Paul Schrade's head
51	Bullet removed from Irwin Stroll
52	Bullet removed from Ira Goldstein
53	Two bullet fragments removed from the head of Elizabeth Evans
54	Bullet removed from William Weisel
55	Three test bullets fired into the water recovery tank at LAPD

Cooper seemed more concerned that "this bullet fragment … looks like a bullet from an exceptionally large revolver." Indeed, a fragment with a diameter of 12mm (.47 inches) had been reported in the autopsy report as having been recovered from inside Kennedy's head. A *fragment* that large would have to have come from a gun much larger than Sirhan's .22 caliber one. Did Cooper realize that was evidence of conspiracy? Others would, as you'll read in later chapters.

Fitts said he would allow the jury to see the actual bullet "fragment" so they would understand how truly small it was. Which "fragment" would he show them, though? The largest one or a more appropriately sized one?

Cooper also objected to showing photos of Robert Kennedy after he was shot, claiming they would not only hurt his client's chances but put images in the head of the Kennedy family that they didn't need to see. But again, was that his chief concern? His concern and Fitts' seemed to dovetail. Neither wanted anything that would suggest a conspiracy to be introduced. They just had different opinions as to how best to avoid that. Fitts told the Judge:

> With reference to the circumstances of the shooting, your Honor, your Honor has heard Karl Uecker and any number of witnesses who attempted to describe what happened; one witness has put the muzzle of the revolver some three or four feet from the Senator's head; others have had it at varying ranges. The only way we can clear up whatever ambiguity there may be there and to show the truth is by the testimony of this witness who, on the basis of the powder tattooing and the experiments that he performed with respect thereto,

will testify that the muzzle range with respect to the Senator's head
was about one inch.

Now I think the prosecution is entitled to present that.

But that made no sense. You can't prove *Sirhan* was within an inch when
all the witnesses said he was further away simply by showing that Kennedy
was shot from an inch. That's assuming your conclusion: there was only one
shooter, so Sirhan had to be an inch away. Sherlock Holmes would have objected
to this faulty logic. If you follow only the evidence presented, Sirhan was placed
a few feet from Kennedy by the most credible witnesses; therefore, there had
to be a second shooter. And Cooper could not have been simply ignorant of
the significance of the distance issue. Remember that before the trial began,
Kaiser, the defense team investigator, had notified Cooper of the fact that no
witness put Sirhan's gun muzzle anywhere near close to an inch from Kennedy.
All witnesses who identified Sirhan as the shooter put his gun more than two
feet from Kennedy.

But Cooper was no Sherlock Holmes and compounded the problem by
agreeing with it:

> Your honor, we have no objection to his testifying that he observed
> these powder burns and we have no objection to his testifying to
> whatever his opinion is, but I don't feel it's necessary to illustrate
> it. *We don't quarrel that it was held within one inch.*

Judge Walker overruled Cooper's objections to the display of Kennedy autopsy
photographs and overruled Cooper's next suggestion that one photo would
suffice and that showing two or more was unnecessary and prejudicial. Was the
Judge deliberately trying to help the prosecution here? Photos of a dead person
always bring up emotions, and numerous studies have shown people to be more
persuaded by their emotions than by their logic.

Fitts showed Wolfer the evidence envelope for People's 55, which contained
three test shots Wolfer claimed he took from the Sirhan gun. These, Wolfer said,
were the bullets he had used to perform a comparison test against the other bullets
to see if they had identical markings, indicating they came from the same gun.

> Now, these riflings are important from the standpoint that different
> manufacturers have different rifling specifications, and they spin right
> and left, and they go anywhere from four, five, six, up to twenty-two
> lands and grooves, and they have a gyroscopic value, and these are
> important also for identification purposes. But even more important

are the imperfections that creep in, and that bullet [he meant gun barrel] produces a series of thousands of scratch marks on this bullet.

Looking at the scratches under the comparison microscope and the lands and grooves of this test bullet being in evidence, if I can have them, the scratches and the lands, the majority of the lands, *I can say that they were fired from this gun and no other gun*, and that is what I attempted to do with each of the exhibits.

Fitts asked if these markings were akin to fingerprints, such that bullets fired from one gun barrel could not match those fired from another gun barrel.

"That is correct," Wolfer said.

Fitts then asked Wolfer if some bullets were "sufficiently impaired so you could not make a comparison under the comparison microscope?"

"They were."

Fitts asked which bullets could not be used for a match, but Wolfer apparently either misheard or misunderstood the question, because he then named the Kennedy neck bullet, the Goldstein bullet, and the Weisel bullet. If Wolfer had correctly stated that the victim bullets could not be matched to Sirhan's gun, he had just made a liar of himself—first claiming a match between the *test* bullets from Sirhan's gun and the victim bullets, and then saying a match could not have been made because the *victim* bullets were "sufficiently impaired" to make the match impossible.

Wolfer gave the wrong evidence number, too. Wolfer had referenced Exhibit No. 56, and Cooper interjected "Pardon me, 54, Item 56?"

Judge Walker responded with "You are correct, Counsel. I am sorry. That is right. It is actually People's Exhibit No. 54, were [sic] fired from this gun and no other gun." The Judge was repeating Wolfer's statement to the jury as if it were a fact, that the bullets *had* been fired from that gun, rather than letting the jury weigh and decide whether what Wolfer said was a true statement. When I sat on a jury, the judge made clear to us jurors that nothing a witness said was necessarily a fact until and unless the jury decided it was a fact. Sworn statements were evidence to be weighed and considered, but not necessarily facts. Here, Judge Walker appeared clearly to be both correcting Wolfer's error and adding his own stamp of approval.

And this was a terrible thing, because William Harper, the criminalist who had warned Cooper not to trust Wolfer before the trial began, discovered *after* this trial that the envelope in which the test bullets had been kept was marked with *a wholly different gun number than either the gun at the trial or the gun turned in by Rafer*. Harper discovered the bullets were in an envelope marked with gun number H18602 when it should have been marked with H53725. The mismatched evidence envelope slipped into the record unnoticed at the time, with Cooper's stipulation and Judge Walker's stamp of approval.

Wolfer then made another misstatement, buried in a mishmash of grammatical errors:

> In the case of People's Exhibit 48, this was a bullet taken from Senator Kennedy, and the bullet was extremely or badly damaged, which is well depicted here in [the photograph] People's 49. This was damaged to the point, and I say that these were Mini-Mag ammunition, which is the same ammunition as previously used in my test, they were Mini-Mag ammunition that was fired from the gun of the same ballistic rifling specification as that of People's No. 6, but because of the damage, I cannot say positively that it was fired from that gun.

"Just a moment, sir," Fitts said, stopping Wolfer to clarify for the jury that Wolfer didn't mean "a bullet" couldn't be matched to Sirhan's gun. "With reference to People's 48, that exhibit consists of *fragments*, does it not, sir?"

"Yes, it does."

Wolfer had said People's 48 had "a bullet," in it, not fragments. Fitts did his best to marry the two in the jury's minds.

"By your testimony, you were using *fragment bullets*?" Fitts suggested, trying to cover Wolfer's error.

"Fragments of People's No. 48," Wolfer said.

"We are talking about fragments of *one* bullet, are we not?" Fitts prompted.

"Yes, we are."

In a later chapter, we'll see that Wolfer may well have meant "a bullet," just as he said, and not the one that produced the fragments. Wolfer may have inadvertently told the truth, without meaning to, at the trial.

Fitts asked Wolfer to discuss the Elizabeth Evans "fragments." Recall how the FBI not only called it a bullet but also said the chain of possession had been broken and that her "bullet" could not be entered into evidence for that reason. Wolfer responded to Fitts that Evans' "fragments" were all from Mini-Mag ammunition but that the rifling characteristics were "very weak" and the "fragments" were "too badly damaged" to make any kind of identification. It sounds more like the bullet didn't match Sirhan's gun or possibly the other bullets from the pantry, so Wolfer turned her bullet into "fragments" to avoid the problem.

The next exchange showed how stage-managed the show for the jury was. Cooper again objected to putting photographs of Kennedy's autopsy into evidence.

> Cooper: I would suggest this, if your Honor please—I would have no objection to his [Wolfer's] testifying from those photographs as

though they were powder tattooing, provided, however, that at a later period of time they were put on the testimony to show that it was in fact powder tattooing.

Judge Walker to Fitts: "Do you have any way of doing that from the pictures?"

Fitts: Well, if the Court please, it seems to me it's asking a little bit too much of anybody to look at a photograph and say—

Judge Walker: Well, I'm just asking you.

Fitts: I don't want to ask him that question because I think it's asking too much. From the pictures, you can't tell whether it's a smudge or whether it's embedded in the skin or what.

Was Fitts worried Wolfer might not recognize those as powder burns?

Judge Walker: He could testify that it resembled that, and another witness could testify that he observed the actual area.

Fitts: Yes, we expect that will come in.

Cooper: I do object, your Honor, to its being received in evidence and shown to the jury until such time as there is testimony that it is powder tattooing.

Judge Walker: He could testify—well, I will allow him to testify they resemble powder burns.

Fitts: Could he testify on the assumption these are powder burns?

Cooper: Yes, I have no objection to that, providing I will move to strike his testimony with respect to that, and the introduction of the photograph, which is the only thing I am objecting to, when that foundation is subsequently made.

Judge Walker: That is, that someone who actually saw the powder burns?

Cooper: And who can testify that there is actually powder tattooing. Yes, your Honor.

Judge Walker: That's the only way you can do it.

Fitts then asked if he could talk to Wolfer. Clearly, Fitts had to clue Wolfer in now on what to say, even though witnesses are not supposed to be coached or led. After that, the scene unfolded exactly as planned.

Fitts drew Wolfer's attention to the "black smudging, which appears on the lobe and the edge of the right ear" and asked "Are you familiar with what that is, sir?"

"I am," Wolfer said. "This is what we call powder tattooing for two purposes—"

"Your Honor," Cooper interjected, "I move to strike the witness' answer."

"That may go out. The jury will disregard it."

Fitts then led Wolfer—so much that at one point Cooper objected and the Judge upheld it—to say he had personally examined Kennedy and found direct evidence of the powder tattooing on Kennedy.

Fitts wanted to get to the distance issue. He got Wolfer to describe how he had fired at pigs' ears "at a 30-degree angle inward and a 50-degree angle upward as per information I had regarding" what Fitts called "the wound tract" in Kennedy's head. The tests were conducted at various distances, with the same type of Mini-Mag, hollow-point ammunition used in the pantry, and the pattern that matched what was seen on Kennedy was made from a distance of one inch. These were the same pigs' ears Thomas Noguchi had requested. The two had worked together to determine the distance. And interestingly, Noguchi was set to testify shortly after. So why didn't the prosecution have Noguchi testify to the distance? Were they worried Noguchi might stray off script and mention that was inconsistent with Sirhan's firing position?

"The weapon [that killed Kennedy] was held approximately one inch away from the Senator's ear at the time it was fired."

Fitts asked if the gun in People's Exhibit 6 had been used.

"No, we did not use this gun. We used a gun which was the exact make and model and *within a very close serial number of this weapon.* At that particular time the gun was in the Court exhibits and was unavailable for us to obtain for the purpose of testing."

Was the gun that was "within a very close serial number of this weapon" the gun with the serial number H58725, the gun Uecker had identified as the gun at the start of the trial? Sirhan's gun was H53725. Gun manufacturers often embed dates of manufacture in the serial number. Given that both guns share "725" at the end, it is possible "725" represents a coded date. If so, then H58725 might have been a "very close serial number" indeed. The gun that Wolfer used for sound tests (and which appeared on the evidence envelope for Wolfer's "test" bullets) was H18602. H18602 does not appear to be a close serial number to H53725.

Due to this and other evidence that will be presented later, I'm convinced that the gun with H58725 was indeed presented in the courtroom, that the record did not contain a typo, and that it was not the gun Rafer turned in to the police after the shooting. That would mean when Wolfer testified that this gun was the one that fired the bullets he presented in court, he may well have been telling the truth on that point. That would also mean Sirhan had been convicted based on demonstrably false evidence.

Fitts next introduced Kennedy's coat into evidence. The coat was missing one arm. Although Wolfer explained he had to cut the coat to fit a mannequin and then sewed it awkwardly by hand together again, no one asked him to explain why the whole left sleeve was still missing. Kennedy was supposed to have been shot only on the right side.

Cooper offered a stipulation to the cutting of the coat if Fitts wanted one. Fitts did, but the way Fitts framed it was very odd, considering Wolfer had just admitted to cutting up the coat:

> With respect to the condition of the coat and the cutting, we would offer to stipulate that at the time Senator Kennedy was removed from the Ambassador Hotel to the Central Receiving Hospital for receiving treatment there at the hands of Dr. Fausten [sic] Bazilauskas and Dr. Kolti that the coat was removed from him and by reasons of the condition, it was cut with scissors in various ways, and the reason it was in this condition accounts for the condition in which Mr. Wolfer received it.

Fitts appeared to have just made a liar of his client, claiming the coat had been cut up before it ever got to Wolfer. Once again, the Judge jumped in to help the prosecution's case:

> Judge Walker: And it accounts for the absence of one sleeve.
> Fitts: I should certainly suppose so. I would have thought it would have had a sleeve at the time it was worn.
> Cooper: The only point is that, obviously, it wasn't done by the defendant.

Note that Fitts did not say "yes" to Walker's response but rather, "I should certainly suppose so." He said something that could not be construed as a direct lie. But who cut the left sleeve off, and more importantly, why did it disappear? If the doctors had removed the sleeve for medical reasons, why was no one asked to testify to this at the trial? And why was the cut sleeve not returned, in a murder case? The rest of the coat was. Did the sleeve contain one hole too many, or in an inconvenient position, perhaps on the left side, when all the other shots in Kennedy's body came in from behind his right side? It's hard to believe that, with so much at stake, an innocent explanation was not conclusively provided in the trial. Cutting a sleeve off for surgery makes sense. Throwing it away, however, does not, in a case of this importance.

Wolfer discussed the five bullet holes found in the coat—three entrance points and two exit points. One bullet passed through the right sleeve just below Kennedy's shoulder seam without entering his body. Two more bullets entered under his armpit, one of passed through Kennedy's chest and exited out "the upper front lapel" of Kennedy's coat. The other bullet lodged in the back of Kennedy's neck.

Fitts asked Wolfer how far the gun had to have been from the coat for these shots. Wolfer said all the shots that hit Kennedy's coat came from a distance of one to six inches at most. The shot just below the right shoulder came from "about one inch away," but the two holes under the arm were within two inches of each other, so it was hard to say if one was fired at closer range than the other.

Under closer questioning, Wolfer indicated the shots under the arm likely came from a distance *that could have been as close as three-quarters of an inch away and not more than three inches away, and of the two, he leaned toward the closer figure.*

Cooper noted that Wolfer had used a gun other than the Sirhan gun in evidence to make the powder tests and asked, might he have gotten a different answer on the distance had he used the actual gun and not a similar gun? Cooper appeared to be hinting to Wolfer that he should widen the distance between the gun and Kennedy. Wolfer either missed or rejected the hint. Wolfer explained that the powder tattooing patterns didn't vary much from gun to gun, so Fitts did a quick redirect of Wolfer on this point.

"There may be some ambiguity with respect to your testimony, Officer Wolfer, as to the range from which the gun was shot and the bullet that went into the head of the Senator was fired. I believe on direct examination it was your testimony that it was approximately one inch, is that correct sir?"

"That is correct. … *I really feel it was closer than an inch*, but I gave you the maximum difference of an inch. I would say three-quarters of an inch tolerance at the inch distance that they had."

"When you use the word 'tolerance' are you saying that you added a quarter of an inch on to what your real opinion is?"

"I would say I added possibly three-quarters of an inch."

"Well, that would be what in adding everything together, would that make an inch and three-quarters?"

Fitts appeared to be deliberately miscalculating the math here, just as Cooper had. But Wolfer's testimony was actually clear on this point. Wolfer said that the shot behind Kennedy's right ear was, in his opinion, made from a distance of *not more than a quarter of an inch* away. He only added the extra three-quarters of an inch as the largest possible margin of error, to give a total maximum distance of one inch.

For the underarm shots, Wolfer said the overlapping patterns indicated that at least one of the two shots came from a distance of from three-quarters of an inch to at most three inches away, but he added another three-inch tolerance to make his maximum estimation of the distance six inches at the most.

In other words, Wolfer's information showed the gun muzzle of the gun that killed Kennedy was *likely never more than three inches from Kennedy for all four shots* that hit him and his clothing, and that the headshot was fired from a point of nearly direct contact, closer to one quarter of an inch than an inch. Whoever shot Kennedy had to have been right beside him. Sirhan never got anywhere near that close, and he was always to the front left of Kennedy, not behind him and to the right, where the shooter had to have been. Kennedy didn't spin around until he had already been shot, and even then, he fell away from, not toward, Sirhan.

In a perfect world, the trial would have ended right there and the charges changed on the spot, as Wolfer essentially proved that Sirhan couldn't have killed Kennedy, even though that was neither Wolfer's nor the prosecution's (and clearly not the Judge's or the defense team's) intention. But the world is far from perfect, and the charade continued for another month.

Sirhan's defense team opened with some background on Sirhan. As a child in Palestine at the time Israel declared independence from its British overseers and waged war against the Palestinians, Sirhan's family was forced to move from their middle-class home to a decrepit two-story building that housed nine families of 50 people, with a single hole in the ground for a toilet. There was no furniture. They stuffed sheets with old clothes to make beds. They received flour, beans, and Mazola corn oil from the United Nations, which was never enough food to satisfy. People died of starvation. Sirhan shared his family's paltry rations with others who had literally "nothing to eat."

Young Sirhan was tasked with fetching water from a well. One time, the bucket he pulled up had a severed hand in it. Another cistern of water wasn't drinkable because there were dead bodies in there. Sirhan's mother, Mary Sirhan, explained how sometimes the family would stand in line and wait half a day just to get water from a truck.

Bombs rained down all around him. Young Sirhan saw a grocer blown up right in front of him. He blacked out from the terror and wouldn't leave the house for two weeks after a horrific incident. In one incident, a man was blown up but his leg got caught by and hung from a steeple on a church. Another time, Sirhan saw "many young girls in [a] truck that were naked, and there was blood running from their breasts, and a big lot of army that was going in," Mary Sirhan had said on the stand. "I don't know what kind of soldiers they were, clapping their hands, saying 'Look what we can do,' and this is what Sirhan and I saw." Another time, Sirhan found a man caught in a barbed-wire fence who had been shot and had blood running from him. Sirhan literally trembled, according to his mother. "I believe he took a long time before he could even stand on his feet."

Sirhan had an older brother named Munir who was run over by a car while playing in the street by someone attempting to escape gunfire. Mary Sirhan described how Sirhan didn't seem to understand the concept of death. He kept

184 A LIE TOO BIG TO FAIL

asking when Munir would come out to play. When Mary Sirhan gave birth to the youngest member of the family, she named him Munir in the hopes of comforting Sirhan.

Another time, Sirhan had seen a neighbor's boy tied to a tree and "whipped, whipped, whipped for many—I don't know how many days they did whip him" by Israelis in front of her neighbor's eyes. Clearly, trauma shaped Sirhan's young life.

Despite this, one of Sirhan's childhood friends, Ziad Hashimeh, told the jury of Sirhan's kindness, even among all the terror. Hashimeh wanted to steal an ice cream cone from a vendor, but Sirhan talked him out of it. "Do not steal, because that man makes very few pastries ... and he has to feed a family, and that is not nice."

Despite the heartbreaking testimony, and despite the fact that six medical professionals, including two initially hired by the prosecution, said Sirhan was clearly suffering from a degree of paranoid schizophrenia that made it impossible for him legally to have the capability to have committed first-degree murder, while only two said Sirhan was sane enough, the jury found Sirhan guilty of murder in the first degree and, after another set of impassioned arguments on both sides, sentenced him to death.

The psychological testimony, at this point in the story, is premature. If Sirhan didn't shoot Kennedy, did he shoot anybody? Was he firing blanks? Did he know what he was doing? The trial put the cart before the horse. After examining two more episodes from the trial, we'll take a more in-depth look at what really happened. Until we understand the nature of the event, we have no way to competently evaluate Sirhan's role in it. We'll return to his mental state when we have a better grounding in the crime itself.

One event from the trial that must be discussed here is commonly misrepresented in other books on this case: Sirhan's outburst where he told Judge Walker, initially outside the hearing of the jury, "I killed Robert Kennedy willfully, premeditatively, with 20 years of malice aforethought." Many journalists have looked at that statement and thought, case closed. The guy confessed. But as noted at the start of this chapter, people sometimes confess to crimes they didn't commit.

There's also much more context to that statement than is generally presented. If someone robs a bank, they're guilty, right? But what if you found out the robber did so to save his child from being killed in front of him? That information changes the context entirely. Suddenly the robber is more victim than criminal. With that example in mind, consider what happened next.

Sirhan's anger had been building for days. He had never fully bought in to his defense team's plans to plead him mentally ill. This tremendously bothered

Sirhan. As we've seen, Sirhan truly had no memory of what had happened and, lacking a motive, invented one: that he was defending Palestine against Kennedy, who was about to send in more bombers.

When the notebooks were to be put into evidence, which Sirhan understood to have been obtained through an illegal search and seizure, as the police had no search warrant, thereby violating his rights, Sirhan insisted on speaking to Judge Walker. He was brought to the Judge's chambers shortly after 9 A.M., where he told the Judge,

> Your Honor, if these notebooks are allowed in evidence, I will change my plea to guilty as charged.
>
> I will do so, sir, not so much that I want to be railroaded into that gas chamber, sir, but to deny you the pleasure, sir, of, after convicting me, turning around and telling the world: 'Well, I put that fellow in the gas chamber, but I first gave him a fair trial,' when you in fact, sir, will not have done so.
>
> The evidence, sir, that was taken from my home was illegally obtained, was stolen by the District Attorney's people. They had no search warrant. I did not give them permission, sir, to do what they did to my home.
>
> My brother Adel had no permission to give them permission to enter my own room and take what they took from my home, from my room.

"If your Honor please," Cooper interjected, "I didn't know that this statement was going to be made. I knew he was going to object to the use of the notebooks, but in the light of his statement, I would like to have a few minutes to talk to him."

"Right," Howard said, "I think that is—"

"No, sir, I'm adamant on this point," Sirhan said.

Cooper asked Sirhan to step outside with him, where they had a brief discussion. When they returned about ten minutes later, Cooper told Judge Walker, "We have him calmed down, temporarily at least, and we don't know when he might blow again."

Cooper, Howard and Walker agreed that if Sirhan made further outbursts in the courtroom, the judge would call a recess immediately and dismiss the jury.

"Now, Mr. Sirhan, let me tell you this," Judge Walker told Sirhan. "The court has ruled on the admissibility of this evidence in court, and, if there is an error, the upper court can reverse this case."

"Yes, I understand."

"You are guided by three excellent attorneys and they have been at this business for many years."

"I understand, sir."

"And I know them personally, at least two, for 30 years. I am not saying that you are going to go to the gas chamber. You are not going to go to the gas chamber unless that is the determination of the jury, and even then, I have an opportunity to set it aside if it is warranted. … [G]uide yourself by your attorneys…. They are doing you an excellent job."

"I understand that."

"So keep that in mind before you come in here and say these things to the court."

"Well, I wanted to say it here because I didn't want to say it in court last night, and I almost blew up."

"I know you did. That is why we recessed early," Walker explained. "I want you to understand that if you plead guilty, before I take a plea from you, I would examine you for at least 20 minutes, and I have to under the law, and you understand that?"

"Yes."

"I have it all worked out, four pages of questions that I will ask you before I will even accept a plea and that is what the law requires."

After the notebooks were introduced, Sirhan was again visibly disturbed, and his upset grew when a superintendent was brought in to testify to Sirhan's failing grades. As mentioned previously, Sirhan had been taking care of his sister, who was dying of leukemia. His failing grades were due to absences, not his classwork.

When Sirhan's lawyers wanted to call Sirhan's mother Mary to the stand, Sirhan again objected. Mary was so distraught herself that Judge Walker ended her testimony early and let her continue the next morning, when she could be more composed.

The final straw came when Parsons showed Sirhan a list of 31 witnesses to be called on his behalf, two of which were two women that Sirhan had appeared to have a crush on, Gwen Gumm and Peggy Osterkamp, as their names appeared frequently throughout his notebooks. Kaiser reported in his book *R.F.K. Must Die* that Sirhan was in some disassociated state at this point, accusing two girls in the courtroom of being Gumm and Osterkamp who were provably not those girls. Regardless, Sirhan blew up. He said he did not want those women inconvenienced on his account.

Cooper told Sirhan if they wouldn't let him give him the defense they felt he needed, they would withdraw from the case. Sirhan was fine with that, as he didn't like the direction his defense was going anyway. Cooper told Judge Walker,

> As a result of this conflict with my client … I should ask to be relieved
> of this case. Except … believing as I do that he has diminished

capacity—not that he's insane—I don't think he is in a position to exercise judgment and therefore I owe him a duty.

But in view of the fact that he has blown up in the courtroom before … in my opinion if we call these witnesses [he] will blow up again….

In his book on the case, Kaiser noted the irony of Cooper arguing his client suffered from diminished mental capacity while expecting him to maintain total decorum during the court proceedings.

Compton warned if Sirhan did this in open court, it could backfire because Sirhan might feel he had won, that he had gotten Cooper off his case. Cooper suggested the Judge could lecture Sirhan, but the Judge had done that and it appeared to have little effect.

Cooper added something else.

"Your Honor, please, there was something I omitted. He said that if we read those exhibits out loud, he would get up and plead guilty, but since they weren't read out loud, he didn't."

The judge didn't want to make a decision on this. It was a no-win situation. Nearly anything that happened next could be grounds for a mistrial, and that was the last thing any of them wanted. "Give yourself some time to think about it with your conferees," Judge Walker advised Cooper. Sirhan was a ticking time bomb and they all knew it.

Sirhan's control didn't last much longer. After lunch on February 28, Sirhan had had enough, and asked to address the Judge "in chambers," a request Judge Walker declined. But the jury was cleared from the room, and Sirhan spoke.

"I at this time, sir, withdraw my original plea of not guilty and submit the plea of guilty as charged on all counts. I also request that my counsel disassociate themselves from this case completely."

"Do I understand—stand up," the Judge admonished Sirhan. "Do I understand that you want to plead guilty to murder in the first degree?"

"Yes, sir, I do."

"All right, and what do you want to do about the penalty?"

"I will offer no defense whatsoever."

"The question is, what do you want to do about the penalty?"

"I will ask to be executed, sir."

Many authors have misrepresented this as a "confession of guilt" from Sirhan. But this was clearly Sirhan's attempt to control the proceedings. He had conceded his guilt from the start, because he had no memory that might clear him of involvement. Everyone said he did it, and he saw no evidence to the contrary, so he believed them. Sirhan wanted to end the trial. He didn't want his mother to suffer. He didn't want people saying he was crazy. He thought by pleading guilty he could end the proceedings and spare the girls the indignity of being questioned. But Sirhan didn't have the power he thought he had.

"Now, I know of nothing in the law that permits a defendant under any circumstances to enter a plea of guilty to murder of the first degree and ask for execution," Judge Walker told him.

"Well, I have, sir," Sirhan responded.

"Well, now, just a minute. Why do you want to do this?"

"I believe, sir, that is my business, isn't it?"

"You just believe it is your business?"

"That is my prerogative."

"No, it isn't. Now, when we come to accepting a plea, you have to give me a reason."

Sirhan, drawing a line from the testimony about his childhood in Palestine to exaggerate how ridiculous he felt his defense was, responded, "I killed Robert Kennedy willfully, premeditatedly, with 20 years of malice aforethought: that is why."

Of course he hadn't planned to kill Kennedy as a four-year-old. Even Judge Walker knew this claim was ludicrous. "Well, the evidence has to be produced here in court," he told Sirhan.

"I withdraw all evidence, sir."

"There is no such procedure."

"To hell with it!" Sirhan exploded in frustration.

Judge Walker told Sirhan if he could not refrain from interrupting the proceedings he would be physically muzzled and strapped to his chair in front of the jury.

Sirhan did not appear to understand and persisted. Kaiser noted that Sirhan appeared to be in some sort of dissociative state throughout this exchange.

"I understand. However, sir, I intend to defend myself pro per. I don't want to be represented by these counsel."

"You have trained counsel. Counsel is staying in the trial."

"What I have said, I don't want anyone to have a trial shoved down my throat, sir, in any way you want. [sic]"

Judge Walker asked Sirhan to describe the elements of a crime of murder and its defenses to prove to Sirhan he did not know enough to represent himself pro per.

"I don't know," Sirhan conceded.

"I find you incapable of representing yourself. Sit down and keep quiet, and if not, I intend to keep you quiet."

"No, sir. I still maintain my original point. I plead guilty to murder and ask to be executed."

"I thought I made it clear. The court will not accept the plea."

"I am sorry," Sirhan said. "I will not accept it."

Sirhan begged the Judge to allow him to talk privately to him in chambers. Judge Walker refused. Cooper then asked if he and counsel could be dismissed: "None of us have any desire to continue representing a client who does not desire our services."

Cooper explained further that Sirhan seemed completely capable of understanding the communications from his defense team. "It is just that there is a very violent difference of opinion as to how the defense should be conducted," Cooper continued. He explained how the defense had enlisted friends, family and Arabic-speaking individuals to attempt to influence Sirhan to accept their advice, to no avail.

"Since the defendant does not desire us to represent him, we are perfectly willing, as a matter of fact, I might say *anxious*, to withdraw from the case and let him either represent himself or be represented by other counsel."

Perhaps suddenly realizing how *that* might sound to history, Cooper said "I want to hasten to add this: Neither one of us wants to desert him.

"We are still willing, if your Honor please, to represent him as conscientiously as we know how. With that, I must leave it up to the court."

Judge Walker refused to allow them to withdraw. Walker added, "I think you have prepared a good defense, if not the only logical defense that could be presented." Given that a clearly conscious decision had been made to avoid all facts that pointed to conspiracy, perhaps that *was* the only logical defense left.

But if Sirhan's defense team could be excused for ignoring evidence of conspiracy for fear that would further risk their client's life, what excuse can we give the prosecution for not only failing to find and prosecute the guilty coconspirators, but provably conspiring to conceal that evidence from the future historical record? That's what happened at a private meeting between the Judge, Fitts and Deputy Chief Robert Houghton of the LAPD five days before Walker made his final ruling on this case.

On May 16, at 1:30 P.M., Fitts, Judge Walker and the LAPD's Chief Houghton met with Emery Hatcher (Chief Deputy, County Clerk's Office), Peter Talmachoff (Division Chief, Criminal Division, County Clerk's Office) and Alice Nishikawa (Clerk for Department 107, where the trial had been held) in the Chambers of Assistant Presiding Judge Charles A. Loring. The goal of the meeting was bizarre. They met to decide which evidence should be kept from the public. If there was nothing to hide, why go to such lengths?

Walker opened the proceedings. "First, perhaps we better take up the [autopsy] photographs."

"There are somewhere in the neighborhood of 130," Fitts said. They weren't entered into evidence but offered for identification only.

"I am willing to seal those subject to order of court, and I think I can put it on some kind of ground," Walker said. "I am going to look at it and find myself some ground to do it."

"I don't think there is going to be too much demand to see these," Fitts responded. "The only people that could do anything are going to be cranks in the first place." "Cranks" was the word Fitts assigned to people who cared enough about history not to trust the victor alone with the telling of it. "Cranks" were those who invested their own time and money to conduct honest investigations into the evidence, without fear or favor. "Cranks" were those who were mentally courageous enough to follow evidence of conspiracy wherever it led.

"Well, those are the people I am worried about," Walker said.

"Well, I sort of thought these people would be the cranks and they want to see them so they can start cranking."

"I will agree with that," Houghton said.

The Clerk pointed out that there were *two* groups of photos, "one consisting of 166 and the other 127 photos."

Houghton offered that "There was a set of photographs of the autopsy which Noguchi's people took, and then there was about half a dozen, it seems to me, of photographs taken by the Los Angeles police officers over there at the Good Samaritan Hospital and you remember those. They were taken prior to any surgery or cutting on the wound, on the head wound, and I think they ought to be categorized in the same group."

Walker was also concerned that the photos were "extremely valuable" and he wanted to ensure they didn't get in any way "mutilated." He worried that if the photos had any damage, it could affect the case on appeal.

Walker then turned to "our second problem. We have got these bullets, we have got the gun, and I have even had a request from some woman that got hit with one of those bullets [Elizabeth Evans]. She wanted it for a souvenir. I have already told her where she can get it."

"What I am trying to do," Walker continued, "is to set up something like this, *that the actual exhibits are not exhibited to these people* in some manner, so they are not mutilated or lost or anything else, because it is easy for those exhibits to get lost in your office and everybody is in a mess. I understand that maybe you could have copies that the public could see." Was Walker suggesting the public be allowed to see a gun that wasn't Sirhan's? Copies of bullets rather than actual bullets?

"I was going to wait until you got through with those exhibits and then we can talk about this other," Houghton said. "We have done a lot of investigating of cases which were not subject to testimony and I think you put in Owens [sic]." Houghton was concerned that the testimony of one strange Reverend Jerry Owen, nicknamed "The Walking Bible" because he claimed he could recite any and every passage from the Bible (a claim he was never able to actually demonstrate). Owen had injected himself into this case by telling the police after the assassination that he had picked up a hitchhiking Sirhan on June 3, 1968, the day before the primary election. For whatever reason, during the trial, although the prosecution and defense discussed Sirhan's activities on June 2 and June 4, they both studiously avoided mention of June 3. According to Owen, Sirhan was accompanied by two others and wanted to buy a horse. The two others later approached Owen, paid him $100 and said bring the horse to the Ambassador Hotel and the rest of the money would be delivered. Owen went instead, he said, to Oxnard to preach that night, taking their money with him and not delivering a horse. (No witness placed Owen in Oxnard that night, and a church he said he was preaching at was closed at that time.) Houghton described the preacher Owen as "one self-seeking son-of-a-bitch." Fitts mentioned that Owen may have had a "kick-back sheet" in the Criminal Investigation and Identification (CII) files, as did witnesses Enrique Rabago, who claimed Sirhan made a derogatory remark about Kennedy the night of the assassination, and Delgado, a name that does not appear in the LAPD's cardfile of the people interviewed. Owen may have played a significant role in these events, as will be discussed in a later chapter.

Walker allayed Houghton's fears that Owen might be exposed. "It was not even put in for identification," Walker clarified. Neither apparently knew that a journalist named Jonn Christian and a former FBI agent named Bill Turner were already hot on Owen's trail.

Houghton then talked of evidence of conspiracy. "There was the Cuban, Duarte, who you are not familiar with, but he got in and he even went on TV [to allege, apparently falsely, that Sirhan had attended a meeting of anti-Castro Cubans and accused Duarte of being with the CIA]; and Jerry Owens [sic], the self-styled preacher; John Fahey—and I think he got some publicity… and I think one or two others, and they might have Virginia Teresi [misspelled Teresa in the transcript]." Teresi had reported having seen Sirhan, or a lookalike, standing at the corner of Melrose and St. Andrew's Place, less than two miles from the Ambassador Hotel, on June 3, the day before the primary, talking to three men in a car, one of which was wearing a holster with a gun. She also saw two rifles leaning against the back seat. But unlike the other witnesses to conspiracy, Teresi admitted right away, when confronted, that she had made the story up. She said she was worried the police wouldn't look into evidence of conspiracy so she provided some herself.

After a discussion about other evidence in the case, Walker returned to the question of making copies of documents available. Hatcher said "Our office could duplicate every single exhibit that could be duplicated and only those that could be duplicated."

"Well, that is all right with respect to physical exhibits like papers all things like that, but we have got the coat [that was cut off of Kennedy], we have the bullets, we have got expended shells, unexpended, and so forth, which are physical."

Judge Loring suggested putting those in "some kind of a plastic or cellophane container that can be seen through without being able to touch them."

"There aren't going to be many people who want to look at those bullets anyway. What can they do with it?" Fitts asked Judge Loring.

"Could your office make copies of all of the other exhibits?" Walker asked Loring.

When assured that was no problem, Walker made it clear this time he wasn't just talking about copying documents. "How about the bullets, guns and other physical things?"

"We could have them photographed, if you would like. We could arrange to have it done," Hatcher told Walker.

"Well, we don't want any of the originals available except to attorneys of record," Walker said, as if he knew there was something to hide.

"Or upon order of court," Loring responded. "If somebody comes in with a valid reason as to why they should see it, and they are responsible people, then we could order it."

Fitts, too, seemed nervous about what people might uncover if they had access to the exhibits. He suggested that "rather than having anybody willy-nilly walking in off the street and coming up and pestering the clerk, it would be nice somehow if they obtained a kind of clearance through the court. I know I am posing a sort of onerous burden," Fitts added.

Loring clearly didn't understand there was anything to hide. "Well, as long as you are dealing only with copies such as photographs of the original documents, what risk is there? Why shouldn't they see copies?"

The clerk mentioned Dr. Pollack's interview with Sirhan. There was no written copy of the interview—only a tape of it, and Pollack's comments on the stand about it.

"Anything not in evidence, I don't see why we have to make it available," Judge Walker said. They discussed protecting not Sirhan's reputation or privacy, but Pollack's. Fitts was also concerned someone might erase it: "If it ever got close enough to a magnet, we don't even have the words."

Houghton had his own concerns. There were a large number of files. "We interviewed a lot of people and you never knew who they were going to talk to. I am sure some of it will leak out. The majority of it has not. Much of it has. Now, we think that nothing in this case should be withheld from the public."

"That is right," Walker said, but given what Walker had just said, one has to believe he agreed with this as a *posture*, not a *policy*.

Houghton said, "We think to put secrecy around this phase of it is just going to open up speculation that is going on with the John Kennedy assassination since we did do, in my opinion, as professional a job of investigation as could have been done anywhere, and I feel that this information should be made available." But he immediately contradicted himself by saying, "Now, we have not yet decided whether we will make the files available yet. We will decide this."

Houghton said there were about 50,000 files and a "final report."

"You need a final, final report," Walker said.

Houghton noted that Attorney General Ramsey Clark wanted a copy of all the LAPD's files placed in the National Archives in Washington. The LAPD had agreed to this so long as there was a mutual policy re how the files could be accessed.

Walker and Loring thought that made sense, and since they weren't the Court's own files, they had no say over them anyway. But Fitts appeared concerned. "I would like to have a little talk with you about this matter," Fitts said to Houghton. Fitts said the District Attorney would be interested in how these files would be made available.

Houghton said he was waiting "to get some kind of final decision from Washington on the files" because he didn't know the National Archives' procedures.

When Fitts suggested that transcripts of the tapes could be made available, Loring said people should be able to hear the tapes, hear the voices, not just read a transcript.

While Houghton seemed more concerned about the logistics of copying and handing off all their files than the actual exposure of them, that may have been a smokescreen for the record. Near the end of their conversation, Houghton asked if they could go off the record, which was deeply ironic considering he had opened by saying everything should be made public and nothing should be held back.

After the off-the-record discussion, Judge Walker said everything was now clear.

Houghton alerted the group to the fact that he knew of at least four books that were soon to be published on the case, three of which alleged a "major conspiracy in this matter and not what the truth is" but immediately followed it up with the need to keep the files under lock and key. "We are going to isolate the files because they are not available to the average person."

Hatcher added, "We advise them that they can procure a copy of a page and that our fee is 50 cents a page. That will stop a lot of them." Adjusting for inflation, 50 cents from 1969 would be roughly $3.53 a page in 2018 dollars.[261] That would indeed be a deterrent, as most researchers do not have a lot of money, having spent their time chasing the truth about our collective past.

To see public officials, on the record, discussing how to hide evidence from the public is disturbing. Democracy can only survive with the consent of an *informed* public. A people deprived of a full and accurate history cannot make

---

261   Per the U.S. Department of Labor's CPI Inflation Calculator at www.bls.gov/data/inflation_calculator.htm.

the necessary course corrections to improve their future condition. As President Abraham Lincoln once said, "Let them know the truth, and the country is safe."[262]

Before 1969 was over, Judge Walker retired; prosecutor Dave Fitts was appointed a judge on the Los Angeles County Superior Court by then-Governor and future president Ronald Reagan; Cooper got the lightest possible sentence—a $1,000 fine—for the stolen transcript incident; Jerry Owen got his own TV show; and *Los Angeles Times* reporter Dave Smith won an award for his coverage of the Sirhan trial.

As with Cooper, Judge Walker had a case hanging over his head at the time of Sirhan's trial. Walker's nephew Erwin M. Walker, a former Army officer who had returned from the horrors of war to become a burglar, had murdered a police officer and had pleaded not guilty by reason of insanity. He had been sentenced to death, but his death sentence had been commuted to life without the possibility of parole in 1961 by Governor Pat Brown. In 1970, the year following Sirhan's trial, Walker's nephew received a new hearing which eventually was heard by the Supreme Court of California, which ordered the lower court to remove the parole restriction in 1974. One of the counsels for the defense was Evelle Younger. One can't help but wonder if there was a quid pro quo there: sink Sirhan's case and Younger will help you rescue your nephew.

In 1970, Governor Reagan appointed Lynn Compton to the California appellate court, Evelle Younger became California's Attorney General, and Younger then appointed Robert Houghton to head the state's Criminal Intelligence and Investigation (CII) bureau.

During the SUS investigation, Sergeant Hernandez, the man who polygraphed all witnesses to any aspect of conspiracy (and told them all they were lying), was promoted to Lieutenant. In 1973, Hernandez left the LAPD and formed Inter-Con, an international security firm, with a contract obtained from NASA. Contrary to propaganda that assured the world NASA was not a spy or warfare agency, NASA has worked closely with both the CIA and the Department of Defense on numerous projects. Inter-Con continues to be an "important security provider" to "Departments of State, Homeland Security, Justice and Defense."[263]

After the trial, the LAPD destroyed the several ceiling panels which had, as Wolfer had told the interagency working group on the case, an "unbelievable" number of holes in them from the shooting. The LAPD also burned more than two thousand photos relating to Sen. Kennedy's assassination in a hospital incinerator. Not all the photos ended up in the incinerator, however. The autopsy

262   *The Wheeling Daily Intelligencer*, April 21, 1865.

263   Inter-Con's description of its services at its website at www.icsecurity.com/sectors/government-and-diplomatic, accessed November 26, 2015.

photos (or presumably copies thereof) found their way into the safe of James Angleton, the man who headed the CIA's large counterintelligence unit and whose most secretive "black op" group had secret files on Lee Harvey Oswald that long predated the assassination of President John F. Kennedy.

The LAPD destroyed the telltale pantry door jambs that the FBI had photographed and labeled as containing "bullet holes" as well. The excuse for the destruction was that they could not fit inside a file cabinet, as if that was the only way evidence was ever stored.

The LAPD created three drafts of its "Final Report," each more redacted than the one before. Perhaps realizing that any information helped the conspiracy angle more than the "lone nut" one, the LAPD, in the end, decided not to release its report or files *ever*.

History, however, had other plans.

REINVESTIGATIONS

"Eventually, reluctantly, against all my instincts
and wishes, I arrived at the melancholy thought that
people who have nothing to hide do not lie, cheat, and
smear to hide it."

WHEN PRESIDENT JOHN F. KENNEDY, MALCOLM X, MARTIN LUTHER King, Jr. and Senator Robert Kennedy were assassinated within a five-year period, the antiwar left in American was essentially beheaded. While some placated themselves with the belief that some or all of these were killed by lone nuts, others began to suspect a coup had transpired in America. All four had spoken out vigorously against the Vietnam War and had promoted the notion that nations were entitled to self-determination. In the years since, presidents have largely supported the neoconservative and neoliberal views that nations should be, essentially, subservient states to America, a view each of these leaders had opposed.

These assassinations threatened America's status as a democracy. As Representative Allard Lowenstein wrote in later years,

> When a series of such events changes the direction of the nation
> and occurs under suspicious circumstances, institutions seem com-
> promised or corrupted and democratic process itself undermined. It
> is natural that many people will then wonder if they know the full
> story of these events, and that there will be a national nervousness
> that more may occur.[264]

---

264   Unpublished manuscript by Allard Lowenstein, provided to the author by Paul Schrade.

Not surprisingly then, a Pew Research Center report that has tracked the public's faith in government for decades shows a deep downward spike that began with the release of the Warren Report at the end of 1964. The Warren Commissioners did nothing to inspire confidence in their report when they locked up their records until 2039, preventing independent review.[265] And despite more than 50 years of information and disinformation to the contrary,[266] a majority of Americans still believe that President John Kennedy was killed by a conspiracy. Far fewer, however, know anything of substance about the assassination of President Kennedy's brother.

After Senator Kennedy's assassination, protests against the government's growing involvement in the Vietnam War became more frequent and more virulent. Antiwar activists were arrested at a Democratic Convention that had been robbed of its likely standard-bearer. Instead of the torch being passed to a new generation, the delegates returned the torch to the previous one with the nomination of President Lyndon Johnson's Vice President, Hubert Humphrey.

In 1969, the last brother who could possibly have reclaimed that torch, Ted Kennedy, became embroiled in an incident on Chappaquiddick Island that resulted in the death of a young campaign worker named Mary Jo Kopechne.[267] The scandal put a bullet in the hopes of many for another Kennedy presidency.

And with the death of two Kennedys and the neutralization of a third, the Vietnam War kicked into high gear. Protestors, failing to stop the war's escalation, in some cases turned to drugs, following Timothy Leary's advice to "tune in, turn on, drop out." After reports surfaced of the now infamous My Lai massacre, in

---

265   Fortunately, the Freedom of Information Act intervened, moving the deadline up several years. And after Oliver Stone's film *JFK* caused a public outcry as the facts screamed out for more serious investigation, a government body was created called the Assassination Records Review Board (ARRB) which sought to release many of the documents well in advance of that original deadline. Many more records were released in 2017. But the CIA continues to withhold records researchers such as former *Washington Post* reporter Jefferson Morley and former intelligence analyst John Newman deem important to the historical record.

266   See Lance deHaven-Smith, *Conspiracy Theory in America* (University of Texas Press, 2013) for coverage of the propaganda war advocating the lone nut position in the JFK assassination and the CIA's subsequent efforts to turn the phrase "conspiracy theory" into a pejorative worthy only of ridicule. See also Jerry Policoff's excellent essay, co-written with Robert Hennelly, "JFK: How the Media Assassinated the Real Story," www. assassinationresearch.com/v1n2/mediaassassination.html.

267   John Dean has never fully explained his comment captured on the Watergate tapes on March 13, 1973, about the 1969 Chappaquiddick incident, where he said "if Kennedy knew the bear trap he was walking into ...." Questioned years later, Dean said only this was related to "Tony U," the nickname of Tony Ulasewicz, a former New York Police Detective who had worked in the NYPD's Bureau of Special Services and Investigations (BOSSI, the intelligence branch). Tony U had been sent to Chappaquiddick ostensibly to investigate what had happened, but allegations were made that he was spotted on the island before news of the accident had been made public. Had Tony U helped set up the accident? Was that why Dean seemed slightly concerned on the tape that there was a financial link to Chappaquiddick in relation to Tony U's employment? The Watergate investigators do not appear to have pursued this information. E. Howard Hunt, who had aided the Watergate burglars, was also on the island after the incident as well, although as with Tony U, some suspected he had been on the island in advance.

which American soldiers brutally massacred the majority of innocent civilians in a Vietnamese hamlet, one very prominent antiwar protestor, John Lennon, the wildly popular songwriter and singer with the rock group The Beatles, refused an award from the British government in protest of its support for the U.S.' war in Vietnam.

A decade later, Lennon would be killed by a gunman. The strange background and behavior of the man arrested, Mark David Chapman, sparked theories that he had been hypnotically manipulated in some way by the CIA. In an eerie similarity to the Sirhan case, Chapman had been standing to Lennon's right, but all the wounds came from Lennon's left, suggesting someone else had fired the shots that killed Lennon. Policemen used the word "programmed" in reference to Chapman's apparent mental state. After the killing, instead of running off, he waited patiently to be caught. Chapman claimed he did it for publicity, but he threw away his best chance at publicity when he accepted a plea bargain.[268]

On May 4, 1970, four students protesting the Vietnam War were killed by the Ohio National Guard on the campus of Kent State University, and nine others were wounded in the fusillade. To some commentators, the country seemed on the verge of a new civil war as the decade started.

In the same year as the Kent State shootings, the first two major books on the Robert Kennedy assassination were published. Each, in very different ways, provided evidence of conspiracy and cover-up. One was *R.F.K. Must Die*, by Robert Blair Kaiser, the man who had traded part of his book advance for a seat on the defense team before and during Sirhan's trial. While Kaiser refused to concede that anyone other than Sirhan had been firing (despite having notified Grant Cooper about the fact that Sirhan had been a few feet in front of Kennedy while Kennedy had been shot from a distance of one inch, behind the right ear), Kaiser did believe that someone had hypnotically programmed Sirhan to do the shooting for reasons that will be clear in a later chapter. But ironically it was the book by LAPD Chief of Detectives Robert Houghton and co-author Theodore Taylor, *Special Unit Senator*, that did more damage to the LAPD's version of events.

---

268   Tony Rennell, "Was John Lennon's murderer Mark Chapman a CIA hitman? Thirty years on, there's an extraordinary new theory," Daily Mail.com, www.dailymail.co.uk/news/article-1335479/Was-John-Lennons-murderer-Mark-Chapman-CIA-hitman-Thirty-years-theres-extraordinary-new-theory.html. The article reviews the book *John Lennon—Life, Times and Assassination*, by Phil Strongman from The Bluecoat Press. Contrary to the article's headline, Strongman's theory was hardly new. Fenton Bresler had promoted the same theory 11 years earlier in his book "Who Killed John Lennon," published by St. Martin's Press. The scope of this book does not allow a serious discussion of the Lennon case, but there are substantial issues that are not adequately addressed by the official story.

Houghton's approach in *Special Unit Senator* was to raise evidence that suggested a conspiracy solely for the purpose of rebutting it. For example, the girl in the polka dot dress was mentioned but quickly explained away as having been Valerie Schulte, even though Schulte could not have been the girl. Schulte had a cast on her leg and therefore couldn't have been seen running down the back steps by Sandra Serrano. She had worn a green dress with yellow lemons on it and therefore could not have been the girl in a white dress with dark polka dots. And where both DiPierro and Serrano had described the girl in the polka dot dress as a dark brunette, Schulte was a light blonde. None of this mattered to Houghton, though, as most of the public did not know these details and were easily fooled. Evidence of conspiracy that could not be so easily waved away, such as the presence of four bullet holes in the pantry door jambs, was simply omitted from Houghton's presentation.

Houghton's book presented another problem for the LAPD as well. While the LAPD refused to release their files to the public, Houghton had already shared the *Special Unit Senator* files with one particular member of the public: his co-author Theodore Taylor.

Taylor told Melanson he was also shocked by *what* was shared with him. Taylor told Melanson, "I had access to some papers that I shouldn't have had access to." When Melanson asked what he meant, Taylor explained:

> They were FBI ... Central Intelligence. [Houghton] said, "For Chrissakes, you know, you're looking at 'em and I'll give 'em to you for 48 hours and then you get 'em back up here [Parker Center] and don't copy anything down from 'em. ... He just turned over everything he had.[269]

Allowing Taylor, a civilian, to see and profit from the LAPD's confidential files eventually undermined the LAPD's claim that the files must be kept secret.

Ironically, it was Houghton's attempt to close the case that provided a tiny piece of evidence that cracked the case wide open, because it launched Bill Harper, the respected Pasadena criminalist who tried to warn Cooper not to trust Wolfer, into the case.

Harper, who was then 69 years old and had testified in more than three hundred cases, had a general interest in the case from a historical perspective. But it was a note in Houghton's book about a 12mm fragment recovered during Kennedy's autopsy that specifically piqued his interest:

---

269   Philip Melanson, *The Robert F. Kennedy Assassination* (New York: S.P.I. Books, 1991), p. 80.

I had some vague recollection at that time that Senator Kennedy had been shot with a twenty-two. Twelve millimeters is quite a lot larger than a [.22's gun barrel]. So this sort of fascinated me ...."[270]

The X-ray section of the autopsy report describes this fragment as follows:

The largest metallic fragment is situated in the petrous ridge and at about the arcuate eminence. This measures 12 mm in transverse dimension, 7 mm in vertical dimension, and approximately 12 mm in anteroposterior dimension.

In other words, this fragment measured 12x7x12 mm. Twelve millimeters is roughly .47 inches, suggesting a .47 caliber gun, not a .22 like Sirhan's, had fired a bullet into Kennedy's brain. A .22 gun has a barrel about 5.6 millimeters in diameter. How then could such a large piece fit through it?

This information, coupled with Harper's knowledge of how untrustworthy Wolfer was, caused Harper in 1970 to take a special camera capable of photographing the bullets in microscopic detail to the Los Angeles County Clerk's office. Harper was allowed to examine and photograph the bullets because Sirhan's attorney at that time gave him permission, even though Harper was not acting on behalf of Sirhan's defense team but on behalf of his own curiosity.

Harper found the "fragment," according to a report by Dave Smith (*Los Angeles Times*, August 16, 1971), was actually a "flattened .22 bullet."[271] If that were true, however, that may well have been a *ninth* bullet—one more than Sirhan's gun could hold. One bullet had already exploded into at least 43 fragments in Kennedy's head. If this had been only a bullet *fragment*, Harper had already stated that was too large to have come from a .22 caliber gun. So it probably *was* a flattened bullet.

Recall how Cooper appeared to have understood the significance of this at the trial, and how Fitts had to lead Wolfer into calling this not a bullet, as Wolfer initially had, but "fragment bullets" And why did Fitts say "fragment bullets" and not "bullet fragments"? Perhaps because there really had been bullets plural, not just fragments, in Kennedy's head, and Fitts knew it, causing his Freudian slip.

As strange as that charge may seem, there is compelling evidence that two bullets entered Kennedy's head. The autopsy report indicates that there were *two bullet tracks* in Robert Kennedy's head diverging from one entry point:

---

270   Statement of William Harper, taken in the Los Angeles County D.A.'s office, on June 10, 1971.

271   Dave Smith, "Sirhan Case—Was there a 2nd Gunman?" *Los Angeles Times*, August 16, 1971.

> There are two bullet tracks. One extends slightly anterior to the vertical dimension (15 degrees). The second extends 30 degrees posterior to the vertical dimension, so that the two tracks diverge by 45 degrees.
>
> In the frontal projection, both tracks extend superiorly toward the vertex at an angle of 30 degrees to the horizontal.[272]

All the bullets or fragments that were removed from Kennedy's head were removed during surgery, while Kennedy was still alive, so the autopsy report did not comment on what was removed, but only what remained: two tracks in the head that diverged by 45 degrees.

Whatever was initially removed from Kennedy's head was originally entered into the LAPD evidence log as items 24 and 25. Yet on the evidence log page, these items appear after item 23 as items 26 and 27. Entries 13–23 on this page were entered by Officer J.A. Roach. Entries 26 and 27, however, were entered by Sergeant Dudley Varney, per a note on the back of this page. Two other items not related to the bullets were logged on a separate sheet as items 24 and 25. See Figure 2 below.

Figure 2: A portion of the LAPD evidence log showing items entered out of sequence by a different person on the same sheet

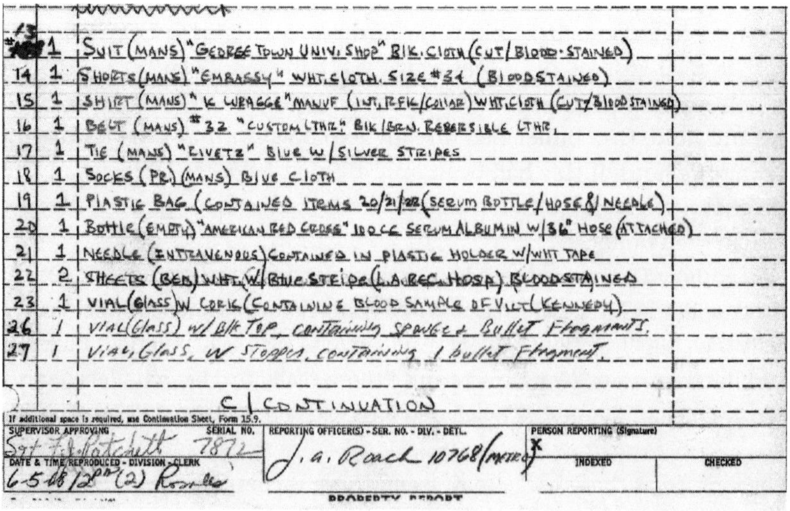

13	1	SUIT (MANS) "GEORGE TOWN UNIV. SHOP" BLK. CLOTH (CUT/BLOOD-STAINED)
14	1	SHORTS (MANS) "EMBASSY" WHT. CLOTH. SIZE #34 (BLOODSTAINED)
15	1	SHIRT (MANS) "K WRAGGE" MANUF (INT. RFK/COLLAR) WHT. CLOTH (CUT/BLOOD STAINED)
16	1	BELT (MANS) #32 "CUSTOM LTHR" BLK/BRN. REVERSIBLE LTHR.
17	1	TIE (MANS) "CIVETZ" BLUE W/SILVER STRIPES
18	1	SOCKS (PR.) (MANS) BLUE CLOTH
19	1	PLASTIC BAG (CONTAINED ITEMS 20/21/22 (SERUM BOTTLE/HOSE & NEEDLE)
20	1	BOTTLE (EMPTY) "AMERICAN RED CROSS" 100 CC SERUM ALBUMIN W/36" HOSE (ATTACHED)
21	1	NEEDLE (INTRAVENOUS) CONTAINED IN PLASTIC HOLDER W/WHT TAPE
22	2	SHEETS (BED) WHT. W/BLUE STRIPE (L.A. REC. HOSP.) BLOODSTAINED
23	1	VIAL (GLASS) W CORK (CONTAINING BLOOD SAMPLE OF VICT (KENNEDY)
26	1	VIAL (GLASS) w/Blk Top, containing sponge & Bullet Fragments.
27	1	Vial, Glass, w Stopper, containing 1 bullet Fragment.

C | CONTINUATION

If additional space is required, use Continuation Sheet, Form 15.9.

SUPERVISOR APPROVING	SERIAL NO.	REPORTING OFFICER(S) - SER. NO. - DIV. - DETL.	PERSON REPORTING (Signature)	
Sgt F.J. Patchett	7872	J. A. Roach 10768 (METRO)	X	
DATE & TIME REPRODUCED - DIVISION - CLERK			INDEXED	CHECKED
6-5-68 / 12 PM (2) [illegible]				

PROPERTY REPORT

Source: Scan of the LAPD evidence log page from the California State Archives

272 See Rose "Lynn" Mangan's self-published *Sirhan Evidence Report*, www.sirhansresearcher.com, for a copy of the relevant autopsy page (p. 17 of the full autopsy report on p. 311 in Mangan's downloadable PDF—marked page 305 by Mangan).

Due to the odd change of writing in a few places in the evidence log, I asked an archivist at the California State Archives to inspect the original document to tell me whether the pages were originals or copies, whether pen or pencil had been used, and if some sort of substance had whited out the initial entries. She sent me clear scans of the requested pages and wrote she believed this sheet was not a copy, that there was no white-out of any kind, and that the writing appeared to have been done in pencil, "although this is inconclusive." That would make sense, because in the photograph of the original document sent to me (Figure 1), you can see the faint outline of what looks be a "24" behind entry 26, as if someone had started to erase it but then just written over it instead. And despite the date on the log being June 5, note that the *first* number in the log appears to have originally been "138," but was changed to "13," indicating this page was either written out of order or possibly *remade* at some later date, either of which would be a violation of the chain of evidence.

There's another problem here. Given that the item numbers of #24 and #25 had been issued by the LAPD Property division and were already written onto the glass vials containing the fragments and the one acknowledged head bullet, why were *those* item numbers changed in the log? Why weren't the items eventually logged as 24 and 25 renumbered instead? Those were on a page by themselves and could more easily have been renumbered. Could there be something in the original items 24 and 25 that necessitated a little obfuscation of that evidence? Bullet fragments needed no obfuscation, suggesting something else may have been originally logged.

And why were two vials used for the bullet fragments instead of one? In all other cases, the fragments from others, such as Paul Schrade, had been entered as a single evidence item, not as two evidence items. Why were two containers used for the fragments of one tiny .22 bullet? Perhaps because originally each had contained a bullet?

Amazing, Wolfer's log supports the hypothesis that two bullets, not one, were found initially. In two successive places in his log, Wolfer wrote of the "bullets" plural, not "bullet fragments," from Kennedy's head. Wolfer made clear distinctions between bullets and fragments elsewhere in his records. And the bullet recovered from Kennedy's neck is not confused with these, as Wolfer made clear distinctions between the bullet from the neck and the "bullets" from the head. Consider, then, these entries excerpted from Wolfer's log, and note how the "bullets" became a "bullet" after Wolfer ran ballistics tests and cleaned the "fatal bullets":

June 13, 1968 - Thursday

    9:30 A.M.   —   Received Items #24 and #25, bullets from Kennedy's head (Lodola, Patchett and MacArthur)

    12:30 P.M.   —   Coroner's office

June 14, 1968 - Friday

    8:00 A.M.   —   Ballistics tests and clean fatal bullets.

    1:00 P.M.   —   Photos taken in color of Kennedy's head bullet by Watson.

June 17, 1968 – Monday

    8:00 A.M.   —   Bullet comparison Kennedy's head.

    12:00 A.M.   —   Cartridge study - CCI Kennedy's bullet weight.

Making these entries even more peculiar was the fact that items 24 and 25 had been removed from Kennedy's head *before* Kennedy died, and on June 5. The neck bullet was not deemed fatal, and given its precarious location in the spine at the back of his neck, was left in place until Kennedy's death and not removed until the autopsy on June 6. So why did it take until *June 13* for the "bullets from Kennedy's head" to reach Wolfer? Where did they go in the interim?

An entry in the evidence log after item 37 in the evidence log appears to answer that question:

> Items 26-34 inclusive were released to F.B.I. Special Agent E. Rhoad
> Richards Jr. Credential #4560 on 6-5-68 3:00pm by Sgt. W. E. Brandt # 10004.

Apparently the two "bullets" went to the FBI before being returned to the detectives at Rampart, who then took the "fatal bullets" to Wolfer. Someone must have realized that *two* bullets was *one bullet too many* for Sirhan to have fired, which would explain why the flattened bullet became a "fragment" in the record and the second "bullet" was replaced with fragments.

Similarly, Wolfer seemed to have forgotten to lie about this at the trial, referring to the 12mm "fragment" as a "bullet," a point on which Fitts had to correct Wolfer by suggesting Wolfer must have meant "fragment bullets."

This would also explain why Cooper had tried so hard to keep the large blow-up of this exhibit from the jury. He claimed it would be prejudicial, but he may also have believed that someone on the jury might have recognized that as a flattened bullet rather than a fragment and wondered about where the other fragments then came from. A bullet doesn't both shatter and flatten. If it shatters, then fragments of the bullets flatten, not the original bullet. If one of the "fragments" was a flattened bullet, the other fragments must have come from a second bullet in the head.

Earlier in this book I mentioned that there could be an innocent explanation for some of the cover-up. But in this instance, it seems clear Wolfer, at least, was aware that two "bullets" was one bullet too many than could be accounted for by Sirhan's gun, because after receiving the "bullets" from "Lodola, Patchett and MacArthur," at 9:30 A.M., Wolfer's next entry in his log was a visit to the coroner's office at 12:30 P.M. He had already finished his muzzle distance tests with Noguchi two days earlier. Why did he need another trip? Was he curious whether Noguchi had figured out that two bullets must have entered the brain?

Satisfied perhaps that Noguchi hadn't, Wolfer then ran ballistics tests, perhaps to determine which bullet to keep and which to lose, after which the "bullets" become a single "bullet" that was then photographed in color. Then Wolfer made a "bullet comparison," meaning a comparison under a microscope between the Kennedy head bullet and a test bullet. If there had been a match, you can be certain that photo would have been taken and used at the trial. That no such photo now exists strongly suggests Wolfer *couldn't* match the bullet—perhaps *either* bullet—to Sirhan's gun.

Next, Wolfer did something related to the bullet's weight. The sum total weight of fragments and the flattened bullet or bullet fragment could not be allowed to exceed the total weight of a single bullet. Was Wolfer here tying up loose ends? The 44 fragments the autopsy report noted are not all in evidence. Many of them were not retrieved from the brain. But might Wolfer have been concerned that the retrieved fragments alone collectively might have exceeded the weight of a single bullet?

Based on the totality of the evidence, it appears two bullets, not one, entered Kennedy's brain from the same near-contact entry point. Bang-bang. That would explain everything that is—and isn't—in Wolfer's records. That would explain why the evidence was stored in two glass vials rather than one. That would explain why the log entries were obfuscated. That would also explain why the evidence went to the FBI. The FBI could hardly have been concerned about bullet fragments. But they would have been very interested in bullets, plural, removed from Kennedy's head. But they would have kept this secret, for reasons that will be clear by the end of this book.

In a footnote to this obfuscation, the items eventually booked as 24 and 25 are listed as photographs and negatives provided to the LAPD by George Ross Clayton. But when Scott Enyart, who, as a teenager, had taken pictures in the pantry during the shooting, took the LAPD to court years later to recover his photos, the LAPD said they had found that Clayton's photos were really Enyart's photos, and that one side of the tag had listed Clayton and the other side had listed Enyart.

Although this sounds like a convenient way to have "found" Enyart's photos, there may be some truth to this. In a report by Officer C. Craig, he claimed George Clayton offered his photos to the LAPD and was then transported with the other witnesses to the Rampart Station to be interviewed. But Clayton wasn't interviewed by the LAPD until October of that year. Enyart was interviewed immediately after the assassination, so maybe the tag really did have both names on it at some point. Likely Craig had met both and had mistakenly merged their two stories into one in his mind, not unlike what witnesses may have done after encountering evidence of multiple shooters, as you will see in the next couple of chapters.[273]

These photos were purportedly stolen from a courier's car at a gas stop on the way between the California State Archives in Sacramento to the courthouse where Enyart's case was in session in Los Angeles. Given that nothing else from the car was stolen, we have to ask who wanted to keep Enyart from receiving these photos, and what the photos may have shown that was worth pilfering in an elaborate operation.[274]

It wouldn't be the first time evidence was sabotaged. Less than two months after the assassination, the LAPD took the extraordinary step of burning some *2,400 photos* from the case in Los Angeles County General's medical-waste incinerator.[275] Why destroy thousands of photos in an incinerator if there was nothing to hide? The LAPD kept *hundreds* of innocuous crowd scene photos that showed no girl in a polka dot dress and no suspicious activities or individuals. Why were *those* photos preserved? Perhaps because those photos had nothing in them that warranted their destruction?

The fragment or flattened bullet that initially launched Harper on his private investigation into the Robert Kennedy assassination soon became the least of the anomalies Harper found in the ballistics evidence.

Harper was the first to note that the test bullets entered into evidence at the trial, which Wolfer swore had come from the gun that shot Kennedy, had been placed in an envelope that bore a *wholly different gun number: H18602.* The Sirhan gun was H53725. Harper realized that if Wolfer's testimony at the trial had been accurate, if the bullets in that envelope truly had matched the gun used in the pantry "and no other," *then the shots that killed Kennedy came from a gun that had no connection to Sirhan whatsoever.*

The gun H18602 had been in the possession of the LAPD at the time of the shooting. Either Wolfer had sworn, accurately, that a gun from the LAPD's lockers

273   LAPD interview of Officer C.C. Craig, September 24, 1968.

274   Court of Appeal, Second District, Division 3, California, *Jamie Scott ENYART, Plaintiff and Respondent, v. CITY OF LOS ANGELES et al., Defendants and Appellants,* No. B108348, Decided: November 29, 1999, caselaw.findlaw.com/ca-court-of-appeal/1223691.html.

275   AP, "Robert Kennedy Assassination Photos Burned," *The New York Times*, April 21, 1988, www.nytimes.com/1988/04/21/us/robert-kennedy-assassination-photos-burned.html.

killed Kennedy, or Wolfer had committed perjury on the stand by connecting bullets from a different gun to Sirhan, or—and this is Wolfer's explanation—he had sealed and dated the envelope but neglected to add the gun number until weeks later, when he claimed he asked someone for the number of the Sirhan gun and was given the wrong gun number.

But Wolfer's explanation makes little sense, as there are literally hundreds of SUS records with the correct gun number (H53725) and none, save this gun envelope and a gun destruction receipt, with the incorrect number (H18602) on it. It's not only possible but vastly more plausible that the reason the number H18602 is on that envelope is because that was, in fact, the actual gun number of the gun from which those "test" bullets were fired.

Harper found numerous other problems with Wolfer's evidence. Harper closely examined the evidence envelope in which Noguchi had placed the bullet from Kennedy's neck. On the envelope, Noguchi had indicated that the bullet within had five grooves. But when Harper examined the neck bullet in evidence, he found six grooves. Had the bullets been switched? Harper was hesitant to draw such a conclusion without more investigation, but he felt the issue deserved an explanation "because bullets don't grow grooves."[276] (At a hearing in 1974, Noguchi claimed he had examined the bullet too hastily, and when he looked at what he believed to be the same bullet years later, he, too, found six grooves on it. It's not clear, however, how closely Noguchi examined the bullet presented in court. He said he saw something reasonably similar to his markings on the bullet.)

Harper also found "no individual characteristics establishing that Exhibit 47 [the Kennedy neck bullet] and Exhibit 54 [the Goldstein bullet] had been fired from the same gun." Harper also noted there was an issue with the rifling angle.

> In fact, my examinations disclosed that bullet Exhibit 47 had a rifling angle [of] approximately 23 minutes (14%) greater than the rifling angle of bullet Exhibit 54. It is, therefore, my opinion that bullets 47 and 54 could not have been fired from the same gun.

Years later, a panel of experts tried to dismiss Harper's findings by claiming he had been looking at imperfect two-dimensional photographs of the bullets. But Harper examined the bullets *by hand, in person, about "twelve or fourteen times, perhaps"*[277] *over a seven-month period.*

On December 28, 1970, Harper completed and signed a notarized affidavit of his findings in the case, which he summarized this way:

---

276   William Harper's testimony at the Baxter Ward hearing in 1974, p. 12.
277   *Ibid.*, p. 3.

(1) Two .22 caliber guns were involved in the assassination.

(2) Senator Kennedy was killed by one of the shots fired from FIRING POSITION B [a position behind Kennedy], fired by a second gunman.

(3) The five surviving victims were wounded by Sirhan shooting from FIRING POSITION A [in front of Kennedy].

(4) It is extremely unlikely that any of the bullets fired by the Sirhan gun ever struck the body of Senator Kennedy.

Harper was a conservative individual, not some wild-eyed conspiracy theorist, hence the cautious wording. He had the requisite background to accurately examine the evidence. For that reason, his December 28, 1970, affidavit caused a firestorm of concern that was not easily answerable.

But Harper appeared to have gotten one thing wrong: there's literally no physical evidence that proves Sirhan fired *any* of the bullets. Wolfer had left behind *not one scintilla of scientific evidence* to prove he had successfully matched *any* of the victim bullets to Sirhan's gun or to any test bullets fired from Sirhan's gun. He kept no photos of these comparisons, despite having a device designed for that purpose in his lab, and the X-rays he *had* taken of the doorframes and ceiling tiles were destroyed. There was literally *no evidence* that would allow anyone to independently verify Wolfer's claims of a match between Sirhan's gun and any of the victim bullets or his assertion that eight and only eight bullets had been fired in the pantry. And a key piece of evidence that did exist, the evidence envelope for the test bullets, had the wrong gun number on it. Someone had clearly fired from Sirhan's vicinity, a point we'll return to in later chapters.

At this point, the LAPD faced a difficult choice. They could either admit there was a conspiracy that they had not solved, and admit that one of their own had fudged the evidence to implicate Sirhan alone, or they could close ranks and double down on their previous statements.

Remember, Wolfer's credibility issues didn't impact solely the Kennedy case. As we saw in a previous chapter, Wolfer was all but accused of perjury in the murder trial of former Los Angeles D.A. Jack Kirschke. One could argue the LAPD closed ranks behind Wolfer every time he was accused of being less than honest in *any* case, *because to admit to fraud in any of them could have meant reopening all of them.*

Given the choice between spending millions to right numerous wrongs, and possibly sending some of their own to jail, or doubling down on the lies, what the LAPD did next was predictable. In the spring of 1971, the LAPD promoted DeWayne Wolfer to the head of its crime lab.

Upon learning of Wolfer's promotion, a local Los Angeles lawyer named Barbara Blehr said what the California Supreme Court would stop just short of saying: that Wolfer had committed perjury. Blehr collected affidavits from experts and attached them to a four-page letter she sent to the Los Angeles Civil Service Commission in an effort to block Wolfer's nomination. She accused Wolfer of having violated, in different cases, six basic precepts of firearms identification, such as these:

> The positive identification of an evidence bullet as having been fired from a particular gun and no other must be based on a comparison of the evidence bullet with a test bullet recovered from the same evidence gun and no other. ...
>
> A single land of the rifling of a firearm can produce only one land impression on a fired bullet.

Blehr wrote that in the Kirschke case, Wolfer had matched "a single land impression on the test bullet with TWO [sic] different land impressions 120 degrees apart on the fatal bullet. This amounts to saying that a single blade of a plow cuts TWO furrows in the ground over which it moves—an obvious impossibility .... His testimony combined with his very esoteric photographic manipulations label his work in this instance nothing but perjury," adding, "Exhibits substantiating these statements are in my possession."

Blehr also referenced the Sirhan case (SC No. A233421) to point out how Wolfer had violated four precepts there, pointing out, as Harper had noted, that the bullet envelope suggested strongly that the test bullets did not come from Sirhan's gun (H53725) but from a wholly separate gun (H18602). "The only possible conclusion," Blehr wrote, "is that two similar guns were being fired at the scene of the crime." And that conclusion, Blehr wrote, "leads unavoidably to the question: which of the two guns fired the fatal bullet?" In regards to the Sirhan case, Blehr commented:

> I find it hard to believe that a man of the professed expertise of Mr. Wolfer could violate four of the basic precepts of his profession in a single case by sheer accident. I am more inclined to believe that these violations were made in response to an overzealous desire to help the cause of the prosecution. The choice seems to be rank incompetence on the one hand or morbid motivation on the other.[278]

In a third case, Blehr accused Wolfer of making "physical alterations of certain inscriptions on three rifle cartridge cases," noting that in the trial testimony,

---

278   Blehr's letter was reprinted in full in the *Los Angeles Free Press*, June 11, 1971.

Wolfer had admitted to altering one of them but denied altering all three. She called this "scurrilous tampering" made in "a vain attempt to make the physical evidence support the prosecution's theory of the murder." In other words, Wolfer had provably altered evidence in a prior case, making it easier to believe he altered evidence in the Kennedy case as well.

Blehr's bold accusations made headlines in Los Angeles. Wolfer responded by filing a libel suit against Blehr for two million dollars. Wolfer must have known that the LAPD and County essentially had little choice but to back him. Indeed, LAPD Chief Edward M. Davis summarily dismissed the charges against Wolfer as nonsense, saying Blehr's charges were simply a "vendetta" and that Wolfer was, in his estimation, "the top expert in the country." What else *would* an LAPD chief say about accusations that not only challenged the official verdict in the Robert Kennedy assassination but could have exposed the LAPD to hundreds of lawsuits from people who might credibly claim they had been wrongfully convicted by Wolfer? Of course he defended the LAPD. But his statement deserves little credibility for that reason, a point journalists should have noted in their reporting.

Ironically, Wolfer's suit ended up doing more damage to him than anything Blehr had charged him with. In the sworn statements he gave for the suit, Wolfer revealed interesting and important information about the bullets in the case. For example, when Wolfer was interviewed by the Board of Inquiry that convened to address Blehr's concerns, he said he did not have gun H18602 until June 10, 1968.[279] Wolfer's log of activities, however, indicated he had conducted a gun test on June 8, when Sirhan's gun had already gone to the Grand Jury.[280] So either Wolfer misstated (or lied about) the date he first had the gun, or he had used a "third" gun on June 8 at California State College at Long Beach for the chronograph tests he performed (speed, rapidity, distance). Wolfer mentioned the "Long Beach State" tests, sans the date, during his deposition in the Blehr case:

> Q: How many guns did you use, other than H18602, and the Sirhan gun 53725, in your testing for sound, muzzle distance, whatever?
> A: I believe this was the only gun that we used.
> Q: What test exactly, did you use?
> A: For the sound test—I am sorry, but that is for the sound test and the muzzle distance test. Those are the only two tests.
> Q: Those were the only two tests that you ran?
> A: No, I am sorry. I did run a test down at Long Beach State on the cc. Those were the three tests that I recall here today.

---

279   Lynn Mangan, Sirhan Evidence Report, transcript from the Board of Inquiry, June 16, 1971.

280   Log of DeWayne Wolfer, LAPD. The entry, which can be viewed at www.maryferrell.org/showDoc. html?docId=99847#relPageId=313&tab=page, reads: "Chronograph tests on mini-mag ammunition — 2" Iver Johnson — California State College at Long Beach."

> Q: And this gun, H18602, was used for all those tests?
>
> A: I believe it was, to the best of my recollection here today. I am not sure.

Recall that during the trial, Wolfer had said he had used a gun that was "within a very close serial number of this weapon" for the muzzle distance powder-burn-pattern tests he had conducted with Coroner Noguchi on June 11.[281] H18602 was *not* a "very close serial number" to H53725. And Wolfer's "I am not sure" leaves the door open to the use of a "third" gun, possibly the gun that was identified by Karl Uecker at the trial with the serial number H58725, a number which was a much closer serial number to the H53725 gun taken from Sirhan and provided by Rafer Johnson to the police after the shooting.

Either way, the fact that the wrong gun number was on an envelope dated days before the gun ostensibly entered the case showed the chain of evidence around the test bullets was, at best, untrustworthy and at worst, the result of sinister machinations.

Wolfer's libel suit against Blehr was ultimately ordered dismissed by conservative California Superior Court Judge David Eagleson, who stated that Blehr's letter was a privileged public record not subject to defamation laws. The ruling came one day before the case went to trial, a trial that would likely have further exposed Wolfer's mishandling of the evidence in the Robert Kennedy case.[282]

Wolfer's appointment also caused concern to Evelle Younger's friend Marshall Houts, who, like Younger himself, was a former FBI and OSS man. A lawyer and a teacher, Houts wrote and taught about the law and medicine. One of Houts' 44 books, *Where Death Delights*, became the inspiration for the popular TV series *Quincy*, starring Jack Klugman.

In a "personal and confidential" letter from Houts to Evelle Younger, who had recently left the D.A.'s office to become California's Attorney General, Houts expressed concerns about Wolfer:

> I have no personal interest in this matter, but do have a deep academic and professional concern over Wolfer's horrendous blunders in the past and those he will commit in the future if he continues on his present assignment. I am also concerned that you and the present District Attorney stand a strong chance of getting burned by Wolfer's misdirected hyperenthusiastic procedures and testimony.[283]

---

281   Although Noguchi did not mention working with Wolfer on these tests in his own book, Wolfer indicated in his log that he conducted these tests with Thomas Noguchi (which Wolfer misspelled "Noguchii").

282   "Dismissal of Suit Ordered," *Los Angeles Times*, December 5, 1973.

283   Letter from Marshall Houts to Evelle Younger, June 26, 1971, found in Harold Weisberg's archive in the "Blehr" folder.

Houts knew the experts cited in Blehr's filing and wrote they were "all men of great integrity and professional competence," adding that charges that their statements were made out of professional jealousy or that the men were out to "get" Wolfer were "totally absurd." Houts added:

> Wolfer suffers from a great inferiority complex for which he compensates by giving the police exactly what they need to obtain a conviction. He casts objectivity to the winds and violates every basic tenet of forensic science and proof by becoming a crusading advocate. This is rationalized as being entirely legitimate since the accused is guilty anyway which makes the social objective worthy of the means required to obtain it. … Unfortunately, there are many Wolfers in this brand of forensic science.[284]

Houts suggested to Younger that Wolfer be "encouraged" to retire, adding that "I know some lawyers who say they will accuse him of perjury and institute every law suit [sic] possible against every possible party defendant if he does receive permanent civil service status."[285]

Harper, Blehr and Houts weren't the only ones expressing concerns about the evidence. Ted Charach, a freelance journalist who had been at the Ambassador Hotel that night, was making a documentary about the case that contradicted the official version of events.

Charach in some ways epitomized the worst caricature of a "conspiracy theorist." He seemed to always be looking for a way to profit personally from the case. He had a rumpled appearance, with pink, pudgy fingers and small eyes that seemed perpetually half-closed. Before Charach tried to sell a film made in the pantry to the LAPD, he showed it to the journalist Fernando Faura. When Faura told Charach he saw nothing of value in the film, Charach said he knew that but hoped the police would buy it anyway.[286] Charach even offered to spy on Jim Garrison's investigation for the LAPD for money, but the LAPD rejected his offer.[287]

---

284   *Ibid.*

285   *Ibid.*

286   Conversation with Fernando Faura, December 19, 2015.

287   Memo from Sgt. Dudley Varney to Lt. Charles Higbie re Charach, August 2, 1968. The LAPD did have a strong interest in Garrison's case. One pantry witness, Richard Lubic, was encouraged to go on at length about what he had learned from a visit to Garrison in New Orleans. Garrison predicted that it would be found that Sirhan had fired "exploding" bullets, as those were rarely used by regular people but were used on John Kennedy and Martin Luther King. Garrison predicted the pattern would hold with Robert Kennedy, and he was correct. For this and many other reasons, Garrison felt the same group had taken out all three leaders. For more information on Jim Garrison's courageous struggle to bring the conspiracy in the JFK case to light, against impossible odds, see Jim DiEugenio, *Destiny Betrayed: JFK, Cuba, and the Garrison Case* (New York: Sheridan Square Press, 1992, first edition, as the second edition represents an extensive rewrite that is less about Garrison and more about other aspects of the case) and Garrison's own book *On the Trail of the Assassins* (New York: Sheridan Square Press, 1988). Oliver Stone's film

But whatever his motives, and despite his unsavory character, Charach did important investigative work in the days when most researchers remained focused on President John Kennedy's assassination and too few were looking into the death of his brother Robert. For example, Charach reinterviewed Karl Uecker, the man who had grabbed Sirhan first during the shooting. Uecker was adamant that Sirhan had not fired the shots that hit Kennedy:

> I was the closest to Senator Kennedy, besides Cesar behind me—Sirhan at no time was firing from behind Senator Robert Kennedy. No! No! Not an inch from Kennedy's head—I don't believe that it was Sirhan's gun firing from back to front in an upward direction. I think I would have seen it. I was the closest one.
>
> In order for Sirhan to get that close to Senator Kennedy from behind he would have had to pass me and he didn't pass me at that point. I had him very tight, pushed against the steam table while Senator Kennedy staggered back and Mr. Schrade dropped to the floor first. So this does not fit with what Mr. Fitts told the jury.[288]

Uecker also told Charach that while they were looking at Sirhan, "many witnesses missed the guard behind me pull up his weapon and drop to the floor. I did see a guard with a drawn gun and told them [sic] he must be crazy to brandish a weapon in the kitchen chaos."[289]

Uecker said that the police never pursued this line of inquiry with him. He also described how Assistant D.A. Buck Compton told him, during a filmed LAPD reenactment, that Uecker couldn't have reacted as fast as he claimed he did. This incensed Uecker, because he was there and knew what he had done. Uecker couldn't help noting that Compton had been appointed by Governor Ronald Reagan "to the Appellate Court, who will now have the judicial authority, we understand, to review the Sirhan case" then under appeal. Uecker said he was certain he had grabbed Sirhan after the second shot, not the fourth shot. He noted that Fitts, too, had been elevated to a position on the California Superior Court after essentially lying to the jury and claiming Uecker had grabbed Sirhan after the *fourth* shot. Fitts clearly understood that if Uecker had grabbed Sirhan after the second shot, then someone else had to have shot Kennedy at least twice, as Kennedy had provably been shot four times from near-contact range.

JFK is based largely on Garrison's account in the latter.

   At a conference on the RFK case at Duquesne University in 2008, Charach said from the stage that he had worked in intelligence. I went up to him later and asked him what intelligence service he had worked for. He looked at me and thought for a minute before saying, "I don't think I should say."

288   Varley Brogan, "Suppressed Evidence: Who Killed Bobby?" *Los Angeles Free Press*, July 3, 1970.
289   *Ibid.*

In addition to Uecker, Charach found a second witness who had seen Cesar with his gun drawn in the pantry at the time of the shooting. Donald L. Schulman, a runner for the Los Angeles television station and CBS affiliate KNXT, had been interviewed by the station's own Ruth Ashton Taylor right after the shooting. Schulman was the first witness to accurately note that Kennedy had been wounded three times. He claimed he saw the bullets hit Kennedy directly. In the first few hours, the story was that only two shots had hit Kennedy, not three. Schulman told the reporter he had seen a guard pull his gun and fire, and that Kennedy had been hit three times.

Charach put Schulman's statements and an interview he had conducted of Cesar, where Cesar revealed himself to be a right-winger who did not like the Kennedys, together with the evidence that Kennedy's shooter had to be standing no further than Kennedy's right side, right where Cesar was standing—the perfect spot from which to fire two shots under his arm—and essentially accused Cesar of being the true assassin of Robert Kennedy.

When Charach made this accusation public in his documentary, Kaiser contacted Cesar and asked him why he didn't sue Charach. Cesar told Kaiser that Charach had no money and it would cost more to sue than he would get in return. But was that his only reason? Suing also exposes one to "discovery," a legal process by which the opposing party can ask wide-ranging questions. And Cesar had provably lied about an important point, claiming he had sold a gun he owned at the time of the assassination months *before* the assassination, when in fact the receipt of the sale showed he had sold it well *after* the assassination. Cesar had also indicated to the buyer there might be an issue with the gun. Cesar also had something else significant to hide, but that's getting ahead of the story.

In his taped 1971 interview, Schulman said he had been interviewed two days or so after the shooting by someone from either the police or FBI. Schulman said he told the police when he had first been interviewed that he had seen other guns, plural, but the policeman taking his statement told him he must have been mistaken, as other witnesses said no one said anything about other weapons, and that Kennedy could only have been shot twice.[290]

In the LAPD summary of Schulman's August, 1968, interview, Sergeant Paul O'Steen wrote that Schulman had been "forced by crowds following Kennedy to go through double doors and was just outside the serving kitchen when he heard noise like firecrackers. Saw woman bleeding and Kennedy on floor. Did not see actual shooting or susp. due to crowd. Saw no woman in polka dot dress.

---

290   Taped interview of Donald Schulman, July 23, 1971, from the California State Archives.

Did not take photos. Thinks he saw three gunshot wounds when he looked at Senator."[291]

O'Steen's summary is misleading on some points and incorrect on others, begging the question of whether that was deliberate. The pantry is "outside" the serving kitchen, which was to the north of the pantry area, but O'Steen makes it sound like Schulman was outside the *pantry*, when he was not.[292] And Schulman's statements made immediately after the shooting and on tape ever since indicate clearly he was right behind and to the right of Kennedy when the shooting began. He saw a man step out and fire a gun, he saw Kennedy hit three times, and he saw a guard fire a gun. Schulman was fuzzy on the sequence. In an interview with the D.A.'s office, Schulman stated he never meant to say that Cesar had shot Kennedy. Schulman explained that he meant his comments as two separate statements, that he saw Cesar pull his gun and fire, and he saw Kennedy hit three times, but that he could never say for certain that Kennedy was hit by the *guard's* gun.[293] But Schulman never said the guard did *not* hit Kennedy, either. He just wasn't *sure* who hit Kennedy, only that multiple guns had been fired.

When Schulman was asked by his interviewer in 1971 if he was "absolutely certain" he had seen the guard fire, Schulman responded, "I'm pretty sure in my mind, yes."[294] He was equally adamant that at the moment of the shooting he had seen at least three different guns drawn in the pantry.[295] He continued to reiterate that point when interviewed a last time in 1975.

If Schulman was correct—and having listened to him on tape, I'm convinced he is telling the truth as he experienced it—where did Cesar's shot go? No stray bullets were found in the pantry, and no one was wounded who was in front of Kennedy. The most logical explanation is that Cesar did, in fact, hit Kennedy. Sirhan was not shot (despite an early and mistaken report that the suspect had been shot in the leg) and no one else in front of Kennedy had been wounded.

In addition to Uecker and Schulman, one more person also reported seeing Cesar with his gun drawn: Richard Lubic. Lubic had told an interviewer he saw a guard in Cesar's position with his gun drawn and pointed at the floor after

---

291   LAPD interview summary of Don Schulman, August 9, 1968.

292   Predictably, the tape of O'Steen's interview is no longer in the record, as I confirmed with the California State Archives. This begs the question of how many other witnesses saw evidence of conspiracy that was simply omitted from the interview summaries, which, along with a few tapes, are all that remain from the LAPD's extensive investigation. Only a few witnesses' statements were transcribed in full. Most were summarized, making it impossible to know what was left out of the witnesses' original statements. (If anyone reading this was a witness to any evidence of conspiracy in the pantry, to a girl in a polka dot dress, or to someone other than Sirhan firing, please contact the California State Archives to see if your witness report is in the record.)

293   Taped interview of Donald Schulman, October 24, 1975, California State Archives.

294   Taped interview of Donald Schulman, July 23, 1971, California State Archives.

295   Schulman made this point in both his 1971 and 1975 taped interviews.

Robert Kennedy fell, which made Lubic upset. Why was the gun pointing toward the fallen Kennedy and not at the suspect? According to Lubic, members of SUS visited his house shortly after that interview and told him not to talk about what he had seen.[296] But Lubic's and Uecker's assertions about the guard with the gun drawn were whispers in a record that had not yet (in Lubic's case) or only barely (in Uecker's case) been made public, whereas Schulman's assertions were made on camera in Charach's publicly shown film, so Schulman was the one that needed discrediting.

Bob Kaiser, perhaps motivated by his own desire to be right about Sirhan being only one shooter, evidently took on this task. Kaiser claimed Schulman had never been in the pantry during the shooting. Kaiser pointed to a list of pantry witnesses the LAPD had compiled and noted Schulman wasn't on it.

But the LAPD's list was provably incomplete, by their own evidence. An obvious example is Queen Rutledge, who was photographed standing on top of a table in the pantry as the wounded Ira Goldstein was carried out. Rutledge, in a taped interview conducted less than three hours after the shooting, described the events in a way that matched all other pantry witness statements. She even saw Kennedy fall into the arms of Vince DiPierro, something that had not yet been made known by any other witness at that early point. But sloppy and inaccurate interview summaries led the LAPD to believe Rutledge was behind a cameraman who was still in the anteroom just outside the pantry when the shots started, so they left Rutledge off the list.[297]

Kaiser also used the statements of two CBS coworkers of Schulman from KNXT who told him Schulman hadn't been in the pantry during the shooting. He even repeated this in his 2008 edition of his book, despite the fact that in the tape of the 1975 interview of Schulman, the LAPD and the D.A.'s office *confirmed* Schulman's presence in the pantry during the shooting, assuring him they knew he was in the pantry. Schulman even had blood on his jacket from the shooting. Of course he was in the pantry.

Now, no one researcher knows *all* the evidence. There are hundreds of hours of tape and hundreds of thousands of pages to read. Everyone misses something. That's the most innocent explanation for Kaiser's assertion that Schulman was not in the pantry. It's not only possible but likely that Kaiser didn't know that evidence confirming Schulman's presence in the pantry existed. That said, CBS

---

296   David Talbot, *Brothers: The Hidden History of the Kennedy Years* (New York: Free Press, 2007), p. 374.

297   The taped interview by the LAPD of Queen Rutledge, June 5, 1968, available from the California State Archives, as well as the FBI interview report of the reporter she apparently talked to, Bob Funk, dated June 24, 1968, puts the lie to the LAPD's interview summary of a follow up interview of Queen E. Rutledge on August 15, 1968. The August LAPD interview report however does note that a picture existed of Rutledge on the table in the pantry. There does not appear to be any sinister motive for leaving her off the list. Rutledge saw nothing that indicated a conspiracy. Her omission appears to be the result of a simple error.

had one of the closest relationships with the CIA of any media organization during this period. According to Carl Bernstein in his landmark *Rolling Stone* article "The CIA and the Media" (October 20, 1977):

> CBS was unquestionably the CIA's most valuable broadcasting asset. CBS President William Paley and Allen Dulles enjoyed an easy working and social relationship. Over the years, the network provided cover for CIA employees, including at least one well-known foreign correspondent and several stringers; it supplied outtakes of newsfilm to the CIA; established a formal channel of communication between the Washington bureau chief and the Agency; gave the Agency access to the CBS newsfilm library; and allowed reports by CBS correspondents to the Washington and New York newsrooms to be routinely monitored by the CIA.

It's possible that someone in the CIA motivated a couple of CBS employees to feed Kaiser that line of baloney and he fell for it.

And that's not the only possible explanation for Kaiser's misinformation. When Kaiser was a correspondent for *Time* magazine in Rome, his bureau chief, William McHale, had been a CIA operative using his *Time* role as a cover. During a stint in Beirut, McHale had provided the CIA with a death list of people to be killed in the coup that set Saddam Hussein on his path to power.[298]

When I asked Kaiser about this a few years back, he expressed disbelief and told me that he didn't believe his chief had been with the CIA, saying *Time*'s management wouldn't have tolerated people on staff working with the CIA. Could Kaiser really not have known that the Time-Life empire of Henry Luce had been one of the closest CIA collaborators at the time, hiring stringers and staffers alike to do their bidding? According to Carl Bernstein, "By far the most valuable of these associations, according to CIA officials, have been with the *New York Times*, CBS and Time Inc." [299] Carl Bernstein elaborated on this point:

> For many years, Luce's personal emissary to the CIA was C.D. Jackson, a Time Inc., vice president who was publisher of *Life* magazine from 1960 until his death in 1964. While a *Time* executive, Jackson coauthored a CIA-sponsored study recommending the reorganization of the American intelligence services in the early 1950s. Jackson, whose

---

298   Said K. Aburish, *Saddam Hussein: The Politics of Revenge* (New York: Bloomsbury Publishing, 2000), pp. 58–59. McHale's brother, Don McHale, was a high-level CIA official, per Aburish. McHale was killed in the plane crash of Enrico Mattei, an Italian oil magnate who challenged the power of the "Seven Sisters" of the Standard Oil empire. Kaiser told me he had originally been scheduled to be on that flight, but that at the last moment he had been pulled from the assignment and the magazine sent McHale instead.

299   Carl Bernstein, "The CIA and the Media," *Rolling Stone*, October 20, 1977.

TimeLife service was interrupted by a one-year White House tour as an assistant to President Dwight Eisenhower, approved specific arrangements for providing CIA employees with TimeLife cover. Some of these arrangements were made with the knowledge of Luce's wife, Clare Boothe.[300]

Kaiser himself had originally been recruited into the Time-Life empire by Clare Boothe Luce.[301] After President John F. Kennedy had been assassinated, C.D. Jackson, then working for *Life* magazine, had purchased the famous Zapruder film which showed Kennedy's head exploding in a way that suggested a shot from the front, while Lee Harvey Oswald had been well behind Kennedy. Jackson and *Life*, after publishing frames from the film—out of order—kept the film hidden from the public for more than a decade. Indeed, it was only when Kaiser's good friend Robert Groden showed a copy of the Zapruder film to the public on the Geraldo Rivera show that the film first saw the light of day. Surely Groden would have clued Kaiser in to Jackson's CIA connections, which had been made public decades before my conversation with Kaiser on this point.

It would be easier to believe Kaiser was covering for the CIA, which had been quietly involved behind the scenes in the LAPD's investigation, as you will see in a later chapter, than to believe that this veteran reporter, decades later, could still have still been so ignorant of the CIA's relationships with Time-Life and CBS. If Kaiser had some relationship with the CIA, that would explain his reliance on two CBS people to attempt to discredit Schulman. It would explain why his first reaction was to encourage Cesar to sue. It would also explain why, over the years, Kaiser attempted to sandbag some of the other researchers who reported on the conspiracy aspects of the Robert Kennedy assassination. For instance, Bill Turner, who co-wrote an excellent book on the case with Jonn Christian, talked of how Kaiser tried to frame Christian on an evidence tampering charge. Turner wrote it off to professional jealousy. But given Kaiser's work for the Luce Press, other interpretations cannot be dismissed out of hand.

On June 4, 1971, Charach filed a lawsuit against the LAPD, Chief Davis, Chief Houghton, and D.A. Evelle Younger for the suppression of their files. He opened by quoting state law:

The people of this state do not yield their sovereignty to the agencies which serve them. The people, in delegating authority, do not give their public servants the right to decide what is good for the people to know and what is not good for them to know. The people insist

---

300   Carl Bernstein, "The CIA and the Media," *Rolling Stone*, October 20, 1977.

301   Thomas Fox, "Robert Blair Kaiser dies at 84 on Holy Thursday," *National Catholic Reporter*, April 3, 2015.

on remaining informed so that they may retain control over the instruments they have created.[302]

Charach charged that each defendant had "deliberately, intentionally and knowingly suppressed facts and evidence within their knowledge and control, and continue to do so, usurping the right of the People to remain informed and on the part of said defendants, and each of them, attempting to decide what is good for the People to know and what is not good for them to know."[303]

With Harper, Blehr and Charach making public affidavits and taking legal steps, and accusations from Don Schulman of a second shooter, Joseph P. Busch, Jr., who was appointed to the role of District Attorney when Younger became the California State Attorney General in 1971, ordered his deputies to investigate the recent charges against Wolfer. Busch announced there would be a press conference in a week but then delayed this twice, presumably because the charges could not immediately be answered, since Wolfer had no evidence to back up his assertions.

In the process of investigating the charges against Wolfer, the D.A.'s office also quietly questioned both Schulman and Cesar, as well as a few others. In other words, while publicly stating otherwise, Busch and his team appeared to be looking to tie up any loose ends regarding a conspiracy, not just to answer the specific charges against Wolfer.

Busch also charged that the evidence in the County Clerk's office might have been tampered with and convened a grand jury in 1971 to look into it, an idea perhaps inspired by Bob Kaiser. In 1971, Kaiser "had been put on the D.A.'s payroll as the house "expert" on the investigation" to "monitor the activities of the 'buffs.'"[304] This would have made little sense, given Kaiser's role with Sirhan's defense team. Why did Busch think he could trust Kaiser? Here again, if Kaiser had some sort of connection with the CIA, that would have made more sense. According to Turner and Christian,

> Kaiser took the position that if the bullets didn't match as Harper claimed, then they probably had been tampered with or possibly even switched by unauthorized persons. It was almost verbatim the line that Busch would soon make public.[305]

---

302   A copy of the lawsuit was reprinted in the August 1970 issue of *Computers and Automation*. The section of the California Code cited was from the Bagley-Keene Open Meeting Act (Section 11120).

303   *Computers and Automation*, August 1970.

304   Turner and Christian, p. 165.

305   Turner and Christian, p. 165.

Harper's findings could have been washed away if the D.A.'s office could prove someone from the outside had gotten in there and switched the bullets. But that effort fell short. As mentioned earlier, Kaiser tried at this point to implicate Jonn Christian with having tampered with evidence, but Christian had already found the evidence against him had been forged, and the case against him was quickly dropped. There was never any evidence that anyone from the *outside* had tampered with the evidence.[306]

The D.A.'s office motive for covering up wrongdoing by Wolfer was similar to the LAPD's. To admit fallibility or deliberate misconduct would open the D.A.'s office to a number of lawsuits over false convictions. Wolfer had presented evidence in many cases over the years. Therefore, to let the D.A. investigate, in essence, itself and its partner agency was, in retrospect, ridiculous. To believe the government can *ever* successfully investigate itself when so much is at stake is to deny the realities of human and bureaucratic nature. Even appointed "special counsels" cannot help, as we will see shortly, because they are appointed by the very bodies involved in the cases they are investigating.

Wolfer's behavior in the Robert Kennedy case was so clearly understood by the rank and file within the LAPD that his name became a term of derision in the years that followed, as the *Los Angeles Times* reported years later:

> "There is a nickname in our profession," one specialist said, for mistakes in which an investigator is too quick to "make" a gun. It is "Wolferism," a reference to DeWayne Wolfer, a one-time LAPD criminalist who misread evidence in the assassination of Sen. Robert F. Kennedy in Los Angeles in 1968....[307]

Nevertheless, despite all the problems with Wolfer's mishandling of the evidence, his lack of any documentation to back up claims of a match between bullets, and his lab's destruction of evidence, Busch officially cleared Wolfer, and Wolfer became head of the LAPD's lab, claiming he was clearly qualified for the job.

---

306   William Turner and Jonn Christian, "The Assassination of Robert F. Kennedy: Is Bobby's Killer Still Loose?" *Hustler*, January 1979. Turner and Christian wrote that the point of the charge of evidence tampering was to discredit not only the evidence but Christian as well. They note "Busch's fall guy was to be Christian, who two years earlier had merely looked at Sirhan's notebooks and other printed documents. The D.A.'s investigators confronted Christin with the exhibit-request slips, but Christian noticed that several exhibit numbers had been added in a different hand. He emphatically pronounced them a 'crude forgery.'" In their book on the case, Turner and Christian made clear it was Bob Kaiser who had tried to implicate Christian in this evidence tampering, but the evidence against Christian had clearly been forged.

307   Bob Baker and Paul Lieberman, "Faulty Ballistics in Deputy's Arrest: Eagerness to 'Make' Gun Cited in LAPD Lab Error," *Los Angeles Times*, 5/22/89, via articles.latimes.com/1989-05-22/news/mn-411_1_firearms-lapd-lab-error-police-officers/2, accessed 6/6/14. I left out the seemingly obligatory phrase "even though the guilt of Sirhan Sirhan was never in doubt" at the end of this quote because it is an uninformed statement, as this volume amply attests.

But wishing didn't make it so. In 1974, Wolfer was reprimanded for "alleged improper conduct" in a case where members of the LAPD apparently tried to pressure the Civil Service Board into appointing specific people to the LAPD's crime lab. In 1980, Chief Daryl Gates suspended Wolfer for 30 working days without pay after an internal investigation revealed he had "failed to provide proper storage and analysis of bullets and other evidence" in another case.[308] And in a strange twist—or not—in later years, Wolfer went on to become the president of the very same Ace Security guard service that had sent Thane Cesar to the Ambassador Hotel the night Robert Kennedy was killed.

There are any number of improbable explanations for Wolfer's behavior. But there is one scenario in which all of this, Wolfer's actions, his protection, and his later employment make sense: Wolfer had deliberately covered up evidence of multiple shooters in an important crime and was protected and rewarded for doing so, regardless of whether he ever knew whom—or what—he was protecting.

On May 15, 1972, Arthur Bremer fired upon the racist, conservative Democratic presidential primary candidate Governor George Wallace during a campaign rally in Laurel, Maryland. As I wrote for *Probe* magazine nearly two decades ago,

> Wallace alone was wounded in nine different places. Three other people were wounded by a bullet apiece. ... The gun found at the scene and presumed to be the only weapon used could only hold five bullets. Looks like someone brought magic bullets to Laurel that day.[309]

The New York Times timidly noted there was "broad speculation on how four persons had suffered at least seven separate wounds from a maximum of five shots." There was an enormous amount of evidence that multiple gunmen had fired upon Wallace that day. But as with the Sirhan case, it was all neatly buttoned up and pinned on a single man, despite the fact that the bullets retrieved from Wallace could not be matched to the gun recovered, and Bremer's fingerprints were not found on the gun he had ostensibly fired. Like Sirhan, Bremer was reported to have had a "silly grin" and to appear "incredibly indifferent to what was going on around him." [310]

Nixon's team had feared Wallace. Wallace was very popular, and had he chosen to run as an independent in the general election, a consideration that was floated at the time, his conservative, racist views would have cut more into Nixon's support than George McGovern's. If anyone had a motive to remove Wallace from the race, it was Nixon and his backers.

---

308   Myrna Oliver, "LAPD Suspends Forensic Chemist: Aide Reprimanded, 6 Others Face Hearing Chief LAPD Chemist Suspended," *Los Angeles Times*, May 31, 1980.

309   Lisa Pease, "Arthur Bremer and George Wallace—It's Déjà Vu all over again," *Probe*, May-June 1999.

310   *Ibid.*

A month later, a "third-rate burglary"[311] at the Democratic National Committee headquarters at the Watergate complex in D.C. by current and former CIA operatives, at the behest of the White House, began a chain of events that would not only cause President Nixon to step down but would launch *five separate investigations* into what the CIA was doing domestically and what its role might have been in assassinations not only abroad but at home as well.[312]

In Los Angeles, a number of independent researchers pursued their own investigations into the case in the 1970s. Lillian Castellano, then in her sixties, was the first to notice the problem with too many bullets in the pantry. She had already been studying the assassination of President Kennedy when Senator Robert Kennedy was killed, so she paid closer attention than most. When she read that there were two bullet holes in the center frame of the swinging doors in the pantry, she recognized immediately those represented two more bullets than Sirhan's gun could hold. The *Los Angeles Free Press* published her findings on May 23, 1969, shortly after Sirhan's trial had ended.

Art Kevin of KMPC did a number of interviews of people with evidence that did not support the official story. While at KHJ Radio, he had upset then-D.A. Evelle Younger by enumerating the evidence that pointed to conspiracy in the Robert Kennedy assassination. Younger had threatened to revoke Kevin's press credentials, but when KHJ backed their reporter and promised to expose Younger's threat, Younger backed down.

While at KMPC, on December 20, 1974, Kevin interviewed Paul Sharaga, the LAPD officer who had set up the command post immediately after the assassination, about what had happened. Sharaga had responded within "less than 30 seconds from the time the call came out" about the shooting. He was just passing the back of the Ambassador Hotel and quickly turned in to the "upper level rear parking lot." There, according to Sharaga, he met a couple whose name he did not remember:

> An older couple, probably in their fifties—fifties to sixties—came running toward me and I stopped them and asked what had happened.

---

311   That was how Ron Ziegler, President Nixon's press secretary, tried to wave away initial reporting of the Watergate break-in. "The Watergate Story," *washingtonpost.com*, www.washingtonpost.com/wp-srv/politics/special/watergate/timeline.html.

312   The Watergate committee devoted a portion of its time to investigate the CIA's apparent role in Watergate, as several of the burglars were current and former CIA operatives. The other four investigations were the Rockefeller Commission (formally, the President's Commission on CIA Activities Within the United States), the Church Committee (formally, the Senate Select Committee to Study Governmental Operations with Respect to Intelligence), the Pike Committee (the House Permanent Select Committee on Intelligence), and the HSCA (the House Select Committee on Assassinations). The last committee focused on who killed President Kennedy and Dr. Martin Luther King, Jr. Allard Lowenstein tried mightily to get the committee to investigate the Robert Kennedy assassination as well, but that effort fell short.

They related that they were outside one of the doors to the Embassy Room, when a couple in their early twenties came rushing out. This couple seemed to be in a state of glee, shouting 'We shot him! We shot him! We killed him!'—The only description I could get out of this couple were that they were in their early twenties. The woman was wearing a polka dot dress.

Sharaga told Kevin he had given the couple's names to the investigating detectives at Rampart and specifically mentioned Bill Jordan. Sharaga then said he broadcast a description of the girl and her male companion. But from the transcript of the broadcasts made by Sharaga and others that night, it appears the only suspect Sharaga called in a description of was his tall, sandy-haired male suspect. In addition, Sharaga told Kevin that, after he had broadcast a description of the girl in the polka dot dress, Inspector Powers came on the air and shut him down. The police transcripts show Powers shut Sharaga down in exactly the manner he described, but after Sharaga had broadcast his description of the tall blond man. I asked audio expert Philip Van Praag if the police tapes could have been altered. No, he said. He explained that all police channels were recorded simultaneously on one big machine, with time checks inside, so it would have been virtually impossible for someone to fake all the channels at the same time. I believe, therefore, that Sharaga conflated two separate events in his head and reported them as a single event.

There *is* a record that indicates Sharaga *did* in fact meet the couple he described. A report of an LAPD interview with Sharaga on September 26, 1968, indicates that Sharaga had met a couple who were extremely upset because they believed they heard a woman run by saying "We shot him, we shot him."[313] When asked who had been shot, the woman indicated Kennedy. Sharaga said the couple had been standing on the balcony outside the Embassy Room. Sharaga also told me when I contacted him by phone years later, and I found him very credible on this point, that he had not heard of Sandra Serrano's story until several years after the assassination. He had not seen her broadcast live, it was never aired again, and he was not involved in Special Unit Senator's investigation. The balcony outside the Embassy Room was a few feet above and east of where Serrano had been on the fire escape. Someone could easily have overheard Serrano's exchange

---

313   LAPD interview of Paul Sharaga, September 26, 1968, SUS files. In a notarized statement obtained by Jim DiEugenio from Bill Turner's files on the case, Sharaga stated that "The LAPD report on the reverse side is not based on any interview of me by any officials in the LAPD at any time. Further, it also contains false and deliberately misleading statements. It is obviously derived from a much longer report personally prepared by me in September of 1968, which disappeared from LAPD files later on under entirely suspicious circumstances." Sharaga was clearly upset by the following statement in the report: "[Sharaga] believes that due to the noise and confusion at the time what was said was misinterpreted, and what was probably said was, 'they shot him.'" As you saw in the passage to which this footnote is attached, that was not what Sharaga believed they had said. Like Serrano, Sharaga recalled the couple had heard the girl say "we shot him, we shot him."

with the girl in the polka dot dress from that location. The report indicates that Sharaga passed the couple's information along to another officer.

In addition, there was *another couple* that appeared to have sparked Sharaga's broadcast of the tall, sandy-haired suspect. Gilman Kraft and his wife Ruth had been near the Ambassador Hotel lobby at the time of the shooting when Kraft's attention was drawn to a 6'2" Caucasian man in his twenties with "long blond hair" who "hurdled a couch" as he ran through the lobby. In a 1992 interview of Kraft,[314] Kraft said that he was a friend of the Kennedys and choked up as he remembered this moment. Asked if the guy pushed him out of the way as he ran by, Kraft said "He didn't, but if we had been in his path he certainly would have." He described the young man as lean, between 20 and 30 years old, with "longish blond hair" and said he "vaulted" over sofas "on his way out toward the back of the Ambassador Hotel—the South Side." This was clearly not Michael Wayne, who had dark curly hair, not long blond hair, and was not that tall.

It appears Kraft's observations formed the basis for Sergeant Paul Sharaga's initial broadcast of a tall, sandy-haired suspect, as Kraft's interview was in a folder with other information about Sharaga.[315] Predictably, the police had written "Do Not Type" on the top of his wife Ruth's LAPD interview report. Both were interviewed at the same time. All interviews were taped initially. Her tape appears to no longer be in existence, but now we likely know what was on it and why the police did not want that information in the record.

I believe Sharaga merged the report from the Kraft couple with the couple he encountered earlier in his mind and reported on separately to other officers. Sharaga's APB on the tall blond man was then cancelled by Inspector Powers in exactly the manner Sharaga described. I believe in all aspects Sharaga told the truth as he remembered it. I just think in his mind he merged two separate stories into one storyline.

During the course of the original investigation and later reinvestigations, several witnesses were threatened in some way. For example, Darnell Johnson, who saw Sirhan shortly before the shooting in a group of four men and a girl in a polka dot dress who appeared to be together, told the police his brakes had been tampered with.[316]

---

314   Phone interview of Gilman Kraft, supplied from Bill Turner's files to Jim DiEugenio, who in turn gave it to me. The interviewer is not listed but was attached to a document signed by Floyd Nelson and Jonn Christian. Given Christian's relationship to Bill Turner (they wrote a book together which was reissued in the wake of the film JFK), it appears this interview of Kraft was conducted by Christian. The date of the interview is October 9, 1992.

315   Jim DiEugenio gave me a "Sharaga" file from Bill Turner's files that contained the Gilman Kraft interview.

316   Darnell Johnson's death threat came from a note by the investigator who interviewed him on his July 24, 1968 SUS interview report, signed by Lt. Manny Pena. The writer tried to dismiss Darnell's observation as being out of whack with other witnesses, but my own research shows Darnell's information lines up neatly with that of several other witnesses, as you will see in a later chapter. The writer added this note: "He states that he has

Another witness, a 17-year-old boy by the name of John Chris Weatherly, had been shot at after telling KHJ-TV newscaster Baxter Ward about knowing a man named Bill Powers who had seen someone who looked like Sirhan in the back of Oliver Brindley "Jerry" Owen's truck on June 3, 1968, the day before the primary election that ended in Kennedy's death. June 3 was a day in Sirhan's life that *no one* at the trial—neither the prosecution nor the defense—wanted to talk about. Ward was impressed by the young man's sincerity and aired the report after changing some names and details to protect him. A few days after the broadcast, someone shot at Weatherly with a high-powered rifle as he arrived home at 3 A.M. in the morning. Jerry Owen, known popularly as "the Walking Bible," had also reported a phone call telling him to "keep your mother___ mouth shut."[317]

And in August 1971, the day before Harper was to testify at Busch's grand jury hearing regarding the ballistics evidence, Harper noticed a car following him home. He tried to lose the car by speeding up but the other car gave chase, following his random turns. Harper heard what sounded like a shot just as his car hit a dip in the road. Had it not been for the dip, the bullet that might have cost him his life dented his bumper instead.[318]

If Sirhan were the only shooter, who cared what these other people found? The threats only make sense if there was, in fact, something to hide, that these people were exposing.

After talking to Weatherly and others, Baxter Ward became so invested in this case that, after being elected to the Los Angeles County Board of Supervisors, as Chairman of the Coroner's committee, he convened a day-long hearing on May 13, 1974, on the ballistics evidence. The purpose of the hearing was not, purportedly, to reopen the case but rather to make recommendations on the handling of ballistics evidence in California going forward. Predictably, Buck Compton, by then an associate justice on the California Court of Appeals, issued a counter-statement with the stated goal of preventing the public "from being deluded into believing persons other than Sirhan were involved in the assassination of Robert Kennedy."[319]

By 1973, the rumors and innuendo surrounding the case had finally compelled New York Congressman Allard Lowenstein to step into the case. He met privately with actor Robert Vaughn, the star of the TV series *The Man From U.N.C.L.E.*, who had taken a personal interest in the case. As Lowenstein described it years later:

---

received threatening phone calls and that someone has tampered with his vehicle brakes which caused him almost to have an accident."

317   LAPD notes of an interview with Jerry Owen, SUS Conspiracy Investigation Files, www.maryferrell.org/showDoc.html?docId=99850&relPageId=94.

318   Turner and Christian, p. 158.

319   Statement of Lynn D. Compton, May 13, 1974.

The truth is that I finally went to that first meeting chiefly because in my closed-mindedness I believed that spending half an hour with people who had gone gaga about the Robert Kennedy case would both prove my open-mindedness and help me persuade a good man to avoid further involvement in such foolishness.

That afternoon at Robert Vaughn's house I saw the autopsy report and discovered that Robert Kennedy had been hit from *behind* by bullets fired at point-blank range.... I thought I had remembered that Sirhan had been *facing* Senator Kennedy and had shot him from a distance of several *feet*, so I assumed that either the autopsy report or my memory was in error. I soon learned that neither was.[320]

Lowenstein also found that, when he discussed this with others, this was a key factor in changing their minds as well.

Everyone was certain that Sirhan was the assassin until they heard what was in the autopsy report. Then there would come a kind of mental double-take: the pain of rethinking the worst of nights, the shock of implications dimly glimpsed; and then the sorting out of what if anything to do next. For most, a quick decision to do nothing, to try to put the matter away again; often a warning that going public about my doubts would be awkward, maybe damaging.[321]

Trying to act through official channels, Lowenstein went to District Attorney Busch "with a list of questions about specific problems that seemed troublesome."[322] But the answers Lowenstein received were "as peculiar as the contradictions in the evidence .... Every official at the D.A.'s office was polite and talked about cooperation, but nobody did anything much with my list except periodically to request another copy." And worse, the answers he received "often turned out to be untrue—not marginally untrue, but enthusiastically, aggressively, and sometimes quite imaginatively untrue."[323] As Lowenstein wrote in 1977,

As events moved on, I found that propaganda campaigns were being concocted that peddled the precise reverse of the facts. Two of these were especially daring and effective: it was repeated constantly that "every eyewitness" had seen Sirhan kill Kennedy (so how could any

320   Allard Lowenstein, "The Murder of Robert Kennedy: Suppressed Evidence of More than One Assassin?" *Saturday Review*, February 19, 1977.

321   Lowenstein's unpublished manuscript, pp. 12–13.

322   Allard Lowenstein, "The Murder of Robert Kennedy: Suppressed Evidence of More than One Assassin?" *Saturday Review*, February 19, 1977.

323   *Ibid.*

rational person doubt that he had done it?); and it was said almost as frequently that there was "only one gun" in the hotel pantry where Kennedy was shot (so how could anyone have fired a second?)—this despite the fact that everyone connected with the case, if very few other people, knew that there was at least one other gun in the precise area from which the bullets that hit Kennedy were fired.[324]

Lowenstein found the most compelling evidence of a second gun was the bullet found in the stage doorframe immediately after the assassination. The finding of the bullet had been captured in a photograph of two policemen pointing at the hole with a caption that stated a "bullet was still in the wood."

Then, too, there were the FBI photos of the doorframes in the pantry's west end captioned "Bullet holes." When Lowenstein asked for a study of the doorframes, he ran into stonewalling that he initially took for bureaucratic delays rather than an attempt at deception. But the delay stretched on for two years, when he was finally told the doorframes had been destroyed years earlier.

In 1973, Herbert Leon MacDonnell, a famous New York criminalistics professor, added fuel to the growing evidence of conspiracy by confirming Harper's interpretation of his evidence. He signed an affidavit that indicated the Kennedy neck bullet (Exhibit 47) and the William Weisel bullet (Exhibit 54) could not have been fired from the same gun and that the Kennedy bullet specifically could not have been fired from Sirhan's gun.

Meanwhile, pantry victim Paul Schrade had been equally puzzled by the evidence, as had one of the more flamboyant members of the D.A.'s office, one who had never been invited into the Robert Kennedy case at the time, former Assistant District Attorney Vincent Bugliosi. Schrade, represented by Bugliosi and Lowenstein, filed a suit against Sirhan and anyone else who might have been shooting in the pantry as a means to force the case back into a courtroom so the evidence of multiple shooters could be properly examined.

As the calls for a new investigation continued, on December 16, 1974, Ron Kessler, a journalist who had written the AP articles with information leaked from the prosecution during Sirhan's trial, and who now worked for the *Washington Post*, interviewed Bill Harper in his home.

Three days later, the *Post* published Kessler's piece, which was clearly designed to dispel any notion of conspiracy in the case in an obvious attempt to forestall any attempt at a reinvestigation. For example, Kessler's article quoted Vince DiPierro as saying "It would be impossible for there to be a second gun. I saw

---

324   *Ibid.*

the first shot. Kennedy fell at my feet. I had a clear view of Kennedy and Sirhan."
But Kessler didn't mention that DiPierro had also put Sirhan's gun muzzle about
three feet from Kennedy, making it impossible for him to have fired *any* of the
shots that hit Kennedy.

Regarding his discussion with Harper, Kessler wrote:

> Under persistent questioning in his home here, Harper admitted
> that what he had previously described as discrepancies between the
> bullets fail to show they were fired from different guns. The evidence
> that would permit matching of the bullets is lacking because of the
> poor condition, Harper said. ...
>
> He said "there's no evidence to show they're different." The
> inability to make a positive identification, said Harper, who is highly
> regarded in law enforcement circles, is not uncommon in the field
> of ballistics.[325]

Kessler's article so outraged Harper that he wrote to Harry Rosenfeld, the
Assistant Managing Editor of the *Post*:

> I have been put in the awkward position of having to call [Ron
> Kessler] a liar, but this is the case. However, in analyzing Kessler's
> article as a whole, there is now no question in my mind—or of many
> newsmen familiar with me and my work—that his was a calculated
> attempt to do what you gentlemen in the press call a "hatchet job"
> on my professional integrity and my findings in this case. Frankly,
> Kessler's efforts strangely parallel those of the authorities in this
> matter, who would have the world believe that all of us daring to
> challenge their untenable position in this matter are either fools or
> charlatans or worse.
>
> Frankly, I should have been suspicious of Kessler's intentions
> when he refused a copy of my entire affidavit before he left after
> our one and only two-hour meeting at my home on December 16th.
> However, I rightfully assumed The Post had given Kessler plenty of
> time to conduct "an intensive investigation" on this case, as your
> December 9th letter represented. I would hardly call three days
> time enough to conduct an intensive investigation on anything as
> complicated as the case at hand.[326]

In response, Ben Bradlee, the editor at the *Post*, sent an Ombudsman to hear

---

325   Ron Kessler, "Expert Discounts RFK 2d-Gun Theory," *The Washington Post*, December 19, 1974.

326   Letter from Bill Harper to Harry Rosenfeld, December 31, 1974.

Harper's side of the story. Bradlee offered to let Harper tell his side of the story, but he refused to retract Kessler's reporting, despite Harper having outlined four specific factual errors in Kessler's work. Harper refused because just posting his rebuttal would make it look like the issue were a difference of opinion instead of a difference in fact.

Always close to the intelligence community, Kessler went on to write books about the CIA, the FBI, and the Secret Service, begging the question of whether Kessler was one of the CIA's assets in the media. In recent years, the Senate's report on torture, the one the CIA tried hard to suppress, included a discussion of Ron Kessler's role in supporting the CIA's side of the story. In a 2014 *Bloomberg* article titled "Was Ron Kessler a CIA journalism asset?", Emily Greenhouse wrote that the Senate's report on the CIA's use of torture, which the CIA tried to suppress, included comments indicating:

> CIA officials had "provided assistance" with Kessler's book, in order to "shape press reporting on the CIA's Detention and Interrogation Program." The Senate report quotes then-Senior Deputy General Counsel John Rizzo saying that the Director of the CIA "blessed" Kessler with agency cooperation. It seems to paint Kessler as something of a chosen mouthpiece, the person in whom the CIA put its faith.[327]

That the CIA used journalists to cover up its actions and to attack the CIA's detractors was first uncovered and documented by both the Church and Pike Committees, investigations by Senate and House committees formed in the wake of the Watergate Committee's and Rockefeller Commission's exposures of the CIA's numerous illegal domestic activities. Carl Bernstein, of the famous Woodward and Bernstein team whose reporting led to the Watergate investigation, wrote what is still the most thorough documentation of the CIA's role of journalists to sway public opinion on matters of importance to the agency. Bernstein also wrote of journalists being used for operational work as well.[328]

Short of a CIA admission, which would never be forthcoming because the CIA never confirms or denies whether people are their employees or assets for obvious reasons, it's impossible to *prove* that Kessler's work on the Robert Kennedy case was similarly supported by the CIA. But it's certainly reasonable to suspect it was, given his history with the agency, which you've seen, and given the CIA's covert involvement in this case, which will be discussed in later chapters.

Bradlee had chosen to run Kessler's hit piece on Harper, wrote Lowenstein, "just as Paul Schrade and I were holding our Los Angeles press conference" to get

---

327   Emily Greenhouse, "Was Ron Kessler a CIA journalism asset?" Bloomberg, www.bloomberg.com/politics/articles/2014-12-11/was-ron-kessler-a-cia-journalism-asset, December 11, 2014
328   Carl Bernstein, "The CIA and the Media," *Rolling Stone*, October 20, 1977.

the case reopened. "The Kessler recanting of the Harper 'contentions' drowned our efforts at a critical juncture."[329]

Lowenstein was scathing in his critique of the *Post* in this episode, noting that "It was not until May 20, 1975, that a careful reader of the *Post* could discover that Mr. Harper had denied the Kessler version of their interview." On May 20, 1975, Lester Hyman, a former chairman of the Democratic Party in Massachusetts, as Lowenstein recounted, "managed to get a letter printed in the *Post* protesting the failure to report Mr. Harper's protests." Hyman noted that the *Post* devoted plenty of space to "the fantasies of the so-called lunatic fringe" but did not devote "equal space" to professionals like "Harper." Hyman lamented that even though some "charlatans" were "involved in the assassination story," that should not have been an excuse "to deter a responsible search for the truth."[330]

The *Post* had been lauded for its reporting on the Watergate break-in. Bob Woodward and Carl Bernstein at the *Post* were credited with forcing President Nixon to step down. But their reporting only scratched the surface of government misdeeds, as events were about to reveal.

On Christmas Eve, 1974, the *New York Times* published an explosive article by Seymour Hersh implicating the CIA in illegal domestic activities. Dealing with this fell to America's first unelected president, former Warren Commission member Gerald Ford, who had received covert CIA donations as a Congressman.[331] Ford had created a commission nicknamed the "Rockefeller Commission" after Ford's similarly unelected Vice President Nelson Rockefeller, whom Ford appointed to oversee it.

The entire commission was so overtly CIA-friendly the press quickly deemed its investigation a "whitewash." Asked at a press event why he had appointed such people, Ford said he needed people who could keep some things secret. The reporters wanted to know what Ford meant. "Like assassinations!" Ford blurted out, adding immediately—but belatedly—"That's off the record."[332] The comment led to a firestorm of publicity. Whom in the U.S. had the CIA assassinated, given that the topic of inquiry was illegal domestic CIA activities? Was Ford worried that the CIA's role in the JFK assassination might be exposed due to his tenure on the Warren Commission?

It's incredibly difficult to investigate the activities of an intelligence agency when secrets aren't put to paper and lies are deliberately spread. But when the target of an investigation has the ability to infiltrate and control the investigation

---

329   Lowenstein manuscript, p. 29.

330   Lowenstein manuscript, p. 29.

331   Larry DuBois and Laurence Gonzales, "The Puppet And The Puppetmasters Uncovering the Secret World of Nixon, Hughes and the CIA," *Playboy*, September 1976.

332   Daniel Schorr, *Clearing the Air* (Boston: Houghton Mifflin Company, 1977), p. 144.

as well as the media narrative, they have power unaccountable to anyone. That's what the Church and Pike Committees and later the House Select Committee on Assassinations faced. The complete disregard the CIA held toward its ostensible overseers in this period was evident to the participants. When questioned by the Church Committee, James Angleton famously said, "It is inconceivable that a secret intelligence arm of the government has to comply with all the overt orders of the government."

Dan Hardway, one of the HSCA's investigators into the CIA's possible role in the JFK assassination, experienced this incredible attitude firsthand, as he recounted in a talk at Duquesne University in 2013:

> I was sent to Jacksonville, FL, with investigator Gaeton Fonzi, to interview Joseph Burkholder Smith, a retired CIA officer. Upon our arrival, we handed him our HSCA credentials, telling him we were there to ask him some questions on behalf of Congress. He flipped the credentials back at us and told us, "So you represent Congress, what the f*** is that to the CIA. You'll be gone in a few years and the CIA will still be here." That really sums up a lot of the problem that we had.[333]

The CIA was not above infiltrating the investigations of others to disrupt them, as Gaeton Fonzi reported in his book *The Last Investigation*. The HSCA found that when Jim Garrison, as District Attorney of New Orleans, was investigating various local figures for potential roles in the plot to kill JFK, the CIA planted several operatives on his staff.[334]

Tactics the CIA used to avoid scrutiny included not just infiltration and refusal, but evidence manipulation as well. Files were stolen. Tapes of a likely Oswald imposter in Mexico City were destroyed. But the CIA also used the much more subtle technique of simply stalling, as the Pike Committee described in their report:

> There were numerous public expressions by intelligence agencies and the Executive that full cooperation would be accorded. ... Despite these public representations, in practice most document access was preceded by lengthy negotiations. Almost without exception, these negotiations yielded something less than complete or timely access.

---

333   When I asked Dan for a copy of his remarks at Duquesne, Dan sent me an article he wrote which, at the time of this writing, had not been published, titled, "The View from the Trenches," © 2013. The text quoted is from that article, which he provided to me by email.

334   Gaeton Fonzi, *The Last Investigation* (New York: Thunder's Mouth Press, 1993), pp. 239, 375.

> In short, the words were always words of cooperation; the reality
> was delay, refusal, missing information, asserted privileges, and on
> and on.[335]

The LAPD and District Attorney's office used the same type of stalling tactics, always hidden under the language of cooperation, much to Lowenstein's dismay. And even when they did investigate, they dismissed any evidence of conspiracy and attempted to explain it away, sometimes with the most ludicrous of explanations.

Consider this particular episode, in which the County offered to search the pantry again—*many years after the crime*—for evidence of additional bullets and bullet holes! In his unpublished manuscript on the Robert Kennedy assassination, Lowenstein wrote:

> Thus did high comedy enter the saga of the continuing effort to
> confuse the public about the facts in the assassination of Senator
> Kennedy. A pantry which had been studied minutely by the authorities
> in the wake of the assassination and had been stripped of relevant
> physical evidence, a pantry which subsequently had been largely
> refurbished by the hotel, inexplicably failed to yield new bullets or
> bullet holes seven and a half years later. ...
>
> Nor was it generally reported that on November 18, 1975, thirty
> days before the great pantry raid, representatives of the District Attor-
> ney and of the Attorney General of the State of California opposed
> in court an effort to question under oath the witnesses who believed
> they had seen the extra bullets. ...
>
> [T]he raid of the pantry was a hoax whose only purpose and
> accomplishment was to confuse the public into believing that ques-
> tions raised by the evidence are being investigated satisfactorily,
> which they are not. To conduct a search for something which cannot
> possible be, and then to announce that it wasn't there as evidence
> that it never existed, is to assume idiots are in the audience.

Remember that the FBI labeled pictures of four holes in the doorframes as "bullet holes." The LAPD had booked the doorframes into evidence. Why would they do that, Lowenstein asked, if they did not have any evidence to examine? And worse, why did the LAPD later destroy them just two months after the trial had ended, along with the ceiling tiles that Wolfer had stated had an "unbelievable" number of holes in them? The LAPD's excuse was that these were not considered evidence because they had not been used at the trial, and they had nowhere to put them.

---

335   Phil Agee, *CIA: The Pike Report* (New York: Spokesman Books, 1977), p.26.

While none of this passed muster with Lowenstein, he was surprised how few people seemed to be able to conceive that the government could be actively covering up a conspiracy in this case:

> What is odd is not that some people thought it was all random, but that so many intelligent people refused to believe that it might be anything else. Nothing can measure more graphically how limited was the general understanding of what is possible in America.[336]
>
> Researchers were the exception. They had dug into the evidence and faced it fearlessly, and saw clearly the dark hand of conspiracy at work. Several openly speculated the CIA was somehow involved in the death of Senator Robert Kennedy as well as his brother.

The year 1975 was a pivotal one for the RFK case. The cover-up had become so threadbare it needed new tailoring. Information about CIA assassination plots uncovered by the Rockefeller Commission, the Church Committee and the Pike Committee, as well as provocative new evidence surfaced by researchers in the John Kennedy and Robert Kennedy assassinations, increased the calls for *both* Kennedy assassinations to be reinvestigated. Paul Schrade and CBS sued for access to the records on the case, Los Angeles City Councilmember Zev Yaroslavsky called for a new investigation, and the Los Angeles County Board of Supervisors, at the prodding of the outspoken Baxter Ward, were also considering further action.

This was the year, too, in which Senator Edward Kennedy indicated support for a new investigation. And there was considerable belief at the time that if Ted ran for president in 1976, he would win. Imagine what a "Kennedy Commission" might have uncovered. "Almost everyone who knows him says he is running," Carl Rowan wrote in an Arkansas paper. In San Antonio, Ralph Blumenfeld wrote:

> The surviving Kennedy brother, Sen. Edward M. Kennedy, said on May 9, 1975, that he would favor a new investigation if there is new evidence in the assassination of his brother Robert or in the assassination five years earlier of his brother John.
>
> "Obviously it is painful for the family," Ted Kennedy said, "but the first consideration ought to be on the basis of what new evidence is available."[337]

---

336   Gary Abrams, "For years, he had his mind on one thing: the assassination of Robert Kennedy. He spent almost every waking hour studying the case, and his apartment was a cross between an RFK shrine and archive. Then, last month, apparently despondent over his failure to reopen the case, Greg Stone killed himself. "The Obsession," *Los Angeles Times*, February 17, 1991, articles.latimes.com/1991-02-17/news/vw-1850_1_jennifer-stone/2.

337   Ralph Blumenfeld, "The Death of RFK," *San Antonio Express*, July 20, 1975.

I met a woman in Seattle who had testified in Executive Session to the Watergate Committee after learning of a plot to kill Ted Kennedy at the Democratic Convention in 1972 if he had become the nominee. The plot involved shooting Kennedy from the air vents. Curiously, in the course of the Watergate investigation, a report surfaced showing CIA asset Bernard Barker asked Miami architect Leonard Glasser to obtain the blueprints to the Convention Hall, and specifically the air conditioning plans. "This was unreal, because what the hell would anybody want them for?"[338] The Watergate committee concluded there was a plan to put a gas into the vents, but a convention hall is huge and the amount of gas required for such a large space would have been prohibitive. Was my informant correct?

And then there was the Jerry Owen case. Owen, the con-man-*cum*-preacher who told the LAPD he'd picked up Sirhan and offered to sell him a horse the night that resulted in Kennedy's assassination, sued KCOP in 1975 for slander over a comment KCOP's John Hopkins made about the cancellation of the TV show Owen had received post-assassination. Hopkins was alleged to have said Owen's show was cancelled "because he was a thief; he has burned down several churches in Arizona; he was involved in the killing of Robert Kennedy, and he is a criminal."[339]

Vince Bugliosi believed there had been a conspiracy in the Robert Kennedy assassination, and he used the Owen case as a means to bring it into a courtroom. Rather than trying to disprove the defamation charge on technical grounds, he chose instead to try to prove Owen really had been involved in a conspiracy that resulted in the killing of Robert Kennedy. Bugliosi joined the defense very late, however, and had little time to prepare. You can imagine how upset the judge was that Bugliosi wanted to suddenly introduce this angle into the case. The judge did all he could to keep the Robert Kennedy questions out of the case.

In the course of preparing for that trial, Bugliosi had been especially struck by the AP photo that stated a bullet was still in the hole of a doorframe at the back of the stage where Kennedy had exited. He worked his contacts to identify the policemen in the photo as Sergeants Robert Rozzi and Charles Wright. Both assured him there had definitely been a bullet in the hole.

Rozzi gave Bugliosi a signed statement stating the object he saw "appeared to be a small-caliber bullet." Turner and Christian described what happened next:

> Bugliosi was approached by Sergeant Phil Sartuche, an SUS veteran
> who was monitoring the proceedings for [LAPD] Chief Ed Davis,

---

338   Washington Post Service, "Architect says Dem break-in figure sought meeting hall data," *Arizona Republic*, June 26, 1972.

339   Myrna Oliver, "Bugliosi Claims Conspiracy in Robert Kennedy Slaying," *Los Angeles Times*, July 31, 1975.

and who had worked with Bugliosi as an investigating officer in the Manson case. "Vince, do you have Rozzi's statement?" Sartuche asked. When Bugliosi said yes, Sartuche wanted to see it, but the lawyer said he didn't have it with him. Sartuche dashed out the nearest exit in such a rush that his service revolver was jostled loose and fell clattering on the floor.

The race was on. Bugliosi hurried to the West Los Angeles Division to try to get a statement from Sergeant Wright before the LAPD could get to him. "I was not quick enough," Bugliosi recounted. "When I arrived I was told Wright was on the phone. Ten minutes later he appeared holding a yellow paper in his hand. The name 'Sartuche' was written on it."[340]

Of course Wright backtracked from his earlier positive identification of the bullet and said he couldn't be sure, now, if it had been a bullet. But he had been quite sure before Sartuche got to him. Unfortunately, not a lot of people are brave enough to tell the truth when their future income depends upon them *not* telling that truth. His reversal must be understood in this light.

In the fall of 1975, pressed for new tests by a joint lawsuit by Paul Schrade and CBS as well as inquiries from the Board of Supervisors and City Council, Los Angeles Superior Court Judge Robert Wenke ordered a panel of experts to reexamine the ballistics evidence in the case. While some saw that as a positive move designed to address the questions of conspiracy, this could also be viewed as a defensive move designed to forestall a larger Congressional investigation, a serious possibility at that point, that might have been unable to ignore the growing evidence of conspiracy.

Judge Wenke appointed seven people to the panel so there could be no tie on any vote. Each person was nominated to Judge Wenke by a different party. The panel members were, in alphabetical order, Stanton O. Berg (chosen by Los Angeles County), Alfred A. Biasotti (chosen by the Los Angeles District Attorney's office), Lowell W. Bradford (chosen by CBS News), Cortlandt Cunningham (chosen by then State Attorney General Evelle Younger), Patrick Garland (chosen as an "Expert at large" representing no one's interests in particular), Charles V. Morton (chosen by Sirhan) and Ralph Turner (chosen by Schrade).[341]

Five of the seven members—all of those not chosen by Schrade or Sirhan— were members of the Association of Firearm and Tool Mark Examiners founded at the February 1969 meeting in Chicago that Wolfer attended immediately

---

340   Turner and Christian, p. 181.
341   Stanton O. Berg, untitled history of the AFTE, afte.org/uploads/documents/berg.pdf, accessed September 6, 2016.

following his trial appearance, and some of them had been present at that meeting.[342]

The panel was given a number of bullets to examine, including bullets purportedly retrieved from Kennedy, Goldstein and Weisel; test bullets fired from Sirhan's gun; and eight bullets the panel fired from Sirhan's gun to test against.

The panel's report stated that two cannelures had been found on the Kennedy neck bullet, and that it was not possible to accurately determine rifling angles on the bullets due to the damage on each bullet. The cannelure discrepancy Harper had found and MacDonnell had confirmed was explained away as having to do with the fact that Harper's Balliscan photographs were in black and white, while the panel's photographs were in color. But that didn't make sense, since Harper had physically examined the bullets by hand *many* times, as we have already seen. It made more sense that the bullets the panel was examining were not the same ones Harper had examined.

"Can't anyone on that panel count?" Harper exploded to Christian after finding out the panel found wood embedded in the two bullets found in Sirhan's car. "They just finished examining the ninth and tenth bullets and don't even know it!"[343]

Harper knew that bullet holes had been found in the pantry after the shooting, which begged the question, where did the bullets go? Bullets don't bore into wood and then throw themselves into reverse and back out! Knowing police as he did, Harper had no trouble assuming the police had dug the bullets out of the wall and planted them in Sirhan's car in an attempt to further link Sirhan to the pantry shooting while simultaneously disposing of evidence that would have proved to be two bullets too many for Sirhan to have fired.

The panelists, however, as had Grant Cooper at Sirhan's trial, accepted the validity of the ballistics evidence without question. They stayed narrowly focused on their task. They could not match the bullets found in Sirhan's car to Sirhan's gun, due to the damage on the bullets. In fact, the panel couldn't match *any* of the bullets from the shooting to Sirhan's gun.

The big finding that the media reported heavily was that the panel could find no evidence that a second gun had been used. The media instantly misreported that as definitive proof that no second gun had been used. Lowell Bradford, the CBS-chosen expert, was particularly upset by this misreporting. Absence of evidence is the not the same thing as evidence of absence. As Bugliosi put it during

---

342   Stanton O. Berg, untitled history of the AFTE, afte.org/uploads/documents/berg.pdf, accessed September 6, 2016.

343   Turner and Christian, p. 177.

his appearance in the Owen case, "It would be like walking down my street and saying I saw no avocados on the street. That doesn't mean there *weren't* any avocados, only that I didn't *see* the avocados."[344]

Oddly enough, a close reading of the panel's report suggests a second gun had *very likely been used*, because while three of the victim bullets could be matched to each other (according to five of the seven experts, with the other two saying only they could not make a positive identification of the victim bullets with each other[345]), *none of the victim bullets could be positively matched to Sirhan's gun. And none of the test bullets fired from Sirhan's gun in 1975 could be matched to Wolfer's test bullets fired in 1968 or any of the other evidence bullets.*

Let me restate that. Not one of the bullets from the pantry could be successfully matched to Sirhan's gun. A match *should* have been possible if the official story had been correct. At the very least, test bullets fired from the gun should have matched the original test bullets fired from Sirhan's gun. But even those did not match. So what happened?

The official explanation for this was that Sirhan's gun had become heavily coated with lead since the time Sirhan fired it in the pantry. But given the gun had been in the sole possession of the court since the time of Wolfer's test firings that implied that someone in an official capacity with the justice system had to have repeatedly fired lead bullets through the barrel, fouling the barrel, an extraordinary development that represented illegal evidence tampering. Since that would lead to the obvious question of why the prosecution felt the need to obscure evidence in their own case, a different explanation had to be concocted: that unnamed cops accessed the evidence and fired Sirhan's gun over the years to make souvenir bullets, a ghoulish and illegal act and one that permanently damaged the evidence in a case under appeal that was guaranteed to receive immense scrutiny.

But does that explanation make sense? The gun was not stored in an LAPD evidence locker where anyone with a friend in the property lab could get to it. It was stored nearly immediately after Wolfer fired the test shots with the County Clerk in a secured area that a cop would have no access to. And remember that Joe Busch's grand jury found no evidence to suggest any of the evidence had been tampered with while in custody.

According to Turner and Christian, "One of the firearms experts later postulated that the leading might have 'grown' within the gun barrel (like

---

344   Turner and Christian, p. 176.

345   FBI copy of the Kranz Report, Part 2 of 3, p. 13, vault.fbi.gov/Robert%20F%20Kennedy%20 (Assassination)%20Robert%2F%20Kennedy%20(Assassination)%20Part%202%20of%203/view, accessed September 11, 2016. The two experts unable to make the match were, perhaps predictably, the two chosen by Sirhan's lawyers and Paul Schrade: Charles Morton and Ralph Turner. All five chosen by CBS and the government entities felt a match could be made.

algae)—a theory completely beyond the comprehension of scientists in the field of metallurgy, we discovered."[346]

There are, of course, two other possible explanations. The first is that someone in an official capacity, like Wolfer, *knew* the bullets would not match the gun and deliberately fouled the barrel while he had it to prevent that secret from being proven. But this seems unlikely, as Wolfer had not yet made any bullet comparisons at the point at which he gave the gun to the Grand Jury so he could hardly have known there would be issues to cover up.

The last explanation is the simplest, and here perhaps Occam's Razor serves us the best. Maybe the reason the barrel was leaded is that none of the copper-jacketed bullets expended in the pantry had been fired from it. Credible witnesses saw Sirhan fire his gun in the pantry. But no witness "saw" him fire *copper-jacketed* bullets, or *any* bullets, for that matter. Bullets move too quickly to be seen with the naked eye. People saw a *flame* coming out of Sirhan's gun and *assumed* that meant a bullet had exited. But Sirhan could have been firing blanks, i.e., slugless cartridges. The numerous witness reports of seeing a tongue of flame come from Sirhan's gun muzzle support this notion, as bullets do not create much of a flash when fired, but blanks or slugless cartridges contain paper that flash-burns when the gun is fired, producing a long, highly visible flame.

If Sirhan had fired blanks, then at least two other shooters had to have been firing in the pantry to account for the sheer number of bullets (seven removed from victims, one lost in the ceiling space, and another four that apparently entered the southern and center pantry doorframes, to be removed and hidden later). If Sirhan had fired blanks, the conspirators would have wanted someone firing from Sirhan's direction to hide this fact. And that appears to be exactly what happened.

It also appears that Wolfer or someone working closely with him in the lab somehow substituted fake bullets for the three victim bullets the panel had matched to each: the Kennedy bullet, the Goldstein bullet, and the Weisel bullet.

This begins to sound like a crazy conspiracy theory. But in fact, there's strong evidence suggesting this is exactly what happened, and the panel's experts all missed it due to a form of misdirection. The panel was so focused on proving matches or mismatches between the bullets that not one of them stopped to verify that the bullets they were comparing were actually the bullets they were purported to be.

In the LAPD's files, there is a mysterious document titled "Confidential Addenda to the Lowenstein Inquiry." The undated, anonymous document from the SUS files states:

---

346   Turner and Christian, p. 189.

This separate addenda contains confidential information relative to the questions submitted by Allard Lowenstein. The information has not been revealed prior to this report and may conflict with previous statements made by the Chief of Police and other officials.

Serious consideration should be given to the release of this information.

There exists a photograph of the Kennedy bullet and a test bullet taken through a comparison microscope showing one Land comparison.

It is not intended to be a bullet striation identification comparison because the lighting and details of the bullet are not displayed in the proper position.

The photograph is an overall photo not shot for striation detail.

The photograph is of a groove made by a Land in the barrel of the gun; the principal area of the photo is referred to as "one Land width." The area on either side of this Land width depicts a partial groove marking.

The fuzzy area on the left side of the photo is due to a deficiency in the optics of the microscope. This defect has existed since the Department first received the microscope and efforts to correct the defect have been unsuccessful.

The defect was a subject in the Kirschke case. The photograph shows identical Land widths between the Kennedy and test bullet. It also shows a comparison area between the shoulders of the Land widths. This comparison area is located approximately in the center of the shoulders.

The existence of this photograph is believed to be unknown by anyone outside of this Department. It should be rebuttal evidence were this case ever to be retried. However, the release of this information at this time would be susceptible to criticism because lay people would in all probability have difficulty deciphering this photograph. The issue as to its not being revealed at an earlier time may further make its authenticity suspect, particularly to the avid, exact assassination buff.[347]

Translation: We have secret evidence we have withheld from the public so we can use it to put calls to conspiracy to rest if the case is ever retried. But people paying attention will challenge its authenticity.

---

347   "Confidential Addenda to the Lowenstein Inquiry," SUS files, viewable at www.maryferrell.org/showDoc.html?docId=99861&relPageId=74&search=addenda, accessed August 25, 2016.

This photograph was presented to Wenke's panel as a comparison of the Kennedy bullet and a test bullet from Sirhan's gun. To a nonexpert who had no access to the physical evidence, this could have been enough to convince the public that Robert Kennedy had been killed by a bullet from Sirhan's gun.

But the experts soon found a serious discrepancy in that assertion. The panel found this photomicrograph, "Special Exhibit 10," showed the Kennedy bullet and the *Goldstein* bullet together, not the Kennedy bullet and a *test* bullet. At best, this only proved that the two bullets came from the same gun, but not necessarily Sirhan's gun.

Was the assertion that one of the bullets was a test bullet a mistake or a lie? One need look no further than Wolfer's log. The day this photo was made, Wolfer logged a "comparison" (meaning photomicrograph) of the Kennedy and Goldstein bullets. The photomicrograph would have been done under the same equipment with which the photograph was ultimately made. There was no log entry for a "comparison" between the Kennedy bullet and a test bullet. And as we saw earlier, Wolfer was deemed by the California Supreme Court to have "negligently presented false demonstrative evidence," so it wouldn't be unreasonable to suggest Wolfer knew it was a lie. Wolfer even admitted in a case referenced by Blehr above that he had physically altered ID markings on a cartridge case (and Blehr suspected he had altered more than the one he admitted to).

The panel was proud to have unmasked this deception of trying to pass another victim bullet off as a test bullet to show a match between the Kennedy neck bullet and Sirhan's gun. But they hadn't looked nearly closely enough, as there was a far more sinister deception they all missed.

Perhaps the panel had been distracted, as September 1975 was an extraordinary month in a year of unusual events. President Gerald Ford survived not one but *two* close-range assassination attempts just 17 days apart, in California. Charles Manson devotee Squeaky Fromme tried to kill him in Sacramento, and FBI informant (and last-minute Secret Service detainee) Sara Jane Moore tried to kill him in San Francisco. The success of either attempt would have finally put a Rockefeller in the White House. Ford's appointed Vice President, Nelson Rockefeller, had tried and failed to win the Republican nomination for president in 1960, 1964, and 1968.[348]

Nelson Rockefeller had been particularly close to the CIA. They worked closely together in Latin America, as detailed in the excellent book *Thy Will Be Done*. In fact, our tax dollars, which pay for the CIA, provided security vetting services to a Rockefeller-owned oil company in Venezuela. And The Rockefeller Brothers Fund

---

348   Squeaky Fromme attempted to kill President Ford in the California State Capitol of Sacramento on September 5, 1975. Sara Jane Moore shot at Ford on September 22, 1975, outside the St. Francis Hotel on Union Square in San Francisco.

helped pay for some of the CIA's worst mind control experiments conducted by Ewen Cameron at the Allan Memorial Institute at McGill University in Montreal, Canada.

And on September 18, 1975, Patty "Tania" Hearst, who had been kidnapped and seduced (the official story) or brainwashed (Hearst's claim) into becoming a member of the Symbionese Liberation Army, was arrested for a robbery in San Francisco after having been kidnapped the year before. Theories that the SLA was a false flag operation by the CIA to discredit the antiwar left were already in circulation, and with some evidence to support them.[349]

But if the panel had been distracted, Sirhan's neighbor Rose "Lynn" Mangan was fixated. She spent years studying the ballistics evidence in this case. Mangan had befriended Harper, who spurred her curiosity when he told the 1975 panel was a "fix" and that the bullets had been switched.

Mangan carefully traced the chain of possession of the Kennedy neck bullet and the Goldstein bullets. She noted when Noguchi recovered it, he had marked the base with his initials and the last two digits of the autopsy case number, TN31. The marking of TN31 on the bullet appears in both the autopsy report and the Grand Jury transcript of Noguchi's testimony.

But when Mangan looked at the markings Patrick Garland had carefully detailed in his inventory list for the panel, she found the "Kennedy" bullet the panel examined was not from Kennedy at all, as the base was marked "DWTN."

One of the reasons to believe Wolfer, and not anyone else, switched the bullets was this marking. Wolfer apparently created the photomicrograph using this bullet. It makes sense he would put his initials on it. It doesn't make sense he wouldn't have noticed that someone else had put his initials on that bullet.

Similarly, Mangan traced the Goldstein bullet through the LAPD's records and found the doctor who removed it had marked it with an "X" on the base. Mangan even called the doctor, and he confirmed to her personally that he had put an "X" on the base of the bullet.[350] But the "Goldstein" bullet the panel examined had *no marking* on its base, so a "6" was added to mark it for the panel's purposes. It strains credulity that someone was able to successfully turn an "X" into a 6 such that no one noticed. Clearly, both the "Kennedy" and "Goldstein" bullets the panel examined were *not* the Kennedy and Goldstein bullets originally recovered.

When Mangan first told me the bullets had been switched, I didn't want to believe it. Such an act was such an incredible cheat, so egregious. So I reviewed the documents in SUS and retraced Mangan's information to confirm this for myself. Yes, Noguchi had listed his marking of TN31 in the autopsy report. Yes, he

349   Peter M. Shane, "The SLA: Revolutionary Irresponsibility," *The Harvard Crimson*, May 29, 1974; Mae Brussell, "The SLA is the CIA," *The Realist*, February 1974. See also *Revolution's End: The Patty Hearst Kidnapping, Mind Control and the Secret History of Donald DeFreeze and the SLA* by Brad Schreiber (New York: Skyhorse Publishing, 2016).
350   Mangan, p. 30.

had confirmed that marking at the Grand Jury hearing. Yes, the panel's version of that bullet was marked DWTN, not TN31. Yes, the Goldstein marking of X by the doctor was right there in the SUS files. But the panel's bullet had a 6 where the X should have been. Mangan was right about the markings at all points. That meant the bullets the panel had investigated were *not* the bullets they had been purported to be. Someone, most likely Wolfer, had faked the bullets and then took a photo of the fake bullets with a built-in lie.

Intelligence operatives well know that if you bury one lie inside another more easily exposed, most people stop digging when they hit the first lie, figuring *that* was the thing you were trying to hide, so the second lie remains protected. The lie was that it was a match between the Kennedy neck bullet and a test bullet. But the deeper lie was that they weren't even the original bullets. Since *neither* bullet matched its original markings, we can only accurately say the bullets in the photo were a fake "Kennedy" bullet and a fake "Goldstein" bullet.

That meant the panel's findings were irrelevant, and that the taxpayers paid for a sham investigation, with one exception. *Even the substituted bullets* had not matched Sirhan's gun. Why?

Under questioning in connection with the Wenke panel's findings, Wolfer stated that he had tried but failed to get the original Sirhan gun back for further testing, as it was securely in the custody of the Grand Jury.[351] So clearly, Sirhan's gun had been sealed into the evidence envelope and sent to the Grand Jury before the bullet mismatch was discovered.

Supporting this is the evidence envelope Garland recorded for the gun. The date on the envelope is June 5, 1968, and the charge was (correctly, at that time) listed as 217 P.C. (the penal code for attempted murder). Kennedy did not die until the wee hours of June 6, after which all records refer to the charge as 187 P.C., the code for homicide. Since Wolfer did not receive the Kennedy neck bullet to compare to other bullets until June 6, he could not have found the discrepancy until then. In other words, he probably would have simply refired Sirhan's gun to make all the fake bullets, but he was unable to because the evidence was no longer in his possession, a good argument for getting the gun away from the police and the crime lab as soon as possible in any shooting.

Could there be an alternative explanation? Dan Moldea has suggested that Patrick Garland's inventory list wasn't meant to list *every* marking on the bullet. But that is simply not true, as the carefully detailed and extensive notes Garland made demonstrate. That was the precise reason for the exercise of creating the

---

351   FBI's copy of the Kranz Report, Part 2 of 3, p. 3, vault.fbi.gov/Robert%20F%20Kennedy%20
(Assassination)%20/Robert%20F%20Kennedy%20(Assassination)%20Part%202%20of%203/view, accessed September 11,
2016. There were multiple revisions to this report over a two-year period. This appears to be the final version.

inventory—to ensure all bullets were fully and completely identifiable as that bullet and no other bullet.

In addition, the end of a .22 bullet is tiny—about the size of the eraser on a Number 2 pencil. If TN31 were inscribed there, it was likely with TN on top and 31 underneath. Similar, DWTN would likely have been inscribed DW on top and TN underneath because it's tough to even write *that* small on the base of a bullet. So it's not possible the bullet read DWTN31 and that Garland had just missed the 31 at the end. And this would have required Noguchi to have left room for Wolfer to add a "DW" before his own remarks.

Switching bullets is a completely illegal act of evidence tampering, but that misses the point. *Bullet switching should have been unnecessary.* If Sirhan had been the lone shooter, all the bullets should have matched each other and the gun. There would have been no reason to switch *any* bullets if Sirhan had fired them all. The very fact that *any* had been switched indicates at least *one* of them came from a gun other than Sirhan's.

Mangan had clearly shown me that *two* bullets had been switched. But five of the seven panel members had matched *three* bullets together (that they couldn't match to Sirhan's gun). That left only two possibilities: either the police had in their custody a gun, not belonging to Sirhan that had been used to shoot Weisel, from which fake Kennedy and Goldstein bullets were later fired, or the Weisel bullet, like the Kennedy and Goldstein bullets before it, had also been switched.

Technically there was a third possibility—the bullets really didn't come from the same gun, and the panel was mistaken in saying they did, *which would also prove a conspiracy*. Let's rule that out, even though several on the panel had ties to the National Security state. Let's assume these seven experts were honest and factual with the evidence they were presented, and that it was the evidence itself that wasn't factual. Why switch the bullets at all if not to make a match?

So which was it? Did the LAPD have a gun that had been used in the pantry in its possession, or had the Weisel bullet, too, been switched? I dug into the records to find this answer for myself.

In Patrick Garland's bullet inventory, the Weisel bullet had "LM" inscribed in its base. One of the panelists, however, noted what appeared to be an "O" on the base of the bullet following the "L" and "M." In the evidence log, the Weisel bullet was recorded as showing a marking of "LMO" on it. So it was at least *possible* that the Weisel bullet hadn't been switched.

But was that the original marking? Examine the evidence log page pictured in Figure 3. Note how the bullet marking "LMO" seems to have been added after the fact between the words "marked" and "for ID." The writing is not in the same size or style as the text immediately before and after it. Note how the "M" is written differently from the other "M"s in this paragraph, suggesting it was entered by a different hand.

Figure 3: Evidence log page except for the Weisel bullet

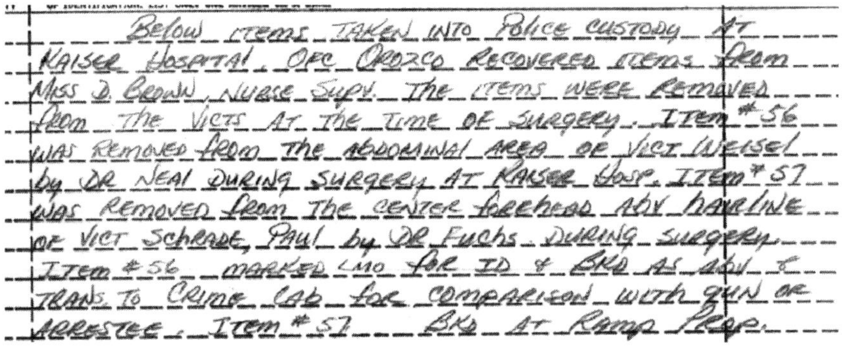

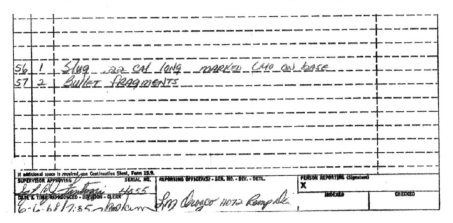

Below items taken into Police custody at
Kaiser Hospital. Ofc Orozco recovered items from
Miss D. Brown, Nurse Supv. The items were removed
from the victs at the time of surgery. Item #56
was removed from the abdominal area of Vict Weisel
by Dr Neal during surgery at Kaiser Hosp. Item #57
was removed from the center forehead abv hairline
of Vict Schrade, Paul by Dr Fuchs during surgery.
Item #56 marked LMO for ID & Bkd as abv &
trans to Crime Lab for comparison with gun of
arrestee. Item #57 Bkd at Ramp Prop.

Source: Scan of the evidence log page from the California State Archives

Note a similar mismatch of M's at the bottom of this same page, as shown in Figure 4. The "M" of LMO is angular, but the "m" of "marked" is rounded.

Figure 4: The bottom of the Weisel bullet evidence page currently in evidence

56	1	Slug .22 cal long marked LMO on base
57	2	Bullet fragments

If additional space is required, use Continuation Sheet, Form 15.9.
SUPERVISOR APPROVING — SERIAL NO. 4455
REPORTING OFFICER(S) - SER. NO. - DIV. - DETL. — Lm Orozco 11072 Ramp Det
PERSON REPORTING (Signature) X
DATE & TIME REPRODUCED - DIVISION - CLERK — 6-6-68 17:35
INDEXED — CHECKED

Source: Scan of the evidence log page from the California State Archives

In addition, the archivist who sent me a photo of the actual log page at my request noted this page "appears to be a copy as the bottom portion of the document is cut off at the left signature." Why would someone store a copy of the original instead of the original, unless the point was to hide an alteration?

In addition, if the Weisel bullet had *not* been switched, one would expect to find a straightforward chain of possession. Instead, this bullet has an inexplicable gap in its evidentiary record.

The SUS summary of Dr. William Neal's interview states that the Weisel bullet was retrieved by Dr. Neal at 2:30 A.M. on June 5 and handed over to Detective Leroy Matthew (L.M.) Orozco of the LAPD an "identifiable lead bullet" on the same day, June 5. There are multiple records indicating Orozco picked up the bullet on June 5. But the bullet wasn't logged into evidence, as item 56, until 5:25 P.M., June 6.

The June 6 date is not a mistake. The evidence log pages before and after this entry were also dated June 6 and in chronological order by time. And another bullet Orozco retrieved, the Kennedy neck bullet, which wasn't pulled from Kennedy's body until June 6, was logged several items earlier, as item 53 with a note that Orozco received it at 9:30 A.M. Orozco signed both sheets—which contained both the date and time of recovery—of the sheets with the Kennedy neck bullet and the Weisel bullet.

Did Detective Orozco hold back the bullet until he could compare it to the one from Kennedy? Had he turned it in on the 5th and the Property Division just sat on it? Could it be that the evidence booking person was simply backlogged? That doesn't seem to be the case, as the Kennedy neck bullet was recovered at 8:40 A.M., given to Orozco by Jordan at 9:30 A.M., and logged into evidence a few minutes later at 9:45 A.M., which makes sense given how close the coroner's location was to Parker Center (a five-minute drive). Everything about that chain of possession seemed legitimate. There was even a note in the evidence log that the crime lab had been contacted so a bullet comparison could be made with the suspect's gun. That is unlikely. I've talked to a few officers from the LAPD and all have assured me that evidence—even in large crimes—is logged immediately and a receipt issued.

Why then did the Weisel bullet, which Orozco appears to have had in his possession before the Kennedy neck bullet, not get entered into the log until 5:26 P.M.? Did Detective Orozco realize that a conspiracy had transpired? Might he have been able to tell by a quick visual comparison that the bullets did not match? Is that why the (apparently substituted) Weisel bullet was logged into evidence about an hour and a half into a five-hour silence in Wolfer's log entries on June 6 between 4 P.M. and 9 P.M.? Did Wolfer fire a new bullet that became the "Weisel" bullet?

There is no log entry to show that Wolfer ever compared the Weisel bullet to test bullets or to the Kennedy neck bullet or any other victim bullet, for that matter. I believe from sheer curiosity, at the very least, he would have. But what if all that needed, too, was an eyeball comparison to note that they didn't match?

Similarly, Wolfer received the Kennedy bullet from "Rampart Detectives" at 3:15 P.M. At 4 P.M. he indicated "End of watch." Then, five hours later, he logged "9 P.M. – Comparison of Kennedy and Goldstein bullet." The only entry following that was his 1 A.M. "End of watch" recorded (again) on the morning of June 7.

Given that the photomicrograph the panel received was dated June 6, it appears that someone, likely Wolfer, *knew* that the *actual* Kennedy and Goldstein bullets didn't match, so he fired two bullets from a gun—and it couldn't have been the Sirhan gun since it had gone to the Grand Jury—and pretended those were the Kennedy bullet and the Goldstein bullet, and then took a picture of them to spring on unsuspecting investigators in some distant year to come. Remember that test bullets had also already been given to the Grand Jury, so those couldn't have been substituted without showing a direct mismatch. The Weisel bullet may also have been forged at this time.

Understand that the Warren Commission's investigation was being questioned seriously at this point in time. Anyone with a brain had to know the assassination of the President's brother would also come upon some vigorous scrutiny within a few years. What better to have in your back pocket than evidence that convincingly, at least to the undiscerning, seemed to dispel notions of conspiracy?

Wolfer may well have ate and napped or run errands during the 4 P.M. to 9 P.M. gap. But he did have five hours to create new bullets, and he had access to another gun, a gun "with a very close serial number," H58725.

If you believe H58725 was just a typo of the Sirhan gun number of H53725, consider the following two pieces of correspondence Lynn Mangan dug up. When Luke McKissack was Sirhan's attorney for a time, he wrote in a letter to Sirhan:

> In case you heard about the fact that the ballistics expert in your case used a different gun for [trial] testimony which was subsequently destroyed and the LAPD is investigating this fact, this is correct, and we are following up on that point.[352]

And a phone report from Captain G. Campbell of his call with Grant Cooper in 1971 reads:

> Cooper stated that to the best of his recollection the gun used by Sirhan to commit his crime was not produced during Wolfer's testimony in the trial ....[353]

---

352   Mangan, postscript in a letter from Sirhan's attorney Luke McKissack to Sirhan, May 31, 1971.
353   Mangan, from Captain G. Campbell's report of a phone call with Grant Cooper, June 8, 1971.

If Wolfer were going to forge bullets from another gun, it makes sense he'd try to get a gun with a "very close serial number" to Sirhan's so that the markings would be very similar. While any gun barrel could have anomalies that made it unique, you would think two guns manufactured close to each other in sequence would be more similar in terms of the barrel than those manufactured far apart in sequence.

The Wenke panel members noted a pronounced "defect" in Sirhan's gun barrel and saw a "similar" defect in the bullets produced, but the more minute markings were different. For these reasons, I'm inclined to believe the victim bullets were "forged" using gun H58725. As noted earlier, given the presence of three identical numbers in the serial number, "725" may have represented the coded date of manufacture. If true, then Sirhan's gun (H53725) and the mystery gun (H58725) could have been only five guns apart coming off the manufacturing line. If there were a defect in the barrel of one gun, the defect may have persisted across a few barrels in sequence, making it an ideal candidate for forging fake victim bullets.

If that were the case, using the H58725 gun in court would have helped Wolfer, because he would have been telling the truth when he said the bullets came from that gun and no other. It would explain why the prosecution had Uecker, who only saw the gun during the struggle, identify the serial number as being correct in court rather than Rafer Johnson, who had the gun in his personal possession before turning it over to the police. It could also mean Wolfer was telling the truth when he said he belatedly asked for the Sirhan gun and was given the wrong gun number. Maybe he really *didn't* have gun H18602 until June 10. Maybe the number on both sets of test bullet envelopes should have read H58725!

If Wolfer was this smart and this foresighted, someone might ask, why didn't he forge the bullet markings on the bases to match? Perhaps he saw no need. After all, in the five years since John Kennedy had been killed, not one researcher had publicly challenged whether the markings on the bullet in evidence as CE 399, the so-called "magic" bullet said to have passed through Kennedy and Gov. Connally while remaining nearly pristine, matched the markings of the bullet as it had originally been logged into custody. It wasn't until decades later that researchers started checking the chain of possession on that bullet and found that the bullet in evidence in the JFK case, too, appeared to have been substituted.[354]

That said, had Wolfer tried to match up the markings, a flip through the evidence log would have shown the marking for only one of the three bullets. There was no indication in the evidence log of the marking on the Kennedy neck bullet or the Goldstein bullet, but there was a marking for the Weisel

---

354   Robert Harris, "The Connally Bullet," jfkhistory.com/bell/bellarticle/BellArticle.html, accessed September 16, 2016.

bullet listed: LMO. That's the only bullet today that has the marking indicated in the original record, but as you just saw, that's likely because the bullet was switched *before* it was entered into the log.

Nailing down exactly who knew about problems with the bullet evidence is problematic, but it's clear that *someone* knew there was an issue with the sheer number of bullets recovered in this case. The Goldstein bullet's evidence sheet has "CONFIDENTIAL" stamped in large letters across the bottom of it. That inscription only appears on two of the log pages—the Goldstein bullet page and the page for item 106, four live rounds of "Super X" ammunition found at the site of Kennedy's speech at Valley College on May 28, 1968, where "CONFIDENTIAL" was handwritten across the bottom in large letters. Perhaps the LAPD kept *all* bullet evidence "confidential" until they could figure out how many bullets they had to account for, disappearing any that put the total over the eight bullets Sirhan's gun was capable of firing.

The Goldstein bullet might prove this hypothesis correct. It was initially logged as evidence item 1, as shown by Wolfer's log. At 1:45 P.M. in Wolfer's log, we find this entry: "Item 1 – 22 cal. slug (Goldstein)." Why, then, in the master evidence log, does the Goldstein item appear as item 113? The log sheet shows clearly this evidence was taken into custody just hours after the shooting, at 4 A.M. on June 5 and received into evidence June 5, 1968 at 5:20 A.M. By rights, this evidence should have been given a much higher log entry. The Kennedy bullet went to the property division first, where it was logged and then given to Wolfer. But the Goldstein bullet appears to have been deliberately kept from the record initially, perhaps because so many bullet holes were found at the scene and initially, the total number of bullets hadn't even been pulled out of bodies yet. Maybe someone knew that recording *any* of the bullets until *all* of them could be accounted for could present a problem.

This could explain how other bullets, such as the one the police told a reporter had been recovered from the pantry doorframe, disappeared from the record. Maybe that bullet had been on a sheet also marked Confidential, and ultimately disposed of when the number of bullets found equaled eight. The press had reported that Goldstein had been shot and that a bullet had been recovered, so the Goldstein bullet could not remain hidden. The four found at the scene of Valley College didn't damage the official story so those didn't need to stay hidden either. But any bullets recovered from the ceiling, walls or doorframes in the pantry would have had to have been kept from the record to keep the bullet count down to eight. That would also explain the delay in the Weisel bullet making it into the official log. It's very possible other bullets were recovered and kept separate on confidential sheets, only to be disposed of when the already-made-public bullet count reached eight.

There's a reason the truth about convoluted matters rarely surfaces. Too few people research cases this closely, and the authorities have worked hard to stay ahead of the revelations so they can find some new "explanation" to wave it away. It's taken me years to find, evaluate, and understand this evidence. Now that this information is being made public, will the media have the guts to report it? Will the LAPD give the case a new investigation? Will Los Angeles County?

I doubt it, after the Kranz Report. The Kranz Report proved that the lies in the Robert Kennedy assassination had become too big to fail, and that any explanation, no matter how insubstantial, would do where the truth could not be told.

After District Attorney Busch died unexpectedly in office in mid-July 1975 at the age of 49, private attorney Thomas F. Kranz approached then acting District Attorney John Howard and said he had always had some concerns about the Robert Kennedy case, and he would like to seek appointment to the role of District Attorney should the County Board of Supervisors find themselves deadlocked over a successor. Howard himself had angled for the D.A.'s job after Busch's death but had been thwarted by Baxter Ward.[355]

After Schrade and CBS filed suit to gain access to the evidence, Howard called Kranz in and asked if he would consider being a special counsel instead, not so much to look into the case but, as Kranz noted, to satisfy the public that there was no cover-up. Kranz wrote:

> The problem confronting Howard, as with Joe Busch, was not the validity of the verdict in the Sirhan case, but the erosion of public confidence in the system of justice in Los Angeles County due to the many questions that were continually being raised in the Sirhan matter.[356]

Howard proposed Kranz serve as "an independent special counsel" who "would work with the District Attorney's office in the preparation and presentation of all evidence in the pending court hearing." But that doesn't sound "independent," does it?

Kranz conducted interviews from January to March in 1976, and drafted a report from March to May 1976. But it took until March 1977 for Kranz to complete the final version. The goal appeared in part to be to head off a Congressional investigation by the House Select Committee on Assassinations. The HSCA had

---

355   Roger M. Grace, "District Attorney Busch Dies, Supervisor Ward Calls Upon Acting D.A. to Resign—Or Else…," *Metropolitan News-Enterprise*, www.metnews.com/articles/2008/perspectives122208.htm, accessed September 11, 2016. According to the article, Howard had recently been charged in a drunk driving incident that had originally been reported as a hit-and-run.

356   The Kranz Report, via the FBI at vault.fbi.gov/Robert%20F%20Kennedy%20%28Assassination%29%20/ Robert%20F%20Kennedy%20%28Assassination%29%20Part%201%20of%203, accessed September 23, 2016.

been pressured by Rep. Lowenstein and others to include an investigation into the Robert Kennedy assassination. Ultimately, the HSCA focused solely on the assassinations of President John Kennedy and Martin Luther King.

Kranz's report, though replete with errors, attempted to explain away all evidence of conspiracy. Kranz's goal was clear: to bolster the official story. It was the County's way of doubling down on the cover-up. That so many books have been and are still being written about this case at the time of this writing indicates that Kranz's report failed.

In fact, in some ways, Kranz's report added to the suspicions that we have not been told the full truth. For example, Kranz inadvertently suggested there were in fact *many more than the three holes* reported by Wolfer in the ceiling tiles, in a statement that at least maps to Wolfer's original comment about how there were an "unbelievable" number of "damn holes" in the ceiling:

> In discussing ceiling panels, Wolfer stated he had found holes that had been made by fragments of fired bullets from Sirhan's weapon. These fragments had exploded, being hollow point Mini-Mag ammunition, and had split as they penetrated the ceiling tiles.[357]

Kranz also made reference to the four bullet holes noted in FBI Special Agent Greiner's report, but noted as well that "in the other 802 pages of the FBI files" there was no other reference to these holes. Well, if the FBI had decided to go along with the LAPD's cover-up, as they clearly did, what would one expect to find? Clearly the caption had been a mistake, not from an evidentiary point of view, but from a political point of view. Finding more bullets than Sirhan's gun would allow meant a conspiracy, and the FBI had already proven willing to cover up the conspiracies in the assassinations of President Kennedy and Martin Luther King. Why would they act any differently in the Robert Kennedy case? (The main reason for this obsequiousness on the part of the FBI will be discussed in a later chapter.) As with the police who told a reporter bullets had been removed from the pantry doorframes, the FBI, at the time of the photos, didn't know there was anything that needed to be covered up, so they just told the truth: bullet holes had been found in the pantry doorframes.

Kranz used for the holes the same logic he had just used about the ceiling panels: since the LAPD said there were seven bullets recovered and one lost in the ceiling space, that meant only eight bullets had been fired, end of story. Any other evidence just had to be wrong, in Kranz's view. That's like saying, since my energy bill this month is $15,000, I must have used $15,000 worth of energy, rather than saying wow, my energy bill is never that high—my bill must be *wrong!* Kranz

---

357   The Kranz Report.

accepted the preposterous notion that kitchen carts had made bullet holes in the pantry doorframes. The kitchen carts had rounded ends, not sharp, .22 caliber bullet-like projections on the ends of them capable of penetrating three-quarter-inch-thick pine wood and burrowing into the post behind the facing. (Someone online floated the notion that the holes had been made by Vince DiPierro based on a comment he had made about poking at a hole in the wall. I showed DiPierro the FBI's photographs of "bullet holes" and asked him specifically if he had made any of those holes. "Oh no," he replied, clearly surprised anyone would suggest that.)

Kranz uncritically accepted the word of every law enforcement official who had every reason to lie, but disbelieved witnesses to conspiracy who had *no* reason to dissemble. The Kranz report was clearly meant to close the door on conspiracy. For example, Kranz noted that the ceiling tiles from the pantry were destroyed because they had no value, without explaining why, then, they had been taken into evidence in the first place. He believed and recorded everything Wolfer said, without challenging him seriously (and without any apparent knowledge of the evidentiary issues raised in this chapter).

Kranz reported that a thorough examination of the pantry had been made in 1975, the "Great Pantry Raid" that Lowenstein had appropriately ridiculed. Kranz seemed satisfied that, having found the pantry devoid of bullet holes a full seven and a half years and many alterations later, none could have been there in 1968. This despite the fact that the man who removed the wood facing from the center of the swinging doors reported not only seeing two holes there but noting that they went through into the center frame of the doors. Kranz rebutted that by noting a second carpenter had inspected the west side of the center panel and hadn't seen exit holes on the west side. In Kranz's view, if bullets didn't go all the way through, bullets hadn't been fired into the pantry doorframe, a nonsequitur that wouldn't have passed muster in a junior high school logic class. Clearly, the bullets made it through the front facing and had lodged themselves into the wood block of the doorframe without passing all the way through, after which they were dug out and hidden from the record. This isn't rocket science.

Kranz commented that he always wondered about where the two bullets with wood embedded in them found in Sirhan's car came from. But he dared not suggest what Harper had naturally assumed, knowing the police as he did: that someone dug them out of the center doorframe and put them in Sirhan's car in a hope to link him to the shooting.

Kranz did the job he set out to do, to write a report designed to instill confidence in the local government. Too bad he didn't try harder to find out what the truth really was.

But our loss was Kranz's gain. Like so many before him, Kranz saw his fortunes rise in the wake of his activities in this case. His online résumé lists his additional positions as "Principal Deputy General Counsel, Department of the Army, Department of Defense, The Pentagon, 1985–1989. Special Assistant to the President [George H.W. Bush], The White House, 1989–1990. Associate Director, Federal Emergency Management Agency, 1990–1992. ... Member, Council of Foreign Relations." He was also a Member of the American Bar Association's "National Security Section," begging the question of how closely he has worked with intelligence agencies over the years.

Lowenstein, who in 1977 was appointed an Ambassador to the United Nations Commission on Human Rights, was disappointed in Kranz's work on the case, to put it mildly:

> Ambitious politicians far more scrupulous than Mr. Kranz have yielded to the temptation to recite fiction as fact at convenient moments, so one doesn't wish to be too harsh about his performance. Nevertheless, he left the case in worse shape than he found it, which was not easy to do. One had the right to hope for something better, but that of course is a summary of this whole distressing history.[358]

As the House Select Committee on Assassinations was enmeshed in its investigations into the JFK and MLK assassinations, Lowenstein not only described what had happened in the Robert Kennedy case but also, presciently, how the cover-ups would be effected in the HSCA as well:

> Despite all the obstacles, new facts have come out about what FBI agents, policemen, and other reputable persons said about the matter of bullets in doorframes, and it seems fair to say that there is now a rebuttable presumption that more than one assassin was involved. But what is even clearer than that is that nobody is making a serious effort to rebut that presumption. The notion seems to be that the presumption can be waited out, that unanswered questions will fade, given time, and that the best way to deal with awkward new facts is to ignore them until they can be denounced as "nothing new" and then dismissed; as if awkward facts somehow become less awkward or less pertinent with age.[359]

---

358   Lowenstein manuscript.
359   Allard Lowenstein, "The Murder of Robert Kennedy: Suppressed Evidence of More than One Assassin?"

Perhaps Lowenstein summed up the mood of all who had looked with honest intentions into the case by this point when he wrote in the *Saturday Review* in 1977:

> I do not know whether Sirhan acting alone murdered Robert Kennedy. I do know what happened when we tried to find out. Eventually, reluctantly, against all my instincts and wishes, I arrived at the melancholy thought that people who have nothing to hide do not lie, cheat, and smear to hide it.[360]

In March 1980, Lowenstein himself was shot and killed in his office by a former protégé, Dennis Sweeney, who claimed, among other crazy-sounding things, that he had received messages in his head broadcast by a CIA transmitter. After Sweeney shot Lowenstein, Sweeney calmly waited in Lowenstein's office to be arrested. He was deemed insane and sentenced to a mental hospital.[361] Like Sirhan before him, Sweeney was deemed to have been a "paranoid schizophrenic with hallucinations and delusions."

According to Robert Vaughn's autobiography, at the time of the shooting, Lowenstein was on the verge of getting a commitment from President Jimmy Carter to reopen an investigation into the Sirhan case if Carter were re-elected to a second term that November. But, as Vaughn put it, "Al died, Carter lost to Reagan, and the official veil of silence over the RFK murder has remained intact."[362]

Saturday Review, February 19, 1977.

360   Allard Lowenstein, "The Murder of Robert Kennedy: Suppressed Evidence of More than One Assassin?" *Saturday Review*, February 19, 1977.

361   Joe Klein, "A Protégé's Story," *New York Times*, June 13, 1982.

362   Robert Vaughn, *A Fortunate Life* (New York: St. Martin's Press, 2008), p. 258.

TOO MANY HOLES

"Police officers framed innocent individuals by planting evidence and committing perjury to gain convictions. Nothing is more inimical to the rule of law than police officers, sworn to uphold the law, flouting it and using their authority to convict innocent people. Innocent men and women pleaded guilty to crimes they did not commit and were convicted by juries because of the fabricated cases against them."

EVERY TIME I SIT IN A COURTROOM FOR JURY DUTY, THE JUDGE admonishes us *not to dismiss circumstantial evidence*, but to treat it the same way we would direct evidence. Several judges have given an example of seeing someone come in from the outside carrying an umbrella and wearing a wet raincoat. It would be reasonable to assume the person had come in from the rain. While it was *possible* that the person had jumped, fully clothed, into a shower to construct an elaborate ruse, without any additional evidence, the *reasonable* conclusion was that the person had just come in from the rain. You didn't have "proof" that the person had been out in the rain, but you could make a logical deduction based on the evidence presented.

In this case, ask yourself if it is reasonable to believe *every* witness to evidence of conspiracy was simply mistaken? That not *one* of the additional bullet holes reported in the pantry were actually bullet holes? That although the shooter had to have been behind Kennedy and all the witnesses who saw both Kennedy and Sirhan during the shooting put them from three to six feet apart, *all* the witnesses were mistaken? It's *possible* that all the other witnesses were randomly mistaken all in the same direction, but it is not *reasonable*.

Each judge has also admonished the would-be jurors that we were to decide for ourselves what the facts of the case were. We were to examine the evidence and testimony presented to determine the facts of the case. The judge stressed it was not the number or quality of witnesses that mattered. "If you believe a single witness," one judge told my October 2016 jury pool, "then you can consider that a fact. You don't judge the evidence by the number of witnesses that report the same thing. If you believe *even one* of them, that is enough for you to consider their statement a fact." Witnesses never have perfect recall of a crime. But in the pantry, enough of them told a consistent picture that what happened starts to become clear. Each judge also made clear that a person's position in life does not matter and should not even enter our minds. A criminal could be telling the truth. A policeman could be lying.

The "official" eight bullets

ONE BULLET LODGED IN EACH OF THE FIVE SHOOTING VICTIMS NOT named Kennedy in the pantry. Kennedy had been shot three times under the arm—one bullet lodged at his spine in the back of his neck, one bullet passed through his chest and exited, and one entered the back of his coat and exited the shoulder without breaking skin. One more bullet entered his head. Seven bullets were recovered from the six victims. But there were three holes in the ceiling that had already been photographed with probes running through them. So Wolfer, the LAPD criminalist, had to do some gymnastics with the bullets to make it so 12 points of entry could be explained by a mere eight bullets. Wolfer claimed that the bullet that exited Kennedy's chest went into the ceiling space and was lost. Wolfer posited that one of the bullets entered the ceiling, hit something, and then ricocheted back down to hit Elizabeth Evans in the forehead. Wolfer claimed the bullet that passed through Kennedy's jacket entered Paul Schrade's head, even though Paul Schrade was behind Kennedy when they were both shot and the bullet passed in a back-to-front trajectory through Kennedy. That's how 12 entry points became eight bullets.

But there was a serious problem, as we've already seen. All the witnesses who saw both Kennedy and Sirhan during the shooting put Sirhan in front of Kennedy. Several witness saw Kennedy put his hands up in front of his face. Clearly, *Kennedy himself perceived a threat from the front* because he threw up his hands to shield his face. It's *possible* that all the witnesses—including Senator Kennedy himself—were wrong on *every* piece of evidence that put Sirhan in front of Kennedy, but for that many people to be wrong all in the same direction is neither logical nor reasonable. What *is* reasonable is to believe that the police and other governmental authorities, having uncovered a conspiracy that put them in a difficult position, chose instead to bury it. And the cover-up started taking place nearly immediately, as we saw when Inspector Powers told Sergeant Sharaga to stop seeking other suspects.

Five more bullets for a total of 13

WE'VE SEEN HOW WITNESSES WITH EVIDENCE OF CONSPIRACY were coerced into changing their statements to conform to the official story of Sirhan as the lone assassin. And most physical evidence that indicated conspiracy was either destroyed or altered. But there is one piece of evidence that just couldn't be explained away, even by the Kranz Report. It concerned Los Angeles County's Chief Administrative Officer, Harry L. Hufford, so much that he wrote the FBI about it in late 1977.

Hufford understood that the excuse that pantry carts had caused the holes in the doorframes would not stand up to historical scrutiny. And any actual bullet hole in the pantry was conclusive evidence of a ninth bullet, one more than Sirhan's gun could hold, which necessarily proved at least two shooters. The pantry doorframes had *four holes* from something that had passed through the doorframe paneling and directly into the doorframe posts. And the official FBI record of the crime scene indicated these were "bullet holes."

Author Dan Moldea has suggested that the only reason these holes were photographed and labeled by the FBI "bullet holes" was because a kitchen worker said these were bullet holes. This despite Moldea's interview with Maynard Davis, a lieutenant with the Los Angeles Sheriff's Office (LASO), who discussed a photo in which LASO's Walter Tew had circled and initialed a hole in the doorframe behind molding that had been pried off. Davis told Moldea that was "SOP" (standard operating procedure) "for officers to identify bullet holes in that matter."[363]

But even if we accept Moldea's strange theory that the FBI would send an amateur photographer who couldn't tell a bullet hole from a dent to the scene of Senator Robert Kennedy's assassination, a case the FBI knew would be scrutinized closely for the next several decades, would that make the kitchen worker's identification any less credible? If at your workplace, after a shooting, fresh holes appeared on a doorframe that you walked through many times a day, wouldn't you be highly qualified to state those were bullet holes formed during the shooting? You might never have seen a bullet hole in your life before or been any kind of an expert. But you would surely recognize a fresh hole where none had previously existed.

To orient you to the items Hufford refers to in his letter, review Figures 5 through 8.

---

363   Moldea's interview of Maynard Davis is Exhibit 35 in the 1992 request for a new grand jury, www.maryferrell.org/showDoc.html?docId=99873.

Figure 5: Drawing of the bullet holes in the pantry doorframes after the wood facing on the doorframes was removed

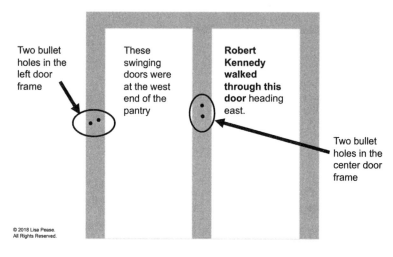

Two bullet holes in the left door frame

These swinging doors were at the west end of the pantry

Robert Kennedy walked through this door heading east.

Two bullet holes in the center door frame

Source: Drawing by Lisa Pease

Figure 6: Drawing overlaid with FBI photos E1 and E2 (after the wood facing on the doorframes was removed). Note that a member of the Los Angeles Sheriff's Office told Dan Moldea it was "standard operating procedure" to circle and initial "bullet holes."

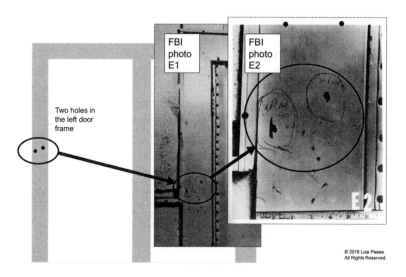

FBI photo E1

FBI photo E2

Two holes in the left door frame

Source: FBI photographs E1 and E2 from the California State Archives overlaid on a drawing by Lisa Pease

Figure 7: Drawing overlaid with FBI photograph E3
and Coroner's photograph

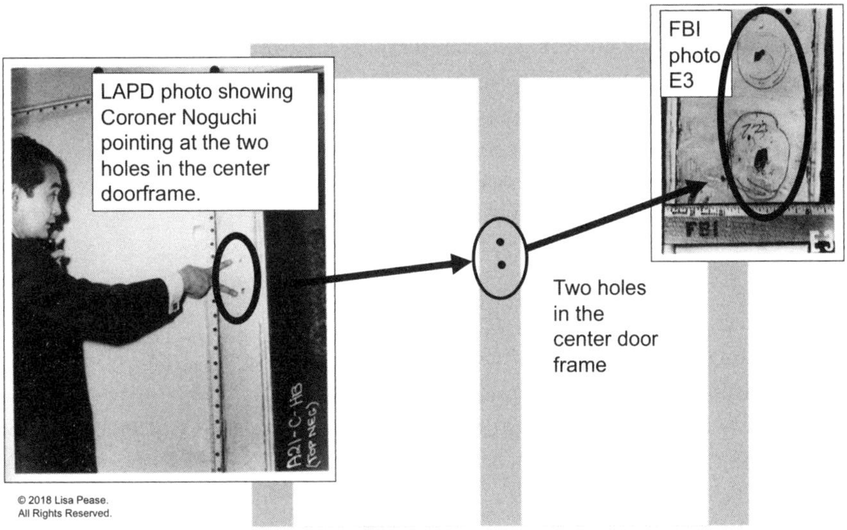

LAPD photo showing
Coroner Noguchi
pointing at the two
holes in the center
doorframe.

FBI
photo
E3

Two holes
in the
center door
frame

Source: Portions of FBI photograph E3 and a photo from the SUS files showing
Thomas Noguchi pointing at the two holes in the center of the doorframe, both
from the California State Archives overlaid on drawing by Lisa Pease

Figure 8: Portion of the FBI document showing the captions for photographs
E1 through E4 (pictures E1–E3 are shown in the pictures above)

RFK Assassination: L.A.F.O. #56-156: Sub File X-1, Volume 1
Current Section: Charts and Photographs Showing Layout of Ambassador Hotel Area Where Shooting Occurred

E-1   View taken inside kitchen serving area showing
doorway area leading into kitchen from the
stage area.   In lower right corner the photo
shows two bullet holes which are circled.   The
portion of the panel missing also reportedly
contained a bullet.

E-2   A close up view of the two bullet holes of
area described above.

E-3   Close up view of two bullet holes which is
located in center door frame inside kitchen
serving area and looking towards direction
of back of stage area.

E-4   Close up view of upper hinge on door leading
into kitchen over from back of stage area.
View shows reported location of another bullet
mark which struck hinge.

Text of Figure 8 retyped for clarity:

E-1 View taken inside kitchen serving area showing doorway area leading into kitchen from the stage area. In lower right corner from the photo shows two bullet holes which are circled. The portion of the panel missing also reportedly contained a bullet.

E-2 A close up view of the two bullet holes of area described above.

E-3 Close up view of two bullet holes which is located in center doorframe inside kitchen serving area and looking towards direction of back of stage area.

E-4 Close up view of upper hinge on door leading into kitchen area from back of stage area. View shows reported location of another bullet mark which struck hinge.

Source: FBI files, Los Angeles Field Office #56-156: Sub File X-1, Volume 1, p. 48.

To reiterate, E-1 and E-2 were photographs of the two bullet holes in the left-hand side of the doorframe. E-3 was a photograph of two *different* bullet holes in the center doorframe.

On November 2, 1977, Hufford, with investigator Robert H. Jackson, tried to quietly close the door on this most obvious evidence of conspiracy. Hufford and Jackson wrote the following to Special Agent Hal Marshall in the FBI's Los Angeles office on Wilshire Boulevard:

In the course of an inquiry by the Los Angeles County Board of Supervisors into certain aspects of the physical evidence at the Senator Robert F. Kennedy assassination, questions have arisen concerning certain FBI photographs. These photographs, purportedly taken by Special Agent Greiner and numbered E-1, E-2, and E-3 and E-4, are captioned "bullet holes."

If these were, in fact, bullet holes, it could be inferred that more than one gun was fired in the pantry during the assassination. Mr. Allard Lowenstein, Ambassador to the United Nations, among others, has maintained that a possibility exists that another assassin was present. Mr. Lowenstein and other critics of the official version have referred to the above photographs as representing the official opinion of the FBI inasmuch as the captions are unequivocal in stating "bullet holes."

If the captions had said possible, probable, or apparent bullet holes, one could assume that no precise examination had taken place at the time the photographs were taken. However, the captions would lead one to believe that a determination had been made by someone with the requisite knowledge and skills.

The dilemma we are faced with is that the photograph captions are being used as evidence of the official FBI position in the absence of any other official stated position.

If more bullets were fired within the pantry than Sirhan Sirhan's gun was capable of holding; we should certainly find out who else was firing. If, in fact, the FBI has no evidence that the questioned holes were bullet holes, we should know that so that the air may be cleared.

It is therefore requested that the official position of the FBI regarding these bullet holes be relayed to this office.[364]

Hufford and Jackson had essentially passed the buck from the County to the FBI, putting the Bureau in an untenable situation. The FBI would either have to deny the expertise of their own employees and go along with the lie, or they'd have to tell a most uncomfortable truth: that the FBI had evidence of a conspiracy but hadn't pursued it. And if they told *that* truth, the FBI would also be in the position of challenging not just their partners at the LAPD and in the County of Los Angeles but the CIA, which had been acting as a covert partner in the assassination investigation, as you'll see later. From that point of view, the obvious choice seems to be the one they took: silence. Professor Philip Melanson and other researchers have sought in vain an official response to Hufford's request, but none has ever surfaced.

By this point, it must be clear to any honest observer that at a bare minimum, 12 bullets had to have been fired in the pantry. Even if we accept Wolfer's scenario that seven bullets entered which victims and the eighth was lost in the ceiling space, we are still left with these four additional "bullet holes."

That these were bullet holes was confirmed by a video I stumbled upon while looking for something else in UCLA's video archives. In a piece of silent footage from a news organization, taken in the pantry in the early hours of June 5, a hand points to two holes in the door post.[365] Leaning next to the post in the video is a piece of the southwest doorframe's molding that had been pried off the post. This is the molding the LAPD later destroyed, so I paid close attention to the few seconds of video showing it. To my knowledge, this is the only picture or video of the door-frame molding in existence. After pointing at the two holes in the door post, the hand pulls the molding before the camera, positions it so the outer portion faces

---

364   Letter from Harry L. Hufford, County Administrative Officer, and Robert H. Jackson, Investigator, to Hal Marshall of the FBI, November 2, 1977, www.maryferrell.org/showDoc.html?docId=99874#relPageId=252&tab=page accessed October 9, 2016.

365   I secured the rights to this video and posted it at vimeo.com/275690516. Source: UCLA Film & Television Archive

the camera, and points to a third dark spot that also could be a bullet hole with a bullet still in it, as the finger points there for some time, indicating it is important. It is clearly not a nail, as the nails in the doorframe are visible in the film along the edges of the wood paneling, and stick out through the back. This dark spot is near the center of the wood, not where a carpenter would place a nail, and whatever is there does not stick out the back. There does not appear to be a hole in the same spot on the wood post behind it, which is also visible in the video as well as in LAPD and FBI photos, so if it were a bullet, it penetrated into the ¾-inch frame, but not into the door post behind it.

Although the possibility of another bullet there is intriguing, what matters is right *below* that third spot. Two small holes appear in the molding that exactly correspond to the two larger holes in the pantry doorframe. In other words, the video shows clearly that something small enough to be a .22 caliber bullet passed through the wood molding of the doorframe and into the post behind. The holes in the door post are bigger than the holes in the paneling that had been on top of the post, indicating someone had dug bullets out from those holes, enlarging the holes in the process.

See Figures 9 through 11 below to see screenshots captured from the author's licensed copy of this video.[366] In Figure 9, note the paneling removed from the doorframe. That wood was ¾" thick, according to the records of Thomas Kranz's investigation. Neither a pencil nor a pantry cart could have penetrated the tiny holes in the wood paneling to create the larger holes found in the doorposts. And whatever entered the posts had to first have passed through the tiny holes in the doorframe. The size of the holes indicates the holes were enlarged, which makes perfect sense if bullets were dug out of them.

Figure 9: A hand points to a possible bullet located in the wood paneling pulled from the southwest door jamb. Circled below the hand are the entry points for the two bullets that penetrated the southwest door jamb.

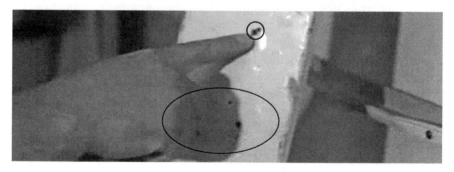

Source: UCLA Film & Television Archive

---

366   *Ibid.*

Figure 10: In the bottom left photo of this composite image, while the finger points toward a third spot on the wood paneling, two spots below it directly line up with the two holes in the door jamb. The top photo on the left shows the paneling that was pulled away from the southwest door jamb leaning against the door jamb from which it was pried.

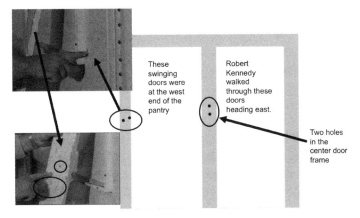

Source: Composite of images from the UCLA Film & Television Archive and a drawing by the author.

Figure 11: Composite of screenshots from the news footage with the drawing and FBI photos. The top left photo shows the doorframe post. The bottom left photo shows the 4'x6' wood paneling that was pulled from the southwest door jamb. The FBI photos E1 and E2 show the exposed door jamb after the wood paneling was pried off.

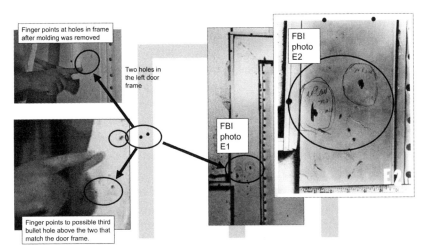

Source: Composite of images from the UCLA Film & Television Archive (left) and California State Archives (right) and a drawing by the author.

Clearly, there were at least two bullet holes in the left side of the southwest pantry doorframe, bringing the provable count of bullets to ten. Let's ignore the possible additional bullet the finger was pointing at for now.

Regarding the two bullet holes in the *center* post, in addition to the FBI photos and captions, we have the word of FBI Special Agent William Bailey of the Los Angeles office. After Bugliosi gave a talk about the Charles Manson case at a college in New Jersey, Bailey, who was then an assistant professor of political science at a nearby college, asked to speak privately to Bugliosi about what he had seen in the pantry. Bailey signed a declaration for Bugliosi stating he and other agents had seen "at least two small caliber bullet holes in the center post of the two doors" in the pantry. "There was no question in any of our minds as to the fact that these were bullet holes and were not caused by food carts or other equipment in the preparation room."[367]

So we have strong evidence that at least 12 bullets had been fired in the pantry. If you add in the bullet that so interested Congressman Lowenstein and Vincent Bugliosi, found by Officers Rozzi and Wright in the doorframe behind the stage, which, being "uphill" from the pantry would have been in line with a shot fired from the pantry, the bullet count reaches 13.

Thirteen shots on tape

AN AUDIO TAPE REDISCOVERED BY BRAD JOHNSON, A CNN INTERnational producer, was made at the time of the shots by freelance reporter Stanislaw Pruszynski, who had inadvertently left his tape recorder on after Kennedy's speech. Johnson sought an audio expert to analyze the tape, and found Philip Van Praag, who had written a book about magnetic media and knew a great deal about various recording equipment. Van Praag analyzed the tape with the help of a computer and found not only 13 distinct shots on the tape but at least two times where two shots came too close together to have been fired by a single gun. After a witness screamed and the overall pantry noise level rose, there may have been more shots, according to Van Praag, but the computer was unable to distinguish them after that point due to the overall noise level.

Other audio experts have disputed Van Praag's findings, and Dan Moldea in particular has ridiculed the notion that 13 shots were fired, but given the rest of evidence, it appears Van Praag's estimate was, if anything, too low, not too high.

---

367   Turner and Christian, p. 383.

Evidence of more than 13 bullets

IN ADDITION TO THE FOUR "BULLET HOLES" IN THE FBI'S PHOTO captions already accounted for, a statement in the description of photograph E1 suggests what would be a *14th bullet*: "The portion of the panel missing also reportedly contained a bullet." The "portion of the panel missing" appears to refer to the paneling shown in the bottom left corner of Figure 11 that had been attached to the leftmost or southernmost door post, which had been pried off after the shooting, likely by the Sheriff's deputies, who were the first on the scene, presumably so they could dig bullets out of the posts behind the paneling.

The pantry footage appears to show this 14th bullet still in the 4x¾" molding. The hand in the pantry footage pauses at the dark spot in the paneling above the two holes that line up with the holes in the post as if to indicate something important. There is no corresponding hole in the door post like there is for the two holes below this dark spot. That the molding was still present indicates the pantry film was taken *before* the FBI made its photos, because the doorframe molding pieces had been removed by the time the FBI photographed the pantry. It's also possible that "the portion of the panel missing" refers to the wall covering, a portion of which had been inexplicably cut away. This is visible in the full "E-1" FBI photo (not shown here).

But even at a solid count of 14 bullets, we may *still* be a few bullets short. Recall how the veteran crime reporter Robert Wiedrich, who had flown in from Chicago and visited the pantry within hours of the shooting, was told by the policeman in the pantry at the time that bullets had been removed from the center doorframe paneling. Wiedrich described seeing an "8-foot strip of molding" that had been "torn by police from the center post of the double doors" from which "a crime laboratory technician's probe" had removed "two .22-caliber bullets that had gone wild."[368] Dan Moldea tracked Wiedrich down in later years to confirm details of his story:

> Clearly, Wiedrich did not realize the significance of what he had written. ... When I finally interviewed Wiedrich—who had not seen the bullets removed—and explained the significance of what he had written for the first time, he paused momentarily and then stood by his story. "That's exactly what happened," Wiedrich insisted. "That's exactly what I saw, and that's exactly what I was told."[369]

---

368   Robert Wiedrich, "'Felt Him Fire Gun,' Hotel Worker Says," *Chicago Tribune*, June 6, 1968.
369   Moldea, p. 263.

If two bullets had been removed from the center divider *molding*, in addition to the two removed from the center divider *post*, that meant 16 bullets had been fired. The Hearst video only shows the molding from the southwest side of the double doors, not the center frame molding. So these could be two *additional* bullets to our 14-bullet count. Angelo DiPierro also swore that a bullet was removed from the center doorframe *molding*, not post, as the post had not yet been exposed at the time Angelo examined it. In an affidavit for Vince Bugliosi in connection with the Owen lawsuit discussed in the previous chapter, Angelo recounted the following:

> After Senator Kennedy had been removed from the pantry, many people, including the police and myself, started to look over the entire pantry area to piece together what had happened. That same morning, while we were still looking around, I observed a small caliber bullet lodged about a quarter of an inch into the wood on the center divider of the two swinging doors. Several police officers also observed the bullet. The bullet was approximately 5 feet 8 or 9 inches from the ground. The reason I specifically recall the approximate height of the bullet location is because I remember thinking at the time that if I had entered the pantry just before the shooting, the bullet may have struck me in the forehead, because I am approximately 5 feet 11½ inches tall. …
>
> I am quite familiar with guns and bullets, having been in the Infantry for 3½ years. There is no question in my mind that this was a bullet and not a nail or any other object. The base of the bullet was round and from all indications, it appeared to be a .22 caliber bullet.[370]

Martin Patruski, during the LAPD's initial re-creation of the crime in the pantry, was told by one of the police officers, who at that early stage could have no idea he was providing evidence of conspiracy, that two bullets had been removed from the center *doorframe*.[371]

There's another possible bullet that was discussed in the previous chapter: the second of the "fatal bullets" from Kennedy's head that Wolfer referred to in his log, the bullet which could have been in the second of the "two bullet tracks" in Kennedy's head as discussed in the previous chapter. The official story is that only one bullet entered Kennedy's skull. But if two did, that could bring the total bullet count to *17 bullets*.

---

370   Turner and Christian, p. 348.

371   Signed statement by Martin Patruski, witnessed in writing by Vincent Bugliosi in his office in December of 1975, www.maryferrell.org/showDoc.html?docId=99873&relPageId=495.

And then there's the missing chunk of the wall to the left of the southwest doorframe. A triangular piece of the paneling is missing, suggesting another bullet or two were found there. In an interview with Dan Moldea, Charles Collier, the civilian photographer for the LAPD's crime lab, said investigators asked him to photograph bullet holes in the walls—"Most of them were in the walls," Collier told Moldea. And lest anyone think Collier had confused the doors with walls, Collier told Moldea there were bullet holes "in the doors, too."[372] Moldea asked how he could be certain he had photographed pictures of bullet holes. Collier told him, "A bullet hole looks like a bullet hole—if you've photographed enough of them."[373]

If there was any bullet hole in any wall outside the doorframes, we're at a possible 17 or 18 bullets, depending on what you believe about Wolfer's references to "fatal bullets," plural, from Kennedy's head. And that's without even examining the somewhat magical trajectory by which the police reduced 12 bullet entry points in its official scenario to eight bullets by having them enter and exit the clothes of one person before lodging in another. For example, the bullet that passed harmlessly through Kennedy's coat at a steep upward angle was supposed to be, in the official account, the bullet that entered Paul Schrade's forehead. But that would only have made sense if Schrade were in front of Kennedy and looking down on him, rather than behind him and looking ahead, as he was. A bullet does not pull a big U-turn in mid-air! No matter how you slice the evidence, there were more bullets fired in the pantry than the police would acknowledge.

Even nine bullets means a conspiracy

YOU DON'T HAVE TO BELIEVE THERE WERE 18 OR EVEN 13 BULLETS to understand that if *a single bullet hole existed in the pantry*, if there was even a single bullet in the doorframes anywhere, we necessarily had at least two shooters, as Sirhan's gun could hold only eight bullets. It would be odd indeed if the veteran crime reporter, the FBI, the LAPD officers, the hotel maître d' and *all* the other witnesses were simply mistaken about *all* of these. That is *possible* in the sense that anything is possible. But it is not the *reasonable* conclusion to be made from of all these accounts.

Seeing this extraordinary count of the bullets makes it more obvious why the LAPD felt the need to label log pages with bullets on them "CONFIDENTIAL."

372   Transcript of Dan Moldea's interview with Charles Collier, December 16, 1989, provided to Sirhan's defense lawyers, via www.maryferrell.org/showDoc.html?docId=99873&search=collier#relPageId=348&tab=page.

373   Dan Moldea, "RFK's Murder A Second Gun?" *Washington Post*, May 13, 1990, via www.washingtonpost.com/archive/opinions/1990/05/13/rfks-murder-a-second-gun/9248e988-9fff-4366-b3e3-2849420b9bf9/, accessed November 13, 2016.

Someone apparently kept careful track of and disposed of any bullets that would make it obvious that more than one gun had been fired in the pantry.

In his book on the case, when he gets to the point where he discusses additional bullet holes in the pantry, Moldea says if the FBI's William Bailey was correct, if he really saw a bullet, "then there is no doubt that at least two guns were fired that night." But Moldea caveats that with the following:

> If Bailey is right, it would mean that DeWayne Wolfer had literally perjured himself on numerous occasions during his sworn statements about whether bullets had been recovered at the crime scene. And Wolfer has hung tough all of these years and even filed a defamation suite, insisting that he found no bullets in the walls and the doorframes of the kitchen pantry. Was he capable of committing this monumental act of obstruction?
>
> To continue to suggest that Wolfer lied is also to suggest that Wolfer, the officers in the SID, and the LAPD wittingly engaged in a conspiracy to permit the escape of Sirhan's co-conspirators. And that defies the evidence, as well as logic.

But Moldea is inaccurate on this point. That assertion does not "defy" the evidence and is in fact well supported by it. And the LAPD did not have to "wittingly engage" in a "conspiracy to permit the escape of Sirhan's co-conspirators" to have ignored evidence of conspiracy. The LAPD *provably* engaged in an act that allowed co-conspirators to escape when Inspector Powers ordered Sharaga to cancel the broadcast of an additional suspect because Rafer Johnson saw only one man. It was simply too soon *not* to pursue every lead, especially when considering Rafer Johnson's account, as Johnson had specifically said he hadn't looked around to see if any other shooters were involved.

We also know that the California Court of Appeals stopped just short of accusing Wolfer of perjury. And numerous people as well as the physical evidence from the crime scene support what Bailey, not Wolfer, contended was there: bullet holes in the doorframes and even, if the LAPD's crime scene photographer was correct, in the walls as well.

The Rampart Scandal

PROVABLY, EVIDENCE IN THIS CASE WAS ALTERED, DESTROYED, and possibly hidden as well. This is where I part ways with Dan Moldea. Moldea has done some solid investigative work, for which all researchers should be grateful, but Moldea has shown himself to be incapable of believing that Wolfer, other members of the LAPD, and the D.A.'s office could have lied about the evidence.

I don't suffer from that same naïveté, perhaps because I have lived in Los Angeles for a few decades and know the LAPD's history. What non-locals may not know is that the very same Rampart Division responsible for collecting bullets, collecting crime evidence, and interviewing dozens of pantry witnesses became embroiled in what became known as the "Rampart Scandal" in the late 1990s.

Although the investigation into the Rampart Division was triggered by the shooting of a black LAPD officer by a white one in 1997, the subsequent investigation quickly broadened into one that exposed a culture of corruption that had been *in place since the 1950s, well before Senator Kennedy was assassinated*. In fact, the investigation revealed the LAPD to be so corrupt it was put into federal receivership for several years.

USC professor Erwin Chemerinsky was asked to provide an independent assessment of the "Rampart Scandal Incident Report and came to the following conclusions:

> Rampart is the worst scandal in the history of Los Angeles. Police officers framed innocent individuals by planting evidence and committing perjury to gain convictions. Nothing is more inimical to the rule of law than police officers, sworn to uphold the law, flouting it and using their authority to convict innocent people. Innocent men and women pleaded guilty to crimes they did not commit and were convicted by juries because of the fabricated cases against them. [374]

Boston University Professor Edwin Delattre echoed Chemerinsky's sentiments in his book *Character and Cops: Ethics in Policing*:

> "Thug code" is a way of life in some police precincts and units. The distinguished former assistant chief of the Los Angeles Police Department, David Dotson, wrote: "[A]t bottom, the problems at the Los Angeles Police Department's Rampart Division are cultural in nature, the result of an institutional mind-set first conceived in the 1950s...." Were that not true, Rampart Division personnel could not possibly have covered up their depravity as long as they did. ...
>
> Those cops told implausible lies about probable cause. Their supervisors either tolerated or encouraged such lies, and the judges who should have known better swallowed the lies without

---

[374]   Erwin Chemerinksy, "An Independent Analysis of the Los Angeles Police Department's Board of Inquiry Report on the Rampart Scandal," *Loyola of Los Angeles Law Review*, January 1, 2001, pp. 549–550.

question. Such a "culture" kills morality completely. Los Angeles County Supervisor Zev Yaroslavsky rightly insists that the Rampart depredations are "a dagger aimed at the heart of constitutional democracy." [375]

Professor Delattre derided the title of the official report on the scandal, the "Rampart Area Corruption Incident," by noting "What police did in the Rampart Division was not mere corruption, and it was no incident."[376] Delattre explained the scope of the scandal was "so heinous and widespread" that nearly one hundred convictions of past cases were overturned and some three thousand cases were up for review. The investigation revealed that LAPD officers "brutalized suspects, submitted false reports, [and] lied in official proceedings."[377]

If you feel someone is guilty, you may not be upset to see the police framing them for a crime they committed. But Chemerinsky challenged us to consider how we would have felt if the police did this to a family member:

> I believe that the challenge for everyone dealing with the Rampart
> scandal in any way is to constantly think that it is our son or daughter,
> or brother or sister, or father or mother, who has been … framed by
> the police planting evidence and lying in court to gain a conviction.[378]

For Moldea or anyone to say officers of the LAPD wouldn't frame an innocent person is simply *ahistorical*. It has happened, often, and especially within—though not limited to—the Rampart Division.

What witnesses heard

ONE QUESTION THAT BOTHERS SOME IS THIS: IF THERE WERE SO many shots in the pantry, how come that many shots weren't reported by witnesses? There are several explanations for this. First, the majority of witnesses didn't realize they were hearing gunshots at first, and those that did were hardly sitting there counting the shots. They were looking for cover, trying to escape, or trying to protect others. And the majority of witnesses didn't even hear the eight shots the police told us must have been fired:

---

375   Edwin J. Delattre, *Character and Cops: Ethics in Policing* (Washington, DC: AEI Press, 2011 ed.), p. 365.

376   Delattre, p. 366.

377   Delattre, p. 365.

378   Erwin Chemerinksy, "An Independent Analysis of the Los Angeles Police Department's Board of Inquiry Report on the Rampart Scandal," *Loyola of Los Angeles Law Review*, January 1, 2001, pp. 549–550.

"When I heard the shots, it sounded like one shot, a pause, then two loud shots. The first shot sounded muffled." – SUS transcript of Earl Williman interview, July 23, 1968

"He was about halfway through the room when he heard six little pops. There was only one shot, a pause, then a burst of shots. His first thought was that an electrical short had occurred as he could see flashes." – SUS interview of Lon Rubin by Collins, Patchett and MacArthur, September 1968

"I heard about five explosions." – Virginia Guy, LAPD interview summary from June 6, 1968

"Then saw flashes and heard firecrackers (hollow-sounding). She heard what sounded like a machine gun—5, 6 or 7 shots." – SUS interview of Pamela Lemke, July 8, 1968

Dick Aubry counted only six shots. Virginia Guy heard three. Delores Beilenson heard three then lost track. Larry Dean heard only five. There are many more who heard less than eight shots. There was certainly no consensus among the earwitnesses as to how many shots were fired.

That said, several witnesses *did* report hearing more than eight shots, and a few mentioned they thought multiple people were firing. Many of the witnesses described the shots as being jumbled together, creating a rapid crackling that sounded like firecrackers. It would have been impossible to determine the exact number of shots if they were fired nearly simultaneously. A few witnesses compared the sound to that of a machine gun because the shots came so rapidly.

The following witnesses heard what each thought was likely more than eight shots, and this is not a complete list:

"In total, he heard what he thought was 10 to 12 shots." – SUS interview report of Booker Griffin, July 25, 1968

"After the Kennedy party had passed, she heard cracking [sic] noises which sounded like exploding firecrackers. She immediately realized, however, that the sounds were gunshot sounds and they were in rapid succession, a total of about 8 or 10 shots." – FBI interview report of Suzanne Locke, June 7, 1968

"At the time of the shooting, he heard between 5 and 10 sharp shots but could not distinguish them as individual reports." – SUS interview of Jesse Unruh, July 21, 1968

"I thought I heard at least about 10 shots, but I know I heard less on the radio, but it sounded like an awful lot. It wasn't one or two. It was a lot of shots." – SUS interview of Estelyn Duffy, June 5, 1968. An abbreviated summary of Duffy's comments in the SUS files includes "Sounded like a whip (shots) 8/10," indicating she told them she heard eight to ten shots.

"He ... heard a string of lighted firecrackers going off. ... When the firecracker sounds had gone off ... he suddenly realized shots had been fired. His reaction was that the shots must have come from an automatic weapon since they were so rapid." – FBI Interview of Michael Rhodes, July 15, 1968

"One witness said those shots came so close together that he could scarcely believe they were fired from one gun. A reporter who heard the shots from an adjoining room said they sounded almost like they came from a machine gun, so short was the burst of fire." – Walter Cronkite on CBS in the early hours after the shooting

"Two or three seconds after Kennedy entered the kitchen, he heard 8 or 9 shots in quick succession. (He thought there had been two guns.)" – LAPD interview summary of Roy Mills, August 9, 1968

"After the third pop I realized it was a gun being fired, it seemed to me that I heard at least 8 or 10 shots." – LAPD interview of Carol Ann Breshears, June 5, 1968

Other guns in the pantry

MOST RESEARCHERS HAVE FIXATED ON THANE EUGENE CESAR, the guard with a gun who was at Kennedy's right elbow just as the shooting broke out, as the only other shooter and co-conspirator. And indeed, it's difficult to imagine Thane Cesar *not* being involved. He was in the perfect position to have been the gunman who killed Kennedy or to have held Kennedy, shielding shooters from view as they fired upon Kennedy from nearly contact range. And every time he talked about what happened in the pantry, his story changed. The kindest thing we can say about Cesar is that he failed utterly in his job. It was his charge to keep the pantry free of interlopers, and he did not. When he took hold of Kennedy's arm, his job became to escort Kennedy safely through the pantry, and he did not. At least three witnesses—Don Schulman, Lisa Urso and Richard Lubic—saw Cesar pull his gun.

"[T]he security guard had a gun and I think he went like this [drawing a gun] or he put it in a holster or something..." – Lisa Urso to Dr. Phil Melanson

"Why would a security guard have his gun pointed toward the

floor, instead of at Sirhan?" – Richard Lubic to David Talbot, recounting
the question on his mind during the shooting[379]

When Lubic asked the LAPD, they told him "Don't bring this up, don't be
talking about this." Lubic was questioned during the trial but not about the guard
with his gun out during the shooting.[380]

Schulman was adamant the guard had fired his gun:

> "I'm pretty doggone sure he fired his gun." – Don Schulman to the
> D.A.'s office in 1971, reiterating his earlier comment that he saw the
> guard fire, made on air immediately after the shooting

Jesus Perez was very near Kennedy when he was shot, but when the police
showed him the gun taken from Sirhan by Rafer, Perez said "No, I think it's
bigger than that." He indicated the gun was about a foot long, hardly the tiny
snub-nosed gun from Sirhan. If someone had a silencer on a revolver, the barrel
would have looked long indeed.[381] The gun Cesar owned at the time, a nine-shot
H&R .22, had a longer nose than the Sirhan gun did. Perez, as you'll recall, was
very fearful when he talked to the police. You'd be fearful too, if you saw a man
in a security uniform commit a crime that was blamed on someone else.

But Cesar did not appear to be the only one who fired a gun in the pantry,
as you'll see in this chapter and the next. For the rest of this chapter, we'll focus
more on where the guns were rather than who was holding them. In the next
chapter, we'll look at potential conspirators.

Witnesses described seeing gunmen other than Cesar and Sirhan, and these
are just a few of many such statements in the record:

> "He saw a man with a gun step out from behind a wall and then he
> heard a shot. … After this first shot, the crowd moved back towards
> the pantry doors in one wave. Then he heard at least eight shots." –
> SUS interview of Ronald John Panda, June 8, 1968
>
> "The guy with the gun could have left. No one seemed to pay
> any attention." – Darnell Johnson to LAPD, 7/24/68
>
> "My God, he had a gun and we let him go by." – Joseph Klein,
> referring to a man leaving the pantry in a hurry while Sirhan was
> being subdued, to LAPD, 7/3/68

---

379   David Talbot, *Brothers: The Hidden History of the Kennedy Years* (New York: Free Press, 2007), pp. 373–374.
380   Talbot, *Brothers*, p. 374.
381   LAPD interview transcript of Jesus Perez, June 5, 1968.

Dr. Marcus McBroom, a psychologist who was one of Kennedy's surrogates on the trail, told a reporter at the *Los Angeles Sentinel* "that he had the distinct impression of a second gunman brushing past him at the same time Sirhan was being pounded into submission by Rosey Grier and Rafer Johnson."[382] McBroom stated in an LAPD interview that although he couldn't see the face of the gunman during the shooting, he saw that the gun was in someone's left hand. Sirhan was right-handed, and the witnesses who identified Sirhan as a gunman said he held the gun in his right hand.

In 1986, McBroom told Paul Schrade about a man who ran out of the pantry with a gun under a newspaper, and how a man in a "pale blue security uniform, a private person" had a gun out "which appeared to be smoking." No guards had pale blue uniforms. But the Ace Security guards had pale gray uniforms.

Frank Burns could have been describing two or even three different shooters when he described what he saw as he followed Kennedy into the pantry:

> As I walked behind him through the kitchen, my eyes were fixed on his back. There were people about me and the crowd seemed to build as I caught up with the Senator. I was standing behind Mr. Kennedy when I heard the noise. It sounded like a string of firecrackers. I focused on an arm and a gun just to my right. It seemed to be close to Senator Kennedy. I felt a burning sensation on my left cheek, then I saw Senator Kennedy falling, turning to his left and holding his arms up. The suspect moved forward into my full view. His arm was extended and aiming the gun slightly downward, firing it. The shots stopped at that time. A lot of people got hold of him.

---

382   "Doctors Heroes, Says Eyewitness," *Los Angeles Sentinel*, June 6, 1968. The LAPD did not believe McBroom was in the pantry. But what McBroom said largely matched what other witnesses have said, and he couldn't have been mimicking them because those statements were kept secret until the LAPD's files were finally released to the public nearly 20 years later. It seems unlikely that Robert Kennedy would choose a fabricator to be one of his surrogates. It's not at all unlikely however, that the LAPD went out of their way to discredit him, just as they did every witness whose account suggested a conspiracy. They showed McBroom a picture of himself in the Embassy Room and said it was taken five seconds after the shooting began. But McBroom had already acknowledged being in the Embassy Room just before the shooting began. He didn't know how many shots had been fired before he realized someone was firing and then he ran into the pantry and saw a gun, a struggle, and evidently felt a possible gunman squeeze past him. McBroom's "statements" were criticized as being inaccurate, when in fact, the police reporter had not accurately summarized what McBroom had said, as he clarified in later interviews. I recommend interested parties look at all his numerous interviews. For example, to the *Sentinel*, McBroom said Kennedy was walking along and "joking about Rosey Grier protecting him." This was mistranslated into an LAPD summary report as McBroom having said that Kennedy was joking to Rosey Grier as he walked through the pantry, and since Rosey Grier hadn't caught up with Kennedy, that was evidence McBroom was lying. *But that wasn't what McBroom had said.* He said Kennedy joked *about* Rosey Grier, not *to* Rosey Grier. There are numerous such twists of people's statements in the LAPD files. That's why the audio tapes have been very valuable. Sadly, no tape of McBroom's statements exist. But that one was clearly misstated by the LAPD, and the misstatement used against him, and it was not the only statement of his twisted and then used inaccurately to "discredit" him. Compare especially McBroom's LAPD interview summary by Collins and Patchett, September 16, 1968, to his earlier FBI interview of July 11, 1968.

How did Burns get a burning sensation on his *left* cheek from a shooter to his *right*? You have to be very near a gun's muzzle to get powder burns. This would make more sense if there were a shooter to his left that had not pulled his focus because he was focused on the arm to his right. And from Burns' description, Sirhan moved "forward" into Burns' view as Burns was "fixed" on Kennedy's back, so he could not have been the shooter to his right or left. It sounds like Burns assumed the shooter to his right was the same as the man in front of him with a gun, a logical assumption only in the absence of the rest of the data. But given that we know Kennedy was shot at near contact range behind the right ear and under his right arm, the person who shot Kennedy would indeed have been to Kennedy's right, not where Sirhan was. Burns may have been sandwiched between two other shooters while noticing Sirhan in front of Kennedy.

Similarly, Boris Yaro was behind Kennedy when he heard the first two shots (after which Uecker and Minasian say Uecker grabbed Sirhan). But Yaro saw "two or three people that had been blocking my view of the Senator disappear, leaving me with a full view of what was happening," a statement Yaro immediately clarified by adding:

> The Senator and the assailant were little more than silhouettes, but the Senator was backing up and putting both if his hands and arms in front of him in what would be best described as a protective effort. The suspect appeared to be lunging at the Senator. ... I didn't realize it was a gun until he started firing again—this time, I could see the flashes from the short-barreled muzzle—I heard no sounds from either man. I felt powder from the weapon strike my face—I knew it was a gun then. I thought I heard more than three shots, in retrospect I know it is more.[383]

Before continuing, the counterargument is that Kennedy was not facing Sirhan but instead facing to the north, exposing his right side to Sirhan. Indeed, Thomas Kranz mistakenly wrote in his report, immediately after quoting Ed Minasian, that "all of these witnesses put Sirhan's firing position to the right and slightly forward of Kennedy." But in Minasian's earliest interview, taken in the wee morning hours after the shooting, Minasian said this:

> I looked up and someone reached around from the—from the front, *it would be to the Senator's left as he was facing him* ... Then at that time I saw Karl grab him and then I jumped across the table and grabbed him .... [Emphasis added.]"[384]

---

383   FBI interview of Boris Yaro, June 7, 1968.
384   LAPD interview transcript of Edward Minasian, June 5, 1968.

A few sentences later Minasian again reiterated Sirhan came at Kennedy *"from his front left."* Minasian saw Paul Schrade fall, and then Senator Kennedy fall. (Several witnesses say Schrade fell before Kennedy, but a few said Kennedy fell before Schrade. Clearly, they went down nearly simultaneously.)

Kennedy himself obviously felt a threat from his front, because he threw his hands up to shield his face. It makes no sense that, facing friendlies he had just shaken hands with, Kennedy would, for no apparent reason, throw his hands up to cover his face. It makes no sense that he could have thrown his hands up at all if he had already been shot. Clearly, Kennedy saw Sirhan shooting at him from the front and threw up his hands in an instinctive motion to protect himself.

So how many shooters were there? How did they escape detection? Or did they? Clearly, people did not just brandish guns. Guns were hidden in some manner, and silencers may have been used to mute the number of gunshots heard. Even so, as you will see in the rest of this chapter and in the next, at least four different gunmen were reported in the pantry: Sirhan, Cesar, a third man on a table who escaped during the shooting, and a fourth man behind Kennedy who ran a gun out of the pantry during the shooting. In the next chapter, you'll meet a possible fifth gunman as well. Remember that once Sirhan fired his gun, all eyes in the room went to his gun, and other gunmen could have been firing without drawing attention. In addition, if they all fired two or three shots at once, it would have been difficult to tell that multiple guns were being fired. It would have sounded like a machine gun, or firecrackers, just as witnesses described.

A few witnesses saw a gun close to Kennedy's head, but none of those witnesses could identify that gunman as Sirhan. Some witnesses reported seeing a hand with a gun reach out from between two cameramen, which is similar to how Jack Ruby approached and shot Lee Harvey Oswald in the police garage in Dallas. He had hidden behind two cameramen and then jumped out when Oswald got close. The pantry shooter's hand was visible, but the face was not, behind the two big men. While witnesses *assumed* this was Sirhan, Lisa Urso, who was within touching distance of Sirhan, right behind him as he pulled a gun and fired, reported no such cameramen in Sirhan's vicinity. Who was hiding between cameramen?

The man to Kennedy's right
and the man on the table

NINA RHODES-HUGHES TOLD ME WHEN I INTERVIEWED HER IN 2012 that she felt there were two shooters, but from what she told me, she seemed to have described, quite unwittingly and without her knowledge, *three* shooters.

Rhodes-Hughes was featured on CNN in 2012 for claiming to have heard 12 to 14 shots in the pantry and for having said that after she told this to the FBI, they altered the shots she heard to eight in her interview summary. Rhodes-Hughes' statement, which she reiterated vigorously to me when I interviewed her in Los Angeles in 2012, was dismissed by a magistrate of the court in response to a filing by Sirhan's lawyers because there were no contemporaneous records from 1968 of her saying she heard more than eight. But given how records have been provably inaccurate in other areas of this case, as well as destroyed, it would not be out of character for evidence of conspiracy that had not yet been made public to have been removed from the record. It also would not have been out of character in the 1960s for someone in the FBI to have altered her statement.

Rhodes-Hughes told CNN and, separately, me, that she heard shots coming from her right, even as she watched a shooter in front of her. She didn't see the shooter to her right. But she felt from the sound that shots were also being fired from a position to her right.

Ronald Panda may have seen this shooter. A few days short of 13 years old, Panda had been a young volunteer for Kennedy. He had been backstage when Kennedy spoke and followed Kennedy into the pantry. He was only 5'2", so he had to jump up to see over the backs of the people around him. Just before he heard the first shot, Panda saw "a man with a gun in his right hand step from behind a wall."[385] The "wall" Panda referred to was likely the dividing wall between the west end of the pantry and the ice machine. There was space between that wall and the ice machine where someone could easily have hid, stepping out when Kennedy got close.

When Panda first contacted the police after seeing Sirhan on TV, he's quoted as having said, "I saw him but I didn't see the gun in his hand."[386] Presumably, this statement referred specifically to Sirhan.

If you put Panda's two statements together, Panda apparently saw a man with a gun *who wasn't Sirhan* step out from behind a wall. Panda knew which one was apprehended because he followed the police as they escorted Sirhan from the hotel. He never said he saw *Sirhan* step from behind the wall. Panda also appears to have seen Sirhan's gun separately from seeing Sirhan, as he described seeing the flame of a gun fired at Kennedy. As discussed earlier, such a flame comes from the burning of paper wads or blanks, not the firing of bullets.[387] So he appears to have seen Sirhan without the gun at some point, the firing of Sirhan's gun

---

385   LAPD interview of Ronald "Roh" Panda, misdated June 8, 1968, as this information is clearly from an interview conducted August 6, 1968. There is a separate document that reflects Panda's comments when he called the LAPD on June 8, 1968.

386   LAPD interview of Ronald Panda, June 8, 1968.

387   LAPD interview of Ronald Panda, August 29, 1968.

at a time when Sirhan's face was blocked from his view, and a gunman who stepped out from next to the ice machine, which would have put that gunman to Rhodes-Hughes' right as she stood behind Robert Kennedy.

When I talked to Rhodes-Hughes shortly after the CNN story aired, she added important information not present in the CNN segment. She was convinced that Sirhan, in a powder-blue suit, was *firing while standing on top of one of the steam tables*, after which he turned and jumped down off the table in one motion.

Rhodes-Hughes was not the only one to make this assertion. Other witnesses had claimed someone was firing from an elevated position, with a knee or body up on the steam table. *But this could not have been Sirhan.* Four credible witnesses put Sirhan on the floor next to the steam table, not kneeling or standing on the steam table. If there was a shooter on the table, and the evidence is strong that there was, as you'll see, it could *not* have been Sirhan.

Sirhan was wearing a light blue velour shirt with a zipper at the neck and blue jeans, not a suit. But several witnesses described a suspicious tall man in a light blue *suit* in the pantry as well who left the scene in the company of a girl in a polka dot dress. Whatever the case, Sirhan could not have been on the table, because four credible witnesses, Lisa Urso, Ed Minasian, Karl Uecker and Vince DiPierro, saw Sirhan standing on the floor when the shooting began. He was only on the table after being pushed there by Karl Uecker. He was never witnessed by anyone *standing and firing* on the table.

Lisa Urso saw Sirhan walk across the pantry from the south side to the north side, in front of Kennedy, and then reach across his body as if to shake his hand before firing at Kennedy instead. She was directly behind Sirhan and close enough to touch him and put Sirhan at least three feet in front of Kennedy, firing slightly upward, which would make sense, as Sirhan was four inches shorter than Robert Kennedy.

Karl Uecker felt rather than saw Sirhan move in front and to the left of him, sliding between Uecker and the steam table, and grabbed Sirhan in a headlock after what Uecker thought was the second shot or the third at the latest.

Edward Minasian saw Sirhan reach around Uecker's left side and fire, just as Urso and Uecker described, at which point Uecker and then Minasian grabbed him.

Vince DiPierro described seeing Sirhan cross from the tray stand at the east end of the ice machine, where he had been held by the girl in the polka dot dress, to a spot near Kennedy, where reached out as if to shake Kennedy's hand and then fired instead.[388]

---

388   LAPD transcripts of taped interviews of Minasian and Uecker, June 5, 1968, and the SUS interview summary of Urso's interview on June 27, 1968, as well as Urso's interview by members of the D.A.'s office, the LAPD and County Supervisor Baxter Ward on August 10, 1977 (www.maryferrell.org/showDoc.html?docId=99873&search=urso#relPageId=696&tab=page).

I queried Rhodes-Hughes extensively on this point, and she said she had not seen the *face* of the man on the table, only the blue coat. From her comments it was clear she had only *assumed* this was the same person as the suspect. Evan Freed, in his taped interview, saw a man in a bright blue sport coat in the pantry that looked remarkably like Sirhan, but was significantly taller. Might Rhodes-Hughes have assumed this was the same man when in fact they were two different people? Rhodes-Hughes was adamant to me about the shots having come from an elevated position, and that is reflected in her contemporaneous FBI interview:

> When the subj [Nina Rhodes] reached the swinging doors to the kitchen from the kitchen anteroom she saw sparking flashes red and orange and heard loud explosions exactly like firecrackers. The subj stated these flashes were approx.. 12 to 16 inches above the level of Senator Kennedy's head. The subj stated she heard 8 explosions in rapid succession (like a string of firecrackers) [Nina disputes this sentence, saying she heard many more than eight shots – LP]. The subj stated that after approximately the third explosion she observed the Senator start to twist and fall to the floor … The subj stated the flashes were still coming from the high elevation where she first saw them. When the flashes stopped she saw what appeared to her as the back of a man wearing a powder blue jacket with his head ducked forward so his head wasn't visible to her. This figure was elevated and in the same position and location where she had seen the flashes come from. The subj. stated the person in the powder blue jacket must have been standing on something as he was much taller than the other people in the room and could be seen by the subj over the heads of numerous people in front of her. … The subj stated the Senator was to the right of center in the room and the flashes came from the left of center in the room.

Richard Lubic thought he saw the shooter with his knee up on the table, but he never saw Sirhan's face until Sirhan was apprehended. He, too, appeared to have simply *assumed* this was Sirhan. And Lubic's statement was also captured nearly contemporaneously in an FBI Airtel from Los Angeles to FBI Director J. Edgar Hoover, dated June 26, 1968. Lubic had entered the pantry just ahead of Kennedy, and was at Kennedy's right shoulder when Kennedy stopped to shake hands. Lubic continued forward a step or two, and then:

> Lubic heard an unidentified voice saying "Kennedy, you son of a bitch," and then heard two shots which sounded to Lubic like shots from a starter pistol at a track meet. Lubic did not identify the source

of the voice and could not immediately determine the source of the pistol shots. He quickly noted, however, an individual with a gun. This individual was located on the left side of the corridor and *had his knee on a small table or air conditioning vent and had lifted himself up on this knee to obtain elevation while shooting.* [Emphasis added.]

Lubic has no recollection of hearing the sounds of additional shots, but recalls seeing the gun and the arm of the assailant and noted the jerk of the gun and the arm apparently caused by the recoil action of this gun. Lubic immediately sought cover behind an ice machine or table in the corridor under the assumption the shooting would continue. Lubic observed the expression in Kennedy's eyes and assumed he was mortally wounded.[389]

After the last sentence quoted above, *nearly all of the next 27 paragraphs over six pages are redacted.* A few redactions show Lubic's name and a few words before returning to the full blackout. What had the FBI hidden behind those redactions? Possibly the other gunman Lubic had identified in the pantry, the guard with his gun pointed at the floor, where Kennedy lay, instead of at the suspect. As we saw earlier, Lubic had told the police that he saw a guard with his gun drawn and pointing at the floor and told David Talbot, the founder and original Editor-in-Chief of Salon.com, that the police told him not to talk about that to anyone. There is no mention of this in his LAPD interview, but I suspect it may be present in the redacted portions of the FBI airtel regarding Lubic's statements.

Lubic's later statements continued to support Rhodes-Hughes' contention that someone was firing from atop or nearly atop a steam table in the pantry. In his August 9, 1968, interview with Sergeants Collins and MacArthur, Lubic thought he saw the shooter on the table as Kennedy turned to "reach across to get that kitchen guy," meaning, to shake the hand of Juan Romero or Jesus Perez. "That's what went on," Lubic said, adding, "Sirhan was on this table," before clarifying that he never saw Sirhan's face. And what he saw didn't match Sirhan's description:

> Q [Collins]: Well, when were you first aware of Sirhan? Did you see him at all prior to the shot?
>
> A [Lubic]: No, I was aware of Sirhan when I looked up and saw Kennedy hit. ...
>
> Q: In your original interview I think you said that you actually— you didn't hear the flash but you heard the shot, and you thought you saw the gun?

---

389   FBI Airtel from Los Angeles to FBI Director J. Edgar Hoover, dated June 26, 1968.

A: No, *I could see the gun. I couldn't see Sirhan's face though.* [Emphasis added.]

Q: All right, now, when you could see the gun, there was obviously a hand holding it—

A: Yeah, I saw this.

Q: Could you distinguish any clothing on it or anything like that?

A: No I—I think he—I think it was a bare hand. I mean, you know, I think he might have had a short-sleeved shirt on. I don't think he had a long-sleeved shirt on or a jacket. I don't know. It looked like he was from behind somebody. There was somebody standing up like this, see, so that to me it looked like he just had, you know, a hand over here. That's why.

Q: You say that you think he stepped from behind somebody?

A: I think—my recollection was that he had one leg on that table like this, on this—one of these tables, *because he seemed to be higher than anybody else, and he had a perfect view of everything.* [Emphasis added.]

Q [MacArthur]: You saw the hand out there, but you didn't see the face, looked like it was coming over somebody?

A: Yeah.

Q: Did you ever see the face, connect the face with the arm and the head and the gun?

A: Oh, yeah, I saw it afterwards.

Q: But that was after you ducked and went over?

A: Yeah, when I was down here, I could see him very—

Q: What was he doing then?

A: He was still shooting the gun.

Q: Oh, okay. In other words you saw—you could identify that he was the one that had the gun?

A: Sure, he still had the gun in his hand because then they jumped on him … You could tell that it was him. I mean I could tell you right now that, you know, the first shot I couldn't tell; but after the crowd started to move and I went down, then you could see him standing right there.

Sirhan had a long-sleeved jacket on, and it is possible he could have pushed up his sleeves before firing. But no other witness reported him having a bare arm when firing. By his own account, Lubic just assumed Sirhan and the gunman were one and the same. It was a logical assumption—Sirhan was provably firing, so it was natural to assume the guy on the table had been Sirhan. But as we just saw, the credible reports from Lisa Urso, Ed Minasian and Karl Uecker dispute this. Uecker talks about pushing Sirhan up against the table when he put him in a headlock after the second shot. He couldn't have pushed Sirhan *up against* the table if Sirhan was already *on* the table. The four witnesses who saw Sirhan at the moment of the initial firing, Lisa Urso, Ed Minasian, Karl Uecker and Vince DiPierro, all have Sirhan on the ground in front of Kennedy when he began firing.

Perhaps the most straightforward witness to a table-top shooter was Harold Burba, the man who testified about Michael Wayne, thinking he was Sirhan, during the Grand Jury. Burba told the FBI in a formal, signed statement:

> I heard what sounded like three shots fairly close, followed by several more at random intervals. They sounded like they came from a cap pistol. I also saw what appeared to be flashes from the shots. At this time I had the impression of someone standing on a table and firing a gun at a downward angle.[390]

George Green, in his live, on-camera televised interview on CBS immediately after the shooting, also said unequivocally the shooter was standing on the table. I must emphasize again: all the witnesses who were able to ID Sirhan correctly as a shooter in the pantry put him on the floor, not on the table.

Ronald Panda saw something similar. "It seemed to him that the suspect was standing on something and he was pointing down."[391] Panda was just days shy of his 13th birthday. When I reached him in 2012 by phone, I asked the now significantly older Panda if he remembered saying the shots had come from an elevated position. "Yes, yes I do," he told me. I asked why he thought the shots had come from an elevated position. Besides having that visual impression, he told me there were other indications. For example, a person next to him had been hit in the upper part of the body, but that person had appeared surrounded such that the shot could only have reached the person via a downward angle.[392] Panda, Lubic and others clearly thought this was Sirhan. But Sirhan was not on any table or tray stacker at the time of the shooting.

Rhodes-Hughes told me the guy in the powder-blue coat she had seen on the table sort of swirled down off the table, turning and covering his face as he rapidly descended from the table. Rhodes-Hughes, like Lubic, had not seen the face of the person on the table. Dick Aubry also had the impression that someone had, as he put it, "jumped" off the table and into the crowd:

> A [Dick Aubry]: I saw two people standing, looked like there was standing on top of the seat, you know how people get on top of things?

---

390   FBI statement from Harold Burba, June 7, 1968.
391   LAPD interview of Ronald Panda, August 29, 1968.
392   Author's interview of Ronald Panda, May 5, 2012.

Q [Sergeant Calkins]: On top of the table?

A: I thought he had jumped—I thought he was just a guy that had jumped down on, you know, fell into the crowd. But then I thought he was being pushed, just everything came into my mind.

In his earliest interview, Aubry made reference to the possibility of an accomplice, even while discounting it:

Q: [D]id you get any indication at all, think about this before you answer it, any indication at all there was anybody helping this assailant that shot the Senator? Was there anybody there? Did you get any indication? Stop and think real—

A: Not—Booker Griffith [*sic* – should be "Griffin"] asked me, should we take after the other cat like this, and my first impulse was to say "yes" but I said—I had come out of the press room then though.

Q: By then it was all over?

A: [Unintelligible, then] oh yes. But Booker said, "Did they get the other guy?"

When Aubry was interviewed again by SUS on July 19, 1968, Aubry's interview summary noted Aubry "noticed a man kneeing [*sic*—kneeling] on the metal table. He was getting down as I passed him. I bumped his knee." According to an SUS progress report's summary of one of Aubry's interviews,

As he [Aubry] walked through the kitchen, he observed a man on the table kneeling; described as a male Caucasian, 25 to 26, small, dark sport coat. This person was getting down from the table as Mr. Aubry walked past him. He was approximately eight feet in front of the Senator when he heard a shot, a pause, then five shots. [393]

In the July interview, Aubry passed the man getting off the table, then heard a shot and turned back to see Kennedy falling. "Two girls in Kennedy dresses brushed by me from between the tables," Aubrey added. He heard only six shots in total: "one shot, a pause, and then five rapid shots."

On NBC's live footage, many witnesses gave indications of two or more gunmen, comments that were not adequately reflected in the FBI's and LAPD's records or later press reports. And several of them thought someone was shooting

---

[393]   RFK LAPD Microfilm, Volume 47 (Progress Reports), "Report on Pandemonium and Hysteria in the Kitchen," August 16, 1968, p. 11.

from an elevated position. As NBC unit manager Jim Marooney reported during the first hour after the shooting:

> I'm getting this from several sources… there were at least five shots fired by a man standing on one of those service trays, which stood about 50 inches off the ground, and he fired down into the Senator. When I finally got up to that point, there was a body behind the Senator, and the Senator was lying in a pool of blood, conscious. … While this was going on, there were at least ten people holding this man … At the same time, someone else was trying to get out the other end, with people running, screaming and chasing after him. I don't know what happened to the one who was running in the other direction but the man who was held against the tray was taken into custody.[394]

Vince DiPierro had reported seeing Sirhan standing on the service tray with a girl in a polka dot dress "holding" him *before* the shooting, but DiPierro saw him get off the tray stand and walk over to the north side of the room near the steam tables, where Lisa Urso saw him and Karl Uecker captured him. There was only one service tray rack reported in the room, and it was positioned at the southeast end of the ice machine, not near the north side where Kennedy was shot. If someone were firing from the service tray rack, it was not Sirhan. If Marooney had confused the steam table with a serving tray, his witnesses were still not describing Sirhan, as Sirhan was on the floor before he was grabbed and thrust onto the table by Karl Uecker and the rest.

Seven years after the shooting, the *San Antonio Express* published a drawing of the pantry that included a caption that read "Gunman stood here on the table." According to the official record, not one gunman was seen on the table until Sirhan was pushed there, and he was not standing there but being piled upon by several men. But as we just saw, there were several witnesses who thought there was a shooter on the table. From where did the *San Antonio Express* of July 22, 1975, get that information?

Another NBC newsman reported that busboy Juan Romero "said that a man whom he described as short, about 5'4", about 35 years old, with curly brown hair, jumped in the air, and fired his handgun down into Kennedy." That description does not match Sirhan. But it did match someone others reported seeing in the pantry, as you will see in the next chapter.

How could someone firing from atop a steam table go unnoticed by all but the small number of witnesses just mentioned? A friend did a magic trick for me

---

394   NBC footage from June 5, 1968, shared with me by Brad Johnson.

once in a restaurant that may have provided the answer. He took a paper napkin, wadded it up, hid it in the palm of his hand, waved his hands around, then opened his hands—both of them. There was no paper in either hand, and he had no sleeves. I felt I'd watched his hands carefully the whole time. Where did it go?

A waiter came by and my friend asked me to stand to his side as he did the same trick for the waiter. After taking the paper, he waved his hands above his head and just threw the paper backward to get rid of it. "But that's so obvious," I said afterwards, asking how I could have missed that. He explained that peripheral vision doesn't extend very far upwards of our normal line of sight. He'd simply put his hands at the highest point above his head, out of my peripheral vision, and disposed of the napkin.

By putting a shooter on the table, you'd almost guarantee that few, if any, witnesses would see the shooter. People were looking straight ahead or down at their feet. Few would have a reason to look up as they crossed the pantry. From a conspirator's point of view, that would be an excellent place to fire from, especially if you could put a shooter there who looked like Sirhan and wore a similar color.

Hidden guns

MOST PEOPLE WHO LOOK INTO THIS CASE ASSUME IF THERE WERE other guns in the pantry, more people would have seen them. Therefore, since only Sirhan's and Cesar's guns were seen (by all but Shulman, who was certain he had seen at least three guns out), there couldn't have been more guns in the pantry. But there are many reasons other guns wouldn't have been seen. What if the gun was in, say, a rolled-up poster? What if the gun were hidden under a busboy's towel? Hidden in a pocket? Fired from within a purse?

What if the gun were disguised in another object? The CIA and other intelligence services around the planet have developed all kinds of guns that do not look like guns. I saw a gun disguised as a cigarette case at the CIA Museum in Washington, D.C., and you can find several variations of a gun hidden in a suitcase on the Internet. The Navy, in World War II, produced a gun hidden inside a glove, triggered by pushing a plunger on the weapon up against the victim's body.[395] In the CIA's now declassified manual of trickery and deception, the CIA's staff magician John Mulholland wrote:

> The objective of the trickster is to deceive the mind rather than the
> eye. ... Even when eyes are misled, the memory may hold something
> that will permit working out how the mystery was accomplished after

---

395   Kim Zetter, "Tools of Tradecraft: More Spy Gear From the CIA, Others," *Wired*, www.wired.com/2011/03/

it is over. When the mind has been deceived, it is almost impossible to work backward and discover the deception.[396]

Guns can also be hidden in cameras. In 1960, a report from the Swiss branch of a Russian trading company alleged that former Gestapo agents, "posing as newspaper men," planned to assassinate the Soviet leader Khrushchev with "a gun hidden in a camera or microphone."[397] The famed filmmaker Alfred Hitchcock used such a device in his 1940 film *Foreign Correspondent*. A man posing as a news photographer kills a dignitary using a gun that looks like a big flash camera. Nina Rhodes-Hughes told me the shots she heard sounded like camera light bulbs popping, and she was not the only witness to say that. Might one of the cameras near Kennedy have concealed a gun?

Hidden or disguised guns aside, several witnesses *did* see not just other guns but other gunmen and reported them, as you'll see in the next chapter.

What did Sirhan fire?

THERE'S ANOTHER PROBLEM WITH THE SHOOTING THAT HAS, TO date, not been adequately addressed. If you were planning a conspiracy, would you even want Sirhan to be firing *real* bullets? Sirhan was not a marksman. A few days at a firing range is not enough to qualify one as an expert. If you were an assassin, would you take a gig if you knew some guy off the street was going to be shooting in your direction? One could argue that the assassination sponsor may simply have not told the shooter behind Kennedy that other people would be firing. But that scenario makes no sense. If you were planning an assassination and knew you'd only have a few seconds to get the job done, would you put one shooter in a position to kill the other shooter before your ultimate target was taken out?

No. A two-shooter scenario is not a reasonable explanation for the evidence. What does make sense, however, maps closely to what witnesses both saw and heard.

A surprisingly large number of witnesses in the pantry thought Sirhan was firing a cap gun, or that balloons were breaking or firecrackers going off. You don't need a cap gun to fire "caps," as Turner and Christian explained in their

cia-spy-tools/, March 25, 2011.

396   H. Keith Melton and Robert Wallace, *The Official C.I.A. Manual of Trickery and Deception* (New York: Harper, 2010), p. 88.

397   Joseph Zullo, "Tighten Guard in Threats on Khrushchev," *Chicago Daily Tribune*, September 22, 1960.

book. You could use "slugless cartridges," cartridges designed to carry paper that flash-burns, not bullets.

Very few people identified the initial sounds as gunshots. It came to them more as a realization as people were hit and blood appeared.

Robin Casden told the police, "It sounded like cap gun shots to me."[398] Richard Drew, a local reporter, told the LAPD, "I heard firecrackers, looked up and saw smoke."[399] Evan Freed heard a "pop noise" like a balloon, then the sound of firecrackers going off.[400] Richard Tuck "heard the sound of what sounded like cap pistols or firecrackers."[401] Virginia Guy, another reporter, thought they sounded "like firecrackers. They sounded like little pops."[402] David Jayne thought the noises were "a flurry" of what "sounded like a string of firecrackers—no pause in the sequence."[403] Irwin Stroll, one of the people wounded during the pantry shooting, remembered seeing the Kennedy procession of people stop. Then "there was [sic] six firecrackers, and I remember screaming out 'Firecrackers,' and then there was smoke."[404] Bob Funk, part of CBS' television crew, had followed Kennedy off the stage, although they were pretty far behind him. "At approximately the swinging doors he heard what sounded like paper cups popping when someone stomps on them. He first realized it was gunfire when he saw plaster fall from the ceiling where a bullet hit."[405]

Booker Griffin heard two sounds he didn't think were shots, and then more than eight shots.[406] A number of qualified witnesses had similar reactions. Even when people knew intellectually they had to be gunshots some were still confused by the sound. One of these was Fred Dutton, who told the LAPD's Captain Hugh Brown,

> My main impression was less the shots than what a small noise they made. As you probably heard, that day before we had big firecrackers thrown onto the car in San Francisco, and that really—I was in the infantry in World War II and I know gunshots, but that was something scary, those damn things. My first reaction was a gun, and then, well, it couldn't be. It's not loud enough. And then I accepted that it was.

Remember how judges routinely admonish would-be jurors that if they believe even *one* witness, that is enough to establish a fact in a court of law? There are

---

398   LAPD interview of Robin Casden, July 1, 1968.
399   LAPD interview of Richard Drew, July 15, 1968.
400   LAPD interview of Evan Freed, June 14, 1968.
401   LAPD interview of Richard Tuck, June 5, 1968.
402   LAPD interview of Virginia Guy, June 5, 1968.
403   LAPD interview of David Jayne, July 29, 1968.
404   LAPD interview of Irwin Stroll, June 14, 1968.
405   FBI interview of Bob Funk, June 21, 1968, dated June 26, 1968.
406   LAPD interview of Booker Griffin, July 25, 1968.

two extremely credible witnesses who thought Sirhan was firing blanks or a cap gun, who were very familiar with guns.

Norbert Schlei had received a law degree from Yale, where he was Editor-in-Chief of the *Yale Law Journal*. He had been a naval officer before being appointed Assistant Attorney General of the United States by President John F. Kennedy in 1962. He was the principal author of the Civil Rights Act. Schlei was a very intelligent, respected person, who was in a position to know about guns. In an on-camera interview broadcast soon after the shooting by local Los Angeles station KTLA, Schlei reported, "It didn't sound like gun shots to me, and I've heard a lot of gun shots. It sounded like a cap pistol or somebody cracking a balloon."[407]

The other highly qualified witness on the point of cap guns was Rafer Johnson, who, as an Olympic Decathalon champion, knew well what a fired cap or blank looked and sounded like. So we should give considerable weight to what Rafer reported right after the shooting. "I thought it was a balloon. I heard the first pop and then I heard about three or four just right after another....I looked, and then the second shot, I saw smoke and saw like something from a—like a—the residue from a bullet or cap, looked like a cap gun throwing off residue."[408]

What kind of residue does a cap gun throw off? Paper residue. A blank or slugless cartridge will give the same result. In both cases, the flame of the paper burning as it comes out of the muzzle is visible, as are tiny bits of paper. Karl Uecker, the maître d' who caught Sirhan in a headlock within the first two or three shots, described seeing nearly exactly that to the Grand Jury: "I saw some paper flying. I don't even remember what it was, paper or white pieces of things."[409]

Supporting the notion that Sirhan was firing blanks was Dick Aubry: "I just saw this blue...like a flash, like maybe something from a firecracker...flash, like a little spark from a....it was just the flashes I saw, I thought somebody threw a firecracker right at him...."[410]

Several other witnesses also thought Sirhan was firing was a cap gun or blanks by the sound alone. Dick Tuck heard "what sounded like cap pistols or firecrackers." He heard at least five shots and then a commotion broke out.[411] Valerie Schulte thought the gun sounded like a "cap gun." Richard Lubic told the FBI he heard two shots "which sounded like shots from a starter pistol at a track meet."[412] And this is still not a complete list of such statements.

The simplest explanation for this is also the best explanation: Sirhan was actually firing blanks, not bullets, in the pantry. This explanation fits everything

---

407   KTLA footage from the Ambassador Hotel, June 5, 1968, viewed by the author at the Museum of Television and Radio in Beverly Hills, now the William Paley Center.

408   LAPD interview transcript of Rafer Johnson, June 5, 1968.

409   Grand Jury testimony of Karl Uecker, June 7, 1968.

410   LAPD interview transcript of Richard Aubry, June 5, 1968.

411   LAPD interview transcript of Dick Tuck, June 5, 1968.

412   FBI interview report of Richard Lubic dated June 27, 1968.

witnesses saw, felt and heard. And if Sirhan were firing blanks, everything else starts to fall into place.

Knowing Sirhan was going to be firing blanks, other conspirators simply had to wait until Sirhan fired his first shot. Then, while everyone else in the pantry froze in shock and fear, assassins moved quickly to get the job done.

This scenario fits all the known evidence. Sirhan was like a magician's assistant, providing the distraction by firing blanks. All eyes went to his gun, leaving the actual assassins to do their job. The actual shooters could have used suppressors and kept their weapons well hidden, perhaps in rolled-up posters or under a newspaper or a busboy's towel. With several people firing at once, it became impossible to tell how many shots are fired. That explains why the shots sounded like firecrackers to such a large number of witnesses.

Firing blanks would have deceived the mind and the eye. The witnesses who saw Sirhan saw him fire the gun. They saw flame come out. Those witnesses were certain Sirhan had fired bullets. Only the earwitnesses who hadn't seen him fire thought he was firing blanks, and then only until Kennedy went down. Then all of them assumed what they had thought were blanks were actually bullets. But it appears the earwitnesses were right the first time.

Remember that the panel of ballistics experts appointed by Judge Wenke could not match any of the victim bullets to Sirhan's gun, and that the victim bullets that matched each other had been switched. If Sirhan fired blanks, that's why the bullets *had* to be switched. The simplest and most logical explanation is that *none of the bullets could be matched to Sirhan's gun because Sirhan had not fired any of those bullets.*

Where did the extra bullets go?

TWO BULLETS WITH WOOD IN THE GROOVES WERE FOUND BY THE police in Sirhan's car. Had they been planted there in the hopes of tying him to the crime, before the police realized there were too many bullets?

Clearly, bullets had been removed. Who took them? In a *Washington Post* article, Dan Moldea recounted how one of the Sheriff's deputies, Thomas Beringer, saw someone in a tuxedo trying to dig a bullet out of a doorframe "with a knife, a silver knife, for a souvenir."[413] But what if the man wasn't after a souvenir? What if the man in the tuxedo was simply part of the clean-up team, present at

---

413   Dan Moldea, "RFK's Murder A Second Gun?" *Washington Post*, May 13, 1990, via www.washingtonpost.com/archive/opinions/1990/05/13/rfks-murder-a-second-gun/9248e988-9fff-4366-b3e3-2849420b9bf9/, accessed November 13, 2016.

the scene of the crime to clean up what the conspirators understood would be evidence of multiple shooters?

The first people on the scene of the crime were Sheriffs, not LAPD, and they appear to have removed bullets from the holes, and then circled and initialed them—standard procedure when a bullet is removed. Where did those bullets go?

It should be clear that we are not dealing with two lone nuts or a small conspiracy between two men. We're dealing with a large operation, and not the kind of thing a couple of right-wingers or mobsters could pull off on their own. This plot required compliance not only with the direct participants, but with the LAPD, the Sheriff's office, the D.A.'s office, state government, the media, and even the FBI. Who had that kind of power in 1968?

The closer you examine the evidence, the more you begin to understand this was a highly sophisticated intelligence operation, with not just shooters but helpers who made sure the shooters could do their jobs and escape undetected.

So who were these team members? And what was Sirhan's actual level of culpability in all of this? Who was orchestrating the plot? And on whose behalf?

SUSPICIOUS OTHERS

"[The person reporting (P/R)] noticed four men and one girl standing between the Venetian Room and the lobby fountain. P/R states one of these men resembled Sirhan B. Sirhan. ... P/R is sure that all these persons were together. ... P/R tackled the suspect and a security officer of the hotel helped subdue the suspect. The officer handcuffed the suspect and took him away. P/R recognized this man as one of the four suspects he observed earlier in the lobby."

PEOPLE OFTEN ASK: HOW DID THE CONSPIRATORS KNOW KENNEDY would be coming through the pantry? The answer they expect to hear is that a member of Kennedy's staff was in on the plot, setting him up from the inside. But the evidence doesn't appear to support that belief.

While the original plan was to take Kennedy downstairs to the overflow crowd in the Ambassador Room below the Embassy Room to say a few words, at every one of his press stops, Kennedy had always talked to the print media. It was understood, then, that at some point, Kennedy would go to the Colonial Room to talk to the print press. And there were only two ways into that room. One was through the lobby area, which would be filled with people, and the other was through the pantry, which opened to a small hallway and then to the Colonial Room. Any other route would have left him more exposed and less protected. The only "change" was that Kennedy's team decided he should talk to the press right after the speech rather than heading downstairs to talk to the overflow crowd first. But this made perfect sense. Fred Dutton described the decision process to Captain Hugh Brown of the LAPD in a phone interview:

> It was a last-minute decision, I would say made within five minutes before the shooting occurred. What had happened was that we'd come down from the Senator's suite through that back way to the

Colonial Ballroom for his statement, and while he was speaking, Bill Barry and I went off on the side and discussed sort of what should be—where we were going next.

Unruh and the local people had suggested—not directly, I got this indirectly—that the Senator should go one flight down where there was an overflow crowd in another ballroom.

I made the decision that the crowd was too rowdy and congested and so forth; it was too late an hour; that he should speak at one place where he already was and then we could go hold the press conference, which was in that press room off of the end of the hallway through the kitchen [the Colonial Room].

That pretty much was the pattern that we had in the other election nights in the primary sites in Nebraska and Indiana and so forth.[414]

So any plotter of intelligence could have deduced that Kennedy would eventually return through the pantry to the Colonial Room, as that was Kennedy's pattern. All the conspirators had to do was wait. And to guarantee they wouldn't be kicked out, they needed press passes. That's why it's important that both Michael Wayne and the girl in the polka dot dress so persistently sought press passes from various people that night. Press passes were like all-access passes and would have been invaluable to conspirators.

Another common fallacy is to assume the conspiracy was necessarily a small one, because otherwise, "someone would have talked." But as you'll see, there *were* those who tried to talk before *and maybe even after* the shooting. No less than four people seemed to have inside knowledge of a plot on the last day of Kennedy's life, as you'll soon see.

The operation might never have succeeded if only two people had been involved. No one knew for sure until the last minute which way Kennedy would go. Although his usual move was to talk to the print press after campaign rallies, would he follow that process this time? What if this time Kennedy *had* decided to forego talking to the printed press and had gone downstairs and never passed through the pantry?

In an assassination plot, you need more than shooters. You need a support team who can help maneuver the shooters into position. Someone had to signal when Kennedy was coming down. What if a shooter or designated patsy is caught moments before the crime? Of course you would put multiple shooters in the room. There even appears to have been a team waiting downstairs as well, had Kennedy gone the other way first.

---

414   LAPD interview transcript of Fred Dutton, September 6, 1968.

Members of the team had even been spotted at earlier Kennedy events. Maybe they had been observing for future reference. Maybe they had tried to kill Kennedy before and failed. This was clearly the conspirators' last best chance to kill Kennedy before the Democratic Convention, where there would be much greater security. And if he got the nomination, as most observers expected he would, the security net would have been tighter still. Kennedy could not be allowed to leave the hotel alive. That's why the plot was large, sophisticated, and efficient.

Six different suspects

IN THE FIRST THREE HOURS AFTER THE ASSASSINATION, THE LAPD'S radio communications referenced *at least six different male suspects.* I say "at least" because only a tiny portion of the radio traffic has been transcribed.

The *first* suspect aired on police radio was not the tall, sandy-haired man that Sharaga broadcast, according to the multi-track transcription made by Philip Van Praag. At 12:28 A.M., call sign 8K1 reported over the police radio: "apparently, the suspect is a male Mexican waiter that supposedly works at the Ambassador."[415] An entry in the LAPD's Emergency Control Center (ECC) journal, entered four minutes later indicated that "possible suspect Jesse Greer" was on his way to the Rampart Station and that the info had come from Jess Unruh.[416] Curiously, one of Fernando Faura's friends in the LAPD tipped him off on the morning of June 5 that a call had come in identifying the shooter as a fry cook at a drive-in at Wilshire and Westwood named "Jesse."[417] Was this the same person? Was the fry cook's full name Jesse Greer? Remember that when Sgt. Jordan was questioning Sirhan after the shooting, before anyone knew Sirhan's identity, Jordan walked in at one point and called him "Jesse." According to Van Praag's transcription, at 12:28 A.M., the person with call sign 3Y65 reported, "according to a radio report,

---

415   Robert J. Joling, J.D. and Philip Van Praag, *An Open & Shut Case*, (United States: JV & CO, LLC, 2008), p. 288.

416   When Faura interviewed a fry cook named Jesse at Tony's Drive In at the corner of Wilshire and Westwood, the 5'8" light-complected Mexican appeared to Faura to be wholly innocent. But when Faura returned to his car, three men were stopped in a "no parking zone" right in front of his car. Faura thought the three of them exchanged looks as he walked up. "The man in the front passenger seat held a walkie-talkie on his lap, the antenna fully extended. His left hand moved to cover it" as Faura approached, "but it was too long. It appeared to be slightly smaller than those used by the police but larger and more solid than those sold to the public." Fernando Faura, *The Polka Dot File on the Robert F. Kennedy Killing* (TrineDay, 2016), p. 19.

When Faura got into his car, he feigned getting out a cigarette but instead took down the license number. When he returned to his office, he called a friend in the police department to have the plate traced, but no record of that plate existed. Faura, pp. 24–25.

417   In what could be just a strange coincidence, or not, Khaiber Khan gave Michael Wayne a ride to the same corner where Tony's Drive In was located, Wilshire and Westwood, on the night of the assassination. See the *SUS Final Report*, in the "Khaiber Khan" section, p. 432.

they have two suspects in custody," so it seems possible that someone named Jesse Greer and Sirhan had both been apprehended, but that Jesse was quietly released.

It would not have been unprecedented for an arrested suspect in an assassination to have been quietly released. When Malcolm X was gunned down in 1965, witnesses reported three attackers. Reporter Jimmy Breslin, who had just happened to be in the audience when Malcolm X was shot (and in the Ambassador Hotel when Kennedy was shot) wrote a front-page article that had a subheading that read, "Police Rescue Two Suspects." Within a few hours, however, the story was reissued in an updated edition with the same story but with a different subheading, "Police Rescue One Suspect." The suspect who got away was ignored, and the second suspect, apprehended but released by the police, was simply written out of that history.

When author Toby Rogers asked Breslin about this years later, Breslin perhaps revealed more than he intended: "Well I was supposed to receive a journalism award in Syracuse that evening, but I got a tip (from the NYPD) that I should go up to Harlem to see Malcolm X speak. I sat way in the back smoking a Pall Mall cigarette." Did someone in the NYPD know Malcolm would be killed that night?

Breslin's reaction to Rogers' next question, about the heading that changed from two suspects to one, suggests Breslin did have some sort of guilty knowledge, if only after the fact. His over-the-top reaction when asked was bizarre, to say the least: "I don't fucking know what is what. I don't know if there was two editions or one. I don't want to remember. I don't want to read it. Fuck it. Who cares! It's 2005!"[418]

Less than 20 seconds after the description of the first suspect, Sgt. Sharaga broadcast his description of a *second* suspect. Sharaga described him as six-foot to six-foot-two, with sandy-colored curly hair, "very thin" in a "light tan shirt."[419]

In the same minute, between 12:28 A.M. and 12:29 A.M., LAPD officers Fedrizzi and De Losh broadcast a suspect description told to them by Andrea Busch and her brother Richard Busch and their friend Richard Ritner about the male and female that seemed to be escaping, where Richard Busch had thrown open the door and the woman hurried past and stopped a few feet away. Fedrizzi and De Losh broadcast a description of this *third male suspect* and a female companion: "No. 1, male Latin, 30 to 35, 5-9½, stocky, wearing a wool hunter's hat with a small brim. No. 2, described as a female Caucasian. No further description."[420]

---

418   Toby Rogers, *The Ganja Godfather: The Untold Story of NYC's Weed Kingpin* (Trine Day, 2015). Just before the passage regarding his conversation with Breslin, Rogers provided pictures of the two different editions with the changing headlines.

419   Robert J. Joling, J.D. and Philip Van Praag, *An Open & Shut Case*, (United States: JV & Co., LLC, 2008), p. 288.

420   SUS Final Report, p. 199.

At 12:34, a *fourth* suspect was reported "being held in the building," meaning the Ambassador Hotel. This was Michael Wayne. Why wasn't he immediately turned over to the police? Instead, he was taken to the office of William Gardner, the man who had hired Ace Guard Services to help with hotel security. This announcement prompted the officer with call sign 114 to broadcast, "One suspect in custody, one suspect inside the building. Is there a supervisor up at the station?"

At 12:36 A.M. a description of the *fifth* suspect, who would turn out to be Sirhan, was broadcast. When Sirhan's description ("male Latin, 25-26, 5-5, bushy hair, dark eyes, light build, wearing a blue jacket and blue levis and blue tennis shoes") was put out again at 1:13 A.M., Sharaga was asked if he had anything to add. That's when Sharaga said that wasn't the description that he put out.

At 12:50, the Intelligence Division log stated that Lt. Sillings reported on television that a 6'4" suspect was in custody. Who was he referring to? Sirhan was a full foot shorter than that. Confusion continued until Inspector Powers got on the radio at 1:43 A.M. to preemptively say Rafer Johnson said there was only one suspect and he didn't want people speculating about a conspiracy.[421]

About 30 minutes later, "114" reported that he "just had a call Sgt. Davis Sherr's office he wants a unit to meet him at 3424 Wilshire in the IBM building. He has a susp he wants interviewed."[422] At 2:13 A.M., an officer transmitted a request to Sharaga at the command post to "send unit to meet Sheriffs at the IBM building to interview subjects."[423] Sharaga agreed to send unit over, and then his communications went down for about 25 critical minutes. It was nearly an hour before word of this now singular *sixth* suspect reappeared. Sharaga asked what the Sheriff's would do with the suspect, who turned out to be Terry Lee Fraser. Rampart said to send the suspect there.

Unlike most of the people seen with Sirhan, Fraser was 5'6", blond-haired and blue-eyed. Fraser had gone with his friends Gary Harmond and Gary Ford to the Ambassador Hotel. Harmond and Fraser said as they parked at the IBM building just west of the hotel around 12:30 A.M., they heard on the car radio that Kennedy had been shot. They walked to the hotel and saw an ambulance pulling away. They went to the Rafferty party to have drinks, but ended up on separate sides of the room. Harmond said he tried to signal Fraser that he wanted to go to the restroom, but Fraser evidently read that as wanting to leave altogether. They had prearranged to meet back at the car, so Fraser went back to the car and waited. When his friends didn't show, Fraser returned to the hotel, but wasn't allowed back in by the cops and was asked to leave. He tried to get to another part of the hotel by sneaking through the bushes but was caught, detained

421   LAPD Radio log, June 5, 1968.
422   LAPD Radio log, June 5, 1968.
423   LAPD Unusual Occurrences Log, June 5, 1968.

briefly at the IBM building, and then transferred to Rampart and interviewed and ultimately released.

While Fraser was likely innocent, the tape of his interview on July 7, 1968, did him no favors. When Thompson said he was arrested around 3 A.M. Fraser corrected him and says "3 A.M.? It was closer to 12:30 A.M." "Right after the shooting?" Thompson asked. "No, wait a minute, when was the shooting?" Fraser asked. When told it was about 12:15 A.M., Fraser moved the time of his apprehension to 1 A.M. Very likely he was just confused. But someone could read his responses as evasive. Without additional evidence, however, I do not believe Fraser was involved. I can't say the same for the other person known to have been apprehended at the hotel that night.

Michael Wayne

MICHAEL WAYNE WAS ONE OF THE MOST SUSPICIOUS CHARACTERS at the hotel that night. Several people noticed him in a negative context. As we have already seen, Wayne was apprehended and handcuffed after being chased from the pantry by people who felt he was involved. One of the Grand Jury witnesses who mistakenly thought he was Sirhan said Wayne appeared to be casing the kitchen as he walked through it. Was his claim that he was just a collector of political memorabilia enough to explain his actions that night? Was he really just running to find a phone when captured?

Michael Wayne was a 21-year-old male Caucasian, 5'8½" tall, weighing a slim 135 pounds. He was wearing a dark sweater over a white shirt and gray pants. He looked a little like Sirhan due to his dark curly hair, but he had noticeably long sideburns (Sirhan didn't have sideburns). Wayne had been born in Manchester, England, and had immigrated to the U.S. in 1951, where he became a citizen in 1960. "He professes to be of Jewish background, but not from the mid-east," Sergeant Varney wrote in his report summary of Wayne.[424] Several witnesses mistook Wayne for Sirhan Sirhan.

Wayne's own account of his actions that night is as follows. Witnesses, however, would flesh out his story in disturbing ways. The LAPD and FBI interviewed Wayne several times and elicited the following story from Wayne.

Wayne worked in the accounts receivable section of the Pickwick Bookstore in Hollywood. He claimed to be an admirer of Robert Kennedy and a collector of political paraphernalia for many years. He had an autograph from President Dwight D. Eisenhower and from Vice President Hubert Humphrey, among others.

---

424   LAPD interview summary of Michael Wayne, July 2, 1968. The rest of this section blends several LAPD interviews with Wayne and an FBI report on Wayne as well. Both agencies interviewed Wayne multiple times.

On May 20, 1968, Wayne went to the Ambassador Hotel, where Senator Kennedy was holding an event. He obtained a PT-109 Kennedy tie clasp from a Kennedy aide, and later "by chance" met the Senator himself on a stairway in the lobby. He introduced himself and shook Kennedy's hand and asked Kennedy if he could exchange the tie clasp he had just been given for the one Kennedy was wearing. They exchanged tie clasps, and Wayne left. Remember this tie clasp. It becomes an important part of the story that follows.

On June 4, Wayne hitchhiked after work at the Pickwick Bookstore to the headquarters of the Republican candidate for California Senator, Max Rafferty, who would lose that night to the Democrat Alan Cranston. There, Wayne picked up various political pins. He then hitchhiked to the headquarters of Thomas Kuchel, the Republican minority whip in the Senate, where he picked up more pins. Given that Wayne was hitchhiking, one wonders where he stored all the pins he was collecting. Wayne had no coat or bag on him at the time he was photographed in handcuffs. One very credible witness thought Wayne did have a coat on when he first saw him.

Someone else from this case stopped at Kuchel's headquarters before heading to the Ambassador Hotel: Sirhan Sirhan.

During his trial, Sirhan described how he came to be at the Ambassador Hotel that night. After he left the shooting range, he stopped at Bob's Big Boy in Pasadena, where he ran into a friend from Pasadena City College whose name was misspelled "Mystery" in the trial transcript but was actually Mistri. The two went to the Pasadena City College Student Center, where Sirhan challenged Mistri to a game of pool but was turned down, because Mistri was looking for work and needed to go home and read through the classified ads. Mistri bought a paper but stopped Sirhan from buying one of his own, giving him all but the want ads Mistri needed. In the paper, Sirhan saw—or thought he saw—an ad for a pro-Israel march in the Miracle Mile section of Wilshire, the same place the Rafferty and Robert Kennedy headquarters were located. Reading about the march triggered deep feelings of resentment, as the Sirhan family's life had been shattered by the Arab-Israeli conflict in 1967. "I had the same emotional feeling, the fire started burning inside of me, sir," when he saw that ad.

Sirhan said that after Mistri turned him down for pool but before he saw the ad, "I was having in my mind to go to the Rosicrucian meeting. I had that in mind, but that was at 8 o'clock or a later time and between this time and the meeting time, I had nothing to do," so he decided to go into Los Angeles and check out the parade.

But Sirhan had misread the ad. The march was on June 5, not June 4. He got so incensed he missed his exit and got lost and had to ask for directions.

Along Wilshire, Sirhan saw "a store with [a] very highly illuminated interior" and thought maybe it had to do with the parade. But it was the headquarters for the Republican Tom Kuchel, who had originally been nominated to the Senate to fill Nixon's place. In 1968, Kuchel was running, unsuccessfully as it turned out, for re-election. Sirhan decided to go in and see what was going on there. As he always did, he left his wallet in his glove box. "I never carried my wallet with me," he explain to Cooper during his trial. None of the Sirhan brothers carried wallets on them.

At Kuchel's headquarters, he found the action "pretty dull, to tell you the truth. At least I thought it was, sir." ("Forgive me, any of the Kuchel supporters here," the ever polite Sirhan said to the jury after this remark.)

There, he heard a couple of boys talking about how there was a "bigger party" down at the Ambassador, so he decided to go check it out. Sirhan walked the five or so blocks west from the Kuchel campaign office to the Ambassador Hotel.

Did Michael Wayne walk with him?

Wayne claimed to have walked to the Kennedy headquarters in Miracle Mile. Both the Kuchel and Kennedy headquarters were on Wilshire Boulevard, with the Ambassador Hotel in between. I find it hard to believe that a political junkie like Wayne would have walked past the Ambassador Hotel, with Kuchel, Rafferty and Kennedy there in person, and chosen instead to continue on for the approximate hour walk it would have taken to reach Kennedy's Miracle Mile headquarters. Given that Wayne had no compunction about hitchhiking, it defies credulity that he would waste an hour walking when he had so many political choices that night. I can't help but believe someone gave him a ride, at least from the Ambassador Hotel at this point.

That Wayne did make it to Kennedy's headquarters was confirmed by the man who drove him from Kennedy's headquarters to the McCarthy headquarters in Westwood, an Iranian man called "the Khaiber Khan," whose real surname appeared to be Goodarzian. Khan's daughter was fingered by a New Yorker the night of the assassination as the girl in the polka dot dress, a story I wrote about in the volume *The Assassinations: Probe Magazine on JFK, MLK, RFK and Malcolm X.* Some have mistakenly written that I had "identified" Khan's daughter as the girl in the polka dot dress, but that was not the case. The point was to show that someone appeared to be framing Khan and his family after the fact. After extensive additional research, I do not consider Khan or his daughter or the numerous volunteers Khan registered to have been any part of the plot. I had speculated at one point that since Khan was under a deportation order, perhaps he had been coerced into some level of involvement, but his deportation was only ordered after the policemen he talked to regarding this case reported him to immigration. The reasons why someone might want to tarnish Khan are amply spelled out in my earlier work. To summarize, Khan had exposed to the U.S. Congress that aid money to Iran was being siphoned into the private accounts of the Pahlavi family and, in some cases, being sent back to people like David Rockefeller and Allen Dulles in multi-hundred-thousand-dollar checks.

Wayne said there were two others in the car with Khan: Khan's girlfriend Maryam Koucham, who was in a cast, and one other man, who has never been identified, but whom Wayne "assumed to be a European newspaper reporter."[425]

According to Khan, when Khan came out of headquarters, Wayne was already in the car, having obtained permission from Koucham to tag along. Wayne asked Khan to go back into the Kennedy headquarters to get him a Kennedy pin. Khan turned him down, but Wayne was "most insistent" and appeared to believe that button would get him into the Kennedy party at the Ambassador Hotel.[426] Wayne's pesky persistence around pins, badges and press passes would draw attention all night.

At McCarthy's headquarters, Wayne picked up McCarthy's book and then hitchhiked to the Beverly Hilton Hotel, where he had the book autographed by McCarthy himself. From there, Wayne caught a ride with "two young Caucasian men and a blonde Caucasian girl" to the Ambassador Hotel, arriving between 8 and 10 P.M." The group drove through the hotel (there was a tunnel under the Embassy Room in the hotel) to the 8th Street parking lot, but they were unable to find parking. Wayne got out of the car before it was parked and said he never saw these people again.

Inside the hotel, Wayne went first to the press room, the Colonial Room, but was refused entrance by a guard there. He then wandered into the hallway between the end of the pantry and the Colonial Room and entered the Colonial Room from this second entrance.

Why was the press room the first place Wayne went? Why didn't he go to the candidate rooms in search of additional memorabilia before whatever was left was all gone? The press room didn't have any campaign buttons. But what the press had would have been invaluable to anyone who was part of the assassination conspiracy: press badges. Those gave people free access to campaign activities anywhere in the hotel. A press badge would have little sentimental value or trade value—but to a conspirator, the badge would be valuable. In the Colonial Room, Wayne obtained a blue and white "Kennedy Election Night Press" badge. Shortly thereafter, Wayne got a woman to give him a green "Kennedy for President" press badge. Wayne then clipped these two badges together with the PT-109 tie clasp from Kennedy that he was wearing.

Wayne next went to the lobby where he found someone handing out posters and took two. Where did the other one go? Did he roll them up together into

425   LAPD interview of Michael Wayne, August 14, 1968.
426   FBI interview of Khaiber Khan taken June 10, 1968 and dated June 12, 1968.

one roll? Did he hand one to someone else at some point? In the photo of him in handcuffs, he appears to be carrying only one poster, and while it's possible both had been rolled together, in a photo of Wayne taken when he was apprehended, there appears to be only one poster, partially unrolled.

Wayne then walked to a room off to the side of the Rafferty Room and collected more buttons. It's a wonder his pockets didn't burst with all that booty. Maybe Wayne had a bag of belongings that he shed somewhere that night. There was a report of a knapsack found in the flowers in the outdoor patio of the Dolphin Court[427] and a report of a knapsack found in a flower pot in the lobby.[428] It's likely this was the same bag, because in both cases the police officer received it from a bellboy or bell captain who had gotten it from a maid. The times of the reports and the original location of the sacks vary, but in both cases the bell person gave the bag to an officer who then gave it to Sergeant McArthur of the LAPD. The contents of this bag have never been revealed. We have only the scrawl of Manny Pena on the cover sheet of one of these accounts saying the owner had been found and the bag returned so "no further invest [sic] needed."

Near the Rafferty Room, Wayne may or may not have had a conversation with Daniel Hall, who told the FBI about an encounter with a man who appeared to fit Wayne's description.

Somewhere between 10 P.M. and 11:30 P.M., while Hall sat in a lounge with a couple of female Republican Committee workers near the Rafferty party's room, a white male, approximately 5'8", with "brown, medium-length hair" wearing a bulky dark sport coat and slacks, came to their table and asked if he could join them.

Hall told the FBI "a bizarre conversation" followed:

> Hall advised that this individual, who spoke with extremely strange vocabulary [sic] but not with an accent, indicated in different sentences that he was for Kennedy and against Rafferty, and then immediately after for Rafferty and against Kennedy. Hall stated that he also advised he was a Bel Air resident, a student at San Fernando Valley State College, a student at Santa Monica City College, and later, not a student at all. Hall advised that the individual in question was carrying a plastic zipper type briefcase containing a bulge which he, Hall, positively believes to have been a gun. Hall stated that he believes this bulge

---

427   LAPD interview of Donald MacEwen, the Bell Captain, June 6, 1968. MacEwen received the bag from "Mary Vaughn, the night clean-up lady" who said he had found it in the flowers of the Dolphin Court. MacEwen said he gave the bag to an officer who in turn gave it to "Lt. McArthur."

428   LAPD interview of Officer E.W. Crosthwaite, September 30, 1968. Crosthwaite said a bellboy had given him the bag, which had originally been found by a maid in a flower pot in "one of the large flower pots in the lobby floor of the hotel" and that he had given it to "Sgt. McArthur," who was "in the kitchen," at 3 A.M.

to have been a gun in that he formerly carried a similar briefcase in which he had a .22 caliber revolver, which made a very similar bulge, when he was [his profession is redacted in the document, but handwritten over the redaction is "an insurance adviser"]. Hall stated this man indicated that he liked to get information from people and intended to find out something about Hall and the two girls.[429]

The man Hall encountered sounds like an intelligence operative, carrying a gun, lying about his background, and attempted to elicit information. But if so, he was a poorly trained one. And if Hall's real job had been as an insurance advisor, there would have been no reason to redact that. Hall may have carried that gun in connection with some intelligence agency assignment himself, something the FBI would be loath to reveal as it would give more credence to his belief there was a gun in the bag.

Oddly enough, another suspect on June 4 would give an equally dishonest, rambling narrative: the woman who spent the day with John Fahey, who told him Kennedy would be taken care of at the winning reception that night. She not only gave him several different names for herself, but also claimed to have lived in a variety of places, changing her story each time Fahey knew anything about each place she mentioned. It was as if Hall's man and Fahey's woman had received the same inadequate training.

A few days later, the FBI reinterviewed Hall, who shared additional information:

> Hall disclosed that as conversation with this individual proceeded it became evident that there was something "strangely wrong" with this man. …
>
> Hall advised that he questioned the individual as to why he liked to get information from people. The unknown male replied, "I have a briefcase here full of information but I have something here (pointing to his briefcase) that's going to make big news tonight. Big news, big news." Hall disclosed that at this time one of the two girls attempted to touch this individual's briefcase but he yanked it roughly from her reach. Hall stated that he asked this man to buy a round of drinks for the table to which he replied, "No, I don't have that kind of money, and I don't like people that have money."

Hall described the man's complexion as "light, possibly pockmarked" and noted he spoke "strangely, however, not with accent, somewhat effeminate" and added that the man's "shoulders seemed somewhat hunched."

429   FBI interview of Daniel Hall, June 12, 1968, dated June 14, 1968.

Wayne's face didn't appear pockmarked in the only two pictures of him I've seen, but his voice was pitched a bit higher than the typical male range and he spoke softly. I could imagine how someone might find that "effeminate." Wayne had no coat on when he was arrested, but the man who tackled Wayne as he was trying to escape, George Clayton, said Wayne was wearing a coat earlier in the night. And if he were carrying a gun in a zippered bag, no doubt he handed it off to someone at some point that night.

Wayne may also have hinted at the assassination to someone other than Daniel Hall and his companions. There are several references to the "electrician's booth" and whether or not Wayne was in it. The police initially thought Hans Bidstrup had talked to Michael Wayne, not Sirhan, in his sound booth. But there are clipped, unclear references that suggest someone had hinted about the upcoming shooting to someone other than Bidstrup in the electrician's booth. On August 12, the LAPD re-interviewed Wayne on this point, but Wayne "was uncertain and did not recall" if he had been in the electrician's booth prior to the assassination.

Whether he was or wasn't the person Daniel Hall spoke to, and whether he did or didn't say something indicating foreknowledge of the assassination in the electrician's booth, Wayne provably lied to people all over the hotel that night, raising the very real prospect that he was in some specific way involved in the assassination story.

After visiting the Rafferty Room, Wayne went upstairs to the Kennedy suite, a floor he could not have gotten onto without the press badges. The hotel staff wouldn't even give out the floor or room number, as it was supposed to be for Kennedy, his associates, and press only. Wayne, however, had no trouble not just getting up there but taking advantage of the situation once he did. At the open bar there he ordered a free scotch and soda. Once there, he recognized Les Gotman, a Kennedy youth coordinator who worked at Kennedy headquarters. Wayne knew exactly where Gotman's desk was, there—"immediately to the right and in the corner as one would enter the Kennedy headquarters."

No one asked Wayne why he had taken note of Gotman's desk. Gotman himself does not appear to have been interviewed. And at no time did Wayne claim to be a volunteer for Kennedy, which is usually the only reason non-staff people enter a political candidate's campaign headquarters. In fact, Wayne's politics were the polar opposite. The fact that he knew the man's name and the precise location of his desk suggests Wayne may have cased the Kennedy headquarters on more than one occasion, which might account for Sirhan sightings at the Kennedy headquarters at times Sirhan could not possibly have been there. In the final days of the campaign, someone had stolen Robert Kennedy's itinerary, listing the times and locations of all his appearances. One of the people in the campaign office had seen someone who looked like Sirhan there and suggested Sirhan had stolen it. Perhaps Wayne had been the culprit.

On Kennedy's floor, Wayne talked to a campaign staff member about the special PT-109 pin that he had gotten from Senator Kennedy and talked the staff member into giving Wayne a *second* PT-109 tie clasp that this staffer was wearing. Most of the people who wore these pins did so in remembrance of John Kennedy. Not Wayne. As you will see, he was of the opposite political persuasion. But looking like a Kennedy loyalist may have gotten him access to places like the pantry.

Was Wayne's role at the Ambassador Hotel that night to pinpoint Kennedy's location and flag others to get into position when Kennedy went down to give his speech? The plotters clearly would have wanted to kill Kennedy *after* his speech because at that point, the cameras would be off. So the plotters would have wanted to know when Kennedy was going to speak so they could plan accordingly. The polls in California closed at 8 P.M. The absolute earliest Kennedy could have given a speech would have been shortly after 8 P.M. But the race was close, so it was a safe bet he wouldn't talk until much later in the night. In addition, the results came in more slowly than ever before due to the newly installed punch-card-counting IBM machines a block away. Not knowing for sure when Kennedy would reach the Embassy Room, the plotters would have wanted someone on the Kennedy floor to alert them when he started to move. Was that Wayne's role? Wayne stayed on the Kennedy floor until Kennedy went down to the Embassy Room to give his speech.

When the Kennedy party descended to the Embassy Room floor, Kennedy and his closest associates got in the freight elevator that emptied into the kitchen and Wayne took a separate elevator with the press (thanks to his press badges). The elevators arrived at nearly the same time. As Kennedy walked through the pantry on his way to the stage to give his victory speech, Wayne stopped him and asked Kennedy to autograph one of the two posters he had obtained earlier.

According to Wayne's account, he waited in the pantry for Kennedy to come back through, but Judy Royer had shooed him out of the area. Wayne told the FBI he left the pantry via the double doors at the east end of the pantry, but as soon as he saw Royer leave, he went back into the pantry.

Robert Klase was also there when Royer asked Wayne to leave the pantry. He told the LAPD that Wayne had told Royer "he had part of an autograph of Senator Kennedy and the Senator told him he would finish signing it when he came back through the kitchen. Judy made him leave the pantry area at that time." Presidential candidates don't sign "half" an autograph and promise to "finish signing" a poster. Did Klase misspeak, or had Wayne lied?

A note in one of Wayne's LAPD interviews states, "Mr. Wayne was brought to our attention by Mr. Charles Winner, who stated a Michael Wayne had spoken to him, in the kitchen area, prior to Senator Kennedy being shot."[430] Charles Winner worked for a PR firm that was supporting Hubert Humphrey, and Wayne tried to get Winner to give him a Humphrey tie clasp. Why did Winner mention Wayne at all? We can't know, because that part of Winner's interview does not appear to exist anymore. The only mention of it is in Wayne's, not Winner's, file. But a clue may exist in the lie detector questions proposed for Wayne. The first question to be asked was, "Did you have prior knowledge that there might be an attempt on Senator Kennedy's life?" This question was not included during the polygraph exam Hernandez gave Wayne. Whether to an electrician, Winner, or someone else, it's clear the police had reason to believe Wayne had made a comment to someone that appeared to indicate foreknowledge of the assassination.

Someone who was not Wayne may have used his name in the pantry, or Fred Droz talked to two men and got the names mixed up, or the LAPD put some false information in an interview report, and these options are not mutually exclusive. Droz told the LAPD that while he was in the pantry he "had a conversation with Michael Wayne. He was wearing a beige, gold sweater and light pants and a Kennedy tie clasp."[431] But this statement about a man in a gold sweater is nowhere to be found on the tape of Droz's interview provided to me by the California State Archives, while everything else in the summary of the interview accurately reflects Droz's taped comments. So either: 1) the tape was edited to exclude this, 2) Droz said this after the tape had been turned off, or 3) Droz never said any such thing, and the LAPD put a deliberate fiction in the record, possibly to attempt to explain away the man in the gold sweater that Sandra Serrano had reported seeing with Sirhan and the girl in the polka dot dress. If Droz talked to anyone in a gold sweater, it was definitely not Wayne, as pictures taken just minutes before and after this conversation show Wayne in a white button-down shirt with the collar open, covered by a dark sweater and light-colored trousers. But if Wayne were part of the plot, someone else involved might have used Wayne's name instead of his own to deflect suspicion. In the Watergate episode, E. Howard Hunt and Frank Sturgis shared an "Edward Hamilton" alias. E. Howard Hunt and James McCord shared the alias "Eduardo" in the anti-Castro community. This is a common intelligence technique to make it harder for others to identify separate individuals in an investigation.

Robert Healy, a reporter for the *Boston Globe*, told the FBI that although he didn't see Sirhan at any point that night, during Kennedy's speech he met

---

430   LAPD interview of Michael Wayne, July 2, 1968.

431   LAPD interview of Fred Droz, June 27, 1968.

someone whose actions he found worth noting. He was approached from inside the Colonial Room by a young white male, 19 years old, 5'8", 135 pounds, with curly dark brown hair. His skin was dark, "possibly of Mexican extraction." The man had a PT-109 clip and wore several badges, including a McCarthy badge and a Peace badge. Despite the man wearing several badges already, Healy said the man was "very persistent" about wanting to get Healy to give him the press badge Healy was wearing around his neck. Healy was surprised that the man had been able to get into the Colonial Room because "security men were positioned at the room's entrance."[432] Healy's description closely matches Wayne. But Wayne didn't need more badges at that point, and as you'll soon see, his claim to be a collector appears phony. Was he asking for co-conspirators? Was this someone else?

Wayne told the LAPD he was in the pantry, standing between the ice machine and the east end of the pantry, when the shots started. Wayne heard noises he did not immediately realize were gunshots and then heard someone say "He's been hit." He suddenly became "aware of the shots. I turned and saw him beginning to move, and men falling on top of a man in a blue shirt." At this point, Wayne ran out of the pantry. Did he hit Virginia Guy on his way out, or did someone else?

As the shooting began, Virginia Guy saw someone she assumed was Sirhan running toward her. Guy was a reporter for *Flare News* in Washington, DC. Due to the crush of people when Senator Kennedy entered the pantry, rather than walking backward to take Kennedy's picture, as she had planned, she walked away from Kennedy. When she heard what "sounded like firecrackers ... like little pops," she turned back to see "people running" and Kennedy "slumping" to the ground.

Then she saw someone "running toward" her who hit her in the mouth with something so hard it chipped her tooth. "He had something dark in his hand," Guy said. "This man was apprehended by Mr. Barry and some other men," Guy said in her June 6 LAPD interview. But in her first interview on June 5, just hours after the shooting, Guy said something different.

"The person was coming toward me and went some way in front of me, and I don't see how he could have done it. But anyway, somehow he like passed in front of me and it was during that time and [sic] I was knocked out of the way and spun around."

The transcript of Guy's interview makes it clear this could not have been Sirhan. She heard something she didn't recognize at first as shots—just little popping sounds. But she turned back to look and saw Kennedy "slumping" to the ground. Someone came hurtling toward her, as she told Sergeant Jack Chiquet:

---

432   FBI interview of Robert Healy, conducted June 19, 1968.

> Guy: [I]t seemed like he passed in front of me, and it was during that time, and I was knocked out of the way and spun around.
>
> Chiquet: By whom or what?
>
> Guy: I thought it was his hands, because it broke my tooth. But I remember that there was something in his hand, but, you see, at that point I wasn't thinking of him being the suspect .... I was just thinking this was some person hurdling [sic] toward me, and I thought they were trying to get me out of the way, because by this time ... it was registering that there was something very radically wrong, but he hurdled [sic] toward me and it was like he was, you know, it seemed like he was hitting at [me when he] probably was pushing ... me out of the way. And I remembered something that appeared to my sight to be dark in his hand.[433]

She said the man "appeared to be Latin," about 22 years old, not "terribly tall" and he looked "crouched in a running position." But Sirhan had stood still, fired, and then been apprehended by Uecker according to DiPierro and Urso as well as Uecker. At no time had he been free to run through the pantry to Guy's position, which she said was at least 10 or 12 feet in front of Kennedy.

Clearly, Guy saw someone who was not Sirhan running toward her, who pushed her out of the way. She was about 10 to 12 feet in front of Kennedy at the time of the shoots. That put her several feet from Sirhan, and he had no such wingspan, even if he was wrestling with people and being thrown around.

Chiquet asked if Guy could say "whether or not it was a gun" and Guy replied, "Well, now that I think back on it, yes, I would say it was a gun." She recalled that the dark thing in his hand may have been "more like silver." Guy was certain Sirhan was the guy who hit her in the mouth, but so many people mistook Michael Wayne for Sirhan she may well have been describing Michael Wayne. And the person she had seen had come diagonally from Kennedy's right side—where Wayne described he had been. Sirhan was to Kennedy's left.

Guy saw something else interesting. As she tried to recreate what she had seen, she said, "I do remember somebody moving off to the right [of Kennedy—her left, as she clarified]. I seem to get an impression of gray. ... [I]t was just a blur of gray moving off to the right ...."[434] Thane Cesar, the guard who had holding Kennedy's right elbow as Sirhan stepped out and fired, was wearing a gray uniform.

By his own admission, Wayne ran out of the east end of the pantry, which would have put him directly in line to collide with Virginia Guy. But this brings up a curious point. No one reported seeing a man carrying a poster or his book in his arms in the pantry at the time of the shooting. If Wayne had all this on him,

---

433   LAPD interview summary of Virginia Guy's 7 A.M. interview on June 5, 1968.
434   Ibid.

wouldn't Guy have noticed and commented on this? Given how much Wayne was carrying a few minutes later when apprehended and arrested, one wonders why no one saw that unless Wayne had set those down somewhere, either inside or outside the pantry, when Kennedy crossed the pantry for the last time.

A few witnesses reported seeing a man who wasn't Sirhan or Michael Wayne running out of the pantry with something that looked like a mostly concealed gun under something draped over his arm. But that's getting ahead of the story.

After he left the pantry, according to Wayne, he picked up several phones in the Colonial Room but couldn't get a line. Oddly, not one of the many press people in the room reported seeing Wayne come in and pick up the phones. Not one of them reported a problem getting a line out. Several heard the shots in the pantry and ran across the hall, so you'd think if someone came running into the press room and started picking up phones, someone would have asked Wayne what had happened. And if Wayne were truly trying to help Kennedy, wouldn't he have asked for help? Wayne said told Sergeant McGann in his first LAPD interview he didn't want to cause a panic.[435] But if the choice is between alerting everyone so everyone can try to help at once, or try to reach the police by yourself, which makes better sense?

Wayne said he next rushed across the Embassy Room foyer to the Gold Room. As Wayne ran across the foyer, according to Wayne, people asked him what had happened and he shouted "I can't say!" Why couldn't he say? If his point was to call for help for Kennedy, why not tell everyone you encountered that Kennedy needed help?

Wayne claimed that in the Gold Room, he asked a busboy where a phone was but the busboy didn't know. Finally, according to Wayne, he ran up to a "Negro security guard," and asked him where a phone was. Augustus Mallard, an African-American guard for Ace Security, was stationed at the Venetian Room at the southeast end of the lobby. According to the FBI's interview summary of Wayne:

> The guard wanted to know why he wanted to phone, and he replied that Kennedy had just been shot, and he wanted to summon aid. The guard appeared to Wayne not to believe what he had heard, and he handcuffed Wayne and took him to some security office in the hotel. Wayne, at this point, was very emotional and crying. The Security Guard advised him of his legal rights, and he remained in the security office about an hour ....[436]

---

435   LAPD interview of Michael Wayne, June 5, 1968.

436   FBI interview of Michael Wayne, July 8, 1968.

Mallard, who handcuffed Wayne, had a very different account of what happened. According to Mallard,

> After midnight, while on duty outside the Venetian Room, Mallard observed an individual come crashing through the crowd, pushing people down, and he heard shouts of "Stop that man." Upon hearing these shouts, Mallard apprehended the individual, who was the source of most of the confusion in the hallway outside the Embassy Room and handcuffed him. Mallard advised the individual turned out to be a reporter for a Los Angeles paper who was trying to get to a telephone and that after he turned this individual over to the Los Angeles Police Department officers, he went home.[437]

Wayne was not a reporter for any Los Angeles paper. Either Wayne lied to Mallard, Mallard lied or misremembered, or someone else had lied or misspoke by volunteering this inaccurate information.

Los Angeles Times photographer Steve Fontanini saw Wayne leave the Colonial Room and run out a short hallway (the hall between the pantry's east end and the Colonial Room's west end) and thought he might be a suspect getting away, so he ran after him. Fontanini was joined in the chase by Mallard. Fontanini said Wayne ran toward the Lautrec Room restaurant, which was south of the Colonial Room and east of the Gold Room. "At this location," Fontanini's LAPD interview report states, "Mr. Wayne ran into a large mirror and was caught by the guard."[438] A young Rafferty supporter named George Clayton also gave chase with Fontanini and tackled Wayne.

So Wayne apparently lied to his FBI interviewer about the way he was apprehended, claiming he ran up to the guard to ask for help when in fact he was apprehended trying to escape the people chasing him. FBI investigators are federal officials. It's actually a very serious crime to lie to a federal official. Wayne could have been charged on that count alone.

And these were hardly Wayne's only lies. Earlier in the night, Betty Barry, wife of the actor Gene Barry (who was also at the Ambassador), noticed a young man with dark curly hair who "was carrying what appeared to be campaign posters or literature." He was trying to get into the Embassy Room from the main entrance. A "Negro uniformed policeman," likely Mallard, "would not let him in." The young man then asked Mrs. Barry if she would help him get into the party in the Embassy Room. When she turned him down, Wayne asked her

---

437   FBI interview of Augustus Mallard, June 9, 1968.

438   I called Steve Fontanini in 2005 in the hopes of obtaining permission to reprint his picture, but at that time, unfortunately, his memory was largely gone. Fontanini didn't even remember taking a picture of Wayne, so I was unable to discuss that with him further.

if he would go to Dick Kline and tell him that Wayne was there, saying "Kline would get him in." Mrs. Barry found Kline, who was Kennedy's Los Angeles area press secretary, but "Kline said he did not know a Wayne and took no action to aid Wayne."[439] In addition, Judy Royer, who knew Wayne by face, if not name, was working with Kline. If Kline and Wayne were in cahoots, surely Kline would have told Royer not to shoo Wayne from the pantry. Clearly, Wayne lied about Kline as well.

One of the pantry victims inadvertently exposed Wayne's cover as a "collector" as being another lie. About "ten seconds before" the shooting, Ira Goldstein, who was about to become one of the shooting victims, talked to a man who had a blue press badge and a green press badge, clipped together with "Senator Kennedy's tie tack," meaning the PT-109 tie tack. Goldstein told the LAPD:

> What happened is, he says to me, "You want to trade press badges?" So, you know, he had a blue press badge, Kennedy Press, and a green one, and I had yellow ones. I said "Yeah, do you have a yellow—blue one [*sic* in the transcript], because I would like to have one of those and I would gladly trade." So he says, "No, I don't." He said, "I have a blue one and a green one and I want to keep them, and this is Senator Kennedy's tie tack I have on here." He had a gold tie tack taped—clipped to both these badges."[440]

The man was about the same height as Ira, 5'8", and weighed about 140. Ira thought he was between the ages of 18 to 24. This sounds like Michael Wayne, and Ira had identified him as Michael Wayne at the trial at Cooper's urging. He was the same height and weight and was wearing the PT-109 tie clasp Kennedy had given him, clasped to the green and blue press badges Wayne had obtained earlier.

But this man *couldn't* have been Michael Wayne, because according to Goldstein the man was wearing "a blue coat" and had "kind of sandy blond hair" that he was "pretty neat" and not curly. Wayne had curly dark hair that could not be mistaken for "sandy blond." And he didn't have a blue coat. He was wearing a dark sweater.

Clearly, the person who was shot had obtained the pin and badges from Wayne, looked somewhat like Wayne, and apparently was using his name as well. It was too close a match in terms of the items and the story behind the tie clasp.

Wayne was wearing only one PT-109 pin at the time of his arrest, clipped to no badges at all, and he reported no badge trades that night—only acquisitions.

<hr>

439   FBI interview of Betty Barry, taken June 21, 1968 and dated June 27, 1968.

440   LAPD interview of Ira Marc Goldstein, June 5, 1968.

Did Wayne lie to the man, giving him the wrong tie clasp and saying he had gotten it from Senator Kennedy? Or had he given away the pin he had gotten from Senator Kennedy, putting the lie to his claim to be a collector?

Not one of Wayne's interviewers ever asked where the other PT-109 pin or press badges went. Wayne described picking them up earlier and clipping them to the PT-109 clasp he got from Kennedy. He described getting a second clasp. But in the pictures of Wayne in handcuffs, he has only one PT-109 clasp, and it was clipped to no other badges. If Wayne were truly a collector, he would not have parted with either PT-109 clasp, especially not the one that Senator Kennedy had worn. It is not unreasonable to conclude that Wayne knew the shooting was to take place, and used one PT-109 pin and the press badges to put another conspirator in place behind Kennedy, thereby shedding his fake credentials in the anticipation of being caught.

The man Goldstein was talking to is important for a second reason. After Goldstein realized he had himself been hit, he saw this same man "laying on the ground, blood all over his head." When asked how the man came to have blood on his head, Goldstein replied, "He was shot."[441] Was this an additional shooting victim? Only three known victims were shot in the head, Kennedy, Schrade and Evans, and this man was none of them. It wasn't a woman, so that eliminated Evans. It wasn't Robert Kennedy, so that left only Schrade. I confirmed with Schrade that he was not wearing these items,[442] and Schrade had dark hair and was significantly taller. So who was the blond guy on the ground, bleeding from the head?

During the Grand Jury hearing, Goldstein made clear the person was definitely not Irwin Stroll. Goldstein told the Grand Jury the man he had been talking to was the young guy who had just been in there. The only young guy who had preceded Goldstein's testimony was Vince DiPierro. At first blush, that made sense. Vince had fallen to the floor and had blood on his glasses. But Vince had not been shot or injured in any way, and the description of the man still didn't fit, so I asked Vince about this. Vince had worn an orange turtleneck that night that he still possessed, complete with a bullet hole in one of the sleeves that the police showed no interest in examining or testing when he told them about it. He had been studying for finals, and when his father called to say get down here and you can see Kennedy, he had rushed right over, wearing blue corduroy pants and no suit coat at all. He did not have any badges on him and the only Kennedy pin of any kind was one he received from John Kennedy, a campaign pin, not a tie-clasp, that Kennedy had given him when he interviewed him for a school paper years earlier. I asked was it possible he had any press badges on?

441   LAPD interview of Ira Marc Goldstein, June 5, 1968.

442   Phone call with Paul Schrade, January 8, 2017.

No, Vince told me. The only thing Vince had that night was a button, a bumper sticker and a poster.

Vince also knew who Ira Goldstein was and was *certain* he hadn't talked to him. "That wasn't me," Vince stated emphatically as I questioned him about each point in Ira's story.[443]

There is another possibility in light of what followed. Could the 5'8" man in the blue suit with sandy hair who Ira indicated was shot near have himself been one of the participants in the conspiracy? Would that explain why no mention of this victim was made anywhere in the media? Had Wayne given this man his badges and clip so this man could gain access to the pantry? Had this man been an assassin who was instantly killed so he could not talk after? Was this perhaps the person Thane Cesar had hit when he fired his gun? Had other conspirators taken him from the room during the pandemonium, when people would have simply assumed he was being taken for medical aid? If we had a complete record of all witness interviews, we might have the answers to these questions. Without that, we can only speculate as to who this was, why Wayne gave him his paraphernalia, and what happened to him.

Wayne's possible participation in the conspiracy is heightened by an account that put him in a group with Sirhan, a girl in a polka dot dress, and three other men at the lobby fountain about a half-hour before Kennedy gave his final speech. Marvene Jones, a former newspaper reporter who was currently volunteering for Max Rafferty's Senate campaign, was manning a desk in the Venetian Room for volunteers when a young white "junior executive type" approached her desk after the shooting and told her,

> Kennedy's been shot. I was back there in that area. There was a man with a gun. *He had helpers.* They did not have guns but they were helping him. I tackled one of them. … *There were two to three helpers.* [Emphasis added.][444]

This man appears to have been George Ross Clayton (incorrectly listed in some places in the files as Gregory Ross Clayton), a Rafferty campaign worker. He was the one who tackled Wayne when he was running through the lobby after the shooting.

Somewhere between about 11 P.M. and 11:30 P.M. on the night of June 4, George Clayton noticed a group of four guys and a girl standing near the fountain in the lobby of the Ambassador Hotel outside the Embassy Room. Clayton's interview summary states:

---

443   Author interview of Vince DiPierro, November 21, 2016.

444   FBI interview of Marvene Jones, dated June 12, 1968.

[The person reporting (P/R)] noticed noticed four men and one girl standing between the Venetian Room and the lobby fountain. P/R states one of these men resembled Sirhan B. Sirhan. ... P/R is sure that all these persons were together. At approximately 12:15 A.M., P/R was en route to the Embassy Room via the Regency Room when he heard firecrackers bursting. Immediately thereafter, P/R observed an unknown male running towards him pushing and shoving people. P/R then heard a newsman yell "stop him." P/R tackled the suspect and a security officer of the hotel helped subdue the suspect. The officer handcuffed the suspect and took him away. P/R recognized this man as one of the four suspects he observed earlier in the lobby.

P/R did not recognize Sirhan's picture until he observed it in Life magazine a few weeks after the assassination. Officers showed P/R a picture of Michael Wayne, after which P/R related that this was the man he subdued. ...

P/R failed to ID Sirhan's mug.[445]

The failure to ID Sirhan from his mug shot for Clayton was not uncommon among witnesses who, by other evidence, had clearly seen Sirhan. Many credible witnesses who could not ID Sirhan from his mug shot were able to identify him from other photos. The mug shot showed Sirhan in a wild state with his hair mussed and his face bruised by the people who tried to subdue him. That's not how Sirhan had looked prior to the shooting.

When Fernando Faura caught up with him, Clayton described an additional "two men, one with an object in his hand," that "appeared to 'flash'" that ran out into the lobby, *one* of which was Michael Wayne. Wayne was "knocking a newspaper photographer all over the table there and some chairs" Clayton told Faura. Clayton said when he called to Mallard for help, "the other guy switched and ran back to the hallway." In other words, a man running from the pantry with Wayne was able to escape while Clayton pursued Wayne.

"The guy had something in his hand?" Faura asked Clayton.

"Yes, that flashed," Clayton reiterated.[446]

The "newsman" Clayton had heard was likely the *Los Angeles Times* news photographer Fontanini. Fontanini and Clayton chased Wayne and were joined by Ace Security guard Augustus Mallard. Clayton succeeded in tackling Wayne, who was then handcuffed by Mallard, a moment Fontanini captured for posterity

445   LAPD interview of "Gregory" [George] Ross Clayton, October 11, 1968.

446   Faura, prepublication version, p. 152.

in a photograph.[447] Fontanini had been especially suspicious of Wayne, and didn't believe Wayne's explanation for running:

> Mr. Fontanini states that Mr. Wayne had stated he ran because he was looking for a telephone. Mr. Fontanini added that there were numerous telephones available in the press room where Mr. Wayne ran from.[448]

When Sergeant Hank Hernandez polygraphed Wayne, he asked him if he were running to find a phone booth, Wayne answered no, and Hernandez deemed his answer honest. But his answer was recorded in writing as "yes" to this question, even though he can clearly be heard answering this question "no" on the audio tape of his session. After completing the polygraph questions, Wayne explained he was looking for a phone, not a phone *booth*, so he had to answer no to the question as worded. But that part of his answer was *not* polygraphed, and it's possible he just lied as soon as the machine was turned off.

The question was also worded differently on the initial list of questions to be posed. The original question was, "Were you being truthful when you said you were running to make a telephone call after Senator Kennedy was shot?" If Wayne had answered that honestly "no" that would have looked bad. And if he answered it as "yes" but the machine showed he was lying, that would also have looked bad. The easy fix was to reword the question to "phone booth," allowing Wayne to give a truthful "no" response, which he was then allowed to clarify immediately after the test was concluded. Whatever the truth, the LAPD essentially lied about Wayne's answer by changing it from "no" to "yes," stripped of the original context.[449] It appeared the LAPD was deliberately trying to help Wayne look innocent.

Did Wayne run a gun out of the pantry? Patricia "Patti" Nelson told the FBI she saw a man running out of the Embassy Room she later identified through photos and video as Michael Wayne. Nelson said Wayne was carrying a package about three and a half feet long and about six inches wide. "From the rear of the package," she told the FBI, "there protruded a piece of wood which appeared to Nelson to be the stock of either a shotgun or a rifle." "She does not know the difference between these two types of guns," her interviewer noted. The interviewer also noted that Nelson saw this man running out of the Embassy

---

447   The California State Archives can provide a copy of this photo. I have a copy, but when I contacted Steve Fontanini in 2005 to attempt to obtain permission to reprint the photo, his memory seemed to be faltering. He didn't recall taking the picture, even though there are numerous records indicating he did, so I did not pursue that further.

448   LAPD interview of Steve Fontanini, June 28, 1968.

449   The audio of Wayne's polygraph session was provided to me by CNN producer Brad Johnson.

Room area before she knew Senator Kennedy had been shot.[450] Her friend Franne Einberg told the LAPD that Patty had mentioned she had seen a man with a "poss[ible] rifle" before Kennedy was shot, probably meaning before she *learned* that Kennedy had been shot. Nelson was with Joseph Thomas Klein and Dennis Weaver, who also identified Michael Wayne as the man they saw.

Klein described seeing something three feet long by three inches wide that was "larger at one end than the other." Like Nelson, Klein did not know anyone was shot. He was in the Palm Room, next to the Venetian room at the Eastern end of the lobby. Klein saw a man with long object, about three feet long and two to three inches wide, "wrapped in a blu material poss cloth or paper. [*sic*]"[451] According to his FBI interview, he did not see a gun in it, and he had a clear view, but he surprised himself later by remembering making the comment to Nelson and Weaver, "My God, he had a gun, and we let him get by."

Weaver, who was standing "within five or six feet" of Nelson said he did not hear Nelson say anything about seeing a gun when the man ran by and did not believe there was a gun in whatever the man was holding. Weaver was "completely amazed" by Patti Nelson's comment re seeing a gun in the rolled-up poster and "dumbfounded" when he heard Klein tell his story.[452]

Another witness who thought Wayne, or a man with a similar description, was carrying something inside a poster, was William Singer:

> I was in the lobby of the Ambassador Hotel right next to the ballroom. Senator Kennedy had just walked away from the podium after his victory speech. Several moments before the commotion started a man came running and pushing his way out of the ballroom past where I was standing. I would describe this man as having Hebrew or some type [*sic*] mid-eastern features, he was approx. 18/22 5-10 thin face, slim, drk swtr or jkt, drk slacks, no tie, firy [*sic*] neat in appearance, nice teeth, curly Arab or Hebrew type hair. He may have been wearing glasses, I'm not sure. I can ID him. He isn't one of the men in the pictures you showed me (Saidallah B. Sirhan or Sirhan Sirhan). This man was in a big hurry and was saying, "Pardon me, please" as he pushed his way out of the crowded ballroom. He was carrying a rolled piece of cardboard, maybe a placard. This placard was approx. 1½ yards long and 4-6" in diameter. I think I saw something black inside. Just as he got pst [*sic*] me I heard screaming and shouting, and I knew something bad had happened. Two men were

---

450   FBI interview report of Patricia Nelson, dated June 10, 1968.

451   LAPD interview of Joseph Thomas Klein, June 7, 1968. There is a nearly illegible copy of this interview in one spot in the files. The legible copy can be found here: www.maryferrell.org/showDoc. html?docId=116655&search=Strain#relPageId=122&tab=page

452   LAPD interview summary of Dennis Weaver, July 1, 1968.

then shouting to "Stop that man." These two men were chasing the first man. I don't know if they caught him.[453]

At the Grand Jury hearing, recall that Harold Burba, the photographer for the Los Angeles Fire Department, discussed seeing the man he said was Sirhan but later realized was Michael Wayne in the pantry as Kennedy passed through to speak onstage. Burba said the man caught his attention because "He appeared to be looking all around him instead of looking ahead, as all the other members [of Kennedy's party] were." Burba noted, "He had an object in his hand as he passed by, and I saw that object in the air" and "wondered about it as he passed by, what was in it."[454] Burba thought he was casing the pantry.

Weaver, Klein and Nelson were taken to the local ABC affiliate station to view footage taken in the pantry before Kennedy was shot. In the footage, Klein and Nelson were certain the man they saw running with the package was Michael Wayne. Weaver could make only a tentative identification.[455] In the pantry, when Kennedy walked through the first time, Wayne had been photographed by Bill Epperidge at the moment when Kennedy stopped to sign Wayne's poster. In the Epperidge photo, the poster Wayne carries is pristine at the end, tightly rolled, about an inch and a half wide at the end. There would have been no way to hide a gun in *that* poster. The (apparently) same poster appears in the photo that Fontanini took, but the edges are crumpled and the roll has loosened to create a hole three or four inches in diameter. It also looks ripped—as if something had been pulled from it in a hurry. There would have been plenty of room inside *that* poster to hide a gun.

Klein and Nelson were only shown the footage during the period in which the Epperidge picture was captured. But if Wayne had a gun at any point, that was not when he had it. The video of Wayne without a gun in his poster at that moment was apparently enough to convince them Wayne never had a gun in his poster at a later point.

Augustus Mallard, who worked for the same security firm Thane Cesar worked for, said that Wayne did not have a gun in the poster when he captured him. I believe that is true, as Clayton never mentioned a gun on Wayne when he tackled him. I believe Wayne's running was designed to pull focus to allow others with guns to get away.

As you will see, *three* suspects ran through the lobby before people in the lobby realized a shooting had occurred. One of these suspects split off from Wayne

453   LAPD interview of William Singer, June 6, 1968.

454   Harold Burba's Grand Jury testimony.

455   FBI internal memo dated June 10, 1968, via www.maryferrell.org/showDoc. html?docId=99631&relPageId=178&tab=page, accessed November 28, 2016.

with something that "flashed" in his hand and ran south down a corridor and out of the hotel toward 8th Street. Another man, a tall blond man, hurdled a couch in the lobby and pushed people over. Maybe Nelson saw the gun stock sticking out of a poster in someone else's hand and confused it with Wayne? Remember how quickly Virginia Guy came to confuse the man who ran at her and chipped her tooth with Sirhan? Witnesses who saw two people sometimes appeared to have conflated two people into a single person.

As the two other men fled from the hotel, the captured Wayne, who had "a look of madness in his eyes as if he had rabies," according to Clayton, kept saying, "'Let me go. Gotta get out of here. Let me go.'"[456] Another witness, Mrs. Abo, the wife of one of the doctors who came to Kennedy's aid in the pantry after the shooting, was running for ice for Kennedy through the lobby past the fountain when she almost bumped into two men bringing someone in handcuffs through the lobby. This had to have been Wayne, as no other person was handcuffed but Sirhan, and he wasn't taken out through the lobby. Mrs. Abo stated that the man who was handcuffed was sporting an "insane grin."[457]

Clayton thought Wayne had been wearing a coat with four flag pins on it. If he was, he had shed it before Fontanini took his picture and taken it off before getting Kennedy's signature on a poster, as neither shows Wayne in a coat. If Wayne had a coat earlier in the night, the first time Clayton saw him, with the group that included Sirhan and the girl at the fountain, then it gives more credence to the notion that Wayne was the man Daniel Hall had talked to, who hinted at something "big" to happen that night, and who appeared to be carrying a gun in a zippered bag.

Faura asked Clayton why he noticed this particular group of people by the fountain in the lobby. Clayton said he feared they were there to cause trouble for the Rafferty party, which was just off the lobby in the Venetian Room, so he kept an eye on them. One of the young men kept pointing toward the Embassy Room, and Clayton knew there was a western entrance to the Venetian Room near the Embassy Room entrance. He feared the group might try to enter the Venetian Room through that western entrance.

Before we continue with Wayne, let's look a bit more closely at the other people who got away while Wayne was being apprehended.

Immediately after the shooting, Samuel Strain saw a five-foot-two or five-foot-three "Filipino" man in a blue turtleneck shirt with black hair and glasses carrying a "bulky package wrapped in blk [sic] paper." As he came across the

---

456   Fernando Faura, *The Polka Dot File on the Robert F. Kennedy Killing* (Waterville, OR: TrineDay, 2016), p. 153.

457   FBI interview of Mrs. Judith Abo, taken and dated July 8, 1968.

lobby from the direction of the pantry with "a black paper over his hand and arm and some type of object underneath," the man said "Excuse" and pushed Strain aside and "walked away fast."[458] Strain thought the man was a male Filipino who looked like the suspect he had seen arrested on TV. To the FBI, Strain added that the man had a beard.[459] Strain said the package he was carrying was "two feet long and six inches wide."

Strain's sighting was also supported by his friend Fred Parrott, who thought the man was 5'7" but confirmed there was a white male with a dark complexion who exited the hotel via the South exit.[460] Parrott, a medical doctor, noted the man was "carrying a rolled up newspaper under his arm" and "appeared to have glassy eyes, as though he were ill."[461]

As with many interviews that hint at additional suspects, Strain's taped interview is absent from the record and the instruction "Do Not Type" (meaning do not transcribe the tape of his interview) is written on his interview summary in the thick pen of Lt. Manny Pena.[462] On an FBI memo noting Parrot's comments, someone hand-wrote, "w/m referred to above is Michael Wayne – he has been interviewed." When I read these statements the first time, I didn't pay attention to Strain's description and believed this was Michael Wayne. It was only after I saw the pictures of Wayne and saw how Strain's sightings of this separate man fit with that of other witnesses that I realized this could not be Michael Wayne. The man was too short, and Wayne did not have a beard. Wayne was not wearing a turtleneck either, but an open collar. Wayne had become the LAPD's catchall, apparently, for any suspect that was not Sirhan.

Strain witnessed this man right after Dr. Marcus McBroom appeared to see the same man leave the pantry. McBroom saw someone furtively move past him in the pantry, carrying what the FBI recorded as a "notebook." As McBroom exited the Embassy Room he ran into Strain, who told him, "My God—he ran right through our fingers." McBroom assumed Strain was referring to the man McBroom had just seen hurrying away. McBroom initially assumed the man was a reporter.[463]

Years later, however, when interviewed by Greg Stone and Paul Schrade in March 1986, Dr. McBroom added additional information. After the shooting, he heard "the first one or two shots" and saw a woman in a polka dot dress run from the pantry yelling "we got him" or "we shot him." McBroom added that "About

458   LAPD phone call report from Samuel Strain, June 5, 1968.

459   FBI interview of Samuel Strain, June 28, 1968 dated July 1, 1968.

460   FBI memo from a redacted special agent to SAC, Los Angeles.

461   FBI interview of Fred Parrott, taken June 20 and dated June 21, 1968.

462   LAPD log of telephone calls received, June 5, 1968, 8:30 P.M., from Samuel T. Strain; LAPD interview of Samuel Strain on June 7, 1968.

463   FBI interview of Dr. Marcus McBroom, taken July 8 and dated July 11, 1968.

this time the man with the gun under a newspaper ran out in a very menacing way." McBroom, Strain and "the man running the ABC camera" all "drew back instinctively" when they "saw the gun, the barrel of the gun." McBroom clarified the gun was not wrapped in a newspaper but just under it, with the newspaper tented at the fold over his arm. "He was ready to literally blast anyone who got in his way," McBroom told them, adding that you could see the barrel clearly.

"I think we were in a state of disbelief," McBroom said in answer to the unasked question of why they let him go without giving chase. McBroom explained he had gone from the euphoria of the California victory to seeing Kennedy shot to seeing Elizabeth Evans bleeding in front of him to seeing the woman in the polka dot dress and the man with the gun run out.[464] The man getting away was wearing "a dark blue suit," according to McBroom's 1986 interview. Clayton, Strain, Parrott and McBroom all appeared to see the same man exiting quickly in a suspicious manner, Clayton saw something "that flashed" in his hand, suggesting metal, and Strain and McBroom thought the man had a gun that was partially covered by something the man was carrying. Due to his proximity to Michael Wayne and due to the fact that both had dark hair, it's possible Patricia Nelson saw the gun butt sticking out of the shorter man's poster roll, not Wayne's.

Ernesto Alfredo Ruiz and Gilman Kraft both reported a tall, sandy-haired or blond man flying through the lobby, shoving people out of the way in a wild fashion. Did they see the same man?

Ernesto Alfredo Ruiz reported that just after midnight, he and his wife tried to get into the Embassy Room where Kennedy was speaking but, presumably seeing the crowd and security at the lobby entrance, decided to wait outside. They stopped at the "waterfall," presumably the large fountain in the lobby. After a few minutes, Ruiz saw a six-foot-tall sandy-haired male, "late 20's," in a blue sport coat and a blue turtleneck shirt come flying out into the lobby with a five-foot-six female, 125 pounds, with "brownish" hair in a white dress with "drk. almost round markings on it."

At first I thought Ruiz's woman might have been Rosemary Kovack, who was wearing a white dress with small black squares that at a distance might have looked round, who ran out the Palm Court at the eastern end of the hotel and told people along the way that Kennedy had been shot. Kovack was with her 5'11", blond-haired, 17-year-old son. Ruiz thought the woman was wearing glasses.

But Ruiz thought the male was older than the female. Rosemary Kovack's age was not listed in her LAPD interview summary, but given that she had a 17-year-old son, she was probably in her late thirties, at least. The woman Ruiz saw looked 21 to 23, and the man she was with was in his late twenties. The summary of Ruiz's interview says he saw the woman and man exit the east end

---

464   Transcript of taped interview with Marcus McBroom by Greg Stone and Paul Schrade, March 9, 1968.

of the hotel, but the map Ruiz drew indicates they ran out the south entrance. The Kovacks had left via the eastern entrance. So apparently, whoever Ruiz saw was not the Kovacks.

Ruiz said the man pushed several people out of his way and that both the man and woman had passed within 30 feet of him in the lobby. The man looked "pale and frightened" and the girl "yelled something" but Ruiz couldn't understand what she said. He learned nearly immediately after they passed him that Kennedy had been shot.

Ruiz followed the police as they escorted Sirhan down the stairs to the west entrance (remember, both the first floor western-facing and second floor eastern-facing entrances were at street level as the ground was higher under the east end of the hotel). As he saw Sirhan being escorted away, Ruiz said the same man in the blue suit returned to where Sirhan was being apprehended and shouted, "let's kill the bastard." Ruiz added that this man "was the only one noticeably in favor of 'getting' the suspect."[465]

As we saw in chapter six, Gilman Kraft had seen a 6'2" male in his twenties with "long blond hair" who "hurdled a couch" and pushed people hard as he "vaulted" over sofas "on his way out toward the back of the Ambassador Hotel—the South Side." I think Ruiz and Kraft may have seen the same man.

Clayton appeared to be the only witness who saw both the man Kraft and Ruiz saw and the man McBroom and Strain saw. Clayton told Faura, "I noticed two youths were running down the hallway that parallels the Venetian Room out to the outdoor patio, and one of the two I recognized as being the tall one in the group" with Sirhan and the girl in the polka dot dress by the fountain.[466]

Olive de Facia may have encountered a witness to an escaping suspect. She had grown tired of waiting for Kennedy to come out and speak and had gotten into her car to leave the hotel. When she turned on the car radio and heard Kennedy had been shot, she went back into the hotel. There, she saw "a tall white, young man" speaking to a policeman. She thought he was about 19 years old. The young man seemed "quite hysterical was telling the policeman something about having chased a man out of the Embassy Room after the shooting and lost him." As her FBI interview summary describes:

> He began to cry and made a motion with his hands which De Facia interpreted to be a measurement or distance that he was trying to explain to the policeman. De Facia said it was her impression that

465   LAPD interview of Ernesto Alfredo Ruiz, June 7, 1968. Ruiz thought she was wearing glasses. If so, this was not the woman in the polka dot dress others had seen with Sirhan that night, as no one else had mentioned glasses. See www.maryferrell.org/showDoc.html?docId=99737#relPageId=4&tab=page, accessed December 13, 2016.

466   Faura, p. 153.

the man was telling the policeman he had chased a man with a long gun out of the building.[467]

This man couldn't have been Michael Wayne, as Wayne didn't escape. Was this the same dark-haired man Strain and McBroom saw? The blond man Gilman Kraft and Ernesto Alfredo Ruiz saw? Or was this a *fourth* man, possibly the one a bystander told Joseph Klein had run out the east entrance, who had then "jumped the hedge outside the hotel" and disappeared into the night?[468]

In any case, Wayne hadn't escaped. Was that part of the plan? After Wayne had been sitting in the hotel's security office for an hour, "two plainclothesmen from the hotel" freed him from custody and took him instead to the witness room, the Gold Room. Neither these men nor their employer were identified, so we have to take Wayne's word that these were plainclothed police officers. From there, according to his FBI report, Wayne "went into the next room, where the NBC television was, and ate some rolls, drank cokes, etc." He was eventually transported to Rampart Station to give his statement. After he gave his statement to the LAPD, the FBI report notes, "he was driven home by them in the Los Angeles Police Department van."

The astute FBI Special Agents Jerome K. Crowe and Roger J. "Frenchy" La Jeunesse added an interesting little comment at the end of their report on Wayne: "He gave no indication whatever that he was displeased with the fact that he had been detained at the hotel."[469] For someone who had been wild-eyed trying to get out and cried in captivity, that's a compelling observation that calls into question Wayne's real role at the Ambassador Hotel.

I don't believe Michael Wayne was a shooter in the pantry. I believe it's more likely his role was that of facilitator and distractor, helping the shooters get into the pantry with press badges, making sure people knew when Kennedy was coming through, and possibly making sure Sirhan was in position. It's also possible, as we've already seen, that he brought a gun into the building and then helped a shooter get it back out of the building.

If Wayne were involved, on whose behalf was he acting? During one of his many interviews, Wayne mentioned shooting a gun with a friend at the Las Vegas Police Rifle Range some three to five years earlier. There are numerous Las Vegas connections to this this case, and while that could indicate to some the involvement of the Mafia, which certainly was active in Las Vegas, the Howard Hughes organization and the CIA (and at that time in Las Vegas, there was little

---

467   FBI interview of Olive de Facia, taken and dated June 15, 1968.
468   LAPD interview of Joseph Thomas Klein, June 7, 1968.
469   FBI report on Michael Wayne, July 6, 1968.

distinction between those two) were also very active in Las Vegas. But it was an extreme right-wing connection that particularly interested the LAPD, if only because the connection demanded an explanation.

Wayne had a business card for Keith Gilbert on him at the time of his arrest. Keith Gilbert was a known militant, racist right-winger who was involved with the radical militia group who called themselves the Minutemen. And although the LAPD would work hard to disprove this, it seems clear that Gilbert apparently had Michael Wayne's card as well. The connection set off alarm bells for Sergeant M. Nielsen, who found the Gilbert card in Wayne's file and showed it to Lieutenant Manny Pena.[470]

In 1965, when Lieutenant Pena commanded the Foothill Detectives Division, 1,400 pounds of stolen dynamite were found in Keith Duane Gilbert's apartment. Gilbert was a former gunshop owner, a right-wing militant and a self-described disciple of Adolf Hitler. He believed white people should have no contact with any other race and that mixed-race children were "not human."[471] Gilbert had been on the run, using a number of aliases to avoid capture, but he was eventually picked up by the Royal Canadian Mounted Police in Ottawa, Canada, and Pena asked to have Gilbert extradited to his jurisdiction.

In a report on the Michael Wayne–Keith Gilbert association in the LAPD's files, no mention is made of why Gilbert had the dynamite or what he planned to do with it. But the story was no secret and had been in the papers at the time: Gilbert had plotted to blow up the Palladium in Hollywood where Martin Luther King, Jr. was to speak to a number of Jewish leaders at a dinner to honor King.

After Nielsen showed Pena the card, Pena assigned Sergeants Dudley Varney and Manuel "Chick" Gutierrez to investigate. When Varney talked to Wayne in July 1968, Wayne did not deny having the card, but said he did not know who Gilbert was or how the card came into his possession.[472]

When William Gardner, the retired Los Angeles police officer who was the Ambassador's security chief, was asked if he had seen the Gilbert card on Wayne at the time of his arrest, he said he had only examined Wayne's wallet long enough to verify Wayne's identity and had not noticed a Gilbert card.[473]

When Gilbert was questioned in San Quentin Prison April 1, 1969, about Wayne and shown pictures of Wayne, he did not recall Wayne's face, but "he stated that he thought he had received the Michael Wayne card from someone at a gun show in Arizona in 1965 or earlier."[474]

---

470   LAPD report titled "Michael Wayne/Keith D. Gilbert Business Card Investigation," July 22, 1969.

471   Maureen O'Hagan and Michael Ko, "Feared Seattle property manager is arrested; dozens of guns seized," *Seattle Times*, February 16, 2005, citing a federal court opinion.

472   LAPD interview of Michael Wayne, July 12, 1968.

473   LAPD interview of William Gardner, June 27, 1969.

474   LAPD report summary of the Wayne-Gilbert investigation, July 22, 1969.

On April 10, 1969, after the trial was long over, Lt. Hernandez administered a polygraph to Michael Wayne. One of the lie detector questions proposed for Michael Wayne was: "Were you truthful when you stated you couldn't remember where you obtained Gilbert's business card?" But this question was never asked.

Naturally, Hernandez told us Wayne's answers showed "no pattern of deception," but the audio tape of the session tells a different story. You can hear the polygraph machine recording in the background. After a series of preliminary questions, Hernandez asked his official questions. "Mike, were you born in California?" Wayne answered "No" and the polygraph continued at its normal level.

"Other than Wayne, have you ever used a different last name?" Wayne responded "No," but that was not entirely true, as he had gone by Wien. Perhaps that is why you can hear the polygraph making a bigger sound here, as if the needle is recording more stress on this answer.

"Did you come here intending to lie to any of my questions?" Hernandez asked. "No," Wayne said, but the polygraph sound is even louder here. Perhaps knowing Wayne would react to this, Hernandez threw in an easy, meaningless question on his list that was not on the original list. "Do you own a dog?" Wayne said no and the polygraph machine quieted.

"Is there anything about the assassination of Senator Kennedy that you're afraid to tell me about?" Wayne answered this and the next several questions "No," but the sound of the polygraph grew louder again. So again, Hernandez asked a question of no consequence: "Are you married?"

The next question was the big one, and Wayne's "No" response brought a lot of action from the polygraph machine. "Do you remember meeting Keith Gilbert?" The next question was asked differently from what Hernandez had written down. Hernandez had written, "Did you and Keith Gilbert know each other previously?" Instead, Hernandez asked, "Do you remember talking to Keith Gilbert?" Again, the polygraph sounded loud here, which is perhaps why Hernandez asked another question that was not on his list. "Did you lie to my last question?" The needle of the polygraph continued to be loud, as if swinging in a wide pattern.

Several other questions were asked, but the next one that drew a big reaction was "Do you remember ever giving one of your business cards to Keith Gilbert?" The needle appeared to swing widely here. Wayne explained he did have business cards in seventh grade. Perhaps that is the Wayne business card in the record, where Wayne spelled his last name Wien and gave an address that is not now in existence in Los Angeles (if it ever was).

The next answer that gets a big reaction is the "Yes" Wayne gave when asked if he was running after Kennedy was shot. At Hernandez's next question, "When you were running inside the Ambassador Hotel, were you running to a phone booth to call for help," Wayne answers "No" on the tape, and the polygraph machine needle can be heard swinging broadly. There is a great deal of distress with this answer. This is the answer recorded in print as "Yes" despite Wayne's clear "No" on the tape.

The next two noticeably loud responses from the polygraph needle came at the question, "Have you ever used a different name than Michael Wayne?" and "In the last two years, have you attended a Minuteman meeting?"

As soon as the test was over, Wayne immediately brought up the "running for a phone booth" question. Wayne said that he wasn't running for a phone *booth*, just a phone, hence his answer. Hernandez, however, had a different question that bothered him. He told Wayne he needn't have said "yes" to the question of whether he had been arrested because that was as a juvenile and he never spent time overnight in a jail cell. Wayne was still concerned about the phone booth question and brought it up again, but Hernandez couldn't seem to care less about Wayne's running from the scene of the crime.

Hernandez asked why Wayne had a reaction to attending a Minuteman meeting and a separate question Hernandez had asked about the Communist party and Students for a Democratic Society (SDS). Wayne made clear he was on the "other side of the fence from SDS." Just before the end of the session, a door opened, then there was silence.

Hernandez probably went to confer with Sergeant Nielsen to ensure all the necessary points had been covered. Nielsen appeared to have been watching the session, as his write-up, not Hernandez's, appears in the LAPD files on this date. At one point, Wayne claimed he had met another man who worked for Kennedy's staff. Sergeant Nielsen noted in his write-up of Wayne's lie detector session, "S.U.S. records reflect no such name." Nielsen overlooked this obvious lie to conclude "Wayne's responses... showed no pattern of deception." [475]

Hernandez returned to the room to ask Wayne one last question. When he was stopped in the Ambassador Hotel, did he have a business card on him? But when Wayne started to answer, Hernandez interrupted him to clarify he meant Keith Gilbert's card, and Wayne again denied knowing Gilbert.

With that, Hernandez was finished. Wayne asked how he'd done. Hernandez said he believed he had been truthful.

Then Wayne tried one more time to talk about running for the phone.

In the Daily Summary of Activities, Sgt. Nielsen, noted, "Wayne's responses were satisfactory… and his answers showed no pattern of deception." In the next paragraph, however, Nielsen notes that on the matter of the accusation that Wayne had Keith Gilbert's card on him and Gilbert had Wayne's, "[Wayne] claimed to have met another man named Michael Wayne who was a member of the Kennedy Staff" but adds "S.U.S. records reflect no such name." In other

---

475   Daily Summary of Activities, April 10, 1969.

words, Wayne appeared to have lied on at least one point. So maybe there was no "pattern" of deception, but provably, Wayne had lied successfully on his test.

Perhaps because the LAPD recognized someone might eventually listen to this tape and still have questions about a connection between Wayne and Gilbert, two months after the polygraph session, Sergeant Gutierrez interviewed Wayne again. He handed Wayne a copy of Keith Gilbert's card and let him examine it.

After "carefully viewing Gilbert's card," Gutierezz wrote in his report, Wayne denied having seen the card or knowing anyone by that name. "He did, however, admit going to a 'Nazi' shop in Glendale with a friend, Robert J. Soto, late in the summer of 1968, after the Kennedy assassination," Gutierrez noted.[476] Wayne didn't remember anyone taking a card from his wallet at any point.

Gutierrez doggedly pursued the issue. The same day he interviewed Michael Wayne for the last time, he also interviewed a man who went by the name Michael Wayne Belcher, but whose real name was Michael Wayne Marousek, who apparently sometimes went by the name Michael Wayne. Gutierrez showed Belcher a "business card bearing the name 'Michael Wayne – Promoter,'" which had been found in Keith Gilbert's apartment. Although Gutierrez's report notes that "copies of Mr. Belcher's old cards, which was [sic] the subject of this investigation and his new business card" were attached to the report, it appears only the new card, which clearly lists his name as Michael Wayne Belcher, is shown in the LAPD files. Perhaps the original "Michael Wayne – Promoter" card, which I have never seen, ended up in the "Kassab Investigation" folder, for Gutierrez had typed at the bottom of Michael Wayne Belcher's LAPD cardfile card, "FOR COMPLETE STORY SEE KASSAB INVESTIGATION."

Throughout the files, there are cryptic references to the "Kassab file" or "the Kassab investigation." This appears to relate to a suggestion to the LAPD from Peter Noyes that Sirhan had been involved with his investigator Michael McCowan in a conspiracy that involved an Arab family by the name of Kassab that had run a massive land scam deal in the San Fernando Valley in the 1960s.

No evidence has ever surfaced that Sirhan or McCowan knew each other at any point before the shooting. I have come to suspect that the LAPD kept "double books" on their investigation into the Kennedy assassination, putting only evidence that had already been made public, evidence that other agencies were aware of, and nonconspiratorial evidence into the files that were eventually made public, and hiding evidence that indicated a conspiracy in "the Kassab investigation" files. Perhaps if such a file were located, we could finally see the missing "Michael Wayne – Promoter" card, instead of the "Michael Wayne Belcher" card that is readily available. Maybe we would also find the missing APB

---

476   LAPD interview of Michael Wayne, June 25, 1969.

for the man in the gold sweater as well as the girl in the polka dot dress that was quoted in Commander Houghton's book but does not appear to be in the files the LAPD provided to the California State Archives as well as a number of the other clearly missing interview summaries and audio tapes.

SUS disbanded a month after Gutierrez's interviews of the two Michael Waynes. "It was said," Bill Turner and John Christian wrote in a footnote in their book on the case, that Gutierrez "had privately voiced doubts" about the LAPD's conclusions about the assassination. Three years later, at the young age of 40, the "physical fitness buff," as Turner and Christian described him, died from a heart attack.[477]

John Khoury

WAYNE WASN'T THE ONLY EXTREME RIGHT-WINGER WHO DREW suspicion at the hotel that night. One of the more interesting characters was the man who was or wasn't there: John Antoine Khoury.

Two people who knew John Khoury reported seeing him at the hotel that night, and one saw him in a group by the lobby fountain while Kennedy was speaking. This was the same fountain where George Clayton had seen a group that included Sirhan and a girl in a polka dot dress talking to Wayne and two other men. Khoury, however, insisted the witnesses couldn't have seen him and had records to prove it. But as with so much of this case, those records don't appear to tell the full story.

Charles Winner, the same man who had brought Michael Wayne to the LAPD's attention, worked for a PR firm named Cerrell Winner & Associates inside the Ambassador Hotel. Two of Winner's employees, Judy Groves and Fred Droz, believed they saw Khoury at the Ambassador Hotel the night of the assassination. Khoury worked in an office in the hotel. He was an auditor, having been promoted from his initial kitchen accountant role when he began employment there in December 1967.

Judy Groves told the police she saw Khoury, whom she had known at California State College at Fullerton, a few times at the hotel that night. She correctly identified Khoury from a photo the police provided. She was with her ex-husband Sanford Groves, who had also been a student at Fullerton.

The first time Groves saw Khoury was inside the Embassy Room sometime between 9 P.M. and 9:30 P.M. At the time, he was just standing there, alone, possibly watching television, as televisions had been set up inside the Embassy Room.

---

477   Turner and Christian, p. 135.

She later saw Khoury around 10:30 P.M. with a group of four or five men who seemed to look about the same—all had suit coats on, all had dark hair, all were of a similar size and shape. They were all "of an uncommon descent—not something that you see commonly." She thought they looked like they "could have been Mediterranean." Khoury seemed to be the one doing the talking. "They were grouped around enough to make me feel that they were talking as a group," Judy told the LAPD. "They seemed to be discussing something. I mean, there was talking going on. They weren't just standing around. They weren't looking around." She saw other people grouped around each other, standing and talking, "but there were gaps between them." With Khoury's group, Groves saw no gaps. "There was no doubt that they were standing as a group, in my mind."[478]

She saw Khoury for the last time at about 11 P.M. talking to a tall, thin man who was about six-foot-two; with sandy, curly hair; about 40 years old; and wearing glasses. They were leaning against a pillar or planter near the fountain in the lobby. She had remembered this sandy-haired man in particular because she had seen him alone several times earlier that night, leaning against the wall, arms folded, observing rather than participating, all over the hotel that night, and suddenly there he was, talking to Khoury. She said he didn't seem to be there celebrating. She didn't think he was a journalist because he didn't have a pad. But he had pulled her attention multiple times that night because he was always alone and seemed to be observing, "just sort of watching over" the events as they unfolded.[479]

Her ex-husband Sanford had also taken political science from Professor Joel Fisher. Sanford told the police he didn't know Khoury well, but at 1 A.M. that night, Sanford called Fisher to tell him Khoury had been at the hotel that night, knowing that Fisher knew Khoury.[480] Did Sanford see Khoury himself? Or had he learned of this from Judy Groves or Fred Droz?

Fred Droz also knew Khoury from their time together at Cal State Fullerton. Droz remembered Khoury particularly from his political science class taught by Professor Fisher. Droz had seen Khoury several times at the Ambassador Hotel before the shooting, as Khoury was employed there, but they were only acquaintances, not friends, and Droz had never spoken to Khoury there. Both had worked at the hotel for the past six months.

Droz felt certain he had seen John Khoury by the fountain in the lobby outside the Embassy Room when Kennedy was giving his speech. There were a

---

478   Audio tape of LAPD interview of Judy Groves, June 28, 1968, provided by the California State Archives.

479   LAPD Interview summary of Judy Groves, June 28, 1968.

480   SUS Final Report, p. 441; LAPD interview of Sanford Groves, July 9, 1968. The interview notes do not say that Groves saw Khoury but do say Groves knew Fisher knew Khoury. It appears some of what Sanford Groves said is now missing. The SUS report writers did not invent material out of whole cloth. The statement about Sanford Groves calling Fisher had to come from somewhere.

lot of people around so Droz couldn't tell if Khoury was with anyone or alone. Droz thought Khoury had been wearing a dark suit, possibly black or navy blue. "Droz states there is no doubt the person he saw was John Khoury," Sergeant Dudley Varney wrote in his interview summary.[481] Droz hadn't given Khoury's appearance at the hotel any thought until Professor Fisher called him the next morning, alarmed.[482]

Professor Fisher remembered seeing Khoury at the Ambassador Hotel when he had visited Droz there a couple of weeks prior to the assassination. Knowing that Khoury was a rabid anti-Kennedy right winger, and having learned that the shooter was a Palestinian, Fisher told Droz that Khoury was also Palestinian and had wanted to go back there during the Six-Day War to help in some way.

Fisher knew Khoury pretty well, as Khoury had been in three of his classes and the two had worked together during a 1966 election as members of the Republican Party.[483]

Fisher told Droz that Khoury had tried to bribe a few teachers to change his grades. Khoury had even tried to bribe Fisher with a new Cadillac to give him a better grade, but Fisher refused. Fisher also received mail from Khoury from all over the world—Paris, Beirut, other places—and that kind of travel has never been cheap. Fisher said Khoury was always "flashing money around" and had a father who "seemed to be fantastically rich," so it made no sense that he'd be working at the Ambassador Hotel.

Upon investigation, the LAPD found Khoury had financial backing from François K. Fakhoury of Beirut, Lebanon.[484] The LAPD also noted that the man who had provided Khoury with essentially a letter of credit in 1962 for his educational expenses had since died.[485]

An associate of Khoury's and a former student of Fisher's named Farid Massouh, who was then attending graduate school in the Political Science department of the University of Chicago, said Khoury was a phony, that he put on a big show of having money that he didn't have. While Massouh and Khoury himself said Khoury liked President John F. Kennedy, Professor Fisher told the LAPD Khoury had made anti-Kennedy remarks during the Arab-Israeli War in June 1967, presumably referring to Senator Robert Kennedy and his support of arms sales to Israel, the very reason given by the defense for Sirhan's acts.[486]

Khoury had been accepted at Hastings Law School and had even been assigned

481   LAPD interview of Fred Droz, June 27, 1968.
482   LAPD interview of Fred Droz, June 27, 1968.
483   LAPD interview of Joel Fisher, July 2, 1968.
484   SUS Progress report on Khoury by Lt. Higbie, July 18, 1968. Francois is misspelled "Flancois" here, but Khoury's Ambassador Hotel employment application shows the name clearly as "François."
485   SUS Progress report on Khoury by Lt. Higbie, July 18, 1968.
486   SUS Final Report, p. 441.

a roommate there, Ralph Johnson. But Khoury never showed up at Hastings. Khoury started classes at Southwestern Law School on a part-time basis instead. Fisher told his interviewer, Sergeant Varney, that Ralph knew a lot about Khoury and would be happy to talk to the police about him,

After Fisher contacted the District Attorney's office and told them about Khoury and the fact that Khoury had been seen at the hotel by Fred Droz, the D.A.'s office asked Khoury in for an interview on June 10, 1968. At that time, Khoury denied being at the hotel and claimed he had been home studying for school until after midnight, when he went to the airport to pick his wife up on an inbound flight from Beirut, Lebanon. His wife was a flight attendant. The part about picking up his wife was true. But he lied about being home at the time.

A few days after Khoury learned someone had reported him being at the hotel that night, Khoury dropped by Droz's office at the Ambassador Hotel, but Droz was out of town. Droz told the police he thought that was weird, as he and Khoury had only ever been acquaintances, not friends. [487] Had Khoury seen Droz at the hotel that night? Did he suspect Droz had identified him to the District Attorney? At that point, Droz hadn't been interviewed, but Fisher had mentioned his name to the District Attorney's office when Fisher was interviewed on June 7, 1968. Had someone inside the D.A.'s office tipped off Khoury?

When the LAPD started looking into Khoury, they found much to be disturbed about. For example, how was Khoury slipping in and out of the country undetected? How could he have sent postcards to Fisher from various places around the world when there were no legal records of his having left or returned to the United States?

Fisher told the LAPD he had received at least two postcards from Khoury during the spring of 1967, one of which was from Mexico. In the spring of 1966 and 1967, Fisher said he'd gotten other cards from Khoury from the Caribbean, Mexico, Paris and Lebanon. [488] Fred Droz remembered that Fisher got cards from Khoury in the summer of 1967 from Cairo, Beirut and Paris. [489] A letter dated "8 July 1968" from Khoury himself to a woman named "Bea," who, from the context of the letter, may have worked for Professor Fisher, states:

> I am leaving tomorrow for Tokyo, Japan on my way to Beirut, Lebanon.
> I shall stay there very shortly and upon seeing the family shall be
> going to France and England on some official business. [490]

Whose "official business" was Khoury conducting? Fakhoury's? In the letter,

---

487   LAPD interview of Fred Droz, June 27, 1968.

488   LAPD interview of Joel Fisher, July 2, 1968.

489   LAPD interview of Fred Droz, June 27, 1968.

490   Khoury letter to "Dear Bea," no further identification, dated July 8, 1967, in the LAPD files.

Khoury asked Bea to have Fisher contact him via a post office box in Vancouver, Canada, care of "Joseph Khoury." For someone who never had any money, that was an extraordinary itinerary, and one that disturbed the LAPD. The LAPD's report on Khoury stated:

> Reports that Khoury traveled to the mid-east, extensively, in 1967, have not been verified. Immigration Dept. Records show his last trip out of the country to have been in December, 1966. An agency in Beirut can find no record of Khoury traveling to that country.[491]

Was the "agency in Beirut" the CIA?

On January 9, 1968, less than a month after Khoury had begun his employment at the Ambassador Hotel, Khoury was arrested on the charge of Grand Theft Auto.[492] Although the details in a County report found in Khoury's LAPD files are sketchy, it appears that after Khoury wrecked his 1967 Cadillac El Dorado, Mrs. Elizabeth Maloof had agreed to lend him her 1966 Cadillac and have his El Dorado repaired and returned to him in exchange for a note for $3,500, to be paid in installments of $115 a month.

Khoury never held title to either vehicle. But Khoury suspected the Maloofs were trying to rip him off, so he "had secretly taken a recording of the conversation with the Maloofs in which they acknowledged his ownership of the vehicle in question." He had already written them two checks and had evidently given Elizabeth Maloof the next check dated January 8, 1968, but she had refused it and told Khoury not to take the car from her premises.

While Sergeant Patrick O'Neil was talking to Mrs. Maloof to see if this really was a theft or not, Mrs. Maloof received a call "and stated that the person calling was the American Embassy from Lebanon requesting her not to sign a complaint."

So although Khoury was a citizen of Lebanon, not the U.S., someone from the *American* Embassy in Lebanon called to intercede on his behalf. It would have made sense for someone from the Lebanese Embassy in the U.S. to intercede, but it made no sense for the *American* Embassy in Lebanon to intercede unless they had a special interest in Khoury, which they would have if he were secretly working for the CIA.

If Khoury were a CIA asset, suddenly everything about his story makes sense. That would explain why he had so much money despite no visible means of support. That would explain how easily he was able to get into and out of the country without leaving a paper trail. That would explain why he felt it was okay to lie to the FBI, a federal crime, which he did on June 27, 1968, when he told

---

491   LAPD.
492   LAPD Progress Report on John Antoine Khoury, July 18, 1968.

the Special Agents who interviewed him that he had gone straight home after he left the Ambassador Hotel.

It would also explain why the LAPD turned to "Goliath" for more information on Khoury. "Goliath" was a code name for the CIA.[493] The CIA responded to several LAPD requests, such as for background information on Sirhan's family from their time in Palestine and any possible traumatic injuries to Sirhan. But to my knowledge, Goliath was only consulted about one possible suspect: John Khoury.

After interviewing Professor Fisher, Fred Droz, Judy Groves, Sanford Groves and Charles Winner, the LAPD asked Khoury back for a second interview on July 15, 1968. At this interview, the LAPD's investigators "explained that his relationship with the shooting was becoming suspicious and that he should provide information that would alleviate that suspicion."[494] In other words, they were asking Khoury essentially for a better alibi.

At Khoury's next interview, he provided new information. Khoury now claimed he had been working the night shift for Globe Security, Inc. at the RCA building in Hollywood from about 6:30 P.M. to midnight on June 4, 1968. Khoury said he hadn't mentioned this before because he didn't want either of his employers to know about the other. Globe Security did not know he worked at the Ambassador Hotel, and the hotel did not know he worked for the security firm.

The SUS Final Report indicates that "Julius Levin, the Chief of Security and Khoury's supervisor" confirmed Khoury's presence at the RCA building, adding that "he recalled that Khoury was at the building at 11:45 P.M."[495] That was odd, because in Khoury's taped interview from July 15, 1968, Khoury mentioned that Levin had left at about 11:30 P.M., begging the question of how he could have verified Khoury's presence any later than that. In addition, on the tape of Khoury's interview, he refers to Levin several times as his "friend" and says the police should call him. But Khoury also said he wrote his own reports, and that he only made rounds at 6 P.M. and 9 P.M. and that other guards made the rounds at 7 P.M. and 8 P.M. (and presumably then at 10 P.M. and 11 P.M. as well). Khoury's shift ended at midnight. Is it possible Khoury checked in for his 9 P.M. rounds and then just left? Levin's incongruous statement and a record written by Khoury himself were the only verifications that he didn't leave the RCA building until midnight.

Perhaps because so many security firms in the United States are owned, founded by or staffed with intelligence officers as a means of cover, the very next day, Captain Brown of the LAPD met "Goliath," i.e., the CIA, and "received background information on John Khoury and associates."[496] (What associates?)

493   John Newman, *Oswald and the CIA* (New York: Carroll & Graf, 1995), p. 253.
494   SUS Final Report, p. 443.
495   SUS Final Report, p. 444.
496   LAPD Daily Summary of Activity, July 16, 1968.

That same day, Lieutenant Higbie reported, "John Khoury has been eliminated as a possible suspect in the Kennedy case."[497] Did the CIA meeting have any influence on the LAPD's decision to accept the word of the man Khoury first introduced as his "friend"[498] as opposed to his boss?

Is it possible that people who knew Khoury well were mistaken? Anything is possible, and people do have lookalikes. But Fred Droz had seen Khoury during his employment at the hotel, so he had seen him fairly recently, and since Judy Groves saw Khoury multiple times that night, it's hard to imagine she got it wrong each time.

Is it possible Khoury and Levin lied? We already know Khoury lied to both the LAPD and the FBI by saying he went home and stayed there until it was time to go to the airport. I believe it is more plausible that Khoury left after checking in for his last round shortly after 9 P.M. went directly to the Ambassador Hotel. I believe that he asked or convinced Levin to cover for him. As we saw earlier, Khoury had no compunction about bribing teachers to get his grades changed.

Even if Khoury lied about not being at the hotel, and even if he also had a relationship with the CIA, that still wouldn't necessarily make him part of any plot to kill Kennedy. The CIA may simply have felt the need to cover for him because the optics looked terrible, especially because the CIA did in fact have "an available pool of assassins" connected with Beirut, Los Angeles and the CIA.

A document from the Los Angeles division of the CIA from October 1976 surfaced during the Church Committee investigation with the subject "Review of ZRRIFLE file" and contained these two entries:

> Tab M – Harold Meltzer
>
> Harold Meltzer with aliases was involved in the rackets with upper echelon "hoodlums" throughout the U.S. … "In 1959 he furnished information to *our QJWIN California office* but has not since cooperated with us. N.B. he has the background and talent for the matter we discussed but it is not known whether he would be receptive.
>
> Tab Y – Hanna Yazbeck
>
> Yazbeck *lived in Beirut and worked for QJWIN's office* intermittently during the past 10 years (dates not given—possibly 51-61.) Yazbeck's chief bodyguard from 50-58 (not named) was a convicted murderer. The bodyguard was murdered. States that Yazbeck has an available pool of assassins. [Emphasis added.][499]

---

497   LAPD Daily Summary of Activity, July 16, 1968.

498   LAPD taped interview of John Khoury, July 15, 1968, California State Archives.

499   NARA Record Number: 104-10308-10287, "Review of ZR Rifle file," October 1976, www.maryferrell.org/showDoc.html?docId=17029. This document was first brought to my attention by Hank Albarelli and is mentioned in his book *A Secret Order: Investigating the High Strangeness and Synchronicity in the JFK Assassination* (Trine Day: 2013).

What QJWIN California office? During the Church Committee, the CIA claimed they had a paid assassin as an employee, a man they would refer to only as QJWIN. They claimed QJWIN served as a "spotter" of talent for the CIA. This document, brought to my attention by author and investigator Hank Albarelli, is the first one I've ever seen that hints that QJWIN was not just a person, but a much larger assassination operation.

In addition, Beirut has long been an important staging ground for the CIA for operations against Syria and Iraq and other leaders in the Middle East. In 1957, the CIA tried, unsuccessfully, to foment a coup in Syria and failed in an attempt to assassinate Nasser in Egypt. David Atlee Phillips, who conducted propaganda and radio operations in the CIA's coups in Guatemala, Indonesia, the Bay of Pigs and Chile, was stationed in Beirut, Lebanon from 1957 to 1958.

In 1958, the CIA successfully prevented the overthrow of King Hussein in Jordan but failed to prevent the overthrow of King Faisal in Iraq by Abdul Karim Kassem. So the CIA enlisted its "Health Alteration Committee" expert Sidney Gottlieb to send Kassem a poisoned handkerchief. Sy Hersh reported that Gottlieb claimed the CIA just wanted to make him sick, not kill him. But Bill Blum, who has a better record of accuracy on matters of interest to the National Security state, reported:

> In February 1960, the Near East Division of the CIA's clandestine services requested that the Agency find a way to "incapacitate" Kassem for "promoting Soviet bloc political interests in Iraq." "We do not consciously seek subject's permanent removal from the scene," said the Near East Division. "We also do not object should this complication develop."[500]

Over the next few years, the CIA worked with, among others, the man who would eventually take over Iraq, Baath Party member Saddam Hussein.[501] Roger Morris recounted in the *New York Times* on the eve of America's latest war in Iraq how the CIA staged the coup in 1963 that led to Kassem's ouster and subsequent assassination:

> As its instrument the CIA had chosen the authoritarian and anti-Communist Baath Party, in 1963 still a relatively small political faction influential in the Iraqi Army. According to Baathist leader Hani Fkaiki, among party members colluding with the CIA in 1962 and 1963 was Saddam Hussein, then a 25-year-old who had fled to Cairo after taking part in a failed assassination of Kassem in 1958.

---

500   William Blum, *Killing Hope: U.S. Military and CIA Interventions Since World War II* (London: Zed Books, 2004), pp. 96–97.

501   "Secrets of his leadership: an interview with Said K. Aburish," www.pbs.org/wgbh/pages/frontline/shows/saddam/interviews/aburish.html

According to Western scholars, as well as Iraqi refugees and a British human rights organization, the 1963 coup was accompanied by a bloodbath. Using lists of suspected Communists and other leftists provided by the CIA, the Baathists systematically murdered untold numbers of Iraq's educated elite—killings in which Saddam Hussein himself is said to have participated. No one knows the exact toll, but accounts agree that the victims included hundreds of doctors, teachers, technicians, lawyers and other professionals as well as military and political figures.[502]

A key figure in the 1963 "death lists" was the *Time* magazine bureau chief in Beirut who later became Robert Blair Kaiser's bureau chief in Rome, William McHale. Would the Beirut branch of the CIA have had an interest in Middle Eastern politics in the wake of the Six-Day War of 1967? Might they have enlisted some assets via the California QJWIN office to help with that?

Clearly, Fred Droz and Judy Groves saw Khoury at the hotel for reasons Khoury and the CIA felt necessary to deny. But even if Khoury were at the hotel and even if he worked for the CIA, that doesn't mean he had anything do with the assassination plot. But when someone provably lies to the FBI and police, we can only speculate about what was behind the lie, and the speculation can take a dark turn. Perhaps he took the assassins to the airport, dropping them off at the terminal outbound for Beirut in the guise of picking his wife up on her inbound flight. Without more information, there remain a number of possibilities that imply guilt as well as innocence.

The Busboy

A SURPRISING NUMBER OF WITNESSES IDENTIFIED SOMEONE AS Sirhan who could not have been Sirhan, because the clothes didn't match what Sirhan was arrested in. Did the conspiracy include a Sirhan double? In both the assassinations of John Kennedy and Martin Luther King, people pretending to be Lee Harvey Oswald or James Earl Ray surfaced at times when the actual Oswald and Ray were provably in other places at the same time. In the last chapter, we saw that Evan Freed reported a dark-haired man in a blue sport coat fleeing the pantry right after the shooting that looked remarkably like Sirhan but was clearly taller. We saw how Harold Burba mistook Michael Wayne for Sirhan at the Grand Jury.

---

502   Roger Morris, "A Tyrant 40 Years in the Making," *The New York Times*, March 14, 2003.

But another man deserves our attention. Several witnesses mistook a slim young man in a white shirt and dark pants, sometimes with a jacket, with some sort of noticeable acne condition (Sirhan's face was clear) and a slight foreign accent, who spoke in a way that sounded effeminate to some, and who may have had a slight stoop. This man was sometimes accompanied by a girl in a polka dot dress. And this may well have been the man Daniel Hall spoke to.

Both Sirhan and a white-topped doppelganger appear to have been seen in the pantry during the shooting as well as in a few places where Kennedy was speaking prior to June 4.

Ernest Vallero told the LAPD and FBI that someone who looked remarkably like Sirhan, of Arabian or Jewish descent, but who had a slight accent and provided him with an Israeli passport, applied for a job as a waiter at the Ambassador Hotel two to three weeks before the assassination. Vallero said the man very closely resembled photographs of Sirhan Sirhan. Vallero said the person became "rather 'nasty' in his speech" when Vallero told him there were no openings.[503] But did he get into the hotel anyway?

Freddy Plimpton, the wife of George Plimpton, who engaged in the struggle with Sirhan, had seen a man with his hand right up to Kennedy's head at the time of the shooting. She could not remember seeing a gun in the man's hand, but felt strongly this was the man who had shot Kennedy. She assumed it was Sirhan, but the description she gave didn't fit:

> He did not seem out of place with these people who were sitting up on the platform. All of them were wearing white, which made me believe he was wearing white. According to people later on, I was told he was not wearing a white shirt, and I'm just very confused about that right now. ... All of them were wearing white kitchen jackets ....[504]

Freddy may have been one of the best witnesses of all because she had been present at the incident in Chinatown where firecrackers went off, sounding like guns, causing the Kennedy party a momentary panic. Freddy explained that she had thought to herself after that incident, if that had been a real shooting, what should she have looked for? So she was paying special attention to Kennedy and saw something that ran counter to the LAPD's narrative.

From her position behind and to the right of Kennedy, she saw someone being pushed up against the steam table who was likely Sirhan, but—and she couldn't

---

503   FBI interview of Ernest Vallero, September 17, 1968.

504   LAPD interview of Freddy Plimpton, June 5, 1968.

say in what sequence things happened—she also saw someone who looked Filipino with his hand right up to Kennedy's head. In other words, she felt she had seen both Sirhan and separately, someone with a hand to Kennedy's head. She did not see a gun in the hand of the person with his hand to Kennedy's head and was puzzled why she didn't see the gun. She said this man "wasn't very big" but appeared to be about 30 years old and said his eyes were squinted nearly shut:

> I saw his hand up next to Robert Kennedy's head. ... I just looked at him and from his position and his posture, just assumed he was the guy who fired. ... All I can say is I knew this guy was shooting Senator Kennedy. I just can't say I saw the gun, no.[505]

If Sirhan had been the man Freddy had seen, no doubt she would have been asked to testify at the Grand Jury and the trial. The distance problem was an issue and anyone who could put Sirhan's hand next to Kennedy's head would have been welcome. But clearly, the police saw the problem in her statement and felt it better not to have her testify. Her husband George Plimpton, who had helped subdue Sirhan and had seen no other suspects, was called. But Freddy appeared to see, even if she didn't understand that at the time, that someone other than Sirhan had shot Kennedy, likely with a concealed gun.

By chance, I met another man who may have seen the same person Freddy Plimpton described. He insisted that Sirhan had been in a white busboy uniform when he shot Kennedy. He did not believe there had been a conspiracy. He showed me a photo proving he was at the Ambassador Hotel that night. I met him while we were both extras on the set of the film *Bobby*, Emilio Estevez's fictional story interspersed with documentary footage of Robert Kennedy that used the assassination as the backdrop. Estevez and his researcher, with whom I had shared some information for the film, pointed me toward this man on the set. His story was strange, but it fit much of what I was learning, so I took down his name and number on a sheet I regrettably never saw again. In a nutshell, here is his story. It's not the kind of story one forgets.

He claimed to be in the pantry during the shooting. He was behind Kennedy and saw a man dressed in a white busboy uniform, whom he was certain was Sirhan, shoot Kennedy. In the aftermath, someone who claimed to be from an Australian television station asked if he could interview him on camera—in Australia. The man thought that was silly because most stations would have had a local Los Angeles affiliate film the interview and then transmit it to them. But in the shock of the situation, he agreed and hopped on the plane. During the long flight, his seatmate, a man who claimed to be an oil industry executive, grilled him about what he had seen in the pantry. When he got to Australia, the

---

interview was very short—just a few minutes—and he was quickly put on a plane back home. He thought that was nuts. Why fly him that far only to interview him on camera for only a few minutes? He believed to the day that I spoke to him he had seen Sirhan wearing a white busboy's uniform. But Sirhan was captured in a blue velour shirt and jeans. Whoever the man in the busboy uniform was, it could not have been Sirhan. Until I read Freddy's and others accounts, I had dismissed his story as simple a case of misremembering Sirhan's clothes. But after a great deal more research, I now wonder if he and Freddy Plimpton saw the actual shooter.

Bill White may have seen this man earlier. He told the LAPD about a "busboy" who aroused his suspicion:

> Inf. additionally stated that he obs. a busboy, described as M-Latin, 5'2", slim build, approx. 18 yrs. of age, wearing a white, buttoned down jacket and dark pants, wandering about the anteroom and anchor desk area of the Embassy Rm., pretending to sweep up cigarette butts. Inf. states however that there were no butts to be picked up, and he does not know if this busboy was genuine or used this activity as a disguise.[506]

The anteroom and anchor desk were immediately behind the stage where Kennedy spoke his last public words, just outside the pantry.

Midge Singer may have seen this man too. About 20 minutes before Kennedy was shot, Midge crossed the pantry on her way to the stairway down to the Ambassador Room. On the way, she bumped her right shoulder "against a man her own height or shorter." She was 5'3". "This man had on a white jacket, dark complexion. She thought it was a busboy." After seeing Sirhan's picture in the papers, she felt that was the man she had bumped into, but was not certain.

One witness shared a story that would explain so much about this evidence. But by the time the FBI went looking for him, the witness had apparently fled.

On June 9, 1968, Winfred Holder, a desk clerk at the Hope Hotel, struck up a conversation at the Cordova Bar with a man who gave his name as John David Wright. Wright was a black man about 28 to 30 years old and approximately 5'6" to 5'8" tall with two gold front teeth.[507] Holder's important information was summarized in the LAPD's Final Report:

---

506   LAPD interview of Bill White, July 18, 1968.
507   FBI interview of Winfred Holder, June 24, 1968, dated June 26, 1968.

> Wright told Holder that he had worked as a kitchen reporter at
> the Ambassador Hotel for two or three months preceding the
> assassination.[508]

Wright described a "kitchen reporter" as one who reports what the kitchen needs. The FBI tried to discount Wright's account by stating there was no such role as a "kitchen reporter" at the Ambassador Hotel and no one employed at the hotel that night by that name. Both of those statements may be true, and Wright may have fabricated those details to explain his presence in a place where he wasn't supposed to be. But Wright could have been telling the truth re this, a truth the Ambassador Hotel would not wish to acknowledge to law enforcement. According to journalist Fernando Faura:

> It is a common practice of California farmers and businessmen to
> hire illegal aliens, known as "mojados" or "wetbacks," and to pay
> them substandard wages. There were "mojados" in the kitchen that
> night. Understandably, no one ever heard from them, except the
> FBI and the police.[509]

Wright might have been working there for cash that night, unofficially, with no record of his employment to be found. Wright had, in fact, worked for the kitchen of the Ambassador Hotel on and off for more than seven years, with the last official date of employment in 1962. So if anyone was positioned to grab a couple of weeks of freelance time off the books and paid in cash, it would have been Wright. And the FBI's assertion that Wright wasn't there and had to have made this up doesn't make sense due to Wright's next comment about a girl and coffee.

> Wright stated that he saw Sirhan in the kitchen several times during
> the evening of June 4, 1968. Sirhan was drinking coffee and a pretty
> girl was with him ... and that the girl with Sirhan had dark hair and
> was "well built."[510]

This information is important because Sirhan's last memory in the pantry before he was choked after the shooting was of pouring coffee for an attractive young woman. But Sirhan's account of the girl was not known at the time the FBI first interviewed Holder. None of the public reports of a girl in a polka dot dress at the time suggested she and Sirhan had coffee together. This information didn't come out until Dr. Bernard Diamond hypnotized Sirhan in January 1969:

508   SUS Final Report, Interview summaries, Winfred Holder entry.

509   Faura, p. 113. Juan Romero was shocked by this when I mentioned this to him and said the
Ambassador Hotel did not employ people off the street. But Faura was certain they had.

510   SUS Final Report, Interview summaries, Winfred Holder entry.

"I recollect giving a girl a cup of coffee. I served myself. I don't remember paying for it ..." ... He remembered meeting a girl, remembered giving her coffee. She looked Armenian. Or Spanish. She said she was tired and sleepy. ...

"The girl kept talking about coffee. She wanted cream. Spanish, Mexican, dark-skinned. When people talk about the girl in the polka dot dress," he figured, "maybe they were thinking of the girl I was having coffee with."[511]

Since neither Wright nor Holder could have gotten this information from any public source at the time Holder reported the conversation, Holder's account of what he heard from Wright gives both of them credence. Wright then described *how* Kennedy was shot:

Wright told Holder that when Senator Kennedy came through the kitchen, he saw one man try to hold the Senator's arm to keep him still and saw Sirhan with the pistol, but did not see him pull the trigger and thought that somebody else did the actual shooting.[512]

This also maps to what the rest of the evidence suggests: Sirhan pulled focus while others did the actual killing. And from what Holder reported, it sounded as if Wright might have been on the periphery of the plot:

Wright also said that the people in the Ambassador kitchen had been talking for two weeks about how they planned the shooting of Kennedy.[513]

The FBI summary of Holder's recollections was more forthcoming:

As Senator Kennedy came through the kitchen, he saw one man try to hold Senator Kennedy's arm to keep him still. This was the man with dark glasses whose picture was in the paper. He saw Sirhan with a pistol, but he did not see him pull the trigger, and he thinks somebody else did the actual shooting of Senator Kennedy.

People in the Ambassador Hotel's kitchen had been talking for two weeks about how they planned the shooting of Senator Kennedy.

He knew a lot that he could not tell or it would be his neck.[514]

---

511   Kaiser, pp. 304–305.
512   SUS Final Report, Interview summaries, Winfred Holder entry.
513   SUS Final Report, Interview summaries, Winfred Holder entry.
514   FBI interview of Winfred Holder, 6/24/68, dated 6/26/68.

Wright made contradictory statements, saying he didn't have to worry about money one minute and then saying he was going to Pensacola (Florida) for a construction job.

Holder was not the only person Wright talked to before leaving town. He told a woman whose name is redacted in the FBI's files a similar story. She told the FBI nearly the same story Holder had, but she added that Wright told her he had told his story to the police, a report the LAPD denied. But that doesn't mean Wright was lying, as the LAPD provably lied about a lot of the evidence in this case, so we cannot take their assertion at face value.

Wright had lived all over, including in Kansas City, where he may have worked for General Motors, although General Motors denied that to the FBI. Curiously, Thane Eugene Cesar's public records and only available email address from a public record company indicated he too worked at General Motors in Detroit, even though Cesar never appeared to have lived in Detroit.

Wright may well have been an itinerant, low-level operative of some kind who perhaps fell in with the wrong crowd in Los Angeles and decided to get out. He apparently checked out of the hotel where he had been staying on June 10, 1968, four days after the assassination.[515]

As bizarre as Wright's account sounded, Marsha Kirz may have seen people discussing the plot at the hotel a little over a week before the assassination. She had attended a luncheon at the Embassy Room on May 28, 1968. Behind the speaker's stage were curtains. Behind the curtain was an anteroom. During the speech, Kirz heard noise coming from behind the stage so she went to the anteroom behind the curtains to see what was going on. There, she saw "four young men talking in a foreign language. The four men were in kneeling positions in a small circular group." She told the LAPD:

> One of the males was holding a pointer (round stick approx. 18" long) and appeared to be giving instructions to the other individuals. This person is described as M/Latin; 23/25, 5-8; 130/40; brown curly bush hair; white dress type shirt with the sleeves rolled up. Blk dress type pants. …
>
> During this period, the other individuals were talking in a foreign language and it appeared they were arguing due to their tone of voice.
>
> Mrs. Kirz observed this activity for two mins. And then indicated to the foursome to lower their voices. At this time, all the persons turned and looked in Mrs. Kirz' direction. The group then quieted down and Mrs. Kirz returned to her table.
>
> Mrs. Kirz thought no more of the matter until she saw the picture

---

515   FBI memo from Special Agent [Redacted] to Special Agent in Charge, Los Angeles, October 1, 1968.

of Sirhan in the newspaper. At this point, she became aware of the fact that one of the individuals in the group strongly resembled Sirhan.[516]

She correctly identified Sirhan from two different photos. One of the men in this group was a man wearing a white busboy-like jacket.[517]

Betty Connolly told the police that right after the shooting, in the lobby outside the Embassy Room, she saw a man in his twenties, about 5'9" with an olive complexion and dark curly hair, wearing a white busboy's jacket and dark pants. This person said to her, "We killed Kennedy," and walked away down the lobby. Right after that, a commotion broke out at the entrance of the Embassy Room, probably because people had only then realized Kennedy had been shot. He had an accent that Connolly thought was Spanish, and Connolly said it was possible she had misheard him. Connolly did not identify this person as Sirhan, however, and the height makes him too tall to be the person Plimpton, White, and the others likely saw.[518]

Actual busboy Juan Romero told FBI Special Agent Bill Bailey that two days before the assassination, two men claiming to be policemen and wearing "Kennedy" signs on chains around their necks asked Romero how they could obtain white kitchen staff jackets. Romero didn't know whether to believe they were policemen, as they offered no identification, but he led them to the supply room where the uniforms were stored, only to find it locked.[519] Perhaps someone got in later that day, because on June 2, during Senator Kennedy's appearance at the Ambassador Hotel and later, the Palm Terrace, a couple of witnesses saw two kitchen helpers with Sirhan—or was it a Sirhan lookalike?

Were *three* men in busboy outfits involved? On Sunday, June 2, Rose Gallegos noticed three "kitchen helpers" standing around outside in the "patio area." The Ambassador Hotel had several patios, and it's not clear which one she meant. Gallegos asked them what they were doing and told them they should get back inside to work. They looked at her for a moment, said nothing, and went inside. After the assassination, Gallegos felt certain the "man in the middle" of these three was Sirhan, "disguised as a kitchen helper," and contacted the FBI by telephone

---

516   LAPD interview of Marsha Kirz, August 6, 1968.

517   LAPD interview of Marsha Kirz, August 6, 1968.

518   LAPD interview of Betty Connolly, October 7, 1968.

519   FBI interview of Juan Romero, June 6, 1968. The names of the two FBI agents who were present for this statement are blacked out in the document I have, but in Bill Turner and Jonn Christian's book, they identify one of the agents as William Bailey. When I talked to Juan Romero as this book was going to press, he did not remember this and wondered if someone else had said this and he reported the incident second-hand.

June 6, 1968.[520] Was the man in the middle really Sirhan? Or was it perhaps the person Freddy Plimpton thought shoot Kennedy, a remarkable lookalike?

Gallegos's daughter Aida Laffredo also remembered seeing three men in white busboy jackets, one of which she identified as Sirhan. One of the men was about 5'10" and about 30 years old, and the other was shorter than Sirhan (5'1", she guessed) and slightly older than Sirhan, 25–30. "All three were wearing white jackets as kitchen help would wear." Laffredo saw these men with Gallegos and placed them near a kitchen door in the ballroom. On Sunday, June 2, Kennedy was speaking at the Cocoanut Grove, not the Embassy Room, so it's not clear which ballroom or which kitchen door she meant.[521]

To Faura, Gallegos said the three men were all wearing black pants and white jackets. She went up to them and addressed them:

> "Are you supposed to be in the hallway? This is the way that the Senator is gonna pass by. Why are you obstructing the way? And they didn't answer. And I says, "I am talking to you. This is the way it's supposed to be. You are supposed to be out of the kitchen.[522]

At this point, the shortest of the three, the man closer to 5'1", told her he didn't speak English. Gallegos thought he looked Mexican, Filipino, or even Hawaiian. His hair was not curly. She thought the man sort of side-eyed her as if trying not to show her his full face. The tall one had glasses, with dark rims. The one Gallegos thought was Sirhan "smiled in such a funny way" that Gallegos told him "You know how to smile but you don't know how to answer?" At that point, the tall one said, "Come on, let's get out of here," and they disappeared into the kitchen. According to Gallegos, the tall man scared her daughter.[523]

The FBI's "X" files may hold a clue to one of these men. When the FBI files on this case were released, they were divided into serials of interviews and FBI memos and communications to and from the FBI Los Angeles Field Office, "Sub H" files of news articles from the media, and "Sub X" files that summarize different parts of the investigation. In these "X" files, the FBI has a section for some unexplained reason named "Investigation concerning Donald David Evangelista, Extra Banquet Waiter at Ambassador Hotel, Los Angeles, From May 17-June 19, 1968." Evangelista had reportedly left town suddenly after June 5, which perhaps was why he was investigated. Other than identifying him as someone who had

---

520   FBI telephone report of Mrs. Rose Julia Gallegos, June 6, 1968. When reporter Fernando Faura questioned Gallegos, he pegged the date as June 4, not June 2, and Gallegos did not correct him, but it's not clear that she paid attention to that part of Faura's question, and there are several records for both her and her daughter that indicate this happened on June 2, not June 4. Faura, p. 65.

521   LAPD interview of Aida Laffredo, December 6, 1968.

522   Faura, p. 66.

523   Faura, pp. 68–71.

cashed a couple of payroll checks from the Ambassador Hotel in years past, the FBI did not get very far. He was the right age and height to be one of the people seen by others. He was in his mid-twenties and 5'8" and had brown curly hair, albeit "light brown." He was of Italian descent and his real name was Donald Wickson. The reason for investigating him was not provided. But knowing now the importance of men dressed as busboys or waiters and people familiar with the kitchen there, I can understand why the FBI performed an investigation.

If Gallegos and her daughter had seen Sirhan on June 2, why wasn't he in the same clothes on June 4? Very likely, Gallegos and her daughter had seen the Sirhan doppelganger on June 2, and he was identically dressed on June 4. Was there a plot to kill Kennedy on June 2? Was the team there scoping out the landscape to plan for the shooting two days later? Was this all some terrible coincidence?

A "coincidence" seems the least likely option in light of what Karen Ross saw.

Karen Ross told the police she had seen a woman who, unbeknownst to Ross, seemed to exactly match the description of the girl seen with Sirhan by both Sandra Serrano and Vincent DiPierro on the night of the primary. On Sunday, June 2, Ross saw a woman in the first row of the Robert Kennedy rally in the Cocoanut Grove. She described her as tall (5'6"), 24–26 years old, husky, with dark blonde hair in a short, puffy flip. She had a round face with almost a double chin and thin eyebrows. She thought the nose might have been "fixed." She wore a white dress with black polka dots the size of a dime, three-quarter-length sleeves, with a ruffle at the neck and cuffs.[524] (Predictably, Lt. Manny Pena had scrawled across the cover sheet of her interview summary, "Don't Type," "Polka Dot Story Serrano Phoney," "Girl in Kitchen I.D. & Int.," "No further Int[erview].")[525]

Given the appearance of the three busboys and the fact that the girl in the polka dot dress as identified by Karen Ross very closely matched the woman that Serrano and DiPierro had seen, it appears there may have been an effort to kill Kennedy the night of June 2 that failed. Perhaps that explains something strange that happened on the night of June 3 in Malibu.

Bugs and tap lines?

AT ABOUT 10 P.M. ON THE NIGHT OF JUNE 3, A WIDOW, WHOSE NAME is redacted in her FBI report, heard someone ring her doorbell in Malibu. She went to the door and without opening it asked who it was. "It's the telephone repairman," a male voice said. "Are you kidding?" the woman asked, given the

524   LAPD interview of Karen Ross, June 6, 1968.
525   LAPD interview of Karen Ross, June 6, 1968.

late hour. "No, I'm not," the man said. The woman became frightened and immediately called the Los Angeles Sheriff's office in Malibu to report the incident. The Sheriffs said there was nothing they could do. The next day, June 4, she learned that Robert Kennedy was staying in the house next door. [526]

When Kennedy was killed on June 5, the woman's son apparently reached out to the FBI, feeling there may have been some connection.[527] In the days before high-tech surveillance, bugs had to be placed manually on phone lines. Was someone attempting to access the phone line from the neighbor's yard in order to better estimate his arrival time at the hotel on June 4, 1968?

Oddly enough, phone repairmen and phone issues showed up at a couple of other key points in the story. At 1:38 A.M., a little more than an hour after the shooting on June 5, the LAPD's "Unusual Occurrence Log" contains this entry: "R unit reporting telephone repairman at Cent. Rec. Hosp. for major repair. R-40 at scene checking out repairman." Central Receiving was the Hospital Kennedy was taken to first, before he was referred to Good Samaritan. It strains credulity there would suddenly, coincidentally be a major telephone failure requiring middle-of-the-night work. It would be far more believable that the conspirators needed to know as much as possible about Kennedy's condition and whether he would survive and made an attempt to get more data, but by the time they got to Central, Kennedy had been moved to Good Samaritan.

An even stranger phone-related entry showed up in the contemporaneous E.C.C. Liaison with Other Agencies log of events. At 4:30 P.M. on June 5, the log states:

> Earlier today, a "Mr. ... Crosby of the American Telephone Co.'s gov't. unit in Arlington, VA. (telephone 703/521-4100)" phoned to advise that the teletype circuit ordered by Defense Dept. into Police Bldg. was soon to be installed. Crosby was advised that LAPD had not approved physical installation of any such teletype equipment, but that circuits could be run to Pac. Tel. Co. terminal strip in Pol. Bldg. if desired; but no physical install of TT machine until approved by LAPD. (Later info. that the circuit and machine now going to Shfs. Jail on Bauchert Street, but this to be discussed more on Thursday by Shfs. Dept.).

Why did the Defense Department need a direct line into police headquarters? And if they needed the police, why was this suddenly rerouted to the Sheriff's jail instead? The LAPD is city government. The Sheriffs answer to Los Angeles County. You don't just move a line randomly from one to another. They are entirely different entities with wholly different missions and personnel.

---

526   FBI memos from redacted to SAC, Los Angeles, dated June 5 and June 7, 1968. The June 5 memo describes an interview of the redacted woman's son, and the June 7 memo reflects a conversation with the woman herself.

527   *Ibid.*

The mention of the jail is the likely clue. Although Sirhan was apprehended by the LAPD, he was soon after transferred to the Sheriff's jail. Arlington is near the CIA's headquarters, and the CIA has, on occasion, used the Defense Department as a cover agency for its actions.

CIA communications to Special Unit Senator did appear in the files as if they had come from a teletype machine, on perforated paper. But it would be hard to believe that a special teletype line was installed just for matters related to Robert Kennedy's assassination. Was someone attempting to tap a communications line in the guise of installing a new line?

Someone signaling?

NOTHING COULD HAVE BEEN MORE IMPORTANT THAN KNOWING when Kennedy was about to enter the pantry. Everyone involved had to get into place. Signals needed to be passed along so the team would know when Kennedy was about to enter. Curiously, a couple of witnesses reported a man that appeared to be "signaling" to someone in a strange way when Kennedy left the stage to head for the pantry. Gloria Farr and her companion Vernon Thompson, who worked for NBC as an electronics technician, saw a man make some sort of signaling motion at the edge of the crepe paper that covered the edges of a platform behind the stage that had a staircase. This was near the stairs that led down to the Ambassador Room below. Originally, the plan had been to take Kennedy out that way, down the staircase to speak to the overflow crowd. But Kennedy always spoke to the press, and that would have necessitated him coming back up to talk to the press and then to go down again and out to the Factory, where the victory party was being held.

Because of this, a row of people with arms linked prevented people from going behind the stage, as Farr found out when she tried to enter that area. She said a man in a "blue wooly [sic] sports coat" prevented her from crossing that line. Thompson was already in the anteroom as Farr was trying to get into it. Just as Kennedy finished his speech, Farr saw something that really struck her:

> There's a man at the top of the stairs, and he pushed the crepe paper aside, looking down underneath the platform and I thought to myself, "I wonder what's under there. I wonder if it's a microphone or what is it." And then he did this a second time just before Vern said to me, "He's leaving through the kitchen." He pushed this crepe paper aside as if he were signalling to someone down there. And the thing that struck me about it was that both Vern and I noticed it and hadn't mentioned it to him until afterwards [sic]. We were on

our way out. They wouldn't let us out and we were sitting in the car waiting and we were talking about it, and I said, "you know, the funniest thing happened." I said, "I saw this man pushing aside the crepe paper." And he said, "Did you see that?" He said, "I did too." And I said "What do you think it was?" And he said "Well, I thought it was maybe someone checking to see if the stairs were pulled out far enough for Senator Kennedy to walk down."[528]

She said the man was on the "first step" that led down from the stage, and the platform edges and stair edges were surrounded with crepe paper that hung to the floor. If someone wanted a good place to hide that will allow them to go either way on a moment's notice, that would have been a great place, as the assassin could move quickly either way. This may sound like a childish way to stage an assassination, but attorney and author Bill Simpich sent me documents showing the CIA at one time had a plan to kill Castro at one point in a kitchen with a guy hidden under some stairs.

And maybe the foot was a signal but not to someone under the stairs. Maybe it was a signal to someone further away—perhaps at the pantry door—that Kennedy was coming. As you will see, it's possible there were assassins both downstairs and upstairs, given how no one could be certain until the last few minutes which way Kennedy would go when he left the stage.

How did Sirhan get into the pantry?

THANE CESAR WAS ONE OF TWO GUARDS FOR MOST OF THE NIGHT charged with keeping people who didn't have the requisite passes *out* of the pantry. Yet Sirhan was allowed to move in and out freely, and was never reported to be wearing passes or badges at any point that night. How was that possible?

Cesar, who had worked only one day for Ace Security before, during the last week in May, did not appear to be checking *anyone* for badges or passes. Only people with press passes were to be allowed in that area, which led to the Colonial Room, the temporary headquarters for members of the printed press. But Dr. Marcus McBroom, who had no press credentials, entered the pantry around 10:30 P.M. on his way to the Embassy Room, and he was far from the only person to get in without credentials.

In the pantry, McBroom noticed a person he later believed to be Sirhan sitting on one of the steam tables. The person wore a pullover top and jeans, so he stood out among the kitchen workers clad in white tops and black pants.

---

528   LAPD transcript of Gloria Farr's interview, June 21, 1968.

Eara Marchman had also been allowed unchallenged into the pantry, despite her lack of credentials, and saw a man she later identified as Sirhan arguing with a uniformed guard by the swinging doors, which was likely Cesar. Her friend Rose Perezsklsy also told the police that Marchman had seen Sirhan arguing with the uniformed guard. Cesar would claim never to have seen or talked to Sirhan before the shooting.[529]

The girl in the polka dot dress

PERHAPS THE MOST INTERESTING OF THE "HELPERS" WAS A GIRL in a polka dot dress that pulled the focus of a surprising number of witnesses. Inspector John Powers told the *Los Angeles Times* that had the girl been found, "she would have been considered a 'principal' in the case."[530]

As we saw in early chapters, Sandra Serrano and Vince DiPierro saw Sirhan in the company of a girl in a white dress with dark polka dots who had a turned-up nose and dark brown hair. DiPierro said the girl appeared to be "holding" Sirhan as he stood on the tray rack along the southern part of the room before crossing north, pulling out a gun and firing at Kennedy. Serrano saw the girl enter the hotel up the southwest fire escape with a man in a gold sweater and Sirhan. Immediately after the shooting, the girl and the guy who was not Sirhan ran back out with the girl saying excitedly, "We shot him," as if it was a good thing.

Dr. Marcus McBroom told the FBI that when he ran into the Embassy Room to find a doctor to help Kennedy, "he remembered seeing a Caucasian female about twenty-five, 5'4", 126 pounds, moving toward the exit." McBroom said the woman "was wearing a white dress with black polka dots and definitely had dark hair." He felt her behavior was unusual because "she appeared much calmer than anyone else in the room, and appeared to be trying to leave the room as soon as possible."[531]

A number of witnesses that night noticed her, allowing us to track her progress through the hotel on June 4th and 5th.

CONRAD SEIM

Photographer Conrad Seim had been approached around 9:30 P.M. by a girl in a white dress with black or navy polka dots with a "funny nose" he thought may have been broken at one time. She was Caucasian, between 25 and 30 years old, approximately 5'5" or 5'6", with short, dark brown hair and an olive complexion.

529   Melanson, p. 313, quoting Dan Moldea's 1987 interview with Cesar.

530   Jerry Cohen, "'Polka Dot' Girl Hunt Called Off,'" *Los Angeles Times*, June 22, 1968.

531   FBI interview summary of Dr. Marcus McBroom, dated July 11, 1968.

She asked him if she could borrow his press pass. He told her no, but she came back up to him again about 15 minutes later to ask again. This description matches that of the girl seen by Sandra Serrano and Vince DiPierro.

DOMINIC GEZZI

Sometime around 11 P.M., Dominic Gezzi noticed two men who appeared to be foreign talking to a girl in a polka dot dress that he thought was Jewish. He said she had a "large nose." The three looked very serious. One of the men was between 5'2" and 5'4" tall. The other male was about 5'10," but Gezzi could not describe him further. When Sirhan was being removed from the hotel, someone grabbed his hair and pulled his head up. When Gezzi saw his face, he was certain this was the short man in the group he had seen earlier.[532]

PAMELA RUSSO

Another witness also saw a woman in a polka dot dress with a nose that drew her attention. Pamela Russo, a Rafferty campaign worker, remembered seeing a girl in a polka dot dress—white with black or dark purple dots—and suggested the girl might have been wearing a wig. She remembered the girl as being about 5'5" or 5'6" with "kind of a bouffant hairdo. It was jet black. It had almost like—you've seen wigs of this sort that are very, very bouffant, they all look the same—they are kind of tucked under, they come a little bit toward the face."

But what Russo really remembered was the girl's nose, as she described to Fernando Faura, the only journalist who seriously pursued the conspiracy angle in the days immediately following the assassination:

> The girl had a long thin nose. It was—it was almost when you looked at it—it looked a little bit crooked. It was thin between the eyes. It came down—it broadened at the nose, and then narrowed again toward the base of the nose, but the nostrils were a little bit wider. This is what I remember. I remember that nose.[533]

At the time Russo saw her, the girl was alone. That may or may not have been the case when Eve Hansen saw her.

532   LAPD interview of Dominic Gezzi, July 18, 1968.

533   Prepublication PDF version of Fernando Faura's book, *The Polka Dot File on the Robert F. Kennedy Killing* (Walterville, OR: Trine Day LLC, 2016), p. 144, provided to the author by Fernando Faura.

EVE HANSEN

Eve Hansen clearly saw the same girl that DiPierro and Serrano saw at the downstairs bar outside the Ambassador Room, called by many the "victory room" that night, as that was the place of the public victory party open to the public. The Embassy Room party was private, intended for campaign workers, the media and donors. The public celebration was held downstairs, with bands and bars aplenty. One such bar was in the foyer just outside the Ambassador Room. And there, Eve Hansen, who was attending the party with her sister Nina Ballantyne, saw something interesting. There was a long bar in the hallway that led into the Ambassador Room, and a shorter bar "around the corner … on the right." Around 10:30 P.M. or 11 P.M., Hansen and Ballantyne had a conversation with a girl in a polka dot dress:

> I was standing at the end of the bar, waiting to be served, and had been standing for a few minutes, and this gal just suddenly popped up alongside of me and my sister and said "You'll never get served there." And I said "Why not?" And she said, "Well I've been standing at the other end of the bar for over a half hour and I couldn't get served, they just won't serve you at this end of the bar." And I said, "You wanna make a bet? Give me your money and tell me what you want" and she gave me a dollar and said she'd like a scotch highball.
>
> This was primarily how come I noticed her, because I'm a scotch drinker, but I like scotch on the rocks when I'm at a public bar, and I said to her, "Why don't you try a scotch on the rocks? You'll get more for your money." So she said, "Okay," and she gave me a dollar for her drink …. And about then, I did get served. …
>
> She was real nice—she was real lively and fun and everything. [534]

After Hansen passed out the drinks and a little chit-chat about the scotch, the girl lifted her glass and said, "Here's to our next president" and Hansen said "I'll drink to that."

> And that was it. There was nothing suspicious. She was a charming kid, girl, I'd say around 25 or so. But the reason we went to the District Attorney's office was because as of Friday noon, nobody—and it was on the radio that the D.A.'s office was looking for a girl in a polka dot dress—nobody had admitted it. And that's when Nina said … that's awfully odd, and maybe we ought to tell the D.A.'s office about it. [535]

Hansen described the girl as Caucasian, with dark brown hair that hit about

---

534   Tape of LAPD interview of Eve Hansen, June 17, 1968.
535   *Ibid.*

at her shoulders with "big poofs" in it, suggesting a bouffant style. She had "a sort of turned-up nose—that's why I described her as being sort of pert, cute, and very vivacious, very talkative." She thought she was 25 or 26, about 5'6" tall. "She had a nice figure," Hansen emphasized. "She wasn't fat and yet she wasn't skinny. She had a nice figure," she repeated. She thought the dress with white with black or navy blue polka dots, and was leaning toward navy blue because she "distinctly remember[ed]" a navy blue belt on the dress. She thought the dots were about the size of a quarter coin. "I think I noticed her hemline because I'm very conscious of that." She hated miniskirts and this dress had a respectable length. "I have no recollection of her having a bag." She probably had brown eyes, Hansen said, "Because I usually notice blue eyes. I have a thing about blue eyes."

Hansen said she had been sitting on the stairs "the girl was supposed to have run down," but she was sitting on the stairs between the backstage area and the Ambassador Room, which were on the northern, Wilshire side of the building, not the stairs were Sandra Serrano was sitting, which was on the southern, 8th Street side of the building. They saw a security guard on those stairs.

When Officer Risen asked Hansen if she saw any men with the girl in the polka dot dress, she said no, but added something interesting that she noticed at the far north end of the short bar around the corner from the main downstairs hallway:

> At the upper end of the bar … where she said she was waiting to be served and they wouldn't serve her, there was just a wall—about six feet beyond the bar, … there were three or four young man of different nationalities just sitting on the floor. And I thought that was very odd, just sitting on the floor. But I didn't notice enough to notice who they were or if she was with them. This was before she popped up.[536]

There was, in fact, something very important here that we will examine in the next chapter. But Officer Risen could not have known that at that early point, so he moved on to ask about the toast the girl had made "to our next president" that the girl had made. "Did she say who?" Risen asked.

"That struck me as odd too," Hansen replied. "She did not say 'Here's to Bobby' … she just said, 'Well, here's a toast to our next president,' and I said, 'I'll drink to that,' thinking of Bobby. And she said, 'Well, I gotta go now,' and just took off."[537]

"Did you see which way she went?" Risen asked.

"She just melted into the crowd," Hansen said.[538]

---

536   *Ibid.*
537   *Ibid.*
538   *Ibid.*

DARNELL JOHNSON'S GROUP

Darnell Johnson described a group of five people that included Sirhan in the pantry just before Kennedy returned from giving his speech. He had the feeling the people were "together." The group contained:

> A white female wearing a white dress, with 25¢ size black polka dots; the dress was fitted, was not a miniskirt but was above the knee; was not a loose shift but was fashionable for the time. She was 23–25 years of age, tall, 5'8," medium build, well built, 145 pounds, long light brown hair, carrying an all-white sweater or jacket, pretty full face, stubby heel shoes in the fashion of the time.
>
> A person whom Johnson identified as Sirhan from photographs shown at the time of this interview and further as the person he saw who was seized immediately following the shooting by persons in the area.
>
> A white male, wearing a light blue washable sport coat, white shirt and tie, 6'1" tall, slim, 30–35 years, blond hair parted far over the left side with the right side long and hanging towards his face like a surfer haircut outdoor type.
>
> A white male, 5'10" tall, 165 pounds, trim, 24–25 years of age, brown, long hair but not hippie, dark coat, darker trousers, white shirt and tie.
>
> A white male, 6'1", tall, slim, darkish brown hair, shiny brown sport coat made of hopsacking, white shirt and tie.[539]

The tall blond man in the light blue sport coat sounds like the man who Nina Rhodes-Hughes saw shooting from the table, and the man Ernesto Ruiz and Gilman Kraft saw run across the lobby at the same time Michael Wayne ran out. These people "were standing in a group between Darnell and the door through which Kennedy came." As Kennedy entered, Darnell, like many other witnesses, thought firecrackers had been set off and was not aware that a gun had been fired, even when he saw a woman "slump against the wall and say 'Oh my God, oh my God.' Johnson saw a photographer "put the lights up to take a picture of the persons standing, and when the lights showed on Sirhan, the photographer said, 'Grab him, that dude has a gun.' This was the first time that Johnson realized there had been a shooting."[540]

At this point, Johnson saw the woman in the polka dot dress and the three other men leave and walk "toward the ballroom from where the Kennedy party had just come." As people seized Sirhan, Johnson said the woman in the polka

---

539   FBI interview of Darnell Johnson taken June 6, 1968.
540   *Ibid.*

dot dress and the man in the "light blue washable sport coat" came back and looked, then left again.

JOSE CARVAJAL

What Darnell Johnson saw maps closely to what Ambassador Hotel busboy Jose Carvajal told reporter Fernando Faura. After the shooting, Carvajal saw a girl in a polka dot dress "run straight into a dead-end hallway."[541] It appears both Carvajal and Darnell Johnson saw the same woman. This makes sense if the woman ran into the employee dining area, thinking she could get through that to the main kitchen, only to find, for whatever reason, she could not. She then turned around and ran back out the south pantry door to join her tall, blue-suited companion. This maps to what Evan Freed and Jack Merritt saw as well.

EVAN FREED AND JACK MERRITT

Evan Freed saw a woman in a polka dot dress and a man wearing a "bright blue" sports coat leave the pantry through separate doors at the east end of the pantry.

There were three exits at the east end of the pantry. One door led south to the Embassy Foyer, a pair of double doors opened east to the Colonial Room across a short hallway, and one door opened to the north to the main kitchen area. A fourth pantry exit in the middle of the north wall led to an employee eating area which may or may not have connected, at least at that point, to the main kitchen. Evan Freed told the LAPD that after the shooting, he had been "pinned against the east wall of the kitchen" by the crowd and saw three people running east toward him, two men and one woman. The woman, wearing a polka dot dress, went out the door to his right (likely one of the two north exits), and a man in blue suit ran out the door to his left (likely the east exit), followed by the third man, who was yelling, "Get him! Get him!"[542] Although Freed said the man he saw had dark hair, he wasn't certain of that. Someone with "surfer" blond hair may well have had dark streaks in his hair as well. Freed also thought the girl had a long dress on, but the color of the man's hair and the length of her polka dot dress weren't important details. What was important is that two people seemed to be escaping just as the shots began.

---

541   Faura, p. 112.

542   LAPD interview of Evan Phillip Freed, June 14, 1968. In later years, an affidavit signed by Freed circulated through the research community that stated Freed had seen a second gunman near Kennedy. But when I contacted Freed and faxed him a copy of that affidavit for comment, he struck out all the parts about the second gunman until the statement matched what was reported in his original report as quoted here. He did not explain how his signature came to be on that other document.

Ace Security guard Jack Merritt reported something similar. He too was at the east end of the pantry at the doors that led to the Colonial Room. He had been near the main doors to the Embassy Room when he heard a woman come from the pantry and scream, "My God, we need a doctor." He ran into the pantry and saw the group of men struggling with Sirhan. But when he first entered the pantry, "he observed two men and a woman walking away from him and out of the kitchen. They seemed to be smiling. He added that the woman was wearing a polka dot dress."[543]

FRANCIS CRITCHELEY

Yet another witness saw a woman leaving the pantry. Francis Critcheley (misspelled Critchley in some records) "assisted a girl early twenties heavy set not fat in a white polka dot dress who was getting shoved in the crowd."

Critcheley described her as having an olive complexion, "similar to Mediterranean Latin" with a "round face," dark hair and eyes that seemed "naturally teardropped shape." She seemed to be in her "early twenties" and was wearing a polka dot dress with a "hi-necked dress."[544] Serrano had described the dress as having "a stand-up collar."[545] She had an "up hairdo blk with an off-center crease in top."[546] Did Critcheley unwittingly help a conspirator escape? She looked "frightened and wide eyed," according to Officer Norris' notes of his conversation with Critcheley.

Earlier that night, Critcheley had spied a different woman in a polka dot dress, but she was about 18 years old and her dress was low-cut and she had a straight-chiseled nose. None of the characteristics of the second woman match the description of the woman DiPierro and Serrano saw, but the first one was a very close match.[547] But the younger woman did seem to match the younger woman in a polka dot dress that other witnesses would report seeing with Sirhan, a point we'll return to later.

BOOKER GRIFFIN

Booker Griffin was yet another witness to a man and a woman in a polka dot dress leaving the pantry right after the shooting while others seemed to be trying to get in.

---

543   SUS Final Report, p. 1069.

544   LAPD Officer Norris' interview notes of Francis Critchley [sic], June 6, 1968; FBI interview of Francis Critcheley (the correct spelling), taken on June 19 and summarized on June 26, 1968.

545   FBI memo quoting the tape of the LAPD interview of Serrano taken June 12, 1968.

546   LAPD Officer Norris' interview notes of Francis Critchley [sic], June 6, 1968.

547   Ibid.

Around 10:30 P.M., Booker Griffin made "negative eye contact" with the man he'd recognize later as Sirhan. He was standing next to a 6'2" Caucasian man, with a lighter complexion than Sirhan's, and a girl in a "predominantly white dress that may have had another color in it." He thought they seemed "totally out of the mood" of the rest of the people in attendance.[548] Griffin saw this trio repeatedly between 11 P.M. and 12 A.M. just before Kennedy was shot. He distinctly remembered Sirhan because he had sneered at him as he went by. A few days later, Booker wrote in the *Los Angeles Sentinel*:

> The man that did the shooting was in the corridor-way as I left [the stage] in advance of the senator. He was there with a tall Caucasian male and a Caucasian female in a white dress. I noticed the man because I had seen him several times before during the evening.
>
> I had seen him first downstairs in the Ambassador Room around 10:15 P.M. I remember distinctly because we had stared each other down. I vaguely remember the girl also with him.
>
> Between 11 and the actual shooting, I traveled between the Embassy Room and press room (using the corridor or where the incident occurred) maybe six or eight times. The last three or four times I noticed the gunman, the girl and the other guy.
>
> When I left the stage and went to the press room the last time before the shooting, there were a few kitchen employees and the gunman and his two friends. I distinctly remember this because the gunman had sneered at me as I went past. This affected me to the point that it stayed on my mind when I sat down in the press room.

Griffin remarked "how we just seemed to dislike each other. It puzzled me." Booker had just started to enter the pantry from the east end when the shooting started. "I had a full view of the room," Griffin wrote, adding,

> I differ very sharply with media reports at this point. I distinctly saw the other man and the girl flee a side corridor heading out of the hotel as I raced to the feet of the fallen senator.
>
> There is no doubt in my mind that on several trips past the trio that they were together.

Griffin tried to pursue them "down that corridor, but couldn't get through." He kept yelling "they're getting away" but no one seemed to pay any attention.[549]

---

548 Melanson, p. 230.
549 Booker Griffin, "Fatalism, Destiny: Fear Now Real," *Los Angeles Sentinel*, June 9, 1968.

Dick Aubrey remembered Griffin saying, "Did they get the other two guys?" In his taped LAPD interview, Griffin noticed the woman because she had sort of a "bubble butt" of the type he saw more commonly on black women than on white women. Griffin said the woman had "blonde bouffant hair." As with the other witnesses, Griffin described these two as leaving through the kitchen area, meaning through one of the northern exits from the pantry. To both the FBI and LAPD, Griffin said the dress had some sort of "colorations" on it. None of Griffin's early interviews, nor Griffin's own article, mention that he saw a girl in a polka dot dress. But we know this to be the case because in a short summary of LAPD witness interviews dated June 7, there is this entry:

> Booker Griffen [*sic*] [phone numbers] Saw Girl Polka Dot Dress

So either Griffin told the police that, or the way he described the girl was enough for the LAPD to believe he had seen "the girl."

The LAPD's Final Report on the case included this outright lie:

> Mr. Griffin observed the shooting from the Colonial Room doorway. He stated he saw a male and a female run from the room. Later he stated that the report of the male and female escaping was a total fabrication on his part.[550]

Griffin never made any such statement. The LAPD statement is the complete fabrication. I've listened to the last interview, on tape, of Griffin, and can verify he said no such thing. When Professor Philip Melanson showed him this statement years later, Griffin's first response was to invoke his lawyer. He was furious the LAPD would make up such a lie about something that never happened. "Law must not perjure itself," Griffin said. Griffin was a trained crime reporter. He knew what he saw and had reported it accurately.

In a curious twist, Griffin had offered to take a lie detector test to prove the veracity of what he was saying, but the police had declined, saying the test was unreliable.[551]

And George Green could have backed him up. He also saw a man he later identified as Sirhan talking to a tall, thin man and a girl in a polka dot dress who had a "good figure." Sirhan caught his attention because he was wearing neither a suit nor a kitchen uniform.[552]

So six people—Darnell Johnson, Carvajal, Critcheley, Freed, Merritt and Griffin saw a girl in a polka dot dress leave the pantry after the shooting in a

---

550   SUS report, p. 977.
551   Melanson, p. 233.
552   Melanson, p. 226.

way that drew their attention. Three of these witnesses noted a tall man with her, and two of those three said the man was wearing a blue suit.

This tall man may well have been the source of Sergeant Sharaga's initial broadcast that was requested cancelled by Inspector Powers.

The man in the maroon coat

SERRANO NEVER SAID THE MAN IN THE GOLD SWEATER SHE SAW on the stairs was wearing a blue coat, so we have to assume that, after leaving the kitchen, the girl went one way and the tall man another. Sandra Serrano saw a woman in a polka dot dress and a man in a gold sweater run out the back fire escape after the shooting. Both of these people had to have run right by the man in the maroon coat who appeared to be holding a radio to his cheek as witnessed by the wives of two television producers.

Serrano had reported hearing six sounds she assumed were backfires from a car until she learned of the shooting. The police conducted tests to show she could not have heard any gunshots from her location. But what if the man in the maroon coat who appeared, according to a witness, to have a radio, was near the outside door? What if she heard the shots over his radio? What if he was their contact at the southwest exit? That might explain why the girl was already shouting "We shot him" before Serrano asked "Who did you shoot?" Maybe the girl was telling their contact in the maroon coat that the operation had been successful. Was the maroon-coated man another helper, making sure the southwest fire escape exit remained open all night, listening to events by radio or coordinating with the team? Someone had to monitor that door to ensure the conspirators could get in and out from that exit. That would explain why the man turned to the two wives of NBC executives to say, "you have seen me here all night," as if trying to establish an alibi.

The man in the gold shirt

SERRANO WASN'T THE ONLY ONE TO SEE A MAN IN A GOLD TOP with Sirhan and a girl in a polka dot dress, as we saw earlier. Jeanette Prudhomme, Irene Gizzie, Kathy Lentine and Katherine Keir all saw a male who looked Latin or Hispanic in a gold-colored top with light pants in the company of Sirhan. The man, like the woman in the polka dot dress, caught their eye because he was not dressed appropriately for the event.

Keir had been standing outside the Sunset Room, which was below the Embassy Room at the south end of the hotel when she saw a young white female "dressed in a polka dot dress, black and white, run from the Sunset Room and down the stairway. The young female was yelling, 'We shot Kennedy.'"[553] As we saw earlier, Keir had also seen Sirhan, or someone who looked just like him, in the company of a man in a short-sleeved, buttoned-down "goldish-colored shirt."

When I talked to Keir in 2016, she confirmed this to me:

> What I remember is my best friend and I were there, and I had seen the woman in the polka dot dress prior to the running down the stairs thing. We had seen her with two guys.[554]

The trio caught her attention because they were shabbily dressed. The guys were in jeans. But everyone else, Keir told me, was "dressed to the nines." Nowadays, Keir said, at political events, people show up in jeans and a T-shirt. "But back then, it was a big deal. I remember some women being dressed in gowns." She and her friend Jeanette Prudhomme (now Jeanette Graves) noticed these people. "We were just being little bitches," Keir joked, explaining that she and her friend made catty comments about their shabby attire, as teenage girls sometimes do.

"I remember walking around and then at some point seeing her [the girl in the polka dot dress] with the two guys. Again, it was the dress. The guys were in jeans and all the men were in suits." I asked Keir if by "Victory Room" she meant the room where the victory party was being held, and she said yes. To my knowledge, there was no room officially named the "Victory Room" at the Ambassador Hotel. The private victory party was being held in the Embassy Room upstairs. The public victory party was being held downstairs in the Ambassador Ballroom.

When I asked Keir if she remembered if the woman was running toward her or away from her, she said she had the impression the woman had been running parallel to her, which would make sense if Keir was standing on the platform outside the Sunset Room facing the 8th Street parking lot (which was up a hill and not well lit, from that angle.) If she were standing at the place where the stairs turned south after first running west, then the girl would have run beside her in a parallel direction.

When she talked to the LAPD, Keir told me she didn't feel that they were taking her seriously about seeing the girl in the polka dot dress: "I definitely had the impression that they didn't believe anything regarding this woman in this dress."[555] Keir remembered being shown mug shots and identifying Sirhan as one of the two men she had seen.

---

553   LAPD interview of Katherine Keir, August 7, 1968.

554   Author interview with Katherine Keir, December 3, 2016.

555   Author interview with Katherine Keir, December 3, 2016. Keir said when she talked to CNN.

Keir told me when Brad Johnson, a CNN International producer, had contacted her, she had neglected to tell Johnson she was on medication and felt mentally "fuzzy." She remembered reading a report indicating she and her friends had somewhat retracted their statements about the girl in the polka dot dress and told me adamantly that wasn't true. When I talked to her at the end of 2016, she was off that medication and quite sharp. I pressed her on this point as well, saying the police considered her saying she heard the woman say "they shot Kennedy" in the second interview a retraction of her having initially reported the woman as having said "we shot Kennedy."

"Yeah, but that doesn't mean she wasn't there," Keir asked, the annoyance palpable in her voice decades later. "And where would I come up with 'we'?" Keir thought the normal thing would have been to assume the woman had said "they shot Kennedy," not "we shot Kennedy." Keir said she didn't remember now, so many years later, exactly what the girl had said, but she urged me to weight her earliest statement over any subsequent one. I read Keir the document Johnson had probably shown her, where the police said she had "retracted" her first statement and said maybe the girl had said "They shot Kennedy" instead of "We shot Kennedy."

"What do you believe you heard?" I asked Keir.

"I believe whatever I told them the first time," Keir reiterated.

Is it possible that Keir heard Serrano's interview before she spoke to the police? No, Keir assured me. Keir and Prudhomme carpooled with a woman from the campaign. They left about 2 A.M., so they could not have heard Serrano's account, which was broadcast live on television, not radio, at around 2 A.M.

Other women

CLEARLY THERE WAS A WOMAN IN A POLKA DOT DRESS WITH Sirhan and another man for much of the night. No wonder Inspector Powers felt she would have been a principal in the case. But this was not the only interesting woman in the case.

There were at least five different women who seemed involved somehow in these events. The first was the woman described with Sirhan by Serrano and DiPierro in the company of Sirhan. The second one was the woman that John Fahey spent the day with, whom you'll soon understand could not be this same woman. The third was a woman who had gone to Kennedy headquarters during the time Fahey was on the road who, like Fahey's woman, seemed to know Kennedy was about to be killed. There was a fourth woman who was also wearing a polka dot dress, but who was skinnier and younger than the woman DiPierro and Serrano saw, and seemed to be in the company of a Sirhan doppelganger. Lastly, a woman in a polka dot dress was seen conversing with a fifth woman who did not seem to speak English (or French, Spanish, or German) but who may have been part of the plot.

There was also a *sixth* woman who seemed to know something about the plot and tried to stop it, as you'll see in a later chapter.

Which of these women did Roy Mills and Bernyce Matthews see?

Roy Mills saw Sirhan in a group in the kitchen area. Around 11:50 P.M., Roy Mills and his friend William Rands wandered into the pantry. Mills noticed a group in the employee dining area just before Kennedy came down to speak. Mills "observed five people in the open room to the left," but maybe he meant right. If he walked east through the pantry, the employee dining area would have been to his left. Walking west, there was no open room to the left. Mills said that four of the people were males and one was female. Mills described one of the males as "a hotel employee," but there is no indication of why he knew or thought that, although a clue may have come from his friend. Rands said Mills used to work at the Ambassador Hotel and knew his way around.[556] Mills was a cook by trade and may well have recognized a kitchen uniform—or perhaps a busboy jacket. But the male Mills noticed the most was the short black-haired male in "very baggy pants." The only thing he could remember about the girl was that she had a yellow press badge on. After the shooting, when Sirhan was brought out, Mills immediately recognized Sirhan as the man with the baggy pants in the group.[557]

Mills remembered seeing Sirhan and a woman talking. "They did not appear to be together, only talking," read his interview summary. All Mills could remember is her dress seemed to be one-piece. Mills was just outside the west end of the pantry when Kennedy walked past him heading into the pantry. Then Mills heard "8 or 9 shots in quick succession" and "thought there had been two guns." When Sirhan was taken out, he recognized Sirhan as the person he had seen talking to the woman in the kitchen.[558]

Like Mills, Bernyce Matthews saw someone she realized after the fact was Sirhan talking to a woman at the hotel. Around 9:40 P.M., Matthews noticed a man in his "late forties" standing about ten feet from her. "She noticed this man because he appeared very grim and didn't seem to be enjoying himself."[559] "A few moments later," Matthews noticed a woman whispering through her cupped hand into Sirhan's ear as they stood outside the Embassy Room. The girl was

556   LAPD interview of William Rands, August 7, 1968.

557   LAPD interview of Roy Mills, June 6.

558   LAPD interview of Roy Mills, August 9, 1968 (the document lists both his June 6 and August 9 date but the bottom date of the typist is August, so presumably this reflects his comments in August).

559   LAPD interview of Bernyce Matthews, April 20, 1969.

talking and the man was nodding. She remembered this because around 10:15 P.M., she saw all three of these people together in the ballroom:

> The two men were squatting on the floor approx. 15 ft south of the entrance to the ballroom. The young girl was standing along approx. 5 ft north of the man. The older man was speaking to the younger man who was acknowledging his conversation by nodding. All three of these persons appeared unconcerned with the activities taking place around them.[560]

Matthews described the girl as 18/20, 5'0", possibly Oriental or Filipino, "very small," about 90 pounds, with long, straight hair. She thought the Sirhan character was 5'8" or 5'9" because she herself was short (5'3") and she had to look up to him. While the investigator added that he smelled alcohol on her breath at the time of the interview, which was many months after the event, Matthews had written the police months earlier, in September of 1968, saying she had seen Sirhan in the company of another man and woman. "I shall never forget the male in particular," Matthews wrote, noting it was "the expression on the man's face that drew my attention to the three of them."[561] This was clearly *not* the 5'6" girl with the "funny nose" and "good figure" others had reported with Sirhan. And this man may not have been Sirhan but one of his doppelgangers.

The girl Matthews saw sounds identical to the girl in the polka dot dress Critcheley had noticed near the Rafferty party in the lobby earlier. He had described the girl as 18 years old, maybe 100 pounds, 5'2", with straight dark hair.[562]

Mary Estrada was interviewed by the LAPD on June 7 and August 22, 1968. In both interviews, she described a group of four males and one female not far from the lobby fountain around 11 P.M. on June 4. She identified one man as Sirhan from a police photo. One of the men was 5'3" and shorter than Sirhan. One was a bit taller than Sirhan but looked very much like him, according to Estrada. (This might have been the man shooting from atop the table that looked like Sirhan.) All were Caucasian and the short one had blond hair. (Could that have been Terry Frasier?) All were dressed too casually for the event. The female, who was wearing a polka dot dress, was leaning her head on Sirhan's shoulder. The woman kept popping in and out of the "room to her left" which was likely the Embassy Room if she was on the south side of the lobby fountain. All of these people were talking to each other when Estrada noticed them. When she and her daughter left the hotel at approximately 11:45 P.M., these people were still

---

560   LAPD interview of Bernyce Matthews, April 20, 1969.

561   Handwritten letter from Bernyce Matthews to the LAPD, September 16, 1968.

562   LAPD interview of Francis Critcheley (misspelled as Critchley in this document), June 6, 1968.

leaning against a wall in the lobby. She noticed them because she had sat with her 12-year-old daughter on the edge of the fountain and expressed embarrassment that they were not more formally dressed. Estrada's daughter then pointed out the group, which included Sirhan in a white T-shirt and jeans, to show they weren't the only ones underdressed.

In her June 7 interview, Estrada said the woman was 5'5" or 5'6", 23 or 24 years old, with brown hair that was possibly a wig, with a slender build and wearing a lot of makeup. Although the age and dress match, neither DiPierro nor Serrano said the woman had a lot of makeup on, and neither described the woman as "slender."

In the summary of Estrada's August 22 interview (which appears to have been mistakenly dated 1969 at the bottom but correctly dated 1968 at the top of the interview summary sheet), Estrada said the girl in the polka dot dress was 18 years old, 120 pounds, 5'4", and wore a lot of makeup. If this memory was accurate, this sounds like the younger, slimmer woman that Bernyce Matthews and Frances Critcheley had seen. And although Estrada had picked out Sirhan's photo as the man she saw with this group, she said he was wearing a dark jacket and denim pants. But Sirhan was wearing a light blue velour shirt over his white T-shirt. Was it possible Estrada had seen both women but only reported one of them each time? Did she really mess up the description in one of these two interviews? Did the police just alter her statements so they wouldn't match the description of the girl in the polka dot dress that Serrano and DiPierro saw?

Southeast of the Embassy Room and Gold Room was the Café Lautrec restaurant. Judy Groves, the woman who had identified Khoury at the hotel, had an encounter with Sirhan or a lookalike and a girl in a polka dot dress. Groves had tried to enter the Embassy Room but was turned away by the guards because the room was already at capacity. Upon overhearing that, a 5'6" young man with a dark complexion and dark hair took her to the restaurant entrance and suggested she enter the Embassy Room through the Lautrec restaurant, but they were stopped at the door by a waiter. No one knew until Kennedy came down which way he would enter the Embassy Room. It's possible someone had scouted Café Lautrec as a possible location to kill and stationed a team there, just in case.

The man Judy talked to was 23 or 24 years old, had a dark olive complexion, spoke with a slight accent and was "wearing a dark coat that was too large for him. He was wearing a white shirt, definitely button type, and no tie." Judy Groves also indicated the man had a pronounced "not terrible but not good" acne condition. [563] Groves said the man's white shirt looked "as though he had slept in it." The man also spoke with a noticeable accent.[564] For these reasons, she

---

563   LAPD interview of Judy Groves, June 28, 1968.

564   Los Angeles County District Attorney's office memo from Clayton Anderson to George Stoner, June 10, 1968.

questioned whether it was Sirhan. Albert Ellis may have seen this man as well. He described a man he thought was Sirhan as having "a fat nose and pimples on his face,"[565] but Sirhan had a clear complexion.

When I read Grove's description of the oversized coat, I wondered if Michael Wayne had given his coat to this man. Wayne was 5'8" and this man was definitely smaller, so it would make sense that the coat would be too large. Maybe this was the man Daniel Hall talked to who may have been carrying a gun in a suitcase. In any case, this acne-faced doppelganger was soon joined by a woman who sounds all too familiar by now.

When Groves and Sirhan's doppelganger stopped at the entrance, they were joined by a girl in a white dress with polka dots and ¾-"inch" (I believe she said or meant "length") bell-type sleeves, 22 to 24 years old, with dark blonde hair done up in a bouffant hairdo, and a fair complexion. Groves described the girl as well-groomed and attractive in an "all-American way."[566] I am a brunette who has been accused of having brown, light brown, dark blonde and dark brown hair, depending on the light, so I understand why there isn't a lot of consistency around the girl's hair color. Different witnesses described her hair color in various ways, but it's clear she was what most people would call a brunette. The ¾-length sleeves and the age make this sound like the woman Serrano and DiPierro saw. Did the women in polka dot dresses trade off guarding Sirhan during the night?

According to Groves, a second woman accompanied the first, but she was about 35 years old, shorter, with darker skin, a slender build, and sharp features that were "otherwise unremarkable." Both women started to talk to the Sirhan doppelganger in a foreign language which Groves knew was not Spanish, German or French,[567] but something with a "staccato" rhythm. Was it Arabic? The darker, older woman did not appear to speak English but the girl in the polka dot dress appeared to be fluent in both languages. Later, Groves saw the darker woman standing alone looking into the Embassy Room from a window near where the television tables were located.

Mary Wall saw a line of people that included Sirhan walking through the Lautrec restaurant around 10 P.M. on June 4. She described Sirhan as a "very ugly person," which could possibly refer to the acne-scarred facial appearance of Sirhan's doppelganger.[568] On the index card entry for Wall in the LAPD files, someone noted that while Mrs. Wall had described clothing that fit what Sirhan was wearing, she had a color TV and might have picked up his clothes from a broadcast.

---

565   LAPD interview of Albert Ellis, August 22, 1968. Ellis also reported hearing a woman yell "We shot him" to his rear as he stood in the Embassy Room, but his position is vague and he didn't get a good glimpse of the woman.

566   Los Angeles County District Attorney's office memo from Clayton Anderson to George Stoner, June 10, 1968.

567   LAPD interview of Judy Groves, June 28, 1968.

568   LAPD synopsis of Mary Wall's taped interview of June 17, 1968.

Terri Trivelli saw a woman in a polka dot dress and a man with dark, curly hair with "an olive complexion with acne" wearing "a light-colored shirt and blue jeans and a dark jacket" walking together through the "Victory Room" downstairs. "She did not hear them talking" but apparently believed they were together.[569]

A couple of people may have seen Serrano's girl in the polka dot dress with either Sirhan or a lookalike at a Kennedy fundraiser a couple of weeks prior to the California primary. Albert (misidentified in some LAPD records as Gilbert) Le Beau, a bartender at Robbie's Restaurant in Pomona, reported seeing a couple of people matching their descriptions.

On May 20th, a fundraiser was held for Senator Kennedy at Robbie's. Le Beau was asked to check tickets on the spiral staircase that led to the banquet room upstairs where the event was held. Nearly immediately after Kennedy arrived, at approximately 12:30 P.M. Le Beau heard a noise. He turned to his left and saw a young woman standing on the third step of the stairway and a male companion who had evidently just jumped the banister to join her, clanging the railing and making the noise that cause Le Beau to turn around. Le Beau's FBI report states that "The young man began pushing the girl with his open left hand and or possibly tan poplin material jacket. The right hand was completely covered by the jacket. Le Beau thought at the time it was odd that the man was carrying a jacket as it was a very hot day." Did the jacket conceal a gun? Le Beau stopped the two and asked for their tickets. The woman responded that they were part of the senator's party and he had just waved them up. Le Beau let them go up. Le Beau told the FBI the man remained silent while the woman spoke. The FBI noted what happened next:

> A few moments later, Le Beau went upstairs, entered through the main door of the banquet hall, and as he did so, he observed the same couple standing by themselves at the left of the main door leaning against the south wall. At this time, Le Beau said he realized that the couple were not part of the Senator's party because they were standing approximately 75 feet from the speaker's stand and there was [sic] a large number of camera and TV men standing between the couple and Kennedy, who was speaking at the time. The couple was practically obscured from the speaker's stand.[570]

Le Beau described the female as 25–30 years old, 5'4" to 5'6" with a "trim nice figure" and shoulder-length light brown hair, wearing a satin blouse. As for

569   LAPD interview of Terri Trivelli, June 6, 1968 and Telephone Interview sheet of this interview with the added date "Polka dot dress info" added to it.

570   FBI interview of Albert Le Beau, June 26, 1968.

the man, he had thought it was Sirhan when he saw his picture in the paper, but when the FBI showed him a picture of Sirhan from three years earlier, Le Beau said the "skin of his face is too smooth." In Sirhan's mug shot, his face was beaten up and scratched, so he looked like he had an acne condition. But that was not what Sirhan looked like *before* he was captured. When Le Beau was asked if he could swear under oath the man was Sirhan, Le Beau "hung his head, stared at the floor for several long moments and then replied, 'No.'"[571] That said, the owner of the restaurant, Mrs. Felecia Maas, had hired a photographer that day, and according to an FBI report, "In one 8x10 photograph of a scene shot outside the restaurant there appears to be a male Latin-type answering the description of Sirhan standing in the crowd."[572] Maybe this was Sirhan. But I doubt it, for this reason. Whatever his faults, Sirhan was, according to the vast majority of reports, unfailingly polite to strangers. When Le Beau walked past the couple, he bumped the man he thought was Sirhan and said "excuse me." According to Le Beau, the person responded, in a surly manner, "why should I?" This just doesn't sound like Sirhan. But it sounds very much like the man who was upset that he couldn't be hired at the hotel as a waiter.[573]

Officer William Schneid saw this same couple when he worked security at Robbie's Restaurant that day. Just before Senator Kennedy and his party went upstairs, Schneid noticed a girl in her mid-twenties trying to get into the kitchen, but someone was not letting her in. Just before Kennedy walked up the stairs, Kennedy said to Schneid, "Officer, let them through," referring to the people waiting in line to have their tickets checked. The crowd surged around him at this and Schneid had to step aside.

At that moment, as Schneid told the FBI, he saw the same girl who had tried to get into the kitchen ducked into a booth on the north side of the staircase. "It was his impression that she was trying to get to someone," possibly the male companion seen with her on the stairs soon after. Schneid remembered this girl and the man with her being detained briefly on the stairs before they were allowed through.

Schneid felt the man bore a resemblance to Sirhan but was not Sirhan. For one, the man was taller. While the man was curly-haired and slim, Schneid pegged the man's height as about 5'6" or 5'7", taller than Sirhan. He put the girl in the 5'4" to 5'7" range and said she was "proportionate," with an "officious" manner. He said her hair was "medium to light brown." This sounds very much like the girl Sandra Serrano and Vince DiPierro saw, who bugged Conrad Seim incessantly for his press pass. But the man she was with

571   *Ibid.*
572   FBI interview of Mrs. Felecia Maas, June 26, 1968.
573   The FBI interview of Le Beau.

did not seem to match the description of Sirhan. This sounds instead like the taller doppelganger.

John Fahey's girl

DID JOHN FAHEY SPEND THE DAY WITH A GIRL WHO LATER donned a polka dot dress? In Chapter 1, we saw how John Henry Fahey met a woman who ended up spending the day with him. She claimed "they" were going to "get Kennedy tonight at the women reception" without explaining what she meant by "they" or "get."

The woman told Fahey she had just come from Beirut. "Is there a Beirut?" Fahey had asked Fernando Faura, not even knowing if that was a city or country.[574] She also mentioned Aqaba and other places in the Middle East. "She had travelled all over through the Arabic countries there," Fahey told Faura.

Faura believed the woman Fahey was with had been the girl in the polka dot dress. Faura had written one of the only news accounts of this girl, so he was familiar with some of the characteristics the police had announced publicly, including that she had a "funny" nose. So when Faura interviewed Fahey, he asked specifically about the girl's nose. Fahey mentioned that the woman had a "hooked" nose "of the fashion where you can realize she was from the Arab world." A "hook nose" is synonymous with a Roman nose, where the nose turns inward and downward, and Fahey also described it as a "Nasser nose," which also describes a nose that curves downward, not upward as Serrano, DiPierro[575] and other witnesses described. That description strongly indicates this was not the woman later seen in a polka dot dress, but some other woman likely involved in the plot.

Faura had taken Fahey to a police artist (who was not then working for the police) and had some pictures drawn which were then fleshed out by another artist and photographed. Faura then sent a representative of his to show the pictures to Vince DiPierro. But years later, when I showed DiPierro the same drawing, he had no reaction to that drawing at all, yet when I showed him a photograph of a voluptuously shaped woman in a polka dot dress (that Faura had staged for his newspaper), DiPierro had a visible and large reaction, as if suddenly remembering something intensely unpleasant. Although Faura quotes his associate's account of DiPierro's identification as having said, "That's the girl," Faura also presents enough evidence to disqualify this, because DiPierro noted several things that didn't fit what he remembered, saying *if* those facial characteristics were *different*, "That's the girl." That's not a solid identification. In addition, Fahey described

---

574   Transcript of Fernando Faura interview of John Fahey, June 12, 1968.
575   Faura, p. 119.

the woman as having dirty blonde hair, but nearly all witnesses to "the" girl in the polka dot dress said she had brunette or dark hair.

In addition, Khaiber Khan, an interesting character I wrote about in *The Assassinations: Probe Magazine on JFK, MLK, RFK and Malcolm X*, saw a man and a woman sitting in a blue Volkswagen in the rear of the Kennedy headquarters on Wilshire on June 3. He saw the same couple the next day, June 4, inside Kennedy's headquarters, but this time, the girl was wearing a "white dress with dark polka dots about the diameter of a penny." It appears then the girl in the polka dot dress was already wearing it while Fahey was still driving with his woman along the coast.[576]

Fahey also said the girl had blue eyes, which looked brown or green at times. Gray eyes can look blue, green or even brown depending on the light and surrounding colors. No one who saw the girl in the polka dot dress noted her eye color, and remember how Eve Hansen said in her taped interview that she had a thing for blue eyes, so if the girl in the polka dot dress had them, she probably would have noticed that. In other words, it appears the girl in the polka dot dress had brown eyes. Blue eyes, dirty blonde hair, and a nose that turned down, not up, means Fahey was not with the same girl Serrano and DiPierro saw in the company of Sirhan. But the fact that she wasn't the same girl doesn't make her any less interesting. It just broadens the number of participants a bit.

In one of Fahey's interviews, he remembered that the woman had shown him a picture of her child,[577] presumably the daughter who was at school on the East Coast.[578] One of the easiest ways to blackmail someone is to threaten their offspring. Many people are brave enough to withstand torture to themselves, but most people would rarely consent to the torture or death of a loved one, especially a child. If the woman had a baby that was not with her, that could explain why she felt compelled to participate in something that was clearly causing her distress. Fahey described how her hands were sweaty and she seemed very nervous.

Fahey also said a few things which led me to believe the woman may have been involved in the world of intelligence. She had a husband stationed or traveling between Guam and Taiwan,[579] which makes it sound like her husband was involved in the military or perhaps military intelligence. She spoke Arabic and English and had traveled extensively in the Middle East. She appeared to lie without compunction, telling Fahey her name was Alice, Virginia, Betty, and several other names, none of which appeared to be her real name. The last

---

576

577   LAPD interview of Ray La Scola, "an MD specializing in hypnotism," September 12, 1968. Faura had taken Fahey to La Scola in the hopes that Fahey would agree to be hypnotized. In the end, Fahey did not want to be hypnotized, but he talked about the girl and how during their conversation she had had shown him a picture of her child.

578   LAPD interview of Chris Gugas, September 13, 1968.

579   LAPD interview of Chris Gugas, September 13, 1968. Gugas was recounting what Fahey had remembered when Gugas gave him a polygraph test.

name she gave him was "Oppenheimer," a German name. But when Fahey spoke a few words in German to her, she did not appear to understand what he was saying. Fahey told Faura the girl claimed her own name as Oppenheimer, but she also showed him a picture of another woman and said *that* woman's name was Oppenheimer. She also referred to a man named Oppenheimer who was an official of the Federal Aviation Agency in Guam.

The woman claimed to have lived in many places, changing her current home each time she picked a place Fahey knew anything about. She said she had to ship a bunch of clothes ahead to Australia, presumably where she was headed next.[580] "She wanted to get out of the country—she was leaving the country,"[581] Fahey had told Hernandez during his polygraph session.

In one of his conversations with Faura, Fahey remembered the woman talking about catching a ride with CAT (Civil Air Transport), a known CIA front, or the Flying Tigers, a CIA-connected airline run by Colonel Claire Chennault. She mentioned having met Claire's wife Anna in New York. In 1968, Anna Chennault was helping Nixon and his backers sabotage President Lyndon B. Johnson's peace efforts in Vietnam so that Johnson could not run on having ended the war there (and so military contractors could continue to make their fortunes there).

Fahey's woman clearly had intelligence connections and appeared to be conflicted about whatever role she was supposed to play. Equally clearly, she was not the same person who had been seen by Serrano and DiPierro later that night.

A large group?

IT SHOULD BE CLEAR BY NOW THIS WAS NOT A QUICK HIT WITH one or two assassins, but a large operation with helpers and others that may have included members of the security force at the hotel.

After the assassination, Second Lieutenant Russell Davis of the U.S. Marine Corps told the FBI he thought he saw the police leading "three short, dark, possibly Puerto Rican, individuals" away when he got off an elevator on the Embassy Room level and saw the post-shooting tumult.[582] Were these just witnesses the police were escorting to its bus? Davis wouldn't have reported it to the FBI if he didn't think it was something more sinister.

Paul Burke, a public defender,[583] called the LAPD at 6:45 A.M. to say he saw "three carloads of Latins or Cubans being directed by a male in a gray uniform

---

580   LAPD interview of John Fahey, September 9, 1968.

581   *Ibid.*

582   FBI interview of Russell Davis, dated June 20, 1969 (yes, after Sirhan's trial was over). Davis was interviewed at the FBI facility at Quantico. This interview can be found in sub file X-8, volume 21.

583   LAPD Complaint Applications Log, 5:45 A.M., June 5, 1968.

in the rear-back-area of the Ambassador Hotel prior to the shooting. States the individual looked hard and surly looking." [584]The men in gray uniforms were from Ace Guard Service. The security men from the hotel had brown uniforms. If a hotel guest had reported this I would have dismissed this. But Burke, as a public defender, had seen a lot of hardened criminals in his time, and felt it worth reporting this group. That's significant.

Foreknowledge

PEOPLE LIKE TO POOH-POOH THE NOTION OF A LARGE OPERATION, saying if so many people were involved, why hasn't anyone talked? The Manhattan Project was kept secret for several years, despite employing many thousands of people. How many secrets have been kept that have never been exposed? We can't answer that. But there's one that we know about, because it is still redacted.

In the wake of the exposure that some of the people participating in the Watergate break-in had CIA backgrounds, in 1973, CIA Director James Schlesinger asked CIA employees to come forward and spill the beans on any illegal operations they knew about. The report put together from these revelations came to be known as the "Family Jewels." Members of the Church and Pike Committee members saw the Family Jewels. A number of people did. But to date, no one has told what's behind the redactions in Family Jewel #1. Although the CIA "released" the Jewels to the public in 2007, Jewel #1 remains, at the time of this writing, redacted. Whatever the CIA's top transgression was, we, the people, still don't know about it. See Figure 12.

---

584   LAPD Telephone Calls Received by Rampart Detective Division, 5 Jun 1968 thru 11 Jun 1968, 7:45 A.M. entry relaying information received from Lt. Lewis of the Intelligence division regarding what "that Att. Paul Burke" had said on the phone.

Figure 12: CIA Family Jewel #1 is still redacted as of November 2017

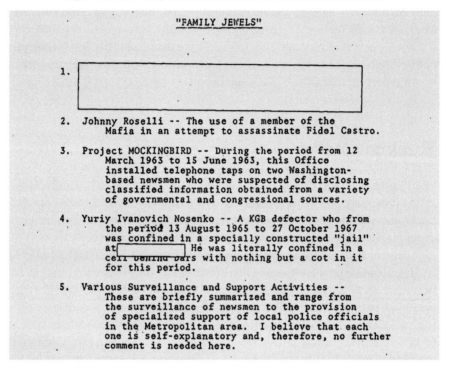

"FAMILY JEWELS"

1.

2. Johnny Roselli -- The use of a member of the
    Mafia in an attempt to assassinate Fidel Castro.

3. Project MOCKINGBIRD -- During the period from 12
    March 1963 to 15 June 1963, this Office
    installed telephone taps on two Washington-
    based newsmen who were suspected of disclosing
    classified information obtained from a variety
    of governmental and congressional sources.

4. Yuriy Ivanovich Nosenko -- A KGB defector who from
    the period 13 August 1965 to 27 October 1967
    was confined in a specially constructed "jail"
    at [   ] He was literally confined in a
    cell behind bars with nothing but a cot in it
    for this period.

5. Various Surveillance and Support Activities --
    These are briefly summarized and range from
    the surveillance of newsmen to the provision
    of specialized support of local police officials
    in the Metropolitan area. I believe that each
    one is self-explanatory and, therefore, no further
    comment is needed here.

When the CIA is involved, big secrets involving large groups of people can be kept forever. If you *can't* keep a secret forever, you can't get a job with the CIA. How is this guaranteed? You sign a vow of secrecy when you join the CIA. You can get fired or lose your pension or be jailed if you lose your pension. That's the official threat. Unofficially, Agency employees feel they could get killed for talking or, worse, that a family member could be made to suffer. Those are successful deterrents.

In addition, people are often chosen to work in such plots because their background makes them "plausibly deniable." The CIA doesn't usually send its employees out to kill someone. It asks its employees to recruit "cut-outs" who in turn hire their own assassins and take the fall if the plot does not succeed. Each person only knows their own small piece of the puzzle, but many don't know what puzzle they are a piece of. They have specific instructions and don't always know the end result of completing those instructions. This is called compartmentalization. That's how CIA and other secret agencies protect their operations from exposure.

Whoever planned this operation, however, didn't do it very well, because the plot was leaking like a sieve before it happened. At least four different people appeared to have some sort of foreknowledge of the events that were about to take place and at least two of them appeared to be trying to stop it.

The first person with foreknowledge was Michael Wayne or whoever was in the electrician's booth. The strange man Daniel Hall talked to who hinted of something big to happen at the hotel may have been this same person in the electrician's booth, so we'll leave the count at one here, even though these may well have been two different people.

The second person who provably displayed foreknowledge was the woman who spent the day with John Fahey who told him that Kennedy would be killed that night.

The third person with possible foreknowledge of a plot was a woman who could not have been Fahey's woman because she was seen in Los Angeles at the same time that Fahey was still on the road with his woman. Christine De Sautels told both the LAPD and FBI that on the afternoon of the primary, as she was about to leave Kennedy's headquarters on Wilshire, a young woman knocked on the window of her car at the curb.

"I know you work in there," the woman said, referring to the Kennedy campaign office. "You've got to take me to the racetrack. Have to inform some people out there to save this country."

De Sautels was on her way to pick someone up and said she couldn't help.

"Don't take me wrong, I don't want to go out there and bet. You have to help me save the country. He is going to be killed," the mystery woman said.

De Sautels suggested the woman go inside to the Kennedy headquarters with her story, but the woman was persistent.

"There are people at Hollywood Park who have to know about this. We've got to keep him from being killed." Given Sirhan's connections to the horse racing world, this comment especially seemed to indicate actual knowledge of the plot rather than some paranoid fantasy, but De Sautels had no way of knowing that at the time.

At this point another woman came up and asked De Sautels to move her car, and while the first woman responded to the second woman, De Sautels drove off. When she came back later that afternoon, she asked around at Kennedy headquarters to see if anyone had seen the woman who had warned of a plot.

De Sautels described the woman as "possibly of Latin descent as she had a dark complexion," mid-twenties, with long brown hair with "blond highlights." She was slender, wearing capris and carrying a notebook "and a large bag-type purse." De Sautels wouldn't have given the woman another thought had Kennedy not been killed that night.[585]

---

585   Conversation recreated from three records: the June 5 LAPD telephone log entry (11:30 A.M. under Wiggins, citing Officer Don Kringen's account of the call, the LAPD interview of "Kristine Destutels" [sic] on June 25, 1968, and the FBI interview of Christine De Sautels.

There was one more person who appeared to know Kennedy would be killed that night: William Crosson.

As we saw in the first chapter, a former Army Sergeant had repeatedly approached the hotel desk where Donald Reinke and Gail Farrar worked to try to warn that Kennedy would be killed. The police and FBI either accidentally or deliberately misrepresented parts of this story.

William Frederick "Billy" Crosson was born May 9, 1922 in Iowa. He married at age 24 in California and had three children, one of which was named Steven William Crosson. (I tried to find Steven, but it appears he died of lung cancer in Ojai in 2002.) Later, Crosson divorced. He died a year and a month after the assassination at the young age of 47, per the Social Security Death Index.

Crosson was arrested by the Venice Division of the LAPD the day after Kennedy was killed, i.e., June 6, 1968. And here is where the story seems to have been deliberately misrepresented.

According to the LAPD's cardfile entry, Crosson was arrested on June 6 for being "plain drunk." The same card indicates a letter by Crosson to Senator Kennedy—written before he was killed—was booked as evidence item 52. I contacted the California State Archives to get a copy of this letter, but was told there were only scraps of paper and nothing that resembled a letter in the evidence envelope. Given how the LAPD had changed evidence that pointed to conspiracy, I wonder if the letter contained something that necessitated its disappearance.

In its summary of Reinke's interview, the LAPD noted that Crosson had been arrested at the Los Angeles International Airport. That was not true. The following is the story reconstructed from the Emergency Control Center (ECC) Log and the LAPD's own final report on the assassination.

Around 11:30 A.M. on June 6, 1968, according to the ECC log, "an unidentified man was arrested by LAPD 100 yards from [the plane that was taking the] Kennedy Family [back home]. He was threatening to kill members of Kennedy family. Susp held at Airport Sub Station." This appears to be untrue, as the Final Report cites an Army Intelligence officer's report that indicated "Crosson had made a remark earlier to a complaining witness that the Senator's airplane had been sabotaged and that he, Crosson, had to get to the Kennedy family to protect them."[586] That sounds more like the man who tried to warn that Kennedy would be killed at the Ambassador Hotel. In the ECC log, there was no such clarification. Indeed, he was described as appearing "psycho" and was "being held for FBI info from det. Tom Nieto—Venice Div." The log did clarify he was arrested at a bar near the airport, not on the tarmac.

And what a story the FBI had to tell. Although Crosson's name does not

---

586   SUS Final Report, p. 288.

appear in the document I'm about to cite, as the subject is redacted, it's clear from the information provided that this person was Crosson.

According to a partially redacted FBI report dated July 16, 1968, Crosson had gone to the FBI the night of May 23, 1968. The FBI writer of the memo, whose name is also redacted, wrote that Crosson had visited the FBI office in Los Angeles on several occasions. "On each visit to the office subject always left some type of material of no value." But the next sentence immediately belies that assertion: "On 5/29/68, the subject [Crosson] was located through investigation by the writer and contacted concerning the items he had left at the FBI office." If he left nothing of value, *why did the FBI go to the trouble of locating him?* "During the telephone conversation," the FBI Special Agent wrote, Crosson offered to work for the FBI, stating he "had been doing work for the CIA for five years and that no one would listen to him." Why wouldn't the CIA listen to him? Perhaps because Crosson told the FBI agent "that Senator Kennedy would be in Los Angeles campaigning and he 'did not want to have another Dallas incident.'"

The FBI Special Agent then asked Crosson if he was making a threat. Crosson denied that he was.

So at least twice before the assassination, to the FBI and on site at the hotel, Crosson had tried to sound the alarm on a plot that eventually came to fruition. If he was just a nut, it was an uncanny coincidence. What the FBI agent put in next made me think it was the writer, not Crosson, who was the nut. The agent wrote, "Subject was arrested by the Venice Division, LAPD, on 6/7/68," an incorrect statement as Crosson had been arrested on June 6, "when he made statements to the effect that he had intended to blow up the plane carrying the body of Senator Kennedy back to New York." But as we saw, both the LAPD and Army Intelligence reported that Crosson was trying to warn that a bomb might blow up the Kennedy plane. In other words, Crosson was trying to protect, not assault, the family.

So clearly, the FBI author of the memo was not factual, whether accidentally or deliberately, in his report. I believe it was for the latter purpose, based on what the agent wrote next:

> [Redacted] VA Hospital, Sepulveda, California, advised her records reflect subject arrested while in Ojai, California, and taken to Camarillo State hospital where he made that statement that he was assigned the task of killing the person who killed Senator Robert F. Kennedy. [Redacted] he was presently at the VA Hospital, Sepulveda, however, she was calling to determine if subject wanted by the FBI.[587]

---

587   FBI memo from [Redacted] to [Redacted], July 16, 1968, found in the L.A. FBI Field Office files, 56-156-1382.

What a bizarre story. He was assigned the task of killing the person who killed Senator Robert F. Kennedy, but then taken to a hospital. Note that the report does not say "mental hospital," but that was my first thought when I saw he had been taken to the VA hospital. Maybe the guy was just crazy.

But maybe he wasn't crazy at all, because there are two historical precedents for such a task. One person claimed to have been tasked with killing the "shooter" (or patsy) before the assassination. Another was tasked with killing shooters after an assassination. And in both cases, the person assassinated was President John F. Kennedy.

On September 20, 1963, a former military officer who had suffered brain damage during the war, Richard Case Nagell, went into a bank, fired two shots into the wall. He didn't want to rob the bank. He wanted to get arrested.

He claimed he was afraid he might be killed for his knowledge of an upcoming plot to kill President Kennedy and knew the safest place he could be was federal custody. Crazy? Or crazy like a fox?

When arrested, Nagell had a document on him that named six CIA officers. Nagell claimed he had been serving as a double-agent for the CIA, pretending to work with a KGB officer in Mexico City. After President Kennedy's assassination, Nagell claimed that he had learned of a plot to kill Kennedy and that the KGB asked him to kill Oswald in the hopes of preventing the plot from taking place. This alone would not be much evidence of anything, but when Nagell was arrested, he had on him the name Richard Fecteau and the notation that Fecteau was CIA at a time when that information was not publicly known.

Fecteau and John Downey had been captured in the 1950s by Chinese Communists while on a mission for the CIA near Manchuria. The CIA denied the two were employees for decades until after the men were returned to the U.S. in the 1970s.

Nagell also had, to the CIA's consternation, the names of six other CIA employees in the paper on him at the time of the arrest. The Director of Security at CIA at the time, Robert L. Bannerman, wrote FBI director J. Edgar Hoover on behalf of CIA Director Richard Helms a request for the FBI to not reveal those names and to let the agency know how those names came to be in Nagell's possession.[588] Nagell was not an agency employee, but he appeared to be a "vest pocket operation," meaning run by a single CIA employee without the knowledge of the rest of the agency, in his dealings. Interested readers should pick up *The Man Who Knew Too Much* for Dick Russell's decades-long pursuit of the truth about Nagell and his story.

Naturally, because such an account implicated the CIA in the assassination

---

588   Letter from R.L. Bannerman on behalf of the CIA Director to The Director, Federal Bureau of Investigation, stamped 1 April 1964, NARA Record Number: 1993.07.26.18:08:25:000590, viewable at www.maryferrell.org/showDoc.html?docId=103975&search=Nagell#relPageId=83&tab=page.

of President Kennedy, CIA defenders claim Nagell was mentally ill or mentally unstable and therefore nothing he said could be believed. But that would not explain how he came to know secret information about several CIA employees.

In the 1990s, the Assassination Records Review Board (ARRB) was created by Congress in the wake of Oliver Stone's film *JFK*, which opened the eyes of many to the evidence of conspiracy in the case. At the end of the film was a note about how many more years the files on the case would remain secret. A public outcry caused Congress to appoint a board to release as many files as possible. The ARRB found Nagell credible and wanted to subpoena tapes and other records he claimed to have kept regarding the actual participants in the plot to kill President Kennedy. But Nagell died in his Los Angeles area home just before the letter reached him.

There is another man who was sent to kill assassins *after* the plot had taken place. In the files of the Church Committee are a number of documents about a man named Roland "Bud" Culligan. He had apparently been set up on a false criminal charge by the CIA to keep him from talking about some of the many covert operations he had been involved with, some of which involved assassinations. He claimed that, among other "Executive Action" plots he had been involved in, he had shot down UN Secretary Dag Hammarskjöld's plane. Hammarskjöld and Kennedy had sided with Patrice Lumumba against the Allen Dulles-Richard Helms faction in the CIA that wanted Lumumba removed so business interests could exploit the rare earth mineral wealth in the Katanga province of Congo.

Feeling burned by the CIA, Culligan reached out to people at various levels of the U.S. government and was eventually given the opportunity to testify, in writing, as to what he knew about assassinations. One task Culligan described was being sent to kill the shooters involved in the assassination of President John F. Kennedy. One way to keep participants in a plot silent forever is simply to kill them after the fact. Culligan claimed he lured the assassins with the promise of a new job, and then killed them at the meeting place. As I explained in my testimony to the recent UN Commission on the Hammarskjöld case, I believe Culligan knew about the CIA's role in the Kennedy assassination but deliberately lied about part of this. He wanted the CIA to know that if he weren't freed from jail, he could tell much more. Soon after this testimony, Culligan was, in fact, freed from jail.

Was Crosson a CIA employee? Was he a contract agent like Culligan? Was he a vest pocket operation, like Nagell appeared to be? Or was Crosson simply crazy and happened to be correct that someone was going to kill Kennedy that night? After all, no one blew up the plane that flew the Kennedy family back to the East Coast. But maybe he wasn't crazy at all. And while he was clearly drinking heavily in the wake of the killing of Kennedy, which he had sought to prevent, neither Reinke nor Farrar said anything about Crosson being drunk when he spoke to them. Maybe he was just an American trying to prevent a tragedy about to happen, who then drank himself into an arrest in his grief.

So now we reach the final and most important question. The sheer number of bullets and bullet holes prove there was a conspiracy. There were numerous people who seemed to play a role in the events of the night. So why has Sirhan maintained to this day that cannot remember any co-conspirators?

There are only two possibilities since brain damage was ruled out early in this case. Either Sirhan is lying, or he is telling the truth. And if he is telling the truth, what caused the hole in his memory?

MIND GAMES

"I find no explanation for Sirhan as satisfactory as the hypothesis that he has been acting and talking under hypnosis or in posthypnotic suggestion."

SO NOW, WE FINALLY COME TO SIRHAN HIMSELF. HE FIRED AT Senator Kennedy and was clearly part of the plot. But what was his level of guilt? Was someone manipulating him?

Sirhan claimed to have no memory of the events in the pantry, and neither the defense psychologist, Dr. Bernard Diamond, nor the prosecution psychologist, Dr. Seymour Pollack, could retrieve a clear memory of the shooting from Sirhan's mind, even after repeated attempts with hypnosis. Medical examinations ruled out the possibility of some physical impediment or brain damage. So why couldn't Sirhan remember?

If Sirhan has been lying all this time, we have to ask, 50 years later, what's the point? He's already in jail for life with no likelihood of parole. Why keep up the charade, if that's all it is? Why not just tell what happened? Who could he be trying to protect? All his family except his youngest brother are now dead.

But if Sirhan were lying, that would also mean he was conscious of the plot. Why, then, would he volunteer to be a patsy in it? Why did he fire no bullets at all in the pantry? This is why it is important to study the ballistics evidence first. Once you understand that if he had fired even a *single* bullet, the police would have kept, not switched, at least *that* bullet, instead of switching *all* the bullets the experts examined in 1975, you begin to understand what really happened.

To suggest Sirhan was lying simply does not fit the physical evidence.

If Sirhan is telling the truth about not remembering the shooting scene in the pantry, what prevents him from remembering? He didn't have brain damage, and no one reported seeing Sirhan drunk. Could Sirhan have been under the influence of a drug? If so, it was nothing the LAPD recognized or, perhaps, wished to acknowledge, because Chief Reddin assured the public Sirhan was not under the influence of any drug.

The most likely cause of Sirhan's memory loss was hypnosis. Some people are more hypnotizable than others, and amnesia can be caused by hypnosis. A hypnotist can also instruct some people to forget what was said under hypnosis. And people in a deep trance often have no conscious memory of what transpired in that state, regardless of whether an instruction to forget was issued. That would explain why Sirhan cannot remember clearly what happened. It would also explain why he doesn't remember being hypnotized. (He couldn't even remember being hypnotized each time Diamond hypnotized him.)

It would explain why Sirhan could not identify any co-conspirators. It would also explain his strange state upon arrest, not understanding fully where he was or even that he had been arrested. It would explain why he couldn't honestly answer if he had a wife or not—he truly couldn't remember. Being in a trance state would also explain his unusually calm and cool demeanor that witnesses noticed during the events in the pantry.

Most researchers on this case who get this far believe that Sirhan was in a hypnotic state or acting out a post-hypnotic command at the time of the firing. But why would any conspirator go to the trouble to program an assassin when so many were readily available for hire? Wouldn't a man in a hypnotic state pose a risk? What if someone inadvertently said something that brought him back out of hypnosis? It's a risky variable.

In addition, using a mind-controlled assassin in a crowd with multiple shooters never made sense to me. What if your mind-controlled puppet missed and killed your more skilled assassin by mistake? That would be a dumb risk to take. And if you were an assassin, would you willingly participate in such an assignment, knowing someone might be firing *real* bullets in your direction but in a hypnotic state? No one in their right mind would agree to participate in such a plot. But if you were told the man firing at you was only firing blanks that would pull focus so you could shoot Kennedy unseen and escape, that's a plot an assassin could be comfortable with.

So what is hypnosis, exactly? Experts disagree on exactly what hypnosis is. Some believe it represents enhanced concentration. Others describe it as a partial sleep state, hence the common appearance of the term "somnambulism" in the literature. The common understanding is that hypnosis is a state in which people are more susceptible to suggestion, but the level of suggestibility varies widely from person to person and by the depth of the trance state. Someone only lightly hypnotized will remember everything that happened under hypnosis. Someone in a deep trance may not remember anything that happened under hypnosis. Experts agree that roughly one in five people, or about 20% of the population, are so susceptible to suggestions under hypnosis that you can get them to perform extraordinary acts that the other 80% of the population would never do.

Just about every hypnotist you ask will tell you authoritatively that people cannot be hypnotized "against their will." But this really isn't the issue. The problem is that people can be hypnotized "without their knowledge." For example, a simple relaxation exercise can be a means to hypnotize someone without their realization that this is occurring.

You will hear that no one can be made to do something under hypnosis that they wouldn't do outside of hypnosis. This is both technically true and dramatically misleading, because people can be tricked under hypnosis into believing the facts are other than they really are. People can be made to do terrible things when they believe that alternate reality. A skilled hypnotist can make a highly suggestible subject do just about anything. Allen Dulles, the infamous CIA chief responsible for creating the CIA's formal mind control programs, described the influence one person could have over another under hypnosis in this manner: "[T]he brain ... becomes a phonograph playing a disc put on its spindle by an outside genius over which it has no control."[589]

In response to the notion that one cannot be made to do something under hypnosis they wouldn't do outside of hypnosis, one of the CIA's hypnosis experts, whose name is still redacted more than 60 years later (and who likely died long ago), wrote:

> Frankly, I now distrust much of what is written by academic experts on hypnotism. Partly this is because many of them appear to have generalized from a very few cases; partly because much of their cautious pessimism is contradicted by Agency experimenters; but more particularly because I *personally have witnessed behavior responses which respected experts have said are impossible to obtain.* In no other field have I been so conscious of the mental claustrophobia of book and lecture hall knowledge. I don't think we have enough evidence to say positively that hypnotism is a practicable covert weapon, but I do say that we'll never know whether it is or is not unless we experiment in the field

---

589   Alan W. Scheflin and Edward M. Opton, Jr., *The Mind Manipulators* (Paddington Press, 1978), p. 437.

where we can learn what is practicable (materially and psychologically)
in a way that no laboratory worker could possibly prove.[590]

Translation: the author of this memo had already seen cases where people
were made to do under hypnosis things they would not do outside of hypnosis.
The author ridiculed academics who claimed such results were not possible. The
author believed that hypnosis was ready to be tested in covert field operations. And
this was *13 years before* Senator Kennedy's assassination. Imagine how much more
skilled the Agency's hypnotists became after an additional 13 years of experience.

Sometimes people in hypnotic states look half asleep, or in some other way
"out of it." You may have noticed this in staged hypnosis demonstrations. But not
all hypnotized subjects will look sleepy or unnatural. Some will appear under
hypnosis exactly the same way they appear when not hypnotized. According to
George Estabrooks, a lifelong experimenter whose prolific contributions on the
subject caused others to call him "the father of modern hypnosis":

> We can coach the subject so that in the trance he will behave exactly
> as in the waking state. Under these circumstances we could defy
> anyone, even a skilled psychologist, to tell whether the subject was
> "asleep" or "awake." There are tests which will tell the story but in
> warfare we cannot run around sticking pins into everyone we meet
> just to see if he is normal.[591]

"Sticking pins" refers to a common test used to determine if someone is
faking being hypnotized. With the proper suggestion, a hypnotist can insert a
pin into the top of a subject's hand and the subject will feel no pain. Someone
who is faking being hypnotized, however, will usually squeal in pain. In fact, a
famous superlawyer of the time, F. Lee Bailey, found something worse than a pin
sticking out of his hand at a hypnosis demonstration at the hands of Dr. William
J. Bryan, as Alison Winter recounted in her book *Memory*:

> F. Lee Bailey ... described meeting Bryan in 1961 in San Francisco at
> one of Belli's popular series of one-day seminars, this one featuring
> Bryan as the main event. Bailey was among a group of volunteers
> Bryan used to demonstrate his technique. He instructed them to
> hold out their right arms. He then described their arms as feeling
> stiff and numb. Suddenly, at a command from Bryan, Bailey became

---

590   Internal CIA memo titled "Hypnosis and Covert Operations," from and to redacted names, dated 5 May
1955, CIA Electronic Reading Room, (FOIA) /ESDN (CREST): 0000140404. Several pages of this document are missing.
591   George Estabrooks, *Hypnotism* (New York: E.P. Dutton & Co., Inc., 1957), pp. 197–198.

aware that a hypodermic needle had been stuck through his hand. Bryan explained that this was an example of hypnotic amnesia. But there was more: there was no blood where the needle had entered the skin. Bryan then told his subjects that they would soon see a slight drop of blood appear "in response to my suggestion." The blood appeared as he spoke. [592]

If Sirhan had been in a trance before, during and after the shooting, that would explain the behavior that others witnessed. To most people, he seemed normal, but to a few who got close to him during or in the hours immediately following the shooting, something seemed terribly off.

Sergeant William Jordan, who saw Sirhan the most in the hours following the shooting, said: "I was impressed by Sirhan's composure and relaxation. He appeared less upset to me than individuals arrested for a traffic violation."[593]

Remember how Assistant District Attorney John Howard found it necessary to ask Sirhan if he knew where he was or that he had been booked? Sirhan had answered, "I don't know." When Howard asked Sirhan "Do you understand where you are?" Sirhan had responded strangely: "As long as you say it." Sirhan then asked if he had been before a judge, and Howard told him he had not, yet. Was Sirhan programmed to respond a certain way until after he had been before a judge? How would one not know if he had been before a judge or not unless there was something seriously wrong with his mind at that point?

Remember too how Sirhan refused to reveal his identity but talked about many other subjects, as if he had been given a post-hypnotic instruction not to divulge his identity (perhaps until after he had seen the judge). Remember how Sirhan was unable to answer if he were married or not.

Sirhan showed abnormal strength in the pantry, which can also be a sign of a hypnotized state. Without the intervention of conscious thought, sometimes the body is capable of extraordinary acts. Remember how Sirhan could tell time, without a watch or any visible clock. All of those are signs one would expect to find in one in a hypnotic state.

In the pantry, during the struggle, several people commented on how unnatural Sirhan's calm demeanor seemed relative to the shooting. George Plimpton, the famous writer (and, as we learned in later years, a CIA asset),[594] was one of the men who tackled Sirhan. In his first interview after the shooting, he said that he couldn't be certain of anything the shooter was wearing, but that he could

---

592   Alison Winter, *Memory: Fragments of a Modern History* (University of Chicago Press, 2012), p. 128.

593   SUS Final Report, p. 312.

594   See Joel Whitney's book *Finks*, which talks about how the CIA co-opted and in some cases corrupted leading intellectual and cultural leaders to serve nefarious purposes. Tom Braden, another CIA asset in this category, was also in the hotel that night. I don't believe Plimpton or Braden had anything to do with the events that transpired.

"tell you all about his eyes," which he described as "dark brown and enormously peaceful," which seemed incongruous in the pandemonium in the pantry.[595]

Vince DiPierro thought Sirhan had a sickly smile. Other witnesses, like Yoshio Niwa, were disturbed that Sirhan was smiling during such a heinous event. Sirhan's unnatural strength—being able to hold off about six men and keeping the gun from professional football player Rosey Grier as long as he did—was also an indicator of hypnosis. Under hypnosis people have demonstrated the ability to do things physically they would not be able to do under ordinary circumstances.

One of the tests to see whether someone is faking being hypnotized or not is to see if the pupils are dilated. People who are faking hypnosis can't make their pupils dilate. But dilated pupils happen naturally under hypnosis. Remember that when Officer Placencia first reported on Sirhan's condition, he had said "His pupils were real wide," a statement he confirmed under oath during the trial.

Not long after Sirhan had seen the judge, in his new cell at the County Jail, Sirhan told Dr. Marcus Crahan that he felt a chill.[596] He later experienced similar chills coming out of Dr. Bernard Diamond's hypnosis. Had Sirhan been given some sort of post-hypnotic command to forget who he was until he was arraigned?

After talking to Sirhan the morning of his arrest, Sheriff Peter Pitchess said Sirhan was "a very unusual prisoner, a young man of apparently complete self-possession, totally unemotional."[597]

One incident often cited as evidence that Sirhan was in a hypnotic trance was when Sirhan gazed unspeaking at a teletype machine. Mary Grohs told Robert Kaiser that Sirhan was:

> Just staring. I'll never forget his eyes. I asked him what he wanted. He didn't answer. I asked him again. No answer. I said that if he wanted the latest figures on Senator Kennedy, he'd have to check the other machine. He still didn't answer. He just kept staring.[598]

When Kaiser asked Grohs if she thought Sirhan was in a trance, she said, "Oh, no, he wasn't under hypnosis,"[599] which we just saw is a pointless observation as you cannot always tell. Kaiser hadn't mentioned hypnosis. He wondered if Grohs had read something about Sirhan being hypnotized during the trial or if she'd been coached. Kaiser said Grohs offered that she thought maybe Sirhan didn't speak English and that's why he didn't respond. Kaiser pointed out Sirhan spoke English just fine at the trial. When he asked again why she thought Sirhan didn't

595   LAPD interview of George Plimpton, June 5, 1968.

596   Kaiser, p. 89.

597   Kaiser, p. 90.

598   Sworn declaration of Robert Blair Kaiser, February 13, 2012.

599   Ibid.

answer, according to Kaiser, Grohs asked, "What was your name again? I want to talk to the police about you. They told me not to say anything about this."[600]

At the trial, Sirhan had an explanation for his behavior, which matched my own experience of the first time I saw a teletype. He was in awe of a typewriter typing by itself. I had a similar experience the first time I saw one, so personally I found that explanation plausible. In addition, Sirhan truly seemed to have no memory of what he did in a hypnotic state, but he remembered the incident with Mary Grohs. So I'm not convinced that incident was evidence of a hypnotic state. But it's interesting that the police were intent about keeping Mary Grohs silent about the incident.

In their attempt to save Sirhan's life, the defense team argued Sirhan was a paranoid schizophrenic who fell into a self-induced trance due to the lights and mirrors in the Ambassador Hotel, a scenario Diamond described to the jury as "absurd, preposterous, unlikely and incredible." How would you like to be defended from the death penalty by a team of lawyers who called their own explanation for your innocence "absurd, preposterous, unlikely and incredible"?

The medical and psychological professionals who examined Sirhan's test results in a battery of psychological tests believed Sirhan had killed Senator Kennedy, so they were predisposed to find signs of a sick mind. Not one expert before the trial was given the results without being told they were Sirhan's, which would have been the only way for someone to have made an unbiased determination. And despite the lengthy presentation of these experts, the jury remained unconvinced that Sirhan was mentally ill. When Sirhan's Rorschach ink blot test results were given to a qualified professional decades later without the results being identified as Sirhan, the professional found no indication of mental illness.[601]

Dr. Eduard Simson-Kallas was the head of the psychological testing program at San Quentin, where Sirhan was initially incarcerated. After spending time with Sirhan, he realized that Sirhan was not schizophrenic and suspected he might have been hypnotically programmed. But prison officials stepped in when they felt Dr. Simson-Kallas was "making a career out of Sirhan." The interference prompted a frustrated Dr. Simson-Kallas to resign, saying "A medical doctor spends as much time with a patient as the disease demands. So does a psychologist."[602]

Dr. Simson-Kallas was also not impressed with Sirhan's defense team's analysis, as Turner and Christian reported:

---

600   *Ibid.*

601   Declaration of Dr. Daniel P. Brown, Ph.D., Exhibit I, Petitioner's Supplemental Brief, 23 Apr 2011, www.maryferrell.org/showDoc.html?docId=146777&search=Exhibit_I#relPageId=43&tab=page.

602   Turner and Christian, p. 201.

382 A LIE TOO BIG TO FAIL

Simson displayed equal indignation when he talked about the testimony of Dr. Diamond and other psychiatrists at the Sirhan trial, which he labeled the "psychiatric blunder of the century." He scoffed at Diamond's self-induction theory, pointing out that it is utterly impossible for a person to place himself in such a deep trance that he suffers an amnesia block. [603]

Simson-Kallas reported that Sirhan was "easily influenced, had no real roots and was looking for a cause," and that the Arab-Israeli conflict could have been used to manipulate him.[604]

Sirhan's original defense team approached his defense backwards. They *assumed* Sirhan was guilty and tried to build an explanation for his guilt that would protect him from the death penalty. Had the defense dealt honestly with the ballistics evidence first, had they realized that not only was Sirhan too far away to have killed Kennedy, but that Sirhan's gun fired none of the bullets recovered from victims in the pantry, necessitating the switching of several bullets, they could have presented an entirely different defense. And that's the generous spin to put on the horrible defense Sirhan was given.

Because numerous studies have shown the brain is still recording during hypnosis, even when amnesia is present, Dr. Diamond hypnotized Sirhan for the defense team in a number of sessions to attempt to get him to recall what happened. The problem was that Diamond believed Sirhan had killed Kennedy, and all his questions had that as an assumption. As a result, Diamond's work on Sirhan was designed to produce a specific result. He wasn't interested in an open-ended investigation into what might have been in Sirhan's mind during the period of the shooting. So Diamond very nearly induced a memory in Sirhan through his work. And Diamond, if he were still alive, would be hard-pressed to deny that, given that he wrote a paper for the *California Law Review* in 1980 that became widely cited in court cases that one can be made to say false things under hypnosis and that courts should bar witnesses who had been hypnotized:

> I believe that once a potential witness has been hypnotized for the purposes of enhancing memory his recollections have been so contaminated that he is rendered effectively incompetent to testify. Hypnotized persons, being extremely suggestible, graft onto their memories fantasies or suggestions deliberately or unwittingly communicated by the hypnotist. After hypnosis the subject cannot differentiate between a true recollection and a fantasy or a suggested

---

603   Turner and Christian, p. 201.
604   Turner and Christian, p. 199.

detail. Neither can any expert trier of fact. This risk is so great, in my view, that the use of hypnosis by police on a potential witness is tantamount to the destruction or fabrication of evidence.[605]

In a footnote to his landmark article, Diamond noted that he was not discussing anything related to the Sirhan case. But it's hard not to listen to the tapes of Diamond and Sirhan and recognize that Diamond should have taken considerably more care with Sirhan.

Whether organically or at the direction of someone else, by 1968, Sirhan had developed a strong belief in the power of the mind. During the 1960s, stories appeared in magazines and newspapers about "psychokinesis," a power to move an object solely with the mind, known colloquially as "mind over matter." Sirhan tried, in his home and out in the world, to affect the actions of inanimate and animate objects.

Sirhan read in a publication from the Rosicrucians that "if you want something, write it down," and you will get it. That became Sirhan's explanation for the appearance of "R.F.K. must die" in his notebook. On the day he wrote that page, he said, he had just learned that Kennedy supported sending bombers to Israel, and that really made him mad. Sirhan claimed he had seen a program on TV about this, but no news or TV show has ever surfaced that could explain where Sirhan got that information on that particular day. Was that the real explanation? More likely, someone induced him to write that through a hypnotic suggestion, and Sirhan tried to explain it after the fact. After that day, though, Sirhan said, "I forgot it all. The idea of killing Kennedy never entered my mind, sir. I just wanted, sir, to stop him from sending planes to Israel," Sirhan told his defense team.[606]

Sirhan didn't understand why he would have focused so much attention on Kennedy in his notebook, rather than what he had always really wanted. Sirhan had always been interested in becoming rich. He'd never expressed an interest in becoming a political martyr until after the assassination, and then he only chose that when the alternative was to say he was crazy.

Sirhan had only questions as to how he happened to be at the hotel that night with a loaded gun:

> "Why did I not go to the races that day? Why did I not like the horses? Why did I go to that range? Why did I save those Mini-Mags? Why did I not expend those bullets? Why did I go to Bob's? Why did Mistri give

---

605   Bernard L. Diamond, "Inherent Problems in the Use of Pretrial Hypnosis on a Prospective Witness."
606   Kaiser, p. 238.

me that newspaper? Why did I drink that night?" As Sirhan rattled
this litany of deeds, he clenched his fists and planted his feet solidly
on the floor as if protesting and resisting—what? "It was," he said,
"*like some inner force.* [Emphasis added.]"[607]

What Sirhan described sounded like a textbook case of hypnotic compulsion. While experts agree that about 20% of the population is highly
hypnotizable, a subset of these people can be manipulated in unsettling ways.
University of California at Berkeley Professor John F. Kihlstrom noted that
"Among those individuals who are most highly hypnotizable, these alterations
in consciousness are associated with subjective conviction bordering on delusion, and an experience of involuntariness bordering on compulsion."[608] And
this compulsion doesn't just persist in the hypnotic state. The compulsion
happens even when the subject is awake, after having received a post-hypnotic
command or trigger.

George Estabrooks, one of the preeminent authorities on hypnosis in the
twentieth century, wrote in his 1947 book *Spiritism* about how difficult it is for
subjects to resist post-hypnotic suggestions, *even when the subject suspects the origin.*
Estabrooks described an experiment which demonstrated this effect:

> One peculiar thing about these post-hypnotic suggestions is their
> compulsive force. One of our greatest modern authorities tried the
> following experiment. He suggested to a subject that after he awoke
> [from hypnosis] and on a given signal he would go to the window,
> cut a pack of cards which was placed there, select the ace of spades
> and give it to the hypnotist. He was then awakened and the signal
> was given.
>
> Now, as it happened, the subject was a graduate student in psy-
> chology at one of our large universities and so was perfectly familiar
> with every phase of hypnotism. On the signal he started for the pack
> of cards and then suddenly stopped.
>
> "You know," he said, "I believe that's a post-hypnotic suggestion."
>
> "What do you want to do?" asked the operator.
>
> "I want to go to that pack of cards, select the ace of spades, and
> give it to you."

607   Kaiser, p. 238.

608   John F. Kihlstrom, "Hypnosis, Memory, and Amnesia," presented at the 75th annual meeting of the
Association for Research in Nervous and Mental Disease, "Biological and Psychological Perspectives on Memory and
Memory Disorders," New York, December 1995. According to the author's webpage with this talk, "An edited version
of the original presentation was published in the *Philosophical Transactions of the Royal Society: Biological Sciences* as part of
a special issue, "Biological and Psychological Perspectives on Memory and Memory Disorders," edited by L.R. Squire
and D.L. Schacter (1997, 372, 1727–1732)," https://www.ocf.berkeley.edu/~jfkihlstrom/.

"You are right. It is a post-hypnotic suggestion. What are you doing to do about it?"

"I'm not going to carry it out."[609]

The hypnotist then bet the subject 50 cents he would not be able to resist the post-hypnotic suggestion. For the next two hours, the subject found himself wandering over to the deck, realizing what he was doing, and stopping himself. By the end of the afternoon, he found himself unable to concentrate on anything else. He went back to the deck, pulled out the ace of spades, and gave it to his hypnotist along with a dollar. "He could obtain no peace of mind," Estabrooks said, "until he had obeyed the suggestion."[610] *And this was someone who was fully aware that he had been hypnotized and recognized the source of his compulsion.* How much more quickly would an unsuspecting subject have given in to the suggestion?

A disturbing phenomenon of hypnosis is how few people, unlike the trained psychological student in the example above, will be unable to attribute their compulsions and actions to the actual cause, because the conscious mind is unaware of suggestion made under hypnosis, as Estabrooks explained:

> One of the most astounding things about the post-hypnotic suggestion is the subject's conviction that he is acting of his own free will. For instance, I tell a subject that he will repeat the alphabet to me backwards on a given signal after awakening. Then I say to him, "Allen, why did you repeat the alphabet to me?
>
> For a moment he is puzzled and then he replies, "Why, as a matter of fact I heard you say about a month ago to someone that the average person couldn't do it backwards and I just wanted to show you I could."[611]

There are numerous examples of this sort in the literature on hypnosis. Unaware of the true source of their behaviors, hypnotized subjects will invent explanations to justify those behaviors.

Sirhan demonstrated this behavior in front of his defense team. At one point, Dr. Bernard Diamond hypnotized Sirhan in his prison cell to demonstrate to his defense attorneys how suggestible Sirhan was. Diamond told the hypnotized Sirhan that when Diamond blew his nose with a large white handkerchief that Sirhan would climb the bars of this prison cell "like a monkey." Diamond brought him out of hypnosis, but the suggestion had been successfully implanted. After

---

609   Estabrooks, *Spiritism*, p. 47.
610   Estabrooks, *Spiritism*, p. 48.
611   Estabrooks, *Spiritism*, pp. 50–51.

a few minutes of discussion, Sirhan suddenly "started climbing the bars of his cell," just as Diamond had suggested he would. Kaiser saw Diamond putting his handkerchief away and knew the signal had been given. Diamond then asked Sirhan what he was doing. Sirhan responded that he was just getting some exercise. Kaiser said it was a plausible enough explanation out of context, but having just seen the suggestion implanted, it seemed undeniable that Sirhan was, in fact, acting out Diamond's suggestion in a post-hypnotic state.

That's why we can't take *any* of Sirhan's statements about why he did anything at home, at the range, or at the Ambassador Hotel or frankly anywhere in the last few months before the assassination, at face value. Maybe Sirhan really had been mesmerized in a normal sense upon seeing a teletype machine typing by itself. But maybe that was just Sirhan's after-the-fact justification for trance behavior. Without more evidence, it's hard to tell if an explanation is real or a false justification to explain away hypnotically induced behavior. Similarly, we have to wonder about all of Sirhan's writings that have been used against him. Any one or many of them may have been written under hypnotic instruction and may not reflect anything within Sirhan's original mind but something planted there by someone else.

The most inexcusable mistake reporters and authors have made has been quoting Sirhan's so-called "courtroom confession" out of context as if it were a true expression of guilt. When Sirhan said *in chambers* with the Judge and his attorneys that he had killed Robert Kennedy "with 20 years malice aforethought," that emotional outburst, which had no basis in reality, appeared to have been inspired by the appearance of two women at the trial, which threw Sirhan into a dissociative state. There were a number of references in Sirhan's notebooks to Peggy Osterkamp, an attractive young blonde woman, and another woman named Gwendolyn Gumm. For some reason, Sirhan thought these two women had appeared in the courtroom, as Kaiser described:

> "I told you not to bring those two girls in here," screamed Sirhan. It was not so much the revelation of his IQ of 89 that triggered Sirhan's rage. Somehow, it was the presence of two girls who had nothing to do with the case.
>
> "Who are you talking about?" I asked.
>
> "Those two girls sitting next to you."
>
> "Who *are* they?"
>
> "As if you didn't know!" cried Sirhan. "One of them is Gwen Gumm and the other is Peggy Osterkamp."
>
> I was dumbfounded. Miss Gumm had visited Cooper's office only the day before. I told him neither of the two ladies was Miss Gumm.

Sirhan called me a liar. One was Peggy Osterkamp and the other was Gwen Gumm, said Sirhan, forcing me to judge that Sirhan was in a kind of paranoid, dissociated state there and then. I went back out to the courtroom and asked the two girls for their identification. One was Sharon Karaalajich, a clerk-typist for the Los Angeles Police Department, and the other was Karen Adams, a beautician from Columbus, Ohio, who was visiting her sister in Los Angeles.[612]

Kaiser wrote the girls' names down and showed them to Sirhan. "Sirhan read it, looked back at the girls and shook his head furiously. He wouldn't be fooled," Kaiser added.[613]

Something about the two girls appeared to trigger something in Sirhan that might have been related to his programming. A similar weirdness happened when Kaiser questioned Sirhan about a random girl from his background:

"And then another time, when that girl was running for campus queen—"

"Don't talk about that, please," said Sirhan.

"Huh?"

"Don't talk about women to me." I was taken aback at the strength of Sirhan's objection to an apparently innocuous question. "Don't talk about women to me." It seemed significant enough to warrant a further probe, and I asked why. "This is political," said Sirhan. "This is politically motivated—" He started to giggle nervously. "This is, heh heh, political, heh heh, politically motivated."

I hadn't implied that Sirhan's relations with girls had had anything to do with the crime, but in Sirhan's mind there was a connection he felt compelled to deny.[614]

Given how the girl in the polka dot dress appeared to be Sirhan's handler at the Ambassador Hotel, this makes sense. Even outside of hypnosis sessions, Sirhan seemed to be acting out a post-hypnotic suggestion not to answer specific questions about women, perhaps because the hypnotist feared if Sirhan answered questions about *a* woman he might also talk about *the* woman who had controlled him in his final moments before the shooting. In fact, Sirhan's *very first words* under full hypnosis by Diamond were, "I don't know any people!"[615] What a strange exhortation to make, unprompted. But it makes sense if Sirhan were hypnotized and the hypnotist had given Sirhan a post-hypnotic instruction to never mention

612   Kaiser, pp. 406–407.
613   Kaiser, p. 407.
614   Kaiser, p. 273.
615   Kaiser, p. 295.

any of the other people connected with the plot, especially the woman in the polka dot dress who appeared to be his handler at the Ambassador Hotel.

Given the evidence that Sirhan was hypnotized, we have to be careful about reading too much into *anything* Sirhan wrote, said, or did before *and after* the assassination. We also have to avoid assumptions about what Sirhan would or wouldn't have done around the time of the assassination as Sirhan clearly was being manipulated. When I talked to Munir about what Sirhan had done the Monday before the primary election, he said that Sirhan would never have hitchhiked, that he would be too proud to do that, and therefore either Jerry Owen had been lying about picking up a hitchhiking Sirhan or he had picked up a lookalike instead. Sirhan denied this as well to his defense team. But if Sirhan were under a hypnotist's control, wasn't it possible the hypnotist compelled Sirhan to hitchhike? When I put the question to Munir in that context, Munir agreed that was perhaps possible and that he had never considered that before.

If someone had the power to hypnotize Sirhan to fire a gun in the pantry when Senator Kennedy came through, they had the power to make Sirhan commit a series of actions that would make him look guilty after the fact. Perhaps it wasn't Sirhan's idea at all to go buy a gun, to fire a gun at a range for hours on June 4, to go to the Ambassador Hotel that night. Perhaps all of that that had been suggested to Sirhan by a hypnotist.

This is also exactly what a veteran of the CIA's mind control programs described to State Department officer John Marks for his seminal book on the government's mind control programs, *The Search for the "Manchurian Candidate."* Mark's confidential CIA informant described to Marks how a hypnotist could, through the skilled application of hypnosis, walk a chosen "patsy" through a series of events, such as "a visit to a store, a conversation with a mailman, picking a fight at a political rally," to lay in a history that could make him look guilty after the fact:

> The subject would remember everything that happened to him but be amnesiac only for the fact that the hypnotist ordered him to do these things. ... The purpose of this exercise is to leave a circumstantial trail that will make the authorities think the patsy committed a particular crime.[616]

So we have to look at the evidence of Sirhan's so-called acts of premeditation with new eyes. Yes, he wrote in his diary, on one page, "R.F.K. must die" over and over, followed inexplicably by "pay to the order of" and "I have never heard"

---

[616]   John Marks, *The Search for the "Manchurian Candidate,"* W. W. Norton, Inc. (New York: 1979), paperback version, p. 204.

among other gibberish. Yes, he went to a shooting range the day of the primary (and a few times prior). Yes, he claimed to have killed Kennedy (a claim he made in the absence of evidence to suggest otherwise, triggered by the presence of two women whom Sirhan thought were two other women). Yes, he had a gun in the pantry. But was any of this entirely of his own volition? It seems not just possible but likely that someone gave Sirhan the hypnotic suggestion to take a gun to the Ambassador Hotel that night.

Over the course of my research, I became fascinated by the question of whether someone could or could not be made to do something through hypnosis that they wouldn't normally do. I not only read a large amount of literature on the subject, but I also sought out and attended various hypnosis demonstrations looking for clues.

In the first act I ever saw, the hypnotist warned the audience afterward not to talk to the people who had been on stage, hypnotized. Why, I wondered? After the show, I immediately sought one out. One tall young man had done all kinds of ridiculous things onstage, so I looked for him afterward. I found him talking to his friends, who had just seen the show. To my surprise, he denied being hypnotized and thought his friends were delusional to suggest he had been. He claimed he'd just been faking going along with the suggestions. But then he denied having done a few of the things we had all just seen him do, and I realized he was the one suffering from a delusion.

An unnerving aspect of hypnosis is its ability to cause people to see hallucinations of things that aren't there. And what's worse is this can happen not only in the hypnotic state but in the waking, post-hypnotic state as well.[617] Apparently, Sirhan entered a hallucination upon a physical cue in the pantry, and what he saw in his hallucination did not match what was really going on. His hallucination prevented him from seeing the reality of what he was doing, as you'll soon see.

At the San Diego County Fair, I personally witnessed an example of someone experiencing a hypnotically induced hallucination. I grabbed a seat early and started chatting with the woman already there in the next seat. During the show, the hypnotist chose her as one of the many people he invited up on the stage. I knew that would be interesting, because after 20 minutes of chat I had a sense of who she was, and she was as normal as could be. During the show, the hypnotist at one point gave her a fake $100 bill that looked like it had come from a game of Monopoly. The hypnotist told her, however, that this was a $25,000 check that she had won. She was very excited on stage, as one might expect in such a stage show. But it's what I saw after the show that really disturbed me.

At the end of the show, the hypnotist appeared to awaken his subjects from hypnosis. But in this case, the woman was still plagued with what could only be

---

617   Estabrooks, *Spiritism*, p. 50.

called a hallucination. I had not seen her when she came off the stage as I wanted to chase down the hypnotist and ask him to comment on the Sirhan case. (The hypnotist got visibly uncomfortable, refused to comment and hurried out of the area.) As I started to leave the area I spotted the woman I had been seated next to. She was wandering around, looking for something or someone. She looked distressed. I went up to her to see if I could help her. She was still holding the fake $100 bill and mumbling to herself. When I got near her I heard her saying, "I have to give this back. I can't keep this." I asked her what she meant. She said, "He gave me this $25,000 check, but I can't keep this. I have to return it to him." I told her to look at what she was carrying. "Can you see this is only play money?" I asked her. She looked right at it and said, "No, this is a $25,000 check. That's too much. I have to return it." I tried for a few minutes to persuade her of the fact that she was carrying only play money, but I was unsuccessful.

It was a frightening sight to behold. She was not a plant. This was not for effect. In all other aspects she appeared to be entirely normal. The show was over and the hypnotist had actually left the area. I had noticed her again after the show only at a distance, and quite by accident. She had not sought me out. Her inability to accurately describe what was in her own hand, long after the show was over and after the hypnotist had already departed the area, convinced me some people could be made to believe just about anything, under hypnosis.

And that's the key to getting people to do something "against their will." If you want someone to do something they wouldn't normally do, you don't suggest it straight out. You don't tell the other person, "take this gun and kill your mother." Hardly anyone would respond to such a direct suggestion. But you could trick the person into believing they are in a different circumstance altogether. You might tell your deeply hypnotized subject instead, "your mother has been kidnapped and an imposter has been substituted in her place. The imposter will look and sound just like your mother. She will know your history, just like your mother. She has even been taught to cry just like your mother. But you must not believe the imposter. Only by killing the imposter can you rescue your real mother." With one of those one-in-five people who are the most susceptible to hypnosis, and with a hypnotist far more skilled than I, conceivably, a person could be made to kill a loved one not so much against their will but without understanding what they were doing.

The CIA's hypnotists, after a number of experiments, came to this same conclusion, as reported in the aforementioned CIA document "Hypnotism and Covert Operations":

> [S]uppose that while under hypnosis a subject is told that a loved one's life is in danger from a maniac and that the only means to rescues is to shoot a person designated as the maniac? Three expert practitioners

(two from universities and the Agency consultant quoted above) say that there is no doubt on the basis of their experience that in such circumstances murder would be attempted. The only requirement is that the proposal be put "in a form and manner acceptable to the subject." Most modern authorities feel that a subject will carry out any suggestion which he can rationalize within the framework of his moral code.

(Currently, there is a murder trial in [redacted] in which the murderer has been judged to have been under hypnosis at the time of the crime. He has been retried, released and the hypnotist tried and convicted. The case is now under appeal. The comment of the three knowledgeable informants was that the hypnotist must have been a rank amateur to have been found out since any experienced operator would have known how to suggest away the fact that he had arranged the crime.) [Parentheses in the original.] [618]

The murder trial the CIA document referred to was that of Palle Hardrup. In 1951, during a botched robbery, Hardrup shot and killed two people. He escaped on a bicycle that belonged to Bjørn Schouw Nielsen. After being arrested, Hardrup insisted for weeks that he had acted alone. But eventually Hardrup realized he had been hypnotized by Nielsen to commit the crimes.[619]

The court-appointed psychiatrist Paul Reiter, "one of Denmark's leading psychiatrists and an expert in hypnosis,"[620] hypnotized Hardrup to get him to remember how he came to commit the crime. He discovered in this manner that Nielsen had been coercively hypnotizing Hardrup over a long period of time and had convinced Hardrup under hypnosis to commit the robbery. In attempting to fulfill the robbery command, Hardrup shot and killed two people.

At first, the police and other authorities thought this was preposterous. To demonstrate how easily hypnotized Hardrup could be, Reiter conducted a hypnotic demonstration in front of law enforcement, doctors and court officials. Nielsen, who had asked to be present, asked Reiter to make Hardrup's arm stiff. Nielsen then stuck a needle under Hardrup's fingernail, presumably to invoke pain and bring Hardrup out of his trance, but Hardrup did not react. Nielsen explained this away by saying Hardrup had Yogi training and noted that the death penalty was at stake. But the jury believed Reiter, and Nielsen was proclaimed guilty of

---

618   Internal CIA memo titled "Hypnosis and Covert Operations," dated 5 May 1955, CIA Electronic Reading Room, (FOIA) /ESDN (CREST): 0000140404. This document is missing pages, but the same document with the missing pages restored can be found at The Black Vault (www.theblackvault.com), which houses the entire batch of the CIA's released MKULTRA files.

619   Lester Davis, "Murder by Hypnosis: The amazing true story behind an almost-perfect crime," *Salt Lake City Tribune*, November 28, 1965.

620   *Ibid.*

"having planned and instigated by influence of various kinds, including suggestions of a hypnotic nature, the commission of the two robberies and homicides
by Hardrup."[621] Nielsen was sentenced to death, and Hardrup was sentenced to
a mental institution. [622] Nielsen appealed his case to the Danish Supreme Court
but lost.

But Nielsen had planted a strong suggestion in Hardrup that would nearly
free him. The relationship between the two men had been cemented over a period
of years together in prison prior to the robbery, and Nielsen had given Hardrup
the hypnotic suggestion that if they were ever separated, he must seek him out
again. True to his programming, Hardrup reinitiated contact with Nielsen. Shortly
thereafter, Hardrup wrote a letter to Nielsen's lawyer saying he had never been
hypnotized and had just fooled everyone. Nielsen sought a new trial based on
this evidence, and the matter "came before a special court in Denmark which
finally rejected his appeal that new, vital evidence had turned up." [623] The special
court "held the charge of hypnosis to be unfounded but held that the applicant
[Nielsen] had planned the crimes and had influenced Hardrup to commit them."[624]
In other words, the court held Nielsen responsible for coercing Hardrup, even
if they doubted this was due to hypnosis. Nielsen's subsequent appeal to the
European Commission on Human Rights in Strasbourg was also a bust. In 1961,
that body rejected Nielsen's appeal and said that Nielsen's human rights had
not been violated.[625] In 1966, Hardrup, the hypnotized one, was released on
probation. Nielsen, the hypnotist, spent the rest of his days in an institution for
the criminally insane. [626] Hardrup, like Sirhan, was, according to Reiter, in that
"highly hypnotizable" segment of the population. [627]

BEYOND THE HARDRUP CASE, NUMEROUS AUTHORITIES ON THE
subject of hypnosis agree that with the right subject and crafty suggestions,
someone could indeed be induced to conduct criminal acts, including murder,

---

621   Council of Europe, European Commission of Human Rights, "Decision of the Commission as to the
Admissibility in respect of application No. 343/57" (hereafter European Commission on Humans Rights Decision),
submitted by Bjørn Schouw NIELSEN against the Government of Denmark," hudoc.echr.coe.int/app/conversion/
pdf?library=ECHR&id=001-158874&filename=NIELSEN%20v.%20DENMARK.pdf, July 6, 1959, accessed via Google July
28, 2017.

622   Jim Kenner, "Killer May Go Free While 'Hypnotist' Serves Life," *Hays Daily News* (Kansas), June 27, 1965.

623   *Ibid.*

624   European Commission on Humans Rights Decision, quoting the judgment from the Special Court.

625   Jim Kenner, "Killer May Go Free While 'Hypnotist' Serves Life," *Hays Daily News* (Kansas), June 27, 1965.

626   Reuters, "2 hypnotists Err—Girl Harmed, 2 Slain" *Chicago Tribune*, December 17, 1966. Two stories
ran under this headline. The other one told how a hypnotist had been fined for leaving a 17-year-old French girl
hypnotized in a saloon who had been found doing strange things in the street. Physicians were unable to bring her
from her trance and the original hypnotist had to be summoned to wake her.

627   *Ibid.*

under hypnosis. These authorities include, but are not limited to, George Estabrooks; Emile Franchel, who had a television show in California in the 1950s called *Adventures in Hypnotism*; Dr. Daniel Brown, who co-wrote one of the modern textbooks on hypnosis; and Santa Clara University law school professor Alan Scheflin, who also has a degree in Counseling Psychology and who has received numerous awards for his work with various psychiatric and psychological organizations. There are now a number of studies showing people will do extreme things to themselves and one another under hypnosis. For this and other reasons, it is illegal to broadcast a hypnotic induction on television, as some members of audience could be inadvertently hypnotized. In fact, stage hypnosis was illegal in several states and countries in the 1960s.[628]

In their book *Snapping*, authors Flo Conway and Jim Siegelman explained the shift in modern thinking about hypnosis:

> As scientists have come to understand hypnosis a little better, most of their earlier beliefs about it have been rudely overturned. The myth of the somnambulant trance state has been shattered—the old notion that a person must be put to sleep to be hypnotized has been categorically disproved. Similarly, the dangling watch fobs and swirling spirals of the stage mesmerist have been shown merely to distract their subjects' attention, rendering them more susceptible to suggestion and command. Gone, too, are *the naïve convictions that hypnosis cannot be put to harmful use and that a person will not perform an act under hypnosis that is contrary to his conscious nature.* Historically, hypnosis practitioners have exercised extreme caution and responsibility in the use of their mysterious skill, *but many admit that, through lies and carefully contrived suggestions, a hypnotist could prompt his subject to commit any action, even a crime, in the firm belief that he was performing the act to accomplish some greater good.* [Emphasis added.][629]

Scheflin elaborated on this point in his declaration for Sirhan's appeal, which was recently denied by the California State Supreme Court. Given that Scheflin also has a degree in Counseling Psychology and has received 14 awards from the American Psychiatric Association, the American Psychological Association, and the Society for Clinical and Experimental Hypnosis, among several others, and given that he has studied the government's experiments into this subject in depth over a period of years, we must give substantial credence to his assertions as stated in his declaration:

---

628   NEA, "Reaction Often Varies," *Raleigh Register* (Beckley, West Virginia), March 21, 1969.

629   Flo Conway and Jim Siegelman, *Snapping: America's Epidemic of Sudden Personality Change* (New York: Stillpoint Press, Second Edition, 2005), p. 82.

People who disbelieve, as I once did, the possibility, under certain special circumstances of enhanced control of the mind do so because 1) they sensibly fear, and thus do not want to accept, the idea that it is possible to control the mind of another person, and 2) they are unfamiliar with the extensive overt and covert scientific literature on this controversial subject. However, those of us who for several decades have studied the scientific research on mind control, and studied the literature on brainwashing, have become reluctant believers.[630]

Beyond the Hardrup case, I found one publicly reported case where someone killed someone else in direct response to a hypnotic suggestion. In December 1923, a policeman was hypnotized during a stage show in Sebenico, Yugoslavia. He was put through various antics before the audience that amused the crowd. Then, the hypnotist gave the policeman a block of wood and told him to shoot the crowd. The policeman tried to shoot the crowd with the block of wood, but when that didn't work, he pulled out his actual gun and fired into the crowd, killing three people and wounding others. "When he learned what he had done, he went mad," said one article.[631] Another article stated that the policeman arrested a few members of the crowd and took them to the police station. The hypnotist had a difficult time removing the hypnotic suggestion from the policeman's mind, noting "it took hours to bring him to his senses."[632] The hypnotist was jailed. The policeman had to be put in an insane asylum.[633] The latter article contained this appropriate warning:

> Fortunately professional exhibitions of hypnotism are not so common in this country [America] as they used to be. They should not be permitted anywhere. Hypnotism is a dangerous power to fool with, and should never be utilized except by a skilled and reputable physician or alienist, for a curative purpose. So used, it may be valuable, though there is always some question about the propriety of putting one's own mind under the control of another person.[634]

---

630   "Exhibit G to Petioner's Reply Brief—Declaration of Alan W. Scheflin, 20 November 2011, Case 2:00-cv-05686-CAS – AJW, Document 180-2, filed 11/20/11, www.maryferrell.org/showDoc. html?docId=146779&relPageId=1&search=Exhibit_G, p. 6.

631   "Hypnotized Policeman," *The Richmond River Express and Casino Kyogle Advertiser* (New South Wales, Australia), trove.nla.gov.au/newspaper/article/122583197?searchTerm=hypnotised&searchLimits, January 2, 1924, accessed September 12, 2017.

632   "Dangerous Hypnotism," *The Town Talk* (Alexandria, Louisiana), January 12, 1924.

633   "Hypnotized Policeman Kills 3; Charmer Jailed," *Pittsburgh Post-Gazette*, December 28, 1923.

634   *Ibid.*

Many of the biggest believers in the power of hypnosis have worked for the U.S. Government. The CIA, Army and Navy have all spent large sums of money trying to find ways to completely control another human being, under project names like Often, Chatter, Chickwit, QKHILLTOP, MKDELTA and the more well-known programs of Bluebird, Artichoke, MKULTRA and MKNAOMI. These programs were uncovered in the wake of the Watergate hearings, which precipitated the Rockefeller Commission, the Church and Pike Committees, and ultimately, a Senate investigation into the CIA's mind control programs.

It's important to note that the CIA's mind control programs began with a lie. The CIA had been conducting biological warfare in Korea during the Korean War in the 1950s. When captured soldiers confessed to this, to hide this war crime, the CIA told the media the men had been "brainwashed" to make untrue accusations against the U.S. government. And then the CIA sent Col. Boris Pash, who led an assassination unit, to ensure the soldiers recanted.[635]

During the Senate's introduction to their report on the CIA's MKULTRA projects, Senator Edward Kennedy, who perhaps had the most personal interest in this matter, said at the conclusion of these efforts:

> The intelligence community of this Nation, which requires a shroud of secrecy in order to operate, has a very sacred trust from the American people. The CIA's program of human experimentation of the fifties and sixties violated that trust. It was violated again on the day the bulk of the agency's records were destroyed in 1973. It is violated again each time a responsible official refuses to recollect the details of the program. The best safeguard against abuses in the future is a complete public accounting of the abuses of the past.[636]

The CIA's awful experiments, one of which famously resulted in the death of government employee Frank Olson, were the result of a decades-long mindset that in the world of spying, anything was justifiable. President Harry S. Truman commissioned a study of government and appointed former president Herbert

---

635   I first learned of the use of biological warfare from Carl McNabb, who stumbled into the wrong mess tent when serving in the Korean War effort. Having learned this highly classified information, he was essentially forced to join the CIA, a place that brought him such unhappiness in later years he attempted suicide. For more information on this still largely suppressed story, start with Jeff Kaye's excellent summary article which refers to two good books on the subject and the International Scientific Commission's report on this matter (which is linked from this article) at shadowproof.com/2015/03/28/book-review-this-must-be-the-place-how-the-u-s-waged-germ-warfare-in-the-korean-war-and-denied-it-ever-since/, accessed September 10, 2017.

636   "PROJECT MKULTRA, THE CIA'S PROGRAM OF RESEARCH IN BEHAVIORAL MODIFICATION," U.S. Senate, Select Committee on Intelligence and Subcommittee on Health and Scientific Research of the Committee on Human Resources, comments of Senator Ted Kennedy, p. 3.

Hoover to what became known as the Hoover Commission. The Hoover Commission Report foreshadowed the mentality of the CIA in such operations:

> It is now clear that we are facing an implacable enemy whose avowed objective is world domination by whatever means and at whatever cost. There are no rules in such a game. Hitherto acceptable long-standing American concepts of "fair play" must be reconsidered. We must develop effective espionage and counterespionage services and must learn to subvert, sabotage, and destroy our enemies by more clever, more sophisticated, and more effective methods than those used against us.[637]

The CIA would use blackmail, sex, drugs and mind control in their efforts to spy on other countries, recruit people into becoming spies or double agents, and ultimately, to convince "unwitting" assets to participate in covert operations. Various accounts hint at a more sinister use of these programs as well: to blackmail American politicians, celebrities, journalists and other opinion leaders who threatened the CIA's hegemony.[638]

George White, one of the CIA's most documented assets in its efforts to use sex, drugs and hypnosis to control others, expressed the feeling of a lot of operatives in this era in a letter he wrote his CIA officer in this projects, Sid Gottlieb:

> I was a very minor missionary, actually a heretic, but I toiled whole-heartedly in the vineyards because it was fun, fun, fun. Where else could a red-blooded American boy lie, kill, cheat, steal, rape, and pillage with the sanction and blessing of the All-Highest?[639]

Such is the mindset of the people involved in such operations. So if anyone thinks no one associated with a government agency would be cruel enough to take a traumatized Christian Palestinian immigrant who was struggling to make it in America and use his own tortured background against him, think of George White.

The best part about using hypnosis in covert operations, from the CIA's point of view, was the ability to guarantee the secrecy of an operation even from the direct participants. As Richard Helms, the director of "plans" in the CIA, i.e., conspiracy plots, told the Church Committee:

---

637   Marks, p. 30.

638   See *Secret Agenda* by Jim Hougan, *Cold Warrior* by Tom Mangold, *The Real CIA* by Miles Copeland, and Part 1 of my article on "James Jesus Angleton and the Kennedy Assassination" in *The Assassinations: Probe Magazine on JFK, RFK, MLK and Malcolm X*.

639   Letter from George White to Sid Gottlieb, quoted in Marks, p. 109.

[T]he clandestine operator, the intelligence operator, is trained to believe that you really can't count on the honesty of your agent to do exactly what you want or to report accurately *unless you own him body and soul*; in other words, unless you have control, is the word of art, over that man, which is so strong that you know darn well he's your fellow. [Emphasis added.][640]

In an effort to gain this complete control over the actions of another, these institutions tried everything they could think of, including sex, blackmail, drugs, hypnosis, and even torture, often in combination. The advantage hypnosis had over all other forms is that the subject would not remember he had been manipulated by someone else.

Richard Helms was particularly involved in the mind control programs, which had been started by his good friend and CIA mentor Allen Dulles. In December 1963, Helms—then the Deputy Director of Plans—wrote an impassioned plea to the current deputy director of the CIA at the time, Lieutenant General Marshall Carter, arguing that the CIA not only needed to conduct "psychochemical" tests on "unwitting" subjects abroad, which the CIA was already doing, but also needed to conduct covert experiments on unwitting subjects in the U.S.:

In the circumstances of potential operational use of this technique, it is virtually certain that the target will be unwitting. … Contacts between the Agency and the police departments in [redacted], for example, could be exploited.[641]

General Carter had previous expressed moral qualms about testing drugs on "unwitting subjects."[642] Helms then said the problem with using prisoners was how many people in law enforcement and the Justice Department would have to be made witting of the agency's role. He suggested instead using the Bureau of Narcotics as "the most practical and secure method available," the implication being that the CIA had a close relationship with that Bureau and that no one would care what was done to a drug addict. In a separate document, which appears to be a follow-up document to this memo, Helms wrote:

We have been unable to devise a better method of pursuing such a program than the one we have with the Narcotics Bureau which [*sic*] *has been completely secure for over eight years* and we have no answer to

---

640   Testimony of Richard Helms to the Church Committee, September 12, 1975, pp. 27–28.

641   "Eyes Only" memo from Richard Helms to the Deputy Director of Central Intelligence [Lt. Gen. Marshall Carter at that time], December 17, 1963.

642   Memorandum for the Record from Inspector General J.S. Earman re the MKULTRA program, November 29, 1963.

the moral issue [of testing drugs and other mind control methods on unwitting subjects].[643]

Helms' document is carefully worded, but strongly suggests the CIA had already achieved operational success with drugs and hypnosis for more than eight years because the first document referenced states the need to "maintain" as opposed to create or develop "an offensive capability."[644]

When John Marks interviewed a veteran of the CIA's MKULTRA mind control programs, the veteran said the CIA did not believe in using mind-controlled assassins and for good reason:

> The MKULTRA veteran maintains that he and his colleagues were not interested in a programmed assassin because they knew in general it would not work and, specifically, that they could not exert total control. "If you have one hundred percent control, you have one hundred percent dependency," he says. "If something happens and you haven't programmed it in, you've got a problem. If you try to put flexibility in, you lose control. To the extent you let the agent choose, you don't have control." He admits that he and his colleagues spent hours running the arguments on the Manchurian Candidate back and forth. "Castro was naturally our discussion point," he declares. "Could you get somebody gung-ho enough that they would go in and get him?" In the end, he states, they decided there were more reliable ways to kill people. "You can get exactly the same thing from people who are hypnotizable by many other ways, and you can't get anything out of people who are not hypnotizable, so it has no use," says Gittinger.[645]

Even so, in June 1960, the Technical Services Staff (TSS) of the CIA, in conjunction with the CIA's Counterintelligence unit, then headed by the notorious James Angleton,[646] launched a joint program of "operational experiments" in hypnosis. "Operational experiments" meant actual counterintelligence operations in the field as opposed to a laboratory or controlled test situation. At the

---

643   "Eyes Only" memo from Richard Helms to the Deputy Director of Central Intelligence [Lt. Gen. Marshall Carter at that time], date not visible in the author's poor copy of this document but likely after December 17, 1963.

644   "Eyes Only" memo from Richard Helms to the Deputy Director of Central Intelligence [Lt. Gen. Marshall Carter at that time], December 17, 1963.

645   Marks, p. 203.

646   See my two-part article on Angleton in *The Assassinations: Probe Magazine on JFK, MLK, RFK and Malcolm X* (Los Angeles: Feral House, 2003) and my speech at the Assassination Archives Research Center conference in 2014 at aarclibrary.org/lisa-pease-james-jesus-angleton-and-the-warren-commission/.

time, according to Marks, "Counterintelligence officials wrote that the hypnosis program could provide a 'potential breakthrough in clandestine technology.'"[647]

James Angleton has been heavily fingered in the story of Lee Harvey Oswald. Angleton had a pre-assassination file on Oswald that was opened—officially, although dates on documents in Oswald's file suggest otherwise—only after the State Department queried CIA about American "defectors" to the Soviet Union. Oswald never actually defected, and after decades of file releases, it now seems Oswald was likely sent to the Soviet Union by the CIA as a false defector as part of a hunt for a mole in the U-2 program. Oswald had intimate knowledge of the U-2, having been a U-2 radar operator. The CIA believed if the Soviets cozied up to Oswald and asked him about the U-2 program, then there was no leak, but if the Soviets ignored Oswald, as they did, then the Soviets already had a better source of information, a mole in the program.

That would explain why Oswald had right-wing friends but was busy espousing a Communist sensibility in staged street altercations and on the radio prior to the assassination of President Kennedy. It would explain why, having announced an intention to "defect" and give up secrets of "special interest" to the Soviets, he believed he would be able to return to the U.S. via a "military hop," something that would have been off-limits to an actual traitor or defector.

Angleton, like his close friend Allen Dulles, had a keen operational interest in the use of hypnosis for counterintelligence (CI) operations. In fact, in July 1963, Angleton's CI staff tried to do an experiment in Mexico City with a "hypnotic consultant" from California. According to John Marks in his book *The Search for the "Manchurian Candidate"*:

> In October 1960 the MKULTRA program invested $9,000 in an outside consultant to develop a way of quickly hypnotizing an unwitting subject. John Gittinger says the process consisted of surprising "somebody sitting in a chair, putting your hands on his forehead, and telling the guy to go to sleep." The method worked "fantastically" on certain people, including some on whom no other technique was effective, and not on others. "It wasn't that predictable," notes Gittinger, who states he knows nothing about the field testing.
>
> The test ... did not take place until July 1963—a full three years after the Counterintelligence experimental program began, during which interval the Agency is claiming that no other field experiments took place. According to a CIA man who participated in this test, the Counterintelligence Staff in Washington asked the CIA station in Mexico City to find a suitable candidate for a rapid induction experiment. The station proposed a low-level agent, whom

---

647   Marks, p. 202.

the Soviets had apparently doubled. A Counterintelligence man flew in from Washington and a hypnotic consultant arrived from California. Our source and a fellow case officer brought the agent to a motel room on a pretext. "I puffed him up with his importance," says the Agency man. "I said the bosses wanted to see him and of course give him more money." Waiting in an adjoining room was the hypnotic consultant. At a prearranged time, the two case officers gently grabbed hold of the agent and tipped his chair over until the back was touching the floor. The consultant was supposed to rush in at that precise moment and apply the technique. Nothing happened. The consultant froze, unable to do the deed. "You can imagine what we had to do to cover-up," says the official, who was literally left holding the agent. "We explained we had heard a noise, got excited, and tipped him down to protect him. He was so grubby for money he would have believed any excuse."[648]

The codename for this project (and other counterintelligence field operations using hypnosis) was ZRALERT. The ZR digraph indicated operations, including the Castro assassination plot ZRRIFLE, that were run by "Staff D" in the CIA, the group that interfaced with the NSA. I once worked with a former NSA staffer who told me the NSA had assassination teams. This would make sense, based on something former CIA officer Joseph Burkholder Smith described in his book *Portrait of a Cold Warrior*. He wrote that anyone who was involved in coup plotting had to talk to Staff D, which he said was a unit within the CIA's counterintelligence unit. If the NSA had assassins, Staff D would be the group that would need them most, for coups. Because the NSA's official stance is that it is entirely an electronic eavesdropping intelligence gathering agency, no Congressional investigation has ever subpoenaed their records in connection with possible other activities, which is unfortunate. For a time, the NSA's budget was larger than the CIA's, but the agency was even more secretive. When it was initially formed, the joke was that "NSA" stood for "No Such Agency."

And who was the hypnotic consultant from California? Did he hypnotize Sirhan? It would not surprise me if there had been a hidden ZR project targeting GPFOCUS, the CIA's codename for Senator Robert Kennedy. (The codename for JFK was GPIDEAL, and the codename for Lee Harvey Oswald was GPFLOOR. No investigation ever sought files from the CIA relative to the Robert Kennedy assassination.)

Angleton kept copies of photographs from Robert Kennedy's autopsy, Carl McNabb, a former CIA operative, told me years ago. Former *Washington Post* reporter Jefferson Morley also noted the same in his book on Win Scott. In a

---

private email, Morley told me that Angleton had believed the Mafia had likely killed Robert Kennedy. But my own research on Angleton showed him to be a skilled disinformationist. This "belief" was likely designed to throw the curious off the scent of the CIA's own role in the killing of Robert Kennedy.

I have found no evidence linking Angleton to the plot, but given Angleton's interest in hypnosis, his contacts in California, and his overall mentality that the CIA should not have to follow the laws of the country, it would not surprise me if he had foreknowledge or were more directly involved.

Estabrooks described in his book *Hypnosis* how he could create multiple personality states in an individual through hypnosis. He'd then program the two states such that one personality wouldn't know what the other one was doing. Estabrooks asked in his book if it was unethical to split personalities in this manner and answered his own question "perhaps," but he felt that anything was justified in war.

Did someone split Sirhan's personality through hypnosis? At the trial, when questioned about a passage in one of Sirhan's notebooks by Grant Cooper, Sirhan's response showed some rudimentary awareness of what some call an "alter," short for "alternate personality," within:

> "That is what you said, isn't it?"
> "That is what I said, but it's not me, sir. It's not Sirhan sitting right here who wrote that."
> "Well, who wrote it?"
> "It's not Sirhan sitting right here who wrote that."
> "Well, who wrote it?"
> "I did."
> "What do you mean it isn't Sirhan writing this?"
> "I can't explain it."

But Estabrooks could have explained this, and the reasons for this, had anyone called him to the stand. In his chapter "Hypnotism and Warfare," Estabrooks described how one could create a "Super Spy" using hypnosis:

> We start with an excellent subject and he must be just that, one of those rare individuals who accepts and who carries through every suggestion without hesitation. ... Then we start to develop a case of multiple personality through the use of hypnotism. In his normal waking state, which we will call Personality A, or PA, this individual will become a rabid communist. He will join the party, follow the party line and make himself as objectionable as possible to authorities.

Note that he will be acting in good faith. He is a communist, or rather his PA is a communist and will behave as such.

Then we develop Personality B (PB), the secondary personality, the unconscious personality, if you wish, although this is somewhat of a contradiction in terms. This personality is rabidly American and anti-communist. It has all the information possessed by PA, the normal personality, whereas PA does not have this advantage. ...

The proper training of a person for this role would be long and tedious, but once he was trained, you would have a super spy compared to which any creation in a mystery story is just plain weak.

My super spy plays his role as a communist in his waking state, aggressively, consistently, fearlessly. But his PB is a loyal American, and PB has all the memories of PA. As a loyal American, he will not hesitate to divulge those memories....[649]

Did this actually work? At the time of the book's first publication in 1943, Estabrooks stated he did not know if this were possible, adding that Milton H. Erickson, a respected hypnotist of the time, "has done excellent work proving to his satisfaction that such uses of hypnotism would be quite impossible," but that other hypnotists "have done excellent work proving the opposite."[650] By 1971, however, Estabrooks asserted that he *had* succeeded in doing this, describing nearly the identical scenario:

During World War II, I worked this technique with a vulnerable Marine lieutenant I'll call Jones. Under the watchful eye of Marine Intelligence I split his personality into Jones A and Jones B. Jones A, once a "normal" working Marine, became entirely different. He talked communist doctrine and meant it. He was welcomed enthusiastically by communist cells, was deliberately given a dishonorable discharge by the Corps (which was in on the plot) and became a card-carrying party member.

The joker was Jones B, the second personality, formerly apparent in the conscious Marine. Under hypnosis, this Jones had been carefully coached by suggestion. Jones B was the deeper personality, knew all the thoughts of Jones A, was a loyal American, and was "imprinted" to say nothing during conscious phases.

All I had to do was hypnotize the whole man, get in touch with Jones B, the loyal American, and I had a pipeline straight into the Communist camp. It worked beautifully for months with this subject,

---

649   Estabrooks, *Hypnotism*, pp. 200–201.
650   Estabrooks, *Hypnotism*, pp. 209–210.

but the technique backfired. While there was no way for an enemy to expose Jones' dual personality, they suspected it and played the same trick on us later.[651]

When I read this the first time, I thought immediately of the young Marine Lee Harvey Oswald who attempted to infiltrate Communist groups while secretly working for the CIA. I wondered if Estabrooks' description could explain both Oswald's pro- and anti-communism stances exhibited during his time in the Marines and after. In the Marines, at the height of the Cold War, Oswald studied Russian, listened to Russian operas and openly talked about Communism. In the ultraconservative Cold War military establishment, the only way that would have been allowed is if the upper brass knew that Oswald was being prepared in some way for a covert mission to the Soviet Union.

While being transferred by the Dallas police, Oswald was assassinated by Jack Ruby. The famous attorney Melvin Belli represented Ruby at his trial. One of Belli's friends, an attorney named Leonard Steinman, suggested in a letter to Belli that Jack Ruby had been acting out a post-hypnotic command when he killed Oswald. Ruby's defense psychiatrist Dr. Louis Jolyon West, who had worked with the CIA on MKULTRA experiments,[652] had argued that Ruby had organic brain damage. Other medical experts disagreed with that diagnosis.[653] Steinman argued Ruby only *appeared* to have brain damage and had instead been hypnotized:

> Mel—the brain damage picture is not the result of previous concussion and physical trauma, but of hypno-conditioning, of induction by suggestion through deep hypnosis of an artificial psychosis. Unlocking this psychosis, of establishing the identity of the hypno-conditioner, requires a dedicated hypnotherapist with an exhaustive knowledge not only of Freudian but Pavlovian principles. Please believe me also that Ruby's explanation of what gave rise to his act, of his feelings of depression and overwroughtness at the President's death, of his feelings for Mrs. Kennedy and the further torment Oswald's trial would cause her, of his chagrin at the anti-Kennedy ads and hate posters—are all confabulations and rationalizing similar to those found in Korsakoff's Syndrome [in which people invent events to correspond to missing memories – LP]; all caused by the hypno-conditioning he was subjected to. In all the cases, the hypno-conditioned victim shows the symptoms of an obsessive-compulsive neurotic

651   George H. Estabrooks, Ph.D., "Hypnosis Comes of Age," *Science Digest*, April 1971, pp. 44–50.

652   AP, "Ruby Hospital Plea is Denied," *The Baytown Sun* (Baytown, TX), April 27, 1964; Marks, p. 63.

653   Charles Patrick Ewing, *Insanity: Murder, Madness, and the Law* (New York: Oxford University Press, 2008), p. 10.

with psychopathic and schizoid components ... all the result of the conditioning process. ...

Do you want to know why Ruby shows a brain syndrome picture? Probably because some toxin was used together with the conditioning. Alcohol. Peyote. Mescaline. LSD-25. To lock the post-hypnotic suggestions firmly in, to prevent Ruby from clearing, from being re-hypnotized by anyone other than the Conditioner. Sound like something out of a piece of fantasy-fiction? Then see "The Manipulation of Human Behavior," 1961, John Wiley & Sons, compiled under the auspices of and sponsored by Uncle Sam's own USAF.... I tell you, Mel, this case is insidious. The theory isn't really a second-line defense. It's what actually happened.[654]

While it's not at all clear that's what happened to Jack Ruby, Bill Turner and Jonn Christian were persuaded that Steinman's thesis likely applied to Sirhan Sirhan:

The Steinman letter was very much on Christian's mind after RFK was shot. That Sirhan might have been programmed through hypnosis sounded like science fiction, but the symptoms began to crop up. CBS cameraman James D. Wilson, who was at the Ambassador when Kennedy was shot, told Turner that he and his colleagues covering the court case had observed that Sirhan seemed permanently depressed "with his mind working in separate compartments."

"I know this sounds silly," Wilson said, "but I find no explanation for Sirhan as satisfactory as the hypothesis that he has been acting and talking under hypnosis or in posthypnotic suggestion."[655]

The presence of Dr. Louis Joylon "Jolly" West in Ruby's trial is interesting. Dr. West had been a professor of psychiatry at the University of Oklahoma at the time of Ruby's trial. He later moved to Los Angeles, where he headed the Neuropsychiatric Institute at UCLA. Dr. West had also been involved in a panel regarding the U.S. airmen captured in Korea which found that sleep deprivation, not brainwashing, along with "the constant fear of harm and the total dependency on their captors, led the airmen into startling and fairly long-lasting personality changes." Dr. West's work prevented the airmen from being court-martialed.[656] But he also may have covered for the CIA's biowarfare experiments by doing so.

---

654   Letter from Leonard L. Steinman, Counsellor at Law, to Melvin Belli, Esq., January 31, 1964, www.maryferrell.org/showDoc.html?docId=10028&relPageId=114, from NARA Record Number PDF version:11206KNARA Record Number: 124-10371-10116, pp. 114–115.

655   Turner and Christian, p. 196.

656   Philip J. Hilts, "Louis J. West, 74, Psychiatrist Who Studied Extremes, Dies," New York Times, January 9, 1999.

In later years, Dr. West examined Patty Hearst, who had committed crimes while a captive of the "Symbionese Liberation Army" or SLA. West made a similar argument—that Hearst's mind had been broken down by her captors. But one of her captors, Donald DeFreeze, had come out of Vacaville, where some of the CIA's MKULTRA experiments had been conducted. In his book *Revolution's End: The Patty Hearst Kidnapping, Mind Control, and the Secret History of Donald DeFreeze* (Skyhorse Publishing, 2016), author Brad Schreiber pointed out that DeFreeze's development of the SLA came about through his association with Colston Westbrook, whose CIA connections had been elucidated briefly in a *New York Times* article.[657] In *Revolution's End*, Schreiber argued, as others have before him, that the SLA was a CIA project to discredit the radical left. Another famous criminal "treated" at the Vacaville facility was Charlie Manson:

> On March 20, 1974, Manson was transferred from Folsom State Prison to CMF to undergo psychiatric treatment. He was treated for "conceptual disorganization" caused by being locked up continually with little or no human contact. In October 1974, he was shipped back to Folsom, but returned in May 1976 with the same diagnosis.[658]

Dr. James Hamilton, a San Francisco psychiatrist who had worked with George White in the OSS, was the "West Coast Supervisor" for Sydney Gottlieb's CIA mind control experiments, including MKSEARCH, the successor program to MKULTRA. MKSEARCH Subproject #3 involved behavioral control experiments on prisoners at Vacaville. As Marks wrote:

> By the early 1960s, [Hamilton] had arranged to get access to prisoners at the California Medical Facility at Vacaville. Hamilton worked through a nonprofit research institute connected to the Facility to carry out, as a document puts it, "clinical testing of behavioral control materials" on inmates. Hamilton's job was to provide "answers to specific questions and solutions to specific problems of direct interest

---

657   John Kifner, "Cinque: A Dropout Who Has Been in Constant Trouble," *New York Times*, May 17, 1974. In the article Kifner wrote:

> The coordinator of the Black Cultural Association was a rotund, fast-talking black man named Colston Westbrook who has since been put on the S.L.A.'s "death list." The group charges that he is a Central Intelligence Agency operative.
> Mr. Westbrook has said that he served in both the Army and the Air Force in Korea, and that he worked in Vietnam for five years for a private contracting firm, Pacific Architects and Engineers.
> Pacific Architects and Engineers has been used as a recruiting pool and cover by the C.I.A. for its Phoenix program, which included assassination teams, according to Bart Osborne of the Fifth Estate, a Washington-based research group of former intelligence personnel who had turned against the Vietnam war. Mr. Osborne was, at one time, a handler of Phoenix teams.

658   Tony Wade, "Charles Manson at the California Medical Facility," *Daily Republic* (Solano, CA), www.dailyrepublic.com/solano-news/local-features/local-lifestyle-columns/charles-manson-at-the-california-medical-facility/, no date, but from the comments, the article went live in July 2017.

to the Agency. In a six-month span in 1967 and 1968, the psychiatrist spent over $10,000 in CIA funds simply to pay volunteers—which at normal rates meant he experimented on between 400 to 1,000 inmates in that time period alone.[659]

Marks added as a footnote to the passage above, "During the late 1960s and early 1970s, it seemed that every radical on the West Coast was saying that the CIA was up to strange things in behavior modification at Vacaville. Like many of yesterday's conspiracy theories, this one turned out to be true."[660]

During Sirhan's trial, both the prosecution and defense psychological experts suggested that if Sirhan were not put to death, he should be transferred to Vacaville. Was someone involved in the MKULTRA program nervous about what someone might find in Sirhan's mind if he were incarcerated elsewhere? Were they eager to continue to put a lock on his mind? In most cases, hypnosis wears off after time. Was there a fear that Sirhan might someday remember what had truly happened in the pantry?

Oddly, the Vacaville reference was missing in the trial pages on file at the California State Archives, which had been copied and posted at the online archive site of MaryFerrell.org. I had to ask an archivist to track down this and other pages that referenced Sirhan's trance state which someone had surreptitiously removed from the trial record. Fortunately, the missing pages were found in the Supreme Court's records and sent to me. The pages that were missing referred to hypnosis, a trance state, and Vacaville.

Lest anyone think the CIA would not be cruel enough to turn human beings into automatons, be aware that the CIA's doctors and psychological experts tried all kinds of crazy things on not only humans but animals. In one particularly gruesome experiment, one of the experimenters tried to cut the head off one monkey and transplant it onto another monkey whose head had been cut off to make room. If this had somehow succeeded, would humans have been next? With the exception of the CIA's asking President Eisenhower for permission to experiment on medical patients and volunteers at the Georgetown University Hospital, a request that was approved in the mid-fifties, the CIA did not ask the president or any other body for permission for its experiments.[661] When the CIA's use of private foundations and nonprofit organizations for funding not just mind control experiments but all sorts of covert activities was exposed in 1967, President Lyndon B. Johnson forbade the CIA from using these institutions for support. That didn't affect their programs, however. The CIA just started funneled

---

659   John Marks, *The Search for the "Manchurian Candidate,"* (New York: W. W. Norton & Company, 1979, p. 215.

660   Marks, *The Search for the "Manchurian Candidate,"* p. 215.

661   Marks, footnote on p. 217.

CIA money through private companies instead, starting with one owned by one of the operatives involved in the experiments.[662]

Whatever the CIA did in its mind control operations must have been truly heinous, because when President Richard Nixon made Helms Ambassador to Iran, essentially firing him from his role as CIA Director, Helms ordered *all documentation on the CIA's mind control programs destroyed.*

Fortunately for history, however, a few documents survived the destruction. These primarily financial documents nonetheless hint at terrifying experiments in brainwashing and mind control. People were subjected to horrific conditions to see if the mind could be reprogrammed through torture, repetitive tapes and recordings, sensory deprivation and other techniques. Some were given combinations of drugs and hypnosis. Tests were conducted on American citizens without their knowledge or consent.

Although the CIA claimed overtly that its mind control operations were meant to help protect U.S. operatives and military personnel from Soviet, Chinese and other countries' control, clearly this was a weapon with offensive potential, as an Agency officer Marks quoted explained:

> Nearly every Agency document stressed goals like "controlling an individual to the point where he will do our bidding *against his will* and *even against such fundamental laws of nature as self-preservation.*" On reading one such memo, an Agency officer wrote to his boss: "If this is supposed to be covered up as a defensive feasibility study, it's pretty damn transparent."[663] [Emphasis added.]

One CIA officer, Morse Allen, used hypnosis on his secretaries to see what he could make them do. In one instance, Allen tried to make a "killer" out of a secretary:

> On February 19, 1954, Morse Allen simulated the ultimate exper- iment in hypnosis: the creation of a "Manchurian Candidate," or programmed assassin. Allen's "victim" was a secretary whom he put into a deep trance and told to keep sleeping until he ordered otherwise. He then hypnotized a second secretary and told her that if she could not wake up her friend, "her rage would be so great that she would not hesitate to 'kill.'" Allen left a pistol nearby, which the secretary had no way of knowing was unloaded. Even though they had earlier expressed a fear of firearms of any kind, she picked up the gun and "shot" her sleeping friend." After Allen brought the

---

662   Marks, p. 218.
663   Marks, p. 25.

"killer" out of her trance, she had apparent amnesia for the event, denying she would ever shoot anyone."[664]

The problem with this experiment, some argue, is that the secretary trusted Allen not to make an assassin out of her and fired the gun in the sure knowledge that she would not have been allowed to fire it if it had been loaded. But if he had loaded the gun, would she have fired anyway? Especially if she trusted him and he had casually mentioned to someone else in front of her that the gun was loaded with blanks (when it wasn't)? The reason this can't be scientifically tested, or reported if such tests have already been performed, is that a successful experiment would result in a murder, and no one would dare brag about that on the record. But as you have already seen, there are plenty of hints that such experiments were successfully conducted.

The CIA wasn't alone in its pursuit of the perfect puppet. The Navy had its own programs, some of which were done in conjunction with the CIA, for years. The Navy's interest was originally focused on finding the perfect truth serum. But soon their interests followed along the lines of the CIA's: to create a mind-controlled assassin.

Some of the Navy's "Manchurian Candidate" programs were revealed by Lt. Commander Thomas Narut at a NATO conference in Oslo, Norway in 1975. Peter Watson, a reporter for the *London Times* who was also a trained psychologist and working on a book on military psychology, interviewed several of the conference participants, including Narut, about what had been discussed at a 1975 conference. What he reported on Sunday, July 6, 1975 in the Sunday edition of the *London Times* made headlines all over the United States the following day.

Watson reported that Narut had described how Navy men were being trained to cope with the stress of killing, and were being forced to watch movies, with their heads clamped so they could not look away. They were shown, for example, films of African youth being circumcised to reduce the troops' qualms about killing Africans. People were being conditioned to think of their enemies as inferior creatures, making them easier to annihilate. Narut describing the programming of soldiers' minds to kill not so much through hypnosis as by repeated conditioning.

Narut mentioned how criminals had been retrieved on occasion from prisons and trained to be assassins. Narut also mentioned that assassins were then assigned to embassies, such as the one in Athens, and that the training took place either at the Naples hospital or at the Navy's neuropsychiatric laboratory in San Diego.

Within 24 hours of Watson's article appearing, Narut was summoned to London to talk to his superior, Admiral Thomas Engen, the U.S. Naval Chief of

---

664   Marks, p. 183.

Staff in Europe. After talking to Admiral Engen, Narut immediately issued a statement saying "The assertion attributed to me that convicted murderers have been assigned to embassies as assassins is totally and blatantly false and absurd."[665] Watson, however, stood by his reporting, stating he obtained this information in private from three or four conference attendees, and that he had obtained other information directly from Narut in a 90-minute interview in his hotel room. In the recantation, the Navy made it sound like Watson talked only briefly to Narut while Narut was getting dressed for dinner. Watson responded that while it was "true we carried on talking while he got ready for dinner," the two had also "talked non-stop for one and a half hours."[666]

In the weeks leading up to the assassination, Sirhan made frequent trips to Corona. What was in Corona, I wondered? I finally drove out there to see for myself. Besides some beautiful stretches of the Santa Ana River, horse farms, and industrial parks, there is a huge Naval Surface Warfare Center (NSWC) there. NSWC is part of the Naval Sea Systems Command. According to the NSWC's website:

> Together, we engineer, build, buy and maintain ships, submarines and combat systems that meet the Fleet's current and future operational requirements.
>
> Naval Sea Systems Command (NAVSEA) is the largest of the Navy's five system commands. With a fiscal year budget of nearly $30 billion, NAVSEA accounts for one quarter of the Navy's entire budget.[667]

Corona is completely landlocked, but there is a lake there nestled largely out of sight among foothills, where naval weapons are presumably tested. Is it possible some of the navy's human weapons along the lines Narut described were developed or tested there as well?

Sirhan apparently frequented Corona in the last months leading up to the assassination. According to LAPD records, Sirhan's name appeared on the roster at the Corona Police Department Firing Range on June 1, 1968 (the Saturday before the California primary election).[668] According to Sirhan's lawyer William Pepper, this was where Sirhan was taught to shoot at human targets.

While privately, the CIA admitted to some successes with their mind control programs, to the public, through its assets, the CIA asserted that no one could

665   Associated Press, "Psychologist denies he said Navy trained assassins," *Arizona Republic*, July 8, 1975.

666   "Navy psychologist denies assassin-training story," *Des Moines Register* (Des Moines, Iowa), July 8, 1975.

667   www.navsea.navy.mil/Who-We-Are/, accessed October 7, 2017.

668   LAPD Progress Report – Pistol and Rifle Range Investigation, www.maryferrell.org/showDoc. html?docId=99734#relPageId=51&tab=page

be hypnotized to do something against their will. Two frequent media voices on this point included one person who has long been exposed as having been associated with the CIA's mind control programs: Dr. Martin T. Orne. The other was Dr. William J. Bryan, who told prostitutes he worked for the CIA, and his friends and associates would seem to suggest this as well. In her book *Memory*, Alison Winter, reached a similar conclusion re Bryan, noting "I have found no solid evidence of government-funded work after the war, but Bryan's published writings certainly mark out an interest that straddles the forensic and the military range of psychological research."[669] Given that the CIA's mind control records were largely destroyed, there may no longer be a way to prove that definitively one way or another.

While Sirhan's defense was being heard by the jury, along with Orne and Bryan, reporter David Shaw quoted Dr. Loyd W. Rowland, who wrote about experiments under hypnosis, including ones where men picked up what they had been told were poisonous snakes, where people had thrown what they had been led to believe was acid in other people's faces on command, and other such experiments. Rowland said, according to Shaw, "The common conception that a hypnotized person will not perform acts that violate his ideas is badly in need of reexamination." But Shaw only quoted Rowland in an attempt to dismiss that same idea, noting, "Most hypnotists bridle at this charge. They say a hypnotized individual's senses are so acute he would realize, subconsciously, that the 'acid' was harmless, that the "rattlesnakes" were not poisonous."[670]

In a letter to Milton Erickson, Rowland asked:

> When are you coming around to the notion that hypnotized persons can be made to harm themselves and others? I think my experiment on this point is conclusive, and I wish that you would duplicate it."[671]

It's worth noting that Erickson, who refused to accede to the notion that someone could be made to do something under hypnosis they would never otherwise do, had also done contract work for the CIA, according to author Hank Albarelli in his book *A Terrible Mistake*. In other words, Erickson may well have had a career-serving reason to advocate this position.

Shaw then turned to Orne and Bryan to refute Rowland, without making his readers aware (if he was even aware himself) of their agency connections. Shaw quoted "Dr. Martin Orne of the Harvard Medical School" as saying, "A subject in an experiment knows he's in a laboratory, no matter what the

---

669   Alison Winter, *Memory: Fragments of a Modern History* (University of Chicago Press, 2012), p. 127.

670   David Shaw, "Hypnotists Claim Suspects Won't Violate Moral Code," *The Arizona Daily Star*, March 1, 1969.

671   Milton H. Erickson, *The Letters of Milton H. Erickson* (Phoenix, AZ: Zeig, Tucker & Theisen, Inc., 2000), p. 215.

hypnotist tells him. … He knows, at least subconsciously, he won't be allowed to kill anyone."[672]

Bryan, then the president of the American Institute of Hypnosis and living in Los Angeles, was even more emphatic on this matter:

> The instant a hypnotist suggests something contrary to your moral code, the rapport between you will be broken. You'll snap out of the trance. [673]

Shaw added Bryan became "infuriated" at the notion that someone could be made to do something against their will under hypnosis:

> "I'm the best hypnotist in the world," he shouts. "Don't you think I'd hypnotize me a bank president and make him give me a couple of million dollars if I could? It just can't be done."[674]

Beyond any possible CIA motive, Bryan's comments were also provably self-serving. Just three months later, Bryan was placed on probation by the California State Board of Medical Examiners "after having been found guilty of having sexual relations" with four women he had hypnotized.[675] Clearly, the Board thought Bryan had some power over the women through hypnosis they would not have given to Bryan outside of hypnosis. Had Bryan admitted that a hypnotist could manipulate others into doing something against their will or moral code, he might have had to face multiple charges of rape.

Bryan was hardly the only one to take advantage of someone under hypnosis. In 1991, psychological examiner Thomas David Remsen received a ten-year prison sentence for raping and fondling a woman he was supposed to be treating for back pain. Clearly, the jury felt she had been hypnotized to participate in acts outside her morality and against her will.

In 2014, a woman wore a hidden camera to her lawyer's office and captured Michael Fine, a 59-year-old divorce attorney, hypnotizing her and then making sexual advances on her. He was given a 12-year prison sentence after pleading guilty to assaulting five other women under similar trances.[676] The defense attorney said these were "strong, intelligent women" to suggest they were consciously participating in the sexual activity. But that just proved that

---

672   David Shaw, "Hypnotists Claim Suspects Won't Violate Moral Code," *The Arizona Daily Star*, March 1, 1969.

673   *Ibid.*

674   *Ibid.*

675   "METROPOLITAN: Yorty Signs Gambling Ordinance," *Los Angeles Times*, June 13, 1969. Bryan was not the only man to take advantage of clients.

676   Kevin Freeman, "Disturbing video released of attorney hypnotizing clients for sexual pleasure," *Fox 8 Cleveland*, January 17, 2017.

even strong, intelligent people can be hypnotized to do things they would not normally do.

A pharmacy assistant who was an amateur hypnotist pleaded guilty in 2015 to fourth-degree assault with sexual motivation after having sexual contact with a woman under hypnosis.[677]

It's clear from all these cases that some people *can* be made to do things under hypnosis that they wouldn't normally do, enough to sue when they figure out how they've been manipulated.

Sex was not the only thing Bryan coerced under hypnosis. Bryan was brought into the Boston Strangler case to hypnotize the only suspect the police had been able to come up with, Albert DeSalvo. Using hypnosis, Bryan apparently coerced the confession of a likely innocent man, according to the research of Susan Kelly in her book *The Boston Stranglers*:

> On March 20 and 21, 1965, [F. Lee] Bailey had brought in hypnoanalyst William Jennings [sic – his middle name was Joseph] Bryan to Bridgewater for the purpose of putting Albert [DeSalvo] into a trance in order to elicit further details of the murders that might be buried in his subconscious mind. In their respective books, Gerold Frank and Bailey offer partial transcripts of these sessions. According to both, Bryan urged Albert to think of the strangling victims as substitutes for his wife, Irmgard, and his daughter, Judy—the true targets of Albert's homicidal rage, Bryan opined. As Frank himself wrote, "those who witnessed the hypnoanalysis wondered how much DeSalvo had been led or influenced by Dr. Bryan, so forceful and domineering." And indeed, Bryan's questions seem to have been highly suggestive: "Each time you strangled, it was because you were killing Judy, isn't it? You were killing Judy ...."[678]

It's not clear if Bryan knew or cared if DeSalvo was innocent. What is clear, after reading both Frank's and Bailey's accounts, is that Bryan essentially put words in DeSalvo's mouth through hypnosis that formed the basis for his so-called "motive." Kelly's book makes a very strong case that another person was instead responsible for these stranglings, not DeSalvo.

If someone can be tricked into confessing to a crime they didn't commit, can someone be tricked into committing a crime without understanding that's what they are doing?

---

677   "State revokes pharmacy worker's license," *TriCity Herald*, March 24, 2015.

678   Susan Kelly, *The Boston Stranglers: The Public Conviction of Albert DeSalvo and the True Story of Eleven Shocking Murders* (New York: Birch Lane Press, 1995), pp. 173–174.

The CIA employed a master magician named John Mulholland who taught operatives the tricks of magic and deception correctly referred to as "the dark arts." People with no literacy in covert operations do not understand the amount of planning and preparation that goes into a covert operation. The original covert operations arm of the agency was called the directorate of "Plans" for this reason. Coups and assassinations require careful, long-term planning. CIA Counterintelligence Chief Angleton said it was as important to plan for the *failure* of an operation as well as its *success*. Nothing could be left to chance. The best foil for an operation was a patsy who didn't know he was one. That was the best way to guarantee the success of an operation. Was that Sirhan's real role, unbeknown to him?

Sirhan has repeatedly been assessed by both defense and prosecution experts as being in the 20% of people who can be the most deeply hypnotized. But was Sirhan programmed to *kill*? Even apart from the physical evidence which proves Sirhan fired no bullets, it appears Sirhan was tricked, through hypnosis and possibly drugs, into being a patsy in the conspiracy to kill Senator Robert Kennedy without his knowledge or consent.

Two TV shows in recent years did experiments designed to parallel Sirhan's case to trick people into being part of an "assassination" plot. While blanks were loaded into the guns, both productions did all they could to convince their hypnotized subjects that the guns in their experiments were loaded and dangerous.

One of the programs was by Derren Brown, an extraordinary British mentalist and hypnotist who has demonstrated over several years the numerous ways someone could be conditioned or programmed to do something extraordinary. As I described in a Salon.com article:

> On Channel 4 in the U.K. ... hypnotist Derren Brown tested this scenario on his TV show "The Experiments." He took a highly hypnotizable subject and, over a two-month period, trained him to shoot and "kill" a celebrity. The subject, however, did not know this was the experiment's goal. Brown gave his subject a two-part trigger that would send him into a hypnotic state: a polka dot pattern and a unique cellphone ring tone. When he saw this pattern and heard the tone, the young man was taught to touch his head to focus his concentration, and then fire a gun at a target on a range. But his final test occurred not at a range, but at a taping of British entertainer Stephen Fry's show. As the subject watched the show from a back row, a hidden camera showed a girl in a polka dot dress enter and sit in front of the subject. The cellphone rang. The girl turned to the subject and whispered, "The target is Stephen Fry." The subject

hesitated a moment, then touched his forehead, opened the case, pulled out a gun loaded with blanks, stood, and fired. Stephen Fry, who was wired with squibs (the exploding fake blood packets used in movies to simulate gunshots), fell down "dead." The hypnotized man showed no reaction at the time. When shown a video of his act later, the subject seemed genuinely surprised at what he had done.[679]

The Discovery Channel subsequently conducted a similar experiment in 2012. After finding a highly hypnotizable person, in a segment called "Brainwashed," experienced hypnotist Tom Silver took an actor and programmed him to "kill" someone. The gun was not loaded, but the actor was told that it was. The actor had also been told the episode was over and that they were done. But then the post-hypnotic trigger was given to pick up a gun and shoot a person. The actor picked up the loaded gun as instructed under hypnosis and fired it at the designated target. As Tom Silver noted:

> I believe hypnosis does have the potential to control someone's mind and actions. … That's something that a lot of hypnotherapists don't want to talk about—it's something they're scared of.[680]

Silver's comments reflect uncommon candor and bravery. Every hypnotist has a vested financial interest in repeating the canard that one cannot be made to do something under hypnosis that they wouldn't normally do. Otherwise, hypnotists could potentially be financially or criminally liable for the actions of their subjects.

There will always be those who refuse to believe the evidence, who insist the subjects in these shows were faking because to believe otherwise makes them personally uncomfortable. But even if the subjects in both shows were faking, what if the gun *had* been loaded, as the subjects in both cases were told? In that case, one could argue, both shows proved you could trick someone into participating in an assassination plot without their knowledge or consent.

In 2017, we had a dramatic real-world example of how people could be tricked into participating in an assassination plot without their knowledge. Two women, thinking they were doing a stunt for a TV show, murdered Kim Jong-nam, the exiled brother of North Korean leader Kim Jong-un. Siti Aisyah, a 25-year-old Indonesian woman, and Doan Thi Huong, a 29-year-old Vietnamese woman, were told they were participating in a prank for TV. They were recruited separately. Both had served as escorts and were open to making a quick $100. They were

679   Lisa Pease, "The other Kennedy conspiracy," *Salon.com*, www.salon.com/2011/11/21/the_other_kennedy_conspiracy/, November 21, 2011.

680   Discovery Channel press release for the "Brainwashed" episode of their *Curiosity* show, press.discovery.com/us/dsc/press-releases/2012/discovery-channels-curiosity-conducts-experim-2123/, October 18, 2012.

given bottles of water to spray in people's faces as the cameras rolled and towels to wipe the water off. They had done this to a few people without harm. But someone had apparently put VX, a highly toxic nerve agent, on the towel with which Thi Huong, according to airport surveillance video, wiped Jong-nam's face.

Aisyah was apparently set up to be the distractor so Thi Huong could get behind Jong-nam to catch him unaware, or so it appears. In video footage, Thi Huong appeared to put a towel over Jong-nam's face. According to Malaysian Police Chief Khalid Abu Bakar, "the woman who accosted Mr. Kim immediately went to wash her hands," suggesting to Bakar that Thi Huong was "very aware" she had used a toxic agent.[681] While this was taken as a sign of guilt, it's also possible she washed her hands simply because she instantly felt the effects as something unpleasant and tried to wash it off without knowing it was fatally toxic. And although the police thought Thi Huong was witting, she showed up two days later at the airport believing she was supposed to do this again for the television show. Would a guilty person do that? Neither woman appeared to know that Jong-nam had died from the attack until after their arrests.[682]

If Thi Huong or higher-level plotters set up Aisyah to take part in an assassination plot not "against her will" but rather "without her conscious knowledge" or understanding of her true role, what level of guilt should be assigned?

Was Sirhan similarly set up, but with the added layer of hypnosis and possibly a drug, to participate in an assassination plot without having any clue that's what he was doing?

Sirhan's current lawyer, William Pepper, gave Dr. Daniel Brown prolonged access to Sirhan to answer that question. Dr. Brown, who co-wrote one of the widely used texts on clinical hypnosis, was allowed to hypnotize Sirhan in a way that had never been done before. Instead of trying to get Sirhan to remember a crime he didn't commit, Brown's technique involved asking open-ended, non-leading questions to encourage Sirhan simply to remember all he could about what happened at the hotel that night.

Various tests have shown that while people may not remember being hypnotized, they do remember what they learned under hypnosis. As Professor Kihlstrom noted, the brain is still recording, even if a hypnotic suggestion to forget has been given:

> Upon termination of hypnosis, some subjects find themselves unable
> to remember the events and experiences which transpired while

---

681   "Kim Jong-nam death: Unravelling the mystery," BBC News, February 25, 2017, www.bbc.com/news/world-asia-39077603.

682   Richard C. Paddock, "Lawyers for Women in Kim Jong-nam Case Say They Were Scapegoated," *The New York Times*, April 13, 2017, www.nytimes.com/2017/04/13/world/asia/kim-jong-nam-assassination-north-korea-malaysia.html?_r=0, accessed June 14, 2017.

they were hypnotized.... This posthypnotic amnesia does not occur unless it has been specifically suggested to the subject, and the memories are not restored when hypnosis is reinduced; thus it is not a form of state-dependent memory. However, it is temporary: upon administration of a pre-arranged cue, the amnesia is reversed and the formerly amnesic subject is able to remember the events perfectly well. Reversibility marks posthypnotic amnesia as a disruption of memory retrieval, as opposed to encoding or storage ....[683]

Accordingly, Dr. Brown had good reason to believe that whatever happened at the hotel was recorded inside Sirhan's mind, and that a good portion of that could be recovered. After six two-day sessions over a three-year period, for a total of 60 hours, using hypnosis, Dr. Brown uncovered a scenario that fits all the known evidence. In the course of his psychological assessment, Dr. Brown noted in a statement for the court:

I directly observed Mr. Sirhan a number of times switch into at least one distinctively different alter personality state, a personality state that responds in robot-like fashion upon cue and adopts the behavior of firing a gun at a firing range. The alter personality state is hereto-fore referred to as "range mode." This altered personality state *only* occurs while Mr. Sirhan is in an [sic] hypnotic or self-hypnotic state, and *only* in response to certain cues. This state never spontaneously manifests. While in this altered personality state Mr. Sirhan shows both a loss of executive control and complete amnesia.[684] [Emphasis in the original.]

Dr. Brown explained that because there was only one state that appeared only on a specific cue and never spontaneously, Sirhan could not be diagnosed as having "dissociative identity disorder," adding the state was "likely the product of coercive suggestive influence and hypnosis."[685] Brown also noted:

His post hypnotic amnesia for suggestions given in or actions per-formed under hypnosis is dramatic. I have written four text books

683   John F. Kihlstrom, "Hypnosis, Memory, and Amnesia," presented at the 75th annual meeting of the Association for Research in Nervous and Mental Disease, "Biological and Psychological Perspectives on Memory and Memory Disorders," New York, December 1995. According to the author's webpage with this talk, "An edited version of the original presentation was published in the Philosophical Transactions of the Royal Society: Biological Sciences as part of a special issue, Biological and Psychological Perspectives on Memory and Memory Disorders, edited by L.R. Squire and D.L. Schacter (1997, 372, 1727–1732)," socrates.berkeley.edu/~kihlstrm/hypnosis_memory.htm.

684   Declaration of Dr. Daniel P. Brown, Ph.D., Exhibit I from Sirhan's appeal by William Pepper, www.maryferrell.org/showDoc.html?docId=146777#relPageId=43

685   Declaration of Dr. Daniel P. Brown, Ph.D., Exhibit I.

on hypnosis, have taught hypnosis to over 3,000 professionals, and have hypnotized over 6,000 individuals over a 40-year professional career. Mr. Sirhan is one of the most hypnotizable individuals I have ever met, and the magnitude of his amnesia for actions not under his voluntary [control] in hypnosis is extreme, more than I have observed in many other highly hypnotizable individuals. [686]

Dr. Brown noted that Sirhan does not have schizophrenia and that the diagnosis at the trial was incorrect. Dr. Brown retested Sirhan and applied a "modern, scientific approach" to the results to come to this conclusion. He also submitted Sirhan's Rorschach test responses to an associate "blind," so that the person didn't know it was Sirhan's results being evaluated. That associate also agreed that there was no evidence of a mental disorder.

Dr. Brown wrote that Dr. Diamond's sessions with Sirhan had been "unduly suggestive." [687] On January 11, 1969, Diamond visited Sirhan in his cell. It was his third visit, and Robert Kaiser was there to observe. Kaiser watched Diamond hypnotize Sirhan and stick a pin in his hand, which did not appear to cause Sirhan pain, indicating he was likely deeply under at this point. Kaiser recounted what happened next:

> "Did anybody pay you to shoot Kennedy? Yes or no."
> Sirhan sighed.
> "I can't hear you."
> "No."
> "No? No one paid you to shoot Kennedy. Did anybody know ahead of time that you were going to do it, Sirhan?"
> "No."[688]

Diamond didn't ask Sirhan an open-ended question like "what happened?" He assumed that Sirhan was the shooter, and that if there were conspirators, Sirhan would have known them. But we saw in the earlier chapters neither of these assumptions proved correct. After a few other questions, Diamond asked Sirhan questions which someone may have programmed Sirhan to specifically avoid answering, as indicated by the pauses, which Kaiser timed.

> "Did you think this all up by yourself?"
> Sirhan paused for five seconds. "Yes," he said."

---

686   Declaration of Dr. Daniel P. Brown, Ph.D., Exhibit I.
687   Declaration of Dr. Daniel P. Brown, Ph.D., Exhibit I.
688   Kaiser, pp. 293–294.

"Yes. You thought this up all by yourself. Did you consult with anybody else, Sirhan?"

"No."

"Are you the only person involved in Kennedy's shooting?"

Sirhan blocked again with a three-second pause. "Yes."

"Yes. Nobody involved at all. Why did you shoot Kennedy?"

Sirhan had no answer. "Why did you shoot him, Sirhan?"

"The bombers," mumbled Sirhan.

"What? The bombers? You mean the bombers to Israel?"

"Yes."

"When did you decide to shoot Kennedy?"

"I don't know."[689]

The pauses Sirhan gave after being asked if he thought up the plan by himself and if others were involved can indicate programming designed to help the person avoid the questions. "Blocking" is an observed phenomenon of what happens when a person has a conflict between what they want to do and what a hypnotic command has ordered them to do.

In his last session with Diamond, in which the prosecution's hypnotist Seymour Pollack took part, after taking Sirhan through a traumatic childhood scene under hypnosis where Sirhan saw a man shot to death in front of him, Diamond turned to the night of Kennedy's assassination, with Pollack and Kaiser listening. He rehypnotized Sirhan, but Sirhan fell so deeply into a trance that Diamond had to work hard to keep Sirhan conscious enough to respond.

Diamond's questions showed an attempt to coercively lead the witness. How could Sirhan know "when he decided" to shoot Kennedy if he not only *never* decided to shoot Kennedy but also *provably never did?* This type of question is a "loaded question" or an "assumptive question" as it assumes something as true that has no basis in fact. We know for a fact that Sirhan did not kill Kennedy. How, then, could he answer such a question? When one uses such a question, discreditation, not fact-finding, is the clear goal.

Note also how Diamond reframed Sirhan's responses as affirmative statements. Again, the questions themselves and Diamond's reiteration of the answers appear to be an attempt to implant and reinforce a belief in Sirhan that he was guilty of the crime. Under hypnosis Diamond reinforced to Sirhan that he had "four Collinses to drink." But if he'd had that much to drink, someone would have noticed it! Sirhan was a small man who rarely drank at all. That amount of alcohol would have been on his breath and visible in his face and eyes. Most people have seen others who had that much to drink and note the redness in the eyes, the flushed face, and other obvious signs of being drunk.

---

689   Kaiser, pp. 302–303.

During each session, Sirhan skipped from seeing someone approaching to being choked. There was clearly some mental block on everything that happened in between. When Diamond tried to get Sirhan to recall what had happened in this missing period, during this final hypnotic session, Diamond again attempted to lead the witness:

> "There is Kennedy, Sirhan. Open your eyes, Sirhan. Sirhan, open your eyes. 'You son of a bitch,' you said, Sirhan."
>
> "He can't. He can't."
>
> "He can't do what?"
>
> "Can't send those bombers."
>
> "He can't send the bombers. You're not gonna let him, are you Sirhan? Hmm?"
>
> "He can't. He can't. He can't. He can't."
>
> "Sirhan! Did you know that Kennedy was coming this way?"
>
> "No."
>
> "Did you expect him?"
>
> "No."
>
> "Sirhan, were you waiting for him?"
>
> "Uhhhh."
>
> "Yes or no, Sirhan?"
>
> "No. Uhhh."
>
> "No. Are you sure you weren't waiting for him?"
>
> "No."
>
> "But you see him now. He's coming now. He's coming down the hall. Look at him, Sirhan. Open your eyes."
>
> "He's running at me."[690]

But of course, Robert Kennedy never ran at Sirhan. Someone who likely had a gun in his hand, however, clearly ran in Sirhan's direction, according to Virginia Guy and other witnesses. And of course, several people ran at Sirhan when they saw he had a gun, but Kennedy wasn't one of them. Diamond kept on, pressing Sirhan in a way more suggestive of implanting rather than recovering a memory:

> "I order you to open your eyes and look at Kennedy. Look at him. There he is. He's coming, Sirhan. He's coming toward you, Sirhan. Don't shake your head."

Was Sirhan shaking his head because that's not what he saw? Sirhan mumbled something that sounded like "Bobby" followed by "Son of a bitch."

---

690   Kaiser, pp. 354–355.

But Sirhan's next statement made it sound like "Son of a bitch" wasn't a term for Kennedy, but more a term of surprise: "What's *he* doing here?" It's also not clear if the "he" Sirhan referred to was Kennedy. If it was, it appears Sirhan was surprised to see Kennedy at that moment, which would hardly fit the story of a man trying to kill Kennedy. But Diamond used this against Sirhan: "You're talking to Kennedy. You call Kennedy a son of a bitch? Sirhan, open your eyes and look at Kennedy."

Diamond continued with Sirhan, who was clearly genuinely upset about Kennedy promising to send bombers to Israel. What had been "he can't" became "you can't" as the session progressed, at which point Diamond, in an effort to nudge Sirhan's memory along, asked, "Are you reaching for your gun, Sirhan?" At this, Sirhan made a grabbing motion across to his left hip with his right hand. Diamond asked Sirhan again, "Are you reaching for your gun?" He followed that up with, "How you gonna stop him?" Diamond prodded Sirhan further:

> Sirhan, open your eyes and look at Kennedy. Sirhan, open your eyes. He's coming. Reach for your gun, Sirhan. It's your last chance, Sirhan. Reach for your gun. Where is your gun? …
>
> Take the gun out of your pants. You've got the gun in your hand now. Let me see you shoot the gun, Sirhan. Shoot the gun. Shoot the gun. Shoot the gun. Sirhan, take the gun and shoot it."[691]

At this, Kaiser noted "Sirhan's right hand pounded climactically on his right thigh—five times. His right forefinger squeezed and twisted three more times in a weakening spasm. Then he was still."[692]

Accordingly, Dr. Brown wrote in his declaration, "I came to the conclusion that Dr. Diamond was unduly suggestive to Mr. Sirhan, in that Dr. Diamond systematically supplied specific suggestions to Mr. Sirhan to fill in the gaps of Mr. Sirhan's memory for the day and evening of the assassination. Such interviewing methods would not meet any current standard of non-suggestive interviewing."

Dr. Brown also found that Sirhan had a "low score on memory suggestibility," which explained why Diamond's efforts did not succeed in implanting a new memory."[693] Dr. Brown believed because of this, Sirhan's memory of what happened was still locked somewhere in his mind. After 60 hours of interviews, this is what Dr. Brown learned:

> Mr. Sirhan was led to the kitchen area by a woman after that woman had received directions from an official at the event. Mr. Sirhan did

---

691   Kaiser, pp. 354–355.

692   Kaiser, p. 355.

693   Declaration of Dr. Daniel P. Brown, Ph.D., Exhibit I. This also neatly disproved Diamond's thesis of 1980 that hypnotizing a witness automatically corrupts the witness, a point courts should consider.

not go with the intent to shoot Senator Kennedy, but did respond to
a specific hypnotic cue given to him by that woman to enter "range
mode," during which Mr. Sirhan automatically and involuntarily
responded with a "flashback" that he was shooting at a firing range
at circle targets. At the time Mr. Sirhan did not know that he was
shooting at people nor did he know that he was shooting at Senator
Kennedy.[694]

Dr. Brown commented, as have many others, that Sirhan's attempt to play
pool with his friend Gaymoard Mistri the night of the assassination "does not
suggest the motivation of an obsessed assassin planning to kill a presidential
candidate that same evening." [695]

One part of Dr. Brown's declaration stunned me, because it coincided with
the downstairs bar episode where the girl in the polka dot dress chatted up Eve
Hansen and Eve's sister Nina Ballantyne, telling them they couldn't get served at
that end of the bar and toasting "our next president" without naming Kennedy.
In his statement, Dr. Brown included a transcript of the portion where Sirhan
recalled wandering into a ballroom where an all-Mexican band was playing. Dr.
Brown assumed this was the Embassy Room upstairs, but in fact the Mexican
band was playing downstairs in the Ambassador Ballroom, which makes sense
with the rest of Sirhan's story.

> I recall a band...all Mexican...the brightness...a lot of people...I'm
> getting tired...I wasn't expecting this...it is getting hot...very hot...I
> want to get a drink. A make-shift bar area...I see a bartender...a white
> smock...he looked Latin...we just nodded...I told him what I wanted...
> *it's like I have a relationship with this guy*...Tom Collins...I drink it while
> I'm walking around...a tall glass... it looks like lemonade glass...I
> want to go back for more... [Tell me everything about the relationship
> with this guy] He looks like in Abbott and Costello...the short one...
> this bartender...he wasn't looking for a sale...he wasn't talkative...it
> is like he's communicating with gestures...a nod after I paid for it.
>
> I'm still looking around...he didn't make it (the drink) right in
> front of me...he made it and brought it over...after that I came back
> again...it was like a routine between us...like I'm more familiar...
> like I'm a regular customer of his...I don't remember seeing him
> before...it seemed like he was a professional...he never initiated
> a conversation but after the second time it was like there was a

---

694   Declaration of Dr. Daniel P. Brown, Ph.D., Exhibit I.
695   Declaration of Dr. Daniel P. Brown, Ph.D., Exhibit I.

> communication between us…like it happened with a nod… [Freely
> recall anything about this communication] It seemed familiar…
> like a return business…when he saw me come back he knew
> what I wanted…it is hard to figure out if he's targeting me or I'm
> targeting him…I don't remember him saying anything like "shoot
> Kennedy" or anything like that…he's just very quiet…we make
> eye contact with a nod…he knows his business…I begin to get
> tired…I sat down on one of the couches…I remember feeling that
> I had to go home…. [All grammar, brackets, ellipses and emphasis
> in the original.] [696]

Perhaps the bartender was giving Sirhan his final hypnotic commands. Or
perhaps he was drugging him, or both, as these options are not mutually exclusive. I have often wondered if the "Tom Collins" drinks that Sirhan thought he
had been drinking could have been drugged drinks. The Senate report on the
CIA's MKULTRA mind control projects described how the behavior of a person
under the influence of barbiturates went through these three stages as the drugs
were increased. Sirhan's behavior, as described by witnesses, would have fit the
description of Plane 2.

> Plane 1: No evident effect, or slight sedative effect.
> Plane 2: Cloudiness, calmness, amnesia. (Upon recovery, the subject
> will not remember what happened at this or "lower" planes or stages.)
> Plane 3: Slurred speech, old thought patterns disrupted, inability
> to integrate or learn new patterns. Poor coordination. Subject becomes
> unaware of painful stimuli. [697]

In the 1950s, the CIA had experimented extensively with both hypnosis
and drugs separately and in combination in their effort to completely control
a person's behavior. CIA documents hint that the right combination had been
found, but the CIA also decided to stop putting on paper anything related to
these efforts. [698] The CIA's records show that the best results were obtained via a

---

696   Declaration of Dr. Daniel P. Brown, Ph.D., Exhibit I.

697   "Project MKULTRA, the CIA's Program of Research In Behavioral Modification," Joint Hearing before
the Select Committee on Intelligence and the Subcommittee on Health and Scientific Research of the Committee
on Human Resources, United States Senate, August 2, 1977, p. 27.

698   See CIA Director Stansfield Turner's August 2, 1977 letter to Senator Daniel Inouye. The Church
committee had reviewed some of the documents on the CIA's "mind control" initiatives, which took place under
projects by the name of Bluebird, Artichoke, MKULTRA, MKNAOMI, MKDELTA, QKHILLTOP and others. In the letter,
Turner refers to the CIA's Inspector General 1963 report on the MKULTRA programs and a note therein which
stated, "Present practice is to maintain no records of the planning and approval of test programs." Turner was
writing because after the Church Committee finished, a new set of documents not previously uncovered, related to
MKULTRA and the other programs, was discovered. When CIA Director Richard Helms had been fired by President

combination of drugs and hypnosis, not just one or the other.

Remember, too, that no one smelled alcohol on Sirhan's breath. And Sirhan's recollection maps to the same downstairs bar where Eve Hansen saw three men sitting in the dark with their backs against the wall near the bar where a girl in a polka dot dress intercepted her when she went to order a drink. Was the girl protecting the operation when she essentially intercepted Hansen and her sister at the bar? Although Hansen paid for the drinks it was the girl, not the bartender, who brought them to her, according to one report.

Maybe this makeshift "bar" wasn't a bar at all, but a staging center for dispatching Sirhan and possibly the others sitting in the dark. It's an intriguing possibility that fits all the evidence without distortion. And remember, the original plan early in the night was for Kennedy to finish his speech at the private Embassy Room party for key campaign operatives and donors, and to proceed downstairs to the public "victory party" in the Ambassador Room. That option would have sent Kennedy down the narrow hallway from the end of the stairs into the Ambassador Room, right past the makeshift bar. It might have been even easier to kill him there than in the pantry. The final route was not set until Kennedy started speaking. But it appears the conspirators had a plan to take him out whichever way he went. That's why I think talk of a security breakdown or a betrayal by a Kennedy insider is simply a distraction. The conspirators just had two plans and apparently at least two different patsies at the ready. The thin, younger woman in the polka dot dress and the acne-faced Sirhan lookalike might have been waiting downstairs with another team of assassins at the ready.

Hans Bidstrup described seeing in Sirhan's milky white drink "a small red object which looked like a piece of red candy" in Sirhan's drink, "round on one side and flat on the other."[699] Bidstrup was not a drinker, and it's very possible he just didn't know what a half a maraschino cherry looked like. On the other hand, bartenders usually use whole cherries, not half cherries, to garnish drinks. When the CIA was experimenting with hypnosis, they often combined drugs with hypnosis, trying to find the perfect combination to make someone wholly pliable, including scopolamine. In a 1993 publication, the CIA discussed a 1955 Soviet plot to drug someone they wished to capture with *candy coated with scopolamine*.[700] In large doses, scopolamine is a toxic poison. But in small quantities, scopolamine produces amnesia, high tolerance to pain, and a reduction of one's willpower, all things that could have aided in the framing of Sirhan that night.

Nixon for refusing to help him cover up the Watergate break-in, Helms had ordered the CIA to destroy all its mind-control-related files. Turner suggested that these recently discovered files, then, had not been hidden from Congress, but had been so well hidden they had not been found when the CIA was actively seeking such records to destroy them, which may or may not have been a true statement.

699   FBI interview of Hans Bidstrup, June 10, 1968, dated June 12, 1968.

700   "Soviet Use of Assassination and Kidnapping," *Center for the Study of Intelligence*, Vol. 19. No. 3, September 22, 1993, via www.cia.gov/library/center-for-the-study-of-intelligence/kent-csi/vol19no3/html/v19i3a01p_0001.htm.

Scopolamine also causes the pupils to dilate, a condition Officer Placencia thought he noticed in Sirhan's eyes upon his arrest. While the older, more experienced Officer White said he did a test which provided Sirhan's eyes were behaving normally, remember that White was also a veteran of the force and would have known that if Sirhan were found to be under the influence of any substance, the jury might not convict him, and may have simply lied about Sirhan's eyes to cover up what Officer Placencia had observed.

After Sirhan drank whatever this mysterious bartender prepared for him, he began to feel very sleepy. He remembered going back to his car to go home, but realized he was too tired to drive. He decided to return to the hotel for coffee but found his way, possibly through a post-hypnotic suggestion, to the same bartender. There, according to Dr. Brown's notes, Sirhan was intercepted by an attractive woman with a polka dot dress who was sitting at the bar talking to the bartender. She overheard Mr. Sirhan asking for coffee and she said that she knew where the coffee was. The woman in the polka dot dress then took Mr. Sirhan by the hand and led him to the anteroom behind the stage where Senator Kennedy was speaking. There they discovered a large silver coffee urn and cups. Sirhan poured coffee, and remembered wondering, "How do I pay for this?" He remembered being very sexually attracted to the woman.

"All of a sudden," Sirhan remembered, they were told to move by some official in a suit, not a uniform, with dark hair and "a big, full face." The man seemed to be "in charge," according to Sirhan. The man pointed them in the direction of the pantry and the girl "acknowledge[d] his instruction."

Earl Williman, an assistant chief set electrician for Desilu Studios (per the FBI, because to the LAPD he said he worked at Universal Studios), appeared to have seen the man that directed Sirhan and the girl to the pantry. In his FBI interview, Williman described entering the anteroom behind the stage during Kennedy's speech. Oddly, a young woman in a beige dress wanted to know what Williman was doing in that area and took his name down. There, Williman noticed a stocky, well-dressed man about 50 years old and six feet tall, with "a fat round face." He appeared to Williman to be Latino, with dark skin and bushy hair.[701]

Williman noted the man was wearing a "polka dot necktie" and remained seated during the time he saw him. [702]

Was the polka dot pattern somehow meaningful to our story? When Derren Brown constructed his test of whether someone could be programmed, the polka dot pattern was the first of two triggers. The hypnotized subject grew alert and followed whatever command followed the sighting of the polka dot pattern. Similarly, in the film *The Manchurian Candidate*, the hypnotically

701   FBI interview of Earl Williman, June 23, 1968, dated June 27, 1968.
702   *Ibid.*

programmed character Raymond Shaw is activated using two triggers. The first trigger was an audio command: "Why don't you pass the time by playing a little solitaire?" At this, Shaw was compelled to find a deck of cards and play solitaire. The second trigger was the Queen of Diamonds card. As soon as he saw this card, he did whatever he was next directed to do, including "go jump in a lake." This was not the fictional imagination of some author who knew nothing about hypnosis. Richard Condon, the author of the book by the same name on which the famous film was based, had done a lot of solid research on hypnosis, including much of the lesser-known literature. In his fictional work, he cited several important nonfiction studies that indicated it is possible to program someone to do just about anything under hypnosis. He was not inventing this scenario from thin air.

Another person wearing a polka dot pattern that night, who met with a tragic death, was Kathy Fulmer. Fulmer, a 19-year-old, was at the pantry doors at the west end, right where Kennedy entered the pantry just before the shooting. She was wearing a polka dot scarf. As the shooting started, she reportedly ran off saying "They shot him. They shot Kennedy."

On June 7, Fulmer went to the police and offered herself up as the girl Sandra Serrano must have seen, but upon viewing her, Serrano denied this.[703]

Just before jury deliberations began in Sirhan's trial, Fulmer was found semi-conscious in a motel. She died at a nearby hospital shortly after her arrival from an overdose of Seconal.[704] No motive for suicide had been found. Just four weeks earlier, Ernie Johnson had told the LAPD that around 8:30 P.M. the night of the primary, he saw a "woman in a polka dot scarf" arguing with another woman in a polka dot dress and a "Mexican" (who was not Sirhan) in the pantry.[705] Might that have been the man in the gold sweater that Serrano and others had seen that night with both Sirhan and the woman in the polka dot dress? Had Fulmer been involved in some way? Might she have been able to signal people in the pantry that Kennedy was coming? Had she been silenced lest the truth surface? Or was it all just a coincidence?

There was another woman wearing a polka dot "kerchief or something" that photographer Bill Epperidge noted. While Fulmer was tall and thin, this woman was short and on the heavy side. Epperidge said this olive-skinned woman in her early twenties tried to push her way into a line that had formed near Kennedy as he was on his way to the stage. Epperidge felt she didn't belong there "and gave her a poke in the ribs to get her out of the way," but the girl was very persistent, and Epperidge poked her a second time. He saw this same girl one more time as

---

703   FBI interview of Sandra Serrano, June 7, 1968, dated June 8, 1968.

704   "Kennedy Case, Suicide Linked," *Los Angeles Times*, April 12, 1969.

705   LAPD interview of Ernie Johnson, March 20, 1969.

Kennedy was exiting the stage through the anteroom. She was standing "to the right just off the platform" as they exited.[706]

A woman in a polka dot dress, a man in a polka dot tie, a woman at the entrance to the pantry in a polka dot scarf and a woman backstage with another polka dot "kerchief" or scarf is interesting. Yet in the hundreds of pictures I've seen from the hotel that night, I've never seen anyone wearing any clothing item with polka dots. Was that by design? Was the polka dot pattern some sort of hypnotic trigger? Was it a way for conspirators to identify each other? Did it perhaps serve both purposes? Did the LAPD destroy photos that showed any people in polka dot patterns because they knew this would be a way to identify conspirators?

After encountering the man behind the stage, according to Dr. Brown's notes of Sirhan's sessions, Sirhan followed the girl into the pantry "like a puppy." He had wanted to go back downstairs to hear the mariachi band but felt compelled to follow the girl instead. In earlier sessions with Diamond, Sirhan had remembered pouring coffee for a girl who looked "Armenian" or of some other Mediterranean nationality. But Sirhan did not at that time remember if the woman was wearing a polka dot dress. Nowhere in Dr. Brown's declaration does he substantiate that the girl who intercepted Sirhan at the bar was wearing a polka dot dress in the statements he quoted, so it is unclear if that was Dr. Brown's assumption or something Sirhan said.

Sirhan followed the girl into the pantry. It was not well lit in there, and she sat on one of the steam tables. He faced her. According to Dr. Brown's declaration, Sirhan remembered:

> I'm still sleepy ... very sleepy ... I was flirting with her. ... Then she sat up on the table facing with her back to the wall...her thighs and legs are right here...I am just looking at her, trying to take her beauty in...I am trying to figure out how to hit on her. That's all I can think about ... I was fascinated with her looks ... She was sitting. I was standing. ... She was busty, looked like Natalie Wood. She never said much. It was very erotic. I was consumed by her. She was a seductress with an unspoken unavailability."[707]

The next thing Sirhan remembered was the girl tapping or pinching him on the shoulder, an unnaturally harsh pinch. "It snapped me out of my doldrums," Sirhan said under Dr. Brown's hypnosis. "She says, 'Look, look, look.'" At this

---

706   FBI interview of Bill Epperidge taken likely on June 17, 1968 (despite what I believe is a mistaken notation that says "dictated June 15, 1968"), dated June 19, 1968.

707   Brown declaration.

point the woman directed his attention to the back of the room, where Kennedy was entering.

The woman put her hand on him and Sirhan at first "thought it was romantic." But he saw the woman was not looking at him but "way above my head." Was she looking at the shooter standing on the table that Harold Burba, George Green and Nina Rhodes-Hughes had seen during the shooting? Sirhan continued:

> I think she had her hand on me…I am not sure if it was her hand or somebody else's…Then I was at the target range…a flashback to the shooting range…I didn't know that I had a gun…there was this target like a flashback to the target range…I thought that I was at the range…I think I shot one or two shots…Then I snapped out of it and thought, "I'm not at the range" … Then, "What is going on?' Then they started grabbing me…I'm thinking, "the range, the range, the range." Then everything gets blurry… I think that's when Uecker grabbed me…after that first or second shot…that was the end of it… It was the wrong place for the gun to be there…I thought it was the range…Then, they broke my finger…Next thing I remember, I was being choked and man-handled. I didn't know what was going on. I didn't realize until they got in a car…later when I saw the female judge I knew that Bobby Kennedy was shot and I was the shooter, but it doesn't come into my memory.[708]

If this is an accurate memory of what Sirhan experienced at that moment, if a jury could be made to understand this, it seems unlikely a jury would find him guilty. Sirhan was like a wind-up doll. At a given signal he believed he was back at the target range, shooting.

Laurie Dusek, an attorney working closely with William Pepper on Sirhan's case, observed with Dr. Brown Sirhan's spontaneous exhibition of "range mode" behavior. Brown described how "Mr. Sirhan automatically took his firing stance, and in an uncharacteristic robot-like voice described shooting at vital human organs." Brown noted that "Following brief re-enactments of 'range mode,' Mr. Sirhan remained completely amnesiac for the behavior."[709] According to Dan Brown's declaration, the first time Sirhan realized he was being charged with killing Robert Kennedy was when he went to the Judge, which fits the scenario I proposed earlier—that Sirhan had been programmed not to come out of his trance until he had been arraigned.

It's not only possible but *probable* that Sirhan was as much a victim of this crime as Robert Kennedy. He was used in someone else's assassination plot without

---

708   Brown declaration.
709   Brown declaration.

his conscious knowledge. Here was a man who had come to America to escape the horrible Israeli-Palestinian conflict and to pursue a better life, only to have his background used against him to set him up as a patsy in the assassination of Senator Kennedy. Given that Sirhan didn't kill anyone in the pantry, given that he didn't even wound anyone in the pantry (because remember, *not even one bullet from the victims could be linked to Sirhan's gun*), I believe if the case were retried, a jury might find Sirhan "not guilty" of any criminal act that night.

If the conspirators wanted to ensure Kennedy didn't leave the hotel alive, were there other possible patsies there that night as well? People who might also have been programmed to forget their role? I have two candidates for alternate patsies: Luis Angel Castillo and Crispin Curiel Gonzales. Gonzales committed suicide in jail, or so we were told, after leaving a note indicating possible foreknowledge of the assassination. And Castillo had apparently already been used by the CIA in a previous assassination attempt against a political figure.

In April 1967, numerous papers around the country ran a UPI story out of Manila that announced that the Philippine National Bureau of Investigation (NBI) had in custody a man who claimed, under truth serum, to have been part of the plot to kill President John F. Kennedy in Dallas. The 24-year-old man was named Luis Angel Castillo. According to the UPI story, Castillo was a "Cuban-trained Communist agent sent to the Philippines to contact Communist guerrillas." Under "hypnotic grilling" and truth serum, Castillo "admitted" that he was in Dallas the day President Kennedy was shot. He had been given a rifle by a man he did not know and told to shoot at the man in the open car. Out of the trance, at a news conference in the Manila NBI office, when asked if he was involved in the JFK assassination plot, Castillo said only, "I don't want to answer that question."[710] Castillo said he was a Cuban agent, sent to the Philippines to contact Communist Huk guerrillas.[711] But in a hypnotic session, Castillo revealed that he worked for the CIA. This part, of course, was never reported in the mainstream media and only came out later due to the research of UCLA professor Richard Popkin, author Dick Russell, author and media activist Jeff Cohen, and a small handful of others.

As ridiculous as this story must have sounded to the general public, CIA officials thought there was possibly some truth to Castillo's story. Castillo was mentioned in the CIA's Inspector General (IG) report in connection with the CIA's plots to assassinate Castro. When one of the authors of the IG report, Scott Breckenridge, was questioned about Castillo's name being in there by the Rockefeller Commission, according to a memo from former Warren Commission and Rockefeller Commission attorney David Belin:

---

710   UPI, "America Claims Took Part in Plot," *Daily World* (Opelousas, La.), April 21, 1967.

711   UPI, "Cuban Agent Claims Part in JFK Plot," *Independent* (Long Beach, Calif.), April 22, 1967.

> In the opinion of Breckenridge, *Castillo's story, as documented in these files, probably cannot be dismissed out of hand as inherently incredible.* Breckenridge still has no present memory of how the team preparing the 1967 IG report on assassination came to be aware of Castillo or what follow-up action, if any, was taken on the basis of these documents. He suggests that another person who worked on the 1967 IG report, Ken Greer, may have worked on this Castillo angle and would be the person to contact for such information. He stated that Greer is now retired and living in Wisconsin. [Emphasis added.] [712]

The mention of Wisconsin was interesting because Castillo claimed to have been programmed by a woman named Jean Bolf (now deceased) in Wisconsin.

> Breckenridge also stated that these files do not indicate whether or not Castillo was ever actually deported to the United States and if so whether the FBI ever interrogated him. (But see item below, *which indicates Castillo returned to Chicago on February 10, 1968, and evaded the authorities.*) Apparently the Agency has no knowledge of Mr. Castillo's present location.[713] [Parenthesis in the original; emphasis added.]

Castillo's story, and the effort to surface it, is worthy of a book on its own. I will only give it scant treatment here. I talked to the man who hypnotized him while he was in prison in the Philippines, Victor Arcega. I asked Arcega how he even got access to this prisoner, and he explained that his brother worked for the NBI and had brought him in to see what he could find out.

Castillo was born in Puerto Rico to Cuban parents, according to the FBI, although a family member said the FBI report was wrong and the father was born in Mexico and the mother in Pennsylvania, and that they met in Chicago. Castillo was in and out of prisons in places that included, besides the Philippines, New Jersey and Missouri.

According to Belin's memo, one of Castillo's arrest reports contained this statement: "There were strong indications of homosexual tendencies on the part of Castillo, and he was described as being of low average intelligence with an unstable personality." Homosexual or not, Castillo married a woman he met when he returned to the United States in February of 1968. When he told her he worked for the CIA, she asked him, "Why use someone as erratic as you?" "That's

---

712   Memo from David W. Belin to Mason Cargill MC, May 19, 1975, formerly classified SECRET, released from the Gerald Ford Library to respected researcher William Kelly, who posted it on his blog at jfkcountercoup. blogspot.com/2012/11/. "On March 23, 1996 I wrote to the Ford Library requesting the ROCKCOM records of Luis Angel Castillo. On February 10, 2000, I received the following document, Kelly wrote.

713   *Ibid.*

the point," he told her. [714] And he's right. The CIA's goal when developing assets was always "plausible deniability"—the ability to instantly distance themselves credibly. Unstable conmen and criminals make excellent recruits for this reason. They know how to evade the law and not get caught, and if caught, the CIA can simply use their past crimes to discredit them.

In 1967, Castillo used the name of a criminal wanted in the Philippines, Antonio Eloriaga-Reyes, and committed a crime. Because he was arrested as Eloriaga-Reyes, he was then deported to the Philippines. (Curiously enough, Crispin Curiel Gonzales used someone else's identity and got himself deported to Mexico. Is this a common intelligence agency technique? A cheap way to get into a foreign country?)

Once his actual identity had been verified, the NBI knew they had someone strange on their hands. The NBI asked Arcega to hypnotize Castillo to see if he could uncover what he was really doing in the Philippines. The NBI feared Castillo might have been sent to kill their president, Ferdinand Marcos.

The CIA had at one time controlled the President of the Philippines. Edward Lansdale, who worked for the CIA in a number of sensitive covert operations, controlled Ramon Magsaysay as a CIA asset and helped propel him to the presidency in 1953. When Magsaysay died in a plane crash in 1957, CIA officer Joseph Burkholder Smith was sent to the Philippines with the admonition to "find another Magsaysay."[715] But the CIA was outspent by political forces in the Philippines when Ferdinand Marcos came to power in 1965. Marcos knew how to play the anti-Communist tune to America to get foreign aid, but then he used that money for other purposes. The CIA had not been able to control Marcos, and given their pattern abroad, this would have been reason enough for the CIA to attempt to assassinate him.

In his book *Gold Warriors*, Sterling Seagrave suggests the CIA discovered gold and other treasures plundered by the Japanese during World War II that had been hidden in the Philippines. The gold and other treasures were used to fund secret "off-the-books" CIA operations through a trust named the Santa Romana Foundation in Lichtenstein. But the CIA wasn't the only one to find the hidden Japanese treasures. Ferdinand Marcos had found some sites too and was busy pilfering the riches for himself. If true, that gave the CIA two reasons to want to take Marcos out. Not only was he not playing by their rules, he was depriving them of future funding. Both reasons give credence to the notion the CIA was trying to assassinate Marcos.

In a "Secret/Sensitive" memo from the CIA's files, from Henry Kissinger to

---

714   Jeff Cohen's interview notes of his conversation with Castillo's unnamed wife, May 1976, provided to me by Jeff Cohen. I met Jeff initially through the organization he founded, Fairness & Accuracy In Reporting. I later learned we both shared a serious and longstanding interest in the truth behind the assassinations of the 1960s.

715   Stanley Karnow, "In the Philippines, the CIA Has Found a Second Home," *Los Angeles Times*, May 7, 1989.

President Nixon, dated March 15, 1973, which is still largely redacted, we find this text:

> You will recall that when the Vice President stopped briefly in the Philippines, President Marcos gave him a file of documents which alleged that several Americans were involved in plotting his assassination. At your direction, CIA has completed its analysis of the documents. Director Schlesinger's conclusions are as follows:[716]

A full page of text is redacted at this point, followed by this:

> We will ask [FBI] Director [L. Patrick] Gray to investigate on a close-hold basis what, if anything, can be done about the American citizen who escaped to this country. We will also send a message to President Marcos informing him that we are investigating the involvement of our citizens.[717]

This appears to be an oblique reference to Luis Castillo and the possibility that he went to the Philippines to kill Marcos. After several more wholly redacted pages, there's a "Secret/Sensitive/Eyes Only" memo from Brent Scowcroft to Mike Dunn titled "Alleged Assassination Plot Against President Marcos." The fact that "Assassination Plot" is singular indicates this is not likely a set of plots but a single plot, and the text confirms this:

> The file of documents which President Marcos gave the Vice President on the alleged plot against his life has been evaluated by the CIA ....[718]

The CIA cleared itself of all responsibility, but that means nothing, as that is what they would have done had they been directly involved.

In extensive notes of his sessions with Castillo, Victor Arcega described how the repetitions of certain words, phrases, letters and numbers would send Castillo immediately into automatic behaviors that were wholly repeatable. Common words like "sand" and "flowers" would elicit strong behaviors. But when words and sequences were chained, new behaviors would appear. If Castillo had been faking everything, he would have had to have had a prodigious memory, able to

716   Memo from Henry A. Kissinger to The President, March 15, 1973, www.cia.gov/library/readingroom/docs/LOC-HAK-296-7-11-4.pdf, accessed September 18, 2017.

717   *Ibid.*

718   Memo from Brent Scowcroft to Mike Dunn, March 26, 1973, www.cia.gov/library/readingroom/docs/LOC-HAK-296-7-11-4.pdf, accessed September 18, 2017.

remember which behavior to exhibit upon which clue. Arcega believed Castillo's behavior was indicative of intense and prolonged hypnotic programming. One coded phrase caused Castillo to put an imaginary gun to his head and pull the trigger, a sight Arcega found highly disturbing. His hypnotic sessions with Castillo took place over the course of several months. When shown a picture of Marcos, Castillo would switch into his own version of "range mode" and fire an imaginary pistol at Marcos. If the picture was marched around the cell Castillo would follow it, shooting his imaginary gun at it, according to Arcega's notes.

The woman in Wisconsin, Jean Bolf, appeared to play a large part in Castillo's programming. Awake and unhypnotized, Castillo suggested Bolf was an attractive woman whom he enjoyed being around. But under hypnosis, Castillo appeared to hate her and felt she was controlling him. Arcega found that when he put Castillo under hypnosis, Castillo awakened at the word "flowers." Bolf's husband Gerald had, at the time of their engagement in 1958, been "stationed in Milwaukee with the Navy."[719]

Castillo seemed to fit the "split personality" described by Estabrooks. The first personality to come out under hypnosis believed himself to be a communist agent. But the deeper personality under hypnosis understood he worked for the CIA.

Castillo returned to the United States in February 1968 and apparently disappeared. Did he reappear in the pantry? Castillo looked so much like Sirhan that J. Edgar Hoover, FBI Director, received an urgent telegram from the Philippines after the assassination of Senator Robert Kennedy that read:

> PHOTOS OF SIRHAN SIRHAN AND [CASTILLO] ALMOST IDENTICAL STOP [CASTILLO] DEPORTED FROM PHILIPPINES 1967 FOR FALSIFI-CATION OF PASSPORT STOP WHILE IN PHILLIPPINES HE CLAIMED TO BE PART OF JOHN KENNEDY ASSASSINATION PLOT STOP PLEASE INFORM PRESENT RESIDENCE AND LOCATION OF [CASTILLO] STOP SEND FINGERPRINTS OF SIRHAN FOR COMPARISON WITH [CASTILLO] STOP[720]

At the time of the assassination, Arcega, who had moved his family to Los Angeles, was working as a proofreader at the *Los Angeles Times*. The night of the assassination, someone showed up at his doorstep to ask if the shooter in the pantry had been Filipino. Arcega briefly considered offering Sirhan's defense team his services as a hypnotist, but feared what he might find. He moved his family to Canada and was still living there when I talked to him years later.

Castillo was clearly programmable. And he had already been exposed in the media, although not as a CIA asset. That part of the story never made the news.

---

719   "News of Society," *Wausau Daily Record-Herald, Wausau, Wisconsin,* January 8, 1958.

720   Telegram from a party whose name and affiliation appear redacted to J. Edgar Hoover, June 7, 1968.

It would have not been out of character, then, for the CIA to consider setting him up to be a patsy in the crime.

Another person who may have been set up to be a patsy or participant in the crime was a young man named Crispin Curiel Gonzales. On July 6, 1968, an AP story reported that a 17-year-old named Crispin Curiel Gonzales had hung himself in a cell in a Juarez hospital. The AP reported that Mexican Federal District Attorney Norberto Salinas had said "the youth was arrested June 17 [1968] after a letter or manuscript fell from his pocket at a concession stand in Juarez. The paper included writings to the effect that the youth had prior knowledge of the slaying of Sen. Kennedy in Los Angeles."[721] Gonzales also indicated he had known Sirhan.

Sirhan's brother Sharif said Sirhan went to the library a lot, that there were two or three libraries he'd visit afternoons or evenings.[722] One of these may have been the Santa Monica Library, because Gonzales claimed to have met Sirhan there. But before he could be questioned extensively on this matter, he allegedly hung himself in a prison cell. Given that not long before this, Gonzales had written his father hinting he might soon be coming into a lot of money, his death may not have been a suicide at all.

Kaiser showed a picture of Gonzales in the newspaper to Sirhan and got no reaction. "Who is he?" Sirhan had asked, and Kaiser told him the story. "Where is he now?" Sirhan asked. When Kaiser explained he had hung himself, Sirhan said "He didn't have to die," leading Kaiser to think Sirhan knew him, although I think Sirhan just felt bad that anyone else had to die for a crime he, at the time, believed he had committed.[723] The FBI's Roger "Frenchy" LaJeunesse confirmed there was some association between Gonzales and Sirhan,[724] but perhaps Sirhan had been in a hypnotic state and therefore didn't remember him.

If Sirhan, Castillo, Gonzales or anyone were programmed to be a patsy by the CIA in an actual assassination plot, would the CIA ever admit to that? No agency of the United States government would leave a paper trail if such an effort was undertaken. No one who might talk would be allowed to live. Witting participants would be threatened, blackmailed or killed to prevent such a secret from leaking. When the CIA was drawing up "Executive Action" plans against Castro and Lumumba, one of the notes they left, that the Church Committee discovered years later, was to put "nothing on paper." So if you are of the mind that if there's no official record, it didn't happen, you are in the naïve segment

---

721   AP, "Bulletins," *The Greenwood Commonwealth*, July 6, 1968, via Newspapers.com.
722   LAPD interview of Sharif Sirhan, June 17, 1968.
723   Kaiser, p. 238.
724   Turner and Christian, pp. 90–92.

of the population that can be too easily persuaded to believe that absence of evidence is evidence of absence. Absence of physical, confirmatory evidence is *exactly what you'd expect* in a covert operation. But there's no absence of circumstantial information, and remember, judges will tell you to treat this the same as you would hard evidence in any case.

At this point, there is extremely strong evidence Sirhan was not only hypnotized but set up to be a patsy without his knowledge. How was Sirhan picked? Who knew he was so highly hypnotizable? Where might Sirhan have first been spotted?

Estabrooks suggested "the hospital as a logical point of contact" when looking for subjects that could be easily hypnotized.[725] Estabrooks wrote that in the context of finding foreigners captured as prisoners of war, so the statement is not directly analogous. But by several accounts, after Sirhan had the accident with the racehorse, something happened to change his personality. Was Sirhan first hypnotized after or maybe even during the time he spent in the hospital in Corona?

When interviewed by Sergeants Sandlin and Strong shortly after the assassination, Sirhan's brother Sharif described not only how seriously Sirhan's personality changed after his fall from the horse, but how Sirhan *disappeared for two weeks* following the accident. [726] It was as if someone had kidnapped Sirhan after he was discovered in the hospital to be highly hypnotizable and started programming him to be some sort of covert asset from that point forward.

When he finally came home, "he had stitches all over on this side here .... Seven or eight stitches," Sharif said, pointing to his right eye. Sirhan also complained of pain in his chest and his right side and other places "from his stomach and his back and his front head and shoulders."[727] It makes sense he would hurt all over after a fall from a horse. It makes less sense he would have that much pain all over two weeks later, after presumably having been treated. Dr. Richard Nelson, who treated him, made his injuries sound very minor.[728] Had he been physically abused or even tortured in some way, without his knowledge?

During the trial of Charlie Manson, for his role in manipulating his supporters into committing the murders of Sharon Tate and Rosemary and Leno LaBianca, Dr. William J. Bryan, who was helping the counsel of Linda Kasabian, one of Manson's followers accused with murder, stated that personality changes were not induced through hypnosis but through torture:

---

725   Estabrooks, *Hypnotism*, p. 207.
726   LAPD interview of Sharif Sirhan, June 17, 1968.
727   *Ibid.*
728   LAPD summary of Dr. Richard Nelson in Progress Report dated September 20, 1968.

If the defense is going to be hypnotism, I don't think the defendants have a chance. No one can be forced under hypnosis to commit murder unless that capacity was already in their essential nature.

But there is another, far more powerful influence which may be seen here—brainwashing. Under long-term confinement, deprivation and brutality, which I understand may have been operative in this case, suggestive influence may be brought to bear which will completely change a personality.[729]

If Sirhan received torture in conjunction with hypnosis at any point, he would likely have no memory of that. The hypnotist present would have seen to that. Sharif told the police that "all the times he was seeing the doctor. ... He had some medicine."

The number of visits Sirhan paid to the doctor related to his fall from the horse seemed excessive compared with the injuries described by Dr. Richard Nelson. According to the LAPD's progress report on this matter, Dr. Nelson described Sirhan's condition as noncritical. His face was covered in dirt and Sirhan was unable to see at first due to the foreign matter in his eyes. But there were no broken bones, just some superficial bruises and cuts at the time of his fall. Dr. Nelson cleaned Sirhan's eyes and treated his wounds and sent him on his way.[730]

Why then, do FBI records show that Sirhan visited a doctor *13 more times over the next year* specifically in relation to the track accident? The FBI reported Sirhan went to the doctor on September 25 and 28, October 26, November 8, and December 10 in 1966, and on February 21, April 6, September 6, October 6, October 9, October 10, November 6, and December 18 in 1967.[731] Either Sirhan was far more seriously hurt during his fall from the horse than any official record has ever stated, or these visits were a cover for some other activity. Was someone using these visits to hypnotically program Sirhan?

In Donald Bain's book *The CIA's Control of Candy Jones*, John Nebel, a radio personality in New York, described how his wife, the famous model Jessica Wilcox, who used the stage name of Candy Jones, became a hypnotically controlled courier for the CIA. She had an "alter" personality called Arlene Grant. Arlene was aware of Candy, but Candy was not aware of Arlene. The description very much mirrors what Estabrooks had described for splitting people into multiple personalities and programming them separately. Her hypnotist, whom Bain called "Gilbert Jensen," worked out of Northern California.

729   Ralph Brighton, AP Science Writer, "Can you Hypnotize Person to Murder?" *Charleston Daily Mail*, December 6, 1969.

730   LAPD Progress Report – Background/Conspiracy Team, www.maryferrell.org/showDoc. html?docId=99734#relPageId=20&tab=page.

731   "Chronology of Events, Life of Sirhan Bishara Sirhan," FBI Los Angeles Field Office, No. 56-156: Volume 12 (Ser. 2576-2725), December 16, 1968.

She visited him regularly and received injections of what she was told were vitamins but were more likely psychotropic drugs to keep her under control.

Was Sirhan given similar injections? The doctor who treated him after the fall, Dr. Richard Nelson, noted that Sirhan seemed terrified of the medical treatments. Had someone already started to medicate him in some way before the accident?

In custody, Sirhan had also exhibited a fear that his prison cell was bugged. Most people outside the covert world do not think along these lines. Given Sirhan's school studies in the top spy languages of German, Russian, and Chinese, and given that he already spoke Arabic and English, Sirhan may have already been on some intelligence agency's radar even before his accident. Anyone who knew Sirhan before the accident at the track could have simply used the accident as the perfect cover to accelerate his programming.

Sharif pinpointed the racetrack accident as the point after which Sirhan's behavior changed dramatically. Sharif was not close to Sirhan. They had barely spoken for the last two years. Sharif emphasized he was not saying any of this to take Sirhan's side or try to make him look less guilty but simply because it was the truth:

> After he fell, we noticed that something went wrong with him because he started to change gradually. Now, we noticed the change not all at one time. It just became gradually, gradually, gradually, little by little, little by little. The last two or three months we couldn't even talk to him or say—he was always, you know, avoiding us, and we tried to avoid him just so that we would pretend, if he wants to do something wrong instead of not to do it, because if we keep after him he might get worse and worse and worse. So we thought it better just to leave him the way he is. Not to bother him, to get out of his way.[732]

Before the fall, Sirhan would do what he was asked. He was "sincere and honest and wanting to do whatever you want him to do," Sharif explained. Before the fall from the horse, he kept his room clean, would mow the lawn when asked, and was generally tidy. "After that, he just didn't care for anything—not his room, not even for himself...."[733] He wouldn't come out to talk to visitors. But he talked to the garbage man. "He stays there and he drinks coffee with them, and whenever they pass by—whoever is at the front door, they say, 'Sir, where's Sirhan; how's Sirhan.' He was so—everyone like, even the neighbors." Sharif was trying to explain that people who interacted with Sirhan generally liked him.

---

732   LAPD interview of Sharif Sirhan, June 17, 1968.

733   *Ibid.*

But after the accident, Sirhan had become so obstinate that Sharif said he feared he would hit Sirhan out of frustration so he had stopped speaking to him. Sharif said Saidallah wasn't talking to Sirhan either, because at one point Sirhan had upset Said, as Sharif called him, and Said had hit Sirhan and the police had been called.

When Sgt. Sandlin asked him who Sirhan's closest friend had been in the last year, Sharif responded, "his bedroom and his books."[734]

Walter Rathke, a groom who had been one of Sirhan's friends when they were working together "at a horse racing farm in Norco," which abuts Corona, also noticed a dramatic change in Sirhan after the accident. He last saw Sirhan at his home in 1967. According to Rathke, Sirhan's mother Mary said, "I just can't talk to that boy anymore." The LAPD's report of Rathke's interview states:

> Rathke states that he too noticed a big difference in Sirhan's personality after his injury. He seemed to be a different person. Sirhan appeared very serious. He did not laugh anymore and was not his jovial self.[735]

But Sirhan was his jovial self at Parker Center, after the shooting. Were Sirhan's moods the result of hypnotic conditioning? Had A and B personalities been created?

Sirhan had joined the Rosicrucian Order AMORC (Ancient and Mystical Order Rosae Crucis) in June 1966, a few months before his fall from the horse in September 1966. On their website, the Rosicrucians explain they are not a religion, that students can be of any religion, and that they offer teachings designed to lead one to enlightenment. But there is something odd about the role of the Rosicrucians in Sirhan's life. It was almost as if someone used his association with the Rosicrucians as a cover to hide Sirhan's trancelike states.

Curiously, the strange woman who spent the day with John Fahey, who wanted to fake a passport and get out of the country before "they" killed Kennedy "at the winning reception" said something about going up north, near San Francisco, for a conference or convention, and that she was a member of the Rosicrucians. The national Rosicrucian headquarters is in San Jose, California.

Mrs. Frances Holland, the "Southern California Grand Counsellor of the Rosicrucian Order" told the FBI on June 12, 1968, that Sirhan had attended the Pasadena chapter meeting on June 4, 1968—the night of the California primary. Holland said

---

734   *Ibid.*
735   LAPD interview of Walter Tom Rathke, February 18, 1969.

she had confirmed this with the supervisor of the Pasadena chapter, Sherman Livingston. Holland noted in the same interview that Livingston and the Master of the chapter, Theodore Stevens, were concerned about the negative publicity stemming from Sirhan's association with the Rosicrucians. So it should surprise no one that when the FBI talked to Livington, he said he had reviewed his notes and found Sirhan appeared at their chapter on May 28, not June 4.[736] This may be the truth, but this may also be a lie to distance the organization from any hint of involvement.

A woman wrote Robert Kennedy in November 1967 saying the Rosicrucian organization "planned to kill off the whole Kennedy family." The woman, whose name is redacted in the FBI report from which this information was taken, "suggested that everyone in the organization be interrogated and jailed."[737] Things that sounded crazy in advance sounded far less crazy after the fact. One wonders what might have happened had the FBI taken that woman's threat seriously and done some investigating.

Oddly enough, there appears to have been a possible Rosicrucian-CIA connection to an assassination that happened in 1948 in Bogotá, Colombia. Jorge Eliécer Gaitán was the Bobby Kennedy of his time, a man who was genuinely concerned about the plight of the poor in his country and who took on his own party which was doing too little to help. In April 1948, Gaitán was assassinated in the street. The killing was blamed on a man named Juan Roa Sierra, who was then killed by an angry mob shortly after. The uprising that followed the assassination, called the *Bogotazo*, is still noted annually.

But mysteries in the case surfaced nearly immediately. Roa had been interested, like Sirhan, in the occult. Like Sirhan, Sierra was a member of the Rosicrucians. Roa had joined at the recommendation of an older German astrologer friend. Some witnesses, including famous author Gabriel García Márquez, heard and saw evidence that Roa may have been a patsy and that the real shooter—or shooters— had gotten lost in the crowd. In his memoir, García Márquez described seeing a man in a gray suit incite the crowd against Roa, "to have a false assassin killed in order to protect the identity of the real one."[738] Colombia even brought in the world-famous Scotland Yard detectives to try to get to the bottom of the matter, but all they found were more questions.

At the time, Colombia was about to host the conference the Ninth Pan-American Conference that launched the Organization of American States, an organization designed ostensibly to keep Communism from taking root in Latin America. One could also argue the organization was set up in part to enhance U.S. business interests in the region.

---

736   FBI interview of Frances Holland, June 12, 1968, dated June 13, 1968. Notes about the FBI's conversation with Livingston appear in Holland's interview report.

737   FBI Airtel from SAC New York to Director, June 13, 1968.

738   Mariú Suárez, *Beyond Homo Sapiens: Enlightened Faith* (Xlibris Corporation: 2011), p. 345.

The assassin was accused of being a Communist at time when America was launching the Cold War, but the people of Colombia rejected that too-easy excuse, as the Communists, post-World War II, had the most to lose from such an action.

Paul Wolf, an attorney who has looked seriously into this case for years, noted the following:

> Roa's own motives can barely be understood. Two theories, now discredited, were put forward shortly after Gaitán's death, which might have made sense if they'd been true. One was that Roa was an illegitimate son of Gaitán's father, that there had been trouble between the two families, and that Gaitán's father had made a settlement to Roa's mother just one month before the assassination. A second theory was that Roa related to the alleged victim of one Gaitán's clients in his criminal law practice, for whom Gaitán had won an acquittal the day before. Although the first director of the CIA, Admiral Roscoe Hillenkoetter, reported this version to a Congressional investigating committee as fact, there is no evidence whatsoever that Roa was related to Gaitán or to any of his clients. Why Admiral Hillenkoetter went with this story, instead of reporting that the CIA was still investigating the matter, is another unsolved mystery.[739]

Several writers on the subject believe the nascent CIA was behind Gaitán's assassination. Gaitán was advocating strongly on behalf of the poor and dispossessed, and a large student movement was backing him. The main reason the CIA overthrew Jacobo Arbenz in Guatemala in 1954 and tried to overthrow Castro throughout the 1960s and 1970s were because these leaders expropriated land from American corporations. Gaitán had advocated along similar lines, as Paul Wolf wrote: "in one of Gaitán's best known works, *The Problem of Land*, he put forth the theory that private land ownership was unnatural—the land itself belonged to everyone."[740]

Greg Parker wrote that a man named John Espirito (or Spirito or Spirrito, depending on the source) confessed to killing Gaitán for the CIA, at the direction of his CIA handler Thomas Elliot, in a documentary:

> Under interrogation following his arrest for counter-revolutionary activities, Espirito made the startling confession that he had played a role in the assassination of Gaitán as part of a CIA operation code-named PANTOMIME. The confession was filmed, and later

---

739   Paul Wolf, "Colombian "Magnicidio" Remains a Mystery After 60 Years," *Counterpunch*, www. counterpunch.org/2008/04/09/colombian-quot-magnicidio-quot-remains-a-mystery-after-60-years/, April 8, 2008.

740   *Ibid.*

used as the basis of a documentary made by the Cuban Institute of Cinematographic Art and Industry. ...

The easiest method of removal was always bribery. According to the confession, Thomas Elliot offered Gaitán a chair in Criminal Law at the Sorbonne in Paris, or alternatively at Rome University. ... These bribes were confirmed by the politician's daughter, Gloria ....[741]

Is it possible someone in the Rosicrucian organization between from the late 1940s through the late 1960s served as a spotter for people who might be susceptible to hypnotic programming? Regardless, Sirhan's doings in Corona and his time with the Rosicrucians seem to be areas that should have been much more thoroughly investigated.

If Sirhan were being programmed from late 1966 forward, to what purpose? In 1966, it was not clear that Robert Kennedy would be running for president in 1968. He had denied that he wanted to run and had just been elected Senator of New York. Was Sirhan originally being programmed to be a courier? An assassin? A patsy? The clues may lie in Sirhan's notebook when juxtaposed with world history at that point in time. Understand that the strangely repetitive items in Sirhan's notebook appear to be "automatic writing," writing produced during a hypnotic session, and not the kind of writing Sirhan did in his waking state. When Dr. Diamond hypnotized Sirhan and asked him to write, Sirhan wrote similar, repetitive phrases. Out of hypnosis, the writing scared Sirhan, as they looked like the ramblings of someone mentally ill. But it seems likely those writings were never the product of Sirhan's own mind, but rather the result of someone else's suggestions.

There were numerous references to Nasser in Sirhan's notebooks. On one strange page Sirhan had written "Long live Nasser" over and over. When Gamel Abdel Nasser came to power in Egypt, he had three goals: "to rid Egypt of foreign influence, and especially of the British; to unite the Arabs; and to bring his people out of feudal backwardness into twentieth century life."[742] But nationalism was regarded, economically, as Communism to the Cold Warriors of the previous century, so both British intelligence and the CIA came up with plots to kill him. One plot involving poisoning a box of chocolates that Nasser was fond of. Although the official version states Nasser died of a heart attack in 1970, some researchers into that case believe there is evidence that Nasser was poisoned or killed. Bud Culligan, the CIA man who claimed to have shot down U.N. Secretary Dag Hammarskjöld's plane in 1961 at the CIA's behest, wrote in a letter that

---

741   Greg Parker, *Lee Harvey Oswald's Cold War: Why the Kennedy Assassination Should be Reinvestigated, Volume 1* (Sydney, Australia: New Disense Press), 2014.

742   "President Nasser dies of heart attack," *The Guardian*, www.theguardian.com/theguardian/2014/sep/29/egypt-president-nasser-dies-archive-1970, from the archives, originally published September 29, 1970.

made its way to the Church Committee files that he had gone to confession after Nasser died, implying he may have killed Nasser as well.[743] Positioning Sirhan as a pro-Nasser, pro-Communist supporter—as some of Sirhan's notebook pages indicate—might have made it easier for him to get close to Nasser, had such a plot progressed.

Another page filled with Nasser references has more disturbing text on it. Along with references to AMORC (the Rosicrucians) and "Di Salvo Die S Salvo" we find, scribbled at the top right, "help me please."[744] Perhaps this is meaningless in the original context, whatever that was. But without other information, it's impossible to avoid the suggestion that some part of Sirhan was aware he was being programmed to do something he didn't want to do, so he begged for help.

On another page we find repetitive entries that say "Ambassador Goldberg must die." Ambassador Arthur Goldberg had been an attorney with the United Steelworkers when President John Kennedy tapped him to be his Secretary of Labor. In October 1962, Arthur Goldberg became Supreme Court Justice Goldberg. He served only two short years and a few months. After President Kennedy was assassinated, President Lyndon B. Johnson convinced Goldberg to take over the UN Ambassador role after Adlai Stevenson died. It is very unusual for someone to voluntarily leave the life-long Supreme Court Justice position, but evidently Johnson convinced Goldberg he might be able, from his position in the UN, to help end the Vietnam War. In 1967, Goldberg tried to do just that as well as broker a peace agreement in the Middle East. Either of those could have been a reason for someone to target Goldberg for assassination. War and conflict are extremely lucrative financial propositions that also provide the CIA tremendous power and freedom of movement.

Whether related to Nasser, Ambassador Goldberg or something entirely unrelated, Sirhan was apparently already being programmed for some other operation when Senator Kennedy announced his intention to run for President. At this point, Sirhan's mission appears to have been redirected.

Was Sirhan programmed to be an assassin? Or was he programmed to be a patsy only? As crazy as it sounds, there is a template for using a patsy in this manner in the CIA's ARTICHOKE files. ARTICHOKE was an outgrowth from the CIA's first mind control project, called Project Bluebird. ARTICHOKE's programs eventually were folded in the larger MKULTRA project umbrella. ARTICHOKE focused extensively on the issue of hypnotic control of another.

743   See my U.N. testimony here, aarclibrary.org/the-hammarskjold-commission-witness-statement-of-lisa-pease/, and see Culligan's statement re Nasser in my article "Midnight in the Congo," *Probe*, Vol. 6 No. 3, March–April, 1999, kennedysandking.com/articles/midnight-in-the-congo-the-assassination-of-lumumba-and-the-mysterious-death-of-dag-hammarskjold.

744   FBI copy of Sirhan's notebook pages, p. 162 (stamped by FBI, with 163 crossed out, begging the question of who deleted which page from where and renumbered).

In 1954, the ARTICHOKE team's first assignment was to answer the following question: "Can an individual of ***** descent be made to perform an act of attempted assassination involuntarily under the influence of ARTICHOKE?"[745] Note the words "involuntary" and "attempted assassination." The goal of this particular exercise was not to program someone to kill, but to see if the Agency could compel an individual to *attempt* an act of assassination. The document noted this act would be a "trigger mechanism for a bigger project."

The description is a near match for the scenario Sirhan seemed programmed to perform: an act of simulated, attempted assassination, involuntarily. Sirhan's act of "attempted assassination" was the trigger mechanism for the "bigger project," which was, in 1968, the actual assassination of Senator Robert F. Kennedy and the subsequent right-wing takeover of the government.

The 1954 ARTICHOKE document described how the individual would be "surreptitiously drugged through the medium of an alcoholic cocktail at a social party, ARTICHOKE applied and the SUBJECT induced to perform the act of attempted assassination at some later date." This also closely matches what appeared to happen to Sirhan. It's possible that Sirhan's drinks were laced with another substance.

The CIA document's author added that "All of the above was to be accomplished at one involuntary uncontrolled social meeting."[746] After the unwitting SUBJECT carried out his act of "attempted assassination," according to the CIA document, "it was assumed the SUBJECT would be taken into custody by the *** [sic] Government and thereby 'disposed of.'"

Was there a back-up plan in case Sirhan managed to escape that involved putting him on a horse? Remember that Angleton once said you plan for the failure of an operation as much as for its success. One of the oddest parts to the Sirhan story was Rev. Jerry Owen's assertion that he picked up Sirhan the day before the primary and that Sirhan wanted to buy a horse, which was to be delivered to the Ambassador Hotel the night of June 4. If Sirhan had somehow managed to escape the crowd at the Ambassador Hotel after the shooting, putting him on a horse pretty much guaranteed he would be shot and killed by police. Owen may have played a prior role in Sirhan's life as well, as you will see shortly. But first, we need to figure out who programmed Sirhan.

Only one hypnotist besides the defense and prosecution experts ever claimed to have hypnotized Sirhan: Dr. William J. Bryan. According to Bill Turner and Jonn Christian, two prostitutes who serviced Bryan regularly said he liked to talk about his famous clients and had mentioned Sirhan. They had assumed

---

745   CIA memo from redacted to redacted, subject: "ARTICHOKE report," dated January 22, 1954, www.cia. gov, www.cia.gov/library/readingroom/docs/DOC_0000140399.pdf.

746   *Ibid.*

he meant he had hypnotized Sirhan after the assassination. But Bryan did not have access to Sirhan then. If he hypnotized him, it would have been before the shooting, not after.

Bryan's name came up in other contexts in this case as well. Bryan called in to the Ray Briem show on KABC shortly after the assassination to suggest that Sirhan had been hypnotized. This would not have been out of character for the egotistical, self-promoting Bryan. In addition, Herb Elsman, who had been in the Venetian Room at the hotel attending the Rafferty party when Kennedy was shot, stated that Joan Simmons, a programmer for KABC Radio, and Hortence Farrchild had information that Sirhan "belonged to a secret hypnosis group." Farrchild said she belonged to a group that practiced self-hypnosis but did not know Sirhan. Simmons said "she stated she knew nothing of a Doctor Bryant [sic] of the American Institute of Hypnosis or Hortence Farrchild." What's interesting here is that the LAPD appears to have deliberately omitted the reference to Dr. William Bryan that Simmons was responding to. Why? Did the LAPD know he was involved and therefore removed all references? This one reference might have slipped through because the name was misspelled "Bryant."[747]

On June 18, 1974, Betsy Langman interviewed Bryan in his office. Langman had a serious interest in the anomalies of this case. She co-wrote an article on the evidence of conspiracy with Alex Cockburn for *Harpers* in 1974. To Langman, Bryan emphatically denied ever having hypnotized Sirhan.

During the interview, Bryan—who was never known for his modesty—told her he was "probably the leading expert in the world" on hypnosis. When she asked if someone could be programmed to kill, Bryan's response was interesting. "They program people to kill all the time—they enlist them in the army, and they tell them that's for their country's own good, and they don't use any hypnosis. They just ... close order drill and so on—but these people believe it—it's for real."[748] Bryan then talked about the Hardrup case and said the reason the hypnotist had such control is the level of access he had to Hardrup, locked up physically. Bryan said to completely brainwash someone involved "a certain amount of physical torture," "long-term hypnosis" and "probably drugs." Under that combination, Bryan explained, "yes, you can brainwash a person to do just about anything."[749]

Bryan talked about Henry Busch, the so-called "Hollywood Strangler," and stated "he was programmed very definitely," and discussed how he had hypnotized him to determine his motive. Busch had been a Korean War veteran and

---

747   LAPD interviews of Herb Elsman, Hortence Farrchild and Joan Simmons. The reference to "Bryant" appears in the SUS interview summary under the "Simmons, Joan" listing.

748   Betsy Langman's interview notes re her discussion with Dr. William J. Bryan, Jr., June 14, 1974, with additional notes writing apparently by Bill Turner after listening to the tape and talking to Langman. The notes are from Bill Turner's files.

749   *Ibid.*

was working at an optical firm when he was arrested as a purse snatcher. But he "suddenly broke down and started babbling to police of strangling three women."[750] One of Busch's strangled victims was found, strangely enough, with a blue polka dot scarf around her neck.[751]

Bryan talked about the Boston Strangler case as well. When Langman asked if someone could be made to commit a murder without their knowledge, Bryan responded by describing a scenario whereby someone could be tricked into being a suicide bomber without their knowledge. The person would be told they were safeguarding important files and to deliver them to a certain person in a certain building. But as soon as they got inside the building, the bomb inside, which the courier had no knowledge of, would be remotely triggered. After the fact, it would appear to the world the person had committed suicide. Interestingly enough, Estabrooks described a similar scenario in his book *Hypnosis*, begging the question of how many such stories we have read about in the media were not "suicide" stories at all.

Bryan got agitated when Langman turned the conversation to Sirhan. She asked if Sirhan could have hypnotized himself. Bryan said the word hypnosis was "meaningless" in the case of self-hypnosis because one could talk oneself into doing anything. Bryan had been so loquacious until Sirhan came into the conversation. "This has been gone over 50 million times," Bryan said, although it hadn't. Only Kaiser's book had been published by that point suggesting Sirhan might have been hypnotized. "If that is all that you have got to interview me about, you are wasting my time and yours. ... It just irks me to hear all this old shit ... that is just ridiculous."[752]

Langman changed the subject until Bryan calmed down a bit, and then she returned to the subject of Sirhan. "Do you feel that Sirhan could have been self-hypnotized?" she asked Bryan. "I'm not going to comment on that case, because I didn't hypnotize him." (No one had suggested at that point that he had.) "Why don't you ask Bernie Diamond? He is the guy who did it." Langman asked again whether he felt Sirhan was *self*-hypnotized but Bryan somehow saw that as another accusation and responded, "I just told you that I didn't hypnotize him."

"I am asking what is your opinion," Langman pressed.

"I don't have one, because I didn't treat him," Bryan said. "You got a lot of misconceptions about hypnosis, and you are going around trying to find some more ammunition to put that same old crap out, that people can be hypnotized into doing all these weird things and so on ... the old Svengali stuff ... and I am not going to be a party to it ... all I say is please don't use my name. I don't want

---

750   AP, "Man Admits Three Slayings," *The Orlando Sentinel*, September 7, 1960.

751   *Ibid.*

752   Langman's notes of Bryan interview.

to be quoted by you at all. … I don't want to be in your article. Because eventually it is going to be laughed at."[753]

And with that, Bryan stormed out of his *own* office, yelling, "This interview is over," leaving Langman behind, puzzled at this extraordinary outburst. If he hadn't programmed Sirhan, why was this such a sore spot with him?

And why *wasn't* Bryan asked to hypnotize Sirhan? Bernard Diamond lived in the San Francisco Bay Area and had to be flown in to testify. Bryan, on the other hand, lived and worked in Los Angeles. Was Bryan initially approached? Did he reject the chance for fear something might give away a connection between him and Sirhan?

One special clue in Sirhan's notebook suggests that whatever Sirhan was writing on some pages in his notebook may have been at the instigation of another. Upside down on the edge of one page of writing is, in the handwriting of another person, the words, "Electronic equipment this appears to be the right amount of preponderance."[754] Whoever was working with Sirhan appeared to be using a machine in connection with the hypnosis. The only hypnotist in the Los Angeles area to have been pictured in a local paper in front of electrical equipment that allowed him to hypnotize people was Dr. William J. Bryan. In 1972, Bryan was pictured by the Associated Press at a console into which he inserted tapes that allowed him to hypnotize and monitor three people at once through the use of closed circuit TV.[755] A book review mentioned Bryan's "offices in San Diego and Los Angeles" and further described Bryan's invention, a hypnosis machine that allowed him to hypnotize several people at once:

> Despite his impressive credentials, Bryan comes off as a kook. He is noted for his BEAR, Bryan Electronic Automated Robot hypnotist, which can "simultaneously hypnotize seven patients in two cities, plug them into and out of their trances, and provide each with personalized therapeutic suggestions while Bryan plays golf or does whatever else turns him on."[756]

The most significant clues, however, are the phonetic references to DeSalvo in Sirhan's diary. On one page in Sirhan's notebook can be found the phrase "God help me" followed by "Salvo Di Di Salvo Die S Salvo." In the middle of the "Long live Nasser" scribblings on another page, "DieSovo"—in quotes—appears

753   *Ibid.*

754   Sirhan's notebook, FBI X-1, Vols. 5 & 6, page 47, www.maryferrell.org/showDoc. html?docId=99658#relPageId=47&tab=page.

755   Associated Press, "Hypnosis—More Than Status Symbol: It's Becoming a Big Part of Sports," *San Antonio Express*, July 2, 1972.

756   Joanne Norris, "These are the Love Doctors," *Independent* (Long Beach, CA), November 17, 1972.

between phrases. The word "cabbage" is nonsensically scribbled above "DieSovo." I suspect "DieSovo" is another phonetic reference to Alberto DeSalvo.

Bryan loved to brag about people he had hypnotized, and Albert DeSalvo, the so-called "Boston Strangler," was one of his most famous subjects. If Bryan hypnotized Sirhan, it would not be out of character in the least for Bryan to have talked about DeSalvo. Adding credence to the notion that Sirhan was hypnotized by Bryan was the fact that he did not recognize "Di Salvo" as referring to anyone or anything when he was outside of a hypnotic state. In the wee hours of the morning after the assassination, Sirhan had asked if the Boston Strangler had been identified. It was not like Sirhan, who followed politics and public events closely, not to know the name of the Strangler. What makes more sense is that Bryan told Sirhan to forget whatever was said in their sessions, so outside of hypnosis, the name was obliterated from Sirhan's mind by Bryan's suggestion, forcing him to ask for the name.

When Bryan died in 1977, the year the House Select Committee on Assassinations was formed to investigate the JFK and MLK assassinations, John Miner, the Los Angeles County deputy district attorney who tried to get Noguchi to change the distance of the head shot from an inch to a foot, was the executor of Bryan's will. Pallbearers included Henry Rothblatt (a key lawyer for the Watergate burglars) and Melvin Belli. If ever there was someone connected enough to pull off a hypnotic tour de force in the Los Angeles area, it was the national-security-state-connected Bryan.

It's curious that two figures often linked to Sirhan's case, Dr. Bryan and Jerry Owen, are linked to the Manson case as well. Bryan was hired to help Linda Kasabian, one of Manson's cult followers, and Owen told police that the day before the killing, he had picked up the caretaker of the property of one of the victims. According to Turner and Christian, Owen had injected himself into the Manson case in a similar fashion to the RFK case:

> [LAPD Captain Hugh] Brown suddenly revealed that the preacher had also injected himself into the Tate-LaBianca murder case. He reported to the Hollywood Division that the day before the killings he had picked up a hitchhiker named William Garretson—the nineteen-year-old caretaker of the Tate estate whom the police held for several days as a suspect before releasing him. Owen said that Garretson was looking for extra work as a dishwasher, and he took the young man to the Carolina Pines restaurant to introduce him to the management.[757]

---

757   Turner and Christian, p. 148. Oddly enough, Owen claimed to have been threatened after reporting his Sirhan contact to the police while using a phone booth in front of the Carolina Pines restaurant. After he left the phone booth and drove into Griffith Park with his friend, boxer Johnny Gray, someone shot at their car. According to Gray, Owen had asked Gray to open the windows moments before and Gray felt the bullets had whizzed right through.

And in what appears to be a disturbing pattern, both Bryan and Owen had links to the 1972 assassination attempt on George Wallace by Arthur Bremer as well.

After her upsetting interview with Bryan, Langman had coffee with one of Bryan's secretaries, who told Langman that right after Arthur Bremer shot at George Wallace, in a case where there appeared to be too many bullets to have come solely from Bremer, and where some of the shots came from positions nearly impossible for Bremer to have attained,[758] Bryan received a call from Maryland related to the shooting.

Bremer's half-sister Gail Aiken was a friend of Jerry Owen, the one who claimed he made a deal to sell a horse to Sirhan the night of the California primary. Los Angeles County Supervisor and former newsman Baxter Ward wrote a letter to his fellow supervisors in 1975 discussing his own encounter with Owen:

> In the summer of 1971 as a broadcaster, I attempted unsuccessfully to contact Owen for an interview. In the spring of 1972, while I was campaigning for political office, Jerry Owen left word at my campaign headquarters that he would like to see me the following day. The call was placed just hours after Governor Wallace had been shot. Owen did not keep the appointment the following day.
>
> A short time after the hearing I conducted last May [1974] into the Senator Kennedy ballistics evidence, Jerry Owen called again, saying he would like to see me to disclose the full story behind the conspiracy.
>
> He came the following day, and I obtained his permission to tape record his conversation. In my opinion, he provided no information beyond what he had stated in 1968 to the authorities and to the press. However, there was one addition: when I questioned him as to why he did not keep our appointment the day after Governor Wallace had been shot, Owen volunteered that he was personal friends with the sister of Arthur Bremer [sic]. ... Owen stated that Gale Bremer [sic—his half-sister was Gail Aiken] was employed by his brother here in Los Angeles for several years and had then just left Los Angeles for Florida because she was continually harassed by the FBI.[759]

Just before the assassination of Senator Kennedy, the perennially penniless Jerry Owen came into a large amount of money. A rugged cowboy who had known Owen for years, Bill Powers, testified in Owen's defamation trial that he had seen

---

758   Lisa Pease, "Bremer and Wallace: It's Déjà vu all over again," *Probe*, Vol. 6 No. 4, viewable at kennedysandking.com/articles/bremer-wallace-it-s-deja-vu-all-over-again.

759   Memorandum from Baxter Ward to fellow supervisors, July 29, 1975, published in the Appendix of *The Assassination of Robert F. Kennedy: The Conspiracy and Coverup*, by William Turner and Jonn Christian. (New York: Thunder's Mouth Press, 1993, originally published by Random House, 1978), p. 374.

Sirhan, or someone who looked remarkably like him, on June 3, the day before the 1968 primary, in the back of a truck he had sold to Jerry Owen previously (but for which Owen had not yet fully paid him). Powers was surprised to see Owen, who never seemed to have much money, driving a fancy Lincoln Continental and carrying a roll of what looked like thousand-dollar bills. When asked whether Owen might have just been carrying a "Montana bankroll" of ones covered by a bill of a higher denomination, Powers had told the jury, "No. Being in the horse business, that is what I carry. No, it wasn't one of those." He told Bugliosi he thought there were 25 to 30 $1,000 bills. "There was a lot of serious money there, yes."[760]

Powers, who managed the Wild Bill Stables in Santa Ana, testified that Jerry Owen had referred to a man named "Sirhan" when discussing getting help for the breaking in of some of his horses. Unimpressed with the work Powers' stable-hand Johnny Beckley had done, Powers told Bugliosi that Owen had mentioned Sirhan to him:

> "Well, he didn't like the way Johnny was handling the horses and was cowboying around," Powers recounted, "and he said he had other people at the [race] track and stuff that could handle horses in the right manner, and the name Sirhan was mentioned."
>
> Q [Bugliosi]. By whom?
> A [Powers]. By Mr. Owen.
> Q. Are you positive about this?
> A. I am *very* positive. [Emphasis in the original.][761]

Asked how he could be so certain, Powers said it was an unusual name, and it was only a short time before Sirhan's name was all over the news. That truck was dusted for fingerprints, as Sgt. Hank Hernandez confirmed to superlawyer George T. Davis, who had a longtime friend and client in Jerry Owen. Powers told Jonn Christian that two men representing themselves as police officers told him Sirhan's fingerprints had been found on the glove compartment and the rear window. This would match Owen's story that Sirhan jumped in the back of Owen's truck (where he presumably touched the rear cab window) and later moved to the passenger seat next to the driver (where he presumably touched the glove compartment). At the time, Sirhan was accompanied by a man in a yellow turtleneck shirt and a "dirty blonde girl."[762]

Johnny Beckley was terrified of Owen and refused to testify against him, which was a shame, because Beckley appeared to be the source for a sighting of Owen riding horses with Sirhan along the Santa Ana River.

---

760   Turner and Christian, p. 13.

761   Turner and Christian, Location p. 12.

762   Turner and Christian, Locations 663, 788, and 1729; Statement of Jerry Owen, taken by the LAPD on June 5, 1968 at the University Detective Division.

While Sirhan was being programmed, someone would have had to keep an eye on him. What's the point of developing a patsy if he moves out of the state, gets arrested before the plot, or falls in love with someone who discovers his programming? What if he had taken a short trip unexpectedly and been out of town when he was supposed to be the patsy in the Kennedy plot? In the weeks leading up to the assassination, someone had to have been keeping Sirhan under a close watch. Maybe Owen was Sirhan's "babysitter," keeping track of him until it was time for the plot to unfold. Maybe that would best explain why Owen suddenly came into a lot of money right before the assassination and got his own TV show soon after.

If Sirhan were being prepared for a very public role in an assassination, it makes sense the conspirators would have staged a sort of "field test" in advance to examine how Sirhan performed under hypnosis. Would he follow instructions? If he were drugged, how much was too much and how much was not enough? Too much and he'd be incoherent and unusable. Too little and he might remember something of what happened. Maybe this explains a strange episode that took place shortly before the assassination.

On May 26, 1968, ten days before Kennedy was killed, a pastor at Methodist Church in Las Vegas claimed a "mumbling, apparently tranquilized Sirhan" walked into his service and annoyed other Sunday worshippers.[763]

"During the service proper, he made loud, unintelligible sounds," Reverend Douglas Harrell had told the *Sun*, "and complained to nearby congregation members about some moral issue while I was preaching my sermon." That sounds exactly like something Sirhan would want to discuss, based on his conversations with the police after his arrest. The pastor said that Sirhan mostly mumbled. "Many times, especially in Las Vegas, odd people happen into the church and try to disrupt things. If the ushers think they are dangerous, they eject them. Sirhan was very tranquil, as if he might have been under the influence of a depressant ...."[764]

The Reverend made clear that Sirhan was no threat to the congregation, which is why he was allowed to remain. "He was subdued, it seemed, and didn't look like the type of person who was capable of harming anyone," Harrell said.[765]

"At a coffee hour after the service, Sirhan came right up to me, his face right up to mine, and introduced himself. He mumbled and tried to say something, but I couldn't understand him," Harrell said, explaining why he was so sure of his identification. "The next time I saw him was on television during the coverage of the Kennedy assassination." The reverend reiterated that he "just didn't seem like the type of person who could commit such a foul act."[766]

763　FBI airtel from SAC, Las Vegas to Director, FBI, June 10, 1968, quoting Ralph Donald, "Pastor Notes Sirhan Vegas Visit," *Las Vegas Sun*, June 10, 1968.

764　*Ibid.*

765　*Ibid.*

766　*Ibid.*

The FBI office in Las Vegas jumped on this story right away and reported it directly to J. Edgar Hoover but not to the LAPD. An FBI agent went to talk to Harrell. Immediately after this, and possibly instigated by the FBI visit, Rev. Harrell "found it necessary to issue a public retraction to be disseminated to all news media." According to the FBI report, Rev. Harrell met the reporter, Ralph Donald, when Donald was the best man at a wedding the pastor had performed the day before the story ran. They had discussed the assassination, and Harrell said he had not specifically identified Sirhan but had simply relayed the story as an example of "kooks" who sometimes showed up in church. He issued a statement claiming the article was erroneous and that he had never made a positive identification of Sirhan. But his "retraction" actually buttressed the reporter's version, as Rev. Harrell noted "there seemed a definite resemblance."[767]

The LAPD did not hear of this incident until nearly a month later. The local Las Vegas police chief and his chief detective sent a joint letter to Chief Reddin, copied to Captain Brown, which said, "We think your office should be alerted to this in case defense counsel brings it up at a later date—then you won't be caught unaware." The LAPD asked the LVPD to interview Harrell, and the LVPD sent an "intelligence detail" in response. Harrell again essentially confirmed the details of the article, disputing only his level of certainty that it was Sirhan. He added that, despite the man's incoherence, he seemed to be "in a tranquil condition" and "was positively not under the influence of alcohol." When shown six photos of various individuals, he picked out a photo of Sirhan and separately, a photo of his brother Adel, but he was not positive of either identification.[768]

Despite the provocative story, neither the FBI nor the LAPD pursued this any further, probably for the reasons discussed in earlier chapters. No one wanted to have to deal with evidence of conspiracy, and Sirhan showing up hypnotized at a church in Las Vegas made it harder to argue that he had accidentally hypnotized himself at the Ambassador Hotel. So like all other evidence of conspiracy, this story quietly disappeared into the deep record.

This chapter is about the manipulation of the mind, and not only Sirhan's. There is a far more insidious and invisible mind control operation at work in this case that continues to this day. That operation is a war for the public's mind on this case, on the assassination of President John F. Kennedy, and other matters where "national security" dictates a story other than the truth must be told.

The CIA was formed from the Office of Strategic Services (OSS), which was itself formed in response to the rise of Nazi propaganda. The OSS' initial goal was to counter such propaganda. So from birth, the CIA was, at the very least,

---

767   "Statement of Local Minister," FBI files, L.A.F.O. No. 56-156: Volume 3 (Ser. 501-750), www.maryferrell. org/showDoc.html?docId=99632&search=Harrell#relPageId=26&tab=page.

768   LAPD interview report of LVPD interview of Rev. Douglas Harrell, typed August 13, 1968.

a propaganda operation. Covert operations, and eventually military control, came in the decades that followed. But the ability to "play" the media to any tune the CIA desired was and remains one of its primary capabilities.

During the nascent days of the CIA, the charming, eccentric and deeply disturbed Frank Wisner played the media like an organ so well that people in the CIA referred to his media contacts as "Wisner's Wurlitzer." In addition, reporters made great spies. People expected them to ask probing questions. They were expected to show up and poke around at crime scenes. No one knew who really wrote their dispatches. Even the editor might not know the content of an article had been supplied by the CIA. So it should surprise no one that journalists, especially those stationed abroad, were heavy recruitment targets for the CIA.

According to Carl Bernstein's landmark exposé "The CIA and the Media," published in the October 20, 1977 issue of *Rolling Stone*, the CIA colluded with ABC, CBS, NBC, the Time-LIFE empire, the *New York Times*, the Copley News Service, AP and other wire services, and other media outlets. The story was met with near media silence. The only organ to address and further the story was the *New York Times*, which focused heavily on the one party Bernstein had gone easy on, his employer during the Woodward-and-Bernstein articles on Watergate, the *Washington Post*. Both articles explained in depth how the CIA's use of the media ran from top to bottom, meaning, sometimes the top executives were in the loop and set the tone for the reporters working below them, but often the CIA's media assets were not known by upper management to be working with the CIA.

During the Church and Pike Committee and the HSCA investigations of the CIA in the 1970s, the CIA fought hard to keep its media operations private. In a showdown to determine who really ran the country, the CIA won when the CIA refused to reveal the extent of their media operations to the people who represent the taxpayers who subsidize those operations. CIA made a deal to show Congress the names of only a few of its assets in exchange for keeping the rest of them secret. Congress should have stood up to the CIA and refused such an offer. But Congress is afraid of the CIA, as Nancy Pelosi made clear during the Senate investigation into the CIA's use of torture (and horrific experiments) on prisoners. When Senator Dianne Feinstein, who has been one of the CIA's staunch defenders in Congress, called the CIA out in 2014 for breaking into the Senate servers to remove documentation on the CIA's torture program, House Minority Leader Nancy Pelosi said at a news conference:

> "I'll tell you, you take on the intelligence community, you're a person of courage, and she does not do that lightly. Not without evidence, and when I say evidence, documentation of what it is that she is putting forth." ...

"You don't fight it [CIA] without a price because they come after you and they don't always tell the truth."

"[Investigating the CIA's breaking into the Committee's computers] may be one of the healthiest things we can do because I know one thing: Whatever it is, the intelligence community writes a report on that, they leave, they write a book on it, all of a sudden it becomes conventional...gossip that that's what happened there and we really have to have the ground truth." [769]

In January 2017, Senate Minority Leader Chuck Schumer echoed Pelosi's warnings about tangling with the CIA:

Let me tell you: You take on the intelligence community—they have six ways from Sunday at getting back at you.[770]

Some people mistakenly think the CIA's use of the media ended after the Church and Pike committee hearings. That's simply not true. The relationships were simply restructured and kept better hidden. In fact, by 1991, the CIA had become so powerful in the media that pretense was no longer necessary. CIA Director Robert Gates laid out, in a memo titled "Greater CIA Openness," how its Public Affairs Office "has relationships with reporters from every major wire service, newspaper, news weekly, and television network in the nation. This has helped us turn some intelligence failure stories into intelligence success stories, and it has contributed to the accuracy of countless others. In many instances, we have persuaded reporters to postpone, change, hold, or even scrap stories that could have adversely affected national security interests or jeopardized sources and methods."

As I said at a conference sponsored by the Wecht Center at Duquesne University in 2013, "It should be clear that any organization that brags about its ability to change 'intelligence failures' into 'intelligence success stories' is, at its heart, an anti-democratic organization. The public simply cannot make intelligent choices about politics when failures are misrepresented as successes. No business could survive such misrepresentation for long. But intelligence agencies get away with it."

Whether Ron Kessler was a CIA asset or just a willing volunteer when he misrepresented Harper's findings in the Robert Kennedy case must remain a

769   Emma Dumain, "Pelosi Praises Feinstein, Calls CIA Director's Statements 'Befuddling,'" *Roll Call*, www.rollcall.com/218/pelosi-praises-feinstein-calls-cia-director-brennan-statements-befuddling/, March 13, 2014, accessed October 21, 2017.

770   Daniel Chaitin, "Schumer warns Trump: Intel officials 'have six ways from Sunday at getting back at you'," *Washington Examiner*, January 3, 2017, www.washingtonexaminer.com/schumer-warns-trump-intel-officials-have-six-ways-from-sunday-at-getting-back-at-you/article/2610823.

matter of conjecture. Whether Dan Moldea's refusal to believe his own carefully researched evidence of conspiracy was the act of a person who did not want to be ridiculed as a conspiracy theorist or the act of someone who chose for whatever reason to protect the CIA must also remain a matter of conjecture, because vehement denials would be expected in either case.

If you want to know how a secret can be kept for more than 50 years, look to who controls the media. That there were multiple shooters in the pantry can be easily discerned by any who took a hard, careful look at the evidence. But most people don't do their own research. They rely on the media to tell them what is true, what they should believe. And faith in the media is a necessary component for a democracy to function.

But it should be clear to political observers that one of the key waves Donald Trump rode to the White House in 2016 was the anger at the mainstream media. People believe they have been lied to about the assassinations of the Sixties and events like 9/11. They read what independent researchers put out, and those accounts don't match what has been reported in the mainstream media. That made them, rightly, question the mainstream's ability to tell the truth about important events.

Donald Trump's cries about "fake news" appealed to a significant segment of people on both the right and the left in America. The news has long been, perhaps now more than ever before, a carefully controlled organ of the government's "soft power." Soft power is what controls you without your knowledge, as opposed to hard power, like a tank with a gun pointed in your direction. But people who understand they are being propagandized do eventually rebel against it. They want more independent voices.

We must always ask whether the CIA is manipulating reporting on important, power-shifting events, because they've already admitted to doing this. Calling others "conspiracy theorists" for raising provably legitimate questions actually endangers our democracy.

Disinformation about key events of modern history directly gave rise to Donald Trump, Breitbart, and media organizations that are willing to at least tackle, however inadequately, topics that the mainstream media considers nearly untouchable, i.e., anything that reeks of misdeeds by government actors.

Fake news, then, is in many ways directly responsible for all flavors of conspiracy theories, from the nuttiest to the most credible. When the truth is kept from people, they will try to put the facts together and draw their own conclusions. Some people do this well, and their efforts should be lauded far more than they are. Others do this very badly, and their theories should be dissected and exposed rather than ignored and ridiculed. Ridiculing or ignoring conspiracy theories gives them power. The appropriate way to attack them is to factually dismantle them, where possible. But those who refuse to believe that *anything* is a conspiracy are as ridiculous as those who believe *everything* is a conspiracy.

The fact that Breitbart and many right-wing media outlets themselves promote fake news is sadly lost on their supporters. But the same happens on the political left. Until both the political left and the political right prioritize truth over fiction in books, in news reports, on the radio and in other places where fictional stories are presented as factual, America's survival as any kind of people-driven democracy remains in serious peril.

It was horrible that Robert Kennedy was taken from us far too soon. It is horrible that one man has borne the guilt for an operation he neither planned nor willingly participated in. It's horrible the conspiracy was so obvious that bullets had to be lost and switched to hide it. And it's horrible that the mainstream media has never dared to tell the people of this country that the government lied to us about what they really found when they looked into this case.

Until the media can deal with the truth of the Robert Kennedy assassination, and until the people can be made aware of the CIA's role in slanting the truth on topics of great importance, America's very survival is in jeopardy. If, as the Bible quotation on the CIA's wall says, "The Truth will Set You Free," then it should be obvious that the lies imprison us. We've come perilously close to losing democracy itself because of fake, CIA-sponsored stories about our history. Should America ever become a dictatorship, the epitaph of our democracy must include the role the mainstream media, by bowing to the National Security state, played in killing it.

MISSION: POSSIBLE

*"In the eyes of posterity it will inevitably seem that,
in safeguarding our freedom, we destroyed it. The vast
clandestine apparatus we built up to prove our enemies'
resources and intentions only served in the end to confuse
our own purposes; that practice of deceiving others for
the good of the state led infallibly to our deceiving ourselves; and that vast army of clandestine personnel built
up to execute these purposes were soon caught up in the
web of their own sick fantasies, with disastrous consequences for them and us."*

THE MORNING OF JUNE 5, 1968, CIA OFFICER JOSEPH BURKHOLDER Smith heard on his car radio that Robert Kennedy had been shot. He was on his way to teach a class to a group of Army officers who were going to Vietnam as part of a joint CIA-Defense Department unit. When Smith arrived, an Army colonel who led the unit Smith was about to teach shocked Smith with the following exhortation:

> "Congratulations," said the colonel, "now it won't be us. You guys are great. Only, for Christ's sake, having your agent use that small-caliber weapon is taking an awful chance. He's not dead yet."[771]

Why did the Army Colonel immediately assume, without any evidence, that the CIA had killed Senator Robert Kennedy? Because he had seen the system from the inside, perhaps more than had Smith, who assured his class, also without evidence, that the CIA *hadn't* killed Kennedy.

After the CIA's operations were exposed in the wake of the Church and Pike Committees, Smith wrote he was shocked to find out how much he didn't know about his employer, despite his many years working for the Agency.[772] But Smith

---

771   Joseph B. Smith, *Portrait of a Cold Warrior* (New York: G.P. Putnam's Sons, 1976), p. 400.
772   *Ibid.*

456 A LIE TOO BIG TO FAIL

continued to defend the Agency against all comers, even when an investigator for the House Select Committee on Assassinations came knocking on his door. As Upton Sinclair once said, "It's impossible to make a man understand something when his salary depends on him not understanding it."

Regardless of whether Smith was shocked or posturing, the Army colonel had a clearer view of how the CIA operated, and the ways in which the CIA's world vision clashed with that of the Kennedys, than most reporters do today.

Some people really can't believe that CIA people would ever do such a thing. Aren't they the ultimate patriots, putting their lives on the line to defend us? It's important to understand that, like the Army colonel, there were a number of people in the military and intelligence establishments who felt the Kennedy brothers were Communist sympathizers or worse, so killing them was, in their minds, an act of patriotism, not treason. That the Kennedys weren't Communists or sympathizers was a difference of fact, not opinion, but when people only listen to lies that support their beliefs, instead of the facts that challenge them, terrible things can happen.

The politics of the Kennedy brothers have been deliberately muddied for that reason: If you believe the Kennedy brothers were of the same mind as the CIA of the time, you'll find it impossible to believe that operatives of the CIA killed both brothers. But if you understand that there was an epic power struggle going on between the Kennedys and the CIA at the time of President Kennedy's death, and that Robert Kennedy's policies would have not only mirrored but exceeded those of his brother's on the left of the political spectrum, the picture of why both Kennedys were killed becomes much clearer.

To fully understand the war between the CIA and the Kennedy administration, we have to understand how the CIA operated prior to the Kennedy administration.

The CIA blackmailed its way into existence

AT THE END OF WORLD WAR II, PRESIDENT HARRY TRUMAN DIS-banded the Office of Strategic Services, the forerunner of the CIA. Many OSS members lost their jobs, and the rest were folded into other remaining government agencies. In 1946, "a group of management advisors" reviewed intelligence information going to President Truman, the Secretary of State and others, and concluded the information could have come from press reports, so why pay for a spy agency. Miles Copeland, one of the founding fathers of the CIA, wrote in veiled language about how the CIA essentially ran an operation to silence critics:

There are several stories in the CIA's secret annals to explain how the dispute was settled, but although they "make better history," as Allen Dulles used to say, they are only half-truths and much less consistent with the ways of government than the true one. Old-timers at the Agency swear that the antiespionage people would almost certainly have won out had it not been for the fact that an Army colonel who had been assigned to the management group charged with the job of organizing the new Agency suborned secretaries in the FBI, the State Department, and the Defense Department and organized them into an espionage network which proved not only the superiority of espionage over other forms of acquiring "humint" (i.e., intelligence on what specific human beings think and do in privacy), but the necessity for its being systematized and tightly controlled. The colonel was fired, as were the secretaries, but by that time General John Magruder, then head of the group that was organizing the CIA, had in his hands a strong argument for creating a professional espionage service and putting it under a single organization.[773]

Copeland explains this effort included the targeting of FBI director J. Edgar Hoover:

Also, thanks to the secretaries and their Army spymaster, he had enough material to silence enemies of the new Agency—including even J. Edgar Hoover, since Magruder was among the very few top bureaucrats in Washington on whom Hoover didn't have material for retaliation.[774]

Hoover had long been accused of having a homosexual relationship with his top aide Clyde Tolson. According to two sources, the blackmail against Hoover included a photograph:

John Weitz, a former officer in the OSS, the predecessor of the Central Intelligence Agency, recalled a curious episode at a dinner party in the fifties. "After a conversation about Hoover," he said, "our host went to another room and came back with a photograph. It was not a good picture and was clearly taken from some distance away, but it showed two men apparently engaged in homosexual activity. The host said the men were Hoover and Tolson ...."

---

773   Miles Copeland, *The Real Spy World* (First Sphere Books edition, 1978), pp. 40–41.

774   Copeland, p. 41.

Weitz told author Anthony Summers his host was none other than James Angleton, the CIA's counterintelligence chief. Gordon Novel also sourced a photo of Hoover having sex with Tolson to Angleton:

> "What I saw was a picture of him giving Clyde Tolson a blowjob," said Novel. "There was more than one shot, but the startling one was a close shot of Hoover's head. He was totally recognizable. You could not see the face of the man he was with, but Angleton said it was Tolson. I asked him if they were fakes, but he said they were real, that they'd been taken with a special lens. They looked authentic to me."[775]

Novel reiterated this same story to me when I talked to him in Las Vegas in 2004. During New Orleans District Attorney Jim Garrison's investigation of the JFK assassination, Garrison told *Playboy* Magazine that Novel worked for the CIA. Novel then sued Playboy for defamation. But in his deposition, Novel opened by claiming immunity under the National Security Act of 1947, the very act which formed the CIA. Hoover didn't want him to pursue the lawsuit, but Angleton did, so Angleton showed Gordon the pictures to get Hoover off his back. "I had the impression that this was not the first time the sex pictures had been used," Novel told Anthony Summers. Novel then approached Hoover while he was having dinner with Tolson at the Mayflower Hotel in Washington D.C. and mentioned he had seen the photos. According to Novel, Hoover nearly choked on his food.[776]

Summers wrote that Meyer Lansky, a Mafia capo, was also shown the pictures of Hoover, which would explain why Hoover was unable to pursue mob prosecutions during his tenure. Former FBI agent Bill Turner quit the FBI in large part due to Hoover's denial that there was such a thing as organized crime. The OSS and the Mafia had worked together during WWII to protect American ports from Nazi agents. That may have been the way the OSS thanked its partner.

John Meier, a top aide to Howard Hughes, told me that Hoover had expressed to him in a private conversation that he was "powerless" against the CIA. If the CIA had blackmail material on Hoover, that would explain why Hoover never blew the whistle on the myriad evidence of conspiracy his FBI agents dug up in both the JFK and RFK assassinations.

Hoover wasn't the only one targeted. Copeland wrote about "Byzantine intrigue" designed to keep Congress in check. Former *Crossfire* host and erstwhile CIA employee Tom Braden was shocked when Allen Dulles repeated back to him one morning a bedroom conversation Braden had had with his wife the night

---

775   Anthony Summers, *Official and Confidential: The Secret Life of J. Edgar Hoover* (New York: Pocket Star Books, 1994), pp. 280–281.

776   Summers, p. 281 and my conversation with Gordon Novel in 2004.

before. Braden confirmed to writer David Wise that Angleton had placed the tap. Braden also described how Angleton would discuss the previous night's "take" with Allen Dulles in the guise of fishing talk.[777] How better to ensure the CIA's survival than to know the secrets of those who might otherwise rein you in? Perhaps that explains why even—and perhaps especially—our elected officials *to this day* are afraid to challenge the CIA.

In 2007, Senator Jay Rockefeller chastised a young reporter named Charles Davis for thinking that, because he was the Senate Intelligence Chairman, he had any power over the CIA:

> DAVIS: Is there anything you could do in your position as Chairman of the Intelligence Committee to find answers about this, if it is in fact going on?
>
> ROCKEFELLER: *Don't you understand the way Intelligence works? Do you think that because I'm Chairman of the Intelligence Committee that I just say I want it, and they give it to me? They control it. All of it. All of it. All the time. I only get, and my committee only gets, what they want to give me.*
>
> DAVIS: Is there any way someone, maybe not you, they can somehow press the administration to find something—if they're doing something that may be illegal—
>
> ROCKEFELLER: I don't know that. I don't know that. I deal with Intelligence. That's it. They tend to avoid us.
>
> DAVIS: Well, what do you think about these allegations?
>
> ROCKEFELLER: I'm not—I don't comment on allegations. I can't. I can't afford to.[778]

Eisenhower failed to exercise oversight

WITH THE ELECTION OF PRESIDENT DWIGHT D. EISENHOWER, THE nascent CIA took an early turn for the worse. The CIA's leaders held the view that America had the right to decide the fate of the rest of the world. In a world with finite resources, whoever controlled oil, the rare earth minerals necessary for plane and computer parts, precious metals like gold and silver, and pipeline and shipping routes for oil and other resources would dominate the world economy.

The CIA and the establishment that supported it had no qualms advocating and executing covert action to overthrow governments whose economic policies did not provide the U.S. an advantage over all other nations in areas with key

---

777   David Wise, *Molehunt* (New York: Avon Books, 1992), pp. 31–32.

778   Audio and text from www.tinyrevolution.com/mt/archives/001436.html, accessed December 31, 2017.

resources. In the present era, we can see clearly now how disastrous those policies were in Latin America, in the Middle East, and everywhere else the CIA has meddled. Iran may never have become a fundamentalist state had the CIA not overthrown the democratically elected Mohammad Mossadegh.

No one epitomized the establishment more than the brothers Allen and John Foster Dulles. These two had both worked for the powerful Wall Street law firm of Sullivan and Cromwell, protecting the corporate interests of clients that included the powerful Rockefeller clan. Together, they ran America's overt and covert foreign policy for eight years. And under them, a tragic number of democratically elected leaders would be overthrown.

In 1951, two men were elected president that would become targets of the nascent CIA: Jacobo Arbenz in Guatemala and Mohammed Mossadegh in Iran. Both men wanted to stop the exploitation of their people by foreign interests, predominantly British and American business interests. Both took steps to nationalize their most valuable resources—oil in Iran and farmland in Guatemala, and both were then labeled "Communists" and overthrown by the CIA in the mid-1950s.

Not all the CIA's coup attempts were successful. The CIA tried and failed to overthrow President Sukarno in Indonesia in 1958. A plot to kill Castro designed to coincide with the Bay of Pigs failed. An attempt to foment a revolution in Albania failed miserably. Amazingly, no matter how massive the failure, the CIA always seemed to be rewarded with increased funding, as if more money would solve the fundamental problem: You can't bully the world into submission. People will eventually stand up for themselves and their country, when pushed to the brink.

From nearly its inception, the CIA acted independently of the president, a legacy from its freewheeling "anything goes" WWII mentality. This became painfully obvious during the administration of President Eisenhower. Eisenhower's warning about the "military-industrial complex" rings hollow in light of the way he facilitated these interests.

In his book *Robert Kennedy and His Times*, Arthur Schlesinger described how people around Eisenhower tried to warn him that the CIA was becoming a monster. In the wake of the CIA's "successful" coups in Iran (1953), Guatemala (1954), President Eisenhower rewarded the CIA with more power and less oversight. Ironically, it was his own Board of Consultants on Foreign Intelligence Activities, which Eisenhower created in 1956, that saw the CIA's "successes" in a different light:

> Almost at once the board had appointed a panel, led by Robert Lovett
> and David Bruce, to take a look at CIA's covert operations. "Bruce was
> very much disturbed," Lovett told the Cuba board of inquiry in 1961.
> "He approached it from the standpoint of 'what right have we to go

barging around into other countries buying newspapers and handing money to opposition parties or supporting a candidate for this, that or the other office?' He felt this was an outrageous interference with friendly countries. ... He got me alarmed, so instead of completing the report in thirty days we look two months or more."

The 1956 report, written in Bruce's spirited style, condemned "the increased mingling in the internal affairs of other nations of bright, highly graded young men who must be doing something all the time to justify their reason for being. ... Busy, moneyed and privileged, [the CIA] likes its 'King Making' responsibility (the intrigue is fascinating—considerable self-satisfaction, sometimes with applause, derives from "successes"—no charge is made for "failures"—and the whole business is very much simpler than collecting covert intelligence on the USSR through the usual CIA methods!)."[779]

Unfortunately, the Board of Consultants was utterly unsuccessful in persuading Eisenhower to shepherd the CIA appropriately:

> The Board of Consultants had no visible impact. Allen Dulles ignored its recommendations. Eisenhower gave it no support. But its testimony demolishes the myth that the CIA was a punctilious and docile organization, acting only in response to express instructions from higher authority. Like the FBI, it was a runaway agency, in this case endowed with men professionally trained in deception, a wide choice of weapons, reckless purposes, a global charter, maximum funds and minimum accountability.[780]

More disturbing was Schlesinger's note that "Bruce and Lovett could discover no reliable system of control" over the CIA. The Operations Coordinating Board (OCB), which Eisenhower created in 1953 to coordinate and implement national security policies between various government agencies, which had power over the CIA, served instead to rubber-stamp CIA's operations. The Bruce-Lovett report noted that "no one, other than those in the CIA immediately concerned with their day to day operation, has any detailed knowledge of what is going on." As Schlesinger wrote:

> With "a horde of CIA representatives" swarming around the planet, CIA covert action was exerting "significant, almost unilateral influences ... on the actual formation of our foreign policies ... sometimes

---

779   Arthur Schlesinger, *Robert Kennedy and His Times* (New York: Houghton Mifflin Company, 1978), p. 455.

780   Schlesinger, p. 458.

completely unknown" to the local American ambassador. "We are sure," the report added, "that the supporters of the 1948 decision to launch this government on a positive [covert] program could not possibly have foreseen the ramifications of the operations which have resulted from it." Bruce and Lovett concluded with an exasperated plea:

"Should not someone, somewhere in an authoritative position in our government, on a continuing basis, be ... calculating ... the long-range wisdom of activities which have entailed our virtual abandonment of the international 'golden rule,' and which, if successful to the degree claimed for them, are responsible in a great measure for stirring up turmoil and raising the doubts about us that exist in many countries of the world today? ... Where will we be tomorrow?[781]

The Bruce-Lovett report was written in 1956. In 1957, the OCB reiterated many of these concerns in another report to President Eisenhower. The CIA's Directorate of Plans, the "black ops" division of the CIA, was singled out for "operating for the most part on an autonomous and free-wheeling basis in highly critical areas." In some cases this had led to "situations which are almost unbelievable because the operations being carried out by the Deputy Director of Plans are sometimes in direct conflict with the normal operations being carried out by the Department of State."

Schlesinger quoted an unnamed "CIA man" who described how in 1957 CIA tried to force the State Department's hand in Indonesia by feeding them increasingly disturbing intelligence reports on the Indonesian leader Sukarno. "When they read enough alarming reports, we planned to spring the suggestion that we should support the colonels." When the Indonesian Ambassador expressed opposition to any plot to overthrow Sukarno, Allen Dulles, the head of the CIA, pressured his brother John Foster Dulles, then head of the State Department, to replace the Ambassador. And while Allen Dulles had "personally promised" to keep the new Ambassador apprised of CIA activity, he did not.

In 1958, the CIA launched an utterly unsuccessful attack on Indonesia that resulted in CIA pilot Allen Pope being captured. This incident was as poorly planned and executed as the Bay of Pigs operation would be three years later. The OCB once again admonished President Eisenhower to rein in the CIA. The OCB expressed similar sentiments again in 1959 and 1960. In January 1961, just before John Kennedy was inaugurated, the board wrote:

We have been unable to conclude that, on balance, all of the covert action programs undertaken by CIA up to this time have been worth

781   Schlesinger, p. 456.

the risk or the great expenditure of manpower, money and other resources involved. In addition, we believe the CIA's concentration on political, psychological and related covert action activities have tended to detract substantially from the execution of its primary intelligence-gathering mission. We suggest, accordingly, that there should be a total reassessment of our covert action policies.

Because the CIA had done a covert psychological assessment of John Kennedy before he took office, they knew he would never approve of the assassination of Patrice Lumumba in the mineral-rich Congo. John Kennedy understood, as few leaders of the American political scene did, that most so-called "Communists" the CIA sought to overthrow were really just nationalists trying to protect their country's resources from the greed of foreign interests. So CIA rushed to foment the assassination of Lumumba before JFK took office.

Senator Frank Church, during the Church Committee hearings, accused the CIA of behaving like a "rogue elephant." Indeed, the only evidence that the CIA ever ran an assassination or coup plot directly under orders of a president came in the Lumumba case. Notetaker Robert Johnson testified to the Church Committee that President Eisenhower had given what appeared to be a direct order to assassinate Lumumba. The Church Committee, despite Johnson's testimony, put ultimate responsibility for Lumumba's death on local rebels under the command of Joseph Sese Seko Mobutu. But Mobutu was, as Andrew Tully baldly put it, the "CIA's man" in the Congo.[782] CIA officer John Stockwell claimed in his book *In Search of Enemies* that another CIA officer drove around with Lumumba's body in the trunk of his car for days after Lumumba's assassination, wondering how best to dispose of the body.[783] As I wrote in the *Probe* magazine article "Midnight in the Congo,"

> From the CIA's own evidence, the CIA sought to entice Lumumba to escape protection. They then monitored his travel, assisted in creating road blocks, and when he was captured, encouraged his captors to turn him over to his enemies. The CIA had a strong relationship with Mobutu when Mobutu had the power to decide Lumumba's fate. And then there are the admissions reported by Stockwell .... How can anyone, in the light of such evidence, claim the CIA was not directly responsible for Lumumba's murder?[784]

782   Andrew Tully, *CIA: The Inside Story* (New York: Crest Books, 1963), p. 184.

783   John Stockwell, *In Search of Enemies: A CIA Story* (New York: Norton, 1978), p. 105.

784   Lisa Pease, "Midnight in the Congo: The Assassination of Lumumba and the Mysterious Death of Dag Hammarskjöld," *Probe*, Vol. 6. No. 3, March-April 1999.

President Kennedy versus the CIA

THIS, THEN, IS THE AGENCY PRESIDENT KENNEDY INHERITED when he was sworn in on January 20, 1961. The CIA had been out of control for a full eight years, despite four years of strong warnings to the previous administration. So it should come as no surprise that Allen Dulles and his cohorts at CIA had no qualms planning the disastrous Bay of Pigs operation. They did not fear the consequences of failure, because there had never been any consequences for previous failures. Any parent understands if you do not punish children for errant behavior, they will continue to repeat that behavior.

The CIA brought President Kennedy the Bay of Pigs operation, which had been planned under the Eisenhower administration, as a *fait accompli*. Less than one hundred days into his administration, President Kennedy believed the CIA and trusted them.

Little did he realize that Allen Dulles *specifically planned for the failure of the Bay of Pigs*, as coffee-stained handwritten notes attested when discovered years later.[785] Dulles knew Kennedy would not improve a U.S.-led invasion. So Dulles planned a failed attack on the assumption that, forced with a choice between saving face or letting a CIA operation go sour, Kennedy would send in reinforcements. As reporter Daniel Schorr explained decades later, "In effect, President Kennedy was the target of a CIA covert operation that collapsed when the invasion collapsed.[786]

But the CIA underestimated President Kennedy. Unlike his predecessor, who was content to let the CIA run foreign policy, JFK thought he was truly the Commander in Chief and refused to provide additional support that he had not previously authorized. And contrary to much of the published history on this incident, Kennedy *had* authorized air cover to protect the landing at the Bay of Pigs. But for whatever reason—intentional or otherwise—the air support showed up an hour late—too late to be of any help.

At this point, Kennedy refused to authorize any *additional* military support, given that the invasion had been sold to him as one that would succeed as a "native" uprising of anti-Castro Cubans. Given the choice between escalation to "win" or de-escalation to prevent outright war with Cuba, JFK chose to de-escalate the situation, a choice for which the CIA never forgave him.

Unlike Eisenhower, Kennedy wanted to impose consequences on the CIA for their lies and behavior. That's why he fired Allen Dulles and Richard Bissell, the Deputy Director of Plans who had personal responsibility for the failed operation. President Kennedy formed the President's Foreign Intelligence Advisory Board

---

785   James Douglass, *JFK and the Unspeakable: Why He Died and Why It Matters* (New York: Simon & Schuster, 2010 edition).

786   Douglass, p. 15, citing Daniel Schorr, *All Things Considered*, March 26, 2001, Hour 1, National Public Radio (NPR).

to oversee the CIA. In the first few months of its existence, the PFIAB met 25 times—more than Eisenhower's board met over a five-year period. And President Kennedy made sure the PFIAB's recommendations were implemented.

But it was another of President Kennedy's moves that likely sealed his own fate. In the wake of the Bay of Pigs disaster, Kennedy transferred, via National Security Action Memoranda (NSAM) 55, 56 and 57, control of paramilitary operations from CIA to the Department of Defense. He realized that such operations should be conducted under strict military chains of command, not through unaccountable secret operations. Kennedy had vowed he would shatter the CIA into a million pieces and scatter it to the winds.[787] This move was a huge step in that direction.

President Kennedy even considered having his brother Robert head the CIA, but Robert thought that was a bad idea for political reasons: he was a Democrat—which would arouse the ire of the Republicans who had just lost the presidency after holding power for eight years—and he feared it might look nepotistic.

The Kennedys held a worldview that put them on a collision course with the covert establishment. They believed in the possibility of peaceful coexistence with the Soviet Union and the right to self-determination of smaller countries. They understood that bullying smaller, poorer nations into submission by economic strangulation and military action was not a viable strategy in the long run. Both Robert and John had traveled the world extensively and had reached out to numerous world leaders in an attempt to understand what their countries needed. The Kennedys understood that providing schools, roads, food and other forms of economic aid, including government-to-government loans that bypassed greedy bankers, was key to laying a foundation for a true peace, as President Kennedy laid out in his landmark speech at American University in June 1963:

> What kind of peace do I mean? … Not a Pax Americana enforced on
> the world by American weapons of war. Not the peace of the grave or
> the security of the slave. I am talking about genuine peace, the kind
> of peace that makes life on earth worth living, the kind that enables
> men and nations to grow and to hope and to build a better life for
> their children. Not merely peace for Americans, but peace for all men
> and women. Not merely peace in our time, but peace for all time.

Both Kennedys were aware how close the world came to nuclear war during the October Missile Crisis of 1962. Both were advocates of nuclear disarmament. President Kennedy spoke about how nuclear weapons not only didn't guarantee peace, but were costlier and less efficient than other tactics. But President Kennedy

---

787   Drew Pearson, "Was JFK Killed in CIA Backfire?", *New Orleans States-Item*, March 3, 1967.

also talked about the role every individual played in bringing peace to the world, a topic few leaders have ever broached:

> Some say that it is useless to speak of world peace or world law or world disarmament—and that it will be useless until the leaders of the Soviet Union adopt a more enlightened attitude. I hope they do. I believe we can help them do it. But I also believe that we must reexamine our own attitude—as individuals and as a Nation—for our attitude is as essential as theirs. And every graduate of this school, every thoughtful citizen who despairs of war and wishes to bring peace, should begin by looking inward—by examining his own attitude toward the possibilities of peace, toward the Soviet Union, toward the course of the cold war and toward freedom and peace here at home.

"Our problems are manmade," the President told the American University audience, "therefore they can be solved by man." Kennedy pointed out he wasn't after a fantasy version of peace, but something both tangible and achievable:

> Genuine peace must be the product of many nations, the sum of many acts. It must be dynamic, not static, changing to meet the challenge of each new generation. For peace is a process—a way of solving problems.
>
> With such a peace, there will still be quarrels and conflicting interests, as there are within families and nations. World peace, like community peace, does not require that each man love his neighbor—it requires only that they live together in mutual toler-ance, submitting their disputes to a just and peaceful settlement. And history teaches us that enmities between nations, as between individuals, do not last forever. ...
>
> Peace need not be impracticable, and war need not be inevitable. By defining our goal more clearly, by making it seem more manageable and less remote, we can help all peoples to see it, to draw hope from it, and to move irresistibly toward it.[788]

"The United States, as the world knows, will never start a war," President Kennedy said as part of his closing argument for a kinder, gentler approach to other nations. But in Vietnam, the U.S. was poised to do just that. President Kennedy found himself in conflict with the CIA over the depth and nature of U.S. involvement in Vietnam, a conflict that spilled over into the papers of the time.

---

[788]   Speech given by President John F. Kennedy at American University.

A CIA coup in America

IN AN ARTICLE HEADLINED "ARROGANT, POWER MAD—THAT'S OUR CIA in Viet Nam," journalist Richard Starnes wrote of how the CIA was failing to obey direct orders from President Kennedy's Ambassador to Vietnam, Henry Cabot Lodge:

> Twice the CIA flatly refused to carry out instructions from Ambassador Henry Cabot Lodge, according to a high U.S. source here.
>
> In one of these instances, the CIA frustrated a plan of action Lodge brought with him from Washington, because the agency disagreed with it.
>
> This led to a dramatic confrontation between Lodge and John Richardson, chief of the huge CIA apparatus here. Lodge failed to move Richardson, and the dispute was bucked back to Washington. Secretary of State Dean Rusk and CIA Chief John A. McCone were unable to resolve the conflict, and the matter is now reported to be awaiting settlement by President Kennedy. ...
>
> Other American agencies here are incredibly bitter about the CIA.
>
> *"If the U.S. ever experiences a 'Seven Days in May' it will come from the CIA, and not the Pentagon,"* one U.S. official commented caustically. ...
>
> *"They represent a tremendous power and total unaccountability to no one...."* ...
>
> One very high American official here, a man who has spent much of his life in the service of democracy, *likened the CIA's growth to a malignancy, and added he was not sure even the White House could control it any longer.* [Emphasis added.][789]

Arthur Krock repeated some of Starnes' charges in his own article, calling on President Kennedy to put an end to the war between the administration and the CIA in a way that both preserved the CIA's secrecy yet held them accountable on these charges.

That same month, Starnes also took Allen Dulles to task for propagandizing in his book *The Craft of Intelligence*:

> In any effective sense of the word as used in a democracy, the CIA's accountability is so vague and amorphous as to be meaningless. The face it turns toward the public when it is under criticism is one of

---

[789]   Richard Starnes, Scripps News Service, "Arrogant, Power Mad—That's our CIA in Viet Nam," *El Paso Herald-Post*, October 2, 1963, p. 27.

sad virtue: CIA, so goes the myth, does not reply to attacks, does not deny stories (however outlandish—or true—they may be), is above the hurly burly of democracy in action.

This, of course, is disingenuous nonsense. The CIA does reply to criticism, violently and vociferously. It does deny and attempt to discredit stories that seek to penetrate its cloak of piety. It moves heaven and earth to unmask the sources of news accounts that shake its cloudy complacency.[790]

Privately, to aides and close friends, President Kennedy evinced a desire to get Americans out of Vietnam. At a press conference on November 14, 1963, Kennedy discussed that, because there was a new government in Vietnam, there was a new need to reassess the American commitment there. "That is our object: to bring Americans home," and transition military action back to the South Vietnamese, Kennedy told the reporters, adding that the purpose of the upcoming Honolulu conference was to figure out how to "pursue these objectives."

After President Kennedy was assassinated, combat troops were introduced into Vietnam and the counterinsurgency effort became an outright war, launched under the false premise that the Vietnamese had attacked the U.S.S. *Maddox* in the Gulf of Tonkin. It took nearly 30 years for that lie to be exposed. But Americans in general and journalists in particular seem unable to see the truth of such lies when they are pronounced by government sources. It was perhaps the ability of both Robert and John Kennedy to see through such lies that ensured their fates.

Cuba

NOWHERE WAS THE TURN AWAY FROM AMERICAN EMPIRE AND toward world peace more prominent than in the way President Kennedy treated Fidel Castro and Cuba in the aftermath of the Cuban Missile Crisis.

After the Bay of Pigs, President Kennedy had assigned Robert Kennedy to oversee what became known as Operation Mongoose, a series of covert actions against Cuba designed to weaken Castro in the hopes of destabilizing him politically. These plots were *not* assassination plots. After the Cuban Missile Crisis, Mongoose was cancelled. As Attorney General, Robert Kennedy had the Justice Department and FBI shut down anti-Castro training camps in Miami, in Louisiana and in other places where CIA assets were trying to start their own revolution. President Kennedy sent journalists William Attwood and Lisa Howard

---

790   Richard Starnes, "Spy Bureau," *The Pittsburgh Press*, October 19, 1963.

as unofficial ambassadors to talk rapprochement with Carlos Lechuga, the UN Ambassador from Cuba.

Richard Helms was tracking these attempts at rapprochement closely. One could make the case that Helms wanted to sabotage these efforts. And perhaps he tried, in the Cuban weapons cache episode.

President Kennedy made clear the only way he'd authorize another action against Cuba would be if Castro were found to be exporting his revolution abroad. So when a large cache of weapons ostensibly from Cuba was found on a beach in Venezuela in November 1963, the CIA was quick to tout this as the proof President Kennedy had been looking for.

Helms grabbed a desk officer and dropped in on Attorney General Robert Kennedy on November 19, 1963, just three days before President Kennedy would be killed in Dallas, "with one of the Belgian-made submachine guns we had filched from the arms cache." How did the CIA know the Belgian weapons had been sold to Cuba? Helms' answer borders on the absurd:

> In an effort to conceal the origin of the weapons, the Cubans had attempted to scrape away the Cuban army shield and serial numbers the guns had originally borne. Fortunately, one of our technicians had developed an acid which, when applied to the filed area, rendered the original markings legible. There was one hitch—the restored markings faded from the blue steel barrier in a matter of seconds. Worse, our acid treatment could be applied only twice before the markings faded permanently away. A complex bit of photography solved the problem.[791]

To me, this read as if the CIA forged photos and then attributed the lack of physical evidence to a chemical process. I was not alone in my skepticism, as you will soon see.

Robert Kennedy took Helms and the desk officer to the Oval Office to talk to the president. President Kennedy asked how the Cubans got three tons of ordnance onto the beach. As Helms wrote:

> Castro's *Fidelistas* had in effect answered the President's question. In the process of getting smartly away from the scene of the crime, the Cubans had overlooked one of their outboard-powered launches.[792]

Down in Venezuela, the same Joseph Burkholder Smith we met earlier didn't believe any of this:

791   Richard Helms, *A Look Over My Shoulder* (New York: Random House, 2003), pp. 226–227.
792   Helms, p. 227.

> "I like the touch about the boat's being sold by Canadians to the Cuban Agrarian Reform Institute. Makes it sound as though Castro's trying to be real spooky, using a cover like the Agrarian Institute to deliver arms," I couldn't resist saying. "How did we actually get weapons there?"[793]

Maps had purportedly been found in connection with the recently arrived cache, but Smith knew those maps had been found months earlier in connection with a wholly separate incident. And the person who "confessed" to being involved in the operation had done so while a prisoner of the security police. As Smith explained:

> There are few prisoners of security police in Latin America who refuse to confess. If they don't confess they usually have died in the process of making up their minds, having thought too long about the matter with their heads under water or something similar.[794]

President Kennedy didn't seem persuaded either, because Helms recorded no positive response, no promised action. Instead, Helms wrote that as the president put the gun back into the travel bag from which it had been retrieved, Helms said, "I'm sure glad the Secret Service didn't catch us bringing this gun in here." Imagine the implied threat. It was almost as if Helms was warning Kennedy he'd better change his mind. But Kennedy grinned and was evidently so concerned with the Venezuelan arms cache that as Helms looked back, "we could see the President signing mail."

That afternoon, Helms wrote, "it occurred to me that I did not have one of the customary autographed photographs of President Kennedy." He called Kenny O'Donnell and arranged to get one. Helms was not a fan of the president. Why did he suddenly want an autographed photo? I got a chill, reading this in Helms' words, because it was almost like Helms was bragging to insiders who would understand that he was signaling he knew JFK would be killed just three days later. Helms was a collector. He wrote a letter to his son on stationery stolen from Hitler. Perhaps Helms couldn't resist obtaining a memento he knew would be unobtainable in three days.

---

793   Smith, p. 383.
794   *Ibid.*

Did the CIA kill JFK?

LIKE SMITH'S UNNAMED ARMY COLONEL, ROBERT KENNEDY UNDER-
stood what the CIA was capable of. When Robert learned of President Kennedy's
assassination in Dallas, he called CIA headquarters to ask a startled officer there
if the CIA were involved. But the officer would not have been able to answer that
accurately either way. He likely wouldn't have known the answer, and couldn't
have told the truth if he had. You can't *get* a job at CIA if you can't keep secrets
forever. And as we saw with Tom Braden earlier, the CIA is always listening. They
bug their own employees. So giving up secrets is too costly to be worth the risk,
unless you have the courage of Edward Snowden or Chelsea Manning.

Robert also called CIA Director John McCone over to Hickory Hill and asked
him the same question. But according to Richard Helms, McCone was never
informed by the people beneath him of the CIA's plots to assassinate Castro. If
they hadn't told him about Castro, why would they tell him if they had killed
Kennedy? McCone was a Kennedy appointee. It makes no sense that the CIA
would have looped McCone in on a plot to kill the man who had given him his
current job.

Even President Harry Truman seemed to have his suspicions. He expressed
concern, exactly one month to the day after the assassination of President
Kennedy, that the CIA was out of control. On December 22, 1963, newspapers
around the country published an opinion piece by President Harry Truman
expressing his regret for how far the CIA had moved from its original mandate.
President Truman wrote:

> I think it has become necessary to take another look at the purpose
> and operations of our Central Intelligence Agency—CIA. …
>
> For some time I have been disturbed by the way the CIA has been
> diverted from its original assignment. It has become an operational
> and at times a policy-making arm of the government. This has led
> to trouble and may have compounded our difficulties in several
> explosive areas.
>
> I never had any thought that when I set up the CIA that [sic] it
> would be injected into peacetime cloak and dagger operations. Some
> of the complications and embarrassment that I think we have expe-
> rienced are in part attributable to the fact that this quiet intelligence
> arm of the president has been so removed from its intended role
> that it is being interpreted as a symbol of sinister and mysterious
> foreign intrigue—and a subject for cold war enemy propaganda. …
>
> [T]he last thing we needed was for CIA to be seized upon as

something akin to a subverting influence in the affairs of other people. ...

I, therefore, would like to see the CIA be restored to its original assignment as the intelligence arm of the president, and whatever else it can properly perform in that special field—and that its operational duties be terminated or properly used elsewhere. ...

There is something about the way the CIA has been functioning that is casting a shadow over our historic position and I feel that we need to correct it.[795]

There's no space in this volume to lay out the case for the CIA's role in President Kennedy's assassination, but it's a strong one. Please see *The Last Investigation* by Gaeton Fonzi, *Oswald and the CIA* by John Newman, *JFK and the Unspeakable* by Jim Douglass, *Destiny Betrayed* by Jim DiEugenio, and my previous book with Jim DiEugenio, *The Assassinations: Probe Magazine on JFK, MLK, RFK and Malcolm X* for some of the strong evidence of the CIA's role in the plot. Here I will attempt only the barest summary of some evidence in that regard.

CIA finance officer James Wilcott told the HSCA and later, anyone who would listen, including his friends, who told Jim Douglass, that Oswald had been a paid agent of the CIA. While Wilcott had never paid him personally, he was told by others that Lee Harvey Oswald had been paid under a CIA project code. Wilcott told the HSCA that he learned from others in the CIA in the days following the assassination that members of the CIA had killed Kennedy.

Originally, said Wilcott, the news of Kennedy's assassination was met with joy in the CIA. The CIA was filled with extreme right-wing hardliners who were thrilled the liberal president had been killed. But when Oswald's history surfaced, the joy faded as employees realized their CIA had killed the president. According to Wilcott:

Not long before going off duty, talk about Oswald's connection with CIA was making the rounds. While this kind of talk was a jolt to me, I didn't really take it seriously then. Very heavy talk continued up to about the middle of January. Based solely on what I heard at the Tokyo Station, I became convinced that the following scenario is true: CIA people killed Kennedy. Either it was an outright project of Headquarters with the approval of McCone or it was done outside,

---

795   Harry S. Truman, "CIA Off-Base as Policy Arm, Founder Truman Says," *The Sunday Press* (Binghamton, NY), December 22, 1963. While some authors have suggested Truman not only did not pen this but did not agree with it, multiple drafts of the article in Truman's own handwriting, and correspondence asserting these same points, prove those assertions to be incorrect. This is a lie that Allen Dulles inserted into a CIA memo in the hopes of discrediting Truman's indictment. But researcher Ray Marcus contacted the Truman Library and tracked down Truman's handwritten drafts of this article as well as letters that reiterate these same concerns re the CIA.

perhaps under the direction of Dulles and Bissell. It was done in retaliation for Kennedy's reneging on a secret agreement with Dulles to support the invasion of Cuba.[796]

There was no secret agreement between President Kennedy and Dulles to support an invasion of Cuba, but it would have been fully in keeping with Allen Dulles' character to make up such a story to blame the victim. More disturbing was Wilcott's assertion of the motive behind the killing of Kennedy:

> The branch chiefs and deputy chiefs, project intelligence officers and operational specialists viewed Kennedy as a threat to the clandestine services. The loss of special privileges, allowances, status and early retirement that come with the CIA cloak-and-dagger job were becoming a possibility, even a probability. The prestigious portions of the bureaucratic dominions, ambitiously sought, might be no more. Adjustment to a less glamorous job in a common profession could be the result.[797]

Remember how George White expressed how fun it was to "kill, cheat, steal, rape, and pillage" with impunity? There really were people who'd rather kill the president than give up that lifestyle, especially when it was tinged with a warped patriotism that made them feel killing Kennedy was a necessary act to prevent the spread of liberalism.

As in the RFK case, one of the bullets in the JFK case—the so-called "magic bullet" or Commission Exhibit (CE) 399—does not appear to be the bullet initially submitted. Three of the people in the chain of possession claimed the bullet currently in evidence was not the bullet they had passed along. A fourth claimed to have seen his initials on the bullet, but independent researchers have confirmed his initials are *not* on the bullet currently in evidence. Why would evidence need to be switched? To cover something up is the obvious answer. To explain a bullet wound that had no bullet in it, for example, an FBI agent actually postulated in the official record that perhaps ice bullets had been used.

Oswald's trip to the Soviet Union is another red flag. His trip was misreported across all media in the days following the assassination of President Kennedy as a "defection" to the Soviet Union. Officially, Oswald was a Marxist-Leninist who defected to the Soviet Union because he believed in the Communist revolution. But after being there a time, he grew disillusioned with the Soviet system and moved back to America. But in fact, Oswald never defected and never renounced

---

796   HSCA executive session testimony of James Wilcott, March 22, 1978.
797   *Ibid.*

his citizenship. Oswald met up with "witting" CIA asset Priscilla Johnson (later, Priscilla McMillan) and other CIA assets during his time there. He offered to give the Soviets something of "special interest," presumably related to the U-2 program, as he had been a radar operator and knew key information, such as the altitude at which the planes flew. He received an enormous amount of money from the Red Cross while he was there, an unusual act that has never been fully explained. Priscilla later wrote the book *Marina and Me* about Lee Harvey Oswald and his wife Marina, a book Marina called a pack of lies.

A few months after Oswald landed in the USSR, Francis Gary Powers' U-2 plane exploded and crashed over the Soviet Union on May 1, 1960. Powers managed to parachute out before the plane crashed. That month, President Dwight D. Eisenhower was set to meet with Soviet Premier Nikita Khrushchev in Paris for a peace summit that could have ended the Cold War. When the plane crashed, the U.S.' first response was to lie about the mission, claiming the plane was on a weather mission and had strayed off course. But the data in the captured wreckage as well as the admissions of pilot Powers made clear the plane had been used in a spy mission. In his 1970 book *Operation Oversight*, Powers wondered if Lee Harvey Oswald had anything to do with the downing of his plane to sabotage the upcoming peace summit.

Others have speculated Oswald's true mission in the USSR was to help the CIA determine if they had a mole in the U-2 program. If the Soviets had no source within the program, then they should have showed interest in Oswald. If they already had a mole in the program, they wouldn't need to talk to Oswald. But the CIA didn't consider that their ploy would be so obvious that the Soviets pegged Oswald as a CIA man from the start, so they weren't interested in him either way. At least, that's what a high-level Soviet intelligence officer named Yuri Nosenko told the CIA upon his defection. (The best account of the Nosenko story can be found in Thomas Mangold's *Cold Warrior*, a biography of James Angleton.) Nosenko's assertions threatened the "Soviets did it" line Angleton and Dulles had used to persuade President Johnson and the Warren Commission to go along with a cover-up of any evidence of conspiracy. Before one of his sessions on a polygraph machine, Nosenko had been anally stimulated against his will, presumably to raise his blood pressure and stress level in order to make him "fail" the test on the machine. According to Mangold, in that session, Nosenko was asked "many more" questions about Oswald than in previous sessions.

In Mexico City, a month before the assassination, the CIA appeared to pre-frame Oswald for the crime. No credible evidence has ever placed Oswald at either the Soviet Embassy or the Cuban Embassy. Someone who was not the person Jack Ruby shot in Dallas gave his name as Lee Oswald at the Cuban

Embassy, according to the Cuban Consul there, Eusebio Azcue. And a conversation that couldn't have happened because the Soviet Embassy was closed that day was apparently falsified for the record by CIA operatives to place Oswald in the company of a Soviet assassin at the Russian Embassy. The media has uncritically reported on Oswald's trip to both embassies without realizing they are essentially repeating a CIA "legend," a false story laid down to protect a CIA operation.

After the assassination, Lee Harvey Oswald was given a paraffin test to determine if there were nitrate on his hands and cheek, which could indicate that he had fired a gun. Paraffin tests had often produced false positives but never a false negative until the FBI got involved, as I noted in an article for Robert Parry's *Consortium News*:

> FBI agents tried and failed to fire Oswald's rifle and not get nitrate on their cheeks, yet Oswald's cheek tested nitrate-free. So Courtlandt Cunningham of the FBI created a scenario that would allow one to fire the rifle and not get nitrate on one's cheek: he used two people, one to clean the weapon between shots and hand it back to the other one.
>
> In that manner, Cunningham was able to tell the Warren Commission it was possible to get a "false negative" reading of nitrate. (The Warren Commission failed to explain why a two-man scenario helped prove Oswald was the "lone" assassin.)[798]

In every test, nitrate was found after firing Oswald's weapon except for the one where the rifle was cleaned between shots and handed back. Author Gerald McKnight discussed how sensitive the nitrate tests were, and how one could not get a false negative simply by washing one's hands and face, as the particles would be so deeply embedded in the skin that the paraffin would pull them from the pores. In his book about the Warren Commission called *Breach of Trust*, McKnight summarized, "Short of spending the afternoon in a Russian steam bath sweating out his pores, the negative results on the paraffin cast of his right cheek argue strongly for his exculpation."[799]

When Congress tried to investigate the CIA's possible role in the JFK assassination in the 1970s, they found the CIA manipulated their investigation to the

---

798   Lisa Pease, "The Lost History of 'J. Edgar,'" *Consortium News*, consortiumnews.com/2011/11/14/the-lost-history-of-j-edgar/, November 14, 2011. Read Cunningham's testimony to the Warren Commission to see this sleight-of-hand maneuver.

799   Gerald McKnight, *Breach of Trust: How the Warren Commission Failed the Nation and Why* (University Press of Kansas, 2005), p. 212.

point where the CIA's role could not be found or investigated properly. The CIA lied, stalled, hid records, disappeared others once found, and generally treated the investigation with a disdain unbefitting any government agency in a democracy.

Robert Kennedy's evolution

THE CIA DID NOT FAIL TO RECOGNIZE HOW, IN THE WAKE OF HIS brother's assassination, Robert Kennedy became somewhat radicalized. He pushed hard to get his brother's Civil Rights legislation passed in 1964. He became especially vocal about the plight of the poor and minorities. He not only visited West Virginia and Eastern Kentucky, he went into the poorest of homes and held diseased babies in his arms. He was emotionally fearless about facing the destitution within the U.S.' borders and worked to do something about it. In New York, he worked with the business community to create the Bedford Stuyvesant Restoration Corporation, the nation's first public-private partnership to raise money that was used to hire the impoverished in projects to improve the neighborhood in which they lived. He opposed cuts to hospitals for veterans and battled Governor Nelson Rockefeller to secure grants for impoverished communities. The word "revolution" became a frequent addition to his public speeches. He opposed the growing power of the National Rifle Association, and proposed warning labels for cigarette packages at a time when Big Tobacco could make or break political careers.

Kennedy understood that race and class were two sides of the same coin. At a meeting in Harlem, for example, Kennedy said, "It is one thing to assure a man the legal right to eat in a restaurant. It is another thing to assure that he can earn the money to eat there."[800]

Abroad, Robert Kennedy was equally outspoken. He went to South Africa to protest apartheid at a time when speaking up for "the Negro," the term of the time, was a political liability. He told Peruvians to stop whining about American oil interest threats and nationalize their oil if they felt that would serve them better.[801] Robert understood that the U.S. could not win a war in Vietnam, and that guerrilla warfare and terrorism were the response to, not the cause of, unbearable circumstances. He did not believe we could simply kill our way to peace, and that the goal of counterinsurgency must be political reform, not body counts. Robert repeated a common theme: "The responsibility of our times is nothing less than revolution," one that would be "peaceful if we are wise enough; humane if we

---

800   John R. Bohrer, *The Revolution of Robert Kennedy* (New York: Bloomsbury Press, 2017), p. 205.

801   Richard Goodwin, *Remembering America*.

care enough; successful if we are fortunate enough."[802] In Chile, after visiting a mine in Concepcion, Robert noted, "If I worked in this mine, I'd be a communist too."[803] Robert Kennedy was the Avenging Angel, bent on protecting the poor and disenfranchised from the exploitation of the rich at every turn.

Daniel Ellsberg, the man who leaked the Pentagon Papers, spoke of how Robert Kennedy knew the U.S. could never win a war in Vietnam. Kennedy made clear he didn't believe we could bomb our way to peace and advocated strongly for winning the hearts and minds through aid programs, not through bombing campaigns.

Ellsberg worked on Robert Kennedy's presidential campaign in 1968. He was shaving when he heard Robert Kennedy had been killed, and "sat on the edge of his bed and sobbed, tears carving tiny paths through the shaving cream on his cheeks."[804] At a 1993 conference at Harvard, Ellsberg described how he had asked Robert Kennedy, after John Kennedy's assassination, whether his brother would have pulled out of Vietnam. Jim DiEugenio remembered how Ellsberg said Robert Kennedy responded:

> In 1993, at the Harvard Conference, Ellsberg attended and he talked about his conversation with Bobby Kennedy on the subject of the war. He asked RFK what his brother was going to do in regards to Vietnam. Kennedy said he cannot say what he would have done, only what he intended to do. And he intended on withdrawing. Ellsberg replied that was good, and JFK was a smart man. Kennedy raised his voice and pounded the table with his fist: "What do you mean, 'smart man'? We were *there*. We saw what happened to the French. We knew what would happen to America. You didn't have to be smart to see that!"[805]

Many authors have said Robert Kennedy supported the war in Vietnam more than his brother did. But the comment above and the context from DiEugenio below shows that to be a mistaken impression:

> I always wondered where Ellsberg got that story he told in 1993. I was not aware [until later] he worked for RFK in 1968. RFK was with his brother in 1951, when JFK visited Vietnam and met with State Department employee Edmund Gullion, who told him that France had no chance of winning the war. Ho Chi Minh had fired up the

802   Bohrer, p. 233.

803   Bohrer, p. 241.

804   Steve Sheinkin, *Most Dangerous: Daniel Ellsberg and the Secret History of the Vietnam War* (New York: Roaring Book Press, 2015), p. 137.

805   Email from Jim DiEugenio to the author, December 8, 2017.

Viet Minh to such a point they would rather die than go back under the yoke of colonialism; France could never win a war of attrition, because the home front would not support it. RFK later said that this discussion with Gullion had a deep impact on John Kennedy's thinking. Apparently, it had an impact on Robert's as well.[806]

In response to Robert Kennedy's outspoken critiques against political and monetary oppressors, students and progressives clamored for him. He was as popular as the Beatles. At times people clawed and ripped at his hands during public appearances to the point where it drew blood.

Robert Kennedy's popularity was deeply concerning to the CIA. In 1968, as the *Washington Post* later reported, "The Central Intelligence Agency considered its spying on American political and civil rights leaders such as Sen. Robert F. Kennedy and the Rev. Martin Luther King Jr. as having the same high priority as its intelligence-gathering on the Soviet Union and Communist China, according to CIA files."[807] Through their illegal domestic spying program run under the codename MHCHAOS, the CIA spied on peace activists, opened their mail, and even infiltrated progressive publications like *Ramparts* magazine and publishers like Grove Press, the outfit that published the paperback version of Robert Blair Kaiser's book *R.F.K. Must Die!*. Grove Press later sued the CIA for $10 million for having "adversely influenced its managerial, editorial and employment policies."[808]

The Castro plots

SOME PEOPLE POINT TO THE CASTRO ASSASSINATION PLOTS AS A reason the CIA would not have killed either Kennedy. Weren't the Kennedys on the same side as the CIA in that regard? No, and this is a point on which so much disinformation has been written I feel compelled to set the record straight.

Yes, Fidel Castro was a thorn in the CIA's side. Not only had Castro taken over the Florida faction's nearest tropical playground, he was flaunting Communist ideas just miles from our shores. Yes, the Kennedys were intent on replacing Castro politically. But no, neither Kennedy ever approved an assassination plot, and the CIA has admitted as much in their internal records and in the testimony of senior officers familiar with the plots. And had the CIA thought either would

806   *Ibid.*
807   Timothy S. Robinson, "At CIA, Domestic and Foreign Spying Had Equal Priority," September 9, 1979.
808   Arnold H. Lubasch, "GROVE SUES CIA.; SEEKS $10 MILLION," *New York Times*, July 17, 1975.

have approved of the plot, there would have been no reason to hide the plots from them, as they provably did.

CIA Director Helms gave his head of anti-Castro operations, Desmond Fitzgerald, permission to lie to his operatives, to claim that he had Robert Kennedy's authority, when they both knew this was not true. Fitzgerald then repeated this lie, and the belief grew within the CIA that Robert Kennedy had authorized the plots. Some CIA people, like Sam Halpern, a high-level aide to Des Fitzgerald, made sure that *this* version of the story reached the media. In fact, nearly every author that has claimed Robert Kennedy was in on the Castro assassination plots sources Halpern. Halpern claimed that Richard Bissell told him Robert Kennedy ordered the CIA to kill Castro. Halpern shot his own credibility in the foot, however, when he lamented to author Jefferson Morley that he and others in the CIA were frustrated because Robert Kennedy urged what he and others felt amounted only to "pinpricks" against Castro. An assassination plot could never be described as a "pinprick."

Bissell, too, would put the lie to Halpern's assertion when he testified to the Church Committee. Bissell admitted no one at the White House had asked him to assassinate Castro. Perhaps Bissell's candor reflected his knowledge that the CIA had conducted its own internal investigation through its Inspector General (IG), J.S. Earman, when news of the CIA's plots to kill Castro first leaked out in Drew Pearson's column in 1967. The IG report concluded Kennedy was out of the loop.

While some have suggested this document was meant to protect Kennedy's role in the plots, that assertion makes no logical sense. If that were the case, the CIA would have leaked it to their media assets and made certain its contents were reported. If the goal was to protect the oval office, why did the CIA go out of its way to suppress this report, which was not released to the public until the 1990s? You don't tell the truth publicly and hide a lie—there would be no point in having told the lie in the first place. But telling a lie publicly while hiding the truth privately is an all-too-common practice, especially for the CIA.

The IG report was clearly a damage control assessment. How many people knew of the plots? What might they say? In the report, the CIA was entirely concerned with protecting its own reputation, not the president's or Robert Kennedy's. That's why the findings of this report were considered so sensitive that the report is prefaced with this information:

> This report was prepared at the request of the Director of Central Intelligence. He assigned the task to the Inspector General on 23 March 1967. The report was delivered to the Director, personally, in installments, beginning on 24 April 1967. The Director returned

this copy to the Inspector General on 22 May 1967 with instructions that the Inspector General:

Retain it in personal, EYES ONLY safekeeping

Destroy the one burn copy retained temporarily by the Inspector General

Destroy all notes and other source materials originated by those participating in the writing of this report

The one stayback burn copy, all notes, and all other derived source materials were destroyed on 23 May 1967.

This ribbon copy is the only text of the report now in existence, either in whole or in part. Its text has been read only by:

Richard Helms, Director of Central Intelligence

J.S. Earman, Inspector General

K.E. Greer, Inspector (one of the authors)

S. [Scott] D. Breckinridge, Inspector (one of the authors)[809]

What was in this report that was so sensitive there was only one "EYES ONLY" "ribbon" copy kept? The Castro plots had been made public already in the very article that spurred this review, so that was hardly the information the CIA wanted to keep hidden. A reading of the report shows clearly that the sensitive information was this: the CIA had attempted to kill Castro behind President Kennedy's back, without his approval. In fact, the first plot was to take place concurrently with the Bay of Pigs operation, but neither Kennedy had been advised of that, according to Scott Breckinridge's Church Committee testimony.[810]

Mid-report, there is a chart of allegations from Pearson's article. Statements from Pearson's article appear on one side with the CIA's response opposite it. Next to the allegation that "Robert Kennedy may have approved an assassination plot," the report's authors wrote "Not true. He was briefed on Gambling Syndicate-Phase One after it was over. He was not briefed on Phase Two."

The CIA reiterated this at the end of the report, where the CIA asked itself, "Can CIA state or imply that it was merely an instrument of policy?" and answered, "Not in this case." In other words, the CIA admitted quietly, in a document never intended to be made public, that it had no authority from the Kennedy administration for the plots:

While it is true that Phase Two was carried out in an atmosphere of intense Kennedy administration pressure to do something about Castro, such is not true of the earlier phase. Phase One was initiated

---

809   CIA's IG report on the Castro assassination plots. You can read the full report here: www.maryferrell. org/showDoc.html?docId=9983#relPageId=3&tab=page.

810   Testimony of Scott Breckinridge to the Church Committee, June 2, 1975.

in August 1960 under the Eisenhower administration. Phase Two is associated in Harvey's mind with the Executive Action Capability, which reportedly was developed in response to White House urgings. Again, Phase One had been started and abandoned months before the Executive Action Capability appeared on the scene.

When Robert Kennedy was briefed on Phase One in May 1962, he strongly admonished Houston and Edwards to check with the Attorney General in advance of any future intended use of U.S. criminal elements. This was not done with respect to Phase Two, which was already well under way at the time Kennedy was briefed.[811]

In other words, Robert Kennedy had not known about or approved the Phase One Mafia-oriented plots (including the assassination plot planned in conjunction with the Bay of Pigs operation) and was only told about such plots after they had *ended*. The CIA deliberately did not tell Robert Kennedy about the Phase Two plots. "Executive Action" is a euphemism for assassination. In the context of the statement in the IG report, it meant an in-house CIA operation, as opposed to the Phase One plots, which had been outsourced to the Mafia.

The CIA might never have told Robert Kennedy about *any* of their plots to kill Castro had not Sam Giancana been arrested for the wiretapping of his girlfriend, who was sleeping with someone else. Giancana had participated in plots to kill Castro. As a favor, then, Robert Maheu, the man the CIA chose to run the Castro plots in Phase One, hired wiretappers to help Giancana out. Robert Kennedy discussed the incident with J. Edgar Hoover as soon as he learned of it. As Hoover wrote:

> The Attorney General told me he wanted to advise me of a situation in the Giancana case which had considerably disturbed him. He stated a few days ago he had been advised by CIA that in connection with Giancana, CIA had hired Robert A. Maheu, a private detective in Washington, D.C., to approach Giancana with a proposition of paying $150,000 to hire some gunmen to go into Cuba to kill Castro. I expressed astonishment at this in view of the bad reputation of Maheu and the horrible judgement in using a man of Giancana's background for such a project. The Attorney General shared the same views. The Attorney General stated that in connection with the "bugging" which had been developed by us in Las Vegas of Phyllis McGuire's residence where Giancana and she were living, CIA admitted that they had assisted Maheu in making this installation

---

811   CIA's IG report on the Castro assassination plots.

and for these reasons CIA was in a position where it could not afford to have any action taken against Giancana or Maheu. The Attorney General informed me he had asked CIA whether they ever cleared their actions in hiring Maheu and Giancana with the Department of Justice before they did so and he was advised by CIA they had not cleared these matters with the Department of Justice. He stated he then issued orders to CIA to never again in the future take such steps without first checking with the Department of Justice.

... The Attorney General stated he felt notwithstanding the obstacle now in the path of prosecution of Giancana, we should still keep after him. He stated of course it would be very difficult to initiate any prosecution against him because Giancana could immediately bring out the fact that the United States Government had approached him to arrange for the assassination of Castro.[812]

Why would the CIA need to inform Robert Kennedy of the plots if he had ordered them? Clearly, he hadn't. And clearly, Robert Kennedy didn't want that to impede the prosecution of Giancana, either.

When Robert Kennedy found out about an assassination plot against Castro, according to two of his top aides, Adam Walinsky and Peter Edelman, he stopped it. When angry students in Lima, Peru, accused Robert Kennedy of being behind the plots, Kennedy responded, "I'm the one who saved him."[813] No doubt he thought he had, because according to Sy Hersh of the *New York Times*:

Mr. [Adam] Walinsky, now a lawyer in private practice in New York, said that Mr. [Robert] Kennedy disclosed that he had received "assurances in writing" from the CIA that the attempted assassination had been aborted. Those assurances came after Mr. Kennedy discussed the issue with high officials of the agency, Mr. Walinsky recalled the then-Senator saying.

"He told us that he had discovered that the CIA had made a contract with the Mafia to hit Castro," Mr. Walinsky said. ...

"I remember him saying, blame myself?" Mr. Edelman recalled. "I didn't start it [the Castro assassination attempt]; I stopped it."[814]

Hersh dropped a little bombshell at the end of this article:

---

812   Memo from J. Edgar Hoover to his top lieutenants, May 10, 1962.

813   Tad Szulc, "The Politics of Assassination," *New York*, June 23, 1975.

814   Sy Hersh, "Aides Say Robert Kennedy Told of CIA Castro Plot," *The New York Times*, March 10, 1975.

Asked why Senator Kennedy did not try to make that information public, Mr. Walinsky said he could only speculate, but he believed the Senator, who was assassinated while seeking the Democratic Presidential nomination, in 1968, planned to take some corrective action toward the CIA if elected to the White House.[815]

The last time a president tried to take "corrective action" against the CIA was in 1963, and that didn't go so well for President Kennedy.

Bill Harvey and Roselli

THE PLOT ROBERT TURNED OFF MAY HAVE BEEN LAUNCHED DURING the Cuban Missile Crisis. Robert found out Bill Harvey was sending CIA teams into Cuba at the height of the crisis. Outraged, Kennedy demanded an explanation. Harvey tried to blame the military, but Robert had already talked to the military and knew this to be a lie. Kennedy was so outraged that the CIA transferred Harvey to Rome, where Harvey may well have plotted his revenge. David Talbot and others have written about Harvey's contacts with various mafia leaders in Italy and Corsica, and how Harvey may have plotted President John Kennedy's assassination there. At the time of this writing, the CIA has refused to release Bill Harvey's travel vouchers for November 1963, more than half a century later. What is the CIA still trying to hide? That Bill Harvey had been in Dallas the day President Kennedy was murdered, as a Harvey associate from Rome asserted?[816]

Whatever Harvey knew about the JFK assassination may have come into play when Johnny Roselli, one of the people involved in the Castro assassination plots, was arrested for a sophisticated system for cheating at cards in the Friars Club case.

In September 1967, Roselli contacted Bill Harvey. He made reference to the Grand Jury session and seemed to believe he would be exonerated in the Friars Club case. Roselli also made sure Harvey knew, in the words of FBI man Sam Papich, who served as a liaison between the FBI and CIA, that Roselli "would never reveal his past relationship with the CIA."[817] But Roselli also mentioned that "someone" might leak something in that regard. In other words, it appeared that Roselli was subtly trying to blackmail the CIA so they would help him by threatening to reveal the Castro assassination plots.

815   Sy Hersh, "Aides Say Robert Kennedy Told of CIA Castro Plot," The New York Times, March 10, 1975.
816   David Talbot, The Devil's Chessboard (New York: HarperCollins, 2015), p. 477.
817   FBI memo from Sam Papich to D.J. Brennan, Jr., October 9, 1967.

Harvey reported this to Howard Osborn of the CIA's Office of Security and then asked a strange question. "Harvey asked if CIA had any ties with Robert Maheu." Maheu had brought Roselli to the CIA, after which Harvey took a liking to him and became his primary contact. Osborn told Harvey he didn't know, which likely wasn't true, and he told Papich the CIA "is not in any way connected with Maheu," which provably wasn't true, as Maheu's contracts with the CIA and renewals thereof are now a matter of public record. It was Maheu's friends in the CIA's Office of Security that involved Maheu in the Castro assassination plots. Maheu then brought in Roselli, whom he knew from Las Vegas. Roselli in turn brought in Sam Giancana.

At the end of his October 1967 memo detailing the conversation between Harvey and Osborn that referenced Roselli, Papich wrote:

> It should be noted that Harvey told Osborn and Papich that the conversation with Roselli lasted approximately one hour. The information volunteered by Harvey certainly does not suggest a conversation of that length. The observation is therefore made that Harvey may not be divulging all that is taking place between him and Roselli. This is strictly speculation.[818]

Roselli wasn't just in trouble over the card cheating. The FBI had determined that Roselli was an illegal alien, whose real name was Filippo Sacco, and was moving to deport him. Two days after the earlier memo, the FBI Special Agent in Charge (SAC) in Los Angeles sent an Airtel to J. Edgar Hoover about the CIA's objections to having Col. Sheffield Edwards testify in the Roselli deportation hearing. "It is again noted that the appearance of Colonel Edwards as a witness would strengthen the case against Roselli," the SAC noted. At a meeting in May 1966, Roselli showed Colonel Edwards a picture of himself as a boy that FBI agents had left in his possession. The FBI felt Colonel Edwards should testify against Roselli and that he could do so without exposing his or Roselli's connection to the CIA. But someone in the CIA was nervous about putting Colonel Edwards on the stand:

> Edwards is age 65, possesses a severe speech impediment and is in poor health.
>
> In view of the foregoing, Los Angeles is not authorized to advise the United States Attorney's Office of Roselli's conversation with Edwards.[819]

---

818   FBI memo from Sam Papich to D.J. Brennan, Jr., October 9, 1967.
819   FBI memo from Hoover to SAC, Los Angeles, October 20, 1967.

In other words, CIA was telling FBI to back down on Roselli. Why? The timing is curious. Someone had already apparently leaked information about the Castro plots to columnist Drew Pearson, possibly superlawyer Edward Morgan. Harvey "made the observation that Morgan obviously was very well informed concerning CIA's past relationship with Roselli. Harvey assumes that Morgan acquired this information from Robert Maheu...."[820] The FBI reiterated Roselli's connection to the CIA's Castro assassination plots in a November 1, 1967 memo.

Was CIA concerned about Roselli's knowledge of their Castro plots? Or might Roselli have known something about another assassination plot? Whatever Roselli and Harvey knew or were planning made CIA Director Richard Helms very nervous and the FBI very interested. D.J. Brennan reported in an FBI memo to Bill Sullivan on November 1, 1967, that two days earlier, Harvey had met with Helms to discuss help for Roselli:

> Helms advised SA [Special Agent] Papich 10/31/67 that he mistrusts Harvey; that he is not going to permit himself or CIA to be blackmailed by anybody; and he has no fear of any threats which may emanate from subject.[821]

Scribbled at the bottom of this memo is a handwritten note saying, "We must be very careful in any meetings with Harvey," to which Hoover wrote, "Right & vigorously press case against Roselli."[822]

In an adjacent, undated FBI communication to Sullivan, apparently from Papich, along with reiterating Helms' desire not to allow the CIA "to be black-mailed by anybody," the author added, "Helms commented that as far as he is concerned the Bureau can treat Harvey as it sees fit."[823]

By March 1968, after a phone call with Harvey, Helms told Papich "that Roselli's case on the West Coast was developing to a point which necessitated some serious thinking on the part of CIA. Harvey...claimed he had a responsibility of protecting CIA interests at the same time was of the strong opinion that the Agency should try to help Roselli."[824] At this point, Helms still didn't see it that way:

> Helms advised that he accepted Harvey's statements as a form of pressure, and he then made it very clear to Harvey that CIA was not making any kind of deal with the subject or anybody else....

820   FBI memo from D.J. Brennan, Jr. to William Sullivan, November 1, 1967.

821   FBI memo from D.J. Brennan, Jr. to William Sullivan, November 1, 1967.

822   FBI memo from D.J. Brennan, Jr. to William Sullivan, November 1, 1967.

823   Undated memo from unnamed source to Sullivan, immediately following the November 1, 1967 in the FBI's volume 1c of Castro-related memos.

824   FBI memo from D.J. Brennan, Jr. to William Sullivan, March 29, 1968.

> Helms confided…that he was not going to be squeezed into any
> position by Harvey, Roselli, or any other individuals."

On April 3, 1968, the FBI had made clear to Harvey that, since Harvey appeared to be acting as a sort of unofficial counsel to Roselli, the FBI could not talk to him about Roselli, "Harvey was visibly shaken and asked, 'What is behind this?'" Harvey stressed that his only goal was to protect the interests of the FBI and CIA:

> He was extremely critical of CIA, maintaining that the Agency
> does not fully appreciate the significance of exposure to potential
> embarrassment.

Was Harvey hinting Roselli knew something about the CIA that was even worse than their Castro assassination plots? It's hard not to read that into what follows in the same memo:

> Harvey briefly commented that some people may forget that this is
> an election year. He followed by stating that Robert Kennedy was
> knowledgeable of the operations which had been devised by CIA
> with the collaboration of Roselli and his cohorts. Although he did
> not so state, Harvey definitely left the implication that Kennedy is in
> an extremely vulnerable position if it were ever publicized that he
> condoned an operation which involved U.S. Government utilization of
> hoodlum elements. Harvey stated that he was not certain if Kennedy
> was privy to the beginnings of the operation, but he definitely was
> cognizant of its existence in the late stages.

Harvey probably believed Kennedy did have knowledge of ongoing plots, although the CIA's report made clear he did not. But more important is what Harvey wasn't saying but seemed to be hinting at: that there was something much more sensitive involving Roselli and the CIA than the Castro plots. Was he providing Helms and the FBI a coded hint about perhaps another assassination plot that involved Roselli, such as the assassination of President Kennedy?

Whatever it was that Harvey was referring to eventually persuaded Helms to change his mind. By mid-April 1968, just weeks before Robert Kennedy would be killed, an FBI teletype reported the CIA had said the following:

> CIA REQUESTED THAT BUREAU NOT DISSEMINATE THIS INFO
> BECAUSE ROSELLI'S CONTACT WITH CIA EXTREMELY SENSITIVE
> COULD BE HARMFUL TO NATIONAL SECURITY INTERESTS.[825]

---

825   FBI "URGENT" teletype from Director to the FBI Los Angeles office, April 11, 1968.

It seems likely Roselli had been involved in a plot more sensitive than the Castro assassination plot, perhaps the assassination of President John Kennedy, and/or that he knew something about the upcoming plot against Senator Robert Kennedy through his close association with Robert Maheu.

Robert Maheu

TWO DIFFERENT SOURCES TOLD ME THAT ROBERT MAHEU HAD BEEN behind the assassination of Robert Kennedy. But even without those sources, Maheu seemed the obvious choice. The assassination of Robert Kennedy required comprehensive planning that clearly included the following:

- Control of the LAPD's investigation
- Control of the D.A.'s investigation
- Control of the Sheriff's deputies (who were the first to arrive at the crime scene)
- Control of Sirhan's defense team
- Access to trained assassins
- Access to a patsy that could be hypnotized into taking the fall for the crime

The CIA had the power to control and provide all of this. But more specifically, Robert Maheu connected directly to every point above. And the source for most of these connections was Maheu himself. In 1992, with Richard Hack, Robert Maheu penned his autobiography *Next to Hughes*. There, he revealed all kinds of information that makes him the most credible high-level suspect for the planner of Robert Kennedy's assassination. He revealed additional information when interviewed by the Church Committee and elsewhere.

Maheu had friends in the deepest, darkest corner of the CIA: the Office of Security, the component that ran the mind control programs and bugged CIA employees to prevent them from leaking to others. He was extremely well-connected at the highest realms of power in the country, had access to nearly unlimited funds, and had provable experience in running assassination plots for the CIA. He had mob contacts through Roselli. The *Mission: Impossible* TV series was said to have been based on his company Robert A. Maheu Associates (RAMA), which fronted for CIA activities and provided cover to CIA employees. Maheu also had friends in the LAPD and Sheriff's office. He had run CIA operations in conjunction with the LAPD in the past.

In his autobiography, Maheu claims he was initially recruited in March 1954 to work for the CIA through the Office of Security. In his testimony to the Church

Committee, however, Maheu set the date of the approach as 1952 or 1953. Jim Hougan, in his book *Spooks*, which has a chapter on Maheu titled "The Master Spook," suggested Maheu may have been working for the CIA even earlier due to other records.

Prior to joining the CIA, Maheu had performed counterespionage assignments in the FBI. He was in the same FBI class as Bill Harvey,[826] who headed the Operation Mongoose plots designed to topple Castro. Bill Harvey ran Staff D, which served as liaison with the Office of Security and the then still-secret National Security Agency (NSA) and the office through which, according to Joseph Burkholder Smith, coup plotters had to be cleared before they could engage in coup operations. Both Harvey and Maheu were close to Roselli. It doesn't appear that Maheu and Harvey were in direct contact in 1968, although Harvey's query to the CIA about Maheu suggests contact may have happened.

At the FBI, Maheu was also classmates with two men who later joined the CIA's Office of Security: Jim O'Connell, who was initially tapped to aid the CIA in killing Lumumba, and Bob Cunningham, who helped cover up the apparent murder of Frank Olson by the CIA (see *A Terrible Mistake*, by Hank Albarelli, for that story).[827] The role of the Office of Security is to ensure the CIA's operations do not get exposed. That's why mole hunts were buried there, and why the CIA chose to stash its super-secret mind control operations there.

O'Connell and Cunningham encouraged Maheu to do "cut-out" work for the CIA. But before Maheu could get in bed with the CIA, he had to get out of bed with Carmine Bellino—another ex-FBI agent—with whom Maheu shared an office. Bellino worked for the Kennedy family, and the CIA wanted nothing to do with the Kennedys. Maheu mistakenly attributes this to the Kennedys' "support" of Sen. Joe McCarthy, claiming inaccurately that the Kennedys supported "McCarthyism" while the CIA fought it.[828] More accurately, the CIA turned against McCarthy when he started accusing a couple of their own of being Communist stooges. And the Kennedys, while anti-Communist, were not pro-witch hunts. Joe McCarthy was a family friend, but even then there were limits. Robert Kennedy did not participate in the smears that McCarthy made. And the oft-repeated misinformation that Robert Kennedy asked Joe McCarthy to be the godfather of Robert's firstborn, Kathleen, is simply not true. Kathleen Kennedy reported in her book *Failing America's Faithful* that her godfather was actually Dr. Danny Walsh, a theology professor credited with converting Thomas Merton to Catholicism.

After working for the CIA's Office of Security for a $500/month retainer (roughly equivalent to $4,500 a month in 2017 dollars) for six months, the CIA

---

826   Bayard Stockton, *Flawed Patriot: The Rise and Fall of CIA Legend Bill Harvey* (Washington, D.C.: Potomac Books, 2006), p. 12.

827   Maheu, p. 40; Bayard Stockton and Tara Stockton, *Flawed Patriot* (Washington: Potomac Books, 2006) p. 12.

828   Maheu, p. 40.

changed his contract to a cash-on-delivery basis, probably because a few months in, a British man who turned out to be an agent for Stavros Niarchos hired Maheu for the equivalent of roughly $55,000 to sink an oil shipping contract between Ari Onassis and Saudi Arabia. Had the contract been allowed to stand, Onassis would have eventually had the shipping contract for all major oil companies. Standard Oil, Mobil, Exxon and the rest would have had to go to Onassis. As Maheu explained, "By regulating the chief source of energy in an oil-dependent world, Onassis would become one of the most powerful men alive, capable of bringing whole governments to their knees."[829] Maheu managed to persuade the Saudi king to break the contract.

During the Onassis case, Maheu employed another former FBI man who was working for the CIA, John Joseph Frank. Frank appears to have been involved in the disappearance and apparent murder of Jesus de Galindez, a vocal critic of Rafael Trujillo at a time when the CIA in general and Frank in particular were aiding and abetting Trujillo's dictatorship. Frank rented the airplane that an Oregon man named Gerald L. Murphy apparently used to fly the kidnapped Galindez to the Dominican Republic. Neither Murphy nor Galindez were seen alive again, and a federal prosecutor charged Frank with being involved, although after the CIA interceded on Frank's behalf, he was not convicted. When asked by the Church Committee if he had employed Frank during 1954, the year documents showed Trujillo first discussed killing Galindez, Maheu refused to answer under the Fifth Amendment on the grounds that he might incriminate himself.

I have often wondered why the CIA turned to Maheu, of all the people it knew, to organize a plot to kill Castro. The obvious answer has always been that Maheu was known for a successful assassination in some previous plot, perhaps the Galindez case. But there were other candidates. He might have arranged the murder of Samuel Rand. John Meier, one of Hughes' close associates late in Hughes' life, called Maheu an "assassin" but clarified he was known for arranging plots, not killing people himself.

When Hughes needed a "fixer," Maheu was recommended to him. At the time, Hughes was living in Bel Air, an upscale private development in the mountains above UCLA.

Hughes was known to admire pretty women. He sometimes had his employees approach such women and offer them a place to stay. Hughes visited some and never even visited others. Some of these "kept" women of course rebelled at being at his beck and call. One of them, Yvonne Shubert, had befriended an actor named Samuel Rand. Hughes wanted Maheu to get rid of Rand. Hughes had called Shubert and told her if she didn't stop seeing Rand, Rand might "have

829   Maheu, p. 44.

his face fixed." [830] The official story is that Rand accidentally killed himself while checking Shubert's gun after it had failed to fire.[831] But prior to this, Maheu, using the pseudonym of Bob Marshall, had invited the actor to visit him in his suite at the Bel-Air Hotel. There, Maheu invited his friend, undersheriff Harold Marlowe, up to the suite. Marlowe casually revealed the gun he was carrying and suggested Rand stay away from Shubert.[832]

Hughes was convinced Maheu had killed Rand, a belief Maheu claimed first surprised, then alarmed him. Maheu called his undersheriff friend Hal Marlowe and asked him to make a ballistics test to prove the bullet came from the actor's own hand and not someone else's. Maheu described this as "a little insurance policy, just in case somebody else thought the way Hughes did."[833]

In 1956, when President Sukarno of Indonesia came to visit the United States, Scott McLeod of the State Department contacted Maheu and asked him to vet hookers for Sukarno from a security standpoint under the CIA's Project Harpstar. Maheu said this was done to "please" Sukarno, but no doubt this was also an attempt to compromise him with photographs and other material for potential blackmail. The problem was, Sukarno's appetite for women was part of his appeal to a segment of the public in Indonesia.

A little over a year later, according to Maheu, he got a call from Sheffield Edwards at CIA, the security officer who oversaw the Bluebird and ARTICHOKE CIA mind control programs. Edwards wanted Maheu to perform another operation relative to Sukarno.[834] Evidently, the Soviets supplied Sukarno with prostitutes too, but one of them was a KGB agent. Edwards was initially asked to contact Maheu by the CIA's Far East Division.[835]

Edwards asked Maheu to make a film purporting to show Sukarno and this Soviet agent having sex to insinuate that Sukarno was under the control of a Soviet agent, to be titled *Happy Days*. "It was never in any way intended to be a 'porno' movie," Maheu wrote.[836] So Maheu contacted Bing Crosby and his brother Larry. "The reason was simple," Maheu explained. "The Company [CIA] liked Bing and Larry's politics and, after doing a security check on them, felt they could be trusted completely."[837]

830   FBI memo from J. Edgar Hoover to SAC Los Angeles dated June 18, 1959, archive.org/stream/ RobertMaheu/1342370-0_-_1_djvu.txt, p. 120.

831   Unnamed *Times* correspondent, "Actor Shoots Self in Head Accidentally," *Los Angeles Times*, June 13, 1959. Rand died the next day.

832   FBI memo from J. Edgar Hoover to SAC Los Angeles dated June 18, 1959, archive.org/stream/ RobertMaheu/1342370-0_-_1_djvu.txt, p. 120.

833   Maheu, p. 139.

834   Maheu, pp. 73–75.

835   NARA Record Number: 104-10122-10346, www.maryferrell.org/showDoc. html?docId=53708&search=Harpstar#relPageId=3&tab=page.

836   Maheu, p. 73.

837   Maheu, p. 73.

Maheu admitted working with the man who was Sheriff at the time of the Robert Kennedy assassination, Peter Pitchess, on *Happy Days* for the CIA, but Maheu omitted mention of the involvement of the LAPD in this episode. Initially, the CIA hoped to find footage they could use from existing pornographic movies, supplied by no less than Police Chief William Parker.[838] It appears Maheu was loath to brag about his connections to the LAPD, which was unusual, as he tended to brag about everything else.

When Maheu worked for Hughes, he hired Jack Hooper to head Howard Hughes' personal security detail. Hooper was "a retired Los Angeles Police Department detective he had used on special assignments since the late 1950s, to supervise overall security."[839]

John Meier

JOHN MEIER WAS A TOP AIDE TO HOWARD HUGHES FROM 1966 TO 1970. He was one of the few people allowed in the room with Hughes. Meier was a computer analyst before and after a stint in the Korean War. He met Howard Hughes in the 1950s, and impressed Hughes. Meier is a charismatic, articulate and obviously intelligent individual with a mischievous sense of humor, so it's easy to see why Hughes would have wanted this man at his side.

Meier did not realize, when he took the job, just how deeply embedded the CIA was within the Hughes organization. For its part, the CIA's nickname for Hughes was "The Stockholder," presumably because so much of his money paid for the operations of "The Company," as the CIA called itself. The CIA was so deeply entwined with the Hughes organization that no less than James Angleton, the 25-year head of the CIA's Counterintelligence unit, spoke at Hughes' small funeral service after he died:

> Howard Hughes! Where his country's interests were concerned, no man knew his target better. We were fortunate to have him. He is a great patriot."[840]

Meier first learned of the CIA's role with Hughes two months after Robert Kennedy was assassinated, in August 1968, when a CIA operative named Michael Merhage, who assumed Meier was also CIA, mentioned his CIA employment. Merhage gave Meier a list of American politicians the CIA wanted to support.

---

838   Bill Blum, *Killing Hope*, p. 102.

839   Donald L. Bartlett and James B. Steele, *Howard Hughes: His Life and Madness*.

840   Michael Drosnin, *Citizen Hughes* (New York: Holt, Rinehart and Winston,1985), p. 458.

The list included former Warren Commissioner and soon-to-be President Gerald Ford. Others on the list included James Eastland, John Tower, Paul Laxalt, Wallace Bennett (father of Robert Bennett, whose Mullen Company PR firm employed E. Howard Hunt, one of the Watergate participants when Hunt was ostensibly "retired"—for the third time[841]—from the CIA.)

When I visited Meier in his home in Canada in the 1990s, he had told me the Robert Kennedy assassination had been organized by Robert Maheu. His proof related to the many daily diaries he had kept all his adult life. At the time, he would not show me nor read to me from his diaries, and I didn't press. But when I visited him again with David Talbot in 2013, Meier read us diary entries that included the following:

> [June 1, 1968] I completed the speech and the supporting background documentation I had prepared for Robert Kennedy on the AEC underground testing programs in Nevada. Spent the morning with George Roth, my research editor on additional background information. At noon, Bob Maheu called and told me to cancel my trip scheduled for Monday, and wait until after the fifth. I was upset and advised him a schedule had already been arranged and I was to meet with Harry Evans and Paul Schrade of the UAW who were assisting Kennedy in his campaign in California. They were also assisting Howard Hughes and myself in stopping the underground testing in Nevada. ...
>
> [June 4, 1968] Maheu called in the morning and said he wanted me to call Don Nixon urgently and ask him to fly to Las Vegas to meet with Maheu on Wednesday the 5th. He wanted me to introduce him, as they had never met. That was the reason Maheu wanted me to stay in Vegas and not fly on to L.A. I left a message for Don Nixon .... He called me at 11 A.M. and advised me that he was very busy and was not able to make the meeting on the 5th. I called Maheu and when he heard Don was not coming out, he told me to call Don back and have him call his brother again. At 3 P.M. Don called me back and I gave him the message to call his brother Richard Nixon. Don was upset that this Maheu would try and run his life!

In a version of Meier's diary that circulated among researchers on the Internet at one point, there is an odd bit included on the June 4 entry that was *not* in the diary as John Meier read it to David and me. In the online version,

841   Jim Hougan, *Secret Agenda: Watergate, Deep Throat and the CIA* (New York: Random House: 1984), p. 6.

there is out-of-place text about the Oregon primary, which had happened the previous week. But this is not on the tape that David Talbot recorded when we talked to Meier. Someone apparently inserted some text out of place in the typed version—either by mistake or perhaps deliberately—to discredit the text.

When Meier was shaving himself around 4 A.M. on June 5, 1968, he learned that Robert Kennedy had been shot in the pantry. He cut himself and frantically tried to reach Paul Schrade and his friend Harry Evans. He had heard that some-one named Evans had also been shot in the pantry, but that was a reference to Elizabeth Evans, not his friend Harry.

Meier read the following passages to me and David from his diary entry of June 6, 1968. Robert Kennedy died in the early hours of June 6:

> Bob Maheu called to ask about the Don Nixon meeting and suggested 8:30 for breakfast at the Desert Inn Country Club. I went to the club. Maheu was all smiles, and Don Nixon walks in all smiles. What followed next had to be seen to be believed. They embraced each other and Don Nixon said, "Well that prick is dead," and Maheu said, "Well it looks like your brother is in now." At the time I did not even know what they were talking about.
>
> Maheu joked that they should now be calling Don Nixon "Mr. Vice President." I still did not realize that Robert Kennedy had died and when they saw that I was unaware Maheu told me, "John, you are out of it. Why don't you go home and Don and I will carry on without you."

Meier was sickened when he learned Kennedy had died. And the news got more disturbing with each passing day. Meier recognized a name in the news that gave him a chill, as he noted in his diary entry for June 13:

> Listening to the radio where they were discussing the RFK assassina-tion and who was shot, etc. They mentioned Thane Cesar who was a security guard at the hotel working for ACE Guard Security and was also employed by Lockheed Aircraft. I remember Thane from his trips to Vegas where he was meeting with numerous gaming people and was introduced to me by Jack Hooper, an associate of Bob Maheu.

Meier told us he had "called someone and discussed the fact that I knew RFK, Paul Schrade, Harry Evans and Thane Cesar—all of whom had been at the Ambassador that night." Thane Cesar was known to Meier because he worked for the Hughes organization at that time. But Meier's inquiries brought a reprisal from Maheu the following day:

> Bob Maheu called and told me to come over to his house at 8:30 P.M. that evening and I did. He was furious and wanted to know why I was checking up on Thane. I was stunned at his anger and he said to me that if I kept discussing this matter, he would see that I was no longer around the Hughes operation.

On June 15, Jack Hooper told Meier "that he was speaking with Bob Maheu and I was never to mention his name or Bel Air Patrol!" What was so sensitive about the Bel Air Patrol?

The answer came not from Meier's diary but from something Carl McNabb, a former CIA operative, had told me long ago. McNabb had told me that he had learned there was some association prior to the assassination between Maheu and Thane Cesar from the time when Cesar had worked for Maheu at Bel Air Patrol. I could never confirm this, as Bel Air Patrol refused to share its records. But a CIA document (discussing the granting of QKENCHANT clearance to Maheu's son Peter) confirms that Maheu was, in fact, one of the owners of Bel Air Patrol. Given that he and Hooper owned a number of security firms together, it seemed likely that Hooper too shared the ownership. If there had been a prior connection between Thane Cesar, Hooper and Maheu through Bel Air Patrol, that would have connected the dots for serious researchers very quickly. It makes sense, then, that Meier would be scared into silence with threats from both Maheu and Hooper. It also might explain why on my first trip to see Meier, Maheu called Meier out of the blue and asked if he needed anything. Meier thought it was so odd that Maheu would have called that day, after not having talked to him for ten years.

On that trip, Meier told me that J. Edgar Hoover had said he knew that Robert Maheu was behind the assassination of Robert Kennedy. In the years after that first trip, I had come to believe Maheu, due to his connections listed earlier, was a credible candidate for the assassination plot's mastermind.

Meier was not the only person to assert that Maheu was behind the assassination. Researcher Steve Gaal gave me another source. His father, a WWII veteran, had been an electrician for the City of Los Angeles, working often at the "Glass House," the nickname for the LAPD's Parker Center. "Sometime between 1977 and 1979," Gaal wrote me:

> Dad and I were talking about the Vietnam War at our house in Highland Park. I said that if RFK had been elected history would have been different. Dad said maybe that was so. Dad then said that he had talked to the detectives at the Glass House and that they had told him Maheu had done it. Dad was a big gossip with hard right wing views. That the detectives talked to Dad is for myself very believable.[842]

---

842   Email from Steven Gaal to Lisa Pease, 2011, as a follow-up to an in-person conversation.

Thane Cesar

IN THE COURSE OF WRITING THIS BOOK, I SUBSCRIBED TO TWO prominent online "public records" database aggregation services. Both listed Thane Eugene Cesar's profession as "Contract Agent" for the Central Intelligence Agency. I wrote one of the two sources to ask where the records came from. The response was "marketing surveys, land deeds, catalog purchases, voter registrations, lawsuit filings, court records, magazine subscriptions, and address changes." I wrote the other database company and asked why they would expose a CIA agent's information. I received no response to that question.

Interestingly, although Cesar himself told the LAPD he worked for Hughes Aircraft in the 1970s, that employer is not on the list from any aggregator, giving the appearance that Cesar's primary employer was the CIA at the time, not the Hughes organization, which would fit what we learned about the Hughes organization in the wake of the Watergate hearings. Hughes had been taken over by a combination of the CIA and a Mormon faction (and the Mormons were, at the time, prized recruits for the CIA as they had to spend a year abroad, were clean-cut, and didn't drink). Cesar's involvement with the CIA has long been suspected, but at the time of this writing, proof that he worked for the CIA has never appeared in any other source.

It's hard to overstate the significance of finding a current or future CIA contract agent holding Kennedy's right arm at the moment of the shooting. Recall how one witness felt someone was "holding" Kennedy in place while someone else shot him in the head. But if that was Cesar's only role, why did he, by his own admission, draw his gun? He claimed he didn't fire it, but he did admit to drawing it. The more reasonable supposition is that Cesar held Kennedy long enough for someone to get off a shot or two to his head, while Cesar fired three shots into Kennedy from behind and to the right—the very position where Cesar was standing. It makes much less sense that Cesar fired all four or five shots into Kennedy. He would have been much more exposed for a head shot. Cesar's body, however, could have hidden his gun from anyone not looking in that exact spot at the moment while Sirhan was quite obviously pulling focus.

Another source for a connection between Thane Cesar and the security arm of the Hughes organization can be found in the book *The Assassination Chain*. Sybil Leek, one of the authors, saw Cesar in Las Vegas in the company of a "hit man for a Florida group":

> [The hit man] always seemed to be near a sturdy, well-built and quite interesting-looking man, but they never spoke. So I asked my Las Vegas friend who this other man was. "He's a professional bodyguard," he

replied; and I remarked that I was looking for a bodyguard myself, he would fit the bill perfectly. "You are too late," said my friend. "He is owned by Howard Hughes and his name is Thane Cesar and he is as tough as they come."[843]

Cesar was apparently not the bodyguard for the hit man, however, as Cesar left the room first and the hit man followed. Perhaps he was simply hanging out with a coworker.

Maheu and Owen

IN MAHEU'S AUTOBIOGRAPHY, MAHEU RECOUNTED AN EPISODE with a religious figure who attempted to blackmail Howard Hughes. When I read it, I was instantly struck by how well this fit, with one exception, "The Walking Bible" Jerry Owen.

Maheu described how Bill Gay, the leading member of the "Mormon Mafia" that controlled access to Howard Hughes, asked Maheu to take care of a blackmailer that may well have been Owen:

> Hughes, according to Gay, was being blackmailed, and the blackmailer, believe it or not, was a minister. He was a man of some standing in the L.A. Community, and had found out that one of his young female parishioners had had an affair with Howard.
>
> Apparently either the girl, or a friend of the girl's, had confessed about the affair, looking for advice. Well, instead of saving the poor girl's soul, this so-called "man of God" decided to turn a tidy profit, and threatened to release what he knew to the press unless he was sufficiently compensated.[844]

The man was asking for "just a few thousand dollars," which Maheu didn't think was that much money, but in the FBI, he had learned that "the worst thing you can do with a blackmailer is pay him. It simply never stops there." So Maheu looked for anything he could use as leverage over this preacher. Maheu went to "Peter Pitchess, an ex-FBI agent and a friend." Pitchess was at that time the undersheriff of L.A. County.

---

843   Sybil Leek and Bert R. Sugar, *The Assassination Chain* (New York: Corwin Books, 1976), p. 243. Punctuation is as it appeared in the original.

844   Maheu, pp. 63–64.

I asked Pete if the minister had any kind of record, and I hit the jackpot. Not only did our blackmailer have a record, he had a record as a pederast! He'd been charged, though never convicted, with molesting young boys. I couldn't wait for my tête-à-tête with the blackmailer now. This was a meeting I thought I might even enjoy.[845]

Although Maheu described the preacher as "unimpressively soft, even a bit effeminate," I wondered if Maheu were deliberately misrepresenting the man to hide the fact that this was Owen. Owen was a big tall menace of a man, a former boxer. In all other aspects, the story matches. He had a long rap sheet and had been accused of having sex with both boys and girls. Whoever, this particular preacher was, Maheu threatened to expose him to the media, which was enough to cause the preacher to back down.

A covert operation

WHAT DOES IT TAKE TO RUN A COVERT OPERATION? NO ONE WOULD entrust an assassination plot of importance to a single individual, even one as experienced as Maheu. It takes careful planning and a well-rehearsed team. As Watergate participants and CIA assets, Eugenio Martinez's and Bernard Barker's information on this point matters. In 1974 they wrote, "…you have a briefing and then you train for the operation. You try to find a place that looks similar and you train in disguise and with the codes you are going to use. You try out the plan many times so that later you have the elasticity to abort the operation if the conditions are not ideal."[846]

Clearly, there was a team at the hotel the night of June 4, 1968. Michael Wayne and a girl in a polka dot dress made it a priority to collect press badges, which could then have been used as "all access" passes so team members could go anywhere in the hotel.

Two women in polka dot dresses seemed to escort two men, one of which was Sirhan Sirhan, and another which looked remarkably like him, but who was wearing a white shirt and black pants and who had a pronounced acne condition. One of these teams was upstairs when Kennedy was killed. It's likely the other team was waiting downstairs near the makeshift bar tended by the man Sirhan felt communicated with him without words, in case Kennedy had gone that

---

845   Maheu, pp. 64–65.

846   Eugenio Martinez and Bernard Barker, "Mission Impossible: the Watergate Bunglers," *Harpers Magazine*, October 1974. On the Internet, the source of this article appears to be misattributed to *Vanity Fair* in 1974.

direction instead. That's why it didn't matter which way Kennedy exited the stage or where he went next. He was not going to be allowed to leave the hotel alive.

Someone had to man the southwest fire escape exit door so that the girl in the polka dot dress and the man in the gold sweater could sneak Sirhan into the hotel that way. Someone had to be sure the door would not be blocked when it came time for the gold-sweatered guy and the girl in the polka dot dress to exit after the deed was done. There was a man in a maroon coat standing near that door all night. Recall how he turned to the wives of two TV executives to say, "You've seen me here all night," as if he were trying to establish an alibi. One of the women saw him holding what looked like a radio to his cheek. Remember that the strange girl who rode with John Fahey up to Oxnard and back said the people following them communicated by radios. If the man in the maroon coat were part of the plot, it suddenly makes sense that the polka dot girl would be yelling "We shot him" as she ran past him and out the back fire escape. She may have simply been alerting her cohort at the back door, not realizing Sandra Serrano and Katie Keir would hear her, and not caring when their escape seemed assured.

Rather than imagining Thane Cesar fired five shots without anyone seeing him, including one or two into Kennedy's head, which would have left him very exposed, it makes more sense that he got off a quick three shots under Kennedy's arm while he held Kennedy firmly in place for the man in a white busboy outfit to make two quick shots to Kennedy's head, possibly with a gun that was disguised or small enough to remain hidden.

With Sirhan firing blanks, someone else had to fire from near Sirhan's position to make it look like Sirhan was firing actual bullets. Harold Burba and Nina Rhodes-Hughes saw someone firing from atop a steam table. The man on the table resembled Sirhan and was dressed in a blue suit. As the shooting began, a short, bearded man ran out, possibly breaking Virginia Guy's tooth in the process. He carried a gun partially hidden under a poster or a newspaper. Michael Wayne pulled focus in the lobby as at least two other people with guns—the short man in the blue suit and a tall sandy-haired man—made their escape.

APBs were issued for several other suspects besides Sirhan before Inspector Powers got on the police radio to make clear he didn't want anyone "to get started on a big conspiracy." At some point, someone reported a kitchen worker named "Jesse Greer" had shot Robert Kennedy. This was possibly the same "Jesse" Fernando Faura tried to track down at the corner of Westwood and Wilshire, the same location from which Wayne had hitchhiked to the Ambassador Hotel.

The police recognized early on there were too many bullets, so they kept those bullets on log sheets marked "confidential." Some discrepancy between bullets was so immediately apparent that Wolfer created a secret photo comparison of two bullets not recovered from actual pantry victims. The LAPD deliberately kept this photo secret for fear a "discerning buff" might detect the fraud, until there was a reinvestigation seven years later. And while the panel did realize there was something off about the bullets, no one on the panel thought to check the current markings on the bullets with the original log entries, which would have shown the bullets were not the original ones recovered in the pantry.

Lt. Manny Pena, the man who had retired from the LAPD the year before to work for the Agency for International Development (AID), which has served as cover for the CIA in many countries, had a serious hold over not just the LAPD's investigation but the FBI's as well. An FBI memo dated June 13 lays out Pena's role and strange request:

> Lt. Manuel S. Pena, who is in charge of the new Los Angeles Police Department (LAPD) group investigating the Kennedy assassination [meaning Special Unit Senator – LP], advised on 6/13/68 that he desires everything the FBI has which might be pertinent to the trial of Sirhan Bishara Sirhan. In particular, Lt. Pena wants statements of people interviewed at the Ambassador Hotel of people placed at the crime scene. He also desires statements of interviews of people of the Kennedy party.
>
> He requested that the LAPD be given the results of any foreign investigation on the background of subject Sirhan and his family, particularly anything of a local nature supporting or eliminating any intra United States or local conspiracy. Lt. Pena advised that it is necessary for him to know whether this information is forthcoming from the FBI or whether the LAPD will have to make its own arrangements to obtain same.
>
> Lt. Pena further advised that there would be no distribution of LAPD material until he personally had a chance to review this material.[847]

So Lt. Pena was demanding the FBI give him all relevant evidence, while pre-screening anything the FBI got in return. And in the LAPD interview summaries, witnesses with evidence of conspiracy were asked if they had talked to the FBI or not, and the answer was recorded carefully in the LAPD's files. So Pena would not withhold records from the FBI that they already knew about, but there are notations in other files that indicate if the FBI had not already interviewed the witness, Pena simply buried the information. The annotations "Do not type," and "No further int[erview]" appear on a number of cover sheets for interview summaries with evidence of conspiracy.

---

847   FBI memo from [Redacted] to SAC, Los Angeles, www.maryferrell.org/showDoc. html?docId=99632&search=bugging#relPageId=75&tab=page, June 13, 1968.

Pena and Hernandez were nearly inseparable during the investigation. When Jerry Owen surfaced in San Francisco in the office of someone powerful enough to raise a stink, Pena and Hernandez flew to San Francisco to talk to the man personally. Hernandez mentioned during one of his sessions having worked with high-level government officials in Venezuela, hardly the type of thing a local law enforcement guy does. And we saw how Pena's own brother talked of how proud Manny was of his service to the CIA.

Sirhan's trial was nothing more than a show trial designed to debunk evidence of conspiracy while ensuring that Sirhan would be put to death. Only the move away from the death penalty in California has kept Sirhan alive to date.

The Wenke panel reinvestigation of the ballistics evidence was a waste of taxpayer money because the bullets had clearly been switched, so none of their conclusions mattered.

Most journalists repeated what government authorities told them about the case without question. Others, including authors as well as journalists, may have been actively part of the cover-up.

Several of those who participated in the cover-up in the law enforcement and legal arenas were rewarded with better jobs or lucrative government contracts. The only Congressman to passionately lobby for a deeper investigation of the Robert Kennedy assassination was shot in his office by a man who claimed the CIA had put voices in his head.

By contrast, on December 19, 2017, Robert Kennedy, Jr. visited Sirhan in prison in the company of Sirhan's attorney Laurie Dusek. Bobby hugged Sirhan, told him he knew he hadn't killed his father, and that he considered him as much a victim as his father. "He's a sweet man," Bobby told me after his visit. Bobby took the time to learn the truth about this case. What he found moved him to action, and rightfully so.

Anyone who has looked closely and honestly at the evidence has realized that more than one person was involved in Robert Kennedy's death. So why can't reporters see this? Why can't the media explain this? Because the media and the government are two sides of the same coin, and those who challenge the government's version of history, as numerous reporters have found out, all too often lose status and sometimes even whole careers. Kristina Borjesson published an anthology of such stories in her book *Into the Buzzsaw*, in which journalists describe how they lost their careers when each of them exposed a truth that the government did not want exposed.

That's why I wrote this book. I knew no journalist would give up 25 years of their life to learn the truth about this event. But the way the CIA took over

America in the 1960s is *the* story of our time, and too few recognize this. We can't fix a problem we can't even acknowledge exists.

Our democracy is hanging by a thread. The propaganda that has arisen to hide the malfeasance of government actors has made it difficult to tell good information from disinformation. There really is such a thing as "fake news," but the news that is fake is sometimes the opposite of news so labeled.

I hope my efforts to expose this crisis are met with the mental courage needed to rescue our country from forces that rely on secrecy and corruption to exist. We cannot have full secrecy and full democracy. You have to sacrifice one to gain something of the other. Our task is to help our elected officials understand this and to support them in tipping the scales toward greater democracy and away from excessive secrecy.

There is a role for secrecy and intelligence activities. But there is a need for much greater transparency, much bolder oversight, tighter control of budgets and operations, and a quicker declassification process. Those who say we need greater secrecy to "protect" democracy are part of the problem, not the solution. What's the point of having a secret intelligence service if there is no democracy left to protect?

If John Kennedy was King Arthur in Camelot, Robert Kennedy was Don Quixote in La Mancha, dreaming an impossible dream of a better life not just for Americans, but for the whole world.

When his dreams collided with the dark forces of greed and lust for power, Robert Kennedy was cut down at the crest of a promise that was never to reach our shores. What washed up instead was a bloody tide of lies from which this country has never recovered.

By refusing to honestly and accurately cover the assassinations of the 1960s, the mainstream media lost so much credibility that during the writing of this book, a reality show star who promoted fictitious conspiracy theories named Donald Trump was elected president. And the Senator most responsible for the latest cover-up of these crimes, former California Attorney General Kamala Harris, may run as his Democratic opponent in 2020.

Kamala Harris turned to Mel Ayton to rebut Sirhan's most recent legal filing. Ayton wrote a book on the case in which he argues Sirhan was the first Palestinian terrorist. He cherry-picked character witnesses to try to show Sirhan was a violent person. But none of the people who spent significant amounts of time with Sirhan before the assassination ever described him that way. Most couldn't believe he had done it since his demeanor was so gentle. Ayton misunderstood the placement of a witness he claimed rebutted Serrano, not realizing that his witness was on the Wilshire side of the hotel, not the 8th Street side where Serrano sat. Ayton had a sound expert listen to the Pruszynski tape. The expert found seven shot sounds and "three possible locations" for the "eighth" shot. To any reasonable, honest person, that means Ayton's expert found ten possible shot sounds—two more than Sirhan's gun could have fired.

When she was the Attorney General, Kamala Harris had the power to call for the reopening of this case based on the evidence. She chose instead the politically safe path of cover-up that vaulted so many others up the ladder in their careers. But our country needs someone with integrity and courage. The last thing we need is yet another president unwilling to rein in the CIA.

In 1966, the British journalist Malcolm Muggeridge, who doubled as a spy and therefore understood quite well what he was talking about, said:

> In the eyes of posterity it will inevitably seem that, in safeguarding our freedom, we destroyed it. The vast clandestine apparatus we built up to prove our enemies' resources and intentions only served in the end to confuse our own purposes; that practice of deceiving others for the good of the state led infallibly to our deceiving ourselves; and that vast army of clandestine personnel built up to execute these purposes were soon caught up in the web of their own sick fantasies, with disastrous consequences for them and us.[848]

The assassinations of the top four leaders of the political left in the five-year period—President John Kennedy in 1963, Malcolm X in 1965, and Martin Luther King, Jr. and Senator Robert Kennedy in 1968—represented nothing less than a slow-motion coup on the political scene. Of the five presidents that ruled over the following 20 years, only one would be a Democrat, and a single-term one at that. Another would be the first unelected president, Gerald Ford, a reward, perhaps, for his participation on the Warren Commission. After Ford appointed Nelson Rockefeller to be his Vice President, two assassination attempts on Ford nearly put a Rockefeller in the White House.

It should be clear to anyone that we cannot fix what is broken without major structural changes. Are secret intelligence agencies compatible with Democracy? Can we ever find the right balance between oversight and secrecy?

Can the police be reformed so that the process of examining evidence of guilt is more transparent? Should all evidence in such cases be made available to the public sooner, so that a resolution may be possible while the guilty parties are still alive and available for prosecution?

---

848   Victor Marchetti, "Propaganda and Disinformation: How the CIA Manufactures History," *Journal of Historical Review, Vol. 9* p. 305, www.ihr.org/jhr/v09/v09p305_marchetti.html.

Perhaps we need an outside body composed of people over whom the government has no leverage to investigate crimes that change the course of our democracy. The government has proven itself incapable of successfully prosecuting itself, not just in this case, but in many cases. And we need different kinds of investigators. It took housewives, students, retired people and former government employees to further our understanding of this case and others like it. It took, in short, conspiracy theorists. Because you can't investigate a conspiracy properly if you can't first imagine that one took place.

People who deride others as conspiracy theorists before first hearing their evidence are part of the problem, not the solution. Yes, there are a lot of junk theories out there. But each assertion should be evaluated on the merits of the evidence presented, not just automatically dismissed by some knee-jerk mindset. Not everything is a conspiracy. But conspiracies happen *every day*. Don't believe me? Ask your local prosecutor.

Every time we turn a blind eye to any cover-up, we enable the next one. Every time we give our trust to a government agency that doesn't deserve it, we enable the worst abuses of that trust. As the poet Maya Angelou said, "When people show you who they are, believe them the first time." The CIA has shown us time and again that they will lie to the American people and violate both national and international laws and create their own policy, even when it is at variance with the democratically elected leader of the United States. Why do we let them get away with this? Who really runs the country when our elected officials are afraid to challenge the CIA?

We have *so much power* when we act collectively. Every time the people cry out with one voice, as they did when Oliver Stone's film *JFK* revealed not only the holes in the government's case but the fact that the government was planning to conceal those records, the people win. The outcry from the public, in the wake of that film, changed the course of history. Congress, through the "JFK Act," created the Assassinations Records Review Board, which declassified many of the files the CIA, FBI, INS and other agencies had withheld from us. You can't plan a trip if you don't know where you are on the map. You can't cure your illness if it's misdiagnosed. The truth about our history is critically important so we can plan a better future.

So what can you do? It's not possible to bring Robert Kennedy back. But there is a way to right one historical wrong, to draw the world's attention to what really happened, to open people's eyes to how the world really works. You can help free Sirhan Sirhan, who is still alive and continues to be up for parole regularly. Now that you know Sirhan didn't kill Robert Kennedy, you need to become an ambassador for the truth in this case. Use the hashtag #FreeSirhan in social media as a statement of awareness. Write your elected officials and send them copies of this book. Write small summaries of key points and forward to media people. Friends don't let friends wallow in ignorance. Arm them with useful information. Make a documentary with your phone's camera. Write a novel to explain this in fictional form. Write a stage play, a screenplay. A simple cartoon of Sirhan with an impossibly long arm circling around Robert Kennedy's body to hit him from behind first drew my serious attention to this case. If we free Sirhan, that could have a profound impact on how people view the government in a way that could promote a number of positive changes. "That's how we're gonna win," as the character Rose said in *The Last Jedi*, "Not fighting what we hate—saving what we love." We may not be able fight all that is wrong. But we can save a man who has spent nearly his entire adult life in jail for a crime he provably didn't commit. That's one wrong we *can* right—and must. When we stand together and speak the truth, all missions become possible.

Robert Kennedy urged us to seek out the "harsh facts" about our country so we could make the country better. This book was my attempt—and yours, by reading it—to heed that call. Kennedy dedicated his last days to serving an impossible dream of an America that was a more generous and compassionate place. He spent the last years of his life tilting at the windmills of greed and self-interest that ultimately cut him down. But his song lives on in all of us who strive, in whatever ways we can, to reach those unreachable stars.

INDEX

Abo, Dr. Stanley 21, 316
Ace Guard Service 7, 16-20, 37, 221, 274, 295, 307, 312, 345, 352, 367, 493
Adair, Randolph 23
Agency for International Development (AID) 98, 499
Aiken, Gail 447
Aisyah, Siti 414
Alarcon, Arthur 92, 120-122, 131
Albarelli, Hank 331, 410, 488
Allen, Morse 407
Ambrose, John 34-36, 101, 115
AMORC (Ancient and Mystical Order Rosae Crucis) 437, 441 (see also Rosicrucians)
Angleton, James 66, 144, 171, 195, 231, 398-401, 413, 442, 458, 474, 491
Arbenz, Jacobo 439, 460
Arcega, Victor 429-432
Arnot, Larry 139, 163-64
ARTICHOKE 395, 422, 441-42, 490
Attwood, William 468
Aubry, Dick 33, 271, 282, 288
Ayton, Mel 501
Azcue, Eusebio 475

Bailey, F. Lee 378, 412
Bailey, William 264, 268, 340
Bain, Donald 435
Bakar, Khalid Abu 415
Ballantyne, Nina 348, 421
Bannerman, Robert L. 372
Barber, John 32, 52
Barker, Bernard 234, 497
Barry, Betty 308
Barry, Bill 15, 20, 292, 305
Bay of Pigs 332, 460-68, 480-81
Bazilauskas, V. Faustin 24, 79-81
Beckley, Johnny 393, 448
Beilenson, Delores 271
Belcher, Michael Wayne 324
Belin 428-29

Belli, Melvin 403-04, 446
Bellino, Carmine 488
Berg, Stanton O. 235-36
Beringer, Tom 32, 289
Berman, Emile Zola "Zuke" 124-26, 141-144, 154, 163, 168
Bernstein, Carl 217-18, 229-30, 451
Beveridge, William 127
Biasotti, Alfred A. 235
Bidstrup, Hans 302, 423
Bissell, Richard 70, 464, 473, 479
Blair, Eric 112
Blehr, Barbara 84, 209-212, 219, 240
Blum, Bill 332, 491
Bohrman, Stan 98
Bolf, Jean 429, 432
Borjesson, Kristina 500
Boston Strangler 44, 412, 444-46
Braden, Tom 379, 458-59, 471
Bradford, Lowell W. 235-36
Bradlee, Ben 228-29
Brandt, William E. 60-61, 204
Breckinridge, Scott 480
Bremer, Arthur 221, 447
Breshears, Carol Ann 272
Breslin, Jimmy 9, 294
Briem, Ray 443
Brown, Daniel 381, 393, 415-417, 420-422
Brown, Derren 413, 424
Brown, Hugh 29, 287-91, 446
Brown, Pat 166, 194
Bruce, David 460-462
Bryan, William J. 378-79, 410-412, 434, 442-447
Buckner, Everett 79, 119-121, 159-162
Bugliosi, Vincent (Vince) 59, 227, 234-236, 264-66, 448
Burba, Harold 77-78, 282, 315, 333, 427, 498
Burke, Paul 367
Burns, Frank 16-23, 140, 155-56, 274-75

Burris, Richard 100-101
Busch, Henry 443
Busch, Jim 22
Busch, Joseph P. 219-20, 226, 249
Butler, Lillian 21-22
Byrne, William Matthew 69, 93

California Law Review 382
Cameron, Donald Ewen 241
Carreon, Henry Adrian 78-79, 161
Carter, Jimmy 69, 253
Carter, Marshall 397-98
Carvajal, Jose 351-355
Casden, Robin 44, 74, 287
Castellano, Lillian 222
Castillo, Luis Angel 428-433
Castro, Fidel 70, 123, 345, 398-400, 428-433, 439, 460, 468-71, 478-489
Cesar, Thane Eugene 7, 11, 16-17, 37-38, 213-221, 272-76, 306, 311-15, 339, 345-46, 493-498
Chambers, Stan 31
Chapman, Mark David 199
Charach, Theodore (Ted) 212-214, 21-19
Chavez, Cesar 11-14
Chemerinsky, Erwin 269-70
Chennault, Anna 366
Chennault, Colonel Claire 366
Chetta, Nicholas (New Orleans Coroner) 170
Chiquet, Jack 40-45, 305-06
Christian, Jonn 32, 99, 191, 218-224, 234-37, 287, 325, 381, 404, 442-48
Christopher, Warren 69, 102
Christopher Commission 102
Church Committee (See also: Pike Committee) 98-102, 222, 229-233, 331-32, 367-373, 395-397, 422, 433, 441, 451-55, 463, 479-80, 487-89

CIA (Central Intelligence
    Agency) 45, 58, 66-71,
    90-103, 109, 123, 144,
    159, 169-171, 191-99,
    217-222, 229-234,
    240-41, 253, 261, 285,
    320, 329-333, 344-45,
    366-73, 377-79, 388-391,
    395-413, 422-23, 428-435,
    439-442, 450-453, 455-469,
    471-478, 479-503
Clark, Alvin 168-69
Clark, Ramsey 31, 69, 168-69,
    193
Clayton, George Ross 20,
    205-06, 302, 308,
    311-318, 325, 361
Cockburn, Alex 443
Cohen, Jeff 428, 430
Collier, Charles 36, 59, 66, 267
Compton, Lynn D. "Buck" 69,
    93, 165-66, 187, 194,
    213, 225
Condon, Richard 425
Connolly, Betty 340
Conway, Flo 393
Cooper, Grant 123-26, 129-38,
    141-53, 155-161,
    163-170, 172-182,
    185-89, 194, 199-204,
    236, 246, 298-401
Copeland, Miles 456-458
Copping, Clarence 127
Corona (California) 143, 162,
    409, 434-40
Crahan, Marcus 61, 380
Critcheley, Francis 352-360
Cronkite, Walter 272
Crosby, Bing 490
Crosson, William F. 6, 370-73
Culligan, Roland "Bud" 373,
    440
Cuneo, Henry 24-25, 44, 57, 67
Cunningham, Courtlandt
    235, 475

Davies, Jack 126
Davis, Edward M. 210, 218, 234
Davis, George 448, 459
Davis, Maynard 37, 257, 295
Davis, Russell 367
Dean, Larry 271
de Facia, Olive 319
DeFreeze, Donald 241, 405
Delattre, Edwin 269-70
DeLoach, Cartha 31
De Losh, L.E. 23, 294

DeSalvo, Albert 44, 412, 445-46
De Sautels, Christine 369
Diamond, Bernard 130, 337,
    375-383, 385-387,
    417-420, 426, 440-45
DiEugenio, Jim 90, 223-24,
    472, 477
DiPierro, Angelo 266
DiPierro, Vincent (Vince) 15-17,
    28, 35, 44-51, 72-74, 92,
    99-100, 115-119, 121,
    133, 150-153, 200, 216,
    227-28, 251, 278, 282-84,
    306, 310, 342, 346-348,
    352, 358-61, 364-366, 380
Douglass, Jim 1, 472
Downey, John 372
Dozier, Paul 59
Drew, Richard 16-17, 287
Droz, Fred 304, 325-33
Duffy, Estelyn 38, 271
Dulles, Allen 71, 171, 217,
    299, 377, 397-99, 457-67,
    472-474
Dulles, John Foster 460
Dusek, Laurie 427, 500
Dutton, Fred 6-7, 15, 287-92

Eagleson, David 211
Eckert, Bill 65-66
Edelman, Peter 482
Edward 17-20, 39, 76, 159, 210,
    233, 275-78, 304, 377,
    395, 430, 471, 485
Edwards, Sheffield 481-90
Einberg, Franne 314
Eisenhower, Dwight D. 218, 296,
    406, 459-464, 474, 481
Elliot, Thomas 439-40
Ellis, Albert 361
Ellsberg, Daniel 69, 477
Eloriaga-Reyes, Antonia 430
Elsman, Herb 443
Engen, Thomas 408-09
En-lai, Chou 70
Enyart, Scott 39, 46, 205-06
Epperidge, Bill 315, 425-26
Erickson, Milton 402, 410
Espirito, John 439
Estabrooks, George 378,
    384-85, 393, 401-403,
    432-35, 444
Estevez, Emilio 335
Estrada, Mary 359-60
Evangelista, Donald David 341
Evans, Elizabeth 17, 54, 79, 97,
    173-78, 190, 256, 310,

318, 493
Evans, Harry 492-93
Evans, Ronald 138

Fahey, John 4-5, 99, 118-19,
    191, 301, 358, 364-69,
    437, 498
Farr, Gloria 344
Farrar, Gail 6, 370-73
Farrchild, Hortence 443
Faura, Fernando 4-5, 99, 117-19,
    212, 293, 312-19, 337,
    341, 347-51, 364-366, 498
FBI 3-5, 15-20, 31-33, 42-43,
    59-61, 77-81, 89-106,
    116-133, 137-39, 154-61,
    168-78, 191, 195, 200-05,
    211-14, 227-32, 240,
    250-52, 257-67, 271-74,
    277-82, 290, 296, 300-08,
    313-20, 329-34, 336-46,
    354, 362-63, 367-72, 424,
    429-38, 447-50, 457-61,
    468, 473-75, 483-486-89,
    496, 499-503
Fecteau, Richard 372
Fedrizzi, J. J. 23, 294
Feinstein, Dianne 451
Fernandez, Richard "Dick" 81
Ferrie, David 170-71
Fine, Michael 411
Fisher, Joel 326-330
Fitts, David 139-141, 148,
    152-156, 159-63, 168,
    170-182, 189-194, 201,
    204, 213
Fontanini, Steve 19-20, 308-16
Fonzi, Gaeton 231, 472
Ford, Gary 295
Ford, Gerald 102, 230, 240,
    295, 429, 492, 502
Ford, Ruby 22
Franchel, Emile 393
Frank, John Joseph 489
Frankenheimer, John 3-9
Fraser, Terry Lee 37, 295-96
Freed, Evan 18, 19, 279, 287,
    333, 351-55
Friars Club 123-24, 483
Fromme, "Squeaky" 240
Fry, Stephen 413-14
Fukuto, Morio 67, 72-76,
    82-83
Fulmer, Cathy 112, 425
Funk, Bob 216, 287

Gaal, Steve 494
Gaitán, Eliécer 438-440
Galindez, Jesus de 489
Gallegos, Rose 340-342
Galloway, Calvin B. 66
Gardner, William 7, 295, 321
Garland, Patrick 235, 241-243
Garner, John 97
Garrison, Jim 90, 170-71, 212, 231, 458
Gates, Robert 452
Gay, Bill 496
Gezzi, Dominic 347
Giancana, Sam 481-84
Gilbert, Keith 321-324, 362
Gindroz, Robert 52-54
Gizzi, Irene 113
Glasser, Leonard 234
Glenn, John 25
Gold, Brent 39
Goldberg, Arthur 441
Goldstein, Ira 17, 67-79, 96, 167, 175-77, 207, 216, 236-43, 246-248, 309-311
Goliath 103, 330
Gonzales, Crispin Curiel 428-33
Goodwin, Richard 3-10
Gotman, Les 302
Gottlieb, Sydney 332, 396
GPFLOOR 400
GPFOCUS 400
GPIDEAL 400
Gray, Patrick 431
Green, George 18, 282, 355, 427
Greer, Jesse 52, 293-94, 498
Greer, Ken 429
Greiner, Al 81, 260
Grier, Roosevelt "Rosey" 15-23, 44, 147, 154-55, 274, 380
Griffin, Booker 17, 33, 271, 283, 287, 353-355
Groden, Robert 218
Grohs, Mary 380-81
Groves, Judy 325-33, 360-61
Gruson, Sydney 171
Gugas, Chris 119, 365-66
Guitierrez 324
Gullion, Edmund 477-78
Gumm, Gwen 186, 386-87
Gutierrez 321, 324-25
Guy, Virginia 148, 271, 287, 305-06, 316, 419, 498

Hall, Daniel 300-302, 316, 334, 361, 369
Halpern, Sam 479
Hamill, Pete 9, 13
Hamilton, James 405
Hammarskjöld, Dag 373
Hansen, Eve 11, 347-349, 365, 421-23
Hardrup, Pelle 391-94, 443
Hardway, Dan 231
Harmond, Gary 295
Harper, William (Bill) 173, 177, 200-12, 219, 225-30, 236, 241, 251
Harrell, Douglas 449-50
Harris, Kamala 501-02
Harvey, Bill 483-88
Hashimeh, Ziad 184
Hatcher, Emery 189-93
Hathaway, Wayne G. 21-22
Healy, Robert 20, 304-05
Hearst, Patty 241, 266, 405
Hegge, Albin 80
Helms, Richard 372-73, 396-398, 407, 422-23, 469-471, 479-86
Hernandez, Enrique "Hank" 99-127, 139-52, 160-64, 194, 304, 313, 322-23, 366, 448, 500
Herrick, Donna 139
Hersh, Seymour "Sy" 230, 332, 482
Holder, Winfred 336-339
Holland, Frances 437-38
Hooper, Jack 491-94
Hoover, J. Edgar 3, 31, 279, 372, 396, 432, 450, 457-58, 481, 484-85, 494
Hoover Commission 396
Hougan, Jim 396, 488, 492
Houghton, Robert A. 23, 29, 42, 64-65, 71, 91-95, 98, 102-104, 129, 189-200, 218
House Select Committee on Assassinations (HSCA) 222, 231, 249-52, 451, 472
Houts, Marshall 211-12
Howard, John 36-44, 49, 67-80, 84, 93, 100-01, 117, 132-33, 145-53, 157, 163, 166-69, 185, 249, 379
Howard, Lisa 468
Huerta, Dolores 12-14
Hufford, Harry L. 257-61

Hughes, Charles 80, 91-93
Hughes, Howard 25, 64, 320, 458, 487-496
Humphrey, Hubert 8-10, 64, 84, 198, 296, 304
Hunt, E. Howard 99, 198, 304, 492
Hussein, Saddam 217, 333
Hyman, Lester 230

INFORM 65
Inter-Con 194
Ivon, Lou 171

Jackson, C.D. 217-18
Jackson, Robert H. 260-61
Jayne, David 287
Johnson, Brad 101, 264, 284, 313, 357
Johnson, Darnell 122, 224, 273, 350-51, 355
Johnson, Ernie 425
Johnson, Lyndon Baines 3, 10, 198, 366, 406, 441
Johnson, Rafer 15, 20-23, 29-31, 34, 39, 44, 51, 79-83, 145-47, 154-55, 161, 177-80, 211, 247, 268-74, 288, 295
Johnson, Ralph 328
Johnson, Robert 463
Johnson McMillan, Priscilla 474
Jones, Marvene 311
Jong-nam, Kim 414-15
Jong-un, Kim 414
Jordan, William 27-29, 36-38, 42-44, 47-55, 66, 128, 158, 223, 245, 293, 379

Kamidoi, E. 54
Karaalajich, Sharon 387
Kasabian, Linda 434, 446
Kassem, Abdul Karim 332
Keir, Katherine "Katie" 113-14, 356-57, 498
Kelly, Susan 412
Kennedy, Edward "Ted" 17, 233, 395
Kennedy, Ethel 6-7, 13-17, 21-25, 57-63, 71, 108, 111, 149
Kennedy, Jackie 62-63
Kennedy, John Fitzgerald (JFK) 171, 198, 212, 230,

247-252, 298, 365, 373,
    400, 428, 446, 458,
    470-77, 483, 503
Kennedy, Kathleen 488
Kennedy, Robert (Bobby), Jr.
    15, 111, 349, 419, 427,
    438, 477, 500
Kennedy, Robert Francis (RFK)
    60-64, 103, 125, 140, 213,
    233, 253, 298, 404, 446,
    458, 473, 477, 493
Kessler, Ron 227-230, 452
Kevin, Art 34, 222-23
Khan, "the Khaiber" 298-99, 365
Khoury, John Antoine 325-33,
    360
Khrushchev, Nikita 286, 474
Kihlstrom, John F. 384, 415
King, Coretta Scott 63
King, Martin Luther, Jr. (MLK)
    1-3, 29, 87-89, 197, 212,
    222, 250, 321, 333, 478,
    502
Kirschke, Jack 36, 42, 47, 94,
    173, 208-09, 239
Kirz, Marsha 339
Kissinger, Henry 430
Klase, Robert 167, 303
Klein, Joan 58
Klein, Joseph 19, 273, 314-15,
    320
Kline, Dick 157, 309
Knight, Stewart 93
Korea 395, 404-05
Koucham, Maryam 299
Kovack, Rosemary 318
Kranz, Thomas F. 237, 249-252,
    257, 275
Krock, Arthur 467
Kuchel, Thomas 297-98

LaBianca, Rosemary and Leno
    434
Laffredo, Aida 341
LaHive, Joseph 21, 31, 38
LaJeunesse, Roger "Frenchy"
    98, 433
Langman, Betsy 99, 443-47
Lansdale, Edward 430
Lansky, Meyer 458
Lardner, George 169-171
La Vallee, Albert 71, 145
Lawrence, John 125-26
Leary, Timothy 198
Le Beau, Albert 362, 412, 446
Lee, William 36, 475
Leek, Sybil 495

Lemke, Pamela 271
Lennon, John 199
Lentine, Kathy 113, 356
Levin, Julius 330-31
Lindblom, Robert 32
Littlefield, Wilbur 122
Locke, Suzanne 271
Lodge, Henry Cabot 467
Loring, Charles A. 189-93
Lovett, Robert 460-462
Lowenstein, Allard 197, 222,
    225-33, 238-39, 250-253,
    260, 264
Lubic, Richard (Dick) 16-18,
    212-16, 272-73, 279-282,
    288
Luce, Clare Booth 218
Lumumba, Patrice 373, 433,
    463, 488
Lynch, William 69, 93

Maas, Felicia 363
MacArthur, James 36, 56,
    204-05, 271, 280-81
MacDonnell, Herbert Leon
    227, 236
Magsaysay, Ramon 430
Maheu, Robert (Bob) Aime 64,
    481-85, 487-97
Mallard, Augustus 20, 307-08,
    312-15
Manchurian Candidate 3, 9,
    159, 388, 398-99,
    406-408, 424
Mangan, Rose "Lynn" 83, 173,
    241-243, 246
Mankiewicz, Frank 57-59,
    62-64
Manson, Charles 235, 240, 264,
    405, 434, 446
Marchman, Eara 346
Marcos, Ferdinand 430-432
Marcus, Eric 128, 345-46, 380,
    472
Marks, John 159, 388, 398-99,
    405-407
Marooney, Jim 284
Márquez, Gabriel García 438
Marshall, Hal 260
Martinez, Eugenio 497
Matthews, Bernyce 358-360
McBroom, Marcus 274,
    317-320, 345-46
McCarthy, Eugene (Senator)
    3, 4, 8, 14, 60, 298-305
McCarthy, Eugene B.
    (FBI Agent) 4

McCarthy, Joe 488
McCone, John 467-72
McCowan, Michael 124, 142,
    324
McDaniel, Sidney 126
McHale, William 217, 333
McKissack, Luke 123, 246
McKnight, Gerald 475
McNabb, Carl (Jim Rose) 66,
    395-400, 494
Meese, Edwin 102
Meier, John 64, 458, 489-494
Melanson, Philip (Phil) 101,
    122, 200, 261, 272, 354
Melendres, A. B. 36, 49
Meltzer, Harold 331
Merhage, Michael 491
Merritt, Jack 18, 351-55
Merton, Thomas 488
Messuri, Felicia 14, 19
MHCHAOS 478
Miller, Liza 113
Mills, Roy 272, 358, 359
Minasian, Edward (Ed) 20, 39,
    40, 75-77, 147, 148, 275,
    276, 278, 281, 282
Miner, John 67-69, 93, 95, 446
Mistri, Gaymoard 297, 383, 421
MKDELTA 395, 422
MKNAOMI 395, 422
MKSEARCH 405
MKULTRA 159, 391, 395,
    397-399, 403, 405, 406,
    422, 441
Mobutu, Joseph Sese Seko 463
Moldea, Dan 22, 23, 32, 242,
    257, 258, 264, 265,
    267-270, 289
Mongoose 468, 488
Monroe, Marilyn 65
Montellano, David 78, 161, 162
Montgomery, Clifford 93
Moore, Sara Jane 240
Morgan, Edward 485
Morley, Jefferson 198, 400,
    401, 479
Morton, Charles V. 235, 237
Mossadegh, Mohammed 460
Muggeridge, Malcolm 502
Mulholland, John 285, 413
Murphy, Fred 7, 11, 38, 47, 48,
    52-55
Murphy, George 36
Murphy, Gerald L. 489

Nagell, Richard Case 372, 373
Narut, Thomas 408, 409

NASA 194

Nasser, Gamel Abdel 70, 332, 364, 440, 441, 445

Naval Surface Warfare Center (NSWC) 409

Neal, William 54, 245

Nebel, John 435

Nelson, Patti 19, 313-316, 318

Nelson, Richard 434-436

Newfield, Jack 1, 2, 7, 9, 87

Newman, John 198, 472

Niarchos, Stavros 489

Nielsen, Bjørn Schouw 391, 392

Nishikawa, Alice 189

Niwa, Yoshio 51, 380

Nixon, Don 492, 493

Nixon, Richard Milhous 3, 10, 14, 64, 84, 87, 221, 222, 230, 366, 407, 423, 431

Noguchi, Thomas 32, 65-69, 82, 95, 156, 174, 180, 205, 207, 211, 241, 243, 259, 446

Nolan, William 31, 93, 95, 122

Nosenko, Yuri 474

Novel, Gordon 458

Noyes, Peter 324

NSA 400, 488

Office of Strategic Services (OSS) 70, 169, 170, 211, 405, 450, 456-458

Olson, Frank 395, 488

Onassis, Ari 489

Orne, Martin T. 410

Orozco, Leroy Matthew (L.M.) 54, 66, 245

Osborn, Howard 484

Osterkamp, Peggy 186, 386, 387

Oswald, Lee Harvey 21, 31, 71, 90, 98, 132, 170, 195, 218, 231, 276, 333, 372, 399, 400, 403, 472-475

Owen, Reverend Jerry "The Walking Bible" 190, 191, 194, 225, 234, 237, 266, 388, 442, 446-449, 496, 497, 500

O'Brien, Larry 64

O'Connell, James (Jim) 488

O'Steen, Paul 214, 215

Paley, William 217, 288

Panda, Ronald 18, 273, 277, 282

PANTOMIME 439

Papich, Sam 483-485

Parker, Greg 439

Parker, William 491

Parrott, Fred 317, 318

Parry, Robert 475

Parsons, Russell 123, 124, 126, 142, 149, 161, 168, 186

Pash, Boris 395

Patrusky, Martin 16, 44, 45, 150

Pearson, Drew 2, 465, 485

Pelosi, Nancy 451, 452

Pena, Manny 98, 99, 103, 104, 116, 117, 122, 172, 224, 300, 317, 321, 342, 499, 500

Pepper, William 409, 415, 427

Perez, Jesus 16, 40, 72, 155, 273, 280

Perezsklsy, Rosa 346

Peters, Henry 127

Pharris, Hugh 170

Phillips, David Atlee 332

Pike Committee 98, 102, 170, 222, 229, 231, 233, 367, 395, 451, 452, 455

Pitchess, Peter 61, 380, 491, 496

Placencia, Arthur 23, 24, 74, 156-158, 380, 424

Plimpton, Freddy 45, 334-336, 341

Plimpton, George 45, 163, 334, 335, 340, 379

Pollack, Seymour 130, 131, 375, 418

Pope, Allen 462

Popkin, Richard 428

Powers, Bill 225, 447, 448

Powers, John 23, 29, 33, 34, 56, 69, 91, 223, 224, 256, 268, 295, 346, 355, 357, 498

Project Bluebird 395, 422, 441, 490

Project Harpstar 490

Prudhomme, Jeanette 113, 356, 357

Pruszynski, Stanislaw 264, 501

QJWIN 331-333

QKENCHANT 494

QKHILLTOP 395, 422

Rabago, Enrique 191

Rafferty, Max 20, 295, 297, 298, 300, 302, 308, 311, 316, 347, 359, 443

Rand, Samuel 489, 490

Rathke, Walter 437

Ray, James Earl 1, 89, 124, 333

Reagan, Ronald 69, 91, 102, 194, 213, 253

Reddin, Tom 56-59, 128, 376, 450

Reiter, Paul 391, 392

Rhodes, Michael 272

Rhodes-Hughes, Nina 122, 276-280, 282, 286, 350, 427, 498

Richards, Rhoad 61, 204

Rittner, Richard 22, 23

Rivera, Geraldo 218

Rockefeller, David 299

Rockefeller, Nelson 230, 233, 240, 476, 502

Rockefeller Commission 102, 222, 229, 230, 233, 395, 428

Rogers, Toby 294

Romero, Juan 16, 17, 28, 44, 51, 148-150, 155, 156, 163, 280, 284, 337, 340

Roselli, Johnny 123, 483-488

Rosenfeld, Harry 228

Rosicrucian 60, 297, 383, 437, 438, 440, 441

Ross, Karen 342

Rozzi, Robert 234, 264

Rubin, Lon 271

Ruby, Jack 21, 132, 276, 403, 404, 474

Ruiz, Ernesto Alfredo 318-320, 350

Russell, Dick 428

Russo, Pamela 347

Rutledge, Queen 216

Saccoman, Michael 162

Salinger, Pierre 25, 31

Sanders, Bernard (Bernie) 87

Santa Romana Foundation 430

Sartuche, Phil 234, 235

Schauer, Richard 131

Scheer, Larry 31

Scheflin, Alan 377, 393

Schlei, Norbert 288

Schlesinger, Arthur 65, 460-462

Schlesinger, James 367

Schneid, William 363, 364

Schrade, Paul 14, 16, 17, 21, 39, 54, 56, 64, 73, 77, 79,

80, 203, 213, 227, 229,
233, 235, 237, 249, 256,
267, 274, 276, 310, 317,
318, 492, 493
Schreiber, Brad 241, 405
Schulberg, Budd 9, 12, 13, 99
Schulman, Donald L. 214-216,
218, 219, 272, 273
Schulte, Valerie 117, 152, 153,
156, 163, 200, 288
Schumer, Chuck 452
Scott, Winston (Win) 66, 400
Scowcroft, Brent 431
Seagrave, Sterling 430
Seim, Conrad 11, 347, 364
Serrano, Sandra (Sandy) 9, 13,
14, 18, 19, 34-36, 40, 41,
49, 91, 99-101, 104-116,
118-122, 133, 139, 141,
152, 200, 223, 304, 342,
346-349, 352, 355, 356,
358, 360, 361, 364-366,
425, 498, 501
Sharaga, Paul 22, 24, 25, 28,
33, 34, 37, 116, 222-224,
256, 268, 293-295
Shaw, Clay 89, 90, 170
Shaw, Raymond 425
Shubert, Yvonne 489, 490
Siegelman, Jim 393
Sierra, Juan Roa 438
Sihanouk, Norodom 70
Sillings, Robert 28, 37, 295
Silver, Tom 414
Simpich, Bill 345
Simson-Kallas, Eduard 381,
382
Sinclair, Upton 456
Singer, Midge 336
Singer, William 19, 314
Sirhan, Adel 60, 92, 141, 172,
185, 450
Sirhan, Mary 183, 184, 186,
437
Sirhan, Munir 60, 183, 184,
388
Sirhan, Sharif 433-437
Sirhan, Sirhan 60, 69, 72-74,
90-97, 100-103, 113,
116-133, 136-145, 147-164,
166-176, 180-189, 191-194,
199-213, 215-221, 224-228,
234-238, 242-253, 255-261,
273-282, 284-291, 293-298,
302-307, 311-317, 319-325,
330, 333-338, 340-347,
350-365, 374-376,
379-392, 400-406, 409,

413, 415-428, 432-438,
440-450, 497-504
Sloan, Larry 172
Smith, Dave 194, 201
Smith, Joseph Burkholder 231,
400, 430, 455, 456, 469,
470, 488
Smith, Steve 14, 21, 57
Spangler, Tom 37
Starnes, Richard 467
Starr, Harry C. 162, 163
Steinman, Leonard 403, 404
Stevens, Theodore 438
Stockwell, John 463
Stone, Greg 233, 318
Stoner, George 93, 361
Strain, Samuel 316-320
Stroll, Irwin 17, 71, 72, 74, 79,
175, 287, 310
Sukarno, President 70, 460,
462, 490
Summers, Anthony (Tony) 458
Sweeney, Dennis 253
Symbionese Liberation Army
(SLA) 241, 405

Talbot, David 273, 280, 483,
492-93
Talmachoff, Peter 189
Tate, Sharon 434, 446
Taylor, Ruth Ashton 214
Taylor, Theodore 41, 199-200
Teresi, Virginia 191
Tew, Walter 32, 257
Thi Huong, Doan 414-15
Thompson, Vernon 344
Thornbrugh, James 120-21
Timanson, Uno 13
Tolson, Clyde 457-58
Trivelli, Terri 113, 362
Trujillo, Rafael 489
Truman, Harry S. 395, 456, 471
Trump, Donald J. 453, 501
TSS (Technical Services Staff)
398
Tuck, Richard (Dick) 287-88
Tully, Andrew 463
Turner, William (Bill) 32,
98-99, 191, 218-220, 224,
234-37, 287, 325, 340,
381, 404, 423, 446-47,
458

U.S.S. *Liberty* 70
Uecker, Karl 16-23, 39-40, 56,
72-76, 145-51, 156, 175,

180, 211-215, 247, 275,
278-84, 288, 306, 427
Underhill, John Garrett (Gary)
70
Unruh, Jesse 13, 16, 21-24,
34, 38, 52, 153-54, 271,
292-93
Urso, Lisa 16-17, 69, 140-41,
272, 276, 278-84, 306

Vacaville 405-06
Vallero, Ernest 334
Vanocur, Sander 14, 35-36, 116
Van Praag, Philip (Phil) 28, 34,
223, 264, 293
Varney, Dudley 202, 296, 321,
327-28
Vaughn, Robert 225

Walinsky, Adam 482-83
Walker, Herbert V. 131-133,
137-143, 152-155,
160-166, 168-170,
174-181, 184-194
Wall, Mary 362
Wallace, George 221, 447
Ward, Baxter 225, 233, 249,
278, 447
Watson, Peter 204, 408-09
Wayne 10-16, 20, 45-47, 78,
121, 140, 150, 166-168,
224, 282, 292-300,
302-318, 320-325, 333,
350, 361, 369, 497
Weatherly, John Chris 225
Weaver, Dennis 314-15
Webb, Gary 171
Weisel, William 17, 96, 175-77,
227, 236-38, 243-248
Weitz, John 457-58
Wenke, Robert 235, 242, 247,
289, 500
West, Andrew 20-21
West, Louis Jolyon 403-405
Westbrook, Colston 405
Weston, Don 22
Whalen, Mary 14, 19
White, George 396, 405, 473
White, Theodore 6, 7
White, Travis 23-24, 71, 80,
156-159, 424
Wickson, Donald 342
Wiedrich, Robert 56, 57, 265
Wilcott, James 472
Williams, Claudia 121
Williams, Ronald 161

Williman, Earl 271, 424

Wilson, James D. (Jim)
17, 404

Winner, Charles 304, 325,
330

Winter, Alison 378, 410

Wirin, Abraham Lincoln
(A.L.) 59, 122

Wolf, Paul 439

Wolfer, DeWayne 32, 59-61,
66, 71, 81-84, 91-97,

104, 129, 147, 172-183,
194, 200-212, 219-221,
232-238, 240-251, 256,
266-269, 498

Woodward, Robert (Bob)
229-30

Wright, Charles 234, 264

Wright, John David 336-339

Yaroslavsky, Zev 233

Yaro, Boris 16, 20, 148, 275

Yashuk, Chester 126

Yazbeck, Hanna 331

Yorty, Sam 59, 91, 92

Younger, Evelle 56, 69, 93,
131, 165-170, 194, 211,
218-222, 235

ZRALERT 400

ZRRIFLE 331, 400